Formal Ethics Opinions 2013–2023

Formal Ethics Opinions 2013–2023

AMERICAN BAR ASSOCIATION

Center for Professional Responsibility

Cover design by ABA Design.

Printed in the United States of America.

28 27 26 25 24 5 4 3 2 1

ISBN: 978-1-63905-459-6

Contents

Formal Ethics Opinions

MEMBERS OF THE STANDING COMMITTEE ON ETHICS AND PROFESSIONAL RESPONSIBILITY 2013–2023

MARK ARMITAGE
Detroit, MI

T. MAXFIELD BAHNER
Chattanooga, TN

JOHN BARKETT
Miami, FL

MELINDA BENTLEY
Jefferson City, MO

ARTHUR BERGER
Washington, DC

LONNIE BROWN
Athens, GA

ROBERT A. CREAMER
Boston, MA

WENDY CHANG
Los Angeles, CA

MATTHEW CORBIN
Olathe, KS

HON. DANIEL CROTHERS
Bismark, ND

ROBINJIT EAGLESON
Lansing, MI

DOUG ENDE
Seattle, WA

BRIAN FAUGHNAN
Memphis, TN

KEITH FISHER
Arlington, VA

CHAUNTIS FLOYD
Alpharetta, GA

PAULA J. FREDERICK, *Chair*
Atlanta, GA

HILARY GERZHOY
Washington, DC

BARBARA GILLERS, *Chair*
New York, NY

BRUCE A. GREEN, *Chair*
New York, NY

ROBERT HIRSHON
Ann Arbor, MI

AMANDA JONES
Chicago, IL

HON. GOODWIN LIU
San Francisco, CA

DONALD R. LUNDBERG
Indianapolis, IN

MYLES LYNK, *Chair*
Tempe, AZ

DAVID MAJCHRZAK
San Diego, CA

THOMAS MASON
Washington, DC

Introduction

The American Bar Association has provided leadership in legal ethics and professional responsibility for more than one hundred years through the adoption of professional standards that serve as models of the regulatory law governing the legal profession. The Standing Committee on Ethics and Professional Responsibility, created in 1913 as the Standing Committee on Professional Ethics, has the authority to advise and assist professional organizations and courts regarding the interpretation of statements of the ethical standards of the profession such as the Model Rules of Professional Conduct and to express and publish its opinions on proper professional conduct. The American Bar Association previously published opinions of the Committee covering the years 1924 through 2013 in a series of bound volumes. This volume is the latest in that series and includes 47 opinions issued from 2013 through 2023. Copies of individual opinions are available through the Center for Professional Responsibility website and Westlaw.

AMERICAN BAR ASSOCIATION
STANDING COMMITTEE ON ETHICS AND PROFESSIONAL RESPONSIBILITY

Formal Opinion 462 **February 21, 2013**

Judge's Use of Electronic Social Networking Media

A judge may participate in electronic social networking, but as with all social relationships and contacts, a judge must comply with relevant provisions of the Code of Judicial Conduct and avoid any conduct that would undermine the judge's independence, integrity, or impartiality, or create an appearance of impropriety.[1]

In this opinion, the Committee discusses a judge's participation in electronic social networking. The Committee will use the term "electronic social media" ("ESM") to refer to internet-based electronic social networking sites that require an individual to affirmatively join and accept or reject connection with particular persons.[2]

Judges and Electronic Social Media

In recent years, new and relatively easy-to-use technology and software have been introduced that allow users to share information about themselves and to post information on others' social networking sites. Such technology, which has become an everyday part of worldwide culture, is frequently updated, and different forms undoubtedly will emerge.

Social interactions of all kinds, including ESM, can be beneficial to judges to prevent them from being thought of as isolated or out of touch. This opinion examines to what extent a judge's participation in ESM raises concerns under the Model Code of Judicial Conduct.

Upon assuming the bench, judges accept a duty to "respect and honor the judicial office as a public trust and strive to maintain and enhance confidence in the legal system."[3] Although judges are full-fledged members of their communities, nevertheless, they "should expect to be the subject of

---

1. This opinion is based on the ABA Model Code of Judicial Conduct as amended by the ABA House of Delegates through August 2012. The laws, court rules, regulations, rules of professional and judicial conduct, and opinions promulgated in individual jurisdictions are controlling.

2. This opinion does not address other activities such as blogging, participation on discussion boards or listserves, and interactive gaming.

3. Model Code, Preamble [1].

public scrutiny that might be viewed as burdensome if applied to other citizens...."[4] All of a judge's social contacts, however made and in whatever context, including ESM, are governed by the requirement that judges must at all times act in a manner "that promotes public confidence in the independence, integrity, and impartiality of the judiciary," and must "avoid impropriety and the appearance of impropriety."[5] This requires that the judge be sensitive to the appearance of relationships with others.

The Model Code requires judges to "maintain the dignity of judicial office at all times, and avoid both impropriety and the appearance of impropriety in their professional and personal lives."[6] Thus judges must be very thoughtful in their interactions with others, particularly when using ESM. Judges must assume that comments posted to an ESM site will not remain within the circle of the judge's connections. Comments, images, or profile information, some of which might prove embarrassing if publicly revealed, may be electronically transmitted without the judge's knowledge or permission to persons unknown to the judge or to other unintended recipients. Such dissemination has the potential to compromise or appear to compromise the independence, integrity, and impartiality of the judge, as well as to undermine public confidence in the judiciary.[7]

There are obvious differences between in-person and digital social interactions. In contrast to fluid, face-to-face conversation that usually remains among the participants, messages, videos, or photographs posted to ESM may be disseminated to thousands of people without the consent or knowledge of the original poster. Such data have long, perhaps permanent, digital lives such that statements may be recovered, circulated or printed years after being sent. In addition, relations over the internet may be more difficult to manage because, devoid of in-person visual or vocal cues, messages may be taken out of context, misinterpreted, or relayed incorrectly.[8]

---

4. Model Code Rule 1.2 cmt. 2.

5. Model Code Rule 1.2. *But see* Dahlia Lithwick and Graham Vyse, "Tweet Justice," SLATE (April 30, 2010), (describing how state judge circumvents ethical rules prohibiting ex parte communications between judges and lawyers by asking lawyers to "de-friend" her from their ESM page when they're trying cases before her; judge also used her ESM account to monitor status updates by lawyers who appeared before her), *article available at* http://www.slate.com/articles/news_and_politics/jurisprudence/2010/04/tweet_justice.html.

6. Model Code, Preamble [2].

7. *See* Model Code Rule 1.2 cmt. 3. *Cf.* New York Jud. Eth. Adv. Op. 08-176 (2009) (judge who uses ESM should exercise appropriate degree of discretion in how to use the social network and should stay abreast of features and new developments that may impact judicial duties). Regarding new ESM website developments, it should be noted that if judges do not log onto their ESM sites on a somewhat regular basis, they are at risk of not knowing the latest update in privacy settings or terms of service that affect how their personal information is shared. They can eliminate this risk by deactivating their accounts.

8. Jeffrey Rosen, "The Web Means the End of Forgetting", N.Y. TIMES MAGAZINE (July 21, 2010) *accessible at* http://www.nytimes.com/2010/07/25/magazine/25privacy-t2.html?pagewanted=all.

A judge who participates in ESM should be mindful of relevant provisions of the Model Code. For example, while sharing comments, photographs, and other information, a judge must keep in mind the requirements of Rule 1.2 that call upon the judge to act in a manner that promotes public confidence in the judiciary, as previously discussed. The judge should not form relationships with persons or organizations that may violate Rule 2.4(C) by conveying an impression that these persons or organizations are in a position to influence the judge. A judge must also take care to avoid comments and interactions that may be interpreted as *ex parte* communications concerning pending or impending matters in violation of Rule 2.9(A), and avoid using any ESM site to obtain information regarding a matter before the judge in violation of Rule 2.9(C). Indeed, a judge should avoid comment about a pending or impending matter in any court to comply with Rule 2.10, and take care not to offer legal advice in violation of Rule 3.10.

There also may be disclosure or disqualification concerns regarding judges participating on ESM sites used by lawyers and others who may appear before the judge.[9] These concerns have been addressed in judicial ethics advisory opinions in a number of states. The drafting committees have expressed a wide range of views as to whether a judge may "friend" lawyers and others who may appear before the judge, ranging from outright prohibition to permission with appropriate cautions.[10] A judge who has an ESM connection with a lawyer or party who has a pending or impending matter before the court must evaluate that ESM connection to determine whether the judge should disclose the relationship prior to, or at the initial appearance of the person before the court.[11] In this regard,

9. *See, e.g.*, California Judges Ass'n Judicial Ethics Comm. Op. 66 (2010) (judges may not include in social network lawyers who have case pending before judge); Florida Sup. Ct. Jud. Eth. Adv. Comm. Op. 2009-20 (2009) (judge may not include lawyers who may appear before judge in social network or permit such lawyers to add judge to their social network circle); Ethics Committee of the Ky. Jud. Formal Jud. Eth. Op. JE-119 (judges should be mindful of "whether on-line connections alone or in combination with other facts rise to the level of 'a close social relationship'" that should be disclosed and/or require recusal); Ohio Sup. Ct. Bd. of Comm'rs on Grievances and Discipline Op. 2010-7 (2010) (judge may have ESM relationship with lawyer who appears as counsel in case before judge as long as relationship comports with ethics rules); South Carolina Jud. Dep't Advisory Comm. on Standards of Jud. Conduct, Op. No. 17-2009 (magistrate judge may have ESM relationship with lawyers as long as they do not discuss anything related to judge's judicial position). *See also* John Schwartz, "For Judges on Facebook, Friendship Has Limits," N.Y. TIMES, Dec. 11, 2009, at A25. *Cf.* Florida Sup. Ct. Jud. Eth. Adv. Comm. Op. 2010-04 (2010) (judge's judicial assistant may add lawyers who may appear before judge to social networking site as long as the activity is conducted entirely independent of judge and without reference to judge or judge's office).

10. *See* discussion in Geyh, Alfini, Lubet and Shaman, JUDICIAL CONDUCT AND ETHICS (5th Edition, forthcoming), Section 10.05E.

11. California Judges Assn. Judicial Ethics Comm. Op. 66 (need for disclosure arises from peculiar nature of online social networking sites, where evidence of connection between

context is significant.[12] Simple designation as an ESM connection does not, in and of itself, indicate the degree or intensity of a judge's relationship with a person.[13]

Because of the open and casual nature of ESM communication, a judge will seldom have an affirmative duty to disclose an ESM connection. If that connection includes current and frequent communication, the judge must very carefully consider whether that connection must be disclosed. When a judge knows that a party, a witness, or a lawyer appearing before the judge has an ESM connection with the judge, the judge must be mindful that such connection may give rise to the level of social relationship or the perception of a relationship that requires disclosure or recusal.[14] The judge must remember that personal bias or prejudice concerning a party or lawyer is the sole basis for disqualification under Rule 2.11 that is not waivable by parties in a dispute being adjudicated by that judge. The judge should conduct the same analysis that must be made whenever matters before the court involve persons the judge knows or has a connection with professionally or personally.[15]

lawyer and judge is widespread but nature of connection may not be readily apparent). *See also* New York Jud. Eth. Adv. Op. 08-176 (judge must consider whether any online connections, alone or in combination with other facts, rise to level of close social relationship requiring disclosure and/or recusal); Ohio Opinion 2010-7 (same).

12. Florida Sup. Ct. Jud. Eth. Adv. Comm. Op. 2010-06 (2010) (judge who is member of voluntary bar association not required to drop lawyers who are also members of that organization from organization's ESM site; members use the site to communicate among themselves about organization and other non-legal matters). *See also* Raymond McKoski, "Reestablishing Actual Impartiality as the Fundamental Value of Judicial Ethics: Lessons from 'Big Judge Davis'," 99 Ky. L.J. 259, 291 (2010-11) (nineteenth century judge universally recognized as impartial despite off-bench alliances, especially with Abraham Lincoln); Schwartz, *supra* note 9 ("Judges do not drop out of society when they become judges.... The people who were their friends before they went on the bench remained their friends, and many of them were lawyers.") (quoting New York University Prof. Stephen Gillers).

13. *See* Ethics Committee of the Ky. Jud. Formal Jud. Eth. Op. JE-119 (2010) (designation as an ESM follower does not, in and of itself, indicate the degree or intensity of judge's relationship with the person).

14. *See, e.g.*, New York Judicial Ethics Advisory Opinion 08-176, *supra* n. 8. *See also* Ashby Jones, "Why You Shouldn't Take It Hard If a Judge Rejects Your Friend Request," Wall St. J. Law Blog (Dec. 9, 2009) ("'friending' may be more than say an exchange of business cards but it is well short of any true friendship"); Jennifer Ellis, "Should Judges Recuse Themselves Because of a Facebook Friendship?" (Nov. 2011) (state attorney general requested that judge reverse decision to suppress evidence and recuse himself because he and defendant were ESM, but not actual, friends), *available at* http://www.jlellis.net/blog/should-judges-recuse-themselves-because-of-a-facebook-friendship/.

15. *See* Jeremy M. Miller, "Judicial Recusal and Disqualification: The Need for a Per Se Rule on Friendship (Not Acquaintance)," 33 Pepperdine L. Rev. 575, 578 (2012) ("Judges should not, and are not, expected to live isolated lives separate from all potential lawyers and litigants who may appear before them.... However, it is also axiomatic that justice, to be justice, must have the appearance of justice, and it appears unjust when the opposing side shares an intimate (but not necessarily sexual) relationship with the judge").

A judge should disclose on the record information the judge believes the parties or their lawyers might reasonably consider relevant to a possible motion for disqualification even if the judge believes there is no basis for the disqualification.[16] For example, a judge may decide to disclose that the judge and a party, a party's lawyer or a witness have an ESM connection, but that the judge believes the connection has not resulted in a relationship requiring disqualification. However, nothing requires a judge to search all of the judge's ESM connections if a judge does not have specific knowledge of an ESM connection that rises to the level of an actual or perceived problematic relationship with any individual.

Judges' Use of Electronic Social Media in Election Campaigns

Canon 4 of the Model Code permits a judge or judicial candidate to, with certain enumerated exceptions, engage in political or campaign activity. Comment [1] to Rule 4.1 states that, although the Rule imposes "narrowly tailored restrictions" on judges' political activities, "to the greatest extent possible," judges and judicial candidates must "be free and appear to be free from political influence and political pressure."

Rule 4.1(A)(8) prohibits a judge from personally soliciting or accepting campaign contributions other than through a campaign committee authorized by Rule 4.4. The Code does not address or restrict a judge's or campaign committee's method of communication. In jurisdictions where judges are elected, ESM has become a campaign tool to raise campaign funds and to provide information about the candidate.[17] Websites and ESM promoting the candidacy of a judge or judicial candidate may be established and maintained by campaign committees to obtain public statements of support for the judge's campaign so long as these sites are not started or maintained by the judge or judicial candidate personally.[18]

Sitting judges and judicial candidates are expressly prohibited from "publicly endorsing or opposing a candidate for any public office."[19] Some ESM sites allow users to indicate approval by applying "like" labels to shared messages, photos, and other content. Judges should be aware that clicking such buttons on others' political campaign ESM sites could be perceived as a violation of judicial ethics rules that prohibit judges from publicly endorsing or opposing another candidate for any public

16. Rule 2.11 cmt. 5.

17. In a recent survey, for judges who stood for political election, 60.3% used social media sites. 2012 CCPIO New Media and Courts Survey: A Report of the New Media Committee of the Conference of Court Public Information Officers (July 31, 2012), *available at* http://ccpio.org/blog/2010/08/26/judges-and-courts-on-social-media-report-released-on-new-medias-impact-on-the-judiciary/.

18. Florida Sup. Ct. Jud. Eth. Adv. Comm. Op. 2010-28 (July 23, 2010).

19. Model Code Rule 4.1(A)(3).

office.[20] On the other hand, it is unlikely to raise an ethics issue for a judge if someone "likes" or becomes a "fan" of the judge through the judge's ESM political campaign site if the campaign is not required to accept or reject a request in order for a name to appear on the campaign's page.

Judges may privately express their views on judicial or other candidates for political office, but must take appropriate steps to ensure that their views do not become public.[21] This may require managing privacy settings on ESM sites by restricting the circle of those having access to the judge's ESM page, limiting the ability of some connections to see others, limiting who can see the contact list, or blocking a connection altogether.

Conclusion

Judicious use of ESM can benefit judges in both their personal and professional lives. As their use of this technology increases, judges can take advantage of its utility and potential as a valuable tool for public outreach. When used with proper care, judges' use of ESM does not necessarily compromise their duties under the Model Code any more than use of traditional and less public forms of social connection such as U.S. Mail, telephone, email or texting.

20. *See* "Kansas judge causes stir with Facebook 'like'," The Associated Press, July 29, 2012, *available at* http://www.realclearpolitics.com/news/ap/politics/2012/Jul/29/kansas_judge_causes_stir_with_facebook__like_.html.

21. *See* Nevada Comm'n on Jud. Disc. Op. JE98-006 (Oct. 20, 1998) ("In expressing his or her views about other candidates for judicial or other public office in letters or other recorded forms of communication, the judge should exercise reasonable caution and restraint to ensure that his private endorsement is not, in fact, used as a public endorsement.").

AMERICAN BAR ASSOCIATION

STANDING COMMITTEE ON ETHICS AND PROFESSIONAL RESPONSIBILITY

Formal Opinion 463 **May 23, 2013**

Client Due Diligence, Money Laundering, and Terrorist Financing

The Model Rules of Professional Conduct and the ABA Voluntary Good Practices Guidance for Lawyers to Detect and Combat Money Laundering and Terrorist Financing ("Good Practices Guidance") are consistent in their ethical principles, including loyalty and confidentiality. The Good Practices Guidance provides information to help lawyers recognize and evaluate situations where providing legal services may assist in money laundering and terrorist financing. By implementing the risk-based control measures detailed in the Good Practices Guidance where appropriate, lawyers can avoid aiding illegal activities in a manner consistent with the Model Rules.[1]

In an effort to combat money laundering and terrorist financing, intergovernmental standards-setting organizations and government agencies have suggested that lawyers should be "gatekeepers" to the financial system.[2] The underlying theory behind the "lawyer-as- gatekeeper" idea is that the lawyer has the capacity to monitor and to control, or at least to influence, the conduct of his or her clients and prospective clients in order to deter wrongdoing.[3] Many have taken issue with this theory[4] and with

---

1. This opinion is based on the ABA Model Rules of Professional Conduct as amended by the ABA House of Delegates through February 2013. The laws, court rules, regulations, rules of professional conduct, and opinions promulgated in individual jurisdictions are controlling.

2. Kevin L. Shepherd, *The Gatekeeper Initiative and the Risk-Based Approach to Client Due Diligence: The Imperative for Voluntary Good Practices Guidance for U.S. Lawyers*, 2010 J. Prof. Law 83, 88 (lawyers are considered "gatekeepers" because they have the ability to furnish access to the various functions that might help criminals move or conceal funds).

3. *See* Press Center, *Treasury Deputy Secretary Stuart Eizenstat House Committee on Banking and Financial Services*, U.S Department of the Treasury (Mar. 9, 2000), http://www.treasury.gov/press-center/press-releases/Pages/ls445.aspx (stating that "[w]e are aggressively pursuing programs aimed at the lawyers, accountants and auditors who function as 'gatekeepers' to the financial system. While legal rules properly insulate professional consultations from overly broad scrutiny and create a zone of safety within which professionals can advise their clients, those rules should not create a cover for criminal conduct.").

the word "gatekeeper." The Rules do not mandate that a lawyer perform a "gatekeeper" role in this context.[5] More importantly, mandatory reporting of suspicion about a client is in conflict with Rules 1.6 and 1.18, and reporting without informing the client is in conflict with Rule 1.4(a)(5). In this opinion we examine the contours of a lawyer's ethical obligations under the Model Rules of Professional Conduct with regard to efforts to deter and combat money laundering.

In August 2010 the ABA's policymaking House of Delegates adopted the *Voluntary Good Practices Guidance for Lawyers to Detect and Combat Money Laundering and Terrorist Financing* ("Good Practices Guidance"),[6] along with a resolution stating that the Association "acknowledges and supports the United States Government's efforts to combat money laundering and terrorist financing." The approved Good Practices Guidance states that it is not intended to be, nor should it be construed as, a statement of the standard of care governing the activities of lawyers in implementing a risk-based approach to combat money laundering and terrorist financing, but rather is intended to serve as a resource that lawyers can use in developing their own voluntary approaches.[7]

Good Practices Guidance policy supports a "risk-based" approach in accord with guidelines developed by the Financial Action Task Force on Money Laundering ("FATF") created by the U.S. and other leading industrialized nations.[8] This approach differs from a rules- based approach that requires compliance with every element of detailed laws, rules, or regulations irrespective of the underlying quantum or degree of risk. The Good Practices Guidance urges lawyers to assess money-laundering and terrorist financing risks by examining the nature of the legal work involved, and where the business is taking place.[9]

4. *Federation of Law Societies of Canada v. Canada (Attorney General)*, 2013 BCCA 147 (2013), *available at* http://www.canlii.org/en/bc/bcca/doc/2013/2013bcca147/2013bcca147.html (striking down Canadian legislation as violating the solicitor-client privilege and interfering with the independence of the Bar).

5. *But see* Rutheford B. Campbell, Jr. & Eugene R. Gaetke, *The Ethical Obligation of Transactional Lawyers to Act as Gatekeepers*, 56 Rutgers L. Rev. 9 (2003).

6. Resolution & Report 116, *Voluntary Good Practices Guidance for Lawyers to Detect and Combat Money Laundering and Terrorist Financing*, American Bar Association (2010), http://www.americanbar.org/content/dam/aba/migrated/leadership/2010/annual/pdfs/116.authcheckdam.pdf. *See generally* Shepherd, *supra* note 2.

7. Resolution & Report 116, *supra* note 6, at 7.

8. *Federation of Law Societies of Canada v. Canada*, *supra* note 4.

9. *See* Michael A. Lindenberger, *Into the Breach: Voluntary Compliance on Money Laundering Gets a Boost from the ABA and Treasury*, ABA Journal (Oct. 2011), *available at* http://www.abajournal.com/magazine/article/into_the_breach_voluntary_compliance_on_money_laundering_gets_a_boost/(quoting the ABA President to encourage lawyers to be more vigilant about combating money laundering by following the Good Practices Guidance so that gatekeeper legislation regulating the legal profession will be unnecessary).

The Model Rules neither require a lawyer to fulfill a gatekeeper role, nor do they permit a lawyer to engage in the reporting that such a role could entail. It would be prudent for lawyers to undertake Client Due Diligence ("CDD")[10] in appropriate circumstances to avoid facilitating illegal activity or being drawn unwittingly into a criminal activity. This admonition is consistent with Informal Opinion 1470 (1981), where we stated that "[a] lawyer cannot escape responsibility by avoiding inquiry. A lawyer must be satisfied, on the facts before him and readily available to him, that he can perform the requested services without abetting fraudulent or criminal conduct and without relying on past client crime or fraud to achieve results the client now wants."[11] Further in that opinion we stated that, pursuant to a lawyer's ethical obligation to act competently,[12] a duty to inquire further may also arise.[13]

An appropriate assessment of the client and the client's objectives, and the means for obtaining those objectives, are essential prerequisites for accepting a new matter or continuing a representation as new facts unfold. Rule 1.2(d) prohibits a lawyer from *knowingly* counseling or assisting a client to commit a crime or fraud. A lawyer also is subject to federal laws prohibiting conduct that aids, abets, or commits a violation of U.S. anti-money laundering laws (*e.g.*, 18 U.S.C. Sections 1956 and 1957) or counter-terrorist financing laws.[14] Thus, for example, lawyers should be mindful of legal restrictions applicable to all persons in the U.S. to avoid providing certain legal services to, and receiving money from, individuals or entities publicly identified by the U.S. Department of the Treasury on its Specially Designated Nationals List ("SDN List").[15] In certain circumstances, checking a client's

---

10. The Good Practices Guidance encourages all lawyers to perform basic CDD by (1) identifying and verifying the identity of each client; (2) identifying and verifying the identity of any "beneficial owner" of the client, defined as the natural person(s) with ultimate control of a client, when such an analysis is warranted from a risk-based standpoint; and (3) obtaining enough information to understand a client's circumstances, business, and objectives. Resolution & Report 116, *supra* note 6, at 9-11.

11. ABA Comm. on Ethics & Prof'l Responsibility, Informal Op. 1470 (1981) [hereinafter ABA Informal Op. 1470]. *See also*, Geoffrey C. Hazard, Jr. & W. William Hodes, The Law of Lawyering: A Handbook on the Model Rules of Professional Conduct § 1.6:403, 199-200 (2d ed. 1990 & Supp. 1998). *Cf.* Monroe H. Freedman, *Personal Responsibility in a Professional System*, 27 Cath. U. L. Rev. 191, 200 (1978) (warning lawyers against "assum[ing] the worst regarding the client's desires").

12. *See* Model Code of Prof'l Responsibility DR 6-101 (1979) (now Rule 1.1).

13. ABA Informal Op. 1470, *supra* note 11.

14. These laws include, for example, the Anti-Terrorism and Effective Death Penalty Act of 1996, Pub. L. No. 104- 132, 110 Stat. 1214; Uniting and Strengthening America by Providing Appropriate Tools Required to Intercept and Obstruct Terrorism (USA PATRIOT) Act of 2001, Pub. L. No. 107-56, 115 Stat. 272; Exec. Order No. 13224, 66 Fed. Reg. 49079 (Sept. 23, 2001).

15. *Specially Designated Nationals List*, U.S. Department of the Treasury, http://www.treasury.gov/resource-center/sanctions/SDN-List/Pages/default.aspx (last visited May 20, 2013).

identity internally within the firm against the SDN List can avoid the risk of unlawful conduct by the lawyer.

The level of appropriate CDD varies depending on the risk profile of the client, the country or geographic area of origin, or the legal services involved.[16] For example, the fact that clients are deemed to be "Politically Exposed Persons," (*e.g.*, domestic or foreign senior government, judicial, or military officials) may justify enhanced due diligence on the part of the lawyer because of the potential for corruption. Clients or legal matters associated with countries that are subject to sanctions or embargoes issued by the United Nations, or those identified by credible sources as having significant levels of corruption or other criminal activity or that provide funds or support to terrorist organizations, may require greater examination. Furthermore, clients who ask that the lawyer handle actual receipt and transmission of funds or those who request accelerated real estate transfers for no apparent reason may also require an extra level of scrutiny.

Once a representation has commenced, a lawyer may terminate it in a number of circumstances in which the lawyer does not *know* for certain the client's plans or whether the client is engaged in criminal or fraudulent activities, but the lawyer has reason to believe that the client is engaging, or plans to engage, in such improper activities. Rule 1.16(b)(2) (Declining or Terminating Representation) states that a lawyer may withdraw from representing a client if "the client persists in a course of action involving the lawyer's services that the lawyer *reasonably believes* is criminal or fraudulent." (Emphasis added).[17]

The Committee believes that the advice derived from the Good Practices Guidance is consistent, and not in conflict, with the ethical obligations of lawyers under the Model Rules. Indeed, the Good Practices Guidance states that "when faced with a situation where the lawyer is compelled to decline or terminate the relationship, the lawyer should comply with the requirements of the applicable rules of professional conduct." [18] Accordingly, lawyers should be conversant with the risk-based measures and controls for clients and legal matters with an identified risk profile and use them for guidance as they develop their own client intake and ongoing client monitoring processes. When in a lawyer's professional judgment aspects of the contemplated representation raise suspicions about its propriety, that lawyer's familiarity with risk-

16. *Supra* note 10.

17. Moreover, Model Rule 1.16 (b)(4) allows a lawyer to withdraw when "the client insists upon taking action that the lawyer considers repugnant or with which the lawyer has a fundamental disagreement."

18. Resolution & Report 116, *supra* note 6, at 38.

based measures and controls will assist in avoiding unwitting assistance to unlawful activities. Indeed, the usefulness of the Good Practices Guidance is an example of the declaration in the Model Rules that "[t]he Rules do not … exhaust the moral and ethical considerations that should inform a lawyer…."[19]

19. Model Rules of Prof'l Conduct, Scope, cmt. 16. *See also* Model Rules of Prof'l Conduct R. 2.1 (explaining that "[i]n rendering advice, a lawyer may refer not only to law but to other considerations such as moral, economic, social and political factors, that may be relevant to the client's situation."); ABA Comm. on Ethics & Prof'l Responsibility, Formal Op. 335 (1974) (stating that in the context of writing opinions for transactions involving sales of unregistered securities, a lawyer should not "accept as true that which he does not reasonably believe to be true.").

AMERICAN BAR ASSOCIATION

STANDING COMMITTEE ON ETHICS AND PROFESSIONAL RESPONSIBILITY

Formal Opinion 464 **August 19, 2013**

Division of Legal Fees With Other Lawyers Who May Lawfully Share Fees With Nonlawyers

Lawyers subject to the Model Rules may work with other lawyers or law firms practicing in jurisdictions with rules that permit sharing legal fees with nonlawyers. Where there is a single billing to a client in such situations, a lawyer subject to the Model Rules may divide a legal fee with a lawyer or law firm in the other jurisdiction, even if the other lawyer or law firm might eventually distribute some portion of the fee to a nonlawyer, provided that there is no interference with the lawyer's independent professional judgment.

This opinion considers whether a lawyer subject to the Model Rules may divide a legal fee with another lawyer or law firm practicing in a jurisdiction where the other lawyer or law firm might eventually distribute some portion of that fee to a nonlawyer.[1] In contemporary practice, lawyers routinely work with lawyers from other law firms, including lawyers and law firms in other jurisdictions, to represent clients in particular matters. The August 2012 amendments to the Model Rules expressly recognize these common arrangements. New Comment [6] to Model Rule 1.1 explains that a lawyer may retain or contract with other lawyers outside the lawyer's own firm to provide or assist in the provision of legal services to a client and describes how a lawyer should approach these relationships with both the client and the other lawyers.[2]

---

1. This opinion is based on the Model Rules of Professional Conduct as amended by the American Bar Association House of Delegates through February 2013. The laws, court rules, regulations, rules of professional conduct, and opinions promulgated in the individual jurisdiction are controlling.

2. Comment [6] to ABA Model Rules Of Prof'l Conduct R. 1.1 reads:

Retaining or Contracting With Other Lawyers

Before a lawyer retains or contracts with other lawyers outside the lawyer's own firm to provide or assist in the provision of legal services to a client, the lawyer should ordinarily obtain informed consent from the client and must reasonably believe that the other lawyers' services will contribute to the competent and ethical representation of the client. See also Rules 1.2 (allocation of authority), 1.4 (communication with client), 1.5(e) (fee sharing), 1.6 (confidentiality), and 5.5(a) (unauthorized practice of law). The reasonableness of the deci-

Sometimes the other lawyers with whom a lawyer may work are admitted and practice in other jurisdictions, both within and outside the United States, a situation that has become more common with the growth of national and international commerce. Those other jurisdictions may have professional conduct rules identical or similar to Model Rules 1.5(e) and 5.4(a), which deal with the allocation of legal fees among lawyers and nonlawyers. But some jurisdictions, like the District of Columbia and the United Kingdom, have rules that differ significantly from Model Rules 1.5(e) and 5.4(a).

Model Rule 1.5(e) permits the division of a legal fee between lawyers who are not in the same firm, but only if: (1) the division is in proportion to the services performed by each lawyer or each lawyer assumes joint responsibility for the representation; (2) the client agrees to the arrangement, including the share each lawyer will receive, and the agreement is confirmed in writing; and (3) the total fee is reasonable. Comment [7] to Model Rule 1.5 explains that a "division of fee" is a single billing to a client covering the fee of two or more lawyers who are not in the same firm; and the comment also notes that this kind of fee arrangement "... facilitates association of more than one lawyer in a matter in which neither alone could serve the client as well...." Inter-firm division of legal fees is clearly contemplated by the Model Rules.

Model Rule 5.4(a) provides generally that "a lawyer or law firm shall not share legal fees with a nonlawyer" but recognizes four distinct exceptions: payments to the survivors or estates of deceased lawyers; payments made under Model Rule 1.17 to purchase the practice of a deceased, disabled or disappeared lawyer; firm compensation and retirement plans; and sharing court- awarded fees with nonprofit organizations. The exception for firm compensation and retirement plans depends on whether the profits being shared are "tied to particular clients or particular matters."[3]

In contrast to the Model Rule, District of Columbia Rule 5.4(b) permits "an individual nonlawyer who performs professional services which assist the organization in providing legal services to clients" to hold an ownership interest in a law firm; and District of Columbia Rule 5.4(a) permits the shar-

---

sion to retain or contract with other lawyers outside the lawyer's own firm will depend upon the circumstances, including the education, experience and reputation of the nonfirm lawyers; the nature of the services assigned to the nonfirm lawyers; and the legal protections, professional conduct rules, and ethical environments of the jurisdictions in which the services will be performed, particularly relating to confidential information.

3. Ellen J. Bennett, Elizabeth J. Cohen & Martin Whittaker, *Annotated Model Rules of Professional Conduct* 461 (7th ed. 2011). *See* Ill. State Bar Ass'n, Advisory Op. 89-05 (1989) (firm profit-sharing plan may include nonlawyer employees provided shares based on overall firm profit and not specific matters); N.Y. State Bar Ass'n Comm. on Prof'l Ethics, Advisory Op. 917 (2012) (firm may pay bonus to nonlawyer marketer based on number of clients obtained through advertising provided amount paid not calculated with respect to fees paid by clients).

ing of legal fees with such persons.[4] ABA Formal Opinion 91-360 (July 11, 1991) addressed the question of what rule should govern a lawyer's conduct when the lawyer is admitted in the District of Columbia and a partner in a District of Columbia firm that includes nonlawyer partners, but is also admitted in another jurisdiction that follows Model Rule 5.4(b), which forbids such partnerships. The opinion concluded that the lawyer "should not be subject to the prohibition of the jurisdiction where the lawyer does not practice" and should follow the rules where the lawyer is engaged in practice. Formal Opinion 91-360 did not directly address fee sharing.

A fee-sharing issue may arise when a lawyer undertakes the representation of a client in a matter that involves the services of another lawyer or law firm governed by different rules. For example, a lawyer in a Model Rules jurisdiction may reasonably conclude that the client requires the assistance of a specific lawyer in a District of Columbia firm, in which a nonlawyer happens

---

4. DC Rules of Prof'l Conduct R. 5.4, Professional Independence of a Lawyer, states that:

(a) lawyer or law firm shall not share legal fees with a nonlawyer, except that:

(1) An agreement by a lawyer with the lawyer's firm, partner, or associate may provide for the payment of money, over a reasonable period of time after the lawyer's death, to the lawyer's estate or to one or more specified persons;

(2) A lawyer who undertakes to complete unfinished legal business of a deceased lawyer may pay to the estate of the deceased lawyer that proportion of the total compensation which fairly represents the services rendered by the deceased lawyer. A lawyer who purchases the practice of a deceased, disabled, or disappeared lawyer may, pursuant to the provisions of Rule 1.17, pay to the estate or other representative of that lawyer the agreed-upon purchase price.

(3) A lawyer or law firm may include nonlawyer employees in a compensation or retirement plan, even though the plan is based in whole or in part on a profit-sharing arrangement;

(4) Sharing of fees is permitted in a partnership or other form of organization which meets the requirements of paragraph (b); and

(5) A lawyer may share legal fees, whether awarded by a tribunal or received in settlement of a matter, with a nonprofit organization that employed, retained, or recommended employment of the lawyer in the matter and that qualifies under Section 501(c)(3) of the Internal Revenue Code.

(b) A lawyer may practice law in a partnership or other form of organization in which a financial interest is held or managerial authority is exercised by an individual nonlawyer who performs professional services which assist the organization in providing legal services to clients, but only if:

(1) The partnership or organization has as its sole purpose providing legal services to clients;

(2) All persons having such managerial authority or holding a financial interest undertake to abide by these Rules of Professional Conduct;

(3) The lawyers who have a financial interest or managerial authority in the partnership or organization undertake to be responsible for the nonlawyer participants to the same extent as if nonlawyer participants were lawyers under Rule 5.1;

(4) The foregoing conditions are set forth in writing.

to hold an ownership interest, on a matter involving federal government contracts because that lawyer is uniquely qualified in such matters. With informed client consent, the two lawyers may work together on the matter. If the requirements of Model Rule 1.5(e) are met, a typical fee arrangement in such matters is for the client to receive a single billing for the work of both lawyers. In this situation, there may be a question whether the lawyer from the Model Rules jurisdiction, by participating in this common inter-firm fee arrangement, shares a legal fee in violation of Model Rule 5.4(a) because the District of Columbia firm's portion of the fee will presumably become part of that firm's overall revenues, revenues from which distributions may ultimately be made to the nonlawyer who holds an ownership interest.

In the situation assumed above, however, the lawyer from the Model Rules jurisdiction does not violate Model Rule 5.4(a). That lawyer divided a legal fee only with "another lawyer," and a lawyer may divide legal fees with a lawyer admitted in another jurisdiction.[5] Any concerns of the lawyer subject to the Model Rules regarding inter-firm division of legal fees should end at that point.

The possibility that the District of Columbia firm may, or may not, eventually "share" some fraction of that firm's portion of the fee with a nonlawyer should not expose the lawyer in the Model Rules jurisdiction to discipline. The lawyer subject to the Model Rules has complied with those rules. The compensation system of the District of Columbia firm does not threaten the application of Model Rule 5.4(a) within the Model Rules jurisdiction, and there is no reason to attempt to enforce Model Rule 5.4(a) in the District of Columbia.[6]

This situation is different from that considered in Formal Opinion 91-360, noted above, which dealt with the prohibition of partnerships with nonlawyers expressed in Model Rule 5.4(b) rather than the fee-sharing provision of Model Rule 5.4(a). However, the conclusions are consistent. Formal Opinion 91-360 decided that a lawyer licensed both in a Model Rules jurisdiction and the District of Columbia should adhere to the restrictions of the jurisdiction where the lawyer actually practiced. The conduct of each lawyer and law firm involved in the current hypothetical situation took place in only one ju-

5. ABA Comm. on Ethics & Prof'l Responsibility, Formal Op. 316 (1967) (not necessary that both lawyers be admitted in same jurisdiction to divide legal fees; lawyer admitted in one jurisdiction is lawyer everywhere for purposes of ethics rules). *See also O'Brien, P.C. v. Snyder*, 601 A.2d 1056, 1058 (Del. 1990) (members of New Jersey bar were "lawyers" for purposes of Delaware Rule 5.4(a)); ABA Comm. on Ethics & Prof'l Responsibility, Formal Opinion 423 (2001) (members of recognized legal profession in foreign jurisdictions are "lawyers" for purposes of Model Rule 5.4.).

6. *See Hoffmann-La Roche Ltd. v. Empagran S.A.*, 542 U.S. 155, 165 (2004) (jurisdiction should not apply its law to judge conduct that occurs only in another jurisdiction when conduct creates no serious risk of interference with first jurisdiction's ability to regulate its own affairs).

risdiction and was permitted there. The lawyer subject to the Model Rules divided a fee only with another lawyer in conformance with the Model Rules; and the District of Columbia firm could choose to allocate its portion of the fee to a compensation plan that included distribution to the nonlawyer holding an ownership interest as authorized by the District of Columbia rules.

In summary, a division of a legal fee by a lawyer or law firm in a Model Rules jurisdiction with a lawyer or law firm in another jurisdiction that permits the sharing of legal fees with nonlawyers does not violate Model Rule 5.4(a) simply because a nonlawyer could ultimately receive some portion of the fee under the applicable law of the other jurisdiction.

This conclusion is consistent with the purposes of the Model Rules because the concerns underlying the prohibition in Model Rule 5.4 are not implicated. As explained in Comment [1] to Model Rule 5.4: "These limitations are to protect the lawyer's independence of professional judgment." The rule protects a lawyer's independent professional judgment by limiting the influence of nonlawyers on the client-lawyer relationship.[7] In the typical situation discussed above, there is no reason to believe that the nonlawyer in the District of Columbia might actually influence the independent professional judgment of the lawyer in the Model Rules jurisdiction, who practices in a different firm, in a different jurisdiction. And that lawyer remains subject to the Model Rules, so this conclusion does not compromise any prohibitions on nonlawyer ownership and fee sharing in the Model Rules jurisdiction.[8]

A contrary conclusion, as noted above, would place the lawyer in the Model Rules jurisdiction at the mercy of the organization and compensation practices of the District of Columbia firm. For example, as discussed above, if the District of Columbia firm's compensation plan that included nonlawyers were not "tied to particular clients or particular matters," then there would be no violation of Model Rule 5.4(a) in any event. And even if the District of Columbia firm's compensation plan permitted it to pay a nonlawyer a portion of fees received that were in fact "tied to particular clients or particular matters," but the firm decided for any reason not to do so in a given year, then there could be no concern for allegedly improper fee sharing for that year. Thus, the exposure of the lawyer in the Model Rules jurisdiction to discipline for improper fee sharing would essentially depend on the organization, bookkeeping practices, and annual compensation decisions of the District of Columbia firm.

Presumably, lawyers in Model Rules jurisdictions could always avoid any potentially improper fee sharing by refusing to work with firms in the

---

7. Bennett et al., *supra* note 3, at 456.

8. This conclusion is also in accord with the only other opinion that has directly addressed the question. *See* Philadelphia Bar Assn. Prof'l Guidance Comm., Advisory Op. 2010-7 (2010) (Pennsylvania law firm may divide legal fee from joint representation of a client with District of Columbia firm which has nonlawyer partner).

District of Columbia or other countries unless the clients themselves separately retained and paid the District of Columbia or foreign law firms. But this tactic would likely annoy clients and add unnecessary complexity to a common arrangement with no constructive purpose.

A contrary conclusion would also unreasonably impair the ability of lawyers to work alongside lawyers in firms that may be best suited to serve a particular client or resolve a particular matter. If a lawyer in a Model Rules jurisdiction cannot work with other lawyers from the District of Columbia or the other jurisdictions where law firms are permitted to share fees with nonlawyers, clients would be deprived of the services of those lawyers with no real benefit to those clients or the legal system.

Finally, this conclusion carries an important limitation. Lawyers must continue to comply with the requirement of Model Rule 5.4(c) to maintain professional independence. Even if the other law firm may be governed by different rules regarding relationships with nonlawyers, a lawyer must not permit a nonlawyer in the other firm to interfere with the lawyer's own independent professional judgment. As noted above, the actual risk of improper influence is minimal. But the prohibition against improper nonlawyer influence continues regardless of the fee arrangement.

AMERICAN BAR ASSOCIATION
STANDING COMMITTEE ON ETHICS AND PROFESSIONAL RESPONSIBILITY

Formal Opinion 465 **October 21, 2013**

Lawyers' Use of Deal-of-the-Day Marketing Programs

Deal-of-the-day or group-coupon marketing programs offer an alternative way to sell goods and services. Lawyers hoping to market legal services using these programs must comply with various Rules of Professional Conduct, including, but not limited to, rules governing fee sharing, advertising, competence, diligence, and the proper handling of legal fees. It is also incumbent upon the lawyer to determine whether conflicts of interest exist. While the Committee believes that coupon deals can be structured to comply with the Model Rules, it has identified numerous difficult issues associated with prepaid deals and is less certain that prepaid deals can be structured to comply with all ethical and professional obligations under the Model Rules.

Introduction

Group-coupon or deal-of-the-day marketing programs have emerged as a new model for advertising and selling goods and services. These marketing programs use websites, email, newspapers, and other tools as vehicles for helping local retailers and service providers to promote their goods and services. Businesses gain an influx of new customers, name and brand exposure through the marketing organization's activities, and the opportunity for increased sales from returning customers and word-of-mouth publicity.[1]

One popular model works as follows: a marketing organization uses a website to advertise deals, allowing anyone interested in receiving notifications of such deals to subscribe to the website's frequent emails. Visitors to the website also may view the deals. The marketing organization works with local businesses to create deals for goods or services that are offered to the marketer's subscribers and visitors. After a threshold number of buyers purchase a deal, the marketing organization and the local business share the

1. This opinion is based on the ABA Model Rules of Professional Conduct as amended by the ABA House of Delegates through February 2013. The laws, court rules, regulations, rules of professional conduct, and opinions promulgated in individual jurisdictions are controlling.

proceeds in an agreed-upon division. Each successful buyer receives a code, coupon, or voucher to obtain the specified good or service, which typically has an expiration date.[2]

Lawyers may seek to obtain new clients through these marketing organizations' activities. However, a lawyer must exercise great care to ensure that both the offer and any resulting representation comply with all obligations under the Model Rules, including avoiding false or misleading statements and conflicts of interest, providing competent and diligent representation, and appropriately handling all money received.[3]

Structuring the Deal to Avoid Ethical Issues

The dictionary definition of a coupon is a "voucher entitling the holder to a discount for a particular product."[4] For example, a coupon clipped from the newspaper may entitle a person to buy a jar of spaghetti sauce for fifty cents less than the usual price, but the buyer has to hand over to the merchant both the coupon and the cost of the sauce, less fifty cents. In contrast, marketing organizations often collect the entire discounted price for a good or service and then provide a code that entitles the bearer to collect the good or service from the merchant without any additional payment.

For a lawyer, the two options described above might be illustrated as follows. Assume a lawyer charges $200 per hour for legal services. The lawyer could sell a coupon for $25 that would entitle the bearer to buy up to five hours of legal services at a fifty-percent discount; in other words, the $25 would allow the bearer to pay only $100 per hour for up to five hours of legal services, potentially saving up to $500. This first option requires the coupon bearer to make additional payment to the lawyer commensurate with the number of hours actually used. Alternatively, the lawyer could sell a deal for $500 that would entitle the buyer to receive up to five hours of legal service (with a value of up to $1,000), but all of the money would be collected by the marketing organization, with no additional payment collected by the lawyer no matter how many of the five hours of legal services were actually used.

---

2. Not all deal-of-the-day marketing programs operate alike and the business model is not static. Therefore, variations to the model described in this opinion may impact how a lawyer uses this type of marketing tool. This opinion does not address marketing programs where the recipient has not initiated contact with the marketing organization and requested notification of deals.

3. State ethics opinions addressing lawyer use of marketing organization websites have reached different conclusions. As one opinion concluded, the situation is "fraught with peril." Indiana State Bar Ass'n Legal Ethics Comm., Advisory Op. 1 (2012).

4. New Oxford American Dictionary 397 (3d ed. 2010).

For ease of reference, this opinion will refer to option one as a coupon deal and to option two as a prepaid[5] deal.[6]

A lawyer must pay careful attention to how a deal-of-the-day offer is structured. As discussed more fully below, a coupon deal can meet the requirements of the Model Rules. Less clear is whether a prepaid deal can be structured to be consistent with the Model Rules. No doubt other structures may arise in the future, and they will have to be carefully assessed on their particular terms.

The Cost of Advertising Does Not Constitute Sharing of a Legal Fee

Model Rule 5.4 prohibits a lawyer, with certain exceptions, from sharing legal fees with nonlawyers. Several state ethics opinions examining lawyers' use of deal-of-the-day marketing programs have concluded that these arrangements do not constitute fee sharing and do comport with the purpose behind Rule 5.4, the protection of lawyers' independent professional judgment, by limiting the influence of nonlawyers on client-lawyer relationships.[7] The Committee generally agrees with the analysis set forth in such state opinions, with one caveat.

It is the opinion of the Committee that marketing organizations that retain a percentage of payments are obtaining nothing more than payment for advertising and processing services rendered to the lawyers who are market-

5. Although this opinion uses the term "prepaid deal" to describe one form of marketing, it should not be confused with a lawyer's participation in for-profit prepaid legal service plans which this Committee found permissible, subject to certain requirements, in ABA Comm. on Ethics and Prof'l Responsibility, Formal Op. 87-355 (1987).

6. These two options are not meant to be exhaustive; rather, they are used to illustrate the types of issues a lawyer must consider in structuring a deal for a marketing program.

7. *See, e.g.*, Maryland State Bar Ass'n Comm. on Ethics, Op. 2012-07 (2012) (where website collects fees upfront and retains percentage of purchase price, arrangement is cost of advertising and not legal fee-splitting arrangement); North Carolina State Bar, Formal Op. 10 (2011) (portion of fee retained by website is merely advertising cost because "it is paid regardless of whether the purchaser actually claims the discounted service and the lawyer earns the fee…"); South Carolina Bar Ethics Advisory Comm., Advisory Op. 11-05 (2011) (website's share of fee paid by purchaser was an "advertising cost" and not sharing of legal fee with nonlawyer). *But see Advertising on Groupon and Similar Deal of the Day Websites*, Alabama State Bar, Formal Op. 2012-01 (2012) (percentage taken by site is not tied in any manner to "reasonable cost" of advertisement, thus use of such sites to sell legal services is violation of Rule 5.4 because legal fees are shared with a nonlawyer); Indiana State Bar Ass'n Legal Ethics Comm., Advisory Op. 1, *supra* note 3 (online providers are being paid to channel buyers of legal work to specific lawyers in violation of advertising and fee sharing rules); Pennsylvania Bar Ass'n, Advisory Op. 2011-27 (2011) (use of deal-of-the-day website is impermissible fee splitting under Rule 5.4); State Bar of Arizona, Formal Op.13-01 (2013) (even if portion retained is reasonable, it constitutes illegal fee sharing because the consumer pays all the money directly to the website versus the lawyer paying fees for advertising out of already earned fees).

ing their legal services. This is particularly true where the lawyer structures the transaction as a coupon deal because, as discussed below, no legal fees are collected by the marketer. The fact that the marketing organizations deduct payment upfront rather than bill the lawyer at a later time for providing the advertising services does not convert the nature of the relationship between the lawyer and the marketing organization from an advertising arrangement into a fee sharing arrangement that violates the Model Rules.

The one caveat is that the percentage retained by the marketing organization must be reasonable. Model Rule 7.2(b)(1) prohibits a lawyer from paying for referrals but allows a lawyer to pay the "reasonable" costs of advertising.[8] If the portion of the price retained by the marketing organization is reasonable given the cost of alternate types of advertising, the fee likely would be deemed to be reasonable. Similarly, if additional services are being provided (e.g., where the marketing organization is being compensated for publishing the lawyer's advertising message to a large group of subscribers that has been developed by the marketing organization, and/or the organization processes payments from the buyers), the fee, even if a significant portion of the purchase price, likely would be considered to be reasonable.

Advertising Must Not Be False or Misleading

Truthful advertising, including that for legal services, is constitutionally protected commercial speech.[9] Rule 7.1, however, provides that lawyers must not make false or misleading statements about their own abilities or services.[10] Lawyers who choose to use deal- of-the-day marketing programs must supervise the statements made to ensure their accuracy and ensure that the substantive content does not include misleading or incomplete offers that run afoul of the restrictions contained in the Model Rules.

Advertising a coupon deal likely presents fewer hurdles than advertising a prepaid deal. As with any advertising, lawyers must exercise care in offering prepaid deals for a specified service. The public, particularly first-time or unsophisticated purchasers of legal services, may not easily discern what legal services they require or what legal services are encompassed in an offer.

---

8. ABA Model Rules of Prof'l Conduct R. 7.2(b)(1) provides in full: "A lawyer shall not give anything of value to a person for recommending the lawyer's services except that a lawyer may pay the reasonable costs of advertisements or communications permitted by this Rule."

9. *Bates v. State Bar of Arizona*, 433 U.S. 350 (1977).

10. ABA Model Rules of Prof'l Conduct R. 7.1 provides in full: "A lawyer shall not make a false or misleading communication about the lawyer or the lawyer's services. A communication is false or misleading if it contains a material misrepresentation of fact or law, or omits a fact necessary to make the statement considered as a whole not materially misleading."

Therefore, care should be taken to draft the advertisements and communications to clearly define the scope of services offered, including whether court costs and/or other expenses are excluded. Whether a coupon deal or prepaid deal is offered, care should be taken to explain under what circumstances the purchase price of a deal may be refunded, to whom, and what amount.

Buyer is Neither a Prospective nor Current Client

Importantly, a lawyer must be careful to communicate the nature of the relationship created, if any, by the purchase of a deal. A person who consults with a lawyer about the possibility of forming a client-lawyer relationship with respect to a matter is a prospective client under Rule 1.18.[11] However, mere purchase of a deal for legal services does not make the buyer either a prospective client or a current client, entitled to the attendant duties owed by the lawyer. Prior to establishing a client-lawyer relationship, it is incumbent upon the lawyer to first determine whether conflicts of interest exist and whether the lawyer can competently handle the particular matter based on the expected scope of representation and the buyer's needs. Therefore, the lawyer's advertisement and communications should explain that until a consultation takes place with the lawyer, no client-lawyer relationship exists and that such a relationship may never be formed if the lawyer determines there is a conflict of interest, the lawyer is unable to provide the required representation, or the lawyer declines representation for some other reason.[12]

Lawyers should recognize that purchased deals generally can be traded or given as gifts. Lawyers must ensure that the coupon or voucher and all materials marketing the lawyer's services contain language cautioning any holder to review all terms of the purchase on the marketing organization's website, including whether the coupon is transferable. There may be some legal services that are not appropriate for transfer or gift giving due to the nature of the services or the marketing program's technical inability to adequately provide necessary information to the lawyer. For example, we noted earlier that it is not clear whether a prepaid deal can be structured to be consistent with the Model Rules. Similarly, it is not clear whether a prepaid deal,

---

11. Indiana State Bar Ass'n Legal Ethics Comm., Advisory Op. 1, *supra* note 3, states that the court could reasonably find that a person who has deposited money with the lawyer or lawyer's agent to form a client-lawyer relationship qualifies as a prospective client under Rule 1.18. Comment [1] to ABA MODEL RULES OF PROF'L CONDUCT R. 1.18 states: "Prospective clients, like clients, may … place documents or other property in the lawyer's custody …"

12. While not all jurisdictions require lawyers to use retainer agreements, such use is advised. If the advertising lawyer expects as part of the deal to require one who is accepted as a client to execute a retainer agreement, that information likely should be disclosed on the website as well.

if it can be structured to comply with ethical requirements, could be transferable. Thus, another decision that the lawyer must make in evaluating the marketing program provider and in structuring a deal-of-the-day marketing program is whether or not the service offered can or should be transferable.

Competent Representation and Diligence

Competent handling of a matter requires a preliminary inquiry into, and analysis of, the factual and legal elements of a problem.[13] A lawyer who is offering deals should limit the type of services and practice area(s) covered in the offer to those in which the lawyer is competent so that individuals can make informed decisions whether to purchase the deal. Then, before establishing a client-lawyer relationship pursuant to a deal purchase, a lawyer must determine whether the services required by the purchaser are within the lawyer's competence. A lawyer offering deals should also specify any limitations on the types of matters the lawyer handles.

Even with proper disclosures, a legal matter may be more complex and require more work than contemplated by the offered deal. The lawyer should assess the amount of time and effort necessary to complete the matter, and, if the offer limits the number of hours of legal services the lawyer is obligated to provide, should address the possibility that the allotted time may expire before the representation is concluded. Where appropriate to the scope of services to be provided, the lawyer has an obligation to communicate[14] the fact that additional services may or will be required to complete the representation beyond those included in the deal, and to advise whether the client will be obligated to pay additional fees in that event, and if so, in what amount or at what hourly rate.[15]

In addition, the lawyer must be careful in establishing the maximum number of deals to be sold by the marketing organization. Businesses have been harmed by overselling deals and then struggling to meet the ensuing demand. For a lawyer, setting too high a cap on the number of deals sold

---

13. *See* ABA Model Rules of Prof'l Conduct R. 1.1 ("A lawyer shall provide competent representation to a client. Competent representation requires the legal knowledge, skill, thoroughness and preparation reasonably necessary for the representation.").

14. *See* ABA Model Rules of Prof'l Conduct R. 1.4(b) ("A lawyer shall explain a matter to the extent reasonably necessary to permit the client to make informed decisions regarding the representation.").

15. At least one state opinion concludes that it would be unethical to charge the client additional fees to complete the representation. North Carolina Bar, Formal Op. 10, *supra* note 7, states that the lawyer's duty of competent representation under Rule 1.1 requires the lawyer to complete the representation without additional fees if the matter requires more time than originally anticipated to satisfy the advertised service. This Committee does not agree that it is *per se* improper to charge additional fees for supplemental services not covered by the terms of the original offer.

could lead to a violation of the Model Rules if the result is excessive work that the lawyer cannot handle promptly, competently, and diligently.[16] The duty to provide competent representation and the duty to act with reasonable diligence and promptness require the lawyer to provide the necessary time and effort appropriate to each case accepted.

Properly Managing Advance Legal Fees

As noted above, deal offers are typically made through marketing organizations that collect payments and retain a portion of those payments for their advertising services. The remainder is transferred to the lawyer, generally in a lump sum, reflecting the number of deals sold without identification of individual purchasers. Whether this lump sum constitutes "legal fees ... paid in advance" within the meaning of Model Rule 1.15(c) depends on the nature of the deal.

If a lawyer offers a coupon deal, the purchase of a coupon merely establishes the discount applicable to the cost of future legal services. No legal fees are involved unless and until a client- lawyer relationship is formed, time is spent, and the discounted legal fees are collected directly by the lawyer. In other words, the funds that a marketing organization collects and forwards from the sale of coupon deals are not legal fees. Thus, the aggregate amount transmitted by the marketing organization from such sales may be deposited into the lawyer's general account. On the other hand, if a transaction is structured as a prepaid deal, then the money that a lawyer receives from the marketing organization constitutes advance legal fees, because the marketing organization collects all of the money to which the lawyer will be entitled for legal services that fall within the terms of the deal. Those advance legal fees need to be identified by purchaser's name and deposited into a trust account.[17] The lawyer who chooses to offer a prepaid deal must make appropriate arrangements with the marketing organization to obtain sufficient information about deal buyers in order to appropriately discharge all obligations associated with handling trust funds. Regardless of whether tracking deal buyers and accounting for prepaid fees may prove difficult when a lawyer uses a marketing organization, the lawyer is still responsible for properly handling advanced legal fees.

---

16. *See* ABA Model Rules of Prof'l Conduct R. 1.3 ("A lawyer shall act with reasonable diligence and promptness in representing a client.").

17. To avoid issues of improper handling of trust funds and fee sharing, a lawyer should be sure that any prepaid deal offer explains to the buyer what percentage is not a legal fee and will be retained by the marketing organization. The Committee does not agree that a lawyer always must return the entire amount of the purchase price, including any portion retained by the marketing organization, if legal services are not rendered for any reason whatsoever. *See* State Bar of Arizona, Formal Op. 13-01, *supra* note 7.

Additionally, deals may be purchased and then never used. So long as the lawyer has offered a coupon deal, the lawyer may retain the proceeds.[18] While some jurisdictions have concluded that retaining funds from an unredeemed deal constitutes an excessive fee under Rule 1.5, the Committee does not agree with these jurisdictions to the extent the lawyer has offered a coupon deal and explained as part of the offer that the cost of the coupon will not be refunded.[19] The Committee does agree that monies paid as part of a prepaid deal likely need to be refunded in order to avoid the Model Rules prohibition of unreasonable fees.[20]

In one jurisdiction, if a deal purchaser decides before the expiration of the deal that he or she does not want to be represented by the lawyer, the purchaser is entitled to discharge the lawyer and receive a full refund of the funds paid.[21] The Committee disagrees with this opinion to the extent the lawyer offers a coupon deal and properly explains as part of the offer that there is no right to obtain a refund of the purchase price of the coupon; in such circumstances, the coupon purchaser waives the right to compel a refund. On the other hand, if the purchaser of a prepaid deal decides, prior to the deal's expiration, that he or she does not want to proceed, the lawyer likely must refund unearned advanced fees to avoid the collection of unreasonable legal fees.[22]

Finally, in the event the lawyer cannot perform legal services in accordance with a deal, such as when a conflict of interest or other ethical impediment prevents representation, the duty to refrain from receipt of an unreasonable fee compels a full refund to the purchaser. This is true for both coupon and prepaid deals. The lawyer cannot avoid this obligation to make a refund by stating otherwise in the offer.

---

18. *See* New York State Bar Ass'n Comm. on Prof'l Ethics, Op. 897 (2011) (lawyer may retain coupon proceeds if buyer never seeks the discounted services).

19. *See* North Carolina Bar, Formal Op. 10, *supra* note 7; Maryland State Bar Ass'n Comm. on Ethics, Op. 2012-07, *supra* note 7. Rule 1.5 of the North Carolina Rules of Professional Conduct prohibits the charging of an "excessive" fee while the Model Rules and the Maryland Lawyers' Rules of Professional Conduct both prohibit the charging of an "unreasonable" fee. However, the Model Rules, the Maryland Rules of Professional Conduct, and the North Carolina Rules of Professional Conduct all use the same factors to determine whether a fee is unreasonable or excessive.

20. A refund might not be required in all circumstances. For example, the Committee can envision a deal that offers a reduced flat rate only for an initial consultation. If the overall cost were modest, and if the offer explained that there would be no refund except for situations of conflict or lawyer unavailability, an unreasonable fee would not arise and no refund would be required.

21. *See* New York State Bar Ass'n Comm. on Prof'l Ethics, Op. 897, *supra* note 18.

22. If the prepaid offer were for a simple service at a modest charge, along the lines of the initial consultation discussed at footnote 20, it is possible no refund would be required, provided proper and full disclosure of a no-refund policy had been made.

In those instances in which a lawyer must refund money from the purchase of a deal, e.g., the lawyer has a conflict and cannot render legal services, the lawyer must refund the entire amount paid, regardless of whether the lawyer is entitled to recoup that portion of the amount that was retained as an advertising fee by the marketing organization. The Committee bases this opinion on the fact that it would be unreasonable to withhold any portion of the amount paid by the purchaser if the lawyer is precluded from providing the proffered services through no fault of the purchaser. The lawyer cannot avoid this obligation to make a full refund by providing otherwise in the offer. On the other hand, if a lawyer is not obligated to give a refund but chooses to do so, e.g., a coupon purchaser has failed to use a coupon deal before it has expired, then the lawyer may choose to refund only the portion of the payment the lawyer received, provided this limitation has been clearly disclosed at the time of purchase.

Conclusion

Offering services through deal-of-the-day or group-coupon marketing programs presents a new way for lawyers to market their services and to provide consumers with legal assistance. Lawyers who make use of this form of advertising, however, must observe their ethical and professional obligations. The Committee believes that coupon deals can be structured to comply with the Model Rules. The Committee has identified numerous difficult issues associated with prepaid deals, especially how to properly manage payment of advance legal fees, and is less certain that prepaid deals can be structured to comply with all ethical and professional obligations under the Model Rules.

AMERICAN BAR ASSOCIATION

STANDING COMMITTEE ON ETHICS AND PROFESSIONAL RESPONSIBILITY

Formal Opinion 466 **April 24, 2014**

Lawyer Reviewing Jurors' Internet Presence

Unless limited by law or court order, a lawyer may review a juror's or potential juror's Internet presence, which may include postings by the juror or potential juror in advance of and during a trial, but a lawyer may not communicate directly or through another with a juror or potential juror.

A lawyer may not, either personally or through another, send an access request to a juror's electronic social media. An access request is a communication to a juror asking the juror for information that the juror has not made public and that would be the type of ex parte communication prohibited by Model Rule 3.5(b).

The fact that a juror or a potential juror may become aware that a lawyer is reviewing his Internet presence when a network setting notifies the juror of such does not constitute a communication from the lawyer in violation of Rule 3.5(b).

In the course of reviewing a juror's or potential juror's Internet presence, if a lawyer discovers evidence of juror or potential juror misconduct that is criminal or fraudulent, the lawyer must take reasonable remedial measures including, if necessary, disclosure to the tribunal.

The Committee has been asked whether a lawyer who represents a client in a matter that will be tried to a jury may review the jurors' or potential jurors'[1] presence on the Internet leading up to and during trial, and, if so, what ethical obligations the lawyer might have regarding information discovered during the review.

Juror Internet Presence

Jurors may and often will have an Internet presence through electronic social media or websites. General public access to such will vary. For example, many blogs, websites, and other electronic media are readily accessible by anyone who chooses to access them through the Internet. We will refer to these publicly accessible Internet media as "websites."

1. Unless there is reason to make a distinction, we will refer throughout this opinion to jurors as including both potential and prospective jurors and jurors who have been empaneled as members of a jury.

For the purposes of this opinion, Internet-based social media sites that readily allow account-owner restrictions on access will be referred to as "electronic social media" or "ESM." Examples of commonly used ESM at the time of this opinion include Facebook, MySpace, LinkedIn, and Twitter. Reference to a request to obtain access to another's ESM will be denoted as an "access request," and a person who creates and maintains ESM will be denoted as a "subscriber."

Depending on the privacy settings chosen by the ESM subscriber, some information posted on ESM sites might be available to the general public, making it similar to a website, while other information is available only to a fellow subscriber of a shared ESM service, or in some cases only to those whom the subscriber has granted access. Privacy settings allow the ESM subscriber to establish different degrees of protection for different categories of information, each of which can require specific permission to access. In general, a person who wishes to obtain access to these protected pages must send a request to the ESM subscriber asking for permission to do so. Access depends on the willingness of the subscriber to grant permission.[2]

This opinion addresses three levels of lawyer review of juror Internet presence:

1. passive lawyer review of a juror's website or ESM that is available without making an access request where the juror is unaware that a website or ESM has been reviewed;
2. active lawyer review where the lawyer requests access to the juror's ESM; and
3. passive lawyer review where the juror becomes aware through a website or ESM feature of the identity of the viewer;

Trial Management and Jury Instructions

There is a strong public interest in identifying jurors who might be tainted by improper bias or prejudice. There is a related and equally strong public policy in preventing jurors from being approached ex parte by the parties to the case or their agents. Lawyers need to know where the line should be drawn between properly investigating jurors and improperly communi-

2. The capabilities of ESM change frequently. The committee notes that this opinion does not address particular ESM capabilities that exist now or will exist in the future. For purposes of this opinion, key elements like the ability of a subscriber to control access to ESM or to identify third parties who review a subscriber's ESM are considered generically.

cating with them.[3] In today's Internet-saturated world, the line is increasingly blurred.

For this reason, we strongly encourage judges and lawyers to discuss the court's expectations concerning lawyers reviewing juror presence on the Internet. A court order, whether in the form of a local rule, a standing order, or a case management order in a particular matter, will, in addition to the applicable Rules of Professional Conduct, govern the conduct of counsel.

Equally important, judges should consider advising jurors during the orientation process that their backgrounds will be of interest to the litigants and that the lawyers in the case may investigate their backgrounds, including review of their ESM and websites.[4] If a judge believes it to be necessary, under the circumstances of a particular matter, to limit lawyers' review of juror websites and ESM, including on ESM networks where it is possible or likely that the jurors will be notified that their ESM is being viewed, the judge should formally instruct the lawyers in the case concerning the court's expectations.

Reviewing Juror Internet Presence

If there is no court order governing lawyers reviewing juror Internet presence, we look to the ABA Model Rules of Professional Conduct for relevant strictures and prohibitions. Model Rule 3.5 addresses communications with jurors before, during, and after trial, stating:

> A lawyer shall not:
>
> (a) seek to influence a judge, juror, prospective juror or other official by means prohibited by law;

---

3. While this Committee does not take a position on whether the standard of care for competent lawyer performance requires using Internet research to locate information about jurors that is relevant to the jury selection process, we are also mindful of the recent addition of Comment [8] to Model Rule 1.1. This comment explains that a lawyer "should keep abreast of changes in the law and its practice, including the benefits and risks associated with relevant technology." *See also* Johnson v. McCullough, 306 S.W.3d 551 (Mo. 2010) (lawyer must use "reasonable efforts" to find potential juror's litigation history in Case.net, Missouri's automated case management system); N. H. Bar Ass'n, Op. 2012-13/05 (lawyers "have a general duty to be aware of social media as a source of potentially useful information in litigation, to be competent to obtain that information directly or through an agent, and to know how to make effective use of that information in litigation"); Ass'n of the Bar of the City of N. Y. Comm. on Prof'l Ethics, Formal Op. 2012-2 ("Indeed, the standards of competence and diligence may require doing everything reasonably possible to learn about jurors who will sit in judgment on a case.").

4. Judges also may choose to work with local jury commissioners to ensure that jurors are advised during jury orientation that they may properly be investigated by lawyers in the case to which they are assigned. This investigation may include review of the potential juror's Internet presence.

(b) communicate ex parte with such a person during the proceeding unless authorized to do so by law or court order;
(c) communicate with a juror or prospective juror after discharge of the jury if:
  (1) the communication is prohibited by law or court order;
  (2) the juror has made known to the lawyer a desire not to communicate; or
  (3) the communication involves misrepresentation, coercion, duress or harassment . . .

Under Model Rule 3.5(b), a lawyer may not communicate with a potential juror leading up to trial or any juror during trial unless authorized by law or court order. *See, e.g., In re Holman*, 286 S.E.2d 148 (S.C. 1982) (communicating with member of jury selected for trial of lawyer's client was "serious crime" warranting disbarment).

A lawyer may not do through the acts of another what the lawyer is prohibited from doing directly. Model Rule 8.4(a). *See also In re Myers*, 584 S.E.2d 357 (S.C. 2003) (improper for prosecutor to have a lay member of his "jury selection team" phone venire member's home); *cf.* S.C. Ethics Op. 93-27 (1993) (lawyer "cannot avoid the proscription of the rule by using agents to communicate improperly" with prospective jurors).

Passive review of a juror's website or ESM, that is available without making an access request, and of which the juror is unaware, does not violate Rule 3.5(b). In the world outside of the Internet, a lawyer or another, acting on the lawyer's behalf, would not be engaging in an improper ex parte contact with a prospective juror by driving down the street where the prospective juror lives to observe the environs in order to glean publicly available information that could inform the lawyer's jury-selection decisions. The mere act of observing that which is open to the public would not constitute a communicative act that violates Rule 3.5(b).[5]

5. Or. State Bar Ass'n, Formal Op. 2013-189 ("Lawyer may access publicly available information [about juror, witness, and opposing party] on social networking website"); N.Y. Cnty. Lawyers Ass'n, Formal Op. 743 (2011) (lawyer may search juror's "publicly available" webpages and ESM); Ass'n of the Bar of the City of N.Y. Comm. on Prof'l Ethics, *supra* note 3 (lawyer may use social media websites to research jurors); Ky. Bar Ass'n, Op. E-434 (2012) ("If the site is 'public,' and accessible to all, then there does not appear to be any ethics issue."). *See also* N.Y. State Bar Ass'n, Advisory Op. 843 (2010) ("A lawyer representing a client in pending litigation may access the public pages of another party's social networking website (such as Facebook or MySpace) for the purpose of obtaining possible impeachment material for use in the litigation"); Or. State Bar Ass'n, Formal Op. 2005-164 ("Accessing an adversary's public Web [sic] site is no different from reading a magazine or purchasing a book written by that adversary"); N.H. Bar Ass'n, *supra* note 3 (viewing a Facebook user's page or following on Twitter is not communication if pages are open to all members of that social media site); San Diego Cnty. Bar Legal Ethics Op. 2011-2 (opposing party's public Facebook page may be viewed by lawyer).

It is the view of the Committee that a lawyer may not personally, or through another, send an access request to a juror. An access request is an active review of the juror's electronic social media by the lawyer and is a communication to a juror asking the juror for information that the juror has not made public. This would be the type of ex parte communication prohibited by Model Rule 3.5(b).[6] This would be akin to driving down the juror's street, stopping the car, getting out, and asking the juror for permission to look inside the juror's house because the lawyer cannot see enough when just driving past.

Some ESM networks have a feature that allows the juror to identify fellow members of the same ESM network who have passively viewed the juror's ESM. The details of how this is accomplished will vary from network to network, but the key feature that is relevant to this opinion is that the juror-subscriber is able to determine not only that his ESM is being viewed, but also the identity of the viewer. This capability may be beyond the control of the reviewer because the notice to the subscriber is generated by the ESM network and is based on the identity profile of the subscriber who is a fellow member of the same ESM network.

Two recent ethics opinions have addressed this issue. The Association of the Bar of the City of New York Committee on Professional Ethics, in Formal Opinion 2012-2[7], concluded that a network-generated notice to the juror that the lawyer has reviewed the juror's social media was a communication from the lawyer to a juror, albeit an indirect one generated by the ESM network. Citing the definition of "communication" from Black's Law Dictionary (9th ed.) and other authority, the opinion concluded that the message identifying the ESM viewer was a communication because it entailed "the process of bringing an idea, information or knowledge to another's perception—including the fact that they have been researched." While the ABCNY Committee

6. *See* Or. State Bar Ass'n, *supra* note 5, fn. 2, (a "lawyer may not send a request to a juror to access non-public personal information on a social networking website, nor may a lawyer ask an agent to do so"); N.Y. Cnty. Lawyers Ass'n, *supra* note 5 ("Significant ethical concerns would be raised by sending a 'friend request,' attempting to connect via LinkedIn.com, signing up for an RSS feed for a juror's blog, or 'following' a juror's Twitter account"); Ass'n of the Bar of the City of N.Y. Comm. on Prof'l Ethics, *supra* note 3 (lawyer may not chat, message or send a "friend request" to a juror); Conn. Bar Ass'n, Informal Op. 2011-4 (friend request is a communication); Mo. Bar Ass'n, Informal Op. 2009-0003 (friend request is a communication pursuant to Rule 4.2). *But see* N.H. Bar Ass'n, *supra* note 3 (lawyer may request access to witness's private ESM, but request must "correctly identify the lawyer . . . [and] . . . inform the witness of the lawyer's involvement" in the matter); Phila. Bar Ass'n, Advisory Op. 2009-02 (lawyer may not use deception to secure access to witness's private ESM, but may ask the witness "forthrightly" for access).

7. Ass'n of the Bar of the City of N.Y. Comm. on Prof'l Ethics, *supra*, note 3.

found that the communication would "constitute a prohibited communication if the attorney was aware that her actions" would send such a notice, the Committee took "no position on whether an inadvertent communication would be a violation of the Rules." The New York County Lawyers' Association Committee on Professional Ethics in Formal Opinion 743 agreed with ABCNY's opinion and went further explaining, "If a juror becomes aware of an attorney's efforts to see the juror's profiles on websites, the contact may well consist of an impermissible communication, as it might tend to influence the juror's conduct with respect to the trial."[8]

This Committee concludes that a lawyer who uses a shared ESM platform to passively view juror ESM under these circumstances does not communicate with the juror. The lawyer is not communicating with the juror; the ESM service is communicating with the juror based on a technical feature of the ESM. This is akin to a neighbor's recognizing a lawyer's car driving down the juror's street and telling the juror that the lawyer had been seen driving down the street.

Discussion by the trial judge of the likely practice of trial lawyers reviewing juror ESM during the jury orientation process will dispel any juror misperception that a lawyer is acting improperly merely by viewing what the juror has revealed to all others on the same network.

While this Committee concludes that ESM-generated notice to a juror that a lawyer has reviewed the juror's information is not communication from the lawyer to the juror, the Committee does make two additional recommendations to lawyers who decide to review juror social media. First, the Committee suggests that lawyers be aware of these automatic, subscriber-notification features. By accepting the terms of use, the subscriber- notification feature is not secret. As indicated by Rule 1.1, Comment 8, it is important for a lawyer to be current with technology. While many people simply click their agreement to the terms and conditions for use of an ESM network, a lawyer who uses an ESM network in his practice should review the terms and conditions, including privacy features—which change frequently—prior to using such a network. And, as noted above, jurisdictions differ on issues that arise when a lawyer uses social media in his practice.

Second, Rule 4.4(a) prohibits lawyers from actions "that have no substantial purpose other than to embarrass, delay, or burden a third person . . ." Lawyers who review juror social media should ensure that their review is purposeful and not crafted to embarrass, delay, or burden the juror or the proceeding.

8. N.Y. Cnty. Lawyers' Ass'n, *supra* note 5.

Discovery of Juror Misconduct

Increasingly, courts are instructing jurors in very explicit terms about the prohibition against using ESM to communicate about their jury service or the pending case and the prohibition against conducting personal research about the matter, including research on the Internet. These warnings come because jurors have discussed trial issues on ESM, solicited access to witnesses and litigants on ESM, not revealed relevant ESM connections during jury selection, and conducted personal research on the trial issues using the Internet.[9]

In 2009, the Court Administration and Case Management Committee of the Judicial Conference of the United States recommended a model jury instruction that is very specific about juror use of social media, mentioning many of the popular social media by name.[10] The recommended instruction states in part:

> I know that many of you use cell phones, Blackberries, the internet and other tools of technology. You also must not talk to anyone at any time about this case or use these tools to communicate electronically with anyone about the case . . . You may not communicate with anyone about the case on your cell phone, through e- mail, Blackberry, iPhone, text messaging, or on Twitter, through any blog or website, including Facebook, Google+, My Space, LinkedIn, or YouTube. . . . I expect you will inform me as soon as you become aware of another juror's violation of these instructions.

These same jury instructions were provided by both a federal district court and state criminal court judge during a three-year study on juries and social media. Their research found that "jury instructions are the most effective tool to mitigate the risk of juror misconduct through social media."[11] As a result, the authors recommend jury instruction on social media "early and often" and daily in lengthy trials.[12]

---

9. For a review of recent cases in which a juror used ESM to discuss trial proceedings and/or used the Internet to conduct private research, read Hon. Amy J. St. Eve et al., *More from the #Jury Box: The Latest on Juries and Social Media*, 12 Duke Law & Technology Review no. 1, 69-78 (2014), *available at* http://scholarship.law.duke.edu/cgi/viewcontent.cgi?article=1247&context=dltr.

10. Judicial Conference Committee on Court Administration and Case Management, *Proposed Model Jury Instructions: The Use of Electronic Technology to Conduct Research on or Communicate about a Case*, USCourts.gov (June 2012), http://www.uscourts.gov/uscourts/News/2012/jury-instructions.pdf.

11. *Id.* at 66.

12. *Id.* at 87.

Analyzing the approximately 8% of the jurors who admitted to being "tempted" to communicate about the case using social media, the judges found that the jurors chose not to talk or write about the case because of the specific jury instruction not to do so.

While juror misconduct via social media itself is not the subject of this Opinion, lawyers reviewing juror websites and ESM may become aware of misconduct. Model Rule 3.3 and its legislative history make it clear that a lawyer has an obligation to take remedial measures including, if necessary, informing the tribunal when the lawyer discovers that a juror has engaged in criminal or fraudulent conduct related to the proceeding. But the history is muddled concerning whether a lawyer has an affirmative obligation to act upon learning that a juror has engaged in improper conduct that falls short of being criminal or fraudulent.

Rule 3.3 was amended in 2002, pursuant to the ABA Ethics 2000 Commission's proposal, to expand on a lawyer's previous obligation to protect a tribunal from criminal or fraudulent conduct by the lawyer's client to also include such conduct by any person.[13]

Model Rule 3.3(b) reads:

> (b) A lawyer who represents a client in an adjudicative proceeding and who knows that a person intends to engage, is engaging or has engaged in criminal or fraudulent conduct related to the proceeding shall take reasonable remedial measures including, if necessary, disclosure to the tribunal.

Comment [12] to Rule 3.3 provides:

> Lawyers have a special obligation to protect a tribunal against criminal or fraudulent conduct that undermines the integrity of the adjudicative process, such as bribing, intimidating or otherwise unlawfully communicating with a witness, juror, court official or other participant in the proceeding, unlawfully destroying or concealing documents or other evidence or failing to disclose information to the tribunal when required by law to do so. Thus, paragraph (b)

13. Ethics 2000 Commission, *Model Rule 3.3: Candor Toward the Tribunal*, American Bar Association, http://www.americanbar.org/groups/professional_responsibility/policy/ethics_2000_commission/e2k_rule33.html (last visited Apr. 18, 2014).

> requires a lawyer to take reasonable remedial measures, including disclosure if necessary, whenever the lawyer knows that a person, including the lawyer's client, intends to engage, is engaging or has engaged in criminal or fraudulent conduct related to the proceeding.

Part of Ethics 2000's stated intent when it amended Model Rule 3.3 was to incorporate provisions from Canon 7 of the ABA Model Code of Professional Responsibility (Model Code) that had placed an affirmative duty upon a lawyer to notify the court upon learning of juror misconduct:

> This new provision incorporates the substance of current paragraph (a)(2), as well as ABA Model Code of Professional Responsibility DR 7-102(B)(2) ("A lawyer who receives information clearly establishing that a person other than the client has perpetrated a fraud upon a tribunal shall promptly reveal the fraud to the tribunal") and DR 7-108(G) ("A lawyer shall reveal promptly to the court improper conduct by a venireperson or juror, or by another toward a venireperson or juror or a member of the venireperson's or juror's family, of which the lawyer has knowledge"). *Reporter's Explanation of Changes, Model Rule 3.3.*[14]

However, the intent of the Ethics 2000 Commission expressed above to incorporate the substance of DR 7-108(G) in its new subsection (b) of Model Rule 3.3 was never carried out. Under the Model Code's DR 7-108(G), a lawyer knowing of "improper conduct" by a juror or venireperson was required to report the matter to the tribunal. Under Rule 3.3(b), the lawyer's obligation to act arises only when the juror or venireperson engages in conduct that is *fraudulent or criminal.*[15] While improper conduct was not defined in the Model Code, it clearly imposes a broader duty to take remedial action than exists under the Model Rules. The Committee is constrained to provide guidance based upon the language of Rule 3.3(b) rather than any expressions of intent in the legislative history of that rule.

14. Ethics 2000 Commission, *Model Rule 3.3 Reporter's Explanation of Changes*, American Bar Association, http://www.americanbar.org/groups/professional_responsibility/policy/ethics_2000_commission/e2k_rule33rem.html (last visited Apr. 18, 2014).

15. Compare Model Rules of Prof'l Conduct R. 3.3(b) (2002) to N.Y. Rules of Prof'l Conduct R. 3.5(d) (2013) ("a lawyer shall reveal promptly to the court improper conduct by a member of the venire or a juror....").

By passively viewing juror Internet presence, a lawyer may become aware of a juror's conduct that is criminal or fraudulent, in which case, Model Rule 3.3(b) requires the lawyer to take remedial measures including, if necessary, reporting the matter to the court. But the lawyer may also become aware of juror conduct that violates court instructions to the jury but does not rise to the level of criminal or fraudulent conduct, and Rule 3.3(b) does not prescribe what the lawyer must do in that situation. While considerations of questions of law are outside the scope of the Committee's authority, applicable law might treat such juror activity as conduct that triggers a lawyer's duty to take remedial action including, if necessary, reporting the juror's conduct to the court under current Model Rule 3.3(b).[16]

While any Internet postings about the case by a juror during trial may violate court instructions, the obligation of a lawyer to take action will depend on the lawyer's assessment of those postings in light of court instructions and the elements of the crime of contempt or other applicable criminal statutes. For example, innocuous postings about jury service, such as the quality of the food served at lunch, may be contrary to judicial instructions, but fall short of conduct that would warrant the extreme response of finding a juror in criminal contempt. A lawyer's affirmative duty to act is triggered only when the juror's known conduct is criminal or fraudulent, including conduct that is criminally contemptuous of court instructions. The materiality of juror Internet communications to the integrity of the trial will likely be a consideration in determining whether the juror has acted criminally or fraudulently. The remedial duty flowing from known criminal or fraudulent juror conduct is triggered by knowledge of the conduct and is not preempted by a lawyer's belief that the court will not choose to address the conduct as a crime or fraud.

Conclusion

In sum, a lawyer may passively review a juror's public presence on the Internet, but may not communicate with a juror. Requesting access to a private area on a juror's ESM is communication within this framework.

16. *See, e.g.*, U.S. v. Juror Number One, 866 F.Supp.2d 442 (E.D. Pa. 2011) (failure to follow jury instructions and emailing other jurors about case results in criminal contempt). The use of criminal contempt remedies for disregarding jury instructions is not confined to improper juror use of ESM. U.S. v. Rowe, 906 F.2d 654 (11th Cir. 1990) (juror held in contempt, fined, and dismissed from jury for violating court order to refrain from discussing the case with other jurors until after jury instructions delivered).

The fact that a juror or a potential juror may become aware that the lawyer is reviewing his Internet presence when an ESM network setting notifies the juror of such review does not constitute a communication from the lawyer in violation of Rule 3.5(b).

If a lawyer discovers criminal or fraudulent conduct by a juror related to the proceeding, the lawyer must take reasonable remedial measures including, if necessary, disclosure to the tribunal.

AMERICAN BAR ASSOCIATION
STANDING COMMITTEE ON ETHICS AND PROFESSIONAL RESPONSIBILITY

Formal Opinion 467 **September 8, 2014**

Managerial and Supervisory Obligations of Prosecutors Under Rules 5.1 and 5.3

Model Rules 5.1 and 5.3 require lawyers with managerial authority and supervisory lawyers, including prosecutors, to make "reasonable efforts to ensure" that all lawyers and nonlawyers in their offices conform to the Model Rules. Prosecutors with managerial authority must adopt reasonable policies and procedures to achieve these goals. Prosecutors with direct supervisory authority must make reasonable efforts to ensure that the lawyers and nonlawyers they supervise comply with the Rules. Where prosecutors have both managerial and direct supervisory authority, they may, depending on the circumstances, be required to fulfill both sets of obligations. The particular measures that managerial and supervisory prosecutors must implement to comply with these rules will depend on a variety of factors, including the size and structure of their offices.

A. Introduction

Prosecutors have special duties under the Model Rules of Professional Conduct. They have "the responsibility of a minister of justice and not simply that of an advocate."[1] They must "refrain from prosecuting a charge that [they know] is not supported by probable cause."[2] They must "make reasonable efforts to assure that the accused has been advised of the right to, and the procedure for obtaining, counsel and has been given reasonable opportunity to obtain counsel."[3] They must "make timely disclosure to the defense" of exculpatory and mitigating evidence.[4] In short, and in words long ago written by the Supreme Court in *Berger v. U.S.*,[5] a prosecutor's duties are "not of an ordinary party to a controversy, but of a sovereignty whose obligation

1. ABA Model Rules of Prof'l Conduct R. 3.8 cmt. [1].
2. ABA Model Rules of Prof'l Conduct R. 3.8(a).
3. ABA Model Rules of Prof'l Conduct R. 3.8(b).
4. ABA Model Rules of Prof'l Conduct R. 3.8(d). For additional special duties of prosecutors, see also ABA Model Rules of Prof'l Conduct R. 3.8(c)-(h) and cmts. [3]-[9].
5. Berger v. United States, 295 U.S. 78 (1935).

to govern impartially is as compelling as its obligation to govern at all; and whose interest, therefore, in a criminal prosecution is not that it shall win a case, but that justice shall be done."[6]

We believe that most prosecutors know and follow the rules of professional conduct. Indeed, the laudable efforts of such prosecutors have provided good examples, cited throughout this opinion. But there are prosecutors who do violate the rules, and for all prosecutors there are special challenges and obligations. This opinion provides guidance on the special challenges and obligations of prosecutors with managerial and supervisory responsibility.[7]

B. ABA Model Rules of Professional Conduct 5.1 and 5.3 Apply to Prosecutors

Rules 5.1 and 5.3 address obligations of lawyers with managerial authority (hereinafter sometimes referred to as "managers") and supervisory lawyers within a "firm" or a "law firm." Rule 1.0(c) defines "firm" or "law firm" to include "lawyers employed in a legal services organization or the legal department of a corporation or other organization." Comment [3] makes clear that government organizations are included.[8] The comments to Rule 5.1 also specifically reference government agencies.[9] Prosecutors' offices are *government* organizations.

Rule 3.8, which specifies the "Special Responsibilities of Prosecutors," also makes clear that prosecutors have supervisory obligations under Rules 5.1 and 5.3. Comment [6] to Rule 3.8 reads, "Like other lawyers, prosecutors

---

6. *Id.* at 88. *See also* ABA Comm. on Ethics & Prof'l Responsibility, Formal Op. 09-454 at fn. 9 ("References in U.S. judicial decisions to the prosecutor's obligation to seek justice date back more than 150 years.") (citations omitted). A "prosecutor" for purposes of this opinion is a lawyer employed by a government agency whose primary responsibility involves the investigation and prosecution of criminal cases and related matters. Where a prosecutor's duties also embrace civil authority, this opinion also applies to that sphere of their work. Federal prosecutors are covered by state ethics rules under the McDade Amendment, 28 U.S.C. §530B.

7. Of course all lawyers--e.g., lawyers in private practice, in public defender offices, and in other state and federal agencies--have supervisory obligations under Rules 5.1 and 5.3. We leave for another day a specific discussion of how Rules 5.1 and 5.3 must be implemented by them. The general obligations described in this opinion with respect to prosecutors, however, apply to lawyers in those offices as well.

8. ABA Model Rules of Prof'l Conduct R. 1.0 cmt. [3] ("[w]ith respect to the law department of an organization, *including the government*, there is ordinarily no question that the members of the department constitute a firm within the meaning of the Rules") (emphasis added).

9. ABA Model Rules of Prof'l Conduct R. 5.1 cmt. [1] ("[p]aragraph (a) [of Rule 5.1] applies to lawyers who have managerial authority over the professional work of a firm. . . . This includes . . . . lawyers having comparable managerial authority in a . . . government agency. . . ").

are subject to Rules 5.1 and 5.3, which relate to responsibilities regarding lawyers and nonlawyers who work for or are associated with the lawyer's office."[10] Finally, ABA Formal Opinion 09-454 emphasizes that these obligations apply to prosecutors: "Any supervisory lawyer in the prosecutor's office and those lawyers with managerial responsibility are obligated to ensure that subordinate lawyers comply with all their legal and ethical obligations."[11]

Formal Opinion 09-454 adds, "[S]upervisors who directly oversee trial prosecutors must make reasonable efforts to ensure that those under their direct supervision meet their ethical obligations of disclosure, and are subject to discipline for ordering, ratifying or knowingly failing to correct discovery violations."[12]

C. Who Has Responsibility Under ABA Model Rules 5.1 and 5.3 in a Prosecutor's Office?

Rules 5.1 and 5.3 set forth three types of responsibility for the conduct of lawyers and nonlawyers "employed or retained by or associated with a lawyer."[13] Paragraph (a) addresses lawyers "with managerial authority."[14] Paragraph (b) pertains to lawyers "having direct supervisory authority over another lawyer" or "having direct supervisory authority over the nonlawyer."[15] Paragraph (c) applies to lawyers who either (i) order or ratify the conduct of another, or (ii) have managerial authority or direct supervisory authority, know of the conduct at a time when its consequences can be mitigated, and fail to take reasonable remedial action.[16] We address each below.

1. Managerial Responsibility

Under paragraph (a), "managerial" lawyers "shall make reasonable efforts to ensure that [their organization] has in effect measures giving reason-

10. Comment [6] to Rule 3.8 gives examples: "Paragraph (f) [of 3.8] reminds the prosecutor of the importance of these [supervisory] obligations in connection with the unique dangers of improper extrajudicial statements in a criminal case." Paragraph 3.8(f) also "requires a prosecutor to exercise reasonable care to prevent persons assisting or associated with the prosecutor from making improper extrajudicial statements, even when such persons are not under the direct supervision of the prosecutor."

11. Formal Op. 09-454, *supra* note 6, at 8 (citing Rules 5.1(a) and (b)). See also the opening summary of Formal Op. 09-454: "Supervisory personnel in a prosecutor's office must take reasonable steps under Rule 5.1 to ensure that all lawyers in the office comply with their disclosure obligation."

12. Formal Op. 09-454, *supra* note 6, at 8 (citing Rules 5.1(b) and (c)).

13. ABA Model Rules of Prof'l Conduct R. 5.1(a) (over lawyers) & R. 5.3(a) (over nonlawyers). With respect to nonlawyers, the obligation is to make sure that the nonlawyer's "conduct is compatible with the professional obligations of the lawyer."

14. ABA Model Rules of Prof'l Conduct R. 5.1(a) & 5.3(a).

15. ABA Model Rules of Prof'l Conduct R. 5.1(b) & 5.3(b).

16. ABA Model Rules of Prof'l Conduct R. 5.1(c) & 5.3(c).

able assurance that all lawyers in the [organization] conform to the Rules of Professional Conduct." Managerial lawyers include "members of a partnership, the shareholders in a law firm organized as a professional corporation and [other lawyers] having comparable managerial authority."[17] This group also includes "lawyers who have intermediate managerial responsibilities."[18] Rule 5.3(a) imposes a corresponding obligation with respect to nonlawyers "employed or retained or associated" with the office.

In a prosecutor's office, managerial lawyers are the top prosecutors and all other prosecutors with managerial or executive functions in the office. This group would include, for example, the District or County or U.S. Attorney him or herself, as well as executive staff, bureau or unit heads, and similarly positioned others who, among other duties, make policies and set procedures for the office as a whole or for individual units. As part of their functions, these individuals may also be direct supervisors under 5.1(b) and 5.3(b) discussed below—depending on the facts and circumstances—but they have overarching special duties under Rules 5.1(a) and 5.3(a).[19]

Managers must make "reasonable efforts" to ensure compliance with the Model Rules of Professional Conduct by all lawyers in the office, including other lawyers with comparable managerial authority. As discussed further in this opinion, "these efforts can take many forms, so long as they are reasonably calculated to eliminate or inhibit violations [of the Rules]."[20]

2. Supervisory Responsibility

Under Rule 5.1(b) "[a] lawyer having direct supervisory authority over another lawyer shall make reasonable efforts to ensure that the other lawyer conforms to the Rules of Professional Conduct." Under Rule 5.3(b) "[a] lawyer having direct supervisory authority over [a] nonlawyer shall make reasonable efforts to ensure that the person's conduct is compatible with the professional obligations of the lawyer." This category "applies to lawyers who have supervisory authority over the work of other lawyers [and nonlawyers] in the [office]" regardless of their status in the organization.

In a prosecutor's office, a "supervisor" is a lawyer who—regardless of his or her position or title in the office hierarchy—directly supervises the

17. ABA Model Rules of Prof'l Conduct R. 5.1 cmt. [1].

18. *Id.*

19. *See* Geoffrey C. Hazard, W. William Hodes & Peter R. Jarvis, The Law of Lawyering §42.4 (3rd Ed., Supp. 2010) [hereinafter Hazard & Hodes] (partners and other managers are "'supervisory' lawyers *per se*"); Restatement of the Law Governing Lawyers (3rd Ed.) §11, at 112 (managerial lawyers have "general supervisory" duties over lawyers and nonlawyers).

20. Hazard & Hodes, *supra* note 19, §42.4.

work of another prosecutor in a particular matter, proceeding, inquiry or other event or series of events involving a case. "Even if a lawyer is not a partner or other general manager, he or she may have direct supervisory authority over another lawyer."[21]

Further, a manager within the meaning of paragraph (a) can also be a supervisor within the meaning of paragraph (b). For example, a unit or bureau chief whose job description consists mainly or principally of executive or managerial functions may also directly supervise individual prosecutors in any proceeding, application, inquiry, investigation, trial, appeal, or other matter. When managers function as direct supervisors, they have obligations under paragraph (b) as well.

The key to responsibility under paragraph (b) is the relationship between the two lawyers in the matter. The supervisory authority "need not be over the entirety of the second lawyer's practice. . . [5.1(b)] would apply to direct supervision in a particular case, to a senior or mid-level [lawyer] with supervisory authority over a junior [lawyer's] work in that or a series of cases, or to one partner [or manager] who has been given supervisory authority over another partner [or manager's] work in a case or practice area."[22]

Finally paragraphs (a) and (b) impose some overlapping duties. For, example, a direct supervisor "has the same responsibility as a partner or manager to assure compliance with the ethical rules by those lawyers under her direct supervisory authority."[23] In fact, as noted in G. Hazard, W. Hodes & P. Jarvis, *The Law of Lawyering* (3rd Ed., 2010 Supplement), Rule 5.1(b) "*is essentially identical to Rule 5.1(a),* except that it applies to all lawyers who have 'direct supervisory authority over another lawyer,' whether or not they are partners or managers or other partner- equivalents" and whatever their practice setting.[24] And, "Rule 5.1(b), like Rule 5.1(a), can require proactive, as distinct from merely reactive or passive, measures."[25]

---

21. Ronald D. Rotunda & John S. Dzienkowski, Legal Ethics: The Lawyer's Deskbook on Professional Responsibility § 5.1-2(b), at 1009 (2014) [hereinafter Rotunda & Dzienkowski] (citing Rule 5.1(b)).

22. Hazard & Hodes, *supra* note 19, §42.5. *See also* ABA Model Rules of Prof'l Conduct R. 5.1 cmt. [5] ("Whether a lawyer has supervisory authority in particular circumstances is a question of fact. Partners and lawyers with comparable authority have at least indirect responsibility for all work being done by the firm, while a partner or manager in charge of a particular matter ordinarily also has supervisory responsibility for the work of other firm lawyers engaged in the matter.").

23. Rotunda & Dzienkowski, *supra* note 21, §5.1-2(b), at 1009.

24. Hazard & Hodes, *supra* note 19, §42.5 (emphasis added).

25. *Id.*

3. Responsibility for Another's Conduct Under ABA Model Rules 5.1(c) and 5.3(c)

Rules 5.1(c) and 5.3(c) make a lawyer responsible for another lawyer's or a nonlawyer's conduct if the lawyer "orders or, with knowledge of the specific conduct, ratifies the conduct involved" or if "the lawyer is a partner or has comparable managerial authority in the [office] where the other lawyer practices [or the nonlawyer is employed], or has direct supervisory authority of the other lawyer [or nonlawyer], and knows of the conduct at a time when its consequences can be avoided or mitigated but fails to take reasonable remedial action."[26]

These obligations supplement the obligations of managers and supervisors under paragraphs (a) and (b), even though they are not directed at supervisors and managers alone. Indeed, the obligations set forth in Rules 5.1(c)(1) and 5.3(c)(1) apply regardless of whether the ordering or ratifying lawyer is a manager or a direct supervisor. But it is important to make clear—as we do here—that a lawyer who is a manager or supervisor may be responsible under Rules 5.1(c) and 5.3(c) even though he or she has no formal or structural relationship to the misbehaving lawyer or nonlawyer.[27]

Rules 5.1(c)(2) and 5.3(c)(2) also impose a duty to avoid or mitigate the consequences of improper conduct if there is an opportunity to do so.[28] A lawyer who is "a partner or has comparable managerial authority . . . or has direct supervisory authority over the other lawyer [or non-lawyer] and knows of [misconduct] at a time when its consequences can be avoided or mitigated" must take "reasonable remedial action."[29]

What constitutes "reasonable remedial action" will depend on the circumstances, but in any event requires "prevention of avoidable consequences" of the misconduct if the manager or supervisor learns of the mis-

---

26. ABA Model Rules of Prof'l Conduct R. 5.1(c) & R. 5.3(c).

27. Restatement of the Law Governing Lawyers, *supra* note 19, §11, at 110 (the obligation of a partner or managerial lawyer to take remedial action as described in 5.1(c) "attaches even if [the partner or managerial lawyer] has no direct supervisory authority over the other lawyer"). *See also* Hazard & Hodes *supra* note 19 §42.6 ("[P]artners and those with comparable managerial authority cannot rely upon the fact that they have, or had, no direct responsibility for or supervisory authority over the lawyer engaged in wrongdoing. Partner status, equivalent managerial status, and direct supervisory authority all equally trigger a responsibility to take remedial action under Rule 5.1(c)(2)"). Further, "most violations of [(c)(1) will] also constitute violations of Rule 8.4(a)"). Hazard & Hodes, *supra* note 19, §42.6. Model Rule 8.4(a) provides that it is "professional misconduct for a lawyer to violate or attempt to violate the Rules of Professional Conduct, knowingly assist or induce another to do so, or do so through the acts of another."

28. *See* ABA Model Rules of Prof'l Conduct R. 5.1(c)(1)-(2) & 5.3(c)(1)-(2). *See also* Hazard & Hodes, *supra* note 19, §42.6.

29. *Id.*

conduct when that can be achieved.[30] Steps to avoid future similar acts may be important for other reasons, but Rules 5.1(c)(2) and 5.3(c)(2) require steps that look back — that will "remedy or mitigate the consequences of [a] violation" that has already occurred. In the case of prosecutors, the immediate turnover of material to the defense might be required.[31] In other instances, reporting the conduct to disciplinary authorities might be required.[32] But the obligation to take reasonable remedial steps "extends to all known violations"—not only those covered by an applicable reporting obligation[33]—and should, in some recognizable measure, remedy or mitigate the consequences of misconduct that has occurred.

D. Background: The Need for Guidance

In recent years, reports, court opinions, and other authorities have drawn attention to prosecutorial misconduct—notwithstanding the many excellent prosecutors who scrupulously follow or exceed the mandates of the Rules of Professional Conduct. These reports, opinions and authorities suggest a need for more guidance.[34] For example, in *Connick v. Thompson*,[35] the Supreme Court reversed a $14 million judgment awarded against the New Orleans Parish District Attorney's Office in favor of John Thompson, an innocent man who spent 18 years in prison—14 of them on death row—because pros-

30. *See, e.g.*, ABA Model Rules of Prof'l Conduct R. 5.1 cmt. [5] ("[a]ppropriate remedial action by a partner or managing lawyer would depend on the immediacy of that lawyer's involvement and the seriousness of the misconduct. A supervisor is required to intervene to prevent avoidable consequences of misconduct if the supervisor knows that the misconduct occurred. Thus if a supervising lawyer knows that a subordinate misrepresented a matter to an opposing party in negotiation, the supervisor as well as the subordinate has a duty to correct the resulting misapprehension"). *See also*, Hazard & Hodes, *supra* note 19, §42.6.

31. *In re* Myers, 584 S.E.2d 357, 362 (S.C. 2003) (Solicitor (a supervising or managerial prosecutor) violated Rule 5.1(c)'s obligation to remediate when he failed to notify the defense lawyer about improper eavesdropping by his subordinates immediately upon learning of the misconduct).

32. Restatement of the Law Governing Lawyers, *supra* note 19, §11 cmt. e.

33. *Id.*

34. *See, e.g.*, Brad Heath & Kevin McCoy, *Prosecutors' Conduct Can Tip Justice Scales*, USA TODAY (September 23, 2010), http://usatoday30.usatoday.com/news/washington/judicial/2010-09-22-federal-prosecutors-reform_N.htm; Joaquin Sapien, *Out of Order: When Prosecutors Cross The Line*, ProPublica, http://www.propublica.org/series/out-of-order (last visited July 6, 2014); Kathleen M. Ridolfi & Maurice Possley, Preventable Error: A Report on Prosecutorial Misconduct in California 1997-2009 (2010), *available at* http://www.veritasinitiative.org/downloads/ProsecutorialMisconduct_Exec_Sum.pdf. *See also* United States v. Olsen, 737 F.3d 625 (9th Cir. 2013) (denying petition for rehearing en banc, Kozinski, Pregerson, Reinhardt, Thomas, and Watford dissenting, writing, "There is an epidemic of *Brady* violations abroad in the land.").

35. Connick v. Thompson, 131 S.Ct. 1350 (2011).

ecutors withheld exculpatory evidence. The majority opinion rejected Mr. Thompson's theory of liability based on 42 U.S.C. §1983,[36] and did not address the Rules. But the opinions in *Connick*—both majority and dissenting—document events that demonstrate the need for guidance on the managerial and supervisory obligations of prosecutors under the Rules of Professional Conduct. And, only one year later in *Smith v. Cain*,[37] the Supreme Court reversed a conviction for *Brady* violations by the same office.[38]

In 2013 the Supreme Court of Oklahoma disciplined a former Assistant District Attorney for the Oklahoma County District Attorney's Office and criticized the District Attorney's office for a lack of managerial and supervisory effectiveness.[39] The Court said:

> We must recognize that the [Assistant District Attorney] was acting under the direction, supervision, and policies of the then elected District Attorney. Responsibility for the respondent's conduct and trial tactics falls partially to the District Attorney as the chief administrator of the office.[40]

The New Orleans and Oklahoma examples alone would justify examination of the obligations of managerial and supervising prosecutors under Rules 5.1 and 5.3. But the frequency of prosecutorial misconduct nationwide documented by, *inter alia,* opinions in criminal cases and disciplinary proceedings reported in the last fifteen years, also underscores this need. These

36. "Thompson alleged that Connick had failed to train his prosecutors adequately about their duty to produce exculpatory evidence and that the lack of training had caused [the District Attorney's Office to fail to disclose certain evidence to Thompson]." *Id.* at 1355. *See* 42 U.S.C. §1983 (1996) provides in relevant part: "Every person who, under color of any statute, ordinance, regulation, custom, or usage, of any State . . . subjects, or causes to be subjected, any citizen of the United States or other person within the jurisdiction thereof to the deprivation of any rights, privileges, or immunities secured by the Constitution and laws, shall be liable to the party injured in an action at law, suit in equity, or other proper proceeding for redress. . . ."

37. Smith v. Cain, 132 S.Ct. 627 (2012) (reversing a murder conviction for *Brady* violation by the New Orleans Parish District Attorney's Office).

38. Brady v. Maryland, 373 U.S. 83 (1963).

39. State ex rel. Oklahoma Bar Ass'n v. Miller, 309 P.3d 108 (Okla. 2013) (assistant prosecutor suspended for 180 days for violations of, *inter alia,* Rules 8.4, 3.8 & 3.4). The Tenth Circuit has also expressed concern about prosecutorial misconduct in the Oklahoma County District Attorney's office. *See* Le v. Mullin, 311 F.3d 1002, 1029 (2002) ("While it is true that any prosecutor will have his share of trial-outcome challenges, over the last fifteen years, the Oklahoma County District Attorney's office has been cited for actions deemed improper, 'egregiously improper,' deceitful and impermissible in striking foul blows, deplorable, 'perhaps inappropriate,' worthy of condemnation, and, in this very case, 'condemned' and 'certainly error.'"; "The prosecution's actions in this case suggest defiance of Oklahoma courts and disregard for Oklahoma law.") (footnotes omitted).

40. State ex rel. Oklahoma Bar Ass'n v. Miller, 309 P.3d at 119.

decisions reveal numerous violations of *Brady* in criminal cases[41] (which are also violations of Rule 3.8), and show other examples of misconduct, e.g., prosecutors using false evidence or failing to correct false statements to the court;[42] prosecutors engaging in other improper courtroom conduct;[43] and

41. *See, e.g.*, Monroe v. Angelone, 323 F.3d 286, 314 (4th Cir. 2003) (failure to reveal leniency agreements with key witness and then stressing absence of such deals in closing statement[s]); Tassin v. Cain, 517 F.3d 770, 781 (5th Cir. 2008) (failure to disclose a "beneficial sentencing agreement that hinged directly on [a government witness's] testimony"; failure to correct misleading statements by the witness regarding the agreement; and, arguing to the jury, on the basis of the misleading testimony, that the witness had no reason to lie) (footnote omitted); Silva v. Brown, 416 F.3d 980, 986 (9th Cir. 2005) (failure to disclose an arrangement where the prosecutor agreed to drop murder charges against the chief prosecution witness in exchange for the witness's agreement to refrain from undergoing a psychiatric evaluation before testifying; "The existence of this deal evidencing the prosecution's concern as to the mental state of [the witness] was obviously impeachment evidence favorable to the defense."); Douglas v. Workman, 560 F.3d 1156, 1174-76 (10th Cir. 2009) (failure to disclose plea deal with witness linking defendant to murder; the witness was "indispensible" to the state's case). *See also* Brad Heath & Kevin McCoy, *supra* note 34 (finding *Brady* violations in many federal cases). Indeed, the failure to turn over exculpatory evidence has been described as the "most common form of [prosecutorial] misconduct cited by courts in overturning convictions." *See* Radley Balko, *The Untouchables: America's Misbehaving Prosecutors, And The System That Protects Them*, HUFFINGTON POST, http://www.huffingtonpost.com/2013/08/01/prosecutorial-misconduct-new-orleans-louisiana_n_3529891.html (last visited July 7, 2014). *See also Rampant Prosecutorial Misconduct*, NY TIMES (Jan. 4, 2014), http://www.nytimes.com/2014/01/05/opinion/sunday/rampant-prosecutorial-misconduct.html?_r=0; Comm. on Prof'l Ethics & Conduct of the Iowa State Bar Ass'n v. Ramey, 512 N.W.2d 569 (Iowa 1994) (indefinitely suspending an experienced prosecutor for making false statements regarding a chain of custody and for failing to disclose exculpatory evidence); Office of Disciplinary Counsel v. Wrenn, 790 N.E.2d 1195 (Ohio 2003) (six month stayed suspension for failing to disclose DNA test results in a child sex abuse case); *In re* Jordan, 913 So. 2d 775, 784 (La. 2005) (deferred three month suspension for failing to disclose *Brady* material in violation of 3.8(d) and 8.4(a); deferral "subject to the condition that any misconduct . . . during a one-year period following [the date of the suspension] may be grounds for making the deferred suspension executory, or imposing additional discipline. . . .") (rehearing denied).

42. *See, e.g.*, Napue v. Illinois, 360 U.S. 264, 265, 269-270 (1959) (failure to correct witness testimony the prosecutor knew to be false); Drake v. Portuondo, 553 F.3d 230, 233, 241-243 (2d Cir. 2009) (knowingly presenting false expert-witness testimony); Hobbs v. Cappelluti, 899 F. Supp. 2d 738 (N.D. Ill. 2012) (helping detective coerce a false video confession and pursuing conviction with the false confession); Dow v. Virga, 729 F.3d 1041 (9th Cir. 2013) (knowingly eliciting and failing to correct a detective's false testimony; "textbook prosecutorial misconduct"); *In re* Jordan, 91 P.3d 1168, 1173-1175 (Kan. 2004) (public censure for prosecutor's, *inter alia*, false statements to the court and failure to disclose evidence in violation of Rules 3.3, 3.4, 3.8, and 8.4).

43. *See, e.g.*, United States v. Perlaza, 439 F.3d 1149, 1172-1173 (9th Cir. 2006) (improper comment that presumption of innocence disappears when jury starts to deliberate); Marshall v. Hendricks, 307 F.3d 36, 65 (3d Cir. 2002), *cert. den.*, 538 U.S. 911 (2003) (improper mischaracterization of defense witness's testimony); State v. Rogan, 984 P.2d 1231, 1249-1250 (Haw. 1999) (forbidding re-prosecution on double jeopardy grounds after mistrial based on prosecutor's impermissible appeals to racial prejudice during summation; discussing Rule 3.8 and ABA PROSECUTION FUNCTION STANDARDS 3-5.8 (3d ed. 1993)).

prosecutors engaging in conduct that would violate, *inter alia*, Rule 4.2,[44] Rule 3.6,[45] Rule 8.4(a), and Rule 8.3(a).[46]

E. Basic Requirements

1. Establishing Office-Wide Policies

To accomplish the goals set forth in Rules 5.1 and 5.3, managers must "establish internal policies and procedures."[47] Generally, these policies and procedures should address confidentiality obligations, how to detect and resolve conflicts of interest,[48] "dates by which actions must be taken in pending matters,"[49] and ways to "ensure that inexperienced lawyers are properly supervised."[50] In the prosecutorial context, these policies and procedures should specifically facilitate compliance with ABA Model Rule 3.8. As we wrote in ABA Formal Opinion 09-454, "Supervisors who directly oversee trial prosecutors must make reasonable efforts to ensure that those under their direct supervision meet their ethical obligations of disclosure and are subject to discipline for ordering, ratifying or knowingly failing to correct discov-

44. *See, e.g.*, United States v. Koerber, 966 F. Supp. 2d 1207 (D. Utah 2013), *app. dismissed*, (10th Cir. 2014) (granting defendant's motion to suppress evidence gained by the prosecutor during interviews that violated Rule 4.2).

45. *See, e.g.*, United States v. Bowen, 269 F.Supp. 2d 546, 568, 574 (E.D. La. 2013) (granting defendants' motion for a new trial based on anonymous comments by prosecutors on a website that was viewed by jurors; noting, *inter alia*, the special duties of prosecutors under Rule 3.8; "[T]he government's actions, and initial lack of candor and credibility thereafter, is like scar tissue that will long evidence infidelity to the principles of ethics, professionalism, and basic fairness and common sense necessary to every criminal prosecution, wherever it should occur in this country."); Lawyer Disciplinary Bd. v. Sims, 574 S.E.2d 795 (W. Va. 2002) (public reprimand for violating Rules 3.6, 3.8, and 8.4(a) by, *inter alia*, making improper statements to the press); Att'y Grievance Comm'n. of Md. v. Gansler, 835 A.2d 548 (Md. 2003) (public reprimand for violating Rules 3.6 and 8.4(a) by making improper extrajudicial statements).

46. *See, e.g.*, *In re* Riehlmann, 891 So. 2d 1239, 1247-1249 (La. 2005) (public reprimand for violating Rule 8.3(a) by failing to report a colleague's suppression of exculpatory evidence).

47. ABA Model Rules of Prof'l Conduct R. 5.1 cmt. [2].

48. *Id.* Situations that may give rise to conflicts for prosecutors include, for example, (i) former-client and revolving-door issues under Rule 1.11, (ii) negotiations for private employment, and (iii) relationships with defense counsel and other lawyers. *See also In re* McKinney, 948 N.E.2d 1154 (Ind. 2011) (prosecutor suspended for 120 days because he prosecuted criminal matters as a part-time prosecutor while, at the same time, pursuing related civil forfeiture cases as a private attorney, where he would earn 25% of the amounts collected in the civil forfeiture cases).

49. R. 5.1 cmt. [2], *supra* note 46. For example, prosecutors should know the timing requirements applicable to investigations and prosecutions so as not to prejudice a matter.

50. *Id.*

ery violations. To promote compliance with Rule 3.8(d) in particular, supervisory lawyers must ensure that subordinate prosecutors are adequately trained regarding this obligation. *Internal office procedures must facilitate such compliance.*"[51] Further, in light of the "intensely difficult ethics issues" that arise for prosecutors, more elaborate procedures may be necessary to ensure compliance.[52]

With respect to nonlawyers, managers must establish policies and procedures that provide for "appropriate instruction and supervision concerning the ethical aspects of their employment . . . [that] . . . take account of the fact that [nonlawyers] do not have legal training and are not subject to professional discipline."[53] These policies and procedures for nonlawyers must, among other things, specifically facilitate compliance with Rule 3.8.

For lawyers and nonlawyers the policies and procedures set by managers should include substantive provisions that reasonably ensure compliance, as mandated by paragraph (a), and procedural provisions identifying specific measures that direct supervisors and other responsible individuals should implement to ensure that the policies and procedures established by the managers will be effectively executed. What those specific measures are will vary, depending on the size and structure of the office; no one size fits all. But some measures must be adopted and implemented. Recommendations for such measures are set forth below.

2. Guidance on Specific Measures

The ABA Standards for Criminal Justice Prosecution Function and Defense Function Standards (the "ABA Standards"), the National District Attorneys Association, National Prosecution Standards published by the National District Attorneys Association (the "District Attorneys Standards"), substantial literature on prosecutorial conduct,[54] and compliance programs implemented by law firms and corporate legal departments in response to the

51. Formal Op. 09-454, *supra* note 6, at 8 (emphasis added) (footnotes omitted).

52. *See, e.g., In re* Myers, 584 S.E.2d 357, 360-361 (S.C. 2003) (public reprimand of the Solicitor for the Eleventh Judicial District for violation of Rule 5.1(b) by failing to ensure that a deputy prosecutor disclosed, *inter alia,* eavesdropping by investigators on a confidential conversation between the defendant and his lawyer; "We hold that . . . the Solicitor's Office is a law office where complex ethical questions arise, which necessitate a more elaborate system to ensure that the attorneys in the Solicitor's Office comply with the Rules [of Professional Conduct]").

53. ABA Model Rules of Prof'l Conduct R. 5.3 cmt. [2].

54. *See, e.g.,* Rachel E. Barkow, *Organizational Guidelines for the Prosecutor's Office,* 31 Cardozo L. Rev. 2089 (2010) (advocating an entity-based compliance approach in prosecutor's offices).

requirements of the Sarbanes-Oxley Act[55] all provide examples of the types of measures that might be adopted. We set forth our recommendations below, based on these and other sources.

a. Training

The ABA Standards recommend that supervising prosecutors train incoming lawyers regardless of their previous experience.[56] We recommend that the training cover the ethical and legal obligations imposed by the Rules of Professional Conduct, including what disclosures and other obligations Rule 3.8 imposes, what public statements may be made under Rules 3.6 and 3.8 (including statements on social media, websites, and blogs), what must be revealed to a tribunal under Rule 3.3, what contacts may be made with represented and unrepresented persons under Rules 4.2 and 4.3, what statements may be made in closing argument, and what conduct by other prosecutors must be reported under Rule 8.3(a). We also recommend that training cover what constitutes *Brady* material. Others have suggested that the initial train-

---

55. Responding to the regulations promulgated by the Securities and Exchange Commission (the "SEC") under Section 307 of the Sarbanes-Oxley Act—which sets forth minimum standards of professional conduct for attorneys—law firms and corporate legal departments adopted internal policies which include but are not limited to distributing written policies describing the up-the-ladder reporting requirements, creating compliance committees and setting up training programs. *See* James L. Sonne, *Sarbanes-Oxley Section 307: A Progress Report on How Law Firms and Corporate Legal Departments Are Implementing SEC Attorney Conduct Rules*, 23 Geo. J. Legal Ethics 859, 864-65, 868-69 (2010).

56. *See* ABA Standards for Criminal Justice, Prosecution Function and Defense Function Standards § 3-2.6 & Commentary (3d ed. 1993) (the "ABA Standards") ("[t]raining programs should be established within the prosecutor's office for new personnel and for continuing education of the staff"; "[e]ven lawyers with extensive experience in the trial of civil cases must undergo new training ... before they can function effectively in the trial of a criminal case"). *See also* National District Attorneys Association, National Prosecution Standards §§ 1-5.3, 1-5.4 (2009) (the "District Attorneys Standards") ("At the time they commence their duties and at regular intervals thereafter, prosecutors should participate in formal training and education programs. Prosecutors should seek out continuing legal education opportunities that focus specifically on the prosecution function . . . . Each prosecutor's office should develop written and/or electronically retrievable statements of policies and procedures that guide the exercise of prosecutorial discretion and that assist in the performance of those who work in the prosecutor's office."). Both the ABA Standards and the District Attorneys Standards state that they are intended only as guides to professional conduct, but the ABA Standards constitute ABA policy. The District Attorneys Standards do not constitute ABA policy. For additional guidance *see, e.g.*, Barry Scheck, *Professional and Conviction Integrity Programs: Why We Need Them, Why They Will Work, and Models for Creating Them*, 31 Cardozo L. Rev. 2215, 2244-46 (describing benefits of "Clear Office-Wide Definitions of What Is or Is Not Brady Material").

ing also address office policies and procedures, technical skills, other relevant substantive law, and court rules.[57] In addition, making office policies and procedures available to all lawyers in hard copy or electronically retrievable format may help ensure compliance. Updating those policies and procedures regularly is advisable.

Supervising lawyers should also provide initial training for nonlawyers who are "employed, retained or associated with" the office. This group would ordinarily include detectives and investigators, forensic experts in the office, paralegals and clerical staff. The training should include education on the ethical and legal obligations of prosecutors and related office procedures, e.g., proper handling, filing, and retention of forms and documents, and the preservation of evidence.[58] The training should be adequate to insure that the conduct of nonlawyers is compatible with the professional obligations of prosecutors.

Training sessions should be offered as frequently as needed to update lawyers and nonlawyers on relevant subjects, for example, when an important decision is rendered that directly bears on a prosecutor's professional obligations. Policies, procedures, and training manuals should also be updated regularly, as events require, and key court decisions on prosecutorial conduct should be circulated with explanatory memos.[59] When a court criticizes the conduct of a lawyer or nonlawyer in the office, supervising prosecutors should consider holding special training or educational sessions as appropriate to avoid any repetition.

---

57. *See* NATIONAL PROSECUTION STANDARDS § 5, Commentary (2009) ("A basic orientation package for assistants could include familiarization with office structure, procedures, and polices; the local court system; the operation of local police agencies; and training in ethics, professional conduct, courtroom decorum, and relations with the court and the defense bar."); CTR ON THE ADMINISTRATION OF CRIMINAL LAW, ESTABLISHING CONVICTION INTEGRITY PROGRAMS IN PROSECUTORS' OFFICES: A REPORT OF THE CENTER ON THE ADMINISTRATION OF CRIMINAL LAW'S CONVICTION INTEGRITY PROJECT, at 17 (2012), available at http://www.law.nyu.edu/sites/default/files/upload_documents/Establishing_Conviction_Integrity_Programs_FinalRepo rt_ecm_pro_073583.pdf [hereinafter CONVICTION INTEGRITY PROJECT REPORT] ("Both new and experienced prosecutors must be trained and educated about their ethical and professional obligations. Ongoing training programs are not an admission that an office has a problem with attorney misconduct; they are a necessary component of reminding prosecutors about their unique job responsibilities.").

58. *See* NATIONAL PROSECUTION STANDARDS § 5, Commentary.

59. For a sample manual, *see, e.g.*, DIST. ATT'YS ASS'N OF THE STATE OF N.Y., "THE RIGHT THING:" ETHICAL GUIDELINES FOR PROSECUTORS, *available at* http://www.daasny.org/Ethics%20Handbook%209.28.2012%20FINAL.pdf (last visited July 3, 2014).

b. Supervision

Effective supervision would require that supervisors keep themselves informed of the status of and developments in pending cases by, for example, requiring periodic written or oral reports on pending cases.[60] Other examples of appropriate measures include: (i) requiring that supervising prosecutors participate in major decisions, e.g., granting immunity, deciding charges, identifying *Brady* material, and, where feasible, documenting the basis for these decisions in writing;[61] (ii) establishing a system of individual oversight of line prosecutors, including during the preparation for and the conduct of trials; (iii) pairing untrained or newly-trained prosecutors with more experienced prosecutors; (iv) holding prosecutors with Rule 5.1(b) and 5.3(b) obligations accountable for the conduct of their subordinates; and (v) designating a specific attorney to oversee the review of files for *Brady* material.

F. Other Recommendations

1. Creating a Culture of Compliance

"[T]he ethical atmosphere of [an organization] can influence the conduct of all its members . . . ."[62] Managers and supervisors in prosecutors' offices should create a "culture of compliance."[63] This can be done by, e.g., (i) emphasizing ethical values and imperatives during the hiring process; [64] (ii) providing incentives for ethical behavior, such as positive reviews, promotions,

60. ABA Model Rules of Prof'l Conduct R. 5.1 cmt. [3] notes managerial lawyers "may not assume that all lawyers associated with the firm will inevitably conform to the Rules." Keeping abreast of the developments in the matters under supervision and requiring such periodic reports are reasonable measures to check any such assumptions. *See In re* Anonymous Member of S. Carolina Bar, 552 S.E.2d 10, 14-15 (S.C. 2001) ("[u]ndoubtably, the supervision of attorneys by other attorneys in their firm is one of the most effective methods of preventing attorney misconduct"; "[w]hen an attorney has allegedly violated Rule 5.1, it is not a complete defense to prove that the attorney did not know about the underlying misconduct. . . . In fact, a complete lack of knowledge can lead to a finding of poor supervision if the subordinate's violation is such that reasonable supervision would have discovered it.").

61. *See generally* Stephanos Bibas, *Prosecutorial Regulation Versus Prosecutorial Accountability*, 157 U. Pa. L. Rev. 959, 1005-06 (2009).

62. ABA Model Rules of Prof'l Conduct R. 5.1 cmt. [3].

63. *See* Barkow, *supra* note 53, at 2116 ("Whether or not an office is responding to a history of misconduct, creating a culture of compliance and ethical behavior is in the interests of prosecutors who head the office.").

64. *See* Conviction Integrity Project Report, *supra* note 56, at 16 (recommending posing ethical hypotheticals and asking "potential hires to discuss key ethical rules or obligations").

and raises; (iii) protecting and rewarding lawyers who fulfill their up-the-ladder duties;[65] (iv) promoting initiatives that make compliance with ethical obligations less demanding for line prosecutors[66] such as "open-file" discovery policies;[67] (v) publicizing ethical compliance reforms and internal policies both within the office and to the public;[68] and (vi) internally disciplining lawyers and reporting lawyers who violate the Rules of Professional Conduct.[69]

2. Enforcing "Up-the-Ladder" Obligations

Prosecutors, like lawyers in other government offices, have obligations under Rule 1.13 to report conduct by an employee or other constituent that is a violation of law that might be imputed to the office.[70] This raises especially

65. See discussion of a prosecutor's up-the-ladder duties, *infra* at Part F2.

66. *See, e.g.*, Formal Op. 09-454, *supra* note 6, at 4 (Rule 3.8 "requires the disclosure of evidence or information favorable to the defense without regard to the anticipated impact of the evidence or information on a trial's outcome. The rule thereby requires prosecutors to steer clear of the constitutional line, erring on the side of caution.") (footnotes omitted).

67. An "open-file" discovery policy includes, for example, the office disclosing all exculpatory evidence of which they are aware, without evaluating materiality, in an effort to avoid both intentional and unintentional withholding of *Brady* evidence. *See* Barkow, *supra* note 53, at 2111 ("Another way of improving transparency and monitoring without imposing substantial costs would be for prosecutors' offices to adopt an 'open-file' discovery process. Many offices already follow open-file policies, and several scholars have touted these policies as a protection against Brady violations.") (footnote omitted); *See also* Conviction Integrity Project Report, *supra* note 56.

68. This provides interested "stakeholders" the opportunity to comment on these policies. *See* Barkow, *supra* note 53, at 2111; Conviction Integrity Project Report, *supra* note 56, at 33-34 (discussing the benefits to prosecutors of publicizing their efforts to curb prosecutorial misconduct).

69. ABA Model Rules of Prof'l Conduct R. 8.3(a) provides: "A lawyer who knows that another lawyer has committed a violation of the Rules of Professional Conduct that raises a substantial question as to that lawyer's honesty, trustworthiness or fitness as a lawyer in other respects, shall inform the appropriate professional authority."

70. *See* ABA Model Rules of Prof'l Conduct R. 1.13(b). R. 1.13 cmt. [9] reads, "The duty defined in the Rule [1.13] applies to governmental organizations." "Up the ladder" obligations are also imposed by the Sarbanes- Oxley rule for lawyers appearing and practicing before the SEC. *See* 17 C.F.R. §§ 205.3(b), 205.4 & 205.5 (2013) (establishing responsibilities for supervisory and subordinate lawyers to report material violations of the Sarbanes-Oxley Act). For a model up-the-ladder policy, see Assoc. of the Bar of the City of New York, Report of the Task Force on the Lawyer's Role in Corporate Governance, App. F (2006), which establishes specific procedures, provides for an appropriate level of confidentiality, prohibits retaliation, requires training on reporting requirements, and provides for annual written certification by all lawyers that they are aware of their obligations and will comply.

complex issues for prosecutors and other lawyers who work in government offices about the identity of their clients and the nature of their obligations.[71] We do not address these Rule 1.13 issues in this opinion. We focus here on how prosecutors might implement their supervisory and managerial obligations under Rules 5.1 and 5.3 by developing an internal system for "up-the-ladder" reporting of violations of the Rules of Professional Conduct whether or not such violations would also trigger the up-the-ladder reporting obligations of Rule 1.13.

Though not addressing Rule 1.13, we recommend that managerial and supervising prosecutors establish a similar system for up-the-ladder reporting concerning possible violations of the Rules of Professional Conduct by lawyers in the office. Such internal reporting procedures would enable managers and supervisors to correct, remedy, and sometimes avoid such violations. A system for this up-the-ladder reporting could include (i) designating a specific attorney or committee to receive reports and address and resolve the issues; [72] (ii) permitting confidential review, as appropriate, to promote increased reporting of potential ethical issues;[73] and (iii) requiring the reporting of any reprimand or other criticism by a judge, as well as written complaints or allegations of ethical misconduct by any person, to a supervising prosecutor or to a prosecutor designated for this purpose.[74] In addition, supervising prosecutors should make clear that any lawyer who knows of a violation of the rules of professional conduct may be required to report that information to a supervising prosecutor, or pursuant to an established up-the-ladder regime instituted to comply with Rules 5.1 and 5.3.

3. Discipline

The training and supervision described in this opinion can be enhanced with appropriate remediation and discipline. For example: (i) imposing sanctions within the office; (ii) requiring remedial education targeted at particular types of misconduct;[75] (iii) intensifying, in appropriate cases, the scrutiny of

---

71. For example, actions by constituents in a prosecutor's office could lead to liability under 42 U.S.C. §1983, as alleged in Connick v. Thompson, 131 S.Ct. 1350 (2011), and might require up-the-ladder reporting under Rule 1.13. So too might the apparent failure to supervise and train in the Oklahoma County District Attorney's office noted by the Tenth Circuit in Le v. Mullin, 311 F.3d 1002 (2002), where the Court said that the prosecutor's actions "suggest defiance of Oklahoma courts and disregard for Oklahoma law." In such instances there could be violations of Rule 1.13 separate from any violations of Rules 5.1 and 5.3.

72. *See* ABA Model Rules of Prof'l Conduct R. 5.1 cmt. [3] ("Some firms, for example, have a procedure whereby junior lawyers can make confidential referral of ethical problems directly to a designated senior partner or special committee.").

73. *Id.*

74. *See* Barkow, *supra* note 53, at 2110.

75. For example, if the office is criticized for a *Brady* violation, appropriate remedial education is imperative.

prosecutors who have engaged in improper conduct or whose conduct has been criticized by a court; (iv) demotion or dismissal; and (v) where appropriate, referring the matter to an outside authority under Rule 8.3(a).[76] It may be effective to have responsibility for in-house review placed with a specific supervisory lawyer or a group of lawyers within the office.[77]

G. Organizational and Structural Variables

Organizational and structural differences, such as the size of an office, the personnel turnover rate, the manner in which cases are prosecuted, the size of caseloads,[78] and the hierarchical structure may have an impact on which of the measures we recommend should be used to ensure compliance. Large offices with several layers of hierarchy may need to establish a formal committee to coordinate and direct the internal reporting of misconduct and the monitoring for ethics violations. Such formalized assignments, on the other hand, are unlikely to be required for small prosecutor's offices that employ 10 to 15 prosecutors, or even fewer. Supervising prosecutors in these smaller offices may make "reasonable efforts" by simply, for example, adopting an open-door policy for reporting misconduct or assigning a specific person in the office to hear such reports.

Direct supervision and monitoring also may vary with organizational and structural differences. For example, some offices assign multiple prosecutors to handle a case and each prosecutor is responsible for only one stage

76. *See, e.g.*, *In re* Brizzi, 962 N.E.2d 1240 (Ind. 2102) (public reprimand for improper public statements); *In re* McKinney, 948 N.E.2d 1154 (Ind. 2011) (120 day suspension for conflict of interest); *In re* Miller, 677 N.E.2d 505 (Ind. 1997) (reprimand for advancing the cause of a civil litigant while serving as a prosecutor). *But see*, Joel B. Rudin, *The Supreme Court Assumes Errant Prosecutors Will Be Disciplined by Their Offices or the Bar: Three Case Studies That Prove That Assumption Wrong*, 80 Fordham L. Rev. 537, 541-42 (2011); ABA Comm. on Ethics & Prof'l Responsibility, Formal Op. 09-454, at 2 ("[D]isciplinary authorities rarely proceed against prosecutors in cases that raise interpretive questions under Rule 3.8(d)"); United States v. Olsen, 737 F.3d 625, 630 (9th Cir. 2013) (Kozinski, Pregerson, Reinhardt, Thomas & Watford dissenting) (denying petition for rehearing en banc) ("[p]rofessional discipline [for Brady violations] is rare").

77. *See* Conviction Integrity Project Report, *supra* note 56, at 16 (discussing creation of "Best Practices Committees"). For an analogous discussion of the benefits of having a general counsel in private firms, *see* Rotunda & Dzienkowski, *supra* note 21, § 5.1-1.

78. High caseloads are a particular risk factor. Whether a caseload is manageable may depend on, *inter alia*, the type and complexity of cases being handled by each lawyer, the experience and ability of each lawyer, and the resources available to support the lawyers. *See also* Va. Standing Comm. on Legal Ethics, Advisory Op. 1798 (2004) (addressing whether a chief prosecutor violates Rule 5.1 when he assigns too high a caseload; "[w]here a supervising attorney assigns a caseload so large as to preclude any hope of the supervised attorney's ethically representing the client (or clients), that supervisor would be in violation of Rule 5.1").

of the process.[79] In these offices, a monitoring scheme is unlikely to be reasonable if no special attention is paid to ensure that important information, such as *Brady* material, is not lost in the transition from prosecutor to prosecutor. The handling of this transition is especially delicate in offices with high turnover rates—much can be lost with frequent transitions. By contrast, where only one prosecutor handles a case from start to finish and through all stages in the process, a different monitoring regime will be appropriate.[80]

H. Conclusion

Prosecutors with managerial authority and supervisory lawyers must make "reasonable efforts to ensure" that all lawyers and nonlawyers in their offices conform to the Rules of Professional Conduct. Prosecutors with managerial authority must adopt reasonable policies and procedures to achieve these goals. Prosecutors with direct supervisory authority must make reasonable efforts to insure that the lawyers and nonlawyers they supervise comply with the Rules. Where prosecutors have both managerial and direct supervisory authority, they may, depending on the circumstances, be required to fulfill both sets of obligations. The particular measures that managerial and supervisory prosecutors must implement to comply with these rules will depend on a variety of factors, including the size and structure of their offices, as set forth in this opinion.

---

79. Don Stemen & Bruce Frederick, *Rules, Resources, and Relationships, Contextual Constrains on Prosecutorial Decision Making*, 31 QUINNIPIAC L. REV. 1, 13 (2013) ("horizontal prosecution" refers to matters handled by "multiple prosecutors, each handling the case at one stage of the process").

80. *Id.* at 12 ("vertical prosecution" refers to matters handled by one prosecutor at all stages). *See also* Formal Op. 09-454, *supra* note 6, at 8 ("[W]hen responsibility for a single criminal case is distributed among a number of different lawyers with different lawyers having responsibility for investigating the matter, presenting the indictment, and trying the case, supervisory lawyers must establish procedures to ensure that the prosecutor responsible for making disclosure obtains evidence and information that must be disclosed. . . . Similarly, procedures must ensure that if a prosecutor obtains evidence in one case that would negate the defendant's guilt in another case, that prosecutor provides it to the colleague responsible for the other case.").

AMERICAN BAR ASSOCIATION
STANDING COMMITTEE ON ETHICS AND PROFESSIONAL RESPONSIBILITY

Formal Opinion 468 **October 8, 2014**

Facilitating the Sale of a Law Practice

When a lawyer or law firm sells a law practice or an area of law practice under Rule 1.17, the seller must cease to engage in the private practice of law, or in the area of practice that has been sold, in the relevant jurisdiction or geographic area. But the selling lawyer or law firm may assist the buyer or buyers in the orderly transition of active client matters for a reasonable period after the closing of the sale. Neither the selling lawyer or law firm nor the purchasing lawyer or law firm may bill clients for time spent only on the transition of matters.

Until 1990, lawyers were unable to sell any part of a law practice except for the physical assets such as furniture, office equipment, and books. Rule 1.17, first adopted in 1990, rejected the traditional prohibition on the sale of a law practice and permitted such transactions under certain conditions, including the condition that the selling lawyer or law firm "ceases to engage in the private practice of law, or in the area of practice" that was sold, in the relevant jurisdiction or geographic area. A question has arisen as to whether a selling lawyer or law firm may nevertheless continue to "practice" to assist the buyer or buyers in the orderly transition of active client matters.

Traditional Prohibition on Sale of a Law Practice

Various reasons were typically given for the traditional prohibition on the sale of a law practice. First, the uniform position of the courts and bar associations was that there was no legally or ethically recognized "good will" in a law practice that a lawyer might sell, pledge, assign, or even give away.[1] This position was reflected in ABA Formal Opinion 266 (June 2, 1945), which stated that the "good will," or intangible going-concern value, of a lawyer's practice was not an asset that either the lawyer or the lawyer's estate could sell because ". . . clients are not merchandise. Lawyers are not tradesmen. They have nothing to sell but personal service. An attempt, therefore, to bar-

1. *See* Charles W. Wolfram, Modern Legal Ethics § 16.2, at 879 (1986).

ter in clients, would appear to be inconsistent with the best concepts of our professional status."

A second reason was concern that the sale of a law practice, whether by the estate or the survivor of a deceased sole practitioner to a lawyer or by a lawyer or law firm to another lawyer or law firm, would constitute an impermissible sharing or division of legal fees. With regard to a sale of a practice by the estate or survivor of a deceased sole practitioner, the pre-1990 provisions of Rule 5.4(a), as well as DR 3-102(A) of the 1969 Model Code of Professional Responsibility, generally prohibited lawyers or law firms from sharing legal fees with nonlawyers, with certain limited exceptions including payments made to the survivors or estates of deceased law firm partners and law firm compensation and retirement plans. Thus, compensation for the "good will" of a sole practitioner's law practice, paid by the purchasing lawyer or law firm to the estate or survivor of the sole practitioner and derived from fees paid by the clients of that practice, was considered an improper sharing of a legal fee with a nonlawyer.[2] With regard to a sale of a practice by a lawyer or law firm to another lawyer or firm, both Rule 1.5(e) and DR 2-107(A) of the Code prohibited the division of legal fees between lawyers who are not in the same firm, with limited exceptions not applicable to the sale of the "good will" of a law practice.

A third reason was the long-established ban on payments by a lawyer to anyone for recommending the lawyer's services, as expressed in DR 2-103(B) of the Code and Rule 7.2(b). When a lawyer sells a practice, the lawyer presumably recommends the buyer to the clients of the practice, and thereby receives payment for those recommendations.

A fourth reason was concern that confidential client information might be disclosed as the result of the sale of a law practice. The 1983 version of the Model Rules did not address this issue. However, EC 4-6 of the Code explained: "The obligation of a lawyer to preserve the confidences and secrets of his client continues after the termination of his employment. Thus a lawyer should not attempt to sell a law practice as a going business because, among other reasons, to do so would involve the disclosure of confidences and secrets."

Whatever the reason or reasons given in any particular situation, it was generally held prior to 1990 that a law practice could not be sold, either by a sole practitioner or a law firm or by the survivor or the estate of a deceased sole practitioner.

---

2. *See, e.g.*, O'Hara v. Ahlgren, Blumenfield & Kempster, 537 N.E.2d 730 (Ill. 1989) (contract with widow to sell practice of deceased sole practitioner violated public policy against fee sharing and would not be enforced).

New Model Rule 1.17

In 1990, the ABA House of Delegates adopted new Model Rule 1.17 that permits the sale of a law practice, including the "good will" of the practice, if the detailed requirements of the rule are followed. According to its sponsors, the new rule was designed to accomplish two goals. The first was to address the disparity of treatment of clients of sole practitioners and clients of law firms when a lawyer responsible for a client matter leaves the practice, by ensuring that client matters handled by sole practitioners are attended to when the sole practitioner leaves practice. Formerly, clients of sole practitioners were left to fend for themselves after their lawyer left the practice because the lawyer had no legal way to sell the practice. Second, the new rule put sole practitioners in a financial position equal to partners of law firms regarding the value of the "good will" of their practice because most jurisdictions had limited a sole practitioner's ability to value his or her practice upon retirement or other cessation of practice to physical assets.[3]

Comment [1] to Rule 1.17 reaffirms the traditional notion that the "... practice of law is a profession, not merely a business. Clients are not commodities that can be purchased and sold at will." However, the black letter of the rule and the remaining comments outline and explain the conditions for the sale of a practice or area of practice, including requirements that the entire practice or an entire area of practice must be sold;[4] that the seller give written notice of the proposed sale to each client;[5] and that the fees charged to the client shall not be increased by reason of the sale.[6]

Another key requirement of Rule 1.17, expressed in paragraph (a) of the black letter and Comments [2] and [3], is that the seller must cease to engage in the private practice of law, or in the area of practice that has been sold, in the relevant geographic area or jurisdiction. Comment [5] explains that if an area of practice is sold and the lawyer otherwise remains in the active practice of law, then "the lawyer must cease accepting any matters in the area of practice that has been sold, either as counsel or co- counsel or by assuming joint responsibility for a matter in connection with the division of a fee with another lawyer as would otherwise be permitted by Rule 1.5(e)."

Comment [11] notes that lawyers participating in the sale of a practice or practice area remain subject to the ethical standards applicable to the involvement of another lawyer in the representation of a client, including,

3. *See* A Legislative History: The Development of the ABA Model Rules of Professional Conduct, 1982-2013, at 383 (Art Garwin ed., 2013).

4. ABA Model R. 1.17(b) & cmt. [6] (2014).

5. ABA Model R. 1.17(c) & cmt. [7] (2014).

6. ABA Model R. 1.17(d) & cmt. [10] (2014).

for example, the seller's obligation to exercise competence in identifying a purchaser qualified to assume the practice and the purchaser's obligation to undertake the representation competently;[7] the obligation to avoid disqualifying conflicts of interest and to secure informed consent where appropriate;[8] and the obligation to protect information relating to the representation.[9]

Comment [12] also explains if approval of the substitution of the purchasing lawyer for the selling lawyer is required by the rules of a tribunal, that approval must be obtained before the matter can be included in the sale.

Other provisions of the Model Rules have been amended to reflect the changes made by Rule 1.17. For example, with respect to the prohibition of the sharing of legal fees with a nonlawyer, Rule 5.4(a)(2) now permits a lawyer who purchases the practice of a deceased, disabled, or disappeared lawyer to pay, pursuant to the provisions of Rule 1.17, the agreed-upon purchase price to the estate or other representative of that lawyer. An exception to the general ban expressed in Rule 7.2(b) on payments for recommending a lawyer to clients was adopted that permits a lawyer to "pay for a law practice in accordance with Rule 1.17." Comment [13] to Rule 1.6 now recognizes that lawyers may need to disclose limited information to each other to detect and resolve conflicts of interest in various situations, including when considering the purchase of a law practice. And Comment [3] to Rule 5.6, which generally prohibits agreements that restrict the right of a lawyer to practice, explains that the rule does not apply to "restrictions that may be included in the terms of the sale of a law practice pursuant to Rule 1.17."

Transition of Client Matters

Neither the black letter nor the comments to Rule 1.17 address the timing of when a seller "ceases to engage" in the private practice of law for purposes of the rule. In particular, there is no discussion of whether a selling lawyer may continue to be involved in the practice to assist in the orderly transition of active client matters. It is clear from Comment [5] that the selling lawyer may no longer accept new matters in the relevant practice or area of practice, and that prohibition should logically take effect immediately upon the closing of the sale. However, given the history and purpose of the rule, as well as the black letter provisions and comments to the rule, it seems reasonable to conclude that the transition of pending or active client matters from a selling lawyer or firm to a purchasing lawyer or firm need not be immediate or abrupt.

For example, one of the purposes stated by the sponsors of new Rule 1.17 was to address the disparity of treatment of clients of sole practitioners and

7. ABA Model R. 1.1 (2014).
8. ABA Model R. 1.7 & 1.0(e) (2014).
9. ABA Model R. 1.6 & 1.9 (2014).

law firms. Lawyers retiring or withdrawing from law firms are not precluded from assisting their former colleagues in the transition of responsibility for pending matters from the retiring or withdrawing lawyer to another firm lawyer. Where appropriate, a selling lawyer or firm should be given a similar opportunity, for a reasonable period of time after the closing of the sale, to assist in the transition of active client matters.

This conclusion is consistent with Comment [12] to Rule 1.17, which notes that if "... approval of the substitution of the purchasing lawyer for the selling lawyer is required by the rules of any tribunal in which a matter is pending, such approval must be obtained before the matter can be included in the sale...." The drafters of this comment anticipated situations where the selling lawyer or firm would need to stay involved to accomplish the transition of a pending matter.

This conclusion is also consistent with Rule 1.16(d), which provides that upon termination of representation, a lawyer "shall take steps to the extent reasonably practicable to protect a client's interests...." The duty to protect the client's interests appears to apply regardless of the reason for the termination of the representation, and should therefore include any steps reasonably necessary to protect the interests of the client, even if those steps must be taken after the sale of a lawyer's practice or area of practice has closed.[10]

The period of time required for the selling lawyer to comply with Comment [12] to Rule 1.17 or Rule 1.16(d) in any particular client representation will necessarily depend on the circumstances, including the rules and rulings of courts or other tribunals in pending matters. It is therefore impractical to propose any prescriptive time limitation for when the selling lawyer "ceases to engage" in the private practice of law in the relevant practice area or jurisdiction following the sale of a law practice or area of law practice, as long as the selling lawyer stops accepting new matters in the practice or area of practice that has been sold and also limits his or her activities to acts reasonably necessary to accomplish the orderly transition of active client matters.

Charging Clients for Time Spent on Transitioning Matters

Finally, neither the selling lawyer or law firm nor the purchasing lawyer or law firm may bill clients for time spent on transition activity that does not advance the representation or directly benefit the client. The clear intent of the black letter and the comment of Rule 1.17 is that clients should not experience any adverse economic impact from the sale of a practice or area of practice. As noted above, Rule 1.17(d) unequivocally states: "The fees charged clients shall not be increased by reason of the sale." And Comment [10] fur-

10. *See also* AMERICAN LAW INSTITUTE, RESTATEMENT (THIRD) OF THE LAW GOVERNING LAWYERS (2000) § 33(1) (in terminating representation, lawyer must take steps to extent reasonably practicable to protect client's interests).

ther explains: "The sale may not be financed by increases in fees charged clients of the practice. Existing arrangements between the seller and the client as to fees and the scope of the work must be honored by the purchaser."

The need to spend time on transition activity arises only because of the sale of a practice or area of practice. Charging clients for time spent implementing the sale, activity that would not have been undertaken but for the sale, constitutes an "increase" in the original fee arrangement between the seller and the client "by reason of the sale." Even if the hourly rate is unchanged, billing for the additional time spent on transitioning matters will necessarily increase the fee otherwise due for the representation.[11] Thus, time spent implementing the sale may not be billed to clients.

The compensation, if any, to the selling lawyer or law firm for time spent on transitioning matters should be a matter of negotiation between the seller and the buyer in determining the consideration for the sale.

Conclusion

The requirement of Rule 1.17(a) that the seller of a law practice or area of practice must cease to engage in the private practice of law, or in the area of practice that has been sold, does not preclude the seller from assisting the buyer or buyers in the orderly transition of active client matters for a reasonable period of time after the closing of the sale. However, neither the selling lawyer or law firm nor the purchasing lawyer or law firm may bill clients for time spent only on the transition of matters.

---

11. *See also* ABA Comm. on Ethics & Prof'l Responsibility, Formal Op. 93-379 (1993) (client should only be charged for legal services performed).

AMERICAN BAR ASSOCIATION
STANDING COMMITTEE ON ETHICS AND PROFESSIONAL RESPONSIBILITY

Formal Opinion 469 **November 12, 2014**

Prosecutors and Debt Collection Companies

A prosecutor who provides official letterhead of the prosecutor's office to a debt collection company for use by that company to create a letter purporting to come from the prosecutor's office that implicitly or explicitly threatens prosecution, when no lawyer from the prosecutor's office reviews the case file to determine whether a crime has been committed and prosecution is warranted or reviews the letter to ensure it complies with the Rules of Professional Conduct, violates Model Rules 8.4(c) and 5.5(a).

Introduction

Debt collection companies are contracting with local prosecutors' offices to use prosecutor letterhead to create and mail collection demand letters. These demand letters typically cite the criminal law allegedly violated (such as making or delivering a check with insufficient funds) and advise the debtor that she/he could avoid the possibility of further action from the prosecutor's office by paying the amount of the debt, and in a significant number of cases, a substantial additional fee to attend a mandatory debtor education course. Typically, no lawyer in the prosecutor's office reviews the case file to determine whether a crime has been committed and prosecution is warranted or reviews the letter to ensure it complies with the Rules of Professional Conduct prior to the mailing.[1]

1. For a full discussion of this country-wide practice, see Jessica Silver-Greenberg, *In Prosecutors, Debt Collectors Find a Partner*, NY TIMES (Sept. 15, 2012), http://www.nytimes.com/2012/09/16/business/in-prosecutors-debt-collectors-find-a-partner.html?pagewanted=all&_r=0; Joel Cohen, *When District Attorneys Become Bill Collectors*, AMERICAN LAWYER (Nov. 19, 2012), http://www.americanlawyer.com/id=1202578727214/When-District-Attorneys-Become-Bill-Collectors?slreturn=20140311111758; Mosi Secret, *Bounced Checks: How Local District Attorneys Get a Cut of the Debt Collection Business*, PROPUBLICA (Mar. 2, 2009), http://www.propublica.org/article/bounced-checks-how-local-das-get-a-cut-of-the-debt-collection-business. While programs vary depending on the terms of the contract between the prosecutor's office and the collection company, one thing does not: prosecutors allow debt collection companies to misrepresent the author and sender of this threatening letter. To review a copy of a debt collection letter issued by collection companies on prosecutor letterhead see *Letter from Bad Check Restitution Program*, NY TIMES (Sept. 16, 2012), http://www.nytimes.com/

The Committee concludes that prosecutors involved in this practice violate Model Rules of Professional Conduct 8.4(c) and 5.5(a).

Application of the Rules of Professional Conduct to Prosecutors: Jurisdictional Statement

There is no question that prosecutors are subject to the rules of professional conduct. As ABA Formal Opinion 97-405, Conflicts in Representing Government Entities (1997), explained, "While lawyers who serve as public officers or employees are singled out for special treatment under a few rules, e.g., Rule 1.11 ('Successive Government and Private Employment') and 3.8 ('Special Responsibilities of a Prosecutor'), it has generally been assumed—correctly in our view—that such lawyers are in most other respects subject to the same obligations in representing their client that apply to lawyers representing private clients."

Prosecutors acknowledge their ethical obligations as lawyers. Most prosecutors fulfill those obligations conscientiously and live up to the even higher responsibility of a minister of justice, as prescribed by Comment [1] to Rule 3.8. However, occasionally practices have taken hold in prosecutors' offices that, while driven by budgetary exigencies, fall short of their higher calling. It is such practices that have created the need for this opinion.

Model Rule 8.4, *Misconduct*

A prosecutor who enters into the type of agreement described in this opinion violates Model Rule 8.4(c), which provides that: "It is professional misconduct for a lawyer to engage in conduct involving dishonesty, fraud, deceit or misrepresentation."

In 1943, the ABA issued Formal Opinion 253, which determined that it would be unethical for a lawyer to allow a client to use the lawyer's stationery to deceive a debtor into believing that the debt had been referred to the lawyer and that the lawyer had written the collection letter. Specifically, the Committee noted that the practice violated Canon 15, which read in part: "The office of attorney does not permit, much less does it demand of him for any client, violation of law or any manner of fraud or chicane. He must obey his own conscience and not that of his client."[2] The Committee explained that a lawyer who allowed a client to send a collection letter on the lawyer's stationery was a party to deception and violated Canon 15. Today, Model Rule 8.4(c) addresses this same conduct.

---

interactive/2012/09/16/business/20120916_DEBT_LETTER.html?ref=business. In 2013, the Oregon legislature passed a state bill prohibiting prosecutors from allowing collection companies to use their letterhead. OR. REV. STAT. §646.639 (2013), *available at* http://www.oregonlegislature.gov/bills_laws/lawsstatutes/2013orLaw0551.pdf.

2. ABA Canons of Prof'l Ethics, Canon 15 (1908).

To the same effect is a joint opinion of the New Jersey Committee on the Unauthorized Practice of Law and Advisory Committee on Professional Ethics, which determined that a lawyer who sold his "name and letterhead to a collection agency in exchange for a monthly fee" violated Rule 8.4(c).[3] The conduct enabled the debt collection agency to deceive the debtor into believing that the lawyer was about to institute proceedings to collect the alleged debt by sending a collection letter on firm stationery, giving the debtor reason to believe that "there has been an evaluation by an attorney of the claim asserted with a determination by the attorney that proceedings to ensure collections are warranted."

Such letters written on prosecutors' letterhead are even more deceptive than the letters dealt with in ABA Formal Opinion 253 and in the New Jersey Joint Opinions 48 and 725. This is because they misuse the criminal justice system by deploying the apparent authority of a prosecutor to intimidate an individual. They carry with them the implication that the prosecutor or associates in the prosecutor's office have reviewed the facts and found that a crime has been committed and criminal prosecution is warranted. To create such a false impression violates Rule 8.4(c).[4]

Model Rule 5.5, *Unauthorized Practice of Law; Multijurisdictional Practice of Law*

Since at least 1932, the ABA Standing Committee on Ethics and Professional Responsibility has written about lawyers working for and with creditors to collect allegedly delinquent debts.[5] Many of these opinions have focused on what is the proper allocation of duties between lawyers and laymen in collection matters to ensure that the lawyer is not aiding in the unauthorized practice of law.

---

3. N.J. Comm. on the Unauthorized Practice of Law & Advisory Comm. on Prof'l Ethics, Joint Ops. 48 & 725 (2012).

4. Believing that ABA Model Rule 8.4(b) addressed the crimes of extortion and compounding a crime, when the ABA adopted the Model Rules in 1983, it deliberately omitted former Disciplinary Rule 7-105(A), which prohibited a lawyer from threatening criminal changes to gain an advantage in a civil matter. *See* ABA Comm. on Ethics & Prof'l Responsibility, Formal Op. 94-383 (1994) (threatening a disciplinary complaint against opposing counsel to gain an advantage in a civil matter may violate Rule 8.4(b) if the conduct is extortion under jurisdiction's law). Therefore, depending on the jurisdiction in which the prosecutor practices, if the threat to file a criminal action meets the jurisdiction's elements of extortion, the prosecutor could also be in violation of Rule 8.4(b). Prosecutors have not been excluded from the application of Rule 8.4(b). In *In re* Gobel, the Supreme Court of Nebraska suspended a lawyer for three months because, while county attorney, he threatened the debtor of a private client that unless a debt was immediately paid, the lawyer would file criminal charges against the debtor. *In re* Gobel, 271 N.W.2d 41(1978).

5. *See* ABA Comm. on Ethics & Prof'l Responsibility, Formal Op. 68 (1932), Formal Op. 253 (1943) & Informal Op. 1368 (1976).

Only a licensed lawyer may practice law, and states prohibit the unlicensed practice to protect consumers. Limiting the practice of law to members of the bar "protects the public against rendition of legal services by unqualified persons"[6] and serves to protect the public from unscrupulous persons' engaging in abusive conduct and misuse of the law. Model Rule 5.5(a) prohibits a lawyer from "assisting another" in practicing law in violation of that jurisdiction's regulations.[7]

The practice of law is defined by state statute and case law.[8] In the collection area, generally, a nonlawyer may negotiate, adjust, and settle a debt on behalf of a creditor, but a nonlawyer cannot give legal advice, institute litigation, or threaten to sue on behalf of another.[9]

The participation by a prosecutor in the conduct described in this opinion, wherein the prosecutor supplies official letterhead to a debt collection company and allows the debt collection company to use it to send threatening letters to alleged debtors without any review by the prosecutor or staff lawyers to determine whether a crime was committed and prosecution is warranted, violates Rule 5.5(a) by aiding and abetting the unauthorized practice of law.[10]

In ABA Formal Opinion 68 (1932), the Committee determined that a lawyer who provided a client corporation with signed letterhead so that the client could write to persons who owed the client money "over the attorney's supposed signature" violated Canon 35 of the ABA Canons of Professional Ethics (1928). The Committee explained that by giving the client signed letterhead, the lawyer delegated his professional functions—which were strictly personal to the lawyer—to a nonlawyer. This conclusion is consistent with state Supreme Court decisions and bar association ethics opinions.[11]

The conduct at issue in this opinion is even more abusive than that in Formal Opinion 68 because it gives the impression that the machinery of the

6. ABA Model R. 5.5, cmt. [2] (2014).

7. *See* ABA Model R. 5.5(a) (2014).

8. ABA Model R. 5.5, cmt. [2] (2014).

9. ABA/BNA Laws. Man. on Prof. Conduct § 21:8011 (ABA/BNA 2011).

10. The Committee has become aware of a similar practice that involves a state overpayment of a benefit to a recipient. In that situation, a prosecutor lends office stationery to a state agency so that the agency's employees can use prosecutor letterhead to threaten criminal prosecution for failure to remit the overpayment. This practice, structured similarly to the one presented, would also violate the Rules of Professional Conduct.

11. *See* Yount v. Zarbell, 135 P.2d 309 (Wash. 1943) (lawyer who lends her signature to collection agent aids in the unauthorized practice of law); *In re* DeVinny, 255 N.W.2d 832 (Minn. 1977) (lawyer who allows collection agency to draft letters to debtors under his signature and who does not review and approve said letters aids unauthorized practice of law); Adams v. Kentucky Bar Ass'n, 843 S.W.2d 898 (Ky. 1991) (Assistant County Attorney aided the unauthorized practice of law when he "delegated authority and responsibility for deciding which parents of students in the Christian County School System would receive"

criminal justice system has been mobilized against the debtor, and that unless the debtor pays the debt, the debtor faces criminal prosecution and possible incarceration.

Conclusion

A prosecutor who provides official letterhead of the prosecutor's office to a debt collection company for use by that company to create a letter purporting to come from the prosecutor's office that implicitly or explicitly threatens prosecution, when no lawyer from the prosecutor's office reviews the case file to determine whether a crime has been committed and prosecution is warranted or reviews the letter to ensure that it complies with the Rules of Professional Conduct, violates Model Rules 8.4(c) and 5.5(a).

---

letter threatening jail for nonpayment of school fees.); *In re* Scheck, 574 N.Y.S.2d 372 (N.Y. 1991) (lawyer who allowed collection company to use his name, letterhead and signature to send letters to debtors without actually reviewing letters sent out under his name aids in unauthorized practice of law); *In re* Hear, 755 N.E.2d 579 (Ind. 2001) (lawyer, who contracted with debt collector to perform services, and failed to make reasonable efforts to ensure that collector's conduct complied with rules of professional conduct, violated Rule 5.3). *See also* Ill. State Bar Ass'n, Op. 85-7 (1985) ("A lawyer may not allow unsupervised lay persons to prepare letters on the lawyer's stationery, with or without the lawyer's signature, if the letter states or implies legal conclusions- i.e., that the addressee is liable for the amount claimed- or threatens litigation if the purported debt is not paid. Such activities would constitute unauthorized practice of law by lay persons . . ."); State Bar of Georgia, Formal Op. 00-2 (2000) ("[A] lawyer is aiding a nonlawyer in the unauthorized practice of law when the lawyer allows a nonlawyer member of his or her staff to prepare and sign correspondence which threatens legal action or provides legal advice or both. Generally, a lawyer is aiding a nonlawyer in the unauthorized practice of law whenever the lawyer effectively substitutes the legal knowledge and judgment of the nonlawyer for his or her own."); L.A. County Bar Ass'n Prof'l Responsibility & Ethics Comm., Op. 522 (2009) ("[A]n attorney may not lend his or her name to be used by an unlicensed person. . . . The power and privileges attendant to the right to practice law may not be delegated to a nonlicensed person . . . To facilitate or assist an unlicensed person such as a legal assistant to engage in the practice of law would constitute aiding and abetting UPL." (internal citations omitted)).

AMERICAN BAR ASSOCIATION

STANDING COMMITTEE ON ETHICS AND PROFESSIONAL RESPONSIBILITY

Formal Opinion 470 **May 20, 2015**

Judicial Encouragement of Pro Bono Service

A state supreme court judge may sign a letter printed on the judge's stationery that is duplicated and mailed by the unified state bar association directed to all lawyers licensed in the state encouraging those lawyers to meet their professional responsibility under Rule 6.1 of the Model Rules of Professional Conduct and provide pro bono legal services to persons in need and to contact the bar association for information about volunteer opportunities.

A unified state bar association has asked a state supreme court justice to sign a letter encouraging lawyers to meet their obligations under Model Rule 6.1, Voluntary Pro Bono Public Service, and provide pro bono legal services to persons in need.[1] The letter will suggest that the recipient contact the bar association for information about volunteer opportunities.

The letter will be sent by the bar association on the justice's stationery to every member of the unified bar. Staff for the unified bar will manage and pay for its printing and mailing. The envelope for each letter to members of the bar will be personalized to the extent it will have the name and address of the bar member, but the salutation of the letter will not be personalized. The bar association will not track whether there is an increase in pro bono participation, nor will it report back to the justice on the responses it receives to the letter.[2]

1. A unified bar association requires all lawyers licensed in the jurisdiction to be members of the association. Thirty states, the District of Columbia, U.S. Virgin Islands, Puerto Rico, Guam, and the Northern Mariana Islands are unified bars.

2. This opinion does not address the situation in which a judge asks a specific lawyer to accept appointment for a specific case. For those matters, see ABA Model Code of Judicial Conduct Rules 1.3, 2.13, 2.4, 3.1(D) and ABA Model Rules of Professional Conduct Rule 6.2.

Encouraging Lawyers to Provide Pro Bono Legal Services

Since their adoption in August 1983, the ABA Model Rules of Professional Conduct have included Rule 6.1, Pro Bono Publico Service. Rule 6.1 explains that lawyers have a "professional responsibility to provide legal services to those unable to pay."[3] The Rule provides that lawyers should aspire to give 50 hours of free or reduced-cost legal services a year.

Rule 6.1 is a strong statement of the ABA's position on the duties of the profession.[4] The ABA Standing Committee on Lawyers' Public Service Responsibility, in its 1993 Report to House of Delegates, explained that Rule 6.1 was a meaningful response to the crisis that exists in providing legal services to the poor.[5]

Rule 3.7 of the ABA Model Code of Judicial Conduct allows judges to participate in organizations concerned with the law, the legal system, or the administration of justice subject to the limitations of Rule 3.1. Rule 3.7(B) reads: "A judge may encourage lawyers to provide pro bono publico legal services."

Comment [5] to Rule 3.7 explains this provision noting permitted conduct:

> . . . a judge may promote broader access to justice by encouraging lawyers to participate in pro bono publico legal services, if in doing so the judge does not employ coercion, or abuse the prestige of judicial office. Such encouragement may take many forms, including providing lists of available programs, training lawyers to do pro bono publico legal work, and participating in events recognizing lawyers who have done pro bono publico work.

Rule 3.7(B) recognizes the symbiosis between lawyers' duties to provide pro bono services under Rule 6.1 of the Rules of Professional Conduct and judges encouraging lawyers to meet the obligations of Rule 6.1. The Reporters' Notes to the Model Code of Judicial Conduct explain that Rule 3.7(B) was a new provision in the 2007 Code designed to encourage judges to "pro-

3. Model Rules of Prof'l Conduct R. 6.1.

4. Model Rules of Prof'l Conduct R. 6.1, cmt. [1].

5. According to the Legal Services Corporation's most recent nationwide study of unmet legal needs, approximately 944,000 people who sought legal help from LSC-funded offices in 2009 were turned away because the offices lacked adequate resources to help. *See* Legal Services Corporation, *Documenting the Justice Gap in America: The Current Unmet Civil Legal Needs of Low-Income Americans* (2009), http://www.lsc.gov/sites/default/files/LSC/pdfs/documenting_the_justice_gap_in_america_2009.pdf.

vide leadership in increasing *pro bono publico* lawyering."[6] Rule 3.7(B) also is consistent with a judge's duties under Rule 1.2 to ensure "public confidence in the independence, integrity, and impartiality of the judiciary . . ." and to "promote access to justice for all."[7]

The facts presented require the Committee to construe the meaning and scope of Rule 3.7(B). This is a matter of first impression for the ABA.

Construing Rule 3.7(B) begins with the text of the Rule.[8] The Committee notes that Rule 3.7(B) is permissive; judges may encourage lawyers to provide pro bono services, but judges are not required to do so. ABA Model Code of Judicial Conduct, Scope, paragraph [2] notes, "Where the Rule contains a permissive term, such as 'may' or 'should' the conduct being addressed is committed to the personal and professional discretion of the judge or candidate in question, and no disciplinary action should be taken for action or inaction within the bounds of such discretion."

Rule 3.7(B) allows judges to "encourage" lawyers to provide pro bono legal services. Although not defined by the Code, the Merriam-Webster Dictionary defines encouragement as making someone more determined, hopeful, or confident; making something more appealing or more likely to happen; and making someone more likely to do something. Comment [5] to Rule notes that judicial encouragement to lawyers "may take many forms, including providing lists of available programs, training lawyers to do pro bono publico legal work, and participating in events recognizing lawyers who have done pro bono publico work."[9]

---

6. "This means that for every client served by an LSC-funded program, at least one eligible person seeking help" was turned away. *Id.* at p. More recent data from a spring 2014 report from the State Bar of Michigan noted three new developments that further threaten the ability of low income people to secure adequate representation. First, the recession has "dramatically increased the number of people in poverty" in Michigan, bringing with it an increase in the number of home foreclosures. Second, "Legal Services Corporation funding was cut 4% for 2011 and 15% for 2012." In Michigan, the results have been devastating for LSC staff. The number of lawyers available was reduced by 26 and three paralegals and more than 15 support staffers were laid off. Two offices have closed. As a result, almost 7,000 fewer matters can be processed. Finally, LSC-funded "programs are projected to face an additional 10% in funding cuts . . ." As a result, even fewer clients will have their needs met. State Bar of Michigan and the Michigan's Legal Services Corporation Funded Providers, *Documenting the Justice Gap in Michigan* (updated Spring 2015), https://www.michbar.org/programs/atj/pdfs/JusticeGap.pdf.

7. Charles E. Geyh & W. William Hodes, Reporters' Notes to the Model Code of Judicial Conduct 70 (2009).

8. Model Code of Judicial Conduct R. 1.2, cmt. [4].

9. "The words of a governing text are of paramount concern, and what they convey, in their context, is what the text means." Antonin Scalia & Bryan A. Garner, Reading Law: The Interpretation of Legal Texts 56 (2012).

The word "including" in Comment [5] means that the actions noted are not an exhaustive list of how a judge might encourage lawyers to provide pro bono, but are examples.[10] Therefore, a judge is not limited to the activities noted in Comment [5] when encouraging lawyers to perform pro bono services. Although signing a letter encouraging lawyers to perform pro bono services is not one of the specific activities listed as permissible in Comment [5], the Committee thinks the Rules do not prohibit a judge from sending the encouraging letter described in this opinion. A judge signing a letter encouraging lawyers to contact the bar association for information on pro bono activities – for a list of available pro bono programs – is consistent with the encouragement listed in Comment [5]. This finding is in accord with a number of ethics opinions from around the country.[11]

Rule 3.7(A)(2) Does Not Prohibit Signing a Letter Encouraging Pro Bono Service

Rule 3.7(A)(2) prohibits a judge from soliciting contributions on behalf of a non-profit organization or governmental entity from anyone other than a family member or another judge over whom the soliciting judge "does not exercise supervisory or appellate authority." Though the Terminology of the Model Code of Judicial Conduct defines "personally solicit" as "a direct request made by a judge or a judicial candidate for financial support or in-kind services, whether made by letter, telephone, or any other means of communication" and "contributions" as including "professional or volunteer services," the Committee concludes that the letter is not a solicitation of a contribution for the reasons stated below.[12] Rather, it is a letter encouraging lawyers to meet their professional responsibility to provide pro bono legal services pursuant to Model Rule of Professional Conduct 6.1.

---

10. Comments to the Rules are designed to provide examples of permitted conduct. *See* Model Code of Judicial Conduct, Scope ¶ [3]. When the ABA House of Delegates adopted the 2007 Model Code of Judicial Conduct, the House also adopted the Comments to the Code.

11. Scalia & Garner, *supra* note 8, at 132.

12. *See* Alabama Jud. Inquiry Comm'n Adv. Op. 04-847 (2004) (judge may send letter asking lawyers to participate in state bar operated pro bono program); Florida Sup. Ct. Jud. Ethics Adv. Op. 2010-13 (2010) (judge may send general solicitation letter to "Members of the Bar" asking lawyers to participate in The Florida Bar's One Campaign for pro bono legal service); Florida Sup. Ct. Jud. Ethics Adv. Op. 2012-26 (2012) (judge may ask a local bar association to host an event at which the judge will ask lawyers to provide pro bono legal services; however, judge must monitor tone and delivery of the request to ensure it is not coercive); Maryland Jud. Ethics Comm. Op. 1996-20 (1996) (judge may write personal letters to lawyers asking lawyers to provide *pro bono* services); Texas Comm. on Jud. Ethics Op. 258 (2000) (board of judges may send letter to lawyers asking lawyers to consider providing

Rule 3.7(A)(2) and (B) can and should be read harmoniously for three reasons. First, "The provisions of a text should be interpreted in a way that renders them compatible, not contradictory."[13] If encouraging lawyers to contact the bar association for a list of pro bono opportunities was solicitation of a contribution under Rule 3.7(A)(2), then Rule 3.7's Comment [5]—which allows judges to "provide lists of available programs"—would be contradictory to Rule 3.7(A)(2).

Second, a contradictory reading would be unreasonable. The Scope section of the Model Code of Judicial Conduct explains, "The Rules of the Model Code of Judicial Conduct are rules of reason that should be applied consistent with constitutional requirements, statutes, other court rules, and decisional law, and with due regard for all relevant circumstances."

Finally, more support for this harmonious reading of paragraphs (A)(2) and (B) can be found in the legislative history of the Model Code. Before the amendments of 2007, the Model Code of Judicial Conduct had no provision specifically allowing judges to encourage lawyers to provide pro bono service. Judicial ethics scholars involved with the ABA Joint Commission to Evaluate the Model Code of Judicial Conduct explained the interplay of the paragraphs. In their report accompanying the revisions, the scholars noted that it was "assumed that participation in organizations that promote *pro bono publico* legal services would generally be permissible under rule 3.7(A)"; nevertheless paragraph (B) was adopted to address encouraging pro bono "whether or not conducted in connection with a particular organization or entity."[14]

Model Rule 3.1, Extrajudicial Activities in General

A judge's extrajudicial activities are also guided by Model Rule 3.1. "Thus, even with respect to activities that are explicitly permitted by Rule 3.7, a judge must always consider whether participating in such activities,

---

pro bono service hours to joint project of local legal service organizations). *See also* Alaska Comm'n on Jud. Conduct Adv. Op. 2004-01 (2004) (judge may not refer lawyers to a particular pro bono program); Kentucky Ethics Comm. of the Judiciary Op. JE-107 (2005) (while a generic letter to the bar is permissible, judge may not urge lawyers to volunteer with a specific pro bono organization). *But see* Michigan Stand. Comm. on Prof'l & Jud. Ethics Op. J-7 (1998) (judge may not solicit individual lawyer to perform pro bono); Nebraska Jud. Ethics Comm. Adv. Op. 02-3 (2002) (judge may not sign recruiting letter for bar association pro bono campaign).

13. Because the Committee concludes that the letter is not a solicitation as prohibited by Rule 3.7(A)(2), it need not address whether there is a difference between a direct solicitation and a general one or how the interpretation of the Florida rules regarding solicitation by the U.S. Supreme Court in Williams-Yulee v. Florida Bar, 135 S.Ct. 1656 (2015) might apply.

14. Scalia & Garner, *supra* note 8, at 180.

would on a more basic level, violate Rule 3.1, such as by leading to frequent disqualification."[15]

Rule 3.1 notes that while judges may engage in extrajudicial activities, they shall not:

> (A) participate in activities that will interfere with the proper performance of the judge's judicial duties;
> (B) participate in activities that will lead to frequent disqualification of the judge;
> (C) participate in activities that would appear to a reasonable person to undermine the judge's independence, integrity, or impartiality;
> (D) engage in conduct that would appear to a reasonable person to be coercive; or
> (E) make use of court premises, staff, stationery, equipment, or other resources, except for incidental use for activities that concern the law, the legal system, or the administration of justice, or unless such additional use is permitted by law.

Interfering with the proper performance of judicial duties

Rule 3.1(A)'s prohibition regarding interference with the proper performance of judicial duties is based on Model Rule 2.1. Model Rule 2.1 explains that a judge must perform the duties of the office and that official duties take precedence over personal and extrajudicial activities. A judge taking time to sign a letter encouraging lawyers to perform pro bono is a de minimis activity that will not interfere with the proper performance of the judge's duties.

In fact Rule 1.2 proclaims one judicial duty is to "act at all times in a manner that promotes public confidence in the independence, integrity, and impartiality of the judiciary, and shall avoid impropriety and the appearance of impropriety." Comment [4] gives an example of such actions explaining, "Judges should . . . promote access to justice for all."

A justice who signs the letter described in this opinion encouraging lawyers to seek out pro bono opportunities by contacting the bar association is promoting access to justice for all, consistent with Comment [4] of Rule 1.2.

Activities that lead to frequent disqualifications

Model Rule 3.1(B) prohibits judges from participating in activities that lead to frequent disqualification. Model Rule 2.11 addresses when a judge must disqualify himself or herself from hearing a matter. The Rule explains, in part, that:

15. ABA Joint Commission to Evaluate the Model Code of Judicial Conduct, Report 200, 119-120 (Feb. 2007), http://www.americanbar.org/content/dam/aba/directories/policy/2007_my_200.authcheckdam.pdf.

> A judge shall disqualify himself or herself in any proceeding in which the judge's impartiality might reasonably be questioned, including but not limited to the following circumstances:
>
> The judge has a personal bias or prejudice concerning a party or a party's lawyer, or personal knowledge of facts that are in dispute in the proceeding.
>
> ******

The Model Code of Judicial Conduct defines impartiality as "an absence of bias or prejudice in favor of, or against, particular parties or classes of parties, as well as maintenance of an open mind in considering issues that may come before a judge."[16] A judge who signs a general appeal letter encouraging lawyers to perform pro bono service does not thereby demonstrate a bias or prejudice toward any particular pro bono organization, the people any organization serves, or the lawyers who undertake that work.[17]

Activities that undermine the judge's independence, integrity, or impartiality

Model Rule 3.1(C) mirrors the language of Model Rule 1.2. That reads, in part, "A judge shall act at all times in a manner that promotes public confidence in the independence, integrity, and impartiality of the judiciary. . ."

The Model Code of Judicial Conduct defines independence as "a judge's freedom from influence or controls" in the decision-making process.[18] A judge must make decisions "independent of inappropriate outside influences."[19] Issues of judicial independence often arise in cases in which a judge has become an advocate for one party in a proceeding.[20] A judge who signs a letter encouraging lawyers to seek out pro bono opportunities by contacting the bar association is not being influenced or controlled in the decision-making process. Instead, the judge is encouraging lawyers to comply with Model Rule of Professional Conduct 6.1 and promoting access to justice for all under Model Code of Judicial Conduct Rule 1.2.

---

16. Geyh & Hodes, *supra* note 6, at 68.
17. Model Code of Judicial Conduct, Terminology.
18. This question also has been addressed in at least two states. Both the Alaska Commission on Judicial Conduct and the Alabama Judicial Inquiry Commission noted with approval that general appeals to participate in pro bono service are permissible and do not raise disqualification issues. Alaska Comm'n on Jud. Conduct Op. 2004-01 (2004) & Alabama Jud. Inquiry Comm'n Adv. Op. 04- 847 (2004).
19. Model Code of Judicial Conduct, Terminology.
20. Annotated Model Code of Judicial Conduct 38 (2d ed. 2010).

The Model Code of Judicial Conduct defines integrity as "probity, fairness, honesty, uprightness, and soundness of character."[21] Probity is defined as complete honesty. Cases in which judges have been disciplined for failure to be honest include matters in which a judge has lied on a resume, deceived medical professionals to gain access to prescription drugs, and lied about attending CLE.[22] Uprightness and sound character cases include patterns of judicial behavior that demonstrate disrespect for the office.[23] A judge who signs a letter encouraging lawyers to seek out pro bono opportunities by contacting the bar association is not behaving unfairly, dishonestly, or disrespectfully. Instead, the judge is encouraging lawyers to comply with Model Rule of Professional Conduct 6.1.

The Model Code of Judicial Conduct defines impartiality as "an absence of bias or prejudice in favor of, or against, particular parties or classes of parties, as well as maintenance of an open mind in considering issues that may come before a judge."[24] Impartiality concerns are addressed in the opinion's discussion of disqualification, *supra*.

Activities that a reasonable person would find coercive

Both Rule 3.1(D) and Comment [5] to Rule 3.7 prohibit a judge from employing coercion while engaged in extrajudicial activities. The caution contained in Rule 3.1(D) was added to the 2007 Model Code of Judicial Conduct

---

21. *See, e.g., In re* Frankel, Karp, No. 12-118, Arizona Comm'n on Jud. Conduct (2012) (two judges disciplined for filing amicus brief in appeal of cases they heard because such action "failed to promote public confidence that judges are to be neutral and impartial and not advocates for particular legal results"); *In re* Graham, No. 09-31, Georgia Jud. Qualifications Comm'n (2010) (judge reprimanded for calling into chambers FBI agents investigating drug case and attacking their credibility and character in matter not assigned to judge and holding a hearing in chambers regarding a matter not before the judge); Disc. Counsel v. Campbell, 931 N.E.2d 558 (Ohio 2010) (judge became a participant in two investigations when he encouraged police to follow up on an issue, questioned defendants, and reviewed a prosecutor's file).

22. Model Code of Judicial Conduct, Terminology.

23. *See In re* DeForest, Nos. 12-266 &12-275, Ariz. Comm'n on Jud. Conduct (2012) (justice of the peace reprimanded for inflating experience and training in on-line biography and on resume); Disc. Counsel v. Ault, 852 N.E.2d 727 (Ohio 2006) (judge got doctors to overprescribe painkilling drugs for his use); *In re* Augustus, 626 S.E.2d 346 (S.C. 2006) (judge lied about attending continuing legal education).

24. *See, e.g., In re* Carpenter, 17 P.3d 91 (Ariz. 2001) (judge removed for 14 Code violations); *In re* Jefferson, 753 So.2d 181 (La. 2000) (judge removed for pattern of conduct, including exceeding contempt power and banning city prosecutor from courtroom and thereafter dismissing 41 criminal cases when no prosecutor was present to proceed); *In re* Seitz, 495 N.W.2d 559 (Mich. 1993) (judge removed for hostile attitude toward employees, abuse of contempt power and other acts); Miss. Comm'n on Jud. Performance v. Spencer, 725 So.2d 171 (Miss. 1998) (judge removed for continuing pattern of offensive sexual comments).

because the ABA Joint Commission to Evaluate the Model Code of Judicial Conduct heard testimony about judges coercing others into supporting extrajudicial activities supported by the judge. The Joint Commission noted that judges using coercion "can be a significant problem in small communities with only one judge or a small number of judges and a small number of lawyers who need to maintain good relations with the judiciary."[25] Although the Model Code of Judicial Conduct does not define coercion or coercive practices, to coerce generally means to make or to get someone to perform some action by using force or threats.[26]

Rule 3.1(D) uses a reasonable person standard to determine whether a judge's conduct is coercive. Comment [4] to Rule 3.1 explains that a judge should avoid actions that risk that "the person solicited would feel obligated to respond favorably . . ." The totality of the facts should be reviewed to determine whether a judge's actions appear coercive to a reasonable person.

In this opinion, a state supreme court justice has been asked to send a general letter, with no personal salutation, to every lawyer in the state encouraging all lawyers to meet their professional responsibility under Rule 6.1 and provide pro bono legal services to those in need. The letter encourages lawyers to contact the state bar for a list of agencies in need. No follow-up monitoring will be conducted by the state bar, the supreme court, or the justice to determine whether every lawyer in the state has provided pro bono services.

Under these facts, the Committee does not think such a letter would be coercive. The letter is not threatening and would not lead a reasonable person to feel obligated to perform pro bono services. Additionally, such a letter would not lead a reasonable person to believe that the lawyer who performs pro bono services is currying favor with the justice because no follow-up will be conducted. The justice will not have knowledge of any lawyer's response to the letter.

At the same time, the Committee can foresee facts under which a letter from a judge urging a lawyer to perform pro bono legal services could be viewed as coercive by a reasonable person. Therefore, factors that a judge should weigh before sending a letter encouraging lawyers to perform pro bono include:

- The number of lawyers who will receive the letter. In smaller jurisdictions or in limited-scope mailings that are targeted at lawyers who

25. Model Code of Judicial Conduct, Terminology.
26. Annotated Model Code of Judicial Conduct 331 (2d ed. 2010).

practice in a particular area of the law, a reasonable person might feel coerced into providing pro bono legal services.

- The number of judges serving the jurisdiction. Again, in smaller jurisdictions with a limited number or only one judge, a lawyer who receives a letter from the judge encouraging that lawyer to provide pro bono legal services could feel coerced into doing so.
- Whether the letter is a personalized correspondence or a general plea to the bar as a whole. A letter in which the recipient lawyer is identified by name in the salutation runs the risk of a reasonable person finding such a letter coercive.
- Whether there will be some kind of post-letter monitoring. A letter in which a judge encourages a lawyer to perform pro bono legal services and then explains that the lawyer's participation, or lack thereof, will be monitored runs the risk of a reasonable person finding such a letter coercive.
- The tone of the letter. A letter in which the justice speaks in aspirational and encouraging language will have a much different impact than a letter that features dictatorial, condescending language.

Incidental Use of Court Resources for Activities that Concern the Law, the Legal System, or the Administration of Justice

Rule 3.1 cautions judges that when they engage in extrajudicial activities they must not use court premises, staff, stationery, equipment or other resources unless permitted by law or such use is incidental and is "for activities that concern the law, the legal system, or the administration of justice." Applying this caution to the facts in this opinion, the Committee notes that the justice's leadership of the state court system could easily be seen as part of the justice's judicial responsibility, and thus writing the letter may not be extrajudicial activity. Even if the activity were deemed to be extrajudicial, no court resources will be used to duplicate or mail the letter and only one piece of the justice's stationery need be used to create the general letter that will be sent to all lawyers in the jurisdiction, which is incidental use.

Model Rule 1.3, Avoiding Abuse of the Prestige of Judicial Office

Abuse of the prestige of judicial office is addressed in Rule 3.7 Comment [5] as well as Model Rule 1.3. We will address them together.

Rule 1.3, Avoiding Abuse of the Prestige of Judicial Office, reads: "A judge shall not abuse the prestige of judicial office to advance the personal or economic interests of the judge or others, or allow others to do so." Before 2007, the Model Code of Judicial Conduct prohibited judges from "lending" the prestige of their office. The Reporters' Notes to the 2007 Code explain that the ABA Joint Commission to Evaluate the Model Code of Judicial Conduct believed the word "abuse" more accurately described the conduct Rule 1.3 sought to prohibit. The goal was to address conduct that exploited the prestige of the office in inappropriate ways.[27] In their report to the House of Delegates, the Commission wrote, "In the Commission's view, the term 'lend' created unnecessary confusion."[28] As a result, the word "lend" was deleted from the rule.

The Committee is of the view that a supreme court justice does not abuse the prestige of judicial office when the justice signs a letter on court stationery encouraging lawyers to meet their professional responsibilities under Rule 6.1 and directing lawyers to the bar association for a list of organizations in need of pro bono assistance.[29]

Model Rule 2.4 External Influences on Judicial Conduct

ABA Model Rule 2.4(C) reads: "A judge shall not convey or permit others to convey the impression that any person or organization is in a position to influence the judge." Comment [1] to Rule 2.4 explains, "Confidence in the judiciary is eroded if judicial decision making is perceived to be subject to inappropriate outside influences." A judge who signs a general appeal letter mentioning no specific organization's need, but instead encouraging lawyers to perform pro bono service and directing lawyers to contact the bar association for a list of pro bono service organizations does not convey the impression that the judge's decisions can be influenced by a pro bono service organization or a person connected to a pro bono service organization. This letter writing activity is completely different than having an ex parte communication with one litigant[30] to a matter or holding separate and specially

---

27. *See* N.M. Adv. Comm. on Code of Jud. Conduct Op. 13-05 (2013) (judge could not preside over a school district's hearing-like truancy proceeding in his courtroom wearing his robes at which the truant student, the student's parents, and school personnel would speak with the judge about the student's truancy. Judge had no jurisdiction to conduct the quasi-hearing and the extra- judicial activity was coercive regardless of beneficial purpose of the actions). Charles Gardner Geyh et al., Judicial Conduct And Ethics §9.04 [2] (5th ed. 2013) (While the specific prohibition on coercive conduct first appeared in the Code of Judicial Conduct in 2007, the prohibition against using intimidation to convince a potential donor into making a contribution is one of the concerns at the heart of the prohibition against soliciting contributions for a charitable organization).

28. Geyh & Hodes, *supra* note 6, at 22-23.

29. ABA Joint Commission to Evaluate the Model Code of Judicial Conduct, *supra* note 14, at 38.

30. *See* Kentucky Ethics Comm. of the Judiciary Op. JE-107 (2005) (when crafting a general letter urging lawyers to perform pro bono, judges should "simply exhort the goodness and desirability of pro bono work" to avoid using the prestige of office). *But see* Nebraska Jud. Ethics Comm. Op. 02-3 (2002) (using the prior standard of "lend the prestige of judicial office").

scheduled evening bond hearings,[31] for which judges have been found to violate Rule 2.4(C). Nor does the judge's letter writing activity permit the bar association or any pro bono organization to convey the impression that it is in a position to influence the judge.

Conclusion

A state supreme court judge may sign a letter printed on the judge's stationery that is duplicated and mailed by the unified state bar association directed to all lawyers licensed in the state encouraging those lawyers to meet their professional responsibility under Rule 6.1 of the Model Rules of Professional Conduct and provide pro bono legal services to persons in need and to contact the bar association for information about volunteer opportunities.

31. Miss. Comm. on Jud. Performance v. Lewis, 913 So.2d 266 (Miss. 1994). 31. *In re* David, 645 S.E.2d 243 (S.C. 2007).

AMERICAN BAR ASSOCIATION
STANDING COMMITTEE ON ETHICS AND PROFESSIONAL RESPONSIBILITY

Formal Opinion 471 **July 1, 2015**

Ethical Obligations of Lawyer to Surrender Papers and Property to which Former Client is Entitled

Upon the termination of a representation, a lawyer is required under Model Rules 1.15 and 1.16(d) to take steps to the extent reasonably practicable to protect a client's interest, and such steps include surrendering to the former client papers and property to which the former client is entitled. A client is not entitled to papers and property that the lawyer generated for the lawyer's own purpose in working on the client's matter. However, when the lawyer's representation of the client in a matter is terminated before the matter is completed, protection of the former client's interest may require that certain materials the lawyer generated for the lawyer's own purpose be provided to the client.

This opinion addresses the ethical duties of a lawyer pursuant to the ABA Model Rules of Professional Conduct, when responding to a former client's request for papers and property in the lawyer's possession that are related to the representation. The opinion does not address a client's property rights or other legal rights to these materials.

A lawyer has represented a local municipality for 10 years pursuant to a contract for legal services. The contract term expired. After publishing a request for proposals, the municipality chose a different lawyer to provide the municipality with future legal services. The municipality requested that the lawyer provide the municipality's new counsel with all files – open and closed. The lawyer has been paid in full for all of the work.[1] The lawyer asks what materials must be provided to the former client.[2]

1. Because the lawyer has been paid in full, this opinion does not address retaining liens.

2. The ABA Model Rules of Professional Conduct do not directly address the length of time a lawyer must preserve client files after the close of the representation. Many jurisdictions provide guidance on this issue through court rule or ethics opinions.

The scope of a lawyer's ethical duty pursuant to the Rules of Professional Conduct to provide a former client with papers and property to which the client is entitled at the termination of the representation arises with regularity. Many jurisdictions, through case law on property rights, agency law, or ethics opinions under the jurisdiction's Rules of Professional Conduct, have examined the question and determined which papers and property a lawyer must return, reproduce, and/or provide to a client. There may be other obligations defined in a jurisdiction's case law or court rules.[3] Lawyers are cautioned to review the law in the jurisdiction in which they practice because lawyers have been disciplined for failing to surrender to the client papers and property to which the client is entitled.[4]

ABA Informal Ethics Opinion 1376 (1977) addressed a lawyer's ethical duty to deliver files to a former client. The opinion interpreted Rule 9-102(B)(4) of the Model Code of Professional Responsibility that read, "A lawyer shall: [P]romptly pay or deliver to the client as requested by the client the . . . properties in the possession if the lawyer which the client is entitled to receive." It concluded: "The attorney clearly must return all of the materials supplied by the client to the attorney. . . . He must also deliver the 'end product' . . . On the other hand, in the Committee's view, the lawyer need not deliver his internal notes and memos which have been generated primarily for his own purpose in working on the client's problem."

That opinion was issued prior to the adoption of the Model Rules of Professional Conduct and prior to advances in technology that have affected virtually all aspects of the practice of law, including how lawyers create, communicate, use, and store materials related to client representations. This opinion clarifies and updates a lawyer's ethical duty to provide a former client with papers and property pursuant to Model Rules of Professional Conduct 1.15 and 1.16, and addresses practical considerations attendant to those obligations.

3. *See*, Corrigan v. Teasdale Armstrong Schlafly Davis & Dicus, 824 S.W.2d 92 (Mo. 1992) (client has a conditional right of access to a lawyer's notes, research, and drafts if the client needs the notes, research, and drafts to understand completed documents).

4. *See In re* Brussow 286 P.3d 1246 (Utah 2012). In Brussow, the respondent represented a client in post-dissolution matters and was publicly sanctioned for refusing to turn over the file to the client. Brussow argued that the client owed him money for the cost of deposition transcripts which the client's second husband agreed to pay. The Utah Supreme Court noted that Utah's Rule 1.16 "differs from the ABA Model Rule in requiring that papers and property considered to be part of the client's file be returned to the client notwithstanding any other laws or fees or expenses." *Id.* at 1252. Brussow was also admonished for failing to account for fees paid in advance. *See also In re* Thai, 987 A.2d 428 (D.C. 2009). Thai delayed returning a client's file and "actively obstructed the efforts of his former client and the successor attorney to obtain the file." *Id.* at 430. Thai was disciplined for violating Rule 1.16 as well as for violations of Rules 1.1, 1.3, and 1.4 involving the same client matter.

Model Rule 1.15 provides that a lawyer must safeguard a client's property and promptly deliver it to the client upon the client's request.[5] By its terms, Rule 1.15 applies to a client's and third party's money and to "other property" that comes into a lawyer's possession in connection with a representation.[6] Although not specifically defined in the Rule, "other property" may be fairly understood to include, for example, (a) tangible personal property, (b) items with intrinsic value or that affect valuable rights, such as securities, negotiable instruments, wills, or deeds and (c) any documents provided to a lawyer by a client.[7] Therefore, as an initial matter, and in the absence of other law[8] or a valid dispute under Rule 1.15(e), the lawyer must return all property of the municipality that the municipality provided in connection with the representation. *See* ABA Informal Ethics Opinion 1376 (1977). This would necessarily include original documents provided by the client.

When a representation ends, ABA Model Rule 1.16(d) mandates that the lawyer take steps that are "reasonably practicable to protect a client's interests . . ."[9] "Reasonable," when used to describe a lawyer's actions "denotes the conduct of a reasonably prudent and competent lawyer."[10] These steps include, but are not limited to, "surrendering papers and property to which the client is entitled."[11]

The Model Rules do not define the "papers and property to which the client is entitled," that the lawyer must surrender pursuant to Rule 1.16(d). Jurisdictions vary in their interpretation of this obligation. A majority of jurisdictions follow what is referred to as the "entire file" approach.[12] In those jurisdictions, at the termination of a representation, a lawyer must surrender papers and property related to the representation in the lawyer's possession

---

5. ABA Model Rule 1.15, Safeguarding Property.

6. ABA Model Rule 1.15(a).

7. This obligation exists with respect to all materials whether in paper or electronic form. *See* ABA Model Rule 1.0(n) defining writing as "a tangible or electronic record of a communication . . . including audio or video recording, and electronic communications." *See also* N.H. Bar Ass'n Advisory Op. 2005-06/3 (2005).

8. *See* ABA Model Rule 1.15, cmt. [4] for a discussion of third party liens. *See* ABA Model Rule 1.16(d) and cmt. [9] and ABA Comm. on Ethics & Prof'l Responsibility, Informal Op. 86-1520 (1986) for a discussion of lawyer retaining liens.

9. ABA Model Rule 1.16, Declining or Terminating Representation.

10. ABA Model Rule 1.0(h), Terminology.

11. ABA Model Rule 1.16(d). This duty applies even when the lawyer believes the client's discharge is unfair. *See* ABA Model Rule 1.16, cmt. [9].

12. *See, e.g.*, Iowa Sup. Ct. Attorney Disciplinary Bd. v. Gottschalk, 729 N.W.2d 812 (2007) (failure to return entire file to client violates disciplinary rules); Alaska Bar Ass'n Ethics Comm. Op. 2003-3 (2003); Ariz. Formal Op. 04-01 (2004); Colo. Bar Ass'n. Formal Op. 104 (1999); D.C. Bar Op. 333 (2005); Or. Bar Ass'n Formal Op. 2005-125 (2005); Va. State Bar Op. 1399 (1990).

unless the lawyer establishes that a specific exception applies and that certain papers or property may be properly withheld.[13] Commonly recognized exceptions to surrender include: materials that would violate a duty of nondisclosure to another person;[14] materials containing a lawyer's assessment of the client;[15] materials containing information, which, if released, could endanger the health, safety, or welfare of the client or others;[16] and documents reflecting only internal firm communications and assignments.[17] The entire file approach assumes that the client has an expansive general right to materials related to the representation and retains that right when the representation ends.

Other jurisdictions follow variations of an end-product approach.[18] These variations distinguish between documents that are the "end-product" of a lawyer's services, which must be surrendered and other material that may have led to the creation of that "end-product," which need not be automatically surrendered. Under these variations of the end-product approach, the lawyer must surrender: correspondence by the lawyer for the benefit of the client;[19] investigative reports and other discovery for which the client has paid;[20] and pleadings and other papers filed with a tribunal. The client is also entitled to copies of contracts, wills, corporate records, and other similar documents prepared by the lawyer for the client. These items are generally considered the lawyer's "end product."

Administrative materials related to the representation, such as memoranda concerning potential conflicts of interest,[21] the client's creditworthiness,

13. This approach is also advocated by the RESTATEMENT (THIRD) OF THE LAW GOVERNING LAWYERS. *See* RESTATEMENT (THIRD) LAW GOVERNING LAWYERS (2000) §46 ("On request, a lawyer must allow a client or former client to inspect and copy any document possessed by the lawyer relating to the representation, unless substantial grounds exist to refuse.")

14. *See, e.g.,* Colo. Bar Ass'n Formal Op. 104 (1999) ("A lawyer has the right to withhold pleadings or other documents relating to the lawyer's representation of other clients that the lawyer used as a model on which to draft documents for the present client."); *In re* Sage Realty Corp. v. Proskauer, Rose, Goetz & Mendelsohn LLP, 689 N.E.2d 879,883 (N.Y. 1997).

15. *See, e.g., In re* Sage Realty Corp. v. Proskauer, Rose, Goetz & Mendelsohn LLP, 689 N.E.2d 879, 883 (N.Y. 1997).

16. RESTATEMENT (THIRD) LAW GOVERNING LAWYERS (2000) §46, cmt. c.

17. *See, e.g.,* Colo. Bar Ass'n Formal Op. 104 (1999); D.C. Bar Op. 333 (2005).

18. Ala. Ethics Comm. Advisory Op. 1986-02 (1986); Ill. State Bar Ass'n Advisory Op. 94-13 (1995); Kan. Bar Ass'n Op. 92-5 (1992); Miss. Bar Formal Op. 144 (1988); Utah State Bar Ass'n Advisory Op. 06-02 (2006).

19. *See, e.g.,* Neb. Lawyer's Advisory Comm. Advisory Op. 12-09 (2012); Ill. State Bar Ass'n Advisory Op. 94-13 (1995).

20. *See, e.g.,* Corrigan v. Teasdale Armstrong Schlafly Davis & Dicus, 824 S.W.2d 92, 98 (Mo. 1992); Neb. Lawyer's Advisory Comm. Advisory Op. 12-09 (2012).

21. Ohio Bd. Comm'rs on Grievances and Discipline Advisory Op. 2010-2 (2010); Colo. Bar Ass'n Formal Op. 104

time and expense records,[22] or personnel matters,[23] are not considered materials to which the client is entitled under the end- product approach. Additionally, the lawyer's personal notes,[24] drafts of legal instruments or documents to be filed with a tribunal,[25] other internal memoranda, and legal research[26] are viewed as generated primarily for the lawyer's own purpose in working on a client's matter, and, therefore, need not be surrendered to the client under the end product approach.

Final documents supersede earlier drafts. Earlier drafts and lawyer notes are part of the process of completing the final draft and, when electronic documents go through a process of continuing changes, it can become difficult or impossible to determine what constitutes a distinct "draft."[27] Thus, drafts and other documents representing work by a lawyer are often of relatively small value to clients and can be burdensome for a lawyer to preserve, catalogue, and maintain.

In ABA Informal Ethics Opinion 1376 (1977), the Committee addressed, under the Code of Professional Responsibility, what properties a lawyer must provide to a client at the conclusion of the representation in a trademark mat-

---

22. Saroff v. Cohen, No. E2008-00612-COA-R3-CV, 2009 WL 482498 , 2009 BL 39364 (Tenn. Ct. App. Feb. 25, 2009) (Invoices for legal work performed are a law firm's business records, not prepared for the client's benefit, and need not be turned over upon client request. Proper procedure for securing this information when client is suing firm is to make a discovery request.).

23. Colo. Bar Ass'n Formal Op. 104 (1999); Alaska Bar Ass'n Ethics Comm. Op. 2003-3 (2003); D.C. Bar Op. 333 (2005).

24. Womack Newspapers Inc. v. Town of Kitty Hawk, 639 S.E.2d 96, 104 (N.C. 2007).

25. Miss. Bar Formal Op. 144 (1988); Utah State Bar Ass'n Advisory Op. 06-02 (2006).

26. Ill. State Bar Ass'n Advisory Op. 94-13 (1995); San Diego Cnty. Bar Ass'n Op. 1984-3 (1984).

27. This opinion does not address a lawyer's obligations to retain specific material relating to a representation in the first instance (whether in paper or electronic form). However, a lawyer's duty under Rule 1.16(d) to "surrender papers and property to which the client is entitled" at the termination of a representation necessarily requires some consideration of this issue. In general, a lawyer's ethical obligation to retain and safeguard material relating to a representation arises pursuant to a lawyer's duties of competence and diligence and will depend on the facts and circumstances of each representation. *See* ABA Model Rule 1.1 and ABA Model Rule 1.3. *See also* Ass'n of the Bar of the City of N.Y. Comm. on Prof'l & Judicial Ethics, Formal Op. 2008-1 (2008); S.C. Bar Formal Op. 15 (2013). Further, a lawyer's decision whether to retain specific material related to a representation, in most cases, ultimately rests in the professional judgment of a lawyer consistent with his or her ethical and legal duties to the client. For example, in most instances, a lawyer will not need to retain non-substantive email communication to a client such as an email confirming a meeting or providing driving directions to the lawyer's office. By contrast, the lawyer likely would need to retain an email to the client in which the lawyer communicates and evaluates a settlement offer from an opposing party. Consistent with duties under the Model Rules, lawyers are encouraged to develop good document management policies.

ter. We advised that the lawyer must provide the client with "end product—the certificates or other evidence of registration of the trademark," searches conducted and paid for, "significant correspondence, applications and materials filed in aid thereof, receipts, documents received from third parties, significant documents filed in the administrative and court proceedings, finished briefs whether filed or not if they pertain to the right of the client to the use or registration of the mark in question." The Committee noted that the lawyer "need not deliver" to the client "internal notes and memos."

The Committee affirms the position taken in Informal Ethics Opinion 1376 as it states the minimum required by the Rules. However, there may be circumstances in individual representations that require the lawyer to provide additional materials related to the representation. For example, when the representation is terminated before the matter is concluded, protection of the client's interest may require the lawyer to provide the client with paper or property generated by the lawyer for the lawyer's own purpose.

As noted above, Model Rule 1.16(d) requires a lawyer to take steps to the extent reasonably practicable to protect a client's interest. Such steps include "surrendering papers and property to which a client is entitled . . ." Comment [9] to Rule 1.16 further clarifies that the lawyer "must take all reasonable steps to mitigate the consequences [of withdrawal] to the client." Although surrendering papers and property which the client is entitled to receive does not necessarily give rise to a client's entitlement under the Rules of Professional Conduct to *all* materials in the lawyer's custody or control related to the representation, at a minimum a lawyer's obligation under the Rules reasonably gives rise to an entitlement to those materials that would likely harm the client's interest if not provided.[28] We agree with Colorado Ethics Opinion 104 (1999) that in this context, unless the law of the jurisdiction provides otherwise, "the ethical entitlement is based on the client's right

28. The Committee recognizes that while Model Rule 1.16(d) specifies "papers and property," many lawyers have moved or are moving to a paperless practice in which few documents are available in tangible form. The use of the term "paper" in Rule 1.16(d) includes all communications noted above, whether tangible or electronic. *See* ABA MODEL RULE 1.0(e) defining writing as a "tangible or electronic record of a communication." While this opinion does not address whether and in what circumstances a lawyer must convert an electronic document into paper for a client or who will bear the cost of this conversion, the Committee agrees with the reasoning in D.C. Bar Op. 357 (2012) which explained, "Lawyers and clients may enter into reasonable agreements addressing how the client's files will be maintained, how copies will be provided to the client if requested, and who will bear what costs associated with providing the files in a particular form; entering into such agreements is prudent and can help avoid misunderstandings."

to access the document related to the representation to enable continued protection of the client's interest."[29]

Therefore, on the facts presented, at a minimum, Rule 1.16(d) requires that the lawyer must surrender to the municipality:

- any materials provided to the lawyer by the municipality;
- legal documents filed with a tribunal—or those completed, ready to be filed, but not yet filed;[30]
- executed instruments like contracts;[31]
- orders or other records of a tribunal;
- correspondence issued or received by the lawyer in connection with the representation of the municipality on relevant issues, including email and other electronic correspondence that has been retained according to the firm's document retention policy;
- discovery or evidentiary exhibits, including interrogatories and their answers, deposition transcripts, expert witness reports and witness statements, and exhibits;
- legal opinions issued at the request of the municipality; and
- third party assessments, evaluations, or records paid for by the municipality.

In contrast, under these facts, it is unlikely that within the meaning of Rule 1.16(d), the client is entitled to papers or other property in the lawyer's possession that the lawyer generated for internal use primarily for the lawyer's own purpose in working on the municipality's matters.[32] This is particularly true for matters that are concluded.

Therefore, under the facts presented, under Rule 1.16(d) the lawyer need not provide, for example, the following to the municipality:

- drafts or mark-ups of documents to be filed with a tribunal;
- drafts of legal instruments;
- internal legal memoranda and research materials;

29. *See also* Corrigan v. Teasdale Armstrong Schlafly Davis & Dicus, 824 S.W.2d 92, 97 (Mo. 1992) ("The purpose of the Rule, however, gives it meaning. The Rule is designed to protect a client's interest. It imposes a duty upon the attorney 'to take steps to protect' a former client's interest. 'Surrendering papers and property to which the client is entitled' is one example of a step an attorney must take to protect that interest. But, this duty 'to surrender papers and property' need not be supported or justified by any property concepts.")

30. ABA Comm. on Ethics & Prof'l Responsibility, Informal Op. 1376 (1977).

31. *Id.*

32. ABA Comm. on Ethics & Prof'l Responsibility, Informal Op. 1376 (1977).

- internal conflict checks;
- personal notes;
- hourly billing statements;
- firm assignments;
- notes regarding an ethics consultation;
- a general assessment of the municipality or the municipality's matter; and
- documents that might reveal the confidences of other clients.

The Committee notes that when a lawyer has been representing a client on a matter that is not completed and the representation is terminated, the former client may be entitled to the release of some materials the lawyer generated for internal law office use primarily for the lawyer's own purpose in working on a client's matter.[33]

In this fact scenario, if the lawyer has materials that are: (1) internal notes and memos that were generated primarily for the lawyer's own purpose in working on the municipality's matter, (2) for which no final product has emerged, and (3) the materials should be disclosed to avoid harming the municipality's interest, then the lawyer must also provide the municipality with these materials. For example, if in a continuing matter a filing deadline is imminent, and as part of working on the municipality's matter the lawyer has drafted documents to meet this filing deadline, but no final document has emerged, then the most recent draft and relevant supporting research should be provided to the municipality.

Finally, as part of the lawyer's duty pursuant to Rule 1.4 to keep the client "reasonably informed about the status of the matter," a lawyer may already have provided much of this information to a former client during the course of the representation. As Comment [4] to Rule

1.4 explains, "A lawyer's regular communication with clients will minimize the occasions on which a client will need to request information concerning the representation." The Committee encourages lawyers to regularly provide clients with information and copies of documents during the course of the matter and encourages lawyers to advise clients to maintain these documents. The fact that copies of certain materials may have been previously provided to a client is not dispositive of whether the lawyer must also provide such materials at the termination of a representation.[34] This fact may

33. A number of jurisdictions approve lawyer generated "summary of facts" or redacted memorandum that essentially provide the "useful" part of the documents to the client while preserving the internal thoughts/impressions of the lawyer as unnecessary for protecting the clients' interests. *See* Ohio Bd. Comm'rs on Grievances and Discipline Advisory Op. 2010-2 (2010).

34. *See generally* Travis v. Comm. on Prof'l Conduct, 306 S.W.3d 3 (Ark. 2009) (the client has no duty to maintain a file on his or her own behalf).

not, however, be dispositive of who—the lawyer or the client—should pay for the time and cost of duplication of such materials upon termination of the representation.[35]

Conclusion

Upon the termination of a representation, a lawyer is required under Model Rules 1.15 and 1.16(d) to take steps to the extent reasonably practicable to protect a client's interest, and such steps include surrendering to the former client papers and property to which the former client is entitled such as materials provided to the lawyer, legal documents filed or executed, and such other papers and properties identified in this opinion. A client is not entitled to papers and property that the lawyer generated for the lawyer's own purpose in working on the client's matter. However, when the lawyer's representation of the client in a matter is terminated before the matter is completed, protection of the former client's interest may require that certain materials the lawyer generated for the lawyer's own purpose be provided to the client.

35. Lawyers are encouraged to explain in their retainer letters who is responsible for the costs of copying and under what circumstances.

AMERICAN BAR ASSOCIATION
STANDING COMMITTEE ON ETHICS AND PROFESSIONAL RESPONSIBILITY

Formal Opinion 472 **November 30, 2015**

Communication with Person Receiving Limited-Scope Legal Services

Under Model Rule 1.2(c), lawyers are authorized to provide limited-scope legal representation. Although not required by Rule 1.2(c), the Committee recommends that lawyers providing limited-scope representation confirm the scope of the representation in writing provided to the client.

Although Rule 4.2 does not require a lawyer to ask a person if he or she is represented by counsel before communicating with that person about the subject of the representation, a lawyer's knowledge that the person has obtained assistance from another lawyer may be inferred from circumstances. If the lawyer has reason to believe that an unrepresented person on the opposing side has received limited-scope legal services, the Committee recommends that the lawyer begin the communication with that person by asking whether that person is or was represented by counsel for any portion of the matter so that the lawyer knows whether to proceed under ABA Model Rule 4.2 or 4.3. When a lawyer has knowledge that a person is represented on the matter to be discussed, the lawyer must obtain the consent of counsel prior to speaking with the person.

If the person states that he or she is or was represented by counsel in any part of a matter, and does not articulate either that the representation has concluded or that the issue to be discussed is clearly outside the scope of the limited-scope representation, the lawyer requesting information should contact the lawyer providing limited-scope services to identify the issues on which the inquiring lawyer may not communicate directly with the person receiving limited- scope services.

The lawyer must comply with Rule 4.2 and communicate with the person's counsel when the communication concerns an issue, decision, or action for which the person is represented. Under Rule 4.3, however, the lawyer may communicate directly with the person on aspects of the matter for which no representation exists. On aspects of the matter for which representation has been completed and the lawyer providing limited-scope services is not expected to reemerge to represent the client, a lawyer may communicate directly with the other person. Communication with a person who received limited-scope legal services about an issue for which representation has concluded should not include inquiries about protected communications between the person and the lawyer providing limited-scope services.

In this opinion the Committee addresses the obligations of a lawyer under ABA Model Rule of Professional Conduct 4.2, *Communication with Person Represented by Counsel,* commonly called the "no contact" rule, and ABA Model Rule of Professional Conduct 4.3, *Dealing with Unrepresented Person,* when communicating with a person who is receiving or has received limited-scope representation under ABA Model Rule of Professional Conduct 1.2, *Scope of Representation and Allocation of Authority Between Client and Lawyer.*[1] We also provide recommendations for lawyers providing limited-scope representation.

Like all the Model Rules of Professional Conduct, Rules 1.2, 4.2, and 4.3 are intended to be rules of reason and must be construed and applied "with reference to the purposes of legal representation and the law itself."[2] In a limited-scope representation, the Model Rules in general, and Model Rule 4.2 specifically, must be interpreted accordingly because limited-scope representations do not naturally fit into either the traditional full-matter representation contemplated by Model Rule 4.2 or the wholly pro se representation contemplated by Model Rule 4.3.

Rule 1.2, Scope of Representation and Allocation of Authority Between Client and Lawyer

Model Rule 1.2(c) reads: "A lawyer may limit the scope of the representation if the limitation is reasonable under the circumstances and the client gives informed consent."[3] Today lawyers increasingly represent clients on a limited-scope basis.

Limited-scope representation may include assisting a litigant who is appearing before a tribunal pro se, by drafting or reviewing one or more documents to be submitted in the proceeding. "This is a form of 'unbundling' of legal services, whereby a lawyer performs only specific, limited tasks instead of handling all aspects of a matter." *See* ABA Formal Ethics Opinion 07-446 (2007).[4]

1. This opinion is based on the Model Rules of Professional Conduct as amended by the American Bar Association House of Delegates through February 2013. The laws, court rules, regulations, rules of professional conduct, and opinions promulgated in the individual jurisdiction are controlling.

2. Model Rules of Prof'l Conduct, Preamble & Scope [14].

3. Model Rules of Prof'l Conduct R. 1.2(c).

4. ABA Formal Op. 07-447 (2007) addressed the scope of representation of a client in a collaborative law setting. In that Opinion, the Committee determined that "[A] lawyer may provide legal assistance to litigants appearing before tribunals 'pro se' and help them prepare written submissions without disclosing or ensuring the disclosure of the nature or extent of such assistance." The Committee rejected the argument that courts are deceived by lawyers who "ghostwrite" legal documents for pro se litigants or that such conduct is "dishonest," noting that the conduct does not mislead the court or any party.

Although limited-scope representation is not restricted to low-income clients or small claims matters, the ABA Ethics 2000 Commission explained that the proposed amendments to Model Rule 1.2(c) and its Comments regarding limited-scope representations were in part "intended to provide a framework within which lawyers may expand access to legal services by providing limited but nonetheless valuable legal services to low- or moderate-income persons who otherwise would be unable to obtain counsel."[5]

Rule 1.2(c) requires a lawyer to secure the informed consent of a client when providing limited-scope services. Informed consent is defined as: "the agreement by a person to a proposed course of conduct after the lawyer has communicated adequate information and explanation about the material risks of and reasonably available alternatives to the proposed course of conduct."[6] The Colorado Bar Association advised in Formal Ethics Opinion 101 that a lawyer providing limited-scope services to a client should "clearly explain the limitations of the representation, including the types of services which are not being provided and the probable effect of limited representation on the client's rights and interests."[7] The D.C. Bar Legal Ethics Committee advised in its Opinion 330 (2005) that the "client's understanding of the scope of the services" is fundamental to a limited-scope representation.[8] Opinion 330 recommended that lawyers reduce such agreements to writing:

> Because the tasks excluded from a limited services agreement will typically fall to the client to perform or not get done at all, it is essential that clients clearly understand the division of responsibilities under a limited representation agreement . . . Particularly in the context of limited-representation agreements, however, a writing clearly explaining what is and is not encompassed within the agreement to provide services will be helpful in ensuring the parties' mutual understanding.[9]

Similarly, the Ethics 2000 Commission recommended adding a formal Comment to Rule 1.2 that a "specification of the scope of representation will normally be a necessary part of the lawyer's written communication of the rate or basis of the lawyer's fee as required by Rule 1.5(b)." However, because the House of Delegates rejected the Commission's parallel proposal to

---

5. A Legislative History: The Development of the ABA Model Rules Of Professional Conduct, 1982-2013, at 59 (Art Garwin ed., 2013).

6. Model Rules of Prof'l Conduct R. 1.0(e).

7. Colorado Bar Ass'n Formal Op. 101 (1998, rev. by addendum 2006).

8. D.C. Bar Op. 330 (2005).

9. *Id.*

amend Rule 1.5(b) — which would have required written fee agreements that included an explanation of the scope of the representation, the basis or rate of the fee, and the expenses for which the client will be responsible — this proposed Rule 1.2 Comment language was not advanced.[10]

Therefore, although not required by Rule 1.2(c), the Committee nevertheless recommends that when lawyers provide limited-scope representation to a client, they confirm with the client the scope of the representation—including the tasks the lawyer will perform and not perform—in writing that the client can read, understand, and refer to later. This guidance is in accord with Model Rule 1.5(b) which explains:

> The scope of the representation and the basis or rate of the fee and expenses for which the client will be responsible shall be communicated to the client, preferably in writing, before or within a reasonable time after commencing the representation, except when the lawyer will charge a regularly represented client on the same basis or rate. Any changes in the basis or rate of the fee or expenses shall also be communicated to the client.

The Committee notes that some state rules of professional conduct require a written agreement when a lawyer provides limited-scope services. *See, e.g.*, Maryland Lawyers' Rules of Professional Conduct, Rule 1.2(c)(3); Missouri Rule of Professional Conduct 1.2(c); Montana Rule of Professional Conduct 1.2(c)(2); and New Hampshire Rule of Professional Conduct 1.2(c) and 1.2(g). Other states explain that a written agreement is preferred. *See* Ohio Rule of Professional Conduct 1.2(c) and Tennessee Rule of Professional Conduct 1.2(c). Additionally, some state rules of civil procedure require a limited-scope appearance filing with the court identifying each aspect of the proceeding to which the limited-scope appearance pertains. *See, e.g.*, Illinois Supreme Court Rule 13(c)(6). Therefore, lawyers providing limited-scope representation are advised to review their state rules to determine whether a written agreement is required for their limited-scope representation.[11]

---

10. A Legislative History, *supra* note 5, at 61-62.

11. Because a tribunal may require disclosure of the scope of the services performed by the lawyer, and because a client receiving limited-scope services may desire to disclose to opposing counsel the scope of services performed by the lawyer, the Committee cautions lawyers providing limited-scope services to draft their limited-scope legal service agreement so that the agreement does not reveal information beyond that necessary for the client, opposing counsel, or the tribunal to determine the scope of the representation. For an example of a limited-scope agreement that lists services to be performed, see Reporter's Notes to Maine Rule of Professional Conduct 1.2 Limited Representation Agreement. The agreement lists 20 categories of legal services.

If a lawyer who is providing limited-scope services is contacted by opposing counsel in the matter, the lawyer should identify the issues on which the inquiring lawyer may not communicate directly with the person receiving limited-scope services. A lawyer providing limited-scope legal services to a client generally has no basis to object to communications between the opposing counsel and the client receiving those services on any matter outside the scope of the limited representation.

These issues would best be resolved at the inception of the client-lawyer relationship by the client giving the lawyer providing limited-scope representation informed consent to reveal to opposing counsel what issues should be discussed with counsel and what issues can be discussed with the client directly.

Model Rule 4.2, Communication with Person Represented by Counsel: Is there a duty to ask?

The ABA ethics rules have included a "no-contact" rule since the 1908 adoption of the ABA Canons of Professional Ethics.[12] Current Model Rule 4.2 reads:

> In representing a client, a lawyer shall not communicate about the subject of the representation with a person the lawyer knows to be represented by another lawyer in the matter, unless the lawyer has the consent of the other lawyer or is authorized to do so by law or a court order.

Model Rule 4.2 protects clients who have chosen to be represented by a lawyer from having another lawyer interfere with the client-lawyer relationship by, for example, seeking uncounseled disclosure of information and/or uncounseled concessions and admissions related to the representation.[13] A

12. ABA Canon 9: "Negotiations with Opposite Party. A lawyer should not in any way communicate upon the subject of controversy with a party represented by counsel; much less should he undertake to negotiate or compromise the matter with him, but should deal only with his counsel. It is incumbent upon the lawyer most particularly to avoid everything that may tend to mislead a party not represented by counsel, and he should not undertake to advise him as to the law." Canon 9 is available at: http://www.americanbar.org/content/dam/aba/migrated/cpr/mrpc/Canons_Ethics.authcheckdam.pdf.

13. Model Rules of Prof'l Conduct R. 4.2, cmt. [1].

lawyer directly communicating with an individual, however, will only violate Rule 4.2 if the lawyer *knows* that the person is represented by another lawyer in the matter to be discussed.[14] "Knows" is defined by the Model Rules as "actual knowledge of the fact in question. A person's knowledge may be inferred from circumstances."[15]

ABA Model Rule 4.3 reads:

> In dealing on behalf of a client with a person who is not represented by counsel, a lawyer shall not state or imply that the lawyer is disinterested. When the lawyer knows or reasonably should know that the unrepresented person misunderstands the lawyer's role in the matter, the lawyer shall make reasonable efforts to correct the misunderstanding. The lawyer shall not give legal advice to an unrepresented person, other than the advice to secure counsel, if the lawyer knows or reasonably should know that the interests of such a person are or have a reasonable possibility of being in conflict with the interests of the client.

Lawyers confronted with a person who appears to be managing a matter *pro se* but may be receiving or have received legal assistance, often are left in a quandary. May the lawyer assume that such persons are proceeding without the aid of counsel and, therefore, speak directly to them about the matter under Model Rule 4.3, or should the lawyer first ask whether they are represented in the matter and then proceed accordingly under either Rule 4.2 or 4.3?

---

14. *See, e.g.*, Okla. Bar Ass'n v. Harper, 995 P.2d 1143 (Okla. 2000) (lawyer did not violate Rule 4.2 without actual knowledge of the representation. "Ascribing actual knowledge to a lawyer based on the facts is not the same as applying the rule under circumstances where the lawyer should have known.").

15. Model Rules of Prof'l Conduct R. 1.0(f).

Interpreting Model Rule 4.2 in July 1995, ABA Formal Ethics Opinion 95-396, noted:

> It would not, from such a practical point of view, be reasonable to require a lawyer *in all circumstances* where the lawyer wishes to speak to a third person in the course of his representation of a client first to inquire whether the person is represented by counsel: among other things, such a routine inquiry would unnecessarily complicate perfectly routine fact-finding, and might well unnecessarily obstruct such fact-finding by conveying a suggestion that there was a need for counsel in circumstances where there was none, thus discouraging witnesses from talking.[16] (Emphasis added.)

Thus, while the black letter of Model Rule 4.2 does not include a duty to ask whether a person is represented by counsel, this Committee reiterates the warning of Comment [8] to Rule 4.2 that a lawyer cannot evade the requirement of obtaining the consent of counsel before speaking with a represented person by "closing eyes to the obvious."[17]

In circumstances involving what appears to be an unrepresented person, but in fact may be a person represented by a lawyer under a limited-scope agreement, a lawyer's knowledge that the person has obtained some degree of legal representation may be inferred from the facts.[18] Such circumstances include, for example: when a lawyer representing a client faces what appears

---

16. ABA Formal Op. 95-396, fn. 39 (1995). Immediately after the release of Formal Opinion 95-396, Rule 4.2, Comment [5] was amended to read: "The prohibition on communications with a represented person only applies, however, in circumstances where the lawyer knows that the person is in fact represented in the matter to be discussed. This means that the lawyer has actual knowledge of the fact of the representation; but such actual knowledge may be inferred from the circumstances. See Terminology. Such an inference may arise in circumstances where there is a substantial reason to believe that the person with whom communication is sought is represented in the matter to be discussed. Thus, the lawyer cannot evade the requirement of obtaining the consent of counsel by closing eyes to the obvious." However, the Ethics 2000 Commission recommended to the ABA House of Delegates that the sentence explaining "inference" be deleted, and the House adopted this recommendation in 2002. According to the "Reporter's Observations" document submitted to the House with the Ethics 2000 Commission resolution, this description of the knowledge requirement was "inconsistent with the definition of 'knows' in Rule 1.0(f), which requires actual knowledge and involves no duty to inquire." *See* A LEGISLATIVE HISTORY, *supra* note 5, at 566, citing ABA House of Delegates Report 401 (Feb. 2002).

17. Model Rules of Prof'l Conduct R. 4.2, cmt. [8].

18. Model Rules of Prof'l Conduct R. 1.0(f) (defining "knows").

to be a pro se opposing party who has filed a pleading that appears to have been prepared by a lawyer or when a lawyer representing a client in a transaction is negotiating an agreement with what appears to be a pro se person who presents an agreement or a counteroffer that appears to have been prepared by a lawyer.[19]

Therefore, the Committee recommends that, in the circumstances where it appears that a person on the opposing side has received limited-scope legal services, the lawyer begin the communication by asking whether the person is represented by counsel for any portion of the matter so that the lawyer knows whether to proceed under ABA Model Rule 4.2 or 4.3. This may assist a lawyer in avoiding potential disciplinary complaints, motions to disqualify, motions to exclude testimony, and monetary sanctions, all of which could impede a client's matter.[20] It is not a violation of the Model Rules of Professional Conduct for the lawyer to make initial contact with a person to determine whether legal representation, limited or otherwise, exists.

If the person discloses representation under a limited-scope agreement and does not articulate either that the representation has concluded (as would be the case if the person indicates that yes, a lawyer drafted documents, but is not providing any other representation), or that the issue to be discussed is clearly outside the scope of the limited-scope representation, then the lawyer should contact opposing counsel to determine the issues on which the inquiring lawyer may not communicate directly with the client receiving limited-scope services.[21]

When the communication concerns an issue, decision, or action for which the person is represented, the lawyer must comply with Rule 4.2 and communicate with the person's counsel.

The lawyer may communicate directly with the person on aspects of the matter for which there is no representation.[22] For these communications,

---

19. *See generally* State Bar of Arizona Op. 05-06 (2005) (filing of documents prepared by lawyer but signed by client receiving limited-scope representation is not misleading because ". . . a court or tribunal can generally determine whether that document was written with a lawyer's help.").

20. *See, e.g.*, Weeks v. Independent School Dist. No. I-89, 230 F.3d 1201 (10th Cir. 2000) (affirming district court's disqualification of lawyer who interviewed members of control group in violation of Rule 4.2).

21. Model Rules of Prof'l Conduct R. 4.2, cmt. [3] ("A lawyer must immediately terminate communication with a person if, after commencing communication, the lawyer learns that the person is one with whom communication is not permitted by this Rule.").

22. Model Rules of Prof'l Conduct R. 4.2, cmt. [4] ("This Rule does not prohibit communication with a represented person ... concerning matters outside the representation.").

the lawyer must comply with Rule 4.3. On aspects of the matter for which representation has been completed and the lawyer providing limited-scope services is not expected to reemerge to represent the client, a lawyer may communicate directly with the other person. We note that Rule 1.6 and the confidentiality of communications between a lawyer and the lawyer's client does not end when the limited representation concludes. Therefore, any communication with a person who received limited- scope legal services about an issue for which representation has concluded should not include inquiries about communications between the person and the lawyer providing limited-scope services.

If at any point in the matter the person—or the lawyer providing the limited-scope representation to that person—notifies the communicating lawyer that the scope of the representation was expanded, the communicating lawyer must act in accordance with Rule 4.2 as to any issues, decisions, or actions implicated by the expansion of the scope of services.

Conclusion

Under Model Rule 1.2(c), lawyers are authorized to provide limited-scope legal representation. Although not required by Rule 1.2(c), the Committee recommends that lawyers providing limited-scope representation confirm the scope of the representation in writing provided to the client.

Although Rule 4.2 does not require a lawyer to ask a person if he or she is represented by counsel before communicating with that person about the subject of the representation, a lawyer's knowledge that the person has obtained assistance from another lawyer may be inferred from circumstances. If the lawyer has reason to believe that an unrepresented person on the opposing side has received limited-scope legal services, the Committee recommends that the lawyer begin the communication with that person by asking whether that person is or was represented by counsel for any portion of the matter so that the lawyer knows whether to proceed under ABA Model Rule 4.2 or 4.3. When a lawyer has knowledge that a person is represented on the matter to be discussed, the lawyer must obtain the consent of counsel prior to speaking with the person.

If the person states that he or she is or was represented by counsel in any part of a matter, and does not articulate either that the representation has concluded or that the issue to be discussed is clearly outside the scope of the limited-scope representation, the lawyer requesting information should contact the lawyer providing limited-scope services to identify the issues on which the inquiring lawyer may not communicate directly with the person receiving limited-scope services.

The lawyer must comply with Rule 4.2 and communicate with the person's counsel when the communication concerns an issue, decision, or action for which the person is represented. Under Rule 4.3, however, the lawyer may communicate directly with the person on aspects of the matter for which no representation exists. On aspects of the matter for which representation has been completed and the lawyer providing limited-scope services is not expected to reemerge to represent the client, a lawyer may communicate directly with the other person. Communication with a person who received limited-scope legal services about an issue for which representation has concluded should not include inquiries about protected communications between the person and the lawyer providing limited-scope services.

AMERICAN BAR ASSOCIATION
STANDING COMMITTEE ON ETHICS AND PROFESSIONAL RESPONSIBILITY

Formal Opinion 473 **February 17, 2016**

Obligations Upon Receiving a Subpoena or Other Compulsory Process for Client Documents or Information

A lawyer receiving a subpoena or other compulsory process for documents or information relating to the representation of a client has several obligations. If the client is available, the lawyer must consult the client. If instructed by the client or if the client is unavailable, the lawyer must assert all reasonable claims against disclosure and seek to limit the subpoena or other initial demand on any reasonable ground. If ordered to disclose confidential or privileged information and the client is available, a lawyer must consult with the client about whether to produce the information or appeal. If the client and the lawyer disagree about how to respond to the initial demand or to an order requiring disclosure, the lawyer should consider withdrawing from the representation pursuant to Model Rule 1.16. If disclosure is ordered and the client is unavailable for consultation, the lawyer is not ethically required to appeal. When disclosing documents and information— whether in response to an initial demand or to an order, and whether or not the client is available—the lawyer may reveal information only to the extent reasonably necessary. The lawyer should seek appropriate protective orders or other protective arrangements so that access to the information is limited to the court or other tribunal ordering its disclosure and to persons having a need to know.

I. Introduction

Recently the Committee was asked to revisit Formal Opinion 94-385 (July 5, 1994) regarding subpoena of a lawyer's files because Model Rule 1.6(b)(6) was adopted in 2002, more than a decade ago (at that time as 1.6(b)(4)). Model Rule 1.6(b)(6) provides: "A lawyer may reveal information relating to the representation of a client to the extent the lawyer reasonably believes necessary to comply with *other law or court order*."[1]

When Formal Opinion 94-385 was issued, Model Rule 1.6(b) permitted a lawyer to disclose confidential information *in only two circumstances*: (i) to prevent certain crimes, and (ii) to establish certain claims or defenses on behalf of the lawyer.[2] Relying in part on then Comment [20], Formal Opinion 94-385 advised that the lawyer "must comply with the final orders of a court or other tribunal of competent jurisdiction requiring the lawyer to give information about a client."[3] The Opinion explained that this "does not mean that the lawyer should be a passive bystander to attempts by a governmental agency—or by any other person or entity for that matter—to examine her files or records."[4] Rather,

> [W]here a government agency serves on the lawyer a subpoena or court order directing the lawyer to turn over to the agency the lawyer's files relating to her representation of the client—the lawyer has a professional responsibility to seek to limit the subpoena, or court order, on any legitimate available ground (such as the attorney-client privilege, work product immunity, relevance or burden), so as to protect documents as to which the lawyer's obligation under Rule 1.6 apply. Only if the lawyer's efforts [at limiting the subpoena or order] are unsuccessful, either in the trial court or in the appellate court (in those jurisdictions where an interlocutory appeal on this issue is permitted), and she is specifically ordered by the court to turn over to the governmental agency documents which, in the lawyer's opinion, are privileged, may the lawyer do so.[5]

---

1. ABA Model Rule 1.6(b)(6) (2015) (emphasis added). The phrase "other law" refers, generally, to statutory or regulatory requirements. *See, e.g.*, State Bar of Michigan Advisory Op. RI-311 (1999) (regulation requiring lawyer to report the names and addresses of clients to the Legal Services Corporation); State Bar of Michigan Advisory Op. RI-54 (1990) (Internal Revenue Code requirement that cash transactions exceeding $10,000.00 be reported to the Internal Revenue Service). Although there is overlap in the two phrases, this opinion addresses principally the obligations of a lawyer who receives a subpoena or other initial demand that is or may be enforced by a court or other tribunal. Throughout this opinion, "subpoena," "demand," "compulsory process," and similar terms are used interchangeably to refer to any initial demand by an entity or person or government agency seeking information protected by Model Rule 1.6(a) that is or may be enforced by compulsory process. "Court" or "tribunal" refers to a court, an arbitrator in a binding arbitration proceeding or a legislative body, and an administrative agency or other body acting in an adjudicative capacity and includes any other "tribunal" within the meaning of Model Rule 1.0(m).
2. *Compare* ABA Model Rule 1.6(b) (1994), *with* ABA Model Rule 1.6(b) (2015).
3. ABA Comm. on Ethics & Prof'l Responsibility, Formal Op. 94-385 (1994), at 2.
4. *Id.*
5. *Id.* at 3 (footnotes omitted).

In the twenty-one years since publication of Formal Opinion 94-385 and the fourteen years since the Ethics 2000 amendments, additional questions have arisen regarding how a lawyer should respond to subpoenas, demands, or other compulsory process for client information and documents. These questions include: If disclosure is to be made, how extensive should it be? What, if any, protective measures should or must the lawyer seek? Are the obligations different when the client is not available for consultation? When the client is available for consultation but responding to the demand is outside the scope of a current representation, how should the lawyer handle retention and fee arrangements? If the client and the lawyer disagree about how to respond—either to the initial demand or after disclosure is ordered—what are the lawyer's obligations? Must the lawyer appeal an adverse decision for a client who is unavailable? Should or may the lawyer provide for these contingencies in retainer letters? This opinion provides guidance on these and related questions. The advice offered here updates and extends the advice offered in Formal Opinion 94-385.

II. Discussion

Rule 1.6(b) permits but does not require a lawyer to disclose information relating to the representation of a client ("[a] lawyer may reveal information") that the lawyer would otherwise be barred from disclosure under Rule 1.6(a).[6] Each of the seven 1.6(b) provisions specifies an exception to the 1.6(a) prohibition, and under each provision disclosure is permitted.[7]

For example, Rule 1.6(b)(6) makes clear that a lawyer cannot argue 1.6(a) bars compliance with a court order. Rule 1.6(a) permits disclosure of information relating to the representation, "if such disclosure is permitted by paragraph (b)," and subparagraph (b)(6) permits the lawyer to disclose information "to comply with other law or court order." A lawyer must obey

6. ABA Model Rule 1.6(a) (2015) provides: "A lawyer shall not reveal information relating to the representation of a client unless the client gives informed consent, the disclosure is impliedly authorized in order to carry out the representation or the disclosure is permitted by paragraph (b)."

7. *See, e.g.*, ABA Model Rule 1.6(b)(1) (2015) (a lawyer *may* reveal confidential information "to prevent reasonably certain death or substantial bodily harm") (emphasis added); ABA Model Rule 1.6(b)(2) (2015) (a lawyer *may* reveal confidential information "to prevent the client from committing a crime or fraud that is reasonably certain to result in substantial injury to the financial interests or property of another and in furtherance of which the client has used or is using the lawyer's services") (emphasis added). ABA Model Rule 1.6(b)(6) is, by its terms, and consistent with (b)(1) through (b)(5), also permissive. *See* ABA Model Rule 1.6(b)(6) (2015) ("[a] lawyer *may* reveal information . . . to comply with . . . a court order") (emphasis added). *See also* A Legislative History: The Development of the ABA Model Rules of Professional Conduct, 1982-2013 130 (Art Garwin ed., 2013); Margaret Love, *The Revised ABA Model Rules of Professional Conduct: Summary of the Work of Ethics 2000*, 15 GEO. J. Legal Ethics 441, 451 (2002).

a court order, subject to any right to move the court to withdraw or modify the order or to appeal the order.[8] But a lawyer facing a court order requiring the disclosure of client confidential information still is faced with complex, critical and fact-intensive questions on how to respond—e.g., what challenges should be considered, what specific information should be disclosed, and what protective measures should be sought. In making these judgments the lawyer must balance obligations inherent in the lawyer's dual role as an advocate for the client and an officer of the court. [9] In doing so, the lawyer should disclose client confidential information only to the extent "the lawyer reasonably believes necessary" to comply with the order.[10] Provision (b)(6) enables—indeed calls upon—the lawyer to make these delicate judgments.

A. Notice and Consultation

The lawyer's obligations of notice and consultation upon receiving a demand for client files and information are essentially the same for current and former clients. First, the lawyer must notify—or attempt to notify—the client.[11] For former clients, the lawyer must make reasonable efforts to reach

8. *See, e.g.*, ABA MODEL RULE 3.4(c) (2015) ("A lawyer shall not . . . knowingly disobey an obligation under the rules of a tribunal"); ABA MODEL RULE 8.4(d) (2015) ("It is professional misconduct for a lawyer to . . . engage in conduct that is prejudicial to the administration of justice"); ABA MODEL RULE 8.4(a) (2015) ("It is professional misconduct for a lawyer to . . . violate or attempt to violate the Rules of Professional Conduct"). *See also* RESTATEMENT OF THE LAW GOVERNING LAWYERS (3d) § 105 (2000) ("In representing a client in a matter before a tribunal, a lawyer must comply with applicable law, including rules of procedure and evidence and specific tribunal rulings.").

9. *See* Dike v. Dike, 448 P.2d 490, 493 (Wash. 1968) (discussing whether a lawyer should be ordered to disclose confidential information the court said, "[I]t is important to recognize that an attorney has a dual role [in this context] — he is both an advocate for his client and an officer of the court . . . . Neither duty can be meaningfully considered independent from the other.").

10. ABA MODEL RULE 1.6 cmt. [16] (2015).

11. *See, e.g.*, State Bar of Michigan Advisory Op. CI-925 (1983) (lawyer must notify client upon receipt of a subpoena for documents relating to the lawyer's representation of the client) (citations omitted); Alaska Bar Ass'n Op. 96-3 (1996) (upon receiving a demand for confidential information or documents, the lawyer should attempt to contact the client concerning the request). *See also* Linda G. Bauer, *Subpoena Savvy: What To Do When Your Client's File is Subpoenaed* (Nov. 2002), www.mass.gov/obcbbo/subpoena.htm (". . . [T]he lawyer should first attempt to contact the former client to determine whether the client consents to the disclosure."); D.C. Bar Op. 14 (1976), at 2 ("an attorney should promptly notify his former client when he receives a subpoena asking for documents that came into his possession during the course of the representation of that former client or documents that affect or may affect that former client"); Pennsylvania Legal Ethics & Prof'l Responsibility Comm. Op. 2002-106 (2003) ("a lawyer may comply with an order issued in a private arbitration to reveal confidential client information, but must first raise the confidentiality issue with the arbitration panel and notify any clients whose confidences are implicated. The lawyer should try to limit the scope and impact of the disclosure.").

the client by, for example, internet search, phone call, fax, email or other electronic communications, and letter to the client's last known address. The specific efforts required to reach particular clients will depend on the circumstances existing when the lawyer receives the demand. But these efforts must be reasonable within the meaning of Model Rule 1.0(h), and should be documented in the lawyer's files.

The lawyer's obligations to the client will differ depending on whether the client is available for consultation. Where the client is available, the lawyer must consult the client about how to respond to the demand.[12] Model Rule 1.4 should guide this consultation.

Rule 1.4 directs the lawyer to "promptly inform the client of any decision or circumstance with respect to which the client's informed consent" is required and to "explain [the] matter to the extent reasonably necessary to permit the client to make informed decisions."[13] Rule 1.6(a) allows the lawyer to disclose information relating to the representation with the client's informed consent. [14] "'Informed consent' denotes the agreement by a person to a proposed course of conduct after the lawyer has communicated adequate information and explanation about the material risks of and reasonably available alternatives to the proposed course of conduct."[15]

---

12. *See* ABA Model Rule 1.6 cmt. [15] (2015) (client consultation is required by Rule 1.4 before responding to an order or demand for information relating to a representation by "a court or by another tribunal or governmental entity"). The protection of 1.6 is provided to former clients through Model Rule 1.9(c)(1) and (2), which provide: "A lawyer who has formerly represented a client in a matter or whose present or former firm has formerly represented a client in a matter shall not thereafter: (1) use information relating to the representation to the disadvantage of the former client except as these Rules would permit or require with respect to a client . . . or (2) reveal information relating to the representation except as these Rules would permit or require with respect to a client." *See also* Swidler & Berlin v. U.S., 524 U.S. 399 (1998) (obligations of confidentiality continue even after the death of a client); Jamaica Pub. Serv. Co. v AIU Ins. Co., 684 N.Y.S.2d 459, 462 (N.Y. 1998) (an attorney owes a "continuing duty" to a former client not to reveal confidences learned in the course of a professional relationship). *See also* ABA Comm. on Ethics & Prof'l Responsibility, Formal Op. 10-456 fn8 ("[t]he lawyer's obligation to protect the attorney-client privilege ordinarily applies when the lawyer is called to testify or provide documents regarding a former client no less than a current client"); Rhode Island Supreme Ct. Ethics Advisory Panel Op. 2013-05, at 3 (2013) (obligations under 1.6 continue even after death of client; even then a "lawyer has a professional responsibility to seek to limit [a] subpoena or court order on any legitimate grounds such as attorney-client privilege, work product immunity, burden or relevance, to protect information to which obligations under Rule 1.6 apply") (citing ABA Formal Opinion 94-385).

13. ABA Model Rule 1.4 (2015).

14. *See* ABA Model Rule 1.6(a) (2015) (prohibiting a lawyer from revealing confidential information unless the client gives "informed consent").

15. ABA Model Rule 1.0(e) (2015).

The content of the consultation will depend on the circumstances. It should include, at a minimum, (i) a description of the protections afforded by Rule 1.6(a) and (b), (ii) whether and to what extent the attorney-client privilege or work product doctrine or other protections or immunities apply, and (iii) any other relevant matter. Other relevant matters include, for example, "to the extent that the disclosure of confidential client information in a civil proceeding may raise potential criminal liability for the client, the consequences should be explained to the client during the consultation process."[16] The lawyer also may need to discuss whether the subpoena or other demand is valid and whether the requested document contains self-incriminatory information that might form the basis of a Fifth Amendment privilege claim against disclosure.

If, after consultation, the client wishes to challenge the demand, the lawyer should, as appropriate and consistent with the client's instructions, challenge the demand on any reasonable ground. If, after making the challenge, the court or other tribunal rules against the motion to withdraw or modify the order or demand for production, "the lawyer must consult with the client about the possibility of appeal to the extent required by Rule 1.4."[17]

If the client decides not to appeal and gives informed consent to disclosure, the lawyer must produce the documents and information consistent with the client's instructions and as described in Part IIC of this opinion.

The lawyer has several options and some obligations if the lawyer and client disagree about how to respond to the initial demand or to an adverse ruling, or if the client wishes to retain new counsel. For a current client, where the initial demand or the appeal is within the scope of the retention, for example, the lawyer may seek to withdraw in compliance with Model Rule 1.16.[18] Where the initial demand or the appeal constitutes a new matter for a current client or relates to a former client and the client wishes to seek other counsel, the lawyer should take reasonable steps to protect the client's interest during the client's search for other counsel.[19]

B. Fee Arrangements

When responding to a demand that is outside the scope of a current retention, or when the demand relates to information and documents of a former client, the lawyer may need to discuss fee and retention arrangements during the consultation. In doing so, however, the lawyer must comply with the relevant rules. For example, under Model Rule 1.5(b) "[t]he scope of the representation and the basis or rate of the fee and expenses for which the

16. *See* Bauer, *supra* note 11.
17. ABA Model Rule 1.6 cmt. [15] (2015).
18. *See* ABA Model Rule 1.16(b)(1), (4), (7) & 1.16(c) (2015).
19. *See* ABA Model Rule 1.16(d) (2015).

client will be responsible shall be communicated to the client, preferably in writing, before or within a reasonable time after commencing the representation, except when the lawyer will charge a regularly represented client on the same basis or rate."[20]

Lawyers also may consider providing for these situations in initial retainer letters by including provisions that (i) the client will keep the lawyer informed on how to reach the client, even after the representation has ended, (ii) in the event the lawyer receives a subpoena or other demand for information protected by Model Rule 1.6, the client will promptly respond to the lawyer's request for instructions, and (iii) the client agrees to pay all reasonable fees and costs associated with any production or judicial proceedings in response to a subpoena or other demand. Even if no fee agreement is reached—either in the initial retainer letter or during a consultation following the lawyer's receipt of the demand—the lawyer nevertheless may be required to challenge the initial demand, as discussed below.[21]

C. Where the Client is Unavailable for Consultation

Where the client is unavailable for consultation after the lawyer has made reasonable efforts to notify the client, the lawyer "*should* assert on behalf of the client all non-frivolous claims that . . . the information sought is protected against disclosure by the attorney-client privilege or other applicable law."[22] The lawyer has this obligation to assert all reasonable objec-

20. ABA Model Rule 1.5(b) (2015).

21. *See, e.g.*, D.C. Bar Op. 288 fn4 (1999) (" . . . [even] if no agreement on fees and expenses is reached regarding the efforts to protect the confidential information [demanded by a subpoena], the lawyer must nevertheless take all ethically required steps to protect the privilege even if not compensated for the services by the client."). A later suit in *quantum meruit* for the services rendered may be available to the lawyer but that is an issue of law beyond the jurisdiction of this Committee. Alternatively, a lawyer may seek to withdraw as appropriate under Rule 1.16.

22. ABA Model Rule 1.6 cmt. [15] (2015) (emphasis added). *See* RESTATEMENT OF THE LAW, *supra* note 8, § 63 cmt. b ("A lawyer generally is required to raise any reasonably tenable objection to another's attempt to obtain confidential client information . . . from the lawyer if revealing the information would disadvantage the lawyer's client and the client has not consented . . ."); Bd. of Prof'l Responsibility of the Supreme Ct. of Tennessee Formal Op. 2014-F-158 (2014) ("[i]n the absence of informed consent of the client, the lawyer must reveal the information or document if ordered to [do] so by the tribunal, but only after the lawyer has raised all non-frivolous objections that the information sought is protected against disclosure by the attorney-client privilege or other applicable law"); D.C. Bar Op. 288 (1999) (" . . . . A lawyer generally is required to raise any reasonably tenable objection to another's attempt to obtain confidential information . . . , unless disclosure would serve the client's interests . . . ." (citations omitted); D.C. Bar Op. 14 (1976) (". . . [W]hen documents are subpoenaed or an effort is otherwise made to compel their disclosure, it is the lawyer's ethical duty to a former client to assert on the former client's behalf every objection or claim of privilege available to

tions and claims when the lawyer receives the initial demand.[23] During the proceeding before the court or other tribunal, the lawyer should explain the lawyer's diligent but unsuccessful efforts to reach the client. If the lawyer is ordered to produce the documents and records, paragraph (b)(6) permits the lawyer to comply with the court order, as discussed below.

D. Complying With the Court Order

As noted, relying in part on then Comment [20], Formal Opinion 94-385 declared that a "lawyer must comply with the *final* orders of a court or other tribunal of competent jurisdiction requiring the lawyer to give information about the client."[24] Other authorities also direct a lawyer to comply with "final" orders of a court or other tribunal.[25] Questions have arisen as to whether the reference to "final order" in Formal Opinion 94-385 and elsewhere requires a lawyer to appeal an adverse ruling when the client cannot be located or is unavailable for consultation.

---

him when to fail to do so might be prejudicial to the client"); Kentucky Bar Ass'n Op. E-315 (1987) (upon receiving a grand jury subpoena for client documents a lawyer "must respond by asserting any privilege (i.e., the attorney-client privilege) . . . .") (citations omitted); New Jersey Advisory Comm. on Prof'l Ethics Op. 145 (1969) (". . . if the client fails to respond to the attorney's letter his silence cannot be construed as consent and it would be improper to turn over copies of the [client's documents absent a court order] . . . .").

23. Appropriate objections and claims may vary with the jurisdiction. In some states, e.g., California, a lawyer may be *required* to raise certain claims or objections. *See, e.g.*, Cal. Evidence Code § 955 (1965) (lawyer who received or made a communication subject to the privilege under this article shall claim the privilege whenever he is present when the communication is sought to be disclosed and is authorized to claim the privilege under subdivision (c) of § 954). In other states, by contrast, a lawyer may be *forbidden* from raising certain objections or claims.

24. ABA Comm. on Ethics & Prof'l Responsibility, Formal Op. 94-385, at 2 (emphasis added). Prior to the adoption of the amendments in 2002, Comment [20] to Model Rule 1.6 also said, a "lawyer must comply with the *final* orders of a court or other tribunal of competent jurisdiction requiring the lawyer to give information about the client." *See* A LEGISLATIVE HISTORY, *supra* note 7, at 129 (emphasis added).

25. *See, e.g.*, Rhode Island Supreme Ct. Ethics Advisory Panel Op. 98-02 (1998) (upon receiving a demand for confidential information a lawyer "has professional responsibility to seek to limit subpoena [sic] or court order on any legitimate ground, such as attorney-client privilege, work product immunity, burden or relevance . . . . The . . . attorney must comply, however, with the *final* orders of a court requiring him/her to produce the documents sought or to give information about the former client" (emphasis added) (citing ABA Formal Opinion 94-385)). *See also* State Bar of Arizona Op. 00-11 (2000) (discussing, *inter alia*, a comment to Arizona RPC 1.6, which says, ""The lawyer must comply with the *final* orders of a court or other tribunal . . . [requiring disclosure]" but noting that "[w]hat constitutes a 'final order' is problematic. Criminal attorneys might well argue that before revealing any such confidential information . . . the lawyer must await a final order by the highest court of appellate review and the mandate is spread relative thereto, if the original order of the lower court is appealed") (emphasis added).

Model Rule 1.6(b)(6) makes no reference to a "final" order. The comments adopted in 2002 make no reference to "final" orders. Comment [15] reads simply, "In the event of an adverse ruling, the lawyer must consult with the client about the possibility of appeal to the extent required by Rule 1.4. Unless review is sought, however, paragraph (b)(6) permits the lawyer to comply with the court's order."[26] The text thus suggests that omitting the reference to "final" orders was meant to relieve the lawyer from the added burden of pursuing an appeal or other "final" disposition, unless appropriate arrangements are made with an available client. The obligation of the lawyer with regard to an appeal is particularly relevant if the client or former client is unavailable.[27]

Requiring a lawyer to take an appeal when the client is unavailable places significant and undue burdens on the lawyer. An appeal costs money and takes time away from other clients. Taking an appeal on behalf of an unavailable client forces the lawyer to act without consultation and direction. While such clients need and deserve protection in response to an initial demand—to avoid improper and unjustified access to information and documents that the rules protect even after the client's death[28]—the balance changes once a court or other tribunal has ruled on the lawyer's initial objection. In the absence of instructions from the client to appeal, the ethics rules do not require a lawyer to shoulder further burdens. Accordingly, a lawyer is not ethically required to take an appeal on behalf of a client whom the lawyer cannot locate after due diligence.[29]

Once a lawyer determines disclosure is appropriate—in response to an initial demand or to an order and whether or not the client is available—the lawyer may produce documents and information "only to the extent the lawyer reasonably believes . . . is necessary . . . ."[30] The lawyer should seek appropriate protective orders and similar arrangements "to the fullest extent practicable."[31] "[D]isclosure should be made in a manner that limits access to the information to the tribunal or other persons having a need to know it . . . ."[32]

---

26. ABA Model Rule 1.6 cmt. [15] (2015).

27. *See* the Reporter's comment in A Legislative History, *supra* note 7, at 132.

28. Swidler & Berlin v. U.S., 524 U.S. 399 (1998) (obligations of confidentiality continue even after the death of a client); Jamaica Pub. Serv. Co. v. AIU Ins. Co., 684 N.Y.S.2d 459, 462 (N.Y. 1998) (an attorney owes a "continuing duty" to a former client not to reveal confidences learned in the course of a professional relationship).

29. When challenging the subpoena or other demand in the first instance the lawyer should explain to the court or other tribunal the lawyer's efforts to locate the client and the client's unavailability.

30. ABA Model Rule 1.6 cmt. [16] (2015).

31. *Id.*

32. *Id.*

III. Conclusion

A lawyer receiving a subpoena or other compulsory process for information or documents relating to the representation of a client has several obligations. If the client is available, the lawyer must consult the client. If instructed by the client or if the client is unavailable, the lawyer must assert all reasonable claims against disclosure and seek to limit the subpoena or other demand on any reasonable ground.

If ordered to disclose confidential or privileged information and the client is available, a lawyer must consult with the client about whether to produce the information or to appeal. If the client and the lawyer disagree about how to respond to the initial demand or to an order requiring disclosure, the lawyer should consider withdrawing pursuant to Model Rule 1.16. If disclosure is ordered and the client is unavailable for consultation, the lawyer is not ethically required to appeal.

When disclosing documents and information—whether in response to an initial demand or to a court order and whether or not the client is available—the lawyer may reveal information only to the extent reasonably necessary. The lawyer should seek appropriate protective orders or other protective arrangements so that access to the information is limited to the tribunal ordering its disclosure and to persons having a need to know.

Where the client is available, the lawyer is not required to act without a fee but arrangements regarding the scope of the work and fee arrangements must conform to the relevant rules.[33] Where the client is unavailable to make retention and fee arrangements, the lawyer is nevertheless required to challenge the demand in the first instance. Lawyers should consider providing for these situations in retainer agreements.

---

33. *See, e.g.*, ABA Model Rule 1.5 (2015).

AMERICAN BAR ASSOCIATION

STANDING COMMITTEE ON ETHICS AND PROFESSIONAL RESPONSIBILITY

FORMAL OPINION 474 **April 21, 2016**

Referral Fees and Conflict of Interest

Rule 1.5(e) allows lawyers who are not in the same firm to divide a fee under certain circumstances. A lawyer who refers a matter to another lawyer outside of the first lawyer's firm and divides a fee from the matter with the lawyer to whom the matter has been referred, has undertaken representation of the client.

Fee arrangements under Model Rule 1.5(e) are subject to Rule 1.7. Unless a client gives informed consent confirmed in writing, a lawyer may not accept a fee when the lawyer has a conflict of interest that prohibits the lawyer from either performing legal services in connection with or assuming joint responsibility for the matter.

When one lawyer refers a matter to a second lawyer outside of the firm and the first lawyer either performs legal services in connection with or assumes joint responsibility for the matter and accepts a referral fee, the agreement regarding the division of fees, including client consent confirmed in writing, must be completed before or within a reasonable time after the commencement of the representation.

The question presented is under what circumstances lawyers may divide a fee when one lawyer refers a matter to another lawyer outside the firm.[1] Our analysis starts with Model Rule 1.5(e), which reads:

> A division of a fee between lawyers who are not in the same firm may be made only if:
>
> (1) the division is in proportion to the services performed by each lawyer or each lawyer assumes joint responsibility for the representation;

1. This opinion is based on the ABA Model Rules of Professional Conduct as amended by the ABA House of Delegates through February 2016. The laws, court rules, regulations, rules of professional conduct, and opinions promulgated in individual jurisdictions are controlling.

(2) the client agrees to the arrangement, including the share each lawyer will receive, and the agreement is confirmed in writing; and

(3) the total fee is reasonable.

Comment [7] to Rule 1.5 explains that lawyers in different firms may divide a legal fee. This practice is often used when the fee is contingent and the division is between a referring lawyer and a trial lawyer.[2]

Model Rule 1.5(e)(1) establishes two different standards for such division of fees: either the division must be in proportion to the services performed or the lawyers must assume joint responsibility for the representation.[3] Thus the Rule permits a lawyer to associate with another lawyer (often a trial lawyer) in a different firm, refer a client to that lawyer, and divide a fee either in proportion to the services performed by each lawyer, or by having each lawyer involved in the representation assume joint responsibility for the matter, provided that the client agrees to the participation of all lawyers involved, including the share each lawyer will receive, the agreement is confirmed in writing, and the total fee is reasonable.[4]

Joint responsibility is not defined by the black letter of Model Rule 1.5(e). However, Comment [7] to Rule 1.5 provides guidance noting that "Joint re-

---

2. Model Rules of Prof'l Conduct R. 1.5 cmt. [7] (2016). *See also* Model Rules of Prof'l Conduct R. 1.1 (2016), which requires a lawyer to provide competent representation. Comment [6] to Rule 1.1 notes that "before a lawyer retains or contracts with other lawyers outside the lawyer's own firm to provide or assist in the provision of legal services to a client, the lawyer should ordinarily obtain informed consent from the client and must reasonably believe that the other lawyers' services will contribute to the competent and ethical representation of the client. . . . The reasonableness of the decision to retain or contract with other lawyers outside the lawyer's own firm will depend upon the circumstances, including the education, experience and reputation of the nonfirm lawyers; the nature of the services assigned to the nonfirm lawyers; and the legal protections, professional conduct rules, and ethical environments of the jurisdictions in which the services will be performed, particularly relating to confidential information."

3. There is wide variation in state adoptions of Model Rule 1.5(e). Some states have eliminated the specific requirement of proportionality or joint responsibility, simply requiring client consent and a reasonable total fee. *See, e.g.*, California Rules of Prof'l Conduct R. 2-200; Connecticut Rules of Prof'l Conduct R. 1.5(e); Delaware Rules of Prof'l Conduct R. 1.5(e); Michigan Rules of Prof'l Conduct R. 1.5(e); Oregon Rules of Prof'l Conduct R. 1.5(d). A limited number of states either prohibit referral fees altogether or have declined to adopt any version of subsection (e). *See, e.g.*, Colorado Rules of Prof'l Conduct R. 1.5(e) & Wyoming Rules of Prof'l Conduct R. 1.5(f). Louisiana Rules of Prof'l Conduct R. 1.5(e) requires the provision of substantive legal services to justify a fee division, which would also appear to preclude fee division solely for a referral. Other states require that a fee division always be accompanied by ongoing joint responsibility, or joint financial responsibility, for the matter. *See, e.g.*, Arizona Rules of Prof'l Conduct R. 1.5(e); Illinois Rules of Prof'l Conduct R. 1.5(e); Wisconsin Rules of Prof'l Conduct R. 20:1.5(e).

4. Model Rules of Prof'l Conduct R. 1.5 cmt. [7] (2016).

sponsibility for the representation entails financial and ethical responsibility for the representation as if the lawyers were associated in a partnership."[5] Implicit in the terms of the fee division allowed by Rule 1.5(e) is the concept that the referring lawyer who divides a legal fee has undertaken representation of the client.[6]

Because the client is represented by both the referring lawyer and the lawyer to whom the client was referred, a referral fee arrangement under Model Rule 1.5(e) subjects both lawyers to the conflict provisions of Rule 1.7.[7] Model Rule 1.7(a) reads:

> (a) Except as provided in paragraph (b), a lawyer shall not represent a client if the representation involves a concurrent conflict of interest. A concurrent conflict of interest exists if:
>
> (1) the representation of one client will be directly adverse to another client; or
>
> (2) there is a significant risk that the representation of one or more clients will be materially limited by the lawyer's responsibilities to another client, a former client or a third person or by a personal interest of the lawyer.

Illustration by Hypothetical: Part One

Application of Rule 1.5, and the relationship between Rules 1.5 and 1.7, can be illustrated using a hypothetical. Assume the following situation: for many years, Lawyer has represented The Flower Shoppe Inc., which is jointly owned by Daisy and Rose. Rose was in a car accident while on a personal errand driving a car owned by The Flower Shoppe. Rose, as a co-owner of

---

5. Model Rules of Prof'l Conduct R. 1.5 cmt. [7] (2016). Comments do not add obligations to the Rules but provide guidance. *See* Model Rules of Prof'l Conduct, Preamble and Scope [14] (2016). The Ethics 2000 Commission is the source of the current language of Comment [7]. *See* A Legislative History: The Development of the ABA Model Rules of Professional Conduct, 1982-2013, at 99 (Art Garwin ed., 2013). The Ethics 2000 Commission relied on ABA Comm. on Ethics & Prof'l Responsibility, Informal Op. 85-1514 for the amendments.

6. *See generally* Connecticut Bar Association Prof'l Ethics Comm., Informal Op. 2013-04 (2013); Maine Bd. of Bar Overseers Op. 145 (1994).

7. The Commission on Evaluation of Professional Standards (commonly referred to as the Kutak Commission) explained, "A fee arrangement [envisioned by this paragraph of Rule 1.5] is subject to the conflict provisions of Rule 1.7 and 1.8." *See* Proposed Final Draft, Model Rules of Professional Conduct 37 (1981). *See also* Illinois State Bar Ass'n, Advisory Op. 90-26 (1991); Massachusetts Bar Ass'n Op. 80-10 (1980); State Bar of Michigan, Informal Op. RI-116 (1992).

the Shoppe, had permission to use the Shoppe vehicle to perform the errand. Rose was not at fault but was injured in the accident. Knowing Lawyer does not practice personal injury law, Rose asked Lawyer to refer her to a personal injury trial lawyer. Lawyer will not assist the trial lawyer in preparation of the case. Rose would like Lawyer to receive a referral fee, and Lawyer wants to accept joint responsibility for the matter. When Rose requests the referral, Lawyer reasonably believes that The Flower Shoppe will not be a party to the matter. Before assuming joint responsibility for the matter, Lawyer must determine whether a conflict of interest exists under Rule 1.7(a).

On the facts presented here, Lawyer can proceed with the referral to the trial lawyer because there is no conflict of interest under Rule 1.7(a). The representation of one client is not directly adverse to another client and there is not a significant risk that the referral of Rose will be materially limited by Lawyer's responsibility to The Flower Shoppe. Thus, the requirements of 1.7(a) are satisfied.[8]

Illustration by Hypothetical: Part Two

Assume again that for many years, Lawyer has represented The Flower Shoppe Inc., which is jointly owned by Daisy and Rose. Rose was in a car accident while on a personal errand driving a car owned by The Flower Shoppe. Rose, as a co-owner of the Shoppe, had permission to use the Shoppe vehicle to perform the errand. Rose was injured. Fault is in dispute. Rose asked Lawyer to refer her to a personal injury trial lawyer. Lawyer will not assist the trial lawyer in the representation. Rose would like Lawyer to receive a referral fee, and Lawyer wants to accept joint responsibility for the matter.

Lawyer recognizes that sometime in the future the other driver in the accident will file a claim against Rose and may file a claim against The Flower Shoppe as owner of the car. If the other driver adds The Flower Shoppe as a party and Lawyer continues to represent The Flower Shoppe, Lawyer believes that there is a significant risk that Lawyer's representation of Rose will be materially limited by Lawyer's responsibilities to The Flower Shoppe and vice versa.[9]

---

8. We assume that when Lawyer conducted the conflict check, Lawyer determined that Lawyer's representation was also not limited by Lawyer's responsibilities to another client, a former client or a third person, or by a personal interest of Lawyer.

9. Model Rules of Prof'l Conduct R. 1.7 cmt. [8] (2016) explains that a conflict of interest exists "if there is a significant risk that a lawyer's ability to consider, recommend or carry out an appropriate course of action for the client will be materially limited as a result of the lawyer's other responsibilities or interests. . . . The mere possibility of subsequent harm does not itself require disclosure and consent. The critical questions are the likelihood that a difference in interests will eventuate and, if it does, whether it will materially interfere with the lawyer's independent professional judgment in considering alternatives

Therefore, in order to receive a referral fee for referring Rose to a trial lawyer, Lawyer must meet the requirements of Model Rule 1.7(b).[10]

Illustration by Hypothetical: Part Three

Assume again that for many years Lawyer has represented The Flower Shoppe Inc., which is jointly owned by Daisy and Rose. Rose was in a car accident while on a personal errand driving a car owned by The Flower Shoppe. Rose, as a co-owner of the Shoppe, had permission to use the Shoppe vehicle to perform the errand. Rose was injured. Fault is in dispute. Rose asked Lawyer to refer her to a personal injury trial lawyer. Lawyer will not assist the trial lawyer in the representation. Rose would like Lawyer to receive a referral fee and Lawyer wants to accept joint responsibility for the matter.

The other driver has filed a claim against Rose and The Flower Shoppe, and Lawyer has determined that Rose's interests in the suit are adverse to The Flower Shoppe's interests. While Lawyer does not expect to represent The Flower Shoppe in the suit, The Flower Shoppe will continue to be Lawyer's client. Lawyer's representation of Rose, through the referral, is a conflict of interest under Rule 1.7(a)(1).[11]

To receive a referral fee for referring Rose to the trial lawyer, Lawyer must meet the requirements of Model Rule 1.7(b).

---

or foreclose courses of action that reasonably should be pursued on behalf of the client." In this hypothetical, the facts provide that Lawyer reasonably believes that there is a significant risk that Lawyer's representation of Rose and The Flower Shoppe will be materially limited by Lawyer's responsibilities to the other. Thus Lawyer's reasonable belief establishes the conflict under Rule 1.7(a)(2).

10. Circumstances at the outset also could make accepting a referral fee improper. Changing a few facts in this hypothetical would prohibit Lawyer from referring Rose to the trial lawyer and receiving a referral fee. For example, if at the outset the other driver sued both Rose and The Flower Shoppe Inc., Lawyer represented The Flower Shoppe in the suit, and Rose and The Flower Shoppe asserted claims against each other, then Lawyer would have a conflict that a client could not consent to. *See* Model Rules of Prof'l Conduct R. 1.7(b)(3) (2016).

11. Model Rules of Prof'l Conduct R. 1.7 cmt. [6] (2016) provides, "Loyalty to a current client prohibits undertaking representation directly adverse to that client without that client's informed consent. Thus, absent consent, a lawyer may not act as an advocate in one matter against a person the lawyer represents in some other matter, *even when the matters are wholly unrelated*. The client as to whom the representation is directly adverse is likely to feel betrayed, and the resulting damage to the client-lawyer relationship is likely to impair the lawyer's ability to represent the client effectively. In addition, the client on whose behalf the adverse representation is undertaken reasonably may fear that the lawyer will pursue that client's case less effectively out of deference to the other client, i.e., that the representation may be materially limited by the lawyer's interest in retaining the current client." (Emphasis added).

Informed Consent to the Conflict

Rule 1.7(b) reads:

> Notwithstanding the existence of a concurrent conflict of interest under paragraph (a), a lawyer may represent a client if:
>
> > (1) the lawyer reasonably believes that the lawyer will be able to provide competent and diligent representation to each affected client;
> >
> > (2) the representation is not prohibited by law;
> >
> > (3) the representation does not involve the assertion of a claim by one client against another client represented by the lawyer in the same litigation or other proceeding before a tribunal; and
> >
> > (4) each affected client gives informed consent, confirmed in writing.

Assuming that Lawyer reasonably believes that Lawyer will be able to provide competent and diligent representation to each affected client, that the representation is not prohibited by law, and that at this time the representation does not involve the assertion of a claim by The Flower Shoppe against Rose in the same litigation, then under Rule 1.7(b)(4) Lawyer must still secure the informed consent, confirmed in writing, of each affected client.[12] Under hypotheticals two and three, Lawyer needs the informed consent of both Rose and The Flower Shoppe to refer Rose to the trial lawyer outside the firm and divide the legal fee.

Informed consent is defined by Model Rule 1.0(e) as "the agreement by a person to a proposed course of conduct after the lawyer has communicated adequate information and explanation about the material risks of and reasonably available alternatives to the proposed course of conduct."[13] Comment [6] to Model Rule 1.0 explains:

> The lawyer must make reasonable efforts to ensure that the client or other person possesses information reasonably adequate to make an informed decision. Ordinarily, this will require communication that

---

12. Model Rules of Prof'l Conduct R. 1.0(b) (2016) explains, "'Confirmed in writing,' when used in reference to the informed consent of a person, denotes informed consent that is given in writing by the person or a writing that a lawyer promptly transmits to the person confirming an oral informed consent."

13. Model Rules of Prof'l Conduct R. 1.0(e) (2016).

> includes a disclosure of the facts and circumstances giving rise to the situation, any explanation reasonably necessary to inform the client or other person of the material advantages and disadvantages of the proposed course of conduct and a discussion of the client's or other person's options and alternatives . . .

Before Rose or The Flower Shoppe can provide informed consent to the conflict of interest, Lawyer must provide both with information about the conflict of interest. For example, if Lawyer is representing The Flower Shoppe in the suit as noted in hypothetical two, and if after Lawyer has referred Rose to the trial lawyer the other driver sues both Rose and The Flower Shoppe Inc. resulting in Rose and The Flower Shoppe Inc. asserting claims against each other, then a conflict under Model Rule 1.7(b)(3) would prohibit representation.[14]

Rule 1.5(e) Fee Disclosures

Rule 1.5(e) requires that a client agree to the fee division and that the agreement be confirmed in writing.[15] The agreement must describe in sufficient detail the division of the fee between the lawyers including the share each lawyer will receive.[16] Rule 1.5(e)(3) mandates that the total fee be reasonable. If a contingent fee is divided between a referring lawyer and another lawyer, the total fee cannot be increased because of the referral.[17]

Rule 1.5(e)(2) uses the future tense in the phrase "including the share each lawyer *will receive*" to describe what the fee division agreement must include, and Comment [7] to Rule 1.5 explains "the client must agree to the arrangement, including the share that each lawyer *is to receive* . . . ." The use of the future tense envisions that the fee division agreement will precede the division of fees. Such an agreement should not be entered into toward the end of such a relationship. Instead, the division of fees must be agreed to either before or within a reasonable time after commencing the representation.[18]

---

14. This opinion does not address whether Lawyer would be required to withdraw from representing both Rose and The Flower Shoppe in hypothetical two, if such a conflict did arise. *See* Model Rules of Prof'l Conduct R. 1.7 cmt. [29] (2016). Nor does this opinion address under what circumstances Lawyer might also be required to repay a referral fee that was already paid to and received by the Lawyer.

15. Model Rules of Prof'l Conduct R. 1.5(e)(2) (2016).

16. *Id.*

17. *See, e.g.*, Illinois State Bar Ass'n, Advisory Op. 90-18 (1990).

18. At least two courts have questioned the efficacy of fee division agreements signed after settlement. Wagner & Wagner, LLP v. Atkinson, Haskins, Nellis, Brittingham, Gladd & Carwile, P.C., 596 F.3d 84, 92 (2d Cir. 2010) (rejecting referring lawyer's argument that "technical" requirement of joint responsibility letter required by New York Rule DR 2-107 could be satisfied by complying "before fees have been paid"; court explained that fee division provision "clearly anticipates compliance with its requirements early on in the representation. . . . More-

Conclusion

Rule 1.5(e) allows lawyers who are not in the same firm to divide a fee under certain circumstances. A lawyer who refers a matter to another lawyer outside of the first lawyer's firm and divides a fee from the matter with the lawyer to whom the matter has been referred, has undertaken representation of the client.

Unless a client gives informed consent confirmed in writing, a lawyer may not accept a fee when the lawyer has a conflict of interest that prohibits the lawyer from either performing legal services in connection with or assuming joint responsibility for the matter.

When one lawyer refers a matter to a second lawyer outside of the firm and the first lawyer either performs legal services in connection with or assumes joint responsibility for the matter and accepts a referral fee, the agreement regarding the division of fees, including client consent confirmed in writing, must be completed before or within a reasonable time after the commencement of the representation.

---

over, the undertaking of joint responsibility is difficult (to say the least) to accomplish, other than as a charade, after a settlement with the defendant has been reached."); Saggese v. Kelley, 837 N.E.2d 699, 706 (Mass. 2005) (while affirming the enforcement of an agreement to divide fees that client agreed to "toward the end of the attorney-client relationship," court holds that after the issuance of the decision, referring lawyer required to disclose fee sharing before the referral is made and secure client's consent in writing). *But see* Cohen v. Brown, 93 Cal. Rptr. 3d 24, 38 (Ct. App. 2009) (California's Rule 2-200 "requires only that the client's consent to a division of fees be given prior to the actual *division* of the fees. It does not require client consent prior to the commencement of work by the associated-in attorney/law firm."). *See also* Model Rules of Prof'l Conduct R. 1.1 cmt. [6] (2016) "before a lawyer retains or contracts with other lawyers outside the lawyer's own firm to provide or assist in the provision of legal services to a client, the lawyer should ordinarily obtain informed consent from the client . . . ."

AMERICAN BAR ASSOCIATION
STANDING COMMITTEE ON ETHICS AND PROFESSIONAL RESPONSIBILITY

Formal Opinion 475 **December 7, 2016**

Safeguarding Fees That Are Subject to Division With Other Counsel

A lawyer may divide a fee with another lawyer who is not in the same firm if the arrangement meets the requirements of Model Rule 1.5(e). When one lawyer receives an earned fee that is subject to such an arrangement and both lawyers have an interest in that earned fee, Model Rules 1.15(a) and 1.15(d) require that the receiving lawyer hold the funds in an account separate from the lawyer's own property, appropriately safeguard the funds, promptly notify the other lawyer who holds an interest in the fee of receipt of the funds, promptly deliver to the other lawyer the agreed upon portion of the fee, and, if requested by the other lawyer, provide a full accounting.

Model Rule 1.5(e) provides for the division of fees between lawyers who are not in the same firm.[1] A division of a fee "is a single billing to a client covering the fee of two or more lawyers who are not in the same firm."[2] Rule 1.5(e) provides that such agreements are permissible only if the division is proportionate to the services performed by each lawyer or both lawyers assume joint responsibility for the representation, the client agrees to the arrangement including the share each lawyer will receive, the arrangement is confirmed in writing, and the total fee is reasonable. Model Rule 1.15(a) provides in pertinent part that a lawyer "shall hold property of ...third persons that is in a lawyer's possession in connection with a representation separate from the lawyer's own property."

When lawyers are dividing a fee pursuant to Rule 1.5(e), a question arises regarding how an earned fee received from a client by one of the lawyers must be handled when both lawyers have an interest in the paid fees. Should the other lawyer who holds an interest in the earned fees be treated

1. This opinion is based on the ABA Model Rules of Professional Conduct as amended by the ABA House of Delegates through August 2016. The laws, court rules, regulations, rules of professional conduct, and opinions promulgated in individual jurisdictions are controlling.

2. MODEL RULES OF PROF'L CONDUCT R. 1.5, cmt. [7] (2016).

as a third person under Rule 1.15? We conclude that for the purposes of a division of fees between lawyers, when one lawyer receives fees on behalf of all lawyers in the matter, the answer is yes.

Model Rule 1.15 provides the answer. It explains in relevant part:

> (a) A lawyer shall hold property of clients or third persons that is in a lawyer's possession in connection with a representation separate from the lawyer's own property. Funds shall be kept in a separate account maintained in the state where the lawyer's office is situated, or elsewhere with the consent of the client or third person. Other property shall be identified as such and appropriately safeguarded. Complete records of such account funds and other property shall be kept by the lawyer and shall be preserved for a period of [five years] after termination of the representation.
>
> . . .
>
> (d) Upon receiving funds or other property in which a client or third person has an interest, a lawyer shall promptly notify the client or third person. Except as stated in this rule or otherwise permitted by law or by agreement with the client, a lawyer shall promptly deliver to the client or third person any funds or other property that the client or third person is entitled to receive and, upon request by the client or third person, shall promptly render a full accounting regarding such property.

Rule 1.15 applies in many situations including fee advances, advances of costs, receipt of settlement funds, holding client funds to which creditors have claims, and fee disputes between the lawyer and the client. Whatever the context, Rule 1.15 requires the safekeeping of any property that comes into the lawyer's possession in connection with the representation of a client[3] in which the client or any "third person" has an interest.

Thus, if two or more lawyers have an agreement that satisfies Rule 1.5 regarding a division of fees, and one lawyer receives a payment that must be divided with the other lawyer pursuant to their agreement, the other lawyer is a

---

3. Rule 1.15(a) explicitly applies to property in the lawyer's possession in connection with a representation of a client. Rule 1.15(d) does not contain this explicit limitation and some authorities have applied Rule 1.15(d) outside the context of a representation of a client. *See, e.g.*, Att'y Grievance Comm'n v. Johnson, 976 A.2d 245 (Md. 2009) (applying what is now Maryland Rule 1.15(d) to facts involving a lawyer serving as a settlement agent for a title company); State Bar of Arizona Comm. on Rules of Prof'l Conduct, Op. 04-03 (2004) (applying Arizona Rule 1.15(d) to facts involving funds delivered to a seller's former divorce lawyer by escrow agent in connection with a home sale in which the lawyer did not represent the former client).

"third person" for purposes of Rule 1.15. However, the designation of a person as a "third person" under Rule 1.15 addressing safekeeping property of others is limited to the purposes of Rule 1.15 (i.e., safekeeping the property of others). It is not necessarily indicative of the status of the person beyond the scope of Rule 1.15 (e.g., a lawyer who is co-counsel and a third person under Rule 1.15 for the purposes of safekeeping property is not a third person for the purposes of Rule 1.6).

The receiving lawyer, therefore, must, under Rule 1.15(a), deposit the funds in which co-counsel holds an interest in an account (typically a trust account) separate from the lawyer's own property.[4] Rule 1.15(d) requires the lawyer who receives the earned fees subject to a division agreement to promptly notify the other lawyer who holds an interest in the fee of receipt of the funds, promptly deliver to the other lawyer the agreed upon portion of the fee, and, if requested by the other lawyer, provide a full accounting.

Finally, if there is any dispute as to the interest of the receiving lawyer and the lawyer with whom the receiving lawyer is dividing a fee, Rule 1.15(e) requires that the receiving lawyer keep the disputed funds separate from the lawyer's own property until the dispute is resolved.

Conclusion

A lawyer may divide a fee with another lawyer who is not in the same firm if the arrangement meets the requirements of Model Rule 1.5(e). When one lawyer receives an earned fee that is subject to such an arrangement and both lawyers have an interest in that earned fee, Model Rules 1.15(a) and 1.15(d) require that the receiving lawyer hold the funds in an account separate from the lawyer's own property, appropriately safeguard the funds, promptly notify the other lawyer who holds an interest in the fee of receipt of the funds, promptly deliver to the other lawyer the agreed upon portion of the fee, and, if requested by the other lawyer, provide a full accounting.

4. Applicable state implementation of Rule 1.15 may require that the funds be deposited into an IOLTA (Interest on Lawyer Trust Accounts) account.

AMERICAN BAR ASSOCIATION

STANDING COMMITTEE ON ETHICS AND PROFESSIONAL RESPONSIBILITY

Formal Opinion 476 **December 19, 2016**

Confidentiality Issues when Moving to Withdraw for Nonpayment of Fees in Civil Litigation

In moving to withdraw as counsel in a civil proceeding based on a client's failure to pay fees, a lawyer must consider the duty of confidentiality under Rule 1.6 and seek to reconcile that duty with the court's need for sufficient information upon which to rule on the motion. Similarly, in entertaining such a motion, a judge should consider the right of the movant's client to confidentiality. This requires cooperation between lawyers and judges. If required by the court to support the motion with facts relating to the representation, a lawyer may, pursuant to Rule 1.6(b)(5), disclose only such confidential information as is reasonably necessary for the court to make an informed decision on the motion.

Withdrawal from a Civil Matter Based on a Client's Failure to Pay Fees[1]

Model Rule 1.16 addresses a lawyer's duties and responsibilities when withdrawing from the representation of a client. Rule 1.16(a) sets forth the circumstances when a lawyer is required to withdraw, and Rule 1.16(b) describes the circumstances when a lawyer may be permitted to withdraw from a representation.[2] Among the permissive reasons, Rule 1.16(b)(5) provides

1. This opinion does not address the additional and unique issues raised when a lawyer seeks to withdraw from representation in a criminal matter. The opinion is based on the ABA Model Rules of Professional Conduct as amended by the ABA House of Delegates through February 2016. The laws, court rules, regulations, rules of professional conduct, and opinions promulgated in individual jurisdictions are controlling.

2. Rule 1.16, paragraphs (a) and (b) read:

> (a) Except as stated in paragraph (c), a lawyer shall not represent a client or, where representation has commenced, shall withdraw from the representation of a client if:
>
> (1) the representation will result in violation of the Rules of Professional Conduct or other law;
>
> (2) the lawyer's physical or mental condition materially impairs the lawyer's ability to represent the client; or
>
> (3) the lawyer is discharged.

that a lawyer may withdraw from representing a client when "the client substantially fails to fulfill an obligation to the lawyer regarding the lawyer's services and has been given reasonable warning that the lawyer will withdraw unless the obligation is fulfilled." Comment [8] to the Rule states: "A lawyer may withdraw if the client refuses to abide by the terms of an agreement relating to the representation, such as an agreement concerning fees or court costs . . . ." In addition, Rule 1.16(b)(6) provides that a lawyer may withdraw where "the representation will result in an unreasonable financial burden on the lawyer or has been rendered unreasonably difficult by the client." As the courts have decided in the cases cited below, if a client fails over time to pay a lawyer's fees, and that failure continues after a lawyer provides a reasonable warning to the client, the lawyer may be permitted to withdraw.[3] In effectuating a withdrawal, a lawyer should do so in a manner that minimizes any prejudice to the client.[4]

The Duty of Confidentiality in Moving to Withdraw, Generally

A permissive withdrawal under Rule 1.16(b) is subject to the requirements of Rule 1.16(c). Rule 1.16(c) provides that when representing a client in a matter before a tribunal,[5] a lawyer must comply with the applicable law of

---

(b) Except as stated in paragraph (c), a lawyer may withdraw from representing a client if:

(1) withdrawal can be accomplished without material adverse effect on the interests of the client;

(2) the client persists in a course of action involving the lawyer's services that the lawyer reasonably believes is criminal or fraudulent;

(3) the client has used the lawyer's services to perpetrate a crime or fraud;

(4) the client insists upon taking action that the lawyer considers repugnant or with which the lawyer has a fundamental disagreement;

(5) the client fails substantially to fulfill an obligation to the lawyer regarding the lawyer's services and has been given reasonable warning that the lawyer will withdraw unless the obligation is fulfilled;

(6) the representation will result in an unreasonable financial burden on the lawyer or has been rendered unreasonably difficult by the client; or

(7) other good cause for withdrawal exists.

3. *See* Restatement (Third) of the Law Governing Lawyers § 32(g) cmt. k (2000). *Cf.* Brandon v. Belch, 560 F.3d 536, 538 (6th Cir. 2009).

4. Model Rules of Prof'l Conduct R. 1.16(d) (2016). *See also* Ronald E. Mallen, Legal Malpractice § 33.71 (2016).

5. "Tribunal" is defined in Rule 1.0(m), and "denotes a court, an arbitrator in a binding arbitration proceeding or a legislative body, administrative agency or other body acting in an adjudicative capacity. A legislative body, administrative agency or other body acts in an adjudicative capacity when a neutral official, after the presentation of evidence or legal argument by a party or parties, will render a binding legal judgment directly affecting a party's interests in a particular matter."

the tribunal in seeking to withdraw.[6] Under the rules of most courts, a motion to withdraw is required when a substitute lawyer does not simultaneously enter an appearance.[7]

In preparing a motion to withdraw a lawyer must consider how the duty of confidentiality under Rule 1.6 may limit the information that can be disclosed in the moving papers.[8] Under Rule 1.6(a), the duty of confidentiality applies broadly to "information relating to the representation," unless the client provides "informed consent," disclosure is "impliedly authorized to carry out the representation," or one of the enumerated exceptions in Rule 1.6(b) applies. The exceptions in paragraph (b) permit disclosures only "to

---

6. ABA Model Rule 1.16(c) states: "A lawyer must comply with applicable law requiring notice to or permission of a tribunal when terminating a representation. When ordered to do so by a tribunal, a lawyer shall continue representation notwithstanding good cause for terminating the representation."

7. *See, e.g.*, ARIZ. R. CIV. P. 5.1(b)(2); CAL. R. APP. P. 8.36; D.C. SUP. CT. R. CIV. P. 101(c); FLA. R. JUD. ADMIN. 2.060; ILL. R. CIV. P. 13; MASS. R. CIV. P. 11(c); N.D. CT. R. 11.2; VA. R. CIV. P. 1:5. Under ABA Model Rule 3.4(c), it is ethical misconduct for a lawyer to "knowingly disobey an obligation under the rules of a tribunal, except for an open refusal based on an assertion that no valid obligation exists."

8. ABA Model Rule 1.6, titled "Confidentiality of Information," provides as follows:

> (a) A lawyer shall not reveal information relating to the representation of a client unless the client gives informed consent, the disclosure is impliedly authorized in order to carry out the representation or the disclosure is permitted by paragraph (b).
>
> (b) A lawyer may reveal information relating to the representation of a client to the extent the lawyer reasonably believes necessary:
>
> (1) to prevent reasonably certain death or substantial bodily harm;
>
> (2) to prevent the client from committing a crime or fraud that is reasonably certain to result in substantial injury to the financial interests or property of another and in furtherance of which the client has used or is using the lawyer's services;
>
> (3) to prevent, mitigate or rectify substantial injury to the financial interests or property of another that is reasonably certain to result or has resulted from the client's commission of a crime or fraud in furtherance of which the client has used the lawyer's services;
>
> (4) to secure legal advice about the lawyer's compliance with these Rules;
>
> (5) to establish a claim or defense on behalf of the lawyer in a controversy between the lawyer and the client, to establish a defense to a criminal charge or civil claim against the lawyer based upon conduct in which the client was involved, or to respond to allegations in any proceeding concerning the lawyer's representation of the client;
>
> (6) to comply with other law or a court order; or
>
> (7) to detect and resolve conflicts of interest arising from the lawyer's change of employment or from changes in the composition or ownership of a firm, but only if the revealed information would not compromise the attorney-client privilege or otherwise prejudice the client.
>
> (c) A lawyer shall make reasonable efforts to prevent the inadvertent or unauthorized disclosure of, or unauthorized access to, information relating to the representation of a client.

the extent the lawyer reasonably deems necessary" to address the purpose of a particular exception. *See* Rule 1.6 Comment [16].[9] For example, in *In re Gonzalez*, 773 A.2d 1026 (D.C. 2001), the respondent was given an informal admonition, not for informing the court that fees were owed by the client, but for also disclosing extraneous and embarrassing client information in connection with the motion. Accordingly, when in doubt, a lawyer should err on the side of non-disclosure.

The more difficult question is when is a lawyer permitted to disclose *any* confidential client information in filing a motion to withdraw, and if so, how much. The tension between a lawyer's obligation to provide the court with sufficient facts to rule on a motion and the lawyer's duty of confidentiality has been characterized in one treatise as "a procedural problem that has no fully satisfactory solution."[10] Ultimately, however, lawyers wishing to withdraw must choose some manner in which to phrase their request for relief.[11]

The Duty of Confidentiality in Motions to Withdraw For Unpaid Legal Fees

Neither Rule 1.6(b) nor the Comments expressly refer to motions to withdraw for unpaid fees. The Comments do, however, recognize that some disclosure of confidential client information otherwise protected by Rule 1.6(a) is permitted in fee-collection suits by lawyers, based on the "claim or defense" exception in Rule 1.6(b)(5).[12] Similarly, motions to withdraw based on

9. ABA Model Rule 1.6, Comment [16] states: "Paragraph (b) permits disclosure only to the extent the lawyer reasonably believes disclosure is necessary to accomplish one of the purposes specified...In any case, a disclosure adverse to the client's interest should be no greater than the lawyer reasonably believes necessary to accomplish the purpose. If the disclosure will be made in connection with a judicial proceeding, the disclosure should be made in a manner that limits access to the information to the tribunal or other persons having a need to know it and appropriate protective orders or other arrangements should be sought by the lawyer to the fullest extent practicable."

10. Geoffrey C. Hazard Jr., W. William Hodes & Peter R. Jarvis, The Law of Lawyering § 21.16 (4th ed. 2015). *See also* Byrd v. Mahaffey, 78 P.3d 671, 676 (Wyo. 2003) ("[A] n artful balance between confidentiality and providing an adequate basis for withdrawal must be maintained by counsel requesting to withdraw.").

11. In ABA Formal Opinion 92-366, the Committee discussed the possibility of a "noisy withdrawal" to avoid assisting client misconduct. That Opinion was issued under a prior version of the Model Rules that did not include exceptions for disclosures to prevent or rectify client crime or fraud in furtherance of which the client used the lawyer's services. Currently, ABA Model Rule 1.6(b)(2) and (b)(3) expressly permit such disclosures.

12. ABA Model Rule 1.6(b)(5) permits disclosures "to establish a claim or defense on behalf of the lawyer in a controversy between the lawyer and a client." Comment [11] states: "A lawyer entitled to a fee for services rendered is permitted by paragraph (b)(5) to prove the services rendered in an action to collect it. This aspect of the rule expresses the principle that the beneficiary of a fiduciary relationship may not exploit it to the detriment of the fiduciary." *See also* the Restatement (Third) of Law Governing Lawyers § 65, stating: "A lawyer may use or disclose confidential information relating to the representation when

a client's failure to pay fees are generally grounded in the same basic right of a lawyer to be paid pursuant to the terms of a fee agreement with a client. Nonetheless, courts have differed widely as to whether any specific information regarding a lawyer's reasons for seeking withdrawal is required in a motion to withdraw, and if so, how much.

Comment [16] to Rule 1.6 provides that a lawyer may disclose information under 1.6(b) only "to the extent the lawyer reasonably believes the disclosure is necessary to accomplish one of the purposes specified." In support of the idea that specific information should not be required with respect to a motion to withdraw for nonpayment of legal fees, Comment [3] to Rule 1.16 states:

> The court may request an explanation for the withdrawal, while the lawyer may be bound to keep confidential the facts that would constitute such an explanation. The lawyer's statement that professional considerations require termination of the representation ordinarily should be accepted as sufficient. Lawyers should be mindful of their obligations to both clients and the court under Rule 1.6 and 3.3.

See also N.Y. State Bar Ass'n Comm. on Prof'l Ethics, Advisory Op. 1057 (2015), 2015 WL 4592234, at *3 ("the Rules anticipate that the court will usually not demand the disclosure of confidential information if the lawyer advises the court that 'professional considerations' require withdrawal").

Notwithstanding this authority, however, many courts have issued decisions that recite details as to the money owed by the clients, the specific legal services performed and related facts, indicating that the court required more from the lawyer than just a statement that the motion to withdraw was motivated by "professional considerations." While the courts in the following cases did not address a lawyer's duty of confidentiality, the decisions demonstrate that these courts found such details pertinent to their assessment of the motions. *See, e.g., In re Franke*, 55 A.3d 713, 724 (Md. Ct. Spec. App. 2012) (vacating trial court's denial of attorney's motion to withdraw based on client's nonpayment of $120,000 in unpaid fees as an abuse of discretion and as wrongly causing attorney "to provide free legal services"); *Team Obsolete Ltd. v. A.H.R.M.A. LTD.*, 464 F. Supp. 2d 164 (E.D.N.Y. 2006) (granting motion to withdraw based on supporting affidavit filed under seal revealing that the moving law firm had a dispute with their client regarding unpaid legal fees); *King v. NAID Inflatables of Newport, Inc.*, 11 A.3d 64, 67 (R.I. 2010) (the Supreme Court of Rhode Island, with the benefit of an *amicus* brief from the

---

and to the extent that the lawyer reasonably believes necessary to permit the lawyer to resolve a dispute with a client concerning compensation or reimbursement that the lawyer reasonably claims the client owes the lawyer."

Rhode Island Bar Association, reversed the trial court's denial of a motion to withdraw by a law firm filed before trial, stating that "the hearing justice did not accord adequate weight to the financial burden that would befall [the law firm] if [it] were required to continue to represent a nonpaying client."); *Brandon v. Blech*, 560 F.3d 536, 538-39 (6th Cir. 2009) (reversing trial court's denial of motion to withdraw for a client's nonpayment of fees, stating: "As other circuits recognize, compelling attorneys to continue representing clients who refuse to pay imposes a severe burden" (quoting then from *Rivera-Domenich v. Calvesbert Law Offices PSC*, 402 F.3d 246, 248 (1st Cir. 2005)); *Fid. Nat'l Title Ins. Co. v. Intercounty Nat'l Title Ins. Co.*, 310 F.3d 537, 540 (7th Cir. 2002) (reversing the denial of a motion to withdraw by a law firm that was owed more than $470,000 in fees, stating that it was "difficult to see why [the law firm] should be obliged to provide them free legal services"); *Reed Yates Farms, Inc. v. Yates*, 526 N.E.2d 1115, 1121 (Ill. App. Ct. 1998) (upholding trial court's granting of a motion to withdraw, stating: "If during the course of litigation attorney fees are not paid when due, an attorney may demand payment of accrued fees and withdraw from the case if the fees are not paid in a reasonably time." [internal citation omitted]); *City of Joliet v. Mid-City Nat'l Bank of Chi.*, 998 F. Supp. 2d 689, 694 (N.D. Ill. 2014) (granting motion to withdraw by lawyers who were owed more than $5 million in fees, explaining that "to force unwilling attorneys to labor free of charge in a civil case where parties are not entitled to free representation is not in the interests of justice").

In *Team Obsolete Ltd. v. A.H.R.M.A. LTD.*, 464 F. Supp. 2d 164 (E.D.N.Y. 2006), the moving lawyer provided the reasons for the motion by submitting an affidavit *in camera*. Opposing counsel sought to unseal the affidavit. The court granted the motion to withdraw for nonpayment and denied the motion to unseal, but expressly ruled that the opposing party was entitled to know that the motion was based on an assertion that the client had failed to pay the agreed-upon fees, stating that it "hereby informs" [the opposing parties] "that the basis for [movant's] motion to withdraw is a dispute regarding AHRMA's failure to pay its legal bills." *Id.* at 165.[13]

Thus, when filing a motion to withdraw a lawyer often will not know whether the court will accept the assertion that "professional considerations" warrant withdrawal, or whether the court will require more information. Under the narrow facts of this opinion, when a judge has sought additional information in support of a motion to withdraw for failure to pay fees, Rule 1.6(b)(5) authorizes the lawyer to disclose information regarding the repre-

---

13. As also indicated in *Team Obsolete*, the procedural rules in that court require that motions to withdraw be accompanied by facts showing a sufficient basis to grant the motion. Local Civil Rule 1.4 of the U.S. District Court for the Eastern District of New York, states that motions to withdraw "may be granted only upon a showing by affidavit or otherwise of satisfactory reasons for withdrawal . . . ." Team Obsolete Ltd. v. A.H.R.M.A. LTD., 464 F. Supp. 2d 164, 166 (E.D.N.Y. 2006).

sentation of the client that is limited to the extent reasonably necessary to respond to the court's inquiry and in support of that motion to withdraw. We turn now to the issues facing judges who are called upon to rule on motions to withdraw based on unpaid fees.

The Judicial Inquiry With Respect to Such a Motion

In ruling on a motion to withdraw, judges seek to balance their need for information about the facts underlying the motion with the client's right to confidentiality.[14] In Formal Opinion 93-370, this Committee addressed the need for judicial sensitivity to lawyers' duty of confidentiality in the context of pretrial settlement discussions with judges, stating: "The judge should be sensitive to these ethical constraints on counsel and sensitive as well to the superior position of authority the judge enjoys with respect to the lawyer . . . ."[15] This need for judicial sensitivity applies as well when the judge is considering a motion to withdraw.

Trial courts have wide discretion when ruling on motions to withdraw. In addition to considering a lawyer's reasons for seeking to withdraw, trial courts also have a duty to consider such matters as the likely impact of a withdrawal on the parties and on the court's control over its calendar. *See generally Laster v. D.C.*, 460 F. Supp. 2d 111, 113 (D.C. 2006) ("[C]ourts may consider the disruptive impact that the withdrawal will have on the prosecution of the case."); *In re Kiley*, 947 N.E.2d 1, 7 (Mass. 2011) ("[T]he judge did not abuse his discretion in refusing to release the Kiley firm from the representation where the case was already three years old, discovery was delayed, and no successor counsel could be found."); *Brandon*, 560 F.3d at 538 (discussing topics of strategically timed or coercive behavior, prejudice); *McDonald v. Shore*, 953 N.Y.S.2d 650, 651 (App. Div. 2012) ("Generally, where the insurer of a defendant in a personal injury action issues a contested disclaimer of coverage in the midst of litigation, it is inappropriate to grant a motion to withdraw by the attorney the insurer has provided for that defendant.") In some jurisdictions the procedural rules provide criteria for the court to consider in ruling on motions to withdraw. *See In re Franke*, 55 A.3d at 722 (quoting Rule 2-132(b) of the Maryland Rules of Civil Procedure, permitting a court to deny a motion to withdraw "if withdrawal of the appearance would cause undue

---

14. The Model Code of Judicial Conduct provides only broad based guidance on this matter. Model Code of Judicial Conduct R. 2.5(A) states: "A Judge shall perform judicial and administrative duties, competently and diligently." Comment [4] to Model Code of Judicial Conduct R. 2.5 states that "[i]n disposing of matters promptly and efficiently, a judge must demonstrate due regard for the rights of the parties to be heard and to have issues resolved without unnecessary cost or delay. A judge should monitor and supervise cases in ways that reduce or eliminate dilatory practices, avoidable delays and unnecessary costs."

15. ABA Comm. on Ethics & Prof'l Responsibility, Formal Op. 93-370, at 4 (1993).

delay, prejudice, or injustice."). *See also Team Obsolete*, 464 F. Supp. 2d at 1662 (Local Civil Rule 1.4.).

In some instances, such as when a motion to withdraw is filed early in a case, a court's decision may be relatively straightforward. In other cases, such as when a matter is complex, extensive discovery has been conducted, and the trial date is approaching, a court's decision may be more difficult. To accommodate the individual facts of any particular case, the scope of information that may be deemed pertinent to a particular withdrawal motion is necessarily one that is left to the trial judge's discretion under applicable law.

As with settlement negotiations, judges should recognize the ethical constraints on lawyers who move to withdraw, and work with the lawyers to obtain the information needed to rule on the motion while cognizant of the lawyer's duties under Rule 1.6. In some instances, judges may conclude that the procedural history and status of the case is sufficient to decide the motion without further inquiry. Or a judge may consider asking the lawyer merely to assure the court that the motion is brought in good faith and without purpose of undue delay. A judge should not require the disclosure of confidential client information without considering whether such information is necessary to reach a sound decision on the motion. When a judge decides that confidential information is required, the judge should consider whether there are ways to reduce or mitigate harm to the client. For example, in *Gonzalez*, the court noted that two means of mitigation are to direct that the disclosures be made under seal and *in camera*[16] and for sensitive or

---

16. By "*in camera*" we mean a submission only to the court under seal, to be reviewed in chambers, with a copy to the client. While opposing counsel or opposing parties do not receive copies of the *in camera* submission, they are nonetheless generally aware that it has been submitted. Opposing counsel and parties do not have the same unconditional or unrestricted right to all information relating to a motion to withdraw as they would with other motions. *See* Mallen, *supra* note 4 (noting that "The adverse party's interest in the submission usually is unrelated to the litigation of the merits and not sufficient to warrant disclosure."). While some may suggest that such submissions violate Model Code of Judicial Conduct Rule 2.9, prohibiting judges from engaging in substantive *ex parte* communications, the Committee does not believe that such *in camera* submissions, when made with full knowledge of the opposing party, are an *ex parte* communication and thus, they do not fall within that prohibition. "An *ex parte* communication is one that excludes any party who is legally entitled to be present or notified of the communication and given an opportunity to respond." Annotated Model Code of Judicial Conduct 176 (2d ed. 2011). The prohibition on *ex parte* communications in MCJC Rule 2.9 is directed mainly to surreptitious contacts of which an adversary has no notice or awareness.

unnecessary information to be redacted.[17] Another option available to the court is to issue a protective order. As discussed below, these approaches, while sometimes useful, will not be appropriate in every case, nor are they "silver bullets" that resolve all issues.

Limiting Disclosures to Mitigate Harm to Clients

Comment [16] to Rule 1.6 provides that disclosures under Rule 1.6(b) are permitted only to the extent the lawyer reasonably believes necessary to accomplish the purpose specified. Of course, where practicable, a lawyer should first seek to persuade the client to take suitable action to remove the need for the lawyer's disclosure. When such persuasion is not practicable or successful, and disclosure of some confidential information is required, "If the disclosure will be made in connection with a judicial proceeding, the disclosure should be made in a manner that limits access to the information to the tribunal or other persons having a need to know it *and appropriate protective orders or other arrangements* should be sought by the lawyer to the fullest extent practicable."[18] Thus, Comment [16] anticipates the use of *in camera* submissions for disclosures where any of Rule 1.6(b)'s exceptions may apply. The situation is similar to discovery disputes over claims of privilege, whereby competing claims are often resolved by a court's review *in camera* of the documents at issue and such procedures can help reconcile the competing issues involved in ruling on motions to withdraw as well.

But while *in camera* submissions are a useful tool, a lawyer's disclosure of client information *in camera* is itself a form of "revealing" under Rule 1.6. It is therefore generally not sufficient under Rule 1.6 for a lawyer to proceed in the first instance by providing confidential information *in camera*, without first attempting to file a withdrawal motion with a formulaic reference to "professional considerations" or a similar term as the grounds for the motion, as suggested in Comment [3] to Rule 1.16. At that point the trial court might grant the motion without further inquiry; it might state that a motion will be denied absent further information; it might request further information; or it may order the lawyer to provide further information.

Thus, in order to comply with Rule 1.6, a lawyer who has a good faith basis for withdrawal under Rule 1.16(b)(5) and/or 1.16(b)(6), and who complies with the applicable procedural prerequisites of the court for such mo-

---

17. The *Gonzalez* court implied that the lawyer's disclosure of information relating to the fee claim, if done *in camera* and with certain redactions, would not have violated Rule 1.6, stating: "[W]e agree with the Board [on Professional Responsibility] that Gonzalez could have submitted his documentation in camera, and that he could also have made appropriate redactions of the material most damaging to his client . . . ." *In re Gonzalez*, 773 A.2d 1026, 1032 (D.C. 2001).

18. Model Rules of Prof'l Conduct R. 1.6 cmt. 16 (2016) (emphasis added).

tions, could: (1) initially submit a motion providing no confidential client information apart from a reference to "professional considerations" or the like;[19] (2) upon being informed by the court that further information is necessary, respond, when practicable, by seeking to persuade the court to rule on the motion without requiring the disclosure of confidential client information, asserting all non-frivolous claims of confidentiality and privilege; and if that fails; (3) thereupon under Rule 1.6(b)(5) submit only such information as is reasonably necessary to satisfy the needs of the court and preferably by whatever restricted means of submission, such as *in camera* review under seal, or such other procedures designated to minimize disclosure as the court determines is appropriate. If the court expressly orders the lawyer to make further disclosure, the exception in Rule 1.6(b)(6) for disclosures required to comply with a court order will apply, subject to the lawyer's compliance with the requirements of Comment [15].[20]

We consider here disclosures only in the context of a motion to withdraw in a civil case based on a client's failure to pay a lawyer's fees. Given the competing rights and responsibilities implicated in such motions, these steps should satisfy a lawyer's ethical duties under Rule 1.6. If a motion to withdraw is based on grounds other than a failure to meet financial obligations, other Rules and principles may apply.

As stated in the Scope section of the Model Rules, "The Rules of Professional Conduct are rules of reason."[21] The Scope section also states: "The Rules presuppose a larger legal context shaping the lawyer's role. That context includes court rules, statutes relating to matters of licensure, law defining specific obligations of lawyers and substantive and procedural law in general."[22]

Conclusion

In moving to withdraw as counsel in a civil proceeding based on a client's failure to pay fees, a lawyer must consider the duty of confidentiality under Rule 1.6 and seek to reconcile that duty with the court's need for suf-

19. Of course a lawyer can recite her compliance with procedural steps, such as prior notice to the client, and can recite the procedural history and status of the case as reflected on the docket and the court's file.

20. *See* ABA Comm. on Ethics & Prof'l Responsibility, Formal Op. 473 (2016), relating to a lawyer's duties when responding to a subpoena or compulsory process to provide privileged information. *See also* Oregon Formal Op. 2011-185 (2011), 2011 WL 11741926, at *2 (Lawyer may reveal information relating to the representation of Client under Oregon RPC 1.6(b)(5), but may only do so to the extent "reasonably necessary" to comply with the court order.) The court's mere statement that the motion will not be granted absent more information is not "a court order" and does not trigger the exception under Rule 1.6(b)(6) until the lawyer has taken steps to prevent or limit disclosure of confidential information.

21. Model Rules of Prof'l Conduct, Scope [14] (2016).

22. *Id.* at [15].

ficient information upon which to rule on the motion. Similarly, in entertaining such a motion, a judge should consider the right of the movant's client to confidentiality. This requires cooperation between lawyers and judges. If required by the court to support the motion with facts relating to the representation, a lawyer may, pursuant to Rule 1.6(b)(5), disclose only such confidential information as is reasonably necessary for the court to make an informed decision on the motion.

AMERICAN BAR ASSOCIATION

STANDING COMMITTEE ON ETHICS AND PROFESSIONAL RESPONSIBILITY

FORMAL OPINION 477R* **May 11, 2017**
Revised May 22, 2017

Securing Communication of Protected Client Information

A lawyer generally may transmit information relating to the representation of a client over the internet without violating the Model Rules of Professional Conduct where the lawyer has undertaken reasonable efforts to prevent inadvertent or unauthorized access. However, a lawyer may be required to take special security precautions to protect against the inadvertent or unauthorized disclosure of client information when required by an agreement with the client or by law, or when the nature of the information requires a higher degree of security.

I. Introduction

In Formal Opinion 99-413 this Committee addressed a lawyer's confidentiality obligations for email communications with clients. While the basic obligations of confidentiality remain applicable today, the role and risks of technology in the practice of law have evolved since 1999 prompting the need to update Opinion 99-413.

Formal Opinion 99-413 concluded: "Lawyers have a reasonable expectation of privacy in communications made by all forms of e-mail, including unencrypted e-mail sent on the Internet, despite some risk of interception and disclosure. It therefore follows that its use is consistent with the duty under Rule 1.6 to use reasonable means to maintain the confidentiality of information relating to a client's representation."[1]

Unlike 1999 where multiple methods of communication were prevalent, today, many lawyers primarily use electronic means to communicate and ex-

*The opinion below is a revision of, and replaces Formal Opinion 477 as issued by the Committee May 11, 2017. This opinion is based on the ABA Model Rules of Professional Conduct as amended by the ABA House of Delegates through August 2016. The laws, court rules, regulations, rules of professional conduct, and opinions promulgated in individual jurisdictions are controlling.

1. ABA Comm. on Ethics & Prof'l Responsibility, Formal Op. 99-413, at 11 (1999).

change documents with clients, other lawyers, and even with other persons who are assisting a lawyer in delivering legal services to clients.[2]

Since 1999, those providing legal services now regularly use a variety of devices to create, transmit and store confidential communications, including desktop, laptop and notebook computers, tablet devices, smartphones, and cloud resource and storage locations. Each device and each storage location offer an opportunity for the inadvertent or unauthorized disclosure of information relating to the representation, and thus implicate a lawyer's ethical duties.[3]

In 2012 the ABA adopted "technology amendments" to the Model Rules, including updating the Comments to Rule 1.1 on lawyer technological competency and adding paragraph (c) and a new Comment to Rule 1.6, addressing a lawyer's obligation to take reasonable measures to prevent inadvertent or unauthorized disclosure of information relating to the representation.

At the same time, the term "cybersecurity" has come into existence to encompass the broad range of issues relating to preserving individual privacy from intrusion by nefarious actors throughout the internet. Cybersecurity recognizes a post-Opinion 99-413 world where law enforcement discusses hacking and data loss in terms of "when," and not "if."[4] Law firms are targets for two general reasons: (1) they obtain, store and use highly sensitive information about their clients while at times utilizing safeguards to shield that information that may be inferior to those deployed by the client, and (2) the information in their possession is more likely to be of interest to a hacker and likely less voluminous than that held by the client.[5]

The Model Rules do not impose greater or different duties of confidentiality based upon the method by which a lawyer communicates with a client.

---

2. ABA Comm. on Ethics & Prof'l Responsibility, Formal Op. 08-451 (2008); ABA Commission on Ethics 20/20 Report to the House of Delegates (2012), http://www.americanbar.org/content/dam/aba/administrative/ethics_2020/20120508_ethics_20_20_final_resolution_and_report_outsourcing_posting.authcheckdam.pdf.

3. *See* Jill D. Rhodes & Vincent I. Polley, The ABA Cybersecurity Handbook: A Resource For Attorneys, Law Firms, and Business Professionals 7 (2013) [hereinafter ABA Cybersecurity Handbook].

4. "Cybersecurity" is defined as "measures taken to protect a computer or computer system (as on the internet) against unauthorized access or attack." Cybersecurity, Merriam Webster, http://www.merriam-webster.com/dictionary/cybersecurity (last visited Sept. 10, 2016). In 2012 the ABA created the Cybersecurity Legal Task Force to help lawyers grapple with the legal challenges created by cyberspace. In 2013 the Task Force published The ABA Cybersecurity Handbook: A Resource For Attorneys, Law Firms, and Business Professionals.

5. Bradford A. Bleier, Unit Chief to the Cyber National Security Section in the FBI's Cyber Division, indicated that "[l]aw firms have tremendous concentrations of really critical private information, and breaking into a firm's computer system is a really optimal way to obtain economic and personal security information." Ed Finkel, Cyberspace Under Siege, A.B.A. J., Nov. 1, 2010.

But how a lawyer should comply with the core duty of confidentiality in an ever-changing technological world requires some reflection.

Against this backdrop we describe the "technology amendments" made to the Model Rules in 2012, identify some of the technology risks lawyers face, and discuss factors other than the Model Rules of Professional Conduct that lawyers should consider when using electronic means to communicate regarding client matters.

II. Duty of Competence

Since 1983, Model Rule 1.1 has read: "A lawyer shall provide competent representation to a client. Competent representation requires the legal knowledge, skill, thoroughness and preparation reasonably necessary for the representation."[6] The scope of this requirement was clarified in 2012 when the ABA recognized the increasing impact of technology on the practice of law and the duty of lawyers to develop an understanding of that technology. Thus, Comment [8] to Rule 1.1 was modified to read:

> To maintain the requisite knowledge and skill, a lawyer should keep abreast of changes in the law and its practice, including the benefits and risks associated with relevant technology, engage in continuing study and education and comply with all continuing legal education requirements to which the lawyer is subject. (Emphasis added.)[7]

Regarding the change to Rule 1.1's Comment, the ABA Commission on Ethics 20/20 explained:

> Model Rule 1.1 requires a lawyer to provide competent representation, and Comment [6] [renumbered as Comment [8]] specifies that, to remain competent, lawyers need to "keep abreast of changes in the law and its practice." The Commission concluded that, in order to keep abreast of changes in law practice in a digital age, lawyers necessarily need to understand basic features of relevant technology and that this aspect of competence should be expressed in the Comment. For example, a lawyer would have difficulty providing competent legal services in today's environment without knowing how to use email or create an electronic document. [8]

6. A Legislative History: The Development of the ABA Model Rules of Professional Conduct, 1982-2013, at 37-44 (Art Garwin ed., 2013).

7. *Id.* at 43.

8. ABA Commission on Ethics 20/20 Report 105A (Aug. 2012), http://www.americanbar.org/content/dam/aba/administrative/ethics_2020/20120808_revised_

III. Duty of Confidentiality

In 2012, amendments to Rule 1.6 modified both the rule and the commentary about what efforts are required to preserve the confidentiality of information relating to the representation. Model Rule 1.6(a) requires that "A lawyer shall not reveal information relating to the representation of a client" unless certain circumstances arise.[9] The 2012 modification added a new duty in paragraph (c) that: "A lawyer shall make reasonable efforts to prevent the inadvertent or unauthorized disclosure of, or unauthorized access to, information relating to the representation of a client."[10]

Amended Comment [18] explains:

> Paragraph (c) requires a lawyer to act competently to safeguard information relating to the representation of a client against unauthorized access by third parties and against inadvertent or unauthorized disclosure by the lawyer or other persons who are participating in the representation of the client or who are subject to the lawyer's supervision. See Rules 1.1, 5.1 and 5.3. The unauthorized access to, or the inadvertent or unauthorized disclosure of, information relating to the representation of a client does not constitute a violation of paragraph (c) if the lawyer has made reasonable efforts to prevent the access or disclosure.

At the intersection of a lawyer's competence obligation to keep "abreast of knowledge of the benefits and risks associated with relevant technology," and confidentiality obligation to make "reasonable efforts to prevent the inadvertent or unauthorized disclosure of, or unauthorized access to, information relating to the representation of a client," lawyers must exercise reasonable efforts when using technology in communicating about client matters. What constitutes reasonable efforts is not susceptible to a hard and fast rule, but rather is contingent upon a set of factors. In turn, those factors

---

resolution_105a_as_amended.authcheckdam.pdf. The 20/20 Commission also noted that modification of Comment [6] did not change the lawyer's substantive duty of competence: "Comment [6] already encompasses an obligation to remain aware of changes in technology that affect law practice, but the Commission concluded that making this explicit, by addition of the phrase 'including the benefits and risks associated with relevant technology,' would offer greater clarity in this area and emphasize the importance of technology to modern law practice. The proposed amendment, which appears in a Comment, does not impose any new obligations on lawyers. Rather, the amendment is intended to serve as a reminder to lawyers that they should remain aware of technology, including the benefits and risks associated with it, as part of a lawyer's general ethical duty to remain competent."

9. Model Rules of Prof'l Conduct R. 1.6(a) (2016).

10. *Id.* at (c).

depend on the multitude of possible types of information being communicated (ranging along a spectrum from highly sensitive information to insignificant), the methods of electronic communications employed, and the types of available security measures for each method.[11]

Therefore, in an environment of increasing cyber threats, the Committee concludes that, adopting the language in the ABA Cybersecurity Handbook, the reasonable efforts standard:

> . . . rejects requirements for specific security measures (such as firewalls, passwords, and the like) and instead adopts a fact-specific approach to business security obligations that requires a "process" to assess risks, identify and implement appropriate security measures responsive to those risks, verify that they are effectively implemented, and ensure that they are continually updated in response to new developments.[12]

Recognizing the necessity of employing a fact-based analysis, Comment [18] to Model Rule 1.6(c) includes nonexclusive factors to guide lawyers in making a "reasonable efforts" determination. Those factors include:

- the sensitivity of the information,
- the likelihood of disclosure if additional safeguards are not employed,
- the cost of employing additional safeguards,
- the difficulty of implementing the safeguards, and
- the extent to which the safeguards adversely affect the lawyer's ability to represent clients (e.g., by making a device or important piece of software excessively difficult to use).[13]

---

11. The 20/20 Commission's report emphasized that lawyers are not the guarantors of data safety. It wrote:

"[t]o be clear, paragraph (c) does not mean that a lawyer engages in professional misconduct any time a client's confidences are subject to unauthorized access or disclosed inadvertently or without authority. A sentence in Comment [16] makes this point explicitly. The reality is that disclosures can occur even if lawyers take all reasonable precautions. The Commission, however, believes that it is important to state in the black letter of Model Rule 1.6 that lawyers have a duty to take reasonable precautions, even if those precautions will not guarantee the protection of confidential information under all circumstances."

12. ABA Cybersecurity Handbook, *supra* note 3, at 48-49.

13. Model Rules of Prof'l Conduct R. 1.6 cmt. [18] (2016). "The [Ethics 20/20] Commission examined the possibility of offering more detailed guidance about the measures that lawyers should employ. The Commission concluded, however, that technology is changing too rapidly to offer such guidance and that the particular measures lawyers should use will necessarily change as technology evolves and as new risks emerge and new security procedures become available." ABA Commission Report 105A, *supra* note 8, at 5.

A fact-based analysis means that particularly strong protective measures, like encryption, are warranted in some circumstances. Model Rule 1.4 may require a lawyer to discuss security safeguards with clients. Under certain circumstances, the lawyer may need to obtain informed consent from the client regarding whether to the use enhanced security measures, the costs involved, and the impact of those costs on the expense of the representation where nonstandard and not easily available or affordable security methods may be required or requested by the client. Reasonable efforts, as it pertains to certain highly sensitive information, might require avoiding the use of electronic methods or any technology to communicate with the client altogether, just as it warranted avoiding the use of the telephone, fax and mail in Formal Opinion 99-413.

In contrast, for matters of normal or low sensitivity, standard security methods with low to reasonable costs to implement, may be sufficient to meet the reasonable-efforts standard to protect client information from inadvertent and unauthorized disclosure.

In the technological landscape of Opinion 99-413, and due to the reasonable expectations of privacy available to email communications at the time, unencrypted email posed no greater risk of interception or disclosure than other non-electronic forms of communication. This basic premise remains true today for routine communication with clients, presuming the lawyer has implemented basic and reasonably available methods of common electronic security measures.[14] Thus, the use of unencrypted routine email generally remains an acceptable method of lawyer-client communication.

However, cyber-threats and the proliferation of electronic communications devices have changed the landscape and it is not always reasonable to rely on the use of unencrypted email. For example, electronic communication through certain mobile applications or on message boards or via unsecured networks may lack the basic expectation of privacy afforded to email communications. Therefore, lawyers must, on a case-by-case basis, constantly analyze how they communicate electronically about client matters, applying the Comment [18] factors to determine what effort is reasonable.

While it is beyond the scope of an ethics opinion to specify the reasonable steps that lawyers should take under any given set of facts, we offer the following considerations as guidance:

1. Understand the Nature of the Threat.

Understanding the nature of the threat includes consideration of the sensitivity of a client's information and whether the client's matter is a higher risk for cyber intrusion. Client matters involving proprietary information in highly sensitive industries such as industrial designs, mergers and acquisi-

---

14. See item 3 below.

tions or trade secrets, and industries like healthcare, banking, defense or education, may present a higher risk of data theft.[15] "Reasonable efforts" in higher risk scenarios generally means that greater effort is warranted.

2. Understand How Client Confidential Information Is Transmitted and Where It Is Stored.

A lawyer should understand how their firm's electronic communications are created, where client data resides, and what avenues exist to access that information. Understanding these processes will assist a lawyer in managing the risk of inadvertent or unauthorized disclosure of client-related information. Every access point is a potential entry point for a data loss or disclosure. The lawyer's task is complicated in a world where multiple devices may be used to communicate with or about a client and then store those communications. Each access point, and each device, should be evaluated for security compliance.

3. Understand and Use Reasonable Electronic Security Measures.

Model Rule 1.6(c) requires a lawyer to make reasonable efforts to prevent the inadvertent or unauthorized disclosure of, or unauthorized access to, information relating to the representation of a client. As Comment [18] makes clear, what is deemed to be "reasonable" may vary, depending on the facts and circumstances of each case. Electronic disclosure of, or access to, client communications can occur in different forms ranging from a direct intrusion into a law firm's systems to theft or interception of information during the transmission process. Making reasonable efforts to protect against unauthorized disclosure in client communications thus includes analysis of security measures applied to both disclosure and access to a law firm's technology system and transmissions.

A lawyer should understand and use electronic security measures to safeguard client communications and information. A lawyer has a variety of options to safeguard communications including, for example, using secure internet access methods to communicate, access and store client information (such as through secure Wi-Fi, the use of a Virtual Private Network, or another secure internet portal), using unique complex passwords, changed periodically, implementing firewalls and anti-Malware/Anti-Spyware/Antivirus software on all devices upon which client confidential information is transmitted or stored, and applying all necessary security patches and updates to operational and communications software. Each of these measures is routinely accessible and reasonably affordable or free. Lawyers may consider refusing access to firm systems to devices failing to comply with these basic

15. *See, e.g.*, Noah Garner, *The Most Prominent Cyber Threats Faced by High-Target Industries*, Trend-Micro (Jan. 25, 2016), http://blog.trendmicro.com/the-most-prominent-cyber-threats-faced-by-high-target-industries/.

methods. It also may be reasonable to use commonly available methods to remotely disable lost or stolen devices, and to destroy the data contained on those devices, especially if encryption is not also being used.

Other available tools include encryption of data that is physically stored on a device and multi-factor authentication to access firm systems.

In the electronic world, "delete" usually does not mean information is permanently deleted, and "deleted" data may be subject to recovery. Therefore, a lawyer should consider whether certain data should *ever* be stored in an unencrypted environment, or electronically transmitted at all.

4. Determine How Electronic Communications About Clients Matters Should Be Protected.

Different communications require different levels of protection. At the beginning of the client-lawyer relationship, the lawyer and client should discuss what levels of security will be necessary for each electronic communication about client matters. Communications to third parties containing protected client information requires analysis to determine what degree of protection is appropriate. In situations where the communication (and any attachments) are sensitive or warrant extra security, additional electronic protection may be required. For example, if client information is of sufficient sensitivity, a lawyer should encrypt the transmission and determine how to do so to sufficiently protect it,[16] and consider the use of password protection for any attachments. Alternatively, lawyers can consider the use of a well vetted and secure third-party cloud based file storage system to exchange documents normally attached to emails.

Thus, routine communications sent electronically are those communications that do not contain information warranting additional security measures beyond basic methods. However, in some circumstances, a client's lack of technological sophistication or the limitations of technology available to the client may require alternative non-electronic forms of communication altogether.

A lawyer also should be cautious in communicating with a client if the client uses computers or other devices subject to the access or control of a third party.[17] If so, the attorney-client privilege and confidentiality of com-

---

16. *See* Cal. Formal Op. 2010-179 (2010); ABA Cybersecurity Handbook, *supra* note 3, at 121. Indeed, certain laws and regulations require encryption in certain situations. *Id.* at 58-59.

17. ABA Comm. on Ethics & Prof'l Responsibility, Formal Op. 11-459, Duty to Protect the Confidentiality of E-mail Communications with One's Client (2011). Formal Op. 11-459 was issued prior to the 2012 amendments to Rule 1.6. These amendments added new Rule 1.6(c), which provides that lawyers "shall" make reasonable efforts to prevent the unauthorized or inadvertent access to client information. *See, e.g.*, Scott v. Beth Israel Med. Center, Inc., Civ. A. No. 3:04-CV-139-RJC-DCK, 847 N.Y.S.2d 436 (Sup. Ct. 2007); Mason v. ILS Tech., LLC, 2008 WL 731557, 2008 BL 298576 (W.D.N.C. 2008);

munications and attached documents may be waived. Therefore, the lawyer should warn the client about the risk of sending or receiving electronic communications using a computer or other device, or email account, to which a third party has, or may gain, access.[18]

5. Label Client Confidential Information.

Lawyers should follow the better practice of marking privileged and confidential client communications as "privileged and confidential" in order to alert anyone to whom the communication was inadvertently disclosed that the communication is intended to be privileged and confidential. This can also consist of something as simple as appending a message or "disclaimer" to client emails, where such a disclaimer is accurate and appropriate for the communication.[19]

Model Rule 4.4(b) obligates a lawyer who "knows or reasonably should know" that he has received an inadvertently sent "document or electronically

---

Holmes v. Petrovich Dev Co., LLC, 191 Cal. App. 4th 1047 (2011) (employee communications with lawyer over company owned computer not privileged); Bingham v. BayCare Health Sys., 2016 WL 3917513, 2016 BL 233476 (M.D. Fla. July 20, 2016) (collecting cases on privilege waiver for privileged emails sent or received through an employer's email server).

18. Some state bar ethics opinions have explored the circumstances under which email communications should be afforded special security protections. *See, e.g.*, Tex. Prof'l Ethics Comm. Op. 648 (2015) that identified six situations in which a lawyer should consider whether to encrypt or use some other type of security precaution:

- communicating highly sensitive or confidential information via email or unencrypted email connections;
- sending an email to or from an account that the email sender or recipient shares with others;
- sending an email to a client when it is possible that a third person (such as a spouse in a divorce case) knows the password to the email account, or to an individual client at that client's work email account, especially if the email relates to a client's employment dispute with his employer...;
- sending an email from a public computer or a borrowed computer or where the lawyer knows that the emails the lawyer sends are being read on a public or borrowed computer or on an unsecure network;
- sending an email if the lawyer knows that the email recipient is accessing the email on devices that are potentially accessible to third persons or are not protected by a password; or
- sending an email if the lawyer is concerned that the NSA or other law enforcement agency may read the lawyer's email communication, with or without a warrant.

19. *See* Veteran Med. Prods. v. Bionix Dev. Corp., Case No. 1:05-cv-655, 2008 WL 696546 at *8, 2008 BL 51876 at *8 (W.D. Mich. Mar. 13, 2008) (email disclaimer that read "this email and any files transmitted with are confidential and are intended solely for the use of the individual or entity to whom they are addressed" with nondisclosure constitutes a reasonable effort to maintain the secrecy of its business plan).

stored information relating to the representation of the lawyer's client" to promptly notify the sending lawyer. A clear and conspicuous appropriately used disclaimer may affect whether a recipient lawyer's duty under Model Rule 4.4(b) for inadvertently transmitted communications is satisfied.

6. Train Lawyers and Nonlawyer Assistants in Technology and Information Security.

Model Rule 5.1 provides that a partner in a law firm, and a lawyer who individually or together with other lawyers possesses comparable managerial authority in a law firm, shall make reasonable efforts to ensure that the firm has in effect measures giving reasonable assurance that all lawyers in the firm conform to the Rules of Professional Conduct. Model Rule 5.1 also provides that lawyers having direct supervisory authority over another lawyer shall make reasonable efforts to ensure that the other lawyer conforms to the Rules of Professional Conduct. In addition, Rule 5.3 requires lawyers who are responsible for managing and supervising nonlawyer assistants to take reasonable steps to reasonably assure that the conduct of such assistants is compatible with the ethical duties of the lawyer. These requirements are as applicable to electronic practices as they are to comparable office procedures.

In the context of electronic communications, lawyers must establish policies and procedures, and periodically train employees, subordinates and others assisting in the delivery of legal services, in the use of reasonably secure methods of electronic communications with clients. Lawyers also must instruct and supervise on reasonable measures for access to and storage of those communications. Once processes are established, supervising lawyers must follow up to ensure these policies are being implemented and partners and lawyers with comparable managerial authority must periodically reassess and update these policies. This is no different than the other obligations for supervision of office practices and procedures to protect client information.

7. Conduct Due Diligence on Vendors Providing Communication Technology.

Consistent with Model Rule 1.6(c), Model Rule 5.3 imposes a duty on lawyers with direct supervisory authority over a nonlawyer to make "reasonable efforts to ensure that" the nonlawyer's "conduct is compatible with the professional obligations of the lawyer."

In ABA Formal Opinion 08-451, this Committee analyzed Model Rule 5.3 and a lawyer's obligation when outsourcing legal and nonlegal services. That opinion identified several issues a lawyer should consider when selecting the outsource vendor, to meet the lawyer's due diligence and duty of supervision. Those factors also apply in the analysis of vendor selection in the context of electronic communications. Such factors may include:

- reference checks and vendor credentials;
- vendor's security policies and protocols;
- vendor's hiring practices;
- the use of confidentiality agreements;
- vendor's conflicts check system to screen for adversity; and
- the availability and accessibility of a legal forum for legal relief for violations of the vendor agreement.

Any lack of individual competence by a lawyer to evaluate and employ safeguards to protect client confidences may be addressed through association with another lawyer or expert, or by education.[20]

Since the issuance of Formal Opinion 08-451, Comment [3] to Model Rule 5.3 was added to address outsourcing, including "using an Internet-based service to store client information." Comment [3] provides that the "reasonable efforts" required by Model Rule 5.3 to ensure that the nonlawyer's services are provided in a manner that is compatible with the lawyer's professional obligations "will depend upon the circumstances." Comment [3] contains suggested factors that might be taken into account:

- the education, experience, and reputation of the nonlawyer;
- the nature of the services involved;
- the terms of any arrangements concerning the protection of client information; and
- the legal and ethical environments of the jurisdictions in which the services will be performed particularly with regard to confidentiality.

Comment [3] further provides that when retaining or directing a nonlawyer outside of the firm, lawyers should communicate "directions appropriate under the circumstances to give reasonable assurance that the nonlawyer's conduct is compatible with the professional obligations of the lawyer."[21] If the client has not directed the selection of the outside nonlawyer vendor, the lawyer has the responsibility to monitor how those services are being performed.[22]

---

20. Model Rules of Prof'l Conduct R. 1.1 cmts. [2] & [8] (2016).

21. The ABA's catalog of state bar ethics opinions applying the rules of professional conduct to cloud storage arrangements involving client information can be found at: http://www.americanbar.org/groups/departments_offices/legal_technology_resources/resources/charts_fyis/cloud-ethics-chart.html.

22. By contrast, where a client directs the selection of a particular nonlawyer service provider outside the firm, "the lawyer ordinarily should agree with the client concerning the allocation of responsibility for monitoring as between the client and the lawyer." Model Rules of Prof'l Conduct R. 5.3 cmt. [4] (2016). The concept of monitoring recognizes that although it may not be possible to "directly supervise" a client directed nonlawyer outside

Even after a lawyer examines these various considerations and is satisfied that the security employed is sufficient to comply with the duty of confidentiality, the lawyer must periodically reassess these factors to confirm that the lawyer's actions continue to comply with the ethical obligations and have not been rendered inadequate by changes in circumstances or technology.

IV. Duty to Communicate

Communications between a lawyer and client generally are addressed in Rule 1.4. When the lawyer reasonably believes that highly sensitive confidential client information is being transmitted so that extra measures to protect the email transmission are warranted, the lawyer should inform the client about the risks involved.[23] The lawyer and client then should decide whether another mode of transmission, such as high level encryption or personal delivery is warranted. Similarly, a lawyer should consult with the client as to how to appropriately and safely use technology in their communication, in compliance with other laws that might be applicable to the client. Whether a lawyer is using methods and practices to comply with administrative, statutory, or international legal standards is beyond the scope of this opinion.

A client may insist or require that the lawyer undertake certain forms of communication. As explained in Comment [19] to Model Rule 1.6, "A client may require the lawyer to implement special security measures not required by this Rule or may give informed consent to the use of a means of communication that would otherwise be prohibited by this Rule."

V. Conclusion

Rule 1.1 requires a lawyer to provide competent representation to a client. Comment [8] to Rule 1.1 advises lawyers that to maintain the requisite knowledge and skill for competent representation, a lawyer should keep abreast of the benefits and risks associated with relevant technology. Rule 1.6(c) requires a lawyer to make "reasonable efforts" to prevent the inadvertent or unauthorized disclosure of or access to information relating to the representation.

A lawyer generally may transmit information relating to the representation of a client over the internet without violating the Model Rules of Professional Conduct where the lawyer has undertaken reasonable efforts to

---

the firm performing services in connection with a matter, a lawyer must nevertheless remain aware of how the nonlawyer services are being performed. ABA Commission on Ethics 20/20 Report 105C, at 12 (Aug. 2012), http://www.americanbar.org/content/dam/aba/administrative/ethics_2020/2012_hod_annual_meeting_105c_filed_may_2012.authcheckdam.pdf.

23. Model Rules of Prof'l Conduct R. 1.4(a)(1) & (4) (2016).

prevent inadvertent or unauthorized access. However, a lawyer may be required to take special security precautions to protect against the inadvertent or unauthorized disclosure of client information when required by an agreement with the client or by law, or when the nature of the information requires a higher degree of security.

AMERICAN BAR ASSOCIATION
STANDING COMMITTEE ON ETHICS AND PROFESSIONAL RESPONSIBILITY

FORMAL OPINION 478 **December 8, 2017**

Independent Factual Research by Judges Via the Internet

Easy access to a vast amount of information available on the Internet exposes judges to potential ethical problems. Judges risk violating the Model Code of Judicial Conduct by searching the Internet for information related to participants or facts in a proceeding. Independent investigation of adjudicative facts generally is prohibited unless the information is properly subject to judicial notice. The restriction on independent investigation includes individuals subject to the judge's direction and control.[1]

I. Introduction

The Internet provides immediate access to an unprecedented amount of information. Internet searches offer a vast array of information on endless topics. Social media sites provide extensive information that users share about themselves and others. Information discovered on the Internet may be highly educational and as useful to judges as judicial seminars and books. But information gathered from an Internet search may not be accurate. It may be biased, unreliable, or false. And, whether truthful or not, information discovered by a judge via the Internet that does not qualify for judicial notice and is not disclosed to the parties is untested by the adversary process.[2]

To help the judiciary navigate the hazards of Internet research, this opinion reviews the ethical parameters under the ABA Model Code of Judicial Conduct for conducting on-line independent fact-finding not tested by the adversary system.[3]

---

1. This opinion is based on the ABA Model Code of Judicial Conduct as amended by the ABA House of Delegates through August 2010. The laws, court rules, regulations, rules of professional and judicial conduct, opinions promulgated in individual jurisdictions and the Code of Conduct for United States Judges may be controlling. In addition, standards for judicial notice are beyond the scope of this opinion and discussed throughout only in general terms.

2. As used in this opinion, the term "judge" refers to "anyone who is authorized to perform judicial functions, including an officer such as a justice of the peace, magistrate, court commissioner, special master, referee, or member of the administrative law judiciary." *See* MODEL CODE OF JUDICIAL CONDUCT, Application § I(B)(2011).

3. Fact gathering over the Internet may occur, for example, via (i) search engines like

II. The ABA Model Code Provisions

The Preamble to the ABA Model Code of Judicial Conduct emphasizes that "[T]he United States legal system is based upon the principle that an independent, impartial, and competent judiciary, composed of men and women of integrity, will interpret and apply the law that governs our society."[4] This system requires that judges' decisions be based upon evidence presented on the record or in open court, and available to all parties. Except for evidence properly subject to judicial notice, a defining feature of the judge's role in an adversarial system is that the judge will "consider only the evidence presented by the parties."[5] Judges must be careful not to undermine this hallmark principle of judicial impartiality, or substitute for the time-honored role of the neutral and detached magistrate someone who combines the roles of advocate, witness, and judge.

A. *Ex Parte* Communications

Canon 2 of the Model Code states that a judge shall perform all duties of judicial office impartially, competently, and diligently.[6] An independent and impartial judiciary ensures the right of litigants to a fair trial. Impartiality is essential for the proper discharge of the judicial function.

Improper *ex parte* or "one-sided" communications undermine the independence and impartiality of the judiciary. Such communications create the appearance of bias or partiality on the part of the judge and, therefore, are precluded under the Model Code.

Model Rule 2.9(A) bars *ex parte* communications except in limited circumstances.[7] It provides: "A judge shall not initiate, permit, or consider ex

---

Google, Yahoo, Bing, Duck Duck Go and others, or (ii) electronic social media that is interactive like Facebook, Twitter, or Instagram. *See, e.g.*, ABA Comm. on Ethics & Prof'l Responsibility, Formal Op. 462 (2013), *Judge's Use of Electronic Social Networking Media* (" 'electronic social media' . . . refer[s] to internet-based electronic social networking sites that require an individual to affirmatively join and accept or reject connection with particular persons") (footnote omitted). This opinion covers all types of Internet searching. In addition, while the opinion addresses independent research by judges on the Internet, some of the principles that are discussed also apply to more traditional research resources.

4. Model Code of Judicial Conduct, Preamble [1] (2011).

5. Charles G. Geyh & W. William Hodes, Reporters' Notes to the Model Code of Judicial Conduct 40 (2009).

6. Model Code of Judicial Conduct, Canon 2, R. 2.2 (a judge shall "perform all duties of judicial office fairly and impartially"); Rule 2.5(A) ("a judge shall perform judicial and administrative duties, competently and diligently").

7. Certain *ex parte* communications are permitted. The Model Code permits *ex parte* communications where they are permitted by law, such as in a settlement conference or certain applications for temporary equitable relief, or to address scheduling or administrative issues, or where the parties consent to permit *ex parte* communication, such as in an *in camera* review. A judge may discuss the case with court personnel. Judges may consult among or with other judges, court staff, and law clerks, *see* Model Code of Judicial Conduct R.

parte communications, or consider other communications made to the judge outside the presence of the parties or their lawyers, concerning a pending or impending matter."[8] The ban on *ex parte* communication ensures that the judge will review and make rulings based only on the facts and evidence presented in the case.

B. Independent Fact Research Precluded

The Model Code's rule on *ex parte* communication includes a provision that specifically addresses independent investigation of facts. Model Rule 2.9(C) states: "A judge shall not investigate facts in a matter independently, and shall consider only the evidence presented and any facts that may properly be judicially noticed." Comment [6] to Rule 2.9 clarifies that the "prohibition against a judge investigating the facts in a matter extends to information available in all mediums, including electronic."[9]

Importantly, Rule 2.9(C) does not preclude legal research. Rule 2.9(C) carefully proscribes independent research of "facts." Judges may conduct legal research beyond the cases and authorities cited or provided by counsel.[10]

Rule 2.9(C) of the Model Code was adopted in 2007 and represents a significant clarification of the independent investigation proscription in the Internet age. Prior to 2007, the Model Code stated the general rule against *ex parte* communications and identified certain exceptions. The 1990 Model Code addressed independent investigation in a brief comment: "A judge

---

2.9(A)(1)-(5) (2011); *id.* at cmt. [5], but as noted below, judges may not have others conduct research that the judge may not conduct.

8. The Model Code of Judicial Conduct defines "impending matter" as "a matter that is imminent or expected to occur in the near future." Model Code of Judicial Conduct, Terminology (2011) (references omitted). A "pending matter" is "a matter that has commenced. A matter continues to be pending through any appellate process until final disposition." *Id.* (references omitted).

9. Thirty-one states have adopted Model Rule 2.9(C) or language substantially similar in their judicial codes. There is no similar provision in the Code of Conduct for United States Judges. For a discussion of independent fact-finding by state and federal judges generally see Hon. David B. Saxe, *"Toxic" Judicial Research*, N.Y. St. B.J. 36 (Sept. 2015); Elizabeth F. Thornburg, *The Curious Appellate Judge: Ethical Limits on Independent Research*, 28 Rev. Litig. 131 (2008). For a discussion of whether federal judges may conduct independent research for purposes of obtaining what they consider to be "background" information if the information does not form the basis for a decision see Rowe v. Gibson, 798 F.3d 622 (7th Cir. 2015). For state-by-state adoption of Rule 2.9(C) see ABA, *CPR Policy Implementation Committee: Comparison of ABA Model Judicial Code and State Variations, Rule 2.9: Ex Parte Communication* (2016), http://www.americanbar.org/content/dam/aba/administrative/professional_responsibility/2_9.authcheckdam.pdf (last visited Nov. 21, 2017).

10. Charles G. Geyh, James J. Alfini, Steven Lubet & Jeffrey M. Shaman, Judicial Conduct and Ethics, §5.04 at 5-25 (5th ed. 2013) ("independent investigation of *the law* has always been permitted" (emphasis in original); judges are "experts on matters of law who are charged with the duty of declaring what the law is"); *see also id.* at 5-24 to 5-25 (further discussion of independent research by judges).

must not independently investigate facts in a case and must consider only the evidence presented."[11] The 2007 change, moving the proscription from a comment to the text of the rule, was explained as follows:

> In the Commission's view . . . the judge's duty to consider only the evidence presented is a defining feature of the judge's role in an adversarial system and warrants explicit mention in the black letter Rules.[12]

C. Judicial Notice of Facts

Rule 2.9(C) of the Model Code permits a judge to consider facts "that may properly be judicially noticed. . . . [U]nlike most provisions of the Code of Judicial Conduct, Rule 2.9(C) incorporates a section of the law extrinsic to the Code; specifically, the law relating to judicial notice."[13]

For purposes of this opinion, Fed. R. Evid. 201(b)(1) and (2) contain an appropriate standard; they permit judicial notice of facts which are "not subject to reasonable dispute" because the facts are "generally known within the trial court's territorial jurisdiction" or "can be accurately and readily determined from sources whose accuracy cannot reasonably be questioned."[14] Judicial notice is "founded on the assumption that certain factual determinations are not subject to reasonable dispute and thus may be appropriately resolved other than by the production of evidence before the trier of fact at trial."[15]

Fed. R. Evid. 201(a) governs judicial notice of "adjudicative facts," not "legislative facts."[16] As the 1972 Advisory Committee Note to Rule 201(a) explains, this "terminology was coined by Professor Kenneth Davis in his article *An Approach to Problems of Evidence in the Administrative Process*, 55 Harv.

---

11. *See* Model Code of Judicial Conduct, Canon 3B(7), cmt. (1990).

12. Annotated Model Code of Judicial Conduct, 194 (3d ed. 2016) (citing Charles G. Geyh & W. William Hodes, Reporters' Notes to the Model Code of Judicial Conduct, *supra* note 5).

13. Minn. Bd. on Jud. Standards Advisory Op. 2016-2 (2016).

14. A judge should be familiar with the jurisdiction's authority on judicial notice. The rules and process, even the definition of judicial notice, vary from jurisdiction to jurisdiction. Many state evidence codes track the language of Federal Rule of Evidence 201. *See* Cal. Evid. Code Ann. § 452; Fla. St. Ann. § 90.202; Ill. R. Evid. 201; Pa. R. Evid. 201; Tex. R. Evid. R. 201. For a discussion of various state standards for judicial notice see O'Quinn v. Hall, 77 S.W.3d 438 (Tex. App. 2003); People v. Davis, 357 N.E.2d 792 (Ill. 1976); *In re* Cervera, 16 P.3d 176 n. 3 (2001); Maradie v. Maradie, 680 So. 2d 538 (Fla. Dist. Ct. App. 1996); Kinley v. Bierly, 876 A.2d 419 (Pa. Super. Ct. 2005).

15. Michael H. Graham, Handbook of Federal Evidence § 201:1 (7th ed. 2015) [hereinafter "Graham"].

16. *See Federal Rules of Evidence Rule 201: Judicial Notice of Adjudicative Facts*, Cornell Legal Information Institute, https://www.law.cornell.edu/rules/fre/rule_201 (last visited Nov. 27, 2017).

L. Rev. 364, 404–407 (1942)." The Advisory Committee Note explains that "adjudicative facts" are those "which relate to the parties" or, more fully:

> When a court or an agency finds facts concerning the immediate parties—who did what, where, when, how, and with what motive or intent—the court or agency is performing an adjudicative function, and the facts are conveniently called adjudicative facts. . . . . Stated in other terms, the adjudicative facts are those to which the law is applied in the process of adjudication. They are the facts that normally go to the jury in a jury case. They relate to the parties, their activities, their properties, their businesses.[17]

"Legislative facts," on the other hand, "do not usually concern the immediate parties but are general facts which help the tribunal decide questions of law and policy and discretion."[18] Research of legislative facts does not raise the same due process concerns as research of adjudicative facts.

Procedural protections generally are built into taking judicial notice. Federal Rule of Evidence 201(e) provides that a party is entitled to be heard, either before or after a court takes judicial notice of a fact. If the court takes judicial notice of adjudicative facts, "[o]n timely request, a party is entitled to be heard on the propriety of taking judicial notice and the nature of the fact to be noticed. If the court takes judicial notice before notifying a party, the party, on request, is still entitled to be heard."[19]

D. Judge's Duty to Supervise

Model Rule 2.9(D) requires that judges take steps to prevent court staff and officials from performing improper independent investigations. The Rule provides: "A judge shall make reasonable efforts, including providing appropriate supervision, to ensure that this Rule is not violated by court staff, court officials, and others subject to the judge's direction and control."[20]

---

17. Kenneth Culp Davis, 2 Administrative Law Treatise 353 § 15.03 *Legislative and Adjudicative Facts* (West 1958).

18. Usery v. Tamiami Trail Tours, Inc., 531 F.2d 224, 245, n. 52 (5th Cir. 1976) (*quoting* Davis, *An Approach to Problems of Evidence in the Administrative Process*, 55 Harv. L. Rev. 364, 402-416 (1942)).

19. Fed. R. Evid. 201(e). *See also* Garner v. Louisiana, 368 U.S. 157, 173 (1961) (citation omitted) ("[U]nless an accused is informed at trial of the facts of which the court is taking judicial notice, not only does he not know upon what evidence he is being convicted, but, in addition, he is deprived of any opportunity to challenge the deductions drawn from such notice or to dispute the notoriety or truth of the facts allegedly relied upon. Moreover, there is no way by which an appellate court may review the facts and law of a case and intelligently decide whether the findings of the lower court are supported by the evidence where that evidence is unknown. Such an assumption would be a denial of due process.")

20. Model Code of Judicial Conduct R. 2.9(D) (2011).

III. Guidelines for Independent Factual Research by Judges Via the Internet

When deciding whether to independently investigate facts on the Internet, the judge should consider:

1. Is additional information necessary to decide the case? If so, this type of information generally must be provided by counsel or the parties, or must be subject to proper judicial notice.
2. Is the purpose of the judge's inquiry to corroborate facts, discredit facts, or fill a factual gap in the record? If the facts are adjudicative, it is improper for a judge to do so.
3. Is the judge seeking general or educational information that is useful to provide the judge with a better understanding of a subject unrelated to a pending or impending case? If so, the inquiry is appropriate. Judges may use the Internet as they would other educational sources, like judicial seminars and books.
4. Is the judge seeking background information about a party or about the subject matter of a pending or impending case? If so, the information may represent adjudicative facts or legislative facts, depending on the circumstances. The key inquiry here is whether the information to be gathered is of factual consequence in determining the case. If it is, it must be subject to testing through the adversary process.

IV. Hypotheticals

The following hypotheticals are offered to provide guidance in determining whether independent research is permissible under the Model Code of Judicial Conduct.

Hypothetical #1: In a proceeding before the judge in a case involving overtime pay, defendant's counsel explains that the plaintiff could not have worked more than 40 hours per week because defendant's restaurant is in an "industrial area" and only open for breaks and lunch during the work-week and not on weekends. The judge is familiar with the area and skeptical of counsel's claims. The judge checks websites like Yelp and Google Maps, which list the restaurant as being open from 7 am to 10 pm, seven days each week. Does this search violate Rule 2.9(C) of the Model Code of Judicial Conduct?

Analysis #1: This search violates Rule 2.9(C) of the Model Code of Judicial Conduct because the restaurant's hours of operation are key to whether the plaintiff could prevail on a claim of unpaid overtime. The judge should ask the parties and their counsel to provide admissible evidence as to the restaurant's hours of operation.

Hypothetical #2: The judicial district in which the judge is assigned has many environmental contamination cases involving allegations that toxic chemicals have been released and have contaminated soil and groundwater. The judge is unfamiliar with this area of environmental law. Before a case is assigned to the judge, the judge reads online background information including articles. Does this action violate Rule 2.9(C) of the Model Code of Judicial Conduct?

Analysis #2: Judges may educate themselves by independent research about general topics of interest, even on topics that may come before the judge. General background learning on the Internet may be analogized to attending judicial seminars or reading books, so long as there is reason to believe the source is reliable. Even general subject-area research is not permissible, however, if the judge is acquiring information to make an adjudicative decision of material fact.[21]

Hypothetical #3: A social media-savvy lawyer just has been appointed to the bench. Before being appointed, this lawyer used social media to conduct extensive background research on potential jurors and opposing parties. The judge has been assigned to hear a complex, multi-party case involving lawyers from out of state. The judge wants to review the social media and websites of each of the parties and of the out-of-state lawyers to learn background information about the parties, to read the lawyers' writings, and to review a list of the lawyers' current and former clients. Does this action violate Rule 2.9(C) of the Model Code of Judicial Conduct?

Analysis #3: While the Model Code of Judicial Conduct does not prohibit a judge from personally participating in electronic social media ("ESM"),[22] a "judge must . . . avoid using any ESM site to obtain information regarding a matter before the judge in violation of Rule 2.9(C)."[23] On-line research to gather information about a juror or party in a pending or impending case is independent fact research that is prohibited by Model Rule 2.9(C).[24]

---

21. *See, e.g.*, Cal. Judges Ass'n Jud. Ethics Comm. Advisory Op. 68 (2013) (judge may research basic principles of medicine or other disciplines prior to being assigned a matter; judge may not investigate relevant facts that are germane to the case); Minn. Bd. on Jud. Standards Advisory Op. 2016-2 at 2 (2016) (a judge is permitted to investigate non-adjudicative facts, including research on the general subject areas of cases coming before the judge, without informing the parties); N.Y. Advisory Comm. on Jud. Eth. Op. 13-32 (2013) (a judge may "consult a disinterested expert on the law with respect to a legal issue that is not currently before the judge, and is not the subject of a pending or impending proceeding with identifiable parties"). *Cf.* Model Rule 2.9(A) ("a judge shall not initiate, permit, or consider *ex parte* communications, or consider other communications made to the judge outside the presence of the parties or their lawyers, concerning a pending or impending matter," except as permitted under the rules); Model Rule 2.9(A)(2) (exception permitting a judge to "obtain the written advice of a disinterested expert on the law applicable to a proceeding before the judge, if the judge gives advance notice to the parties of the person to be consulted and the subject matter of the advice to be solicited, and affords the parties a reasonable opportunity to object and respond to the notice and to the advice received").

22. *See* ABA Comm. on Ethics & Prof'l Responsibility, Formal Op. 462 at 2 (2013).

23. *Id.*

24. A judge may perform independent research to determine if a lawyer is authorized to practice in the jurisdiction, however, as this is not an adjudicative fact.

Gathering information about a lawyer is a closer question. The judge's information-gathering about a lawyer may be permissible if it is done merely to become familiar with counsel who appear before the court similar to how a judge may have, in the past reviewed a legal directory like Martindale Hubbell, or to determine whether the lawyer is authorized to practice in the jurisdiction. However, the judge's independent research about a lawyer is not permitted if it is done to affect the judge's weighing or considering adjudicative facts. If an otherwise permissible review results in a judge obtaining information about the existence or veracity of adjudicative facts in the matter, the judge should ask the parties to address the facts in the proceeding through evidentiary submissions.[25]

Hypothetical #4: A trial judge presiding over an owner's claim for insurance coverage heard testimony from competing experts about their investigation and opinions about the cause of a fire that destroyed plaintiff's property. While preparing findings of fact and conclusions of law the judge received summaries her law clerk created from journals and articles on the proper techniques and analysis for investigating fires of unknown origin. Does this action violate Rule 2.9(C) of the Model Code of Judicial Conduct?

Analysis #4: By searching the Internet for journals and articles on investigating fires, the law clerk engaged in an improper independent factual investigation. The method and extent of the expert's investigation is an issue in dispute, *i.e.*, an adjudicative fact. The respective experts' investigative methods related directly to the weight and credibility given to testimony concerning an adjudicative fact, and fall within the prohibition in Rule 2.9(C). The trial court, therefore, could not properly take judicial notice of these facts as being "not subject to reasonable dispute" because they are neither "generally known within the trial court's jurisdiction" nor can they be "accurately and readily determined from sources whose accuracy cannot reasonably be questioned." Fed. R. Evid. 201(b). If the summaries addressed material facts in dispute and the judge used the summaries to make findings of fact without allowing the parties to test the factual content of the summaries through

---

25. Two examples should suffice to make the point. The California Judges Association Judicial Ethics Committee Opinion 68 (2013) explained that a judge may not independently examine a state bar website to determine whether a potential juror is a lawyer to satisfy the judge's concern about that potential juror's veracity in responding to a question at *voir dire*. Instead the judge should "raise the concerns with counsel and ask them to engage in follow-up factual research with respect to this potential juror." In NYC Medical and Neurodiagnostic, P.C. v. Republic Western Insurance Co., 798 N.Y.S.2d 309 (Appellate Term 2nd and 11th Dist. 2004), the New York Appellate Term reversed the trial court's order denying the defendant insurer's motion to dismiss, in part because the trial judge conducted independent factual research on the Internet. The judge used the Internet to access websites, including the New York State Department of Insurance website, to investigate whether the defendant was licensed to do business in the state because the plaintiff did not provide adequate proof on this issue.

evidentiary submissions, the judge violated Model Rule of Judicial Conduct 2.9(A) by considering *ex parte* information, and violated Rule 2.9(D) by failing to require that the law clerk act in a manner consistent with the judge's obligations under the Code.[26]

Hypothetical #5: To render an accurate decision in a pending matter, a judge needs to know whether a party is or was the subject of other judicial proceedings. The judge searches the court's electronic files of the other cases and the facts of each case, including sealed information. The search reveals several other cases, some pending and some concluded and some within and some outside the judge's jurisdiction. Does the judge's search violate Rule 2.9(C) of the Model Code of Judicial Conduct?

Analysis #5: Model Rule 2.9(C) does not prohibit consideration of "facts that may properly be judicial noticed." For example, a judge may take judicial notice of a guilty plea entered before the judge in a previous case[27] and of other court records maintained by the clerk of the court in which the judge sits.[28] Court records can be judicially noticed for their factual existence, and the occurrence and timing of matters like hearings held and pleadings filed, but not for the truth of allegations or findings therein.[29] "[T]he law treats dif-

---

26. As noted previously, Model Rule 2.9(A) provides that "[a] judge shall not initiate, permit, or consider ex parte communications . . . ." Model Rule 2.9(D) provides, "A judge shall make reasonable efforts, including providing appropriate supervision, to ensure that this Rule is not violated by court staff, court officials, and others subject to the judge's direction and control."

Disqualification is an additional risk that may arise from independent research in a pending case. Model Rule 2.11(A)(1) states that a "judge shall disqualify" him or herself when the judge has "personal knowledge of facts that are in dispute in the proceeding." Knowledge is "actual knowledge of the fact in question. A person's knowledge may be inferred from circumstances." Model Rules of Prof'l Conduct, Terminology (2017). A judge likely has "personal knowledge" of facts that the judge has independently researched and found reliable. *See also* Annotated Model Code of Judicial Conduct (2d ed. 2011) ("Independent investigations by a judge . . . may provide a judge with personal knowledge of disputed facts, which is a special ground for judicial disqualification") (citations omitted).

27. *See* People v. Davis, 357 N.E.2d 792, 793-94 (Ill. 1976) (judicial notice of a conviction based upon a guilty plea in the same court before the same judge "falls squarely within the judicially noticeable category of facts 'capable of immediate and accurate demonstration by resort to easily accessible sources of indisputable accuracy'").

28. Ill. Jud. Ethics Comm. Op. 2016-02 (2016) (at sentencing, court may access county court files to review convicted criminal defendant's criminal case history "so long as the established procedural safeguards for taking judicial notice are adhered to"); Minn. Bd. of Jud. Standards, Advisory Op. 2016-2 (2016) (judge hearing *ex parte* order for protection may, under certain circumstances, take judicial notice of facts in Minnesota State Court Information Service).

29. Professional Engineers v. Department of Transportation, 936 P.2d 473, 496 (Cal. S. Ct. 1997) (construing a state Constitution's civil service provision that was later superseded by constitutional amendment; Ardaiz, J. dissenting, "judicial notice of findings of fact does not mean that those findings of fact are true, but, rather, only means that those findings of fact were made") (citations omitted);

ferent portions of the files and records differently."[30] Standards of judicial notice require the judge to give notice and an opportunity to be heard either before or after taking judicial notice. Again, each judge should determine the law of judicial notice in the applicable jurisdiction.

Even when reviewing court records, however, a judge should be mindful of the following caution, from Illinois Judicial Ethics Opinion 2016-02:

> the particular judge's competence to navigate the computerized court records is essential . . . only facts which are 'not subject to reasonable dispute' are the proper subject of judicial notice. The judge must be confident that his or her review will lead to *accurate* information. For example, indexes of computerized court records are likely to contain individuals with the same name; is the inquiring judge capable of finding the appropriate records and accurately matching them to the party in question? Judges must be aware of their own skills and, more importantly, their limitations . . . .

Documents that are sealed may not be reviewed. That would be independent research disclosing information about a party to which both sides do not have access or even know exist. Reviewing sealed documents is improper under Rule 2.9(C) of the Model Code of Judicial Conduct.[31]

V. Conclusion

The Internet provides useful tools for discovering vast amounts of information. Searching reliable sources on the Internet may reveal information that educates, informs, and enlightens the judiciary, not unlike judicial seminars and printed materials.

Information properly subject to judicial notice is well within the judge's discretion to search and use according to the applicable law. On the other hand, adjudicative facts that are needed to determine an issue in a case, but

---

Doyle v. People, 343 P.3d 961, 963 (Colo. S. Ct. 2015) ("Because the resolution of a factual matter at issue in a prior judicial proceeding, unlike the occurrence of the legal proceeding or other court action itself, does not become an indisputable fact within the contemplation of CRE 201 merely as a result of being reflected in a court record, the trial court erred in taking judicial notice that the defendant failed to appear in court on a particular day"); *see also* GRAHAM, *supra* note 15 § 201:3 for a full discussion of judicial notice of court records.

30. Minn. Bd. of Jud. Standards Advisory Op. 2016-2 (2016) *citing In re* Welfare of D.J.N., 568 N.W.2d 170, 175 (Minn. Ct. App. 1997).

31. Wash. Ethics Advisory Comm. Op. 13-07 (2013) ("a judicial officer in a juvenile matter may not *sua sponte* review public and/or sealed records [maintained by the courts] unless such review is authorized by law"; "[i]f a party to a proceeding requests the court to review [the records] but such review is not expressly allowed by law, then the court should allow the other party or parties to be heard").

which are not properly subject to judicial notice, may not be researched without violating Rule 2.9(C). Stated simply, a judge should not gather adjudicative facts from any source on the Internet unless the information is subject to proper judicial notice. Further, and within the guidelines set forth in this opinion, judges should not use the Internet for independent fact-gathering related to a pending or impending matter where the parties can easily be asked to research or provide the information. The same is true of the activities or characteristics of the litigants or other participants in the matter.

AMERICAN BAR ASSOCIATION

STANDING COMMITTEE ON ETHICS AND PROFESSIONAL RESPONSIBILITY

FORMAL OPINION 479 **December 15, 2017**

The "Generally Known" Exception to Former-Client Confidentiality

A lawyer's duty of confidentiality extends to former clients. Under Model Rule of Professional Conduct 1.9(c), a lawyer may not use information relating to the representation of a former client to the former client's disadvantage without informed consent, or except as otherwise permitted or required by the Rules of Professional Conduct, unless the information has become "generally known."

The "generally known" exception to the duty of former-client confidentiality is limited. It applies (1) only to the use, and not the disclosure or revelation, of former-client information; and (2) only if the information has become (a) widely recognized by members of the public in the relevant geographic area; or (b) widely recognized in the former client's industry, profession, or trade. Information is not "generally known" simply because it has been discussed in open court, or is available in court records, in libraries, or in other public repositories of information.

Introduction

Confidentiality is essential to the attorney-client relationship. The duty to protect the confidentiality of client information has been enforced in rules governing lawyers since the Canons of Ethics were adopted in 1908.

The focus of this opinion is a lawyer's duty of confidentiality to former clients under Model Rule of Professional Conduct 1.9(c). More particularly, this opinion explains when information relating to the representation of a former client has become generally known, such that the lawyer may use it to the disadvantage of the former client without violating Model Rule 1.9(c)(1).

The Relevant Model Rules of Professional Conduct

Model Rule 1.6(a) prohibits a lawyer from revealing information related to a client's representation unless the client gives informed consent, the disclosure is impliedly authorized to carry out the representation, or the disclosure is permitted by Model Rule 1.6(b).[1] Model Rule 1.9 extends lawyers' duty of confidentiality to former clients. Model Rules 1.9(a) and (b) govern

---

1. Model Rules of Prof'l Conduct R. 1.6(a) (2017) [hereinafter Model Rules].

situations in which a lawyer's knowledge of a former client's confidential information would create a conflict of interest in a subsequent representation. Model Rule 1.9(c) "separately regulates the use and disclosure of confidential information" regardless of "whether or not a subsequent representation is involved."[2]

Model Rule 1.9(c)(2) governs the *revelation* of former client confidential information. Under Model Rule 1.9(c)(2), a lawyer who formerly represented a client in a matter, or whose present or former firm formerly represented a client in a matter, may not reveal information relating to the representation except as the Model Rules "would permit or require with respect to a [current] client." Lawyers thus have the same duties not to *reveal* former client confidences under Model Rule 1.9(c)(2) as they have with regard to current clients under Model Rule 1.6.

In contrast, Model Rule 1.9(c)(1) addresses the *use* of former client confidential information. Model Rule 1.9(c)(1) provides that a lawyer shall not use information relating to a former client's representation "to the disadvantage of the former client except as [the Model] Rules would permit or require with respect to a [current] client, or when the information has become *generally known*."[3] The terms "reveal" or "disclose" on the one hand and "use" on the other describe different activities or types of conduct even though they may—but need not—occur at the same time. The generally known exception applies only to the "use" of former client confidential information. This opinion provides guidance on when information is generally known within the meaning of Model Rule 1.9(c)(1).[4]

The Generally Known Exception

The generally known exception to the use of former-client information was introduced in the 1983 Model Rules.[5] The term is not defined in Model Rule 1.0 or in official Comments to Model Rule 1.9. A number of courts and other authorities conclude that information is *not* generally known merely because it is publicly available or might qualify as a public record or as a matter of public record.[6] Agreement on when information *is* generally known has been harder to achieve.

---

2. Ellen J. Bennett et al., Annotated Model Rules of Professional Conduct 190 (8th ed. 2015).

3. Model Rules R. 1.9(c)(1) (2017) (emphasis added).

4. *See id.* at cmt. 9 (explaining that "[t]he provisions of this Rule are for the protection of former clients and can be waived if the client gives informed consent").

5. *See* Ronald D. Rotunda & John S. Dzienkowski, Legal Ethics: The Lawyer's Deskbook on Professional Responsibility § 1.9, at 534 (2017–2018) (explaining that the language was originally part of Model Rule 1.9(b), and was moved to Model Rule 1.9(c) in 1989).

6. *See, e.g.*, Pallon v. Roggio, Civ. A. Nos. 04-3625(JAP), 06-1068(FLW), 2006 WL 2466854, at *7 (D. N.J. Aug. 24, 2006) ("'Generally known' does not only mean that the informa-

tion is of public record. . . . The information must be within the basic understanding and knowledge of the public. The content of form pleadings, interrogatories and other discovery materials, as well as general litigation techniques that were widely available to the public through the internet or another source, such as continuing legal education classes, does not make that information 'generally known' within the meaning of Rule 1.9(c)." (citations omitted)); Steel v. Gen. Motors Corp., 912 F. Supp. 724, 739 (D. N.J. 1995) (in a discussion of Rule 1.9(c)(2), stating that the fact that information is publicly available does not make it 'generally known'); *In re* Gordon Props., LLC, 505 B.R. 703, 707 n.6 (Bankr. E.D. Va. 2013) ("'Generally known' does not mean information that someone can find."); *In re* Anonymous, 932 N.E.2d 671, 674 (Ind. 2010) (stating in connection with a discussion of Rule 1.9(c)(2) that "the Rules contain no exception allowing revelation of information relating to a representation even if a diligent researcher could unearth it through public sources" (footnote omitted); *In re* Tennant, 392 P.3d 143, 148 (Mont. 2017) (explaining that with respect to the Rule 1.9(c) analysis of when information is considered to be generally known, the fact that "the information at issue is generally available does not suffice; the information must be within the basic knowledge and understanding of the public;" protection of the client's information "'is not nullified by the fact that the circumstances to be disclosed are part of a public record, or that there are other available sources for such information, or by the fact that the lawyer received the same information from other sources'") (citations omitted)); Turner v. Commonwealth, 726 S.E.2d 325, 333 (Va. 2012) (Lemons, J., concurring) ("While testimony in a court proceeding may become a matter of public record even in a court denominated as a 'court not of record,' and may have been within the knowledge of anyone at the preliminary hearing, it does not mean that such testimony is 'generally known.' There is a significant difference between something being a public record and it also being 'generally known.'"); N.Y. State Bar Ass'n Comm. on Prof'l Ethics Op. 1125, 2017 WL 2639716, at *1 (2017) (discussing lawyers' duty of confidentiality and stating that "information is not 'generally known' simply because it is in the public domain or available in a public file" (reference omitted)); Tex. Comm. on Prof'l Ethics Op. 595, 2010 WL 2480777, at *1 (2010) ("Information that is a matter of public record may not be information that is 'generally known.' A matter may be of public record simply by being included in a government record . . . whether or not there is any general public awareness of the matter. Information that 'has become generally known' is information that is actually known to some members of the general public and is not merely available to be known if members of the general public choose to look where the information is to be found."); Rotunda & Dzienkowski, *supra* note 5, § 1.9-3, at 554 (stating that Model Rule 1.9 "deals with what has become generally known, not what is publicly available if you know exactly where to look"); *see also* Dougherty v. Pepper Hamilton LLP, 133 A.3d 792, 800 (Pa. Super. Ct. 2016) (questioning whether an FBI affidavit that was accidentally attached to a document in an unrelated proceeding and was thus publicly available through PACER was "actually 'generally known,'" since "a person interested in the FBI affidavit 'could obtain it only by means of special knowledge'" (citing Restatement (Third) of the Law Governing Lawyers § 59, cmt. d). *But see* State v. Mark, 231 P.3d 478, 511 (Haw. 2010) (treating a former client's criminal conviction as "generally known" when discussing a former client conflict and whether matters were related); Jamaica Pub. Serv. Co. v. AIU Ins. Co., 707 N.E.2d 414, 417 (N.Y. 1998) (applying former DR 5-108(a)(2) and stating that because information regarding the defendant's relationship with its sister companies "was readily available in such public materials as trade periodicals and filings with State and Federal regulators," it was "generally known"); State ex rel. Youngblood v. Sanders, 575 S.E.2d 864, 872 (W. Va. 2002) (stating that because information was contained in police reports it was "generally known" for Rule 1.9 purposes); Restatement (Third) of the Law Governing Lawyers § 59 cmt. d (2000) ("Information contained

A leading dictionary suggests that information is generally known when it is "popularly" or "widely" known.[7] Commentators have essentially endorsed this understanding of generally known by analogizing to an original comment in New York's version of Rule 1.6(a) governing the protection of a client's confidential information. The original comment distinguished "generally known" from "publicly available."[8] Commentators find this construct "a good and valid guide"[9] to when information is generally known for Rule 1.9(c)(1) purposes:

> [T]he phrase "generally known" means much more than publicly available or accessible. It means that the information has already received widespread publicity. For example, a lawyer working on a merger with a Fortune 500 company could not whisper a word about it during the pre-offer stages, but once the offer is made—for example, once AOL and Time Warner have announced their merger, and the Wall Street Journal has reported it on the front page, and the client has become a former client—then the lawyer may tell the world. After all, most of the world already knows. . . .
>
> [O]nly if an event gained considerable public notoriety should information about it ordinarily be considered "generally known."[10]

Similarly, in discussing confidentiality issues under Rules 1.6 and 1.9, the New York State Bar Association's Committee on Professional Ethics ("NYSBA Committee") opined that "information is generally known only if it is known to a sizeable percentage of people in 'the local community or in the trade, field or profession to which the information relates.'"[11] By contrast, "[I]nformation is not 'generally known' simply because it is in the public domain or available in a public file."[12] The Illinois State Bar Association likewise reasoned that information is generally known within the meaning of Rule 1.9 if it constitutes "'common knowledge in the community.'"[13]

---

in books or records in public libraries, public-record depositories such as government offices, or publicly accessible electronic-data storage is generally known if the particular information is obtainable through publicly available indexes and similar methods of access.").

7. THE AMERICAN HERITAGE DICTIONARY OF THE ENGLISH LANGUAGE 732 (4th ed. 2009).

8. *See* ROY D. SIMON & NICOLE HYLAND, SIMON'S NEW YORK RULES OF PROFESSIONAL CONDUCT ANNOTATED 685 (2017) (discussing former comment 4A to New York Rule 1.6).

9. *Id.*

10. *Id.*

11. N.Y. State Bar Ass'n, Comm. on Prof'l Ethics, Op. 991, at ¶ 20 (2013).

12. *Id.* at ¶ 17.

13. Ill. State Bar Ass'n. Advisory Op. 05-01, 2006 WL 4584283, at *3 (2006) (quoting RESTATEMENT (SECOND) OF AGENCY § 395 cmt. b (1958)). The Illinois State Bar borrowed this definition from section 395 of the Restatement (Second) of Agency, which excludes such in-

As the NYSBA Committee concluded, information should be treated differently if it is widely recognized in a client's industry, trade, or profession even if it is not known to the public at large. For example, under Massachusetts Rule of Professional Conduct 1.6(a), a lawyer generally is obligated to protect "confidential information relating to the representation of a client."[14] Confidential information, however, does not ordinarily include "information that is generally known in the local community or in the trade, field or profession to which the information relates."[15] Similarly, under New York Rule of Professional Conduct 1.6(a), a lawyer generally cannot "knowingly reveal confidential information . . . or use such information to the disadvantage of a client or for the advantage of the lawyer or a third person,"[16] but "confidential information" does not include "information that is generally known in the local community or in the trade, field or profession to which the information relates."[17] Returning to Model Rule 1.9(c)(1), allowing information that is generally known in the former client's industry, profession, or trade to be used pursuant to Model Rule 1.9(c)(1) makes sense if, as some scholars have urged, the drafters of the rule contemplated that situation.[18]

A Workable Definition of Generally Known under Model Rule 1.9(c)(1)

Consistent with the foregoing, the Committee's view is that information is generally known within the meaning of Model Rule 1.9(c)(1) if (a) it is widely recognized by members of the public in the relevant geographic area; or (b) it is widely recognized in the former client's industry, profession, or trade. Information may become widely recognized and thus generally known as a result of publicity through traditional media sources, such as

---

formation from confidential information belonging to a principal that an agent may not use "in violation of his duties as agent, in competition with or to the injury of the principal," whether "on his own account or on behalf of another." RESTATEMENT (SECOND) OF AGENCY § 395 & cmt. b (1958).

14. MASS. RULES OF PROF'L CONDUCT R. 1.6(a) (2017).

15. *Id.* at cmt. 3A.

16. N.Y. RULES OF PROF'L CONDUCT R. 1.6(a) (2017).

17. *Id.* at cmt. [4A] ("Information is generally known in the local community or in the trade, field or profession to which the information relates is also not protected, unless the client and the lawyer have otherwise agreed. Information is not 'generally known' simply because it is in the public domain or available in a public file").

18. *See* GEOFFREY C. HAZARD, JR. ET AL., THE LAW OF LAWYERING § 14.16, at 14-48 (2016) (discussing generally known and saying, "It seems likely that both the Kutak Commission and the Ethics 2000 Commission . . . had in mind situations in which a lawyer has worked with a company in various legal contexts, learned considerable information about its products and practices, and later seeks to use this information in connection with [the] representation of an adverse party in an unrelated lawsuit or transaction of some kind").

newspapers, magazines, radio, or television; through publication on internet web sites; or through social media. With respect to category (b), information should be treated as generally known if it is announced, discussed, or identified in what reasonable members of the industry, profession, or trade would consider a leading print or online publication or other resource in the particular field. Information may be widely recognized within a former client's industry, profession, or trade without being widely recognized by the public. For example, if a former client is in the insurance industry, information about the former client that is widely recognized by others in the insurance industry should be considered generally known within the meaning of Model Rule 1.9(c)(1) even if the public at large is unaware of the information.

Unless information has become widely recognized by the public (for example by having achieved public notoriety), or within the former client's industry, profession, or trade, the fact that the information may have been discussed in open court, or may be available in court records, in public libraries, or in other public repositories does not, standing alone, mean that the information is generally known for Model Rule 1.9(c)(1) purposes.[19] Information that is publicly available is not necessarily generally known. Certainly, if information is publicly available but requires specialized knowledge or expertise to locate, it is not generally known within the meaning of Model Rule 1.9(c)(1).[20]

Conclusion

A lawyer may use information that is generally known to a former client's disadvantage without the former client's informed consent. Information is generally known within the meaning of Model Rule 1.9(c)(1) if it is widely recognized by members of the public in the relevant geographic area or it is

---

19. *See In re* Gordon Props., LLC, 505 B.R. 703, 707 n.6 (Bankr. E.D. Va. 2013) ("'Generally known' does not mean information that someone can find. It means information that is already generally known. For example, a lawyer may have drafted a property settlement agreement in a divorce case and it may [be] in a case file in the courthouse where anyone could go, find it and read it. It is not 'generally known.' In some divorce cases, the property settlement agreement may become generally known, for example, in a case involving a celebrity, because the terms appear on the front page of the tabloids. 'Generally known' does not require publication on the front page of a tabloid, but it is more than merely sitting in a file in the courthouse."); *In re* Tennant, 392 P.3d 143, 148 (Mont. 2017) (holding that a lawyer who learned the information in question during his former clients' representation could not take advantage of his former clients "by retroactively relying on public records of their information for self-dealing"); Rotunda & Dzienkowski, *supra* note 5, § 1.9-3, at 554 (explaining that Model Rule 1.9(c)(1) "deals with what has become generally known, not what is publicly available if you know exactly where to look"); *see also supra* note 6 (citing additional cases and materials).

20. *See* Restatement (Third) of the Law Governing Lawyers § 59 cmt. d (2000) (stating, *inter alia,* that information is not generally known "when a person interested in knowing the information could obtain it only by means of special knowledge").

widely recognized in the former client's industry, profession, or trade. For information to be generally known it must previously have been revealed by some source other than the lawyer or the lawyer's agents. Information that is publicly available is not necessarily generally known.

AMERICAN BAR ASSOCIATION

STANDING COMMITTEE ON ETHICS AND PROFESSIONAL RESPONSIBILITY

Formal Opinion 480 **March 6, 2018**

Confidentiality Obligations for Lawyer Blogging and Other Public Commentary

Lawyers who blog or engage in other public commentary may not reveal information relating to a representation, including information contained in a public record, unless authorized by a provision of the Model Rules.[1]

Introduction

Lawyers comment on legal topics in various formats. The newest format is online publications such as blogs,[2] listserves, online articles, website postings, and brief online statements or microblogs (such as Twitter®) that "followers" (people who subscribe to a writer's online musings) read. Lawyers continue to present education programs and discuss legal topics in articles and chapters in traditional print media such as magazines, treatises, law firm white papers, and law reviews. They also make public remarks in online informational videos such as webinars and podcasts (collectively "public commentary").[3]

Lawyers who communicate about legal topics in public commentary must comply with the Model Rules of Professional Conduct, including the

1. This opinion is based on the ABA Model Rules of Professional Conduct as amended by the ABA House of Delegates through August 2016 [hereinafter the "Model Rules"]. The laws, court rules, regulations, rules of professional conduct and opinions promulgated in individual jurisdictions are controlling.

2. A "blog" is commonly understood to be a website consisting of written entries (posts) regularly updated and typically written in an informal or conversational style by an individual or small group. As recently described in a California State Bar advisory opinion, "[b]logs written by lawyers run the gamut from those having nothing to do with the legal profession, to informational articles, to commentary on legal issues and the state of our system of justice, to self-promotional descriptions of the attorney's legal practice and courtroom successes to overt advertisements for the attorney or her law firm." State Bar of Cal. Comm'n on Prof'l Responsibility & Conduct Op. 2016-196 (2016).

3. These are just examples of public written communications but this opinion is not limited to these formats. This opinion does not address the various obligations that may arise under Model Rules 7.1-7.5 governing advertising and solicitation, but lawyers may wish to consider their potential application to specific communications.

Rules regarding confidentiality of information relating to the representation of a client. A lawyer must maintain the confidentiality of information relating to the representation of a client, unless that client has given informed consent to the disclosure, the disclosure is impliedly authorized to carry out the representation, or the disclosure is permitted by Rule 1.6(b). A lawyer's public commentary may also implicate the lawyer's duties under other Rules, including Model Rules 3.5 (Impartiality and Decorum of the Tribunal) and 3.6 (Trial Publicity).

Online public commentary provides a way to share knowledge, opinions, experiences, and news. Many online forms of public commentary offer an interactive comment section, and, as such, are also a form of social media.[4] While technological advances have altered how lawyers communicate, and therefore may raise unexpected practical questions, they do not alter lawyers' fundamental ethical obligations when engaging in public commentary.[5]

Duty of Confidentiality Under Rule 1.6

Model Rule 1.6(a) provides:

> A lawyer shall not reveal information relating to the representation of a client unless the client gives informed consent, the disclosure is

4. Lawyers should take care to avoid inadvertently forming attorney-client relationships with readers of their public commentary. Although traditional print format commentary would not give rise to such concerns, lawyers interacting with readers through social media should be aware at least of its possibility. A lawyer commenting publicly about a legal matter standing alone would not create a client-lawyer relationship with readers of the commentary. *See* Model Rule 1.18 for duties to prospective clients. However, the ability of readers/viewers to make comments or to ask questions suggests that, where practicable, a lawyer include appropriate disclaimers on websites, blogs and the like, such as "reading/viewing this information does not create an attorney-client relationship."

Lawyer blogging may also create a positional conflict. *See* D.C. Bar Op. 370 (2016) (discussing lawyers' use of social media advising that "[c]aution should be exercised when stating positions on issues, as those stated positions could be adverse to an interest of a client, thus inadvertently creating a conflict.") *See also* Ellen J. Bennett, Elizabeth J. Cohen & Helen W. Gunnarsson, Annotated Model Rules of Professional Conduct 148 (8th ed. 2015) (addressing positional conflicts). *See also* Stephen Gillers, Regulation of Lawyers: Problems of Law and Ethics 50-51 (11th ed. 2018) ("[S]ocial media presence can pose a risk for attorneys, who must be careful not to contradict their firm's official position on an issue in a pending case"). This opinion does not address positional conflicts.

5. *Accord* D.C. Bar Op. 370 (2016) (stating that a lawyer who chooses to use social media must comply with ethics rules to the same extent as one communicating through more traditional forms of communication).

impliedly authorized in order to carry out the representation or the disclosure is permitted by paragraph (b).

As Comment [2] emphasizes, "[a] fundamental principle in the client-lawyer relationship is that, in the absence of the client's informed consent, the lawyer must not reveal information relating to the representation."

This confidentiality rule "applies not only to matters communicated in confidence by the client but also to all information relating to the representation, whatever its source."[6] In other words, the scope of protection afforded by Rule 1.6 is far broader than attorney-client privileged information.

Unless one of the exceptions to Rule 1.6(a) is applicable, a lawyer is prohibited from commenting publicly about any information related to a representation. Even client identity is protected under Model Rule 1.6.[7] Rule 1.6(b) provides other exceptions to Rule 1.6(a).[8] However, because it is highly unlikely that a disclosure exception under Rule 1.6(b) would apply to a lawyer's public commentary, we assume for this opinion that exceptions arising under Rule 1.6(b) are not applicable.[9]

---

6. Model Rules of Prof'l Conduct R. 1.6 cmt. [3] (2017). There is also a general principle noted in the Restatement (Third) of the Law Governing Lawyers that "[c]onfidential client information does not include what a lawyer learns about the law, legal institutions such as courts and administrative agencies, and similar public matters in the course of representing clients." American Law Institute, Restatement of the Law (Third) The Law Governing Lawyers §59, cmt. e (1998). It is beyond the scope of this opinion to define what specific elements will be considered to distinguish between protected client information and information about the law when they entwine.

7. *See* Wis. Op. EF-17-02 (2017) ("a client's identity, as well as a former client's identity, is information protected by [Rule 1.6]"); State Bar of Nev. Comm'n on Ethics and Prof'l Responsibility Formal Op. 41, at 2 (2009) ("Even the mere identity of a client is protected by Rule 1.6."); State Bar of Ariz. Comm. on the Rules of Prof'l Conduct Op. 92-04 (1992) (explaining that a firm may not disclose list of client names with receivable amounts to a bank to obtain financing without client consent). *See also* Model Rules of Prof'l Conduct R. 7.2 cmt. [2] (2017) & N.Y. Rules of Prof'l Conduct R. 7.1(b)(2) (requiring prior written consent to use a client name in advertising). *But see* Cal. Formal Op. 2011-182 (2011) ("…[I]n most situations, the identity of a client is not considered confidential and in such circumstances Attorney may disclose the fact of the representation to Prospective Client without Witness Client's consent.") (*citing to* LA County Bar Ass'n Prof'l Responsibility & Ethics Comm'n Op. 456 (1989)).

8. *See* Model Rules of Prof'l Conduct R. 1.6(b)(1)-(7) (2017).

9. For ethical issues raised when a lawyer is participating in an investigation or litigation and the lawyer makes extrajudicial statements, see *infra* at page 6.

Significantly, information about a client's representation contained in a court's order, for example, although contained in a public document or record, is *not* exempt from the lawyer's duty of confidentiality under Model Rule 1.6.[10] The duty of confidentiality extends generally to information related to a representation whatever its source and without regard to the fact that others may be aware of or have access to such knowledge.[11]

A violation of Rule 1.6(a) is not avoided by describing public commentary as a "hypothetical" if there is a reasonable likelihood that a third party may ascertain the identity or situation of the client from the facts set forth in the hypothetical.[12] Hence, if a lawyer uses a hypothetical when offering

10. *See* ABA Formal Op. 479 (2017). *See also In re* Anonymous, 932 N.E.2d 671 (Ind. 2010) (neither client's prior disclosure of information relating to her divorce representation to friends nor availability of information in police reports and other public records absolved lawyer of violation of Rule 1.6); Iowa S. Ct. Attorney Disciplinary Bd. v. Marzen, 779 N.W.2d 757 (Iowa 2010) (all lawyer-client communications, even those including publicly available information, are confidential); Lawyer Disciplinary Bd. v. McGraw, 461 S.E.2d 850 (W. Va. 1995) ("[t]he ethical duty of confidentiality is not nullified by the fact that the information is part of a public record or by the fact that someone else is privy to it"); State Bar of Ariz. Op. 2000-11 (2000) (lawyer must "maintain the confidentiality of information relating to representation even if the information is a matter of public record"); State Bar of Nev. Op. 41 (2009) (contrasting broad language of Rule 1.6 with narrower language of Restatement (Third) of the Law Governing Lawyers); Pa. Bar Ass'n Informal Op. 2009-10 (2009) (absent client consent, lawyer may not report opponent's misconduct to disciplinary board even though it is recited in court's opinion); Colo. Formal Op. 130 (2017) ("Nor is there an exception for information otherwise publicly available. For example, without informed consent, a lawyer may not disclose information relating to the representation of a client even if the information has been in the news."); *But see In re* Sellers, 669 So. 2d 1204 (La. 1996) (lawyer violated Rule 4.1 by failing to disclose existence of collateral mortgage to third party; because "mortgage was filed in the public record, disclosure of its existence could not be a confidential communication, and was not prohibited by Rule 1.6"); Hunter v. Va. State Bar, 744 S.E.2d 611 (Va. 2013) (rejecting state bar's interpretation of Rule 1.6 as prohibiting lawyer from posting on his blog information previously revealed in completed public criminal trials of former clients). See discussion of *Hunter, infra*, at note 20.

11. ABA Comm. on Ethics & Prof'l Responsibility, Formal Op. 04-433 (2004) ("Indeed, the protection afforded by Rule 1.6 is not forfeited even when the information is available from other sources or publicly filed, such as in a malpractice action against the offending lawyer.")

12. Model Rules of Prof'l Responsibility R. 1.6 cmt. [4] (2017). The possibility of violating Rule 1.6 using hypothetical facts was discussed in ABA Formal Opinion 98-411, which addressed a lawyer's ability to consult with another lawyer about a client's matter. That opinion was issued prior to the adoption of what is now Rule 1.6(b)(4) which permits lawyers to reveal information relating to the representation of a client to the extent the lawyer reasonably believes necessary to secure legal advice about the lawyer's compliance with these Rules. However, the directive provided in Formal Opinion 98-411 remains sound, namely, that a lawyer use caution when constructing a hypothetical. For an illustrative case, see *In re* Peshek, M.R. 23794, 2009 PR 00089 (Ill. 2010). Peshek was suspended for sixty days for violating Rule 1.6. Peshek served as a Winnebago County Public defender for about 19 years. After being assaulted by a client, Peshek began publishing an Internet blog, about

public commentary, the hypothetical should be constructed so that there is no such likelihood.

The salient point is that when a lawyer participates in public commentary that includes client information, if the lawyer has not secured the client's informed consent or the disclosure is not otherwise impliedly authorized to carry out the representation, then the lawyer violates Rule 1.6(a).[13] Rule 1.6 does not provide an exception for information that is "generally known" or contained in a "public record."[14] Accordingly, if a lawyer wants to publicly reveal client information, the lawyer[15] must comply with Rule 1.6(a).[16]

First Amendment Considerations

While it is beyond the scope of the Committee's jurisdiction to opine on legal issues in formal opinions, often the application of the ethics rules interacts with a legal issue. Here lawyer speech relates to First Amendment speech. Although the First Amendment to the United States Constitution guarantees individuals' right to free speech, this right is not without

---

a third of which was devoted to discussing her work at the public defender's office and her clients. Peshek's blog contained numerous entries about conversations with clients and various details of their cases, and Peshek referred to her clients by either first name, a derivative of their first name, or their jail ID number, which were held to be disclosures of confidential information in violation of Rule 1.6. She was suspended from practice for 60 days.

13. We again note that Rule 1.6(b) provides other exceptions to Rule 1.6(a).

14. Model Rule 1.9 addresses the duties lawyers owe to former clients. Rule 1.9(c)(1) permits a lawyer, who has formerly represented a client, to use information related to the representation that has become generally known to the disadvantage of a former client, and Rule 1.9(c)(2) prohibits a lawyer from revealing information relating to the representation except as the Rules permit or require with respect to a current client. This opinion does not address these issues under Model Rule 1.9. The generally known exception in Rule 1.9(c)(1) is addressed in ABA Formal Opinion 479.

15. Lawyers also have ethical obligations pursuant to Rules 5.1 and 5.3 to assure that lawyers and staff they supervise comply with these confidentiality obligations.

16. In addition to the requirements of Rules 1.6(a), a lawyer may consider other practical client relations and ethics issues before discussing client information in public commentary to avoid disseminating information that the client may not want disseminated. For instance, Model Rule 1.8(b) reads: "A lawyer shall not use information relating to representation of a client to the disadvantage of the client unless the client gives informed consent, except as permitted or required by these Rules." Rule 1.8(b) could be read to suggest that a lawyer may use client information if it *does not* disadvantage a client. The lawyer, nevertheless, has a common-law fiduciary duty not to profit from using client information even if the use complies with the lawyer's ethical obligations. *See* Restatement of the Law (Third) The Law Governing Lawyers § 60(2) (1998) ("a lawyer who uses confidential information of a client for the lawyer's pecuniary gain other than in the practice of law must account to the client for any profits made"). *Accord* D.C. Bar Op. 370 (2016) ("It is advisable that the attorney share a draft of the proposed post or blog entry with the client, so there can be no miscommunication regarding the nature of the content that the attorney wishes to make public. It is also advisable, should the client agree that the content may be made public, that the attorney obtain that client's consent in a written form.")

bounds.[17] Lawyers' professional conduct may be constitutionally constrained by various professional regulatory standards as embodied in the Model Rules, or similar state analogs. For example, when a lawyer acts in a representative capacity, courts often conclude that the lawyer's free speech rights are limited.[18]

The plain language of Model Rule 1.6 dictates that information relating to the representation, even information that is provided in a public judicial proceeding, remains protected by Model Rule 1.6(a).[19] A lawyer may not voluntarily disclose such information, unless the lawyer obtains the client's informed consent, the disclosure is impliedly authorized to carry out the representation, or another exception to the Model Rule applies.[20]

---

17. *See* Gregory A. Garbacz, *Gentile v. State Bar of Nevada: Implications for the Media*, 49 Wash. & Lee L. Rev. 671 (1992); D. Christopher Albright, *Gentile v. State Bar: Core Speech and a Lawyer's Pretrial Statements to the Press*, 1992 BYU L. Rev. 809 (1992); Kathleen M. Sullivan, *The Intersection of Free Speech and the Legal Profession: Constraints on Lawyers' First Amendment Rights*, 67 Fordham L. Rev. 569 (1998). *See also* Brandon v. Maricopa City, 849 F.3d 837 (9th Cir. 2017) (when a lawyer speaks to the media in her official capacity as an attorney for county officials, such speech involves her conduct as a lawyer and therefore is not "constitutionally protected citizen speech").

18. *See In re* Snyder, 472 U.S. 634 (1985) (a law license requires conduct "compatible with the role of courts in the administration of justice"); U.S. Dist. Ct. E. Dist. of Wash. v. Sandlin, 12 F.3d 861 (9th Cir. 1993) ("once a lawyer is admitted to the bar, although he does not surrender his freedom of expression, he must temper his criticisms in accordance with professional standards of conduct"); *In re* Shearin, 765 A.2d 930 (Del. 2000) (lawyers' constitutional free speech rights are qualified by their ethical duties); Ky. Bar Ass'n v. Blum, 404 S.W.3d 841 (Ky. 2013) ("It has routinely been upheld that regulating the speech of attorneys is appropriate in order to maintain the public confidence and credibility of the judiciary and as a condition of '[t]he license granted by the court.'" [citing *Snyder*]); State ex rel. Neb. State Bar Ass'n v. Michaelis, 316 N.W.2d 46 (Neb. 1982) ("A layman may, perhaps, pursue his theories of free speech or political activities until he runs afoul of the penalties of libel or slander, or into some infraction of our statutory law. A member of the bar can, and will, be stopped at the point where he infringes our Canons of Ethics.").

19. *See* ABA Formal Op. 479 (2017). See also cases and authorities cited *supra* at note 10.

20. One jurisdiction has held that a lawyer is not prohibited from writing a blog that includes information relating to a representation that was disclosed in an open public judicial proceeding after the public proceeding had concluded. In Hunter v. Virginia State Bar, 744 S.E.2d 611 (Va. 2013) the Supreme Court of Virginia held that the application of Virginia Rule of Professional Conduct 1.6(a) to Hunter's blog posts was an unconstitutional infringement of Hunter's free speech rights. The Committee regards *Hunter* as limited to its facts. Virginia's Rule 1.6 is different than the ABA Model Rule. The Virginia Supreme Court rejected the Virginia State Bar's position on the interpretation and importance of Rule 1.6 because there was "no evidence advanced to support it." But see *People vs. Isaac* which acknowledges *Hunter* but finds a violation of Colorado Rule 1.6. We note, further, that the holding in *Hunter* has been criticized. *See* Jan L. Jacobowitz & Kelly Rains Jesson, *Fidelity Diluted: Client Confidentiality Give Way to the First Amendment & Social Media in Virginia State Bar ex rel. Third District Committee v. Horace Frazier Hunter*, 36 Campbell L. Rev. 75, 98-106 (2013).

At least since the adoption of the ABA Canons of Ethics, the privilege of practicing law has required lawyers to hold inviolate information about a client or a client's representation beyond that which is protected by the attorney-client privilege. Indeed, lawyer ethics rules in many jurisdictions recognize that the duty of confidentiality is so fundamental that it arises before a lawyer–client relationship forms, even if it never forms,[21] and lasts well beyond the end of the professional relationship.[22] It is principally, if not singularly, the duty of confidentiality that enables and encourages a client to communicate fully and frankly with his or her lawyer.[23]

Ethical Constraints on Trial Publicity and Other Statements

Model Rule 3.5 prohibits a lawyer from seeking to influence a judge, juror, prospective juror, or other official by means prohibited by law. Although using public commentary with the client's informed consent may be appropriate in certain circumstances, lawyers should take care not to run afoul of other limitations imposed by the Model Rules. [24]

Lawyers engaged in an investigation or litigation of a matter are subject to Model Rule 3.6, Trial Publicity. Paragraph (a) of Rule 3.6 (subject to the exceptions provided in paragraphs (b) or (c)) provides that:

> A lawyer who is participating or has participated in the investigation or litigation of a matter shall not make an extrajudicial statement that the lawyer knows or reasonably should know will be disseminated by means of public communication and will have a substantial likelihood of materially prejudicing an adjudicative proceeding in the matter.

---

21. *See* Model Rules of Prof'l Conduct R. 1.18(b) (2017) (Even when no client–lawyer relationship ensues, a lawyer who has had discussions with a prospective client shall not use or reveal information learned in the consultation except as permitted by the Rules). *Implementation Chart on Model Rule 1.18*, American Bar Ass'n (Sept. 29, 2017), https://www.americanbar.org/content/dam/aba/administrative/professional_responsibility/mrpc_1_18.authcheckdam.pdf.

22. *See* Model Rules of Prof'l Conduct R. 1.9 (2017); *see also* D.C. Bar Op. 324 (Disclosure of Deceased Client's Files) (2004); Swidler & Berlin v. United States, 524 U.S. 399 (1998). *See also* Gillers, *supra* note 4, at 34 ("[w]hether the [attorney-client] privilege survives death depends on the jurisdiction but in most places it does").

23. See generally Preamble to ABA Model Rules for a general discussion of the purposes underlying the duty of confidentiality. *See also* Geoffrey C. Hazard Jr. & W. William Hodes, The Law of Lawyering, §§ 9.2 & 9.3 at 9-6, 9-14 (3d ed. Supp. 2012).

24. *See, e.g.*, *In re* Joyce Nanine McCool 2015-B-0284 (Sup. Ct. La. 2015) (lawyer disciplined for violation of Rule 3.5 by attempting to communicate with potential jurors through public commentary); *see also* The Florida Bar v. Sean William Conway, No. SC08-326 (2008) (Sup. Ct. Fla.) (lawyer found to have violated Rules 8.4(a) and (d) for posting on the internet statements about a judge's qualifications that lawyer knew were false or with reckless disregard as to their truth or falsity).

Thus any public commentary about an investigation or ongoing litigation of a matter made by a lawyer would also violate Rule 3.6(a) if it has a substantial likelihood of materially prejudicing an adjudicative proceeding in the matter, and does not otherwise fall within the exceptions in paragraphs (b) or (c) of Model Rule 3.6.[25]

Conclusion

Lawyers who blog or engage in other public commentary may not reveal information relating to a representation that is protected by Rule 1.6(a), including information contained in a public record, unless disclosure is authorized under the Model Rules.

---

25. Pa. Bar Ass'n Formal Op. 2014-300 (2014) (lawyer involved in pending matter may not post about matter on social media). This opinion does not address whether a particular statement "will have a substantial likelihood of materially prejudicing an adjudicative proceeding" within the meaning of Model Rule 3.6.

AMERICAN BAR ASSOCIATION
STANDING COMMITTEE ON ETHICS AND PROFESSIONAL RESPONSIBILITY

Formal Opinion 481 **April 17, 2018**

A Lawyer's Duty to Inform a Current or Former Client of the Lawyer's Material Error

Model Rule of Professional Conduct 1.4 requires a lawyer to inform a current client if the lawyer believes that he or she may have materially erred in the client's representation. Recognizing that errors occur along a continuum, an error is material if a disinterested lawyer would conclude that it is (a) reasonably likely to harm or prejudice a client; or (b) of such a nature that it would reasonably cause a client to consider terminating the representation even in the absence of harm or prejudice. No similar obligation exists under the Model Rules to a former client where the lawyer discovers after the attorney-client relationship has ended that the lawyer made a material error in the former client's representation.

Introduction

Even the best lawyers may err in the course of clients' representations. If a lawyer errs and the error is material, the lawyer must inform a current client of the error.[1] Recognizing that errors occur along a continuum, an error

1. A lawyer's duty to inform a current client of a material error has been variously explained or grounded. For malpractice and breach of fiduciary decisions, *see, e.g.*, Leonard v. Dorsey & Whitney LLP, 553 F.3d 609, 629 (8th Cir. 2009) (predicting Minnesota law and concluding that "the lawyer must know that there is a non-frivolous malpractice claim against him such that there is a substantial risk that [his] representation of the client would be materially and adversely affected by his own interest in avoiding malpractice liability" (internal quotation marks omitted)); Beal Bank, SSB v. Arter & Hadden, LLP, 167 P.3d 666, 673 (Cal. 2007) (stating that "attorneys have a fiduciary obligation to disclose material facts to their clients, an obligation that includes disclosure of acts of malpractice"); RFF Family P'ship, LP v. Burns & Levinson, LP, 991 N.E.2d 1066, 1076 (Mass. 2013) (discussing the fiduciary exception to the attorney-client privilege and stating that "a client is entitled to full and fair disclosure of facts that are relevant to the representation, including any bad news"); *In re* Tallon, 447 N.Y.S.2d 50, 51 (App. Div. 1982) ("An attorney has a professional duty to promptly notify his client of his failure to act and of the possible claim his client may thus have against him.").

For disciplinary decisions, *see, e.g.*, Fla. Bar v. Morse, 587 So. 2d 1120, 1120–21 (Fla. 1991) (suspending a lawyer who conspired with his partner to conceal the partner's malpractice from the client); *In re* Hoffman, 700 N.E.2d 1138, 1139 (Ind. 1998) (applying Rule 1.4(b)). *See*

is material if a disinterested lawyer would conclude that it is (a) reasonably likely to harm or prejudice a client; or (b) of such a nature that it would reasonably cause a client to consider terminating the representation even in the absence of harm or prejudice.

If a material error relates to a former client's representation and the lawyer does not discover the error until after the representation has been terminated, the lawyer has no obligation under the Model Rules to inform the former client of the error. To illustrate, assume that a lawyer prepared a contract for a client in 2015. The matter is concluded, the representation has ended, and the person for whom the contract was prepared is not a client of the lawyer or law firm in any other matter. In 2018, while using that agreement as a template to prepare an agreement for a different client, the lawyer discovers a material error in the agreement. On those facts, the Model Rules do not require the lawyer to inform the former client of the error. Good business and risk management reasons may exist for lawyers to inform former

---

also Ill. State Bar Ass'n Mut. Ins. Co. v. Frank M. Greenfield & Assocs., P.C., 980 N.E.2d 1120, 1129 (Ill. App. Ct. 2012) (finding that a voluntary payments provision in a professional liability insurance policy was "against public policy, since it may operate to limit an attorney's disclosure [of his potential malpractice] to his clients").

For ethics opinions, *see, e.g.*, Cal. State Bar Comm. on Prof'l Responsibility & Conduct Op. 2009-178, 2009 WL 3270875, at *4 (2009) [hereinafter Cal. Eth. Op. 2009-178] ("A lawyer has an ethical obligation to keep a client informed of significant developments relating to the representation. . . . Where the lawyer believes that he or she has committed legal malpractice, the lawyer must promptly communicate the factual information pertaining to the client's potential malpractice claim against the lawyer to the client, because it is a 'significant development.'" (citation omitted)); Colo. Bar Ass'n, Ethics Comm., Formal Op. 113, at 3 (2005) [hereinafter Colo. Op. 113] ("Whether a particular error gives rise to an ethical duty to disclose [under Rule 1.4] depends on whether a disinterested lawyer would conclude that the error will likely result in prejudice to the client's right or claim and that the lawyer, therefore, has an ethical responsibility to disclose the error."); Minn. Lawyers Prof'l Responsibility Bd. Op. 21, 2009 WL 8396588, at *1 (2009) (imposing a duty to disclose under Rule 1.4 where "the lawyer knows the lawyer's conduct may reasonably be the basis for a non-frivolous malpractice claim by a current client that materially affects the client's interests"); 2015 N.C. State Bar Formal Op. 4, 2015 WL 5927498, at *2 (2015) [hereinafter 2015 N.C. Eth. Op. 4] (applying Rule 1.4 to "material errors that prejudice the client's rights or interests as well as errors that clearly give rise to a malpractice claim"; N.J. Sup. Ct. Advisory Comm. on Prof'l Ethics Op. 684, 1998 WL 35985928, at *1 (1998) [hereinafter N.J. Eth. Op. 684] (discussing Rules 1.4 and 1.7(b) and requiring disclosure "when the attorney ascertains malpractice may have occurred, even though no damage may yet have resulted"); N.Y. State Bar Ass'n Comm. on Prof'l Ethics Eth. Op. 734, 2000 WL 33347720, at *3 (2000) [hereinafter N.Y. Eth. Op. 734] (discussing the prior Code of Professional Responsibility and concluding that the inquirer had a duty to tell the client that it made "a significant error or omission that may give rise to a possible malpractice claim"); Sup. Ct. of Prof'l Ethics Comm. Op. 593, 2010 WL 1026287, at *1 (2010) [Tex. Eth. Op. 593] (opining that the lawyer must also terminate the representation and applying Texas Rules 1.15(d), 2.01, and 8.04(a)(3)). *See also* RESTATEMENT (THIRD) OF THE LAW GOVERNING LAWYERS § 20 cmt. c (2000) (requiring disclosure where the conduct "gives the client a substantial malpractice claim against the lawyer").

clients of their material errors when they can do so in time to avoid or mitigate any potential harm or prejudice to the former client. Indeed, many lawyers would likely choose to do so for those or other individual reasons. Those are, however, personal decisions for lawyers rather than obligations imposed under the Model Rules.

The Duty to Inform a Current Client of a Material Error

A lawyer's responsibility to communicate with a client is governed by Model Rule 1.4.[2] Several parts of Model Rule 1.4(a) potentially apply where a lawyer may have erred in the course of a current client's representation. For example, Model Rule 1.4(a)(1) requires a lawyer to promptly inform a client of any decision or circumstance with respect to which the client's informed consent may be required. Model Rule 1.4(a)(2) requires a lawyer to "reasonably consult with the client about the means by which the client's objectives are to be accomplished." Model Rule 1.4(a)(3) obligates a lawyer to "keep a client reasonably informed about the status of a matter." Model Rule 1.4(a)(4), which obliges a lawyer to promptly comply with reasonable requests for information, may be implicated if the client asks about the lawyer's conduct or performance of the representation. In addition, Model Rule 1.4(b) requires a lawyer to "explain a matter to the extent reasonably necessary to permit the client to make informed decisions regarding the representation." More broadly, the "guiding principle" undergirding Model Rule 1.4 is that "the lawyer should fulfill reasonable client expectations for information consistent with the duty to act in the client's best interests, and the client's overall requirements as to the character of representation."[3] A lawyer may not withhold information from a client to serve the lawyer's own interests or convenience.[4]

Determining whether and when a lawyer must inform a client of an error can sometimes be difficult because errors exist along a continuum. An error may be sufficiently serious that it creates a conflict of interest between the lawyer and the client. Model Rule 1.7(a)(2) provides that a concurrent conflict of interest exists if "there is a significant risk that the representation of one or more clients will be materially limited by . . . a personal interest of the lawyer." Where a lawyer's error creates a Rule 1.7(a)(2) conflict, the client needs to know this fact to make informed decisions regarding the representation, including whether to discharge the lawyer or to consent to the conflict of interest. At the other extreme, an error may be minor or easily correctable with no risk of harm or prejudice to the client.

---

2. Model Rules of Prof'l Conduct R. 1.4 (2018) ("Communication") [hereinafter Model Rules].
3. *Id.* cmt. 5.
4. *Id.* cmt. 7.

Several state bars have addressed lawyers' duty to disclose errors to clients.[5] For example, in discussing the spectrum of errors that may arise in clients' representations, the North Carolina State Bar observed that "material errors that prejudice the client's rights or claims are at one end. These include errors that effectively undermine the achievement of the client's primary objective for the representation, such as failing to file the complaint before the statute of limitations runs."[6] At the other end of the spectrum are "nonsubstantive typographical errors" or "missing a deadline that causes nothing more than delay."[7] "Between the two ends of the spectrum are a range of errors that may or may not materially prejudice the client's interests."[8] With respect to the middle ground:

> Errors that fall between the two extremes of the spectrum must be analyzed under the duty to keep the client reasonably informed about his legal matter. If the error will result in financial loss to the client, substantial delay in achieving the client's objectives for the representation, or material disadvantage to the client's legal position, the error must be disclosed to the client. Similarly, if disclosure of the error is necessary for the client to make an informed decision about the representation or for the lawyer to advise the client of significant changes in strategy, timing, or direction of the representation, the lawyer may not withhold information about the error.[9]

Another example is contained in the Colorado Bar Association's Ethics Committee in Formal Opinion 113, which discusses the spectrum of errors that may implicate a lawyers' duty of disclosure. In doing so, it identified errors ranging from those plainly requiring disclosure (a missed statute of limitations or a failure to file a timely appeal) to those "that may never cause harm to the client, either because any resulting harm is not reasonably foreseeable, there is no prejudice to a client's right or claim, or the lawyer takes corrective measures that are reasonably likely to avoid any such prejudice."[10] Errors by lawyers between these two extremes must be analyzed individually. For example, disclosure is not required where the law on an issue is unsettled and a lawyer makes a tactical decision among "equally viable alternatives."[11] On the other hand, "potential errors that may give rise to an ethical duty to disclose include the failure to request a jury in a pleading (or

5. *See supra* note 1 (listing authorities).
6. 2015 N.C. Eth. Op. 4, *supra* note 1, 2015 WL 5927498, at *2.
7. *Id.*
8. *Id.*
9. *Id.*
10. Colo. Op. 113, *supra* note 1, at 3.
11. *Id.*

pay the jury fee), the failure to include an acceleration provision in a promissory note, and the failure to give timely notice under a contract or statute."[12] Ultimately, the Colorado Bar concluded that whether a particular error gives rise to an ethical obligation to disclose depends on whether the error is "material," which further "depends on whether a disinterested lawyer would conclude that the error will likely result in prejudice to the client's right or claim."[13]

These opinions provide helpful guidance to lawyers, but they do not—just as we do not—purport to precisely define the scope of a lawyer's disclosure obligations. Still, the Committee believes that lawyers deserve more specific guidance in evaluating their duty to disclose errors to current clients than has previously been available.

In attempting to define the boundaries of this obligation under Model Rule 1.4, it is unreasonable to conclude that a lawyer must inform a current client of an error only if that error may support a colorable legal malpractice claim, because a lawyer's error may impair a client's representation even if the client will never be able to prove all of the elements of malpractice. At the same time, a lawyer should not necessarily be able to avoid disclosure of an error absent apparent harm to the client because the lawyer's error may be of such a nature that it would cause a reasonable client to lose confidence in the lawyer's ability to perform the representation competently, diligently, or loyally despite the absence of clear harm. Finally, client protection and the purposes of legal representation dictate that the standard for imposing an obligation to disclose must be objective.

With these considerations in mind, the Committee concludes that a lawyer must inform a current client of a material error committed by the lawyer in the representation. An error is material if a disinterested lawyer would conclude that it is (a) reasonably likely to harm or prejudice a client; or (b) of such a nature that it would reasonably cause a client to consider terminating the representation even in the absence of harm or prejudice.

A lawyer must notify a current client of a material error promptly under the circumstances.[14] Whether notification is prompt will be a case- and fact-specific inquiry. Greater urgency is required where the client could be harmed by any delay in notification. The lawyer may consult with his or her

---

12. *Id.*

13 *Id.* at 1, 3.

14. *See* N.J. Eth. Op. 684, *supra* note 1, 1998 WL 35985928, at *1 ("Clearly, RPC 1.4 requires prompt disclosure in the interest of allowing the client to make informed decisions. Disclosure should therefore occur when the attorney ascertains malpractice may have occurred, even though no damage may yet have resulted."); 2015 N.C. Eth. Op. 4, *supra* note 1, 2015 WL 5927498, at *4 ("The error should be disclosed to the client as soon as possible after the lawyer determines that disclosure of the error to the client is required."); Tex. Eth. Op. 593, *supra* note 1, 2010 WL 1026287, at *1 (requiring disclosure "as promptly as reasonably possible").

law firm's general counsel, another lawyer, or the lawyer's professional liability insurer before informing the client of the material error.[15] Such consultation should also be prompt. When it is reasonable to do so, the lawyer may attempt to correct the error before informing the client. Whether it is reasonable for the lawyer to attempt to correct the error before informing the client will depend on the facts and should take into account the time needed to correct the error and the lawyer's obligation to keep the client reasonably informed about the status of the matter.

When a Current Client Becomes a Former Client

As indicated earlier, whether a lawyer must reveal a material error depends on whether the affected person or entity is a current or former client. Substantive law, rather than rules of professional conduct, controls whether an attorney-client relationship exists, or once established, whether it is ongoing or has been concluded.[16] Generally speaking, a current client becomes a former client (a) at the time specified by the lawyer for the conclusion of the representation, and acknowledged by the client, such as where the lawyer's engagement letter states that the representation will conclude upon the lawyer sending a final invoice, or the lawyer sends a disengagement letter upon the completion of the matter (and thereafter acts consistently with the letter);[17] (b) when the lawyer withdraws from the representation pursuant to Model Rule of Professional Conduct 1.16; (c) when the client terminates the representation;[18] or (d) when overt acts inconsistent with the continuation of the attorney-client relationship indicate that the relation-

15. *See* Model Rules R. 1.6(b)(4) (2018) (permitting a lawyer to reveal information related to a client's representation "to secure legal advice about the lawyer's compliance with these Rules").

16. United States v. Williams, 720 F.3d 674, 686 (8th Cir. 2013); Rozmus v. West, 13 Vet. App. 386, 387 (U.S. App. Vet. Cl. 2000); *see also* Model Rules Scope cmt. 17 (2018) (explaining that "for purposes of determining the lawyer's authority and responsibility, principles of substantive law external to these Rules determine whether a client-lawyer relationship exists").

17. *See* Artromick Int'l, Inc. v. Drustar Inc., 134 F.R.D. 226, 229 (S.D. Ohio 1991) (observing that "the simplest way for either the attorney or client to end the relationship is by expressly saying so"); *see also, e.g.*, Rusk v. Harstad, 393 P.3d 341, 344 (Utah Ct. App. 2017) (concluding that a would-be client could not have reasonably believed that the law firm represented him where the lawyer had clearly stated in multiple e-mails that the law firm would not represent him).

18. A client may discharge a lawyer at any time for any reason, or for no reason. White Pearl Inversiones S.A. (Uruguay) v. Cemusa, Inc., 647 F.3d 684, 689 (7th Cir. 2011); Nabi v. Sells, 892 N.Y.S.2d 41, 43 (App. Div. 2009); Model Rules R. 1.16 cmt. 4; *see also* Stephen Gillers, Regulation of Lawyers: Problems of Law and Ethics 77 (11th ed. 2018) ("Clients, it is said, may fire their lawyers for any reason or no reason.") (citations omitted).

ship has ended.[19] If a lawyer represents a client in more than one matter, the client is a current client if any of those matters is active or open; in other words, the termination of representation in one or more matters does not transform a client into a former client if the lawyer still represents the client in other matters.

Absent express statements or overt acts by either party, an attorney-client relationship also may be terminated when it would be objectively unreasonable to continue to bind the parties to each other.[20] In such cases, the parties' reasonable expectations often hinge on the scope of the lawyer's representation.[21] In that regard, the court in *National Medical Care, Inc. v. Home Medical of America, Inc.*,[22] suggested that the scope of a lawyer's representation loosely falls into one of three categories: (1) the lawyer is retained as general counsel to handle all of the client's legal matters; (2) the lawyer is retained for all matters in a specific practice area; or (3) the lawyer is retained to represent the client in a discrete matter.[23]

For all three categories identified by the *National Medical Care* court, unless the client or lawyer terminates the representation, the attorney-client relationship continues as long as the lawyer is responsible for a pending matter.[24] With respect to categories one and two above, an attorney-client relationship continues even when the lawyer has no pending matter for the client because the parties reasonably expect that the lawyer will handle all matters for the client in the future as they arise.[25] In the third category, where

---

19. *See, e.g.*, Artromick Int'l, Inc., 134 F.R.D. at 230–31 (determining that a man was a former client because he refused to pay the lawyer's bill and then retained other lawyers to replace the first lawyer); Waterbury Garment Corp. v. Strata Prods., 554 F. Supp. 63, 66 (S.D.N.Y. 1982) (concluding that a person was a former client because the law firm represented him only in discrete transactions that had concluded and the person had subsequently retained different counsel).

20. Artromick Int'l, Inc., 134 F.R.D. at 229.

21. *Id.* at 229–30.

22. No. 00-1225, 2002 WL 31068413 (Mass. Super. Ct. Sept. 12, 2002).

23. *Id.* at *4.

24. *Id.*; *see also* Model Rules R. 1.3 cmt. 4 (2018) (stating that unless the relationship is terminated under Model Rule 1.16, the lawyer "should carry through to conclusion all matters undertaken for a client").

25. *See* Berry v. McFarland, 278 P.3d 407, 411 (Idaho 2012) (explaining that "[i]f the attorney agrees to handle any matters the client may have, the relationship continues until the attorney or client terminates the relationship"); *see also* Model Rules R. 1.3 cmt. 4 (2018) (advising that "[i]f a lawyer has served a client over a substantial period in a variety of matters, the client sometimes may assume that the lawyer will continue to serve on a continuing basis unless the lawyer gives notice of withdrawal").

a lawyer agrees to undertake a specific matter, the attorney-client relationship ends once the matter is concluded.[26]

Although not identified by the *National Medical Care* court, another type of client is what might be called an episodic client, meaning a client who engages the lawyer whenever the client requires legal representation, but whose legal needs are not constant or continuous. In many such instances, the client reasonably expects that the professional relationship will span any intervals and that the lawyer will be available when the client next needs representation.[27] If so, the client should be considered a current client. In other instances, it is possible that the attorney-client relationship ended when the most recent matter concluded.[28] Whether an episodic client is a current or former client will thus depend on the facts of the case.

The Former Client Analysis Under the Model Rules

As explained above, a lawyer must inform a current client of a material error under Model Rule 1.4. Rule 1.4 imposes no similar duty to former clients.

Four of the five subparts in Model Rule 1.4(a) expressly refer to "the client" and the one that does not—Model Rule 1.4(a), governing lawyers' duty

26. Simpson v. James, 903 F.2d 372, 376 (5th Cir. 1990); Berry, 278 P.3d at 411; *see also* Revise Clothing, Inc. v. Joe's Jeans Subsidiary, Inc., 687 F. Supp. 2d 381, 389–90 (S.D.N.Y. 2010) (noting that an attorney-client relationship is ordinarily terminated by the accomplishment of the purpose for which it was formed); Thayer v. Fuller & Henry Ltd., 503 F. Supp. 2d 887, 892 (N.D. Ohio 2007) (observing that an attorney-client relationship may terminate when the underlying action has concluded or when the attorney has exhausted all remedies and declined to provide additional legal services); Model Rules R. 1.16 cmt. 1 ("Ordinarily, a representation in a matter is completed when the agreed-upon assistance has been concluded.").

27. *See, e.g.*, Parallel Iron, LLC v. Adobe Sys. Inc., C.A. No. 12-874-RGA, 2013 WL 789207, at *2–3 (D. Del. Mar. 4, 2013) (concluding that Adobe was a current client in July 2012 when the law firm was doing no work for it; the firm had served as patent counsel to Adobe intermittently between 2006 and February 2012, and had not made clear to Adobe that its representation was terminated); Jones v. Rabanco, Ltd., No. C03-3195P, 2006 WL 2237708, at *3 (W.D. Wash. Aug. 3, 2006) (reasoning that the law firm's inclusion as a contact under a contract, the law firm's work for the client after the contract was finalized, and the fact that the client matter was still open in the law firm's files all indicated an existing attorney-client relationship); Stephen Gillers, Regulation of Lawyers: Problems of Law and Ethics 78-79 (11th ed. 2018) ("Lawyers might believe that a client is no longer a client if they are doing no work for it at the moment and haven't for a while. . . . [A] firm may have done work for a client two or three times a year for the past five years, creating a reasonable client expectation that the professional relationship continues during the intervals and that the lawyer will be available the next time the client needs her.").

28 *See, e.g.*, Calamar Enters., Inc. v. Blue Forest Land Grp., Inc., 222 F. Supp. 3d 257, 264–65 (W.D.N.Y. 2016) (rejecting the client's claim of an attorney-client relationship where the relationship between the law firm and the client had been dormant for three years; despite the fact that the attorney-client relationship had not been formally terminated, it ended when the purpose of the parties' retainer agreement had been completed).

to respond to reasonable requests for information—is aimed at responding to requests from a current client. Model Rule 1.4(b) refers to "the client" when describing a lawyer's obligations. Nowhere does Model Rule 1.4 impose on lawyers a duty to communicate with former clients. The comments to Model Rule 1.4 are likewise focused on current clients and are silent with respect to communications with former clients. There is nothing in the legislative history of Model Rule 1.4 to suggest that the drafters meant the duties expressed there to apply to former clients.[29] Had the drafters of the Model Rules intended Rule 1.4 to apply to former clients, they presumably would have referred to former clients in the language of the rule or in the comments to the rule. They did neither despite knowing how to distinguish duties owed to current clients from duties owed to former clients when appropriate, as reflected in the Model Rules regulating conflicts of interest.[30]

Because Model Rule 1.4 does not impose on lawyers a duty to communicate with former clients,[31] it is no basis for requiring lawyers to disclose material errors to former clients.

The California State Bar's Committee on Professional Responsibility and Conduct reached a similar conclusion with respect to California Rule of Professional Conduct 3-500, which states that "[a] member [of the State Bar of California] shall keep a client reasonably informed about significant developments relating to the employment or representation, including promptly complying with reasonable requests for information and copies of significant documents when necessary to keep the client so informed." In concluding that a lawyer had no duty to keep a former client informed of significant developments in the representation, and specifically the former client's possible malpractice claim against the lawyer, the Committee focused on the fact that the lawyer and the former client had "terminated their attorney-client relationship" and on Rule 3-500's reference to a "client," meaning a current client.[32]

Finally, in terms of possible sources of an obligation to disclose material errors to former clients, Model Rule 1.16(d) provides in pertinent part that, upon termination of a representation, "a lawyer shall take steps to the extent reasonably practicable to protect a client's interests, such as giving rea-

29. AM. BAR ASS'N CTR. FOR PROF'L RESPONSIBILITY, A LEGISLATIVE HISTORY: THE DEVELOPMENT OF THE ABA MODEL RULES OF PROFESSIONAL CONDUCT, 1982–2013, 71–78 (Arthur H. Garwin ed., 2013).

30. *Compare* MODEL RULES R. 1.7 (2018) (addressing current client conflicts of interest), *with* MODEL RULES R. 1.9 (2018) (governing former client conflicts of interest).

31. *See* Sup. Ct. of Ohio, Bd. of Comm'rs on Grievances & Discipline Adv. Op. 2010-2, 2010 WL 1541844, at *2 (2010) (explaining that Rule 1.4 "applies to ethical duties regarding communication *during a representation*" (emphasis added)); Va. State Bar Comm. on Legal Ethics Eth. Op. 1789, 2004 WL 436386, at *1 (2004) (stating that "*[d]uring the course of the representation*, an attorney's duty to provide information to his client is governed by Rule 1.4(a)") (emphasis added)).

32. Cal. Eth. Op. 2009-178, *supra* note 1, 2009 WL 3270875, at *6.

sonable notice to the client, allowing time for employment of other counsel, surrendering papers and property to which the client is entitled and refunding any advance payment of fee[s] or expense[s] that has not been earned or incurred." This provision does not create a duty to inform former clients of material errors for at least two reasons. First, the wording of the rule demonstrates that the error would have to be discovered while the client was a current client, thereby pushing any duty to disclose back into the current client communication regime. Second, Model Rule 1.16(d) is by its terms limited to actions that may be taken upon termination of the representation or soon thereafter; it cannot reasonably be construed to apply to material errors discovered months or years after termination of the representation.

Conclusion

The Model Rules require a lawyer to inform a current client if the lawyer believes that he or she may have materially erred in the client's representation. Recognizing that errors occur along a continuum, an error is material if a disinterested lawyer would conclude that it is (a) reasonably likely to harm or prejudice a client; or (b) of such a nature that it would reasonably cause a client to consider terminating the representation even in the absence of harm or prejudice. The lawyer must so inform the client promptly under the circumstances. Whether notification is prompt is a case- and fact-specific inquiry.

No similar duty of disclosure exists under the Model Rules where the lawyer discovers after the termination of the attorney-client relationship that the lawyer made a material error in the former client's representation.

AMERICAN BAR ASSOCIATION
STANDING COMMITTEE ON ETHICS AND PROFESSIONAL RESPONSIBILITY
321 N. Clark Street, Chicago, Illinois 60654-4714 Telephone (312) 988-5328
CHAIR: Barbara S. Gillers, New York, NY
■ John M. Barkett, Miami, FL ■ Wendy Wen Yun Chang, Los Angeles, CA
■ Hon. Daniel J. Crothers, Bismarck, ND ■ Keith R. Fisher, Arlington, VA
■ Douglas R. Richmond, Chicago, IL ■ Michael H. Rubin, Baton Rouge, LA
■ Lynda Shely, Scottsdale, AZ ■ Elizabeth C. Tarbert, Tallahassee, FL ■ Allison Wood, Chicago, IL

CENTER FOR PROFESSIONAL RESPONSIBILITY:
Dennis A. Rendleman, Ethics Counsel ■ Mary McDermott, Associate Ethics Counsel

AMERICAN BAR ASSOCIATION
STANDING COMMITTEE ON ETHICS AND PROFESSIONAL RESPONSIBILITY

Formal Opinion 482 **September 19, 2018**

Ethical Obligations Related to Disasters

The Rules of Professional Conduct apply to lawyers affected by disasters. Model Rule 1.4 (communication) requires lawyers to take reasonable steps to communicate with clients after a disaster. Model Rule 1.1 (competence) requires lawyers to develop sufficient competence in technology to meet their obligations under the Rules after a disaster. Model Rule 1.15 (safekeeping property) requires lawyers to protect trust accounts, documents and property the lawyer is holding for clients or third parties. Model Rule 5.5 (multijurisdictional practice) limits practice by lawyers displaced by a disaster. Model Rules 7.1 through 7.3 limit lawyers' advertising directed to and solicitation of disaster victims. By proper advance preparation and planning and taking advantage of available technology during recovery efforts, lawyers can reduce their risk of violating the Rules of Professional Conduct after a disaster.

Introduction[1]

Recent large-scale disasters highlight the need for lawyers to understand their ethical responsibilities when those events occur. Extreme weather events such as hurricanes, floods, tornadoes, and fires have the potential to destroy property or cause the long-term loss of power. Lawyers have an ethical obligation to implement reasonable measures to safeguard property and funds they hold for clients or third parties, prepare for business interruption, and keep clients informed about how to contact the lawyers (or their successor counsel). Lawyers also must follow the advertising rules if soliciting victims affected by a disaster.

Much information is available to lawyers about disaster preparedness. The American Bar Association has a committee devoted solely to the topic and provides helpful resources on its website.[2] These resources include prac-

1. This opinion is based on the ABA Model Rules of Professional Conduct as amended by the ABA House of Delegates through August 2018. The laws, court rules, regulations, rules of professional conduct and opinions promulgated in individual jurisdictions are controlling.

2. ABA Committee on Disaster Response and Preparedness, https://www.americanbar.org/groups/committees/disaster.html (last visited Sept. 6, 2018). ABA Committee on Di-

tical advice on (i) obtaining insurance, (ii) types and methods of information retention, and (iii) steps to take immediately after a disaster to assess damage and rebuild. Lawyers should review these and other resources and take reasonable steps to prepare for a disaster before one strikes the communities in which they practice. Lawyers should also review their disaster preparedness plans when a disaster threatens. Included within disaster planning, and of particular importance for sole practitioners, is succession planning so that clients and others know where to turn if a lawyer dies, is incapacitated, or is displaced by a disaster.

Despite the wealth of information available on preparing for a disaster and on the practical steps a lawyer should take to preserve the lawyers' and the clients' property and interests after a disaster, there is a dearth of guidance on a lawyer's ethical responsibilities (i) when a disaster threatens, and (ii) after a disaster occurs.[3] This opinion addresses the lawyers' obligations in these circumstances.[4]

A. Communication

Model Rule 1.4 requires lawyers to communicate with clients.[5] One of the early steps lawyers will have to take after a disaster is determining

---

saster Response and Preparedness, *Surviving a Disaster A Lawyer's Guide* (Aug. 2011), https://www.americanbar.org/content/dam/aba/events/disaster/surviving_a_disaster_a_lawyers_guide_to_disaster_planning.authcheckdam.pdf.

3. There are three ethics opinions from state bars on a lawyer's obligations after a disaster: N.Y. City Bar Ass'n Formal Op. 2015-6 (2015) advises lawyers to notify clients of destruction of client files in a disaster if the destroyed documents have intrinsic value (such as a will) or if the lawyer knows the client may need the documents; La. Advisory Op. 05-RPCC-005 (2005) advises lawyers on providing pro bono assistance through a hotline or both; and State Bar of Cal. Standing Comm. on Prof'l Responsibility & Conduct, Formal Op. 2004-166 (2004) advises lawyers not to participate in a mass disaster victims chat room because it is intrusive, but not because it is prohibited as in-person solicitation.

4. This opinion focuses primarily on the obligations of managers and supervisors within the meaning of Rule 5.1, recognizing that lawyers practice in a variety of contexts, including solo offices, small firms, large firms, government agencies and corporate offices. Subordinate lawyers may rely on the reasonable decisions of managers and supervisors on how to address the ethical obligations this opinion describes. Some of the obligations may be reasonably delegated or assigned to specific lawyers within a firm or organization. Methods of compliance with the obligations may vary depending on the practice context in which they arise. In addition, lawyers employed by governmental or other institutional entities may be subject to requirements imposed by law, or the policies of those entities. Reasonable implementation of the obligations described in this opinion satisfies the Model Rules. Opinion 467 provides examples of how to comply with obligations under several Model Rules in a variety of practice settings. *See* ABA Comm'n on Ethics & Prof'l Responsibility, Formal Op. 467 (2014).

5. Model Rules of Prof'l Conduct R. 1.4 (2018) provides:

(a) A lawyer shall:

(1) promptly inform the client of any decision or circumstance with respect to which the client's informed consent, as defined in Rule 1.0(e), is required by these Rules;

the available methods to communicate with clients. To be able to reach clients following a disaster, lawyers should maintain, or be able to create on short notice, electronic or paper lists of current clients and their contact information. This information should be stored in a manner that is easily accessible.[6]

In these early communications clients will need to know, for example, if the lawyer remains available to handle the client's matters, or, alternatively, if the lawyer is unavailable because of the disaster's effects, and may need to withdraw. In a situation in which a disaster is predicted, for example, with a hurricane or other extreme weather event, lawyers should consider providing clients with methods by which the lawyer may be reached in the event that emergency communication is necessary. Information about how to contact the lawyer in the event of an emergency may be provided in a fee agreement or an engagement letter.[7]

In identifying how to communicate with clients under these circumstances, lawyers must be mindful of their obligation under Rule 1.1 to keep abreast of technology relevant to law practice[8] and Rule 1.6(c)'s requirement "to make reasonable efforts to prevent the inadvertent or unauthorized dis-

---

(2) reasonably consult with the client about the means by which the client's objectives are to be accomplished;

(3) keep the client reasonably informed about the status of the matter;

(4) promptly comply with reasonable requests for information; and

(5) consult with the client about any relevant limitation on the lawyer's conduct when the lawyer knows that the client expects assistance not permitted by the Rules of Professional Conduct or other law.

(b) A lawyer shall explain a matter to the extent reasonably necessary to permit the client to make informed decisions regarding the representation.

6. This opinion addresses a lawyer's ethical responsibilities. Lawyers should take similar steps to maintain communication with their own colleagues and staff. It is also good practice for a lawyer to maintain and update this information on a secure Internet website after the disaster so that colleagues and support staff will have a centralized location to find contact information. For information about the appropriate methods for storing electronic or paper records, lawyers may consult the ABA Committee on Disaster Response and Preparedness website. Also, many state bars and courts provide information on disaster preparedness.

7. Practical problems a lawyer may wish to consider in advance include whether (i) landline phones will be out of service, (ii) the U.S. Postal Service will be impaired, and (iii) electronic devices will lose battery power.

8. ABA Model Rule 1.1 provides, "A lawyer shall provide competent representation to a client. Competent representation requires the legal knowledge, skill, thoroughness and preparation reasonably necessary for the representation." Comment [8] to Rule 1.1 provides: ". . . [A] lawyer should keep abreast of changes in the law and its practice, including the benefits and risks associated with relevant technology . . . ."

closure of, or unauthorized access to, information relating to the representation of the client."[9]

B. Continued Representation in the Affected Area

Lawyers who continue to provide legal services in the area affected by a disaster have the same ethical obligations to their clients as before the disaster, although they may be able to provide advice outside their normal area of expertise.[10]

Lawyers may not be able to gain access to paper files following a disaster.[11] Consequently, lawyers must evaluate in advance storing files electronically so that they will have access to those files via the Internet if they have access to a working computer or smart device after a disaster. If Internet access to files is provided through a cloud service, the lawyer should (i) choose a reputable company, and (ii) take reasonable steps to ensure that the confidentiality of client information is preserved, and that the information is readily accessible to the lawyer.[12]

---

9. As this Committee has previously noted, lawyers may transmit confidential information over the Internet if the lawyer has made reasonable efforts to prevent accidental or unauthorized access to the information. *See* ABA Comm. on Ethics & Prof'l Responsibility, Formal Op. 477R (May 22, 2017). *See also* Alaska Bar Ass'n Op. 98-2 (1998); State Bar of Ariz. Formal Op. 97-04 (1997); State Bar of Cal. Standing Comm. on Prof'l Responsibility & Conduct, Formal Op. 2010-179 (2010); D.C. Bar Op. 281 (1998); Del. State Bar Ass'n Comm. on Prof'l Ethics Op. 2001-2 (2001); Haw. State Ethics Comm'n Formal Op. 40 (2001); Ill. State Bar Ass'n Advisory Op. 96-10 (1997); Iowa State Bar Ass'n Op. 15-01 (2015); N.C. State Bar Op. RPC 215 (1995); State Bar Ass'n of N.D. Advisory Op. 97-09 (1997); Ohio Bd. of Cmss'rs on Grievances & Discipline Op. 99-2 (1999); S.C. Bar Advisory Op. 97-08 (1997); Prof'l Ethics Comm. State Bar of Tex. Op. 648 (2015); Utah State Bar Advisory Op. 00-01 (2000); Vt. Advisory Op. 97-5 (1997); Wash. State Bar Ass'n Advisory Op. 2175 (2008).

10. Comment [3] to Rule 1.1 allows: "In an emergency a lawyer may give advice or assistance in a matter in which the lawyer does not have the skill ordinarily required where referral to or consultation or association with another lawyer would be impractical. Even in an emergency, however, assistance should be limited to that reasonably necessary in the circumstances. Ill-considered action under emergency conditions can jeopardize the client's interest."

11. Rule 1.15 requires that lawyers take reasonable steps to preserve trust account records and documents and property of clients and third parties when a lawyer has notice of an impending disaster. *See also* subsection (E), *infra*, for a discussion of a lawyer's obligations when files are lost or destroyed in a disaster.

12. Lawyers must understand that electronically stored information is subject to cyberattack, know where the information is stored, and adopt reasonable security measures. They must conduct due diligence in selecting an appropriate repository of client information "in the cloud." Among suggested areas of inquiry are determining legal standards for confidentiality and privilege in the jurisdiction where any dispute will arise regarding the cloud computing services. *See* ABA Comm. on Ethics & Prof'l Responsibility, Formal Op. 477R (May 22, 2017) (Lawyer may send client information over the Internet if lawyer makes reasonable efforts to prevent inadvertent or unauthorized access, but may be required to take special security precautions when required by an agreement with the client or by law, or when the nature of the

information requires a higher degree of security); Ala. State Bar Op. 2010-02 (2010) (Lawyer may outsource storage of client files through cloud computing if they take reasonable steps to make sure data is protected); State Bar of Ariz. Formal Op. 09-04 (2009) (Lawyer may use online file storage and retrieval system that enables clients to access their files over the Internet, as long as the firm takes reasonable precautions to protect the confidentiality of the information; in this case, proposal would convert files to password-protected pdf documents that are stored on a Secure Socket Layer server (SSL) which encodes the documents); State Bar of Cal. Standing Comm. on Prof'l Responsibility & Conduct, Formal Op. 2012-184 (2012) (Lawyer may operate virtual law office "in the cloud" as long as the lawyer complies with all ethical duties such as confidentiality, competence, communication, and supervision; lawyer should check vendor credentials, data security, how information is transmitted, whether through other jurisdictions or third-party servers, the ability to supervise the vendor; and the terms of the contract with the vendor); Fla. Bar Op. 12-3 (2013) (Lawyers may use cloud computing if they take reasonable precautions to ensure that confidentiality of client information is maintained, that the service provider maintains adequate security, and that the lawyer has adequate access to the information stored remotely); Ill. State Bar Ass'n Op. 16-06 (2016) (Lawyer may use cloud-based service to store client files as long as the lawyer "takes reasonable measures to ensure that the client information remains confidential and is protected from breaches"; lawyer should engage in due diligence in choosing the provider, including reviewing industry norms, determining the provider's security precautions such as firewalls, password protection and encryption, the provider's reputation and history, asking about any prior breaches, requiring that the provider follow confidentiality requirements, requiring that the data is under the lawyer's control, and requiring reasonable access if the contract terminates or the provider goes out of business); Iowa State Bar Ass'n Op. 11-01 (2011) (Due diligence a lawyer should perform before storing files electronically with a third party using SaaS (cloud computing) includes whether the lawyer will have adequate access to the stored information, whether the lawyer will be able to restrict access of others to the stored information, whether data is encrypted and password protected, and what will happen to the information in the event the lawyer defaults on an agreement with the third party provider or terminates the relationship with the third party provider); State Bar of Nev. Formal Op. 33 (2006) (Lawyer may store client files electronically on a remote server controlled by a third party as long as the firm takes precautions to safeguard confidential information such as obtaining the third party's agreement to maintain confidentiality); New York City Bar Report, *The Cloud and the Small Law Firm: Business, Ethics and Privilege Considerations* (Nov. 2013), https://www2.nycbar.org/pdf/report/uploads/20072378-TheCloudandtheSmallLawFirm.pdf; N.Y. State Bar Ass'n Op. 842 (2010) (Permissible to use an online computer data storage system to store client files provided the attorney takes reasonable care to maintain confidentiality; lawyer must stay informed of both technological advances that could affect confidentiality and changes in the law that could affect privilege); State Bar Ass'n of N.D. Advisory Op. 99-03 (1999) (Permissible to use electronic online data service to store files as long as the lawyer properly protects confidential client information, perhaps via password protected storage); Pa. Bar Ass'n Op. 2011-200 (2011) ("An attorney may ethically allow client confidential material to be stored in 'the cloud' provided the attorney takes reasonable care to assure that (1) all such materials remain confidential, and (2) reasonable safeguards are employed to ensure that the data is protected from breaches, data loss and other risks"); S.C. Bar Advisory Op. 86-23 (1988) (A lawyer can store files in a storage facility operated by a third party if the lawyer ensures that confidentiality is maintained); Tenn. Formal Op. 2015-F-159 (2015) (Lawyer may store information in the cloud if the lawyer takes reasonable measures to protect the information); Vt. Advisory Op. 2010-6 (2010) (Lawyers may use cloud computing if they take reasonable steps to ensure confidentiality of information and that information is accessible).

As part of the obligation of competence under Rule 1.1 and diligence under Rule 1.3, lawyers who represent clients in litigation must be aware of court deadlines, and any extensions granted due to the disaster. Courts typically issue orders, usually posted on their websites, addressing extensions.[13] Lawyers should check with the courts and bar associations in their jurisdictions to determine whether deadlines have been extended.

Lawyers also must take reasonable steps in the event of a disaster to ensure access to funds the lawyer is holding in trust. A lawyer's obligations with respect to these funds will vary depending on the circumstances. Even before a disaster, all lawyers should consider (i) providing for another trusted signatory on trust accounts in the event of the lawyer's unexpected death, incapacity, or prolonged unavailability and (ii) depending on the circumstances and jurisdiction, designating a successor lawyer to wind up the lawyer's practice.[14] Lawyers with notice of an impending disaster should take additional steps. For example, a transactional lawyer should review open files to determine if the lawyer should transfer funds to a trust account that will be accessible after the disaster or even attempt to complete imminent transactions prior to the disaster if practicable.

A disaster may affect the financial institution in which funds are held, or the lawyer's ability to communicate with the financial institution. Consequently, lawyers should take appropriate steps in advance to determine how they will obtain access to their accounts after a disaster. Different institutions may have varying abilities to recover from a disaster.[15] After a disaster,

---

13. *See, e.g.*, Sup. Ct. of Fla. Administrative Order No. AOSC17-57 (2017), http://www.floridasupremecourt.org/clerk/adminorders/2017/AOSC17-57.pdf (extending time periods in the wake of Hurricane Irma); N.D. Sup. Ct. Administrative Order 20 (2011), http://www.ndcourts.gov/court/rules/administrative/ao20.htm (staying deadlines due to flooding); N.D. Sup. Ct. Rules Section 6, Emergency Procedural Rule, Administrative Rule, or Administrative Order, *available at* http://www.ndcourts.gov/court/rules/administrative/ao20.htm (last visited Sept. 4, 2018); Sup. Ct. of Texas Emergency Order Suspending Criminal Court Proceedings in the Wake of Hurricane Harvey (2017), http://www.txcourts.gov/media/1438759/179091.pdf; Supreme Court of Texas Emergency Order on Statutes of Limitations in Civil Cases in the Wake of Hurricane Harvey (2017), http://www.txcourts.gov/media/1438804/179098.pdf.

14. *See* Model Rules of Prof'l Conduct R. 1.1 & 1.3 (2018). Designating a successor and adding trusted signatories are good practices that may already be in place as part of normal succession planning. Some states require designation of a successor counsel or inventory lawyer. *See, e.g.*, Rules Regulating the Fla. Bar R. 1-3.8(e), Iowa Ct. Rule 39.18(1), Me. Bar R. 32(a), and Mo. R. 4-1.3 cmt. [5] & R. 5.26. Some states permit voluntary designation, including California, Delaware, Idaho, South Carolina, and Tennessee. *See Mandatory Successor Rule Chart* (June 2015), ABA, https://www.americanbar.org/content/dam/aba/administrative/professional_responsibility/mandatory_successor_rule_chart.authcheckdam.pdf. Lawyers should also be aware that, in most jurisdictions, a power of attorney to handle law firm affairs will be insufficient because it expires on the principal's death.

15. The rules do not require a lawyer to place funds in a large or national financial institution. *See* Model Rules of Prof'l Conduct R. 1.15 (2018). However, a prudent lawyer

a lawyer must notify clients or third persons for whom the lawyer is holding funds when required disbursements are imminent and the lawyer is unable to access the funds, even if the lawyer cannot access the funds because the financial institution itself is inaccessible or access is beyond the lawyer's capability.[16]

C. Withdrawal from Representation After a Disaster

Lawyers whose circumstances following a disaster render them unable to fulfill their ethical responsibilities to clients may be required to withdraw from those representations. Rule 1.16(a)(1) requires withdrawal if representation will cause the lawyer to violate the rules of professional conduct. Rule 1.16(a)(2) requires withdrawal if "the lawyer's physical or mental condition materially impairs the lawyer's ability to represent the client," for example, if the lawyer suffers severe injury or mental distress due to the disaster. Rule 1.16(b)(7) allows termination of the representation when the lawyer has "other good cause for withdrawal." These conditions may be present following a disaster. In determining whether withdrawal is required, lawyers must assess whether the client needs immediate legal services that the lawyer will be unable to timely provide. Lawyers who are unable to continue client representation in litigation matters must seek the court's permission to withdraw as required by law and court rules.[17]

D. Representation of Clients by Displaced Lawyers in Another Jurisdiction

Some lawyers may either permanently or temporarily re-locate to another jurisdiction following a disaster. Their clients and other residents of the lawyers' home jurisdiction may relocate to the same jurisdiction, or elsewhere, and still require legal services. Although displaced lawyers may be able to rely on Model Rule 5.5(c) allowing temporary multijurisdictional practice to provide legal services to their clients or displaced residents, they should not assume the Rule will apply in a particular jurisdiction. Comment [14] to Rule 5.5 provides:

> . . . lawyers from the affected jurisdiction [by a major disaster] who seek to practice law temporarily in another jurisdiction, but in which they are not otherwise authorized to practice law, should consult the Model Court Rule on Provision of Legal Services Following Determination of Major Disaster.

---

in a disaster-prone area should inquire about a financial institution's disaster preparedness before placing funds there. The lawyer must comply with IOLTA requirements regardless of which financial institution the lawyer chooses.

16. Model Rules of Prof'l Conduct R. 1.4 and 1.15(d) (2018).

17. Model Rules of Prof'l Conduct R. 1.16(c) (2018).

Displaced lawyers who wish to practice law in another jurisdiction may do so only as authorized by that other jurisdiction. Subdivision (c) of the ABA Model Court Rule on Provision of Legal Services Following Determination of Major Disaster provides:

> Following the determination of a major disaster in another United States jurisdiction, a lawyer who is authorized to practice law and who principally practices in that affected jurisdiction, and who is not disbarred, suspended from practice or otherwise restricted from practice in any jurisdiction, may provide legal services in this jurisdiction on a temporary basis if permitted by order of the highest court of the other jurisdiction. Those legal services must arise out of and be reasonably related to that lawyer's practice of law in the jurisdiction, or area of such other jurisdiction, where the major disaster occurred.[18]

This ABA Model Court Rule further provides that lawyers:

- are required to register with the Supreme Court in the state where they are temporarily allowed to practice;
- are subject to the disciplinary authority in the jurisdiction of the Supreme Court in the state where they are temporarily allowed to practice; and
- must cease practice within 60 days after the Supreme Court in the state where they are temporarily allowed to practice determines the conditions of the disaster have ended.[19]

E. Loss of Files and Other Client Property

Some lawyers located in an area affected by a disaster may have their files destroyed. Lawyers who maintain only paper files or maintain electronic files

18. Full text of the ABA Model Court Rule on Provision of Legal Services Following Determination of Major Disaster (2007) can be found at: https://www.americanbar.org/content/dam/aba/migrated/2011_build/professional_responsibility/model_rule_disaster_katrina.authcheckdam.pdf. The ABA Standing Committee on Client Protection Chart on State Implementation of the ABA Model Court Rule on Provision of Legal Services Following Determination of Major Disaster (Sept. 8, 2017) can be found at: https://www.americanbar.org/content/dam/aba/administrative/professional_responsibility/katrina_chart.authcheckdam.pdf.

19. *See* ABA Model Court Rule Provision of Legal Services Following Determination of Major Disaster, *supra* note 17. For an example, see the emergency order entered by the Supreme Court of Texas in 2017, permitting the temporary practice of Texas law by lawyers displaced from their home jurisdictions after Hurricane Harvey. The Court adopted requirements and limitations similar to those in the ABA Model Court Rule. *See* Court of Texas Amended Emergency Order After Hurricane Harvey Permitting Out-of-State Lawyers to Practice Texas Law Temporarily, Misc. Docket No. 17-9101 (Aug. 30, 2017), *available at* http://www.txcourts.gov/media/1438820/179101.pdf.

solely on a local computer or local server are at higher risk of losing those records in a disaster. A lawyer's responsibilities regarding these files vary depending on the nature of the stored documents and the status of the affected clients.

Under the lawyer's duty to communicate, a lawyer must notify current clients of the loss of documents with intrinsic value, such as original executed wills and trusts, deeds, and negotiable instruments.[20] Lawyers also must notify former clients of the loss of documents and other client property with intrinsic value. A lawyer's obligation to former clients is based on the lawyer's obligation to safeguard client property under Rule 1.15.[21] Under the same Rule, lawyers must make reasonable efforts to reconstruct documents of intrinsic value for both current and former clients, or to obtain copies of the documents that come from an external source.[22]

A lawyer need not notify either current or former clients about lost documents that have no intrinsic value, that serve no useful purpose to the client or former client, or for which there are electronic copies. The lawyer must respond honestly, however, if asked about those documents by either current or former clients.[23]

The largest category of documents will fall in the middle; i.e., they are necessary for current representation or would serve some useful purpose to

---

20. *See* Model Rules of Prof'l Conduct R. 1.4 (2018); N.Y. City Bar Ass'n Formal Op. 2015-6 (2015); *See also* ABA Comm. on Ethics & Prof'l Responsibility, Informal Op. 1384 (1977) (Lawyer should not dispose of client property without client consent, should not destroy information that would be useful to the client if the statute of limitations has not run, should not destroy information that the client may need and is not otherwise easily accessible by the client, should exercise discretion in determining which information might be particularly sensitive or require longer retention than others, should retain trust account records, should protect confidentiality in the destruction of any files, should review files before destruction to determine if portions should be retained, and should retain an index of destroyed files); State Bar of Cal. Standing Comm. on Prof'l Responsibility & Conduct, Formal Op. 2001-157 (2001) (Regarding destruction of closed files, indicating that property of the client such as original documents (like wills) is subject to bailment law or other statute, lawyers may not destroy other file materials without making reasonable efforts to obtain client consent, lawyers may not destroy items required to be retained by law, lawyers may not destroy items if destruction would prejudice the clients' interests, and criminal case files should not be destroyed while the client is living); State Bar of Mich. Op. R-12 (1991) (Lawyers must give notice to clients regarding file destruction after 1998, files before 1998 may not be destroyed without reasonable efforts to notify the client, and lawyers are not required to notify clients of file destruction if the lawyer maintains a copy of the documents on microfilm (excluding original documents of the client or if destruction of the documents would prejudice the client's interests)). Lawyers should note that in some states, the client may be entitled to all substantive documents in the file at the client's request. *See e.g.*, State Bar of Ariz. Op. 15-02 (2015).

21. *See also* N.Y. City Bar Ass'n Formal Op. 2015-6 (2015).

22. Lawyers should consider returning all original documents and documents with intrinsic value created by the lawyer as a result of the representation to clients at the end of representation to avoid this situation.

23. *See* Model Rules of Prof'l Conduct R. 8.4(c) (2018); N.Y. City Bar Ass'n Formal Op. 2015-6 (2015).

the client. For current clients, lawyers may first attempt to reconstruct files by obtaining documents from other sources. If the lawyer cannot reconstruct the file, the lawyer must promptly notify current clients of the loss. This obligation stems from the lawyer's obligations to communicate with clients and represent them competently and diligently.[24] A lawyer is not required either to reconstruct the documents or to notify former clients of the loss of documents that have no intrinsic value, unless the lawyer has agreed to do so despite the termination of the lawyer-client relationship.[25]

ABA Model Rule 1.15(a) also requires lawyers to keep complete records accounting for funds and property of clients and third parties held by the lawyer and to preserve those records for five years after the end of representation. A lawyer whose trust account records are lost or destroyed in a disaster must attempt to reconstruct those records from other available sources to fulfill this obligation.

To prevent the loss of files and other important records, including client files and trust account records, lawyers should maintain an electronic copy of important documents in an off-site location that is updated regularly.[26] Although not required, lawyers may maintain these files solely as electronic files, except in instances where law, court order, or agreement require maintenance of paper copies, and as long as the files are readily accessible and not subject to inadvertent modification or degradation.[27] As discussed above,

24. *See* Model Rules of Prof'l Conduct R. 1.1, 1.3 & 1.4 (2018); N.Y. City Bar Ass'n Formal Op. 2015-6 (2015).

25. Lawyers should consider including in fee agreements or engagement letters the understandings between the lawyer and the client about how the lawyer will handle documents once the representation is ended. In addition, lawyers should consult statutes, common law, and court rules that may also govern the retention of client files.

26. Model Rules of Prof'l Conduct R. 1.1 (2018); Model Rules of Prof'l Conduct R. 1.3 (2018).

27. ABA Comm. on Ethics & Prof'l Responsibility, Formal Op. 477R (May 22, 2017) (Lawyer may send client information over the Internet if lawyer makes reasonable efforts to prevent inadvertent or unauthorized access, but may be required to take special security precautions when required by an agreement with the client or by law, or when the nature of the information requires a higher degree of security); ABA Comm. on Ethics & Prof'l Responsibility, Informal Op. 1127 (1970) (Lawyers may use company that stores attorney files on computer as long as the company is set up so that the material is available only to the particular attorney to whom the files belong and the employees of the company; lawyers must take care to choose an appropriate company that has procedures to ensure confidentiality and to admonish the company that confidentiality of the files must be preserved); State Bar of Ariz. Op. 07-02 (2007) (Lawyer may not destroy original client documents after converting them to electronic records without client consent, but may destroy paper documents if they are only copies); State Bar of Cal. Standing Comm. on Prof'l Responsibility & Conduct 2001-157 (2001) (Electronic records may be insufficient if originals are not accurately reproduced, and some documents cannot be copied by law); Fla. Bar Op. 06-1 (2006) (Lawyers may, but are not required to, store files electronically unless: a statute or rule requires retention of an original document, the original document is the property of the client, or destruction of a paper document adversely affects the client's in-

lawyers may also store files "in the cloud" if ethics obligations regarding confidentiality and control of and access to information are met.

---

terests; files stored electronically must be readily reproducible and protected from inadvertent modification, degradation or destruction); Me. Bd. of Overseers Op. 185 (2004) (Lawyers may maintain closed files electronically, rather than paper copies, if they are accessible to the client); Me. Bd. of Overseers Op. 183 (2004) ("If an attorney dispenses with the retention of paper files in favor of computerized records, the attorney must be mindful that the obligation to the client may require the attorney to maintain the means to provide copies of those records in a format that will make them accessible to both the attorney and the client in the future. Because the attorney is obligated to ensure that the client is able to make informed decisions regarding the disposition of the file and also must take care in destroying files to be sure that useful information is retained, an attorney will need to consider how new hardware or software will impact future access to old computerized records."); Mo. Informal Advisory Op. 127 (2009) (Lawyer may keep client's file in exclusively electronic format except documents that are legally significant as originals and intrinsically valuable documents and providing that the appropriate software to access the information is maintained for the time period the file must be retained); State Bar of Mich. Op. R-5 (1989) (File storage via electronic means should be treated carefully to ensure confidentiality by limiting access to law firm personnel); N.J. Advisory Comm. on Prof'l Ethics Decisions Op. 701 (2006) (Documents may be stored electronically if sufficient safeguards to maintain confidentiality of the documents, particularly if they are stored outside the law firm, except for documents that are client property such as original wills, trusts, deeds, executed contracts, corporate bylaws and minutes); N.Y. County Lawyers Ass'n Op. 725 (1998) (General opinion on the ethical obligation to retain closed files, including that it may be proper for a lawyer to retain only electronic copies of a file if "the evidentiary value of such documents will not be unduly impaired by the method of storage"); N.Y. State Bar Ass'n Comm. on Prof'l Ethics Op. 680 (1996) (Although some items in a client's file may be stored electronically, some documents (such as original checkbooks, check stubs, cancelled checks, and bank statements) are required by the rules to be kept in original form; documents stored electronically should be stored in "read-only" form so they cannot be inadvertently destroyed or altered; and records must be readily produced when necessary); N.C. State Bar Op. RPC 234 (1996) (Closed client files may be stored electronically as long as the electronic documents can be converted to paper copies, except for "original documents with legal significance, such as wills, contracts, stock certificates, etc."); S.C. Bar Advisory Op. 02-14 (2002) (General opinion on disposition of closed files when one member of a two-member firm retires, discussing various situations and notes that files may be placed on computer or other electronic media; Note: In South Carolina, the files are the property of the client); S.C. Bar Advisory Op. 98-33 (1998) (The committee declined to give an opinion on electronic retention of closed files as a legal question, but indicated there was no prohibition against retaining documents in electronic format as long as doing so did not adversely affect the client's interests and as long as the lawyer took reasonable precautions to make sure that third parties with access to the electronic records kept the records confidential); Va. State Bar Op. 1818 (2005) (Lawyer can maintain client files in electronic format with no paper copies as long as the method of record retention does not adversely affect the client's interests); Wash. State Bar Ass'n Op. 2023 (2003) (Lawyer may have firm file retention policy in which original documents are provided to the client and the lawyer keeps only electronic copies of file materials as long as documents "with intrinsic value" or that are the property of the client cannot be destroyed without client permission); State Bar of Wis. Op. E-00-3 (2000) (If lawyer has stored files electronically, lawyer should provide client copies on disk at client's request. However, lawyer can bill client for time/expense if required to obtain information in format client wants. Attorney does not need to provide client with internal memos, personal notes, and the like).

F. Solicitation and Advertising

Lawyers may want to offer legal services to persons affected by a disaster. The existence of a disaster, however, does not excuse compliance with lawyer advertising and solicitation rules.[28] Of particular concern is the possibility of improper solicitation in the wake of a disaster. A lawyer may not solicit disaster victims unless the lawyer complies with Model Rules 7.1 through 7.3.[29] "Live person-to-person contact" that is generally prohibited means "in-person, face-to-face, live telephone and other real-time visual or auditory person-to-person communications, where the person is subject to a direct personal encounter without time for reflection,"[30] and a significant motive for the lawyer's doing so is pecuniary gain.[31] In addition to ethical prohibitions, lawyers should be aware that there may be statutory prohibitions that may apply.[32]

Lawyers may solicit in-person to offer pro bono legal services to disaster victims, because the lawyer's motive does not involve pecuniary gain.[33] Additionally, lawyers may communicate with disaster victims in "targeted" written or recorded electronic material in compliance with Rules 7.1 through 7.3. Lawyers also should be mindful of any additional requirements for written or recorded electronic solicitations imposed by particular jurisdictions.[34]

G. Out-Of-State Lawyers Providing Representation to Disaster Victims

Lawyers practicing in jurisdictions unaffected by the disaster who wish to assist by providing legal services to disaster victims must consider rules

---

28. *See* Model Rules of Prof'l Conduct R. 7.1–7.5 (all of these Rules were amended in August 2018).

29. *See* Model Rules of Prof'l Conduct R. 7.3 (2018). *See also* The Florida Bar v. Wolfe, 759 So. 2d 639 (Fla. 2000) (Lawyer suspended for one year for soliciting clients by passing out brochures in affected areas in wake of tornados); State Bar of Cal. Standing Comm. on Prof'l Responsibility & Conduct, Formal Op. 2004-166 (2004) (Solicitation of prospective clients in mass disaster victim chat room is not considered in person solicitation but nevertheless is prohibited because it is "intrusive").

30. Model Rules of Prof'l Conduct R. 7.3 cmt. [2] (2018). Rule 7.3(b) contains some exceptions, and Rule 7.3(c) contains an additional prohibition. Both should be consulted.

31. *Id.*

32. *See, e.g.*, Fla. Stat. §877.02 (Prohibiting solicitation on behalf of lawyers by hospitals, police, tow truck operators, insurance adjusters); 49 U.S.C. §1136(g)(2) (Prohibiting lawyer solicitation within 45 days of an air transportation accident).

33. Model Rules of Prof'l Conduct R. 7.3(a); La. Bd. of Ethics Op. 05-RPCC-005 (2005) (Lawyer may solicit disaster victims in person to provide pro bono legal services). Providing pro bono legal services is encouraged by, inter alia, Model Rules 6.1 and 6.2.

34. *See, e.g.*, Rules Regulating the Fla. Bar R. 4-7.18(b)(2) (requiring contrasting "advertisement" mark on envelope and enclosures; statement of qualifications and experience; information on where the lawyer obtained the information prompting the written solicitation; and specified first sentence, among others).

regulating temporary multijurisdictional practice.[35] Out-of-state lawyers may provide representation to disaster victims in the affected jurisdiction only when permitted by that jurisdiction's law or rules, or by order of the jurisdiction's highest court.

The ABA Model Court Rule on Provision of Legal Services Following Determination of Major Disaster[36] provides that the Supreme Court of the affected jurisdiction must declare a major disaster and issue an order that allows lawyers in good standing from another jurisdiction to temporarily provide pro bono legal services in the affected jurisdiction through a non-profit bar association, pro bono program, legal services program, or other organization designated by the courts.[37] The Model Court Rule also requires those lawyers to register with the courts of the affected jurisdiction, and subjects those lawyers to discipline in the affected jurisdiction.[38]

Conclusion

Lawyers must be prepared to deal with disasters. Foremost among a lawyer's ethical obligations are those to existing clients, particularly in maintaining communication. Lawyers must also protect documents, funds, and other property the lawyer is holding for clients or third parties. By proper advance preparation and taking advantage of available technology during recovery efforts, lawyers will reduce the risk of violating professional obligations after a disaster.

Dissent: Keith R. Fisher dissents.

---

35. Model Rules of Prof'l Conduct R. 5.5 (c), cmt. [14] (2018): "Lawyers desiring to provide pro bono legal services on a temporary basis in a jurisdiction that has been affected by a major disaster, but in which they are not otherwise authorized to practice law, as well as lawyers from the affected jurisdiction who seek to practice law temporarily in another jurisdiction, but in which they are not otherwise authorized to practice law, should consult the Model Court Rule on Provision of Legal Services Following Determination of Major Disaster."

Most states have adopted some form of ABA Model Rule 5.5 on Multijurisdictional Practice. A chart on state implementation of ABA Multijurisdictional Practice Policies compiled by the ABA may be found at: https://www.americanbar.org/content/dam/aba/administrative/professional_responsibility/recommendations.authcheckdam.pdf.

36. ABA Model Court Rule on Provision of Legal Services Following Determination of Major Disaster, *available at* https://www.americanbar.org/content/dam/aba/images/disaster/model_court_rule.pdf (last visited Sept. 7, 2018). The ABA Chart on State Implementation of ABA Model Court Rule on Provision of Legal Services Following Determination of Major Disaster can be found at: https://www.americanbar.org/content/dam/aba/administrative/professional_responsibility/katrina_chart.authcheckdam.pdf.

37. Providing pro bono legal services in this situation would assist the lawyer in meeting the suggested goal of 50 hours per year set forth in Model Rule 6.1(a).

38. As noted above, the Supreme Court of Texas issued an emergency order in 2017 after Hurricane Harvey following the ABA Model Court Order. *See supra* note 18.

AMERICAN BAR ASSOCIATION

STANDING COMMITTEE ON ETHICS AND PROFESSIONAL RESPONSIBILITY

Formal Opinion 483 **October 17, 2018**

Lawyers' Obligations After an Electronic Data Breach or Cyberattack

Model Rule 1.4 requires lawyers to keep clients "reasonably informed" about the status of a matter and to explain matters "to the extent reasonably necessary to permit a client to make an informed decision regarding the representation." Model Rules 1.1, 1.6, 5.1 and 5.3, as amended in 2012, address the risks that accompany the benefits of the use of technology by lawyers. When a data breach occurs involving, or having a substantial likelihood of involving, material client information, lawyers have a duty to notify clients of the breach and to take other reasonable steps consistent with their obligations under these Model Rules.

Introduction[1]

Data breaches and cyber threats involving or targeting lawyers and law firms are a major professional responsibility and liability threat facing the legal profession. As custodians of highly sensitive information, law firms are inviting targets for hackers.[2] In one highly publicized incident, hackers infiltrated the computer networks at some of the country's most well-known law firms, likely looking for confidential information to exploit through insider trading schemes.[3] Indeed, the data security threat is so high that law enforce-

1. This opinion is based on the ABA Model Rules of Professional Conduct as amended by the ABA House of Delegates through August 2018. The laws, court rules, regulations, rules of professional conduct and opinions promulgated in individual jurisdictions are controlling.

2. *See, e.g.*, Dan Steiner, *Hackers Are Aggressively Targeting Law Firms' Data* (Aug. 3, 2017), https://www.cio.com (explaining that "[f]rom patent disputes to employment contracts, law firms have a lot of exposure to sensitive information. Because of their involvement, confidential information is stored on the enterprise systems that law firms use. . . . This makes them a juicy target for hackers that want to steal consumer information and corporate intelligence."); *See also Criminal-Seeking-Hacker' Requests Network Breach for Insider Trading*, Private Industry Notification 160304-01, FBI, Cyber Division (Mar. 4, 2016).

3. Nicole Hong & Robin Sidel, *Hackers Breach Law Firms, Including Cravath and Weil Gotshal*, Wall St. J. (Mar. 29, 2016), https://www.wsj.com/articles/hackers-breach-cravath-swaine-other-big-law-firms-1459293504.

ment officials regularly divide business entities into two categories: those that have been hacked and those that will be.[4]

In Formal Opinion 477R, this Committee explained a lawyer's ethical responsibility to use reasonable efforts when communicating client confidential information using the Internet.[5] This opinion picks up where Opinion 477R left off, and discusses an attorney's ethical obligations when a data breach exposes client confidential information. This opinion focuses on an attorney's ethical obligations after a data breach,[6] and it addresses only data breaches that involve information relating to the representation of a client. It does not address other laws that may impose post-breach obligations, such as privacy laws or other statutory schemes that law firm data breaches might also implicate. Each statutory scheme may have different post-breach obligations, including different notice triggers and different response obligations. Both the triggers and obligations in those statutory schemes may overlap with the ethical obligations discussed in this opinion. And, as a matter of best practices, attorneys who have experienced a data breach should review all potentially applicable legal response obligations. However, compliance with statutes such as state breach notification laws, HIPAA, or the Gramm-Leach-Bliley Act does not necessarily achieve compliance with ethics obligations. Nor does compliance with lawyer regulatory rules *per se* represent compliance with breach response laws. As a matter of best practices, lawyers who have suffered a data breach should analyze compliance separately under every applicable law or rule.

Compliance with the obligations imposed by the Model Rules of Professional Conduct, as set forth in this opinion, depends on the nature of the cyber incident, the ability of the attorney to know about the facts and cir-

---

4. Robert S. Mueller, III, *Combatting Threats in the Cyber World Outsmarting Terrorists, Hackers and Spies*, FBI (Mar. 1, 2012), https://archives.fbi.gov/archives/news/speeches/combating-threats-in-the-cyber-world-outsmarting-terrorists-hackers-and-spies.

5. ABA Comm. on Ethics & Prof'l Responsibility, Formal Op. 477R (2017) ("Securing Communication of Protected Client Information").

6. The Committee recognizes that lawyers provide legal services to clients under a myriad of organizational structures and circumstances. The Model Rules of Professional Conduct refer to the various structures as a "firm." A "firm" is defined in Rule 1.0(c) as "a lawyer or lawyers in a law partnership, professional corporation, sole proprietorship or other association authorized to practice law; or lawyers employed in a legal services organization or the legal department of a corporation or other organization." How a lawyer complies with the obligations discussed in this opinion will vary depending on the size and structure of the firm in which a lawyer is providing client representation and the lawyer's position in the firm. *See* MODEL RULES OF PROF'L CONDUCT R. 5.1 (2018) (Responsibilities of Partners, Managers, and Supervisory Lawyers); MODEL RULES OF PROF'L CONDUCT R. 5.2 (2018) (Responsibility of a Subordinate Lawyers); and MODEL RULES OF PROF'L CONDUCT R. 5.3 (2018) (Responsibility Regarding Nonlawyer Assistance).

cumstances surrounding the cyber incident, and the attorney's roles, level of authority, and responsibility in the law firm's operations.[7]

I. Analysis

A. Duty of Competence

Model Rule 1.1 requires that "A lawyer shall provide competent representation to a client. Competent representation requires the legal knowledge, skill, thoroughness and preparation reasonably necessary for the representation."[8] The scope of this requirement was clarified in 2012, when the ABA recognized the increasing impact of technology on the practice of law and the obligation of lawyers to develop an understanding of that technology. Comment [8] to Rule 1.1 was modified in 2012 to read:

> To maintain the requisite knowledge and skill, a lawyer should keep abreast of changes in the law and its practice, *including the benefits and risks associated with relevant technology*, engage in continuing study and education and comply with all continuing legal education requirements to which the lawyer is subject. (Emphasis added.)[9]

In recommending the change to Rule 1.1's Comment, the ABA Commission on Ethics 20/20 explained:

> Model Rule 1.1 requires a lawyer to provide competent representation, and Comment [6] [renumbered as Comment [8]] specifies that, to remain competent, lawyers need to 'keep abreast of changes in the law and its practice.' The Commission concluded that, in order to keep abreast of changes in law practice in a digital age, lawyers necessarily need to understand basic features of relevant technology and that this aspect of competence should be expressed in the Comment. For example, a lawyer would have difficulty providing com-

7. In analyzing how to implement the professional responsibility obligations set forth in this opinion, lawyers may wish to consider obtaining technical advice from cyber experts. ABA Comm. on Ethics & Prof'l Responsibility, Formal Op. 477R (2017) ("Any lack of individual competence by a lawyer to evaluate and employ safeguards to protect client confidences may be addressed through association with another lawyer or expert, or by education.") *See also, e.g., Cybersecurity Resources*, ABA Task Force on Cybersecurity, https://www.americanbar.org/groups/cybersecurity/resources.html (last visited Oct. 5, 2018).

8. Model Rules of Prof'l Conduct R. 1.1 (2018).

9. A Legislative History: The Development of the ABA Model Rules of Professional Conduct, 1982-2013, at 43 (Art Garwin ed., 2013).

petent legal services in today's environment without knowing how to use email or create an electronic document.[10]

In the context of a lawyer's post-breach responsibilities, both Comment [8] to Rule 1.1 and the 20/20 Commission's thinking behind it require lawyers to understand technologies that are being used to deliver legal services to their clients. Once those technologies are understood, a competent lawyer must use and maintain those technologies in a manner that will reasonably safeguard property and information that has been entrusted to the lawyer. A lawyer's competency in this regard may be satisfied either through the lawyer's own study and investigation or by employing or retaining qualified lawyer and nonlawyer assistants.[11]

1. Obligation to Monitor for a Data Breach

Not every cyber episode experienced by a lawyer is a data breach that triggers the obligations described in this opinion. A data breach for the purposes of this opinion means a data event where material client confidential information is misappropriated, destroyed or otherwise compromised, or where a lawyer's ability to perform the legal services for which the lawyer is hired is significantly impaired by the episode.

Many cyber events occur daily in lawyers' offices, but they are not a data breach because they do not result in actual compromise of material client confidential information. Other episodes rise to the level of a data breach, either through exfiltration/theft of client confidential information or through ransomware, where no client information is actually accessed or lost, but where the information is blocked and rendered inaccessible until a ransom is paid. Still other compromises involve an attack on a lawyer's systems, destroying the lawyer's infrastructure on which confidential information resides and in-

10. ABA Commission on Ethics 20/20 Report 105A (Aug. 2012), http://www.americanbar.org/content/dam/aba/administrative/ethics_2020/20120808_revised_resolution_105a_as_amended.authcheckdam.pdf. The 20/20 Commission also noted that modification of Comment [6] did not change the lawyer's substantive duty of competence: "Comment [6] already encompasses an obligation to remain aware of changes in technology that affect law practice, but the Commission concluded that making this explicit, by addition of the phrase 'including the benefits and risks associated with relevant technology,' would offer greater clarity in this area and emphasize the importance of technology to modern law practice. The proposed amendment, which appears in a Comment, does not impose any new obligations on lawyers. Rather, the amendment is intended to serve as a reminder to lawyers that they should remain aware of technology, including the benefits and risks associated with it, as part of a lawyer's general ethical duty to remain competent."

11. Model Rules of Prof'l Conduct R. 5.3 (2018); ABA Comm. on Ethics & Prof'l Responsibility, Formal Op. 477R (2017); ABA Comm. on Ethics & Prof'l Responsibility, Formal Op. 08-451 (2018); *See also* Jill D. Rhodes & Robert S. Litt, The ABA Cybersecurity Handbook: A Resource for Attorneys, Law Firms, and Business Professionals 124 (2d ed. 2018) [hereinafter ABA Cybersecurity Handbook].

capacitating the attorney's ability to use that infrastructure to perform legal services.

Model Rules 5.1 and 5.3 impose upon lawyers the obligation to ensure that the firm has in effect measures giving reasonable assurance that all lawyers and staff in the firm conform to the Rules of Professional Conduct. Model Rule 5.1 Comment [2], and Model Rule 5.3 Comment [1] state that lawyers with managerial authority within a firm must make reasonable efforts to establish internal policies and procedures designed to provide reasonable assurance that all lawyers and staff in the firm will conform to the Rules of Professional Conduct. Model Rule 5.1 Comment [2] further states that "such policies and procedures include those designed to detect and resolve conflicts of interest, identify dates by which actions must be taken in pending matters, account for client funds and property and ensure that inexperienced lawyers are properly supervised."

Applying this reasoning, and based on lawyers' obligations (i) to use technology competently to safeguard confidential information against unauthorized access or loss, and (ii) to supervise lawyers and staff, the Committee concludes that lawyers must employ reasonable efforts to monitor the technology and office resources connected to the internet, external data sources, and external vendors providing services relating to data[12] and the use of data. Without such a requirement, a lawyer's recognition of any data breach could be relegated to happenstance—and the lawyer might not identify whether a breach has occurred,[13] whether further action is warranted,[14] whether employees are adhering to the law firm's cybersecurity policies and procedures so that the lawyers and the firm are in compliance with their ethical duties,[15] and how and when the lawyer must take further action under other regulatory and legal provisions.[16] Thus, just as lawyers must safeguard and monitor the security of paper files and actual client property, lawyers utilizing tech-

12. ABA Comm. on Ethics & Prof'l Responsibility, Formal Op. 08-451 (2008).

13. Fredric Greene, *Cybersecurity Detective Controls—Monitoring to Identify and Respond to Threats*, ISACA J., Vol. 5, 1025 (2015), *available at* https://www.isaca.org/Journal/archives/2015/Volume-5/Pages/cybersecurity-detective-controls.aspx (noting that "[d]etective controls are a key component of a cybersecurity program in providing visibility into malicious activity, breaches and attacks on an organization's IT environment.")

14. Model Rules of Prof'l Conduct R. 1.6(c) (2018); Model Rules of Prof'l Conduct R. 1.15 (2018).

15. *See also* Model Rules of Prof'l Conduct R. 5.1 & 5.3 (2018).

16. The importance of monitoring to successful cybersecurity efforts is so critical that in 2015, Congress passed the Cybersecurity Information Sharing Act of 2015 (CISA) to authorize companies to monitor and implement defensive measures on their information systems, and to foreclose liability for such monitoring under CISA. Automated Indicator Sharing, https://www.us-cert.gov/ais (last visited Oct. 5, 2018); *See also* National Cyber Security Centre "Ten Steps to Cyber Security" [Step 8: Monitoring] (Aug. 9, 2016), https://www.ncsc.gov.uk/guidance/10-steps-cyber-security.

nology have the same obligation to safeguard and monitor the security of electronically stored client property and information.[17]

While lawyers must make reasonable efforts to monitor their technology resources to detect a breach, an ethical violation does not necessarily occur if a cyber-intrusion or loss of electronic information is not immediately detected, because cyber criminals might successfully hide their intrusion despite reasonable or even extraordinary efforts by the lawyer. Thus, as is more fully explained below, the potential for an ethical violation occurs when a lawyer does not undertake reasonable efforts to avoid data loss or to detect cyber-intrusion, and that lack of reasonable effort is the cause of the breach.

2. Stopping the Breach and Restoring Systems

When a breach of protected client information is either suspected or detected, Rule 1.1 requires that the lawyer act reasonably and promptly to stop the breach and mitigate damage resulting from the breach. How a lawyer does so in any particular circumstance is beyond the scope of this opinion. As a matter of preparation and best practices, however, lawyers should consider proactively developing an incident response plan with specific plans and procedures for responding to a data breach.[18] The decision whether to adopt a plan, the content of any plan, and actions taken to train and prepare for implementation of the plan, should be made before a lawyer is swept up in an actual breach. "One of the benefits of having an incident response capability is that it supports responding to incidents systematically (i.e., following a consistent incident handling methodology) so that the appropriate actions are taken. Incident response plans help personnel to minimize loss or theft of information and disruption of services caused by incidents."[19] While every lawyer's response plan should be tailored to the lawyer's or the law firm's specific practice, as a general matter incident response plans share common features:

> The primary goal of any incident response plan is to have a process in place that will allow the firm to promptly respond in a coordinated manner to any type of security incident or cyber intrusion. The incident response process should promptly: identify and evaluate any potential network anomaly or intrusion; assess its nature and scope; determine if any data or information may have been accessed or compromised; quarantine the threat or malware; prevent

17. ABA Comm. on Ethics & Prof'l Responsibility, Formal Op. 477R (2017).

18. *See* ABA Cybersecurity Handbook, *supra* note 11, at 202 (explaining the utility of large law firms adopting "an incident response plan that details who has ownership of key decisions and the process to follow in the event of an incident.").

19. *NIST Computer Security Incident Handling Guide*, at 6 (2012), https://nvlpubs.nist.gov/nistpubs/specialpublications/nist.sp.800-61r2.pdf.

> the exfiltration of information from the firm; eradicate the malware, and restore the integrity of the firm's network.
>
> Incident response plans should identify the team members and their backups; provide the means to reach team members at any time an intrusion is reported, and define the roles of each team member. The plan should outline the steps to be taken at each stage of the process, designate the team member(s) responsible for each of those steps, as well as the team member charged with overall responsibility for the response.[20]

Whether or not the lawyer impacted by a data breach has an incident response plan in place, after taking prompt action to stop the breach, a competent lawyer must make all reasonable efforts to restore computer operations to be able again to service the needs of the lawyer's clients. The lawyer may do so either on her own, if qualified, or through association with experts. This restoration process provides the lawyer with an opportunity to evaluate what occurred and how to prevent a reoccurrence consistent with the obligation under Model Rule 1.6(c) that lawyers "make reasonable efforts to prevent the inadvertent or unauthorized disclosure of, or unauthorized access to, information relating to the representation of the client."[21] These reasonable efforts could include (i) restoring the technology systems as practical, (ii) the implementation of new technology or new systems, or (iii) the use of no technology at all if the task does not require it, depending on the circumstances.

3. Determining What Occurred

The Model Rules do not impose greater or different obligations on a lawyer as a result of a breach involving client information, regardless of whether the breach occurs through electronic or physical means. Just as a lawyer would need to assess which paper files were stolen from the lawyer's office, so too lawyers must make reasonable attempts to determine whether electronic files were accessed, and if so, which ones. A competent attorney must make reasonable efforts to determine what occurred during the data breach. A post-breach investigation requires that the lawyer gather sufficient information to ensure the intrusion has been stopped and then, to the extent reasonably possible, evaluate the data lost or accessed. The information gathered in a post-breach investigation is necessary to understand the scope of the intrusion and to allow

---

20. Steven M. Puiszis, *Prevention and Response: A Two-Pronged Approach to Cyber Security and Incident Response Planning*, The Prof'l Lawyer, Vol. 24, No. 3 (Nov. 2017).

21. We discuss Model Rule 1.6(c) further below. But in restoring computer operations, lawyers should consider whether the lawyer's computer systems need to be upgraded or otherwise modified to address vulnerabilities, and further, whether some information is too sensitive to continue to be stored electronically.

for accurate disclosure to the client consistent with the lawyer's duty of communication and honesty under Model Rules 1.4 and 8.4(c).[22] Again, how a lawyer actually makes this determination is beyond the scope of this opinion. Such protocols may be a part of an incident response plan.

B. Duty of Confidentiality

In 2012, amendments to Rule 1.6 modified both the Rule and the commentary about a lawyer's efforts that are required to preserve the confidentiality of information relating to the representation of a client. Model Rule 1.6(a) requires that "A lawyer shall not reveal information relating to the representation of a client" unless certain circumstances arise.[23] The 2012 modification added a duty in paragraph (c) that: "A lawyer shall make reasonable efforts to prevent the inadvertent or unauthorized disclosure of, or unauthorized access to, information relating to the representation of a client."[24]

Amended Comment [18] explains:

> Paragraph (c) requires a lawyer to act competently to safeguard information relating to the representation of a client against unauthorized access by third parties and against inadvertent or unauthorized disclosure by the lawyer or other persons who are participating in the representation of the client or who are subject to the lawyer's supervision. *See* Rules 1.1, 5.1 and 5.3. The unauthorized access to, or the inadvertent or unauthorized disclosure of, information relating to the representation of a client does not constitute a violation of paragraph (c) if the lawyer has made reasonable efforts to prevent the access or disclosure.

Recognizing the necessity of employing a fact-based analysis, Comment [18] to Model Rule 1.6(c) includes nonexclusive factors to guide lawyers in making a "reasonable efforts" determination. Those factors include:

- the sensitivity of the information,
- the likelihood of disclosure if additional safeguards are not employed,
- the cost of employing additional safeguards,
- the difficulty of implementing the safeguards, and

---

22. The rules against dishonesty and deceit may apply, for example, where the lawyer's failure to make an adequate disclosure—or any disclosure at all—amounts to deceit by silence. *See, e.g.*, Model Rules of Prof'l Conduct R. 4.1 cmt. [1] (2018) ("Misrepresentations can also occur by partially true but misleading statements or omissions that are the equivalent of affirmative false statements.").

23. Model Rules of Prof'l Conduct R. 1.6(a) (2018).

24. *Id.* at (c).

- the extent to which the safeguards adversely affect the lawyer's ability to represent clients (e.g., by making a device or important piece of software excessively difficult to use).[25]

As this Committee recognized in ABA Formal Opinion 477R:

> At the intersection of a lawyer's competence obligation to keep "abreast of knowledge of the benefits and risks associated with relevant technology," and confidentiality obligation to make "reasonable efforts to prevent the inadvertent or unauthorized disclosure of, or unauthorized access to, information relating to the representation of a client," lawyers must exercise reasonable efforts when using technology in communicating about client matters. What constitutes reasonable efforts is not susceptible to a hard and fast rule, but rather is contingent upon a set of factors.

As discussed above and in Formal Opinion 477R, an attorney's competence in preserving a client's confidentiality is not a strict liability standard and does not require the lawyer to be invulnerable or impenetrable.[26] Rather, the obligation is one of reasonable efforts. Rule 1.6 is not violated even if data is lost or accessed if the lawyer has made reasonable efforts to prevent the loss or access.[27] As noted above, this obligation includes efforts to monitor for breaches of client confidentiality. The nature and scope of this standard is addressed in the ABA Cybersecurity Handbook:

> Although security is relative, a legal standard for "reasonable" security is emerging. That standard rejects requirements for specific security measures (such as firewalls, passwords, or the like) and instead adopts a fact-specific approach to business security obligations that requires a "process" to assess risks, identify and implement appropriate security measures responsive to those risks, verify that the

25. Model Rules of Prof'l Conduct R. 1.6 cmt. [18] (2018). "The [Ethics 20/20] Commission examined the possibility of offering more detailed guidance about the measures that lawyers should employ. The Commission concluded, however, that technology is changing too rapidly to offer such guidance and that the particular measures lawyers should use will necessarily change as technology evolves and as new risks emerge and new security procedures become available." ABA Commission Report 105A, *supra* note 9, at 5.

26. ABA Cybersecurity Handbook, *supra* note 11, at 122.

27. Model Rules of Prof'l Conduct R. 1.6, cmt. [18] (2018) ("The unauthorized access to, or the inadvertent or unauthorized disclosure of, information relating to the representation of a client does not constitute a violation of paragraph (c) if the lawyer has made reasonable efforts to prevent the access or disclosure.").

measures are effectively implemented, and ensure that they are continually updated in response to new developments.[28]

Finally, Model Rule 1.6 permits a lawyer to reveal information relating to the representation of a client if the disclosure is impliedly authorized in order to carry out the representation. Such disclosures are permitted if the lawyer reasonably believes that disclosure: (1) is impliedly authorized and will advance the interests of the client in the representation, and (2) will not affect a material interest of the client adversely.[29] In exercising this discretion to disclose information to law enforcement about the data breach, the lawyer must consider: (i) whether the client would object to the disclosure; (ii) whether the client would be harmed by the disclosure; and (iii) whether reporting the theft would benefit the client by assisting in ending the breach or recovering stolen information. Even then, without consent, the lawyer may disclose only such information as is reasonably necessary to assist in stopping the breach or recovering the stolen information.

C. Lawyer's Obligations to Provide Notice of Data Breach

When a lawyer knows or reasonably should know a data breach has occurred, the lawyer must evaluate notice obligations. Due to record retention requirements of Model Rule 1.15, information compromised by the data breach may belong or relate to the representation of a current client or former client.[30] We address each below.

1. Current Client

Communications between a lawyer and current client are addressed generally in Model Rule 1.4. Rule 1.4(a)(3) provides that a lawyer must "keep the client reasonably informed about the status of the matter." Rule 1.4(b) provides: "A lawyer shall explain a matter to the extent reasonably necessary to permit the client to make informed decisions regarding the representation." Under these provisions, an obligation exists for a lawyer to communicate with current clients about a data breach.[31]

---

28. ABA Cybersecurity Handbook, *supra* note 11, at 73.

29. ABA Comm. on Ethics & Prof'l Responsibility, Formal Op. 01-421(2001) (disclosures to insurer in bills when lawyer representing insured).

30. This opinion addresses only obligations to clients and former clients. Data breach, as used in this opinion, is limited to client confidential information. We do not address ethical duties, if any, to third parties.

31. Relying on Rule 1.4 generally, the New York State Bar Committee on Professional Ethics concluded that a lawyer must notify affected clients of information lost through an online data storage provider. N.Y. State Bar Ass'n Op. 842 (2010) (Question 10: "If the lawyer learns of any breach of confidentiality by the online storage provider, then the lawyer must investigate whether there has been any breach of his or her own clients' confidential information, notify any affected clients, and discontinue use of the service unless the lawyer receives assurances that any security issues have been sufficiently remediated.") (*citations omitted*).

Our conclusion here is consistent with ABA Formal Ethics Opinion 95-398 where this Committee said that notice must be given to clients if a breach of confidentiality was committed by or through a third-party computer vendor or other service provider. There, the Committee concluded notice to the client of the breach may be required under 1.4(b) for a "serious breach."[32] The Committee advised:

> Where the unauthorized release of confidential information could reasonably be viewed as a significant factor in the representation, for example where it is likely to affect the position of the client or the outcome of the client's legal matter, disclosure of the breach would be required under Rule 1.4(b).[33]

A data breach under this opinion involves the misappropriation, destruction or compromise of client confidential information, or a situation where a lawyer's ability to perform the legal services for which the lawyer was hired is significantly impaired by the event. Each of these scenarios is one where a client's interests have a reasonable possibility of being negatively impacted. When a data breach occurs involving, or having a substantial likelihood of involving, material client confidential information a lawyer has a duty to notify the client of the breach. As noted in ABA Formal Opinion 95-398, a data breach requires notice to the client because such notice is an integral part of keeping a "client reasonably informed about the status of the matter" and the lawyer should provide information as would be "reasonably necessary to permit the client to make informed decisions regarding the representation" within the meaning of Model Rule 1.4.[34]

The strong client protections mandated by Model Rule 1.1, 1.6, 5.1 and 5.3, particularly as they were amended in 2012 to account for risks associated with the use of technology, would be compromised if a lawyer who experiences a data breach that impacts client confidential information is permitted to hide those events from their clients. And in view of the duties imposed by these other Model Rules, Model Rule 1.4's requirement to keep clients "reasonably informed about the status" of a matter would ring hollow if a data breach was somehow excepted from this responsibility to communicate.

Model Rule 1.15(a) provides that a lawyer shall hold "property" of clients "in connection with a representation separate from the lawyer's own property." Funds must be kept in a separate account, and "[o]ther property shall be identified as such and appropriately safeguarded." Model Rule 1.15(a) also provides that, "Complete records of such account funds and

---

32. ABA Comm. on Ethics & Prof'l Responsibility, Formal Op. 95-398 (1995).

33. *Id.*

34. Model Rules of Prof'l Conduct R. 1.4(b) (2018).

other property shall be kept by the lawyer. . . ." Comment [1] to Model Rule 1.15 states:

> A lawyer should hold property of others with the care required of a professional fiduciary. Securities should be kept in a safe deposit box, except when some other form of safekeeping is warranted by special circumstances. All property that is the property of clients or third persons, including prospective clients, must be kept separate from the lawyer's business and personal property.

An open question exists whether Model Rule 1.15's reference to "property" includes information stored in electronic form. Comment [1] uses as examples "securities" and "property" that should be kept separate from the lawyer's "business and personal property." That language suggests Rule 1.15 is limited to tangible property which can be physically segregated. On the other hand, many courts have moved to electronic filing and law firms routinely use email and electronic document formats to image or transfer information. Reading Rule 1.15's safeguarding obligation to apply to hard copy client files but not electronic client files is not a reasonable reading of the Rule.

Jurisdictions that have addressed the issue are in agreement. For example, Arizona Ethics Opinion 07-02 concluded that client files may be maintained in electronic form, with client consent, but that lawyers must take reasonable precautions to safeguard the data under the duty imposed in Rule 1.15. The District of Columbia Formal Ethics Opinion 357 concluded that, "Lawyers who maintain client records solely in electronic form should take reasonable steps (1) to ensure the continued availability of the electronic records in an accessible form during the period for which they must be retained and (2) to guard against the risk of unauthorized disclosure of client information."

The Committee has engaged in considerable discussion over whether Model Rule 1.15 and, taken together, the technology amendments to Rules 1.1, 1.6, and 5.3 impliedly impose an obligation on a lawyer to notify a current client of a data breach. We do not have to decide that question in the absence of concrete facts. We reiterate, however, the obligation to inform the client does exist under Model Rule 1.4.

2. Former Client

Model Rule 1.9(c) requires that "A lawyer who has formerly represented a client in a matter or whose present or former firm has formerly represented a client in a matter shall not thereafter . . . reveal information relating to the representation except as these Rules would permit or require with respect to a client."[35] When electronic "information relating to the representation" of a

35. Model Rules of Prof'l Conduct R. 1.9(c)(2) (2018).

former client is subject to unauthorized access, disclosure, or destruction, the Model Rules provide no direct guidance on a lawyer's obligation to notify the former client. Rule 1.9(c) provides that a lawyer "shall not . . . reveal" the former client's information. It does not describe what steps, if any, a lawyer should take if such information is revealed. The Committee is unwilling to require notice to a former client as a matter of legal ethics in the absence of a black letter provision requiring such notice.[36]

Nevertheless, we note that clients can make an informed waiver of the protections in Rule 1.9.[37] We also note that Rule 1.16(d) directs that lawyers should return "papers and property" to clients at the conclusion of the representation, which has commonly been understood to include the client's file, in whatever form it is held. Rule 1.16(d) also has been interpreted as permitting lawyers to establish appropriate data destruction policies to avoid retaining client files and property indefinitely.[38] Therefore, as a matter of best practices, lawyers are encouraged to reach agreement with clients before conclusion, or at the termination, of the relationship about how to handle the client's electronic information that is in the lawyer's possession.

Absent an agreement with the former client lawyers are encouraged to adopt and follow a paper and electronic document retention schedule, which meets all applicable laws and rules, to reduce the amount of information relating to the representation of former clients that the lawyers retain. In addition, lawyers should recognize that in the event of a data breach involving former client information, data privacy laws, common law duties of care, or contractual arrangements with the former client relating to records retention, may mandate notice to former clients of a data breach. A prudent lawyer will consider such issues in evaluating the response to the data breach in relation to former clients.[39]

3. Breach Notification Requirements

The nature and extent of the lawyer's communication will depend on the type of breach that occurs and the nature of the data compromised by the breach. Unlike the "safe harbor" provisions of Comment [18] to Model Rule 1.6, if a post-breach obligation to notify is triggered, a lawyer must make the

---

36. *See* Discipline of Feland, 2012 ND 174, ¶ 19, 820 N.W.2d 672 (Rejecting respondent's argument that the court should engraft an additional element of proof in a disciplinary charge because "such a result would go beyond the clear language of the rule and constitute amendatory rulemaking within an ongoing disciplinary proceeding.").

37. *See* Model Rules of Prof'l Conduct R. 1.9, cmt. [9] (2018).

38. *See* ABA Ethics Search Materials on Client File Retention, https://www.americanbar.org/content/dam/aba/administrative/professional_responsibility/piles_of_files_2008.pdf (last visited Oct.15, 2018).

39. *Cf.* ABA Comm. on Ethics & Prof'l Responsibility, Formal Op. 482 (2018), at 8-10 (discussing obligations regarding client files lost or destroyed during disasters like hurricanes, floods, tornadoes, and fires).

disclosure irrespective of what type of security efforts were implemented prior to the breach. For example, no notification is required if the lawyer's office file server was subject to a ransomware attack but no information relating to the representation of a client was inaccessible for any material amount of time, or was not accessed by or disclosed to unauthorized persons. Conversely, disclosure will be required if material client information was actually or reasonably suspected to have been accessed, disclosed or lost in a breach.

The disclosure must be sufficient to provide enough information for the client to make an informed decision as to what to do next, if anything. In a data breach scenario, the minimum disclosure required to all affected clients under Rule 1.4 is that there has been unauthorized access to or disclosure of their information, or that unauthorized access or disclosure is reasonably suspected of having occurred. Lawyers must advise clients of the known or reasonably ascertainable extent to which client information was accessed or disclosed. If the lawyer has made reasonable efforts to ascertain the extent of information affected by the breach but cannot do so, the client must be advised of that fact.

In addition, and as a matter of best practices, a lawyer also should inform the client of the lawyer's plan to respond to the data breach, from efforts to recover information (if feasible) to steps being taken to increase data security.

The Committee concludes that lawyers have a continuing duty to keep clients reasonably apprised of material developments in post-breach investigations affecting the clients' information.[40] Again, specific advice on the nature and extent of follow up communications cannot be provided in this opinion due to the infinite number of variable scenarios.

If personally identifiable information of clients or others is compromised as a result of a data beach, the lawyer should evaluate the lawyer's obligations under state and federal law. All fifty states, the District of Columbia, Guam, Puerto Rico, and the Virgin Islands have statutory breach notification laws.[41] Those statutes require that private or governmental entities notify individuals of breaches involving loss or disclosure of personally identifiable information.[42] Most breach notification laws specify who must comply with the law, define "personal information," define what constitutes a breach, and provide requirements for notice.[43] Many federal and state agencies also have confidentiality and breach notification requirements.[44] These regulatory schemes have the potential to cover individuals who meet particular statu-

40. State Bar of Mich. Op. RI-09 (1991).

41. National Conference of State Legislatures, *Security Breach Notification Laws* (Sept. 29, 2018), http://www.ncsl.org/research/telecommunications-and-information-technology/security-breach-notification-laws.aspx.

42. *Id.*

43. *Id.*

44. ABA Cybersecurity Handbook, *supra* note 11, at 65.

tory notice triggers, irrespective of the individual's relationship with the lawyer. Thus, beyond a Rule 1.4 obligation, lawyers should evaluate whether they must provide a statutory or regulatory data breach notification to clients or others based upon the nature of the information in the lawyer's possession that was accessed by an unauthorized user.[45]

III. Conclusion

Even lawyers who, (i) under Model Rule 1.6(c), make "reasonable efforts to prevent the . . . unauthorized disclosure of, or unauthorized access to, information relating to the representation of a client," (ii) under Model Rule 1.1, stay abreast of changes in technology, and (iii) under Model Rules 5.1 and 5.3, properly supervise other lawyers and third-party electronic-information storage vendors, may suffer a data breach. When they do, they have a duty to notify clients of the data breach under Model Rule 1.4 in sufficient detail to keep clients "reasonably informed" and with an explanation "to the extent necessary to permit the client to make informed decisions regarding the representation."

---

45. Given the broad scope of statutory duties to notify, lawyers would be well served to actively manage the amount of confidential and or personally identifiable information they store beyond any ethical, statutory, or other legal obligation to do so. Lawyers should implement, and follow, a document retention policy that comports with Model Rule 1.15 and evaluate ways to limit receipt, possession and/or retention of confidential or personally identifiable information during or after an engagement.

AMERICAN BAR ASSOCIATION

STANDING COMMITTEE ON ETHICS AND PROFESSIONAL RESPONSIBILITY

Formal Opinion 484 **November 27, 2018**

A Lawyer's Obligations When Clients Use Companies or Brokers to Finance the Lawyer's Fee

Lawyers may refer clients to fee financing companies or brokers in which the lawyers have no ownership or other financial interests provided they comply with Model Rules 1.2(c), 1.4(b), 1.5(a) and (b), 1.6, 1.7(a)(2), and 1.9(a). If a lawyer were to acquire an ownership or other financial interest in a finance company or brokerage and thereafter refer clients to that entity to finance the lawyer's fees, the lawyer would be entering into a business transaction with a client, or obtaining a security or pecuniary interest adverse to the client, or both. In that instance, the lawyer would also be required to comply with Model Rule 1.8(a).[1]

I. Introduction

Some clients may be unable to afford lawyers' fees absent some form of accommodation or assistance. For example, a criminal defense or family law client may be unable to afford a lawyer's flat fee at the outset of a representation.[2] The client may be able to afford the lawyer's fee, however, if the client can finance the fee through a loan from a third-party. Or, a client may simply wish to finance a lawyer's fee rather than pay a lump sum. In some instances, the client may be able to obtain a loan from a bank or other traditional financial institution, but in other cases that option will not be available. In the latter situation, the client may want to finance the lawyer's fee through

1. This opinion is based on the ABA Model Rules of Professional Conduct as amended by the ABA House of Delegates through August 2018. The laws, court rules, regulations, rules of professional conduct and opinions promulgated in individual jurisdictions are controlling.

2. A client in such a situation may wish to pay the lawyer's fee by credit card if possible; numerous jurisdictions permit lawyers to accept credit cards to pay fees with certain conditions. *See, e.g.*, ABA Comm. on Ethics & Prof'l Responsibility, Formal Op. 00-419 (2000) (rejecting the reasoning in prior opinions regarding the use of credit cards to pay for non-professional services and merchandise, "the Committee accepted, per se, the propriety of using credit cards to pay legal fees"); Ill. State Bar Ass'n Advisory Op. 14-01 (2014), 2014 WL 2434670, at *2; N.Y. State Bar Ass'n, Comm. on Prof'l Ethics Op. 1112 (2017), 2017 WL 527372 at *1; Or. State Bar Ass'n, Bd. of Gov'rs Op. 2005-172 (2005), 2005 WL 5679599, at *1.

a finance company. This raises the following questions: (a) whether the lawyer may refer the client to a finance company that will likely loan the client money to pay the lawyer's fees, or (b) whether the lawyer may refer the client to a broker who will assist the client in obtaining fee financing. Lawyers have reported several fee financing scenarios.

First, a lawyer may know of a finance company in which the lawyer has no ownership or other financial interest. An interested client applies for a loan for the lawyer's full fee with the finance company, which determines whether to make a loan, the amount of any loan, the interest rate on the loan, and the amount of any financing fee (which reportedly ranges between 5–15%). If the finance company approves the loan, it deposits the full loan amount in the lawyer's bank account, less the financing fee. The lawyer receives nothing from the finance company for the client's participation other than the fee payment; the loan to the client is non-recourse as to the lawyer. The lawyer's fee agreement with the client explains the arrangement. Absent other circumstances permitting or requiring the lawyer to terminate the attorney-client relationship, the lawyer will continue to represent the client even if the client defaults on the loan.[3]

Second, the lawyer agrees to pay an initial fee to the finance company in exchange for the right to submit loan applications from clients. The lawyer has no financial or other interest in the finance company, and the finance company makes all decisions about whether to loan funds to the client, in what amount, and on what terms. The client is solely responsible for repaying any loan; the loan is non-recourse as to the lawyer. The finance company pays the loan proceeds directly to the lawyer, minus a 10% finance fee.[4]

Third, the lawyer knows of a finance company in which the lawyer has no ownership or other interest. The lawyer negotiates a fee with a client consistent with the lawyer's customary practice. "In appropriate circumstances," the lawyer may inform a client of the possibility of financing the fee through the finance company.[5] If the client is interested in financing the fee, the lawyer provides the client with additional information about the financing plan. The client then completes the company's printed credit application in the lawyer's office and the lawyer sends the application to the company. If the company approves the credit application, it will establish a credit facility for the payment of the lawyer's fees up to the credit limit established by the company. The lawyer periodically submits vouchers to the finance company for services rendered to the client. The client must approve the vouch-

3. Fla. State Bar Ass'n, Comm. on Prof'l Ethics Op. 16-2 (2016), 2016 WL 8648795, at *1 [hereinafter Fla. Ethics Op. 16-2] (describing such an arrangement).

4. Ill. State Bar Ass'n Advisory Op. 92-9, at 1 (1993) (outlining this arrangement).

5. Or. State Bar Ass'n, Bd. of Gov'rs Op. 2005-133, 2005 WL 5679557, at *1 [hereinafter Or. Ethics Op. 2005-133].

ers. If the client approves a voucher, the finance company pays the lawyer the amount of the voucher minus a 10% service charge (up to the client's unused credit limit). The client must repay the amount of each voucher plus interest at a rate comparable to the interest rates banks charge for credit cards. The finance company also requires the client to deposit funds in a reserve account to reduce the finance company's risk of default.

Fourth, the lawyer knows of a finance company in which the lawyer has no ownership or other interest. The lawyer gives clients a link to the finance company's website or posts the link on the lawyer's website, either of which directs clients to the finance company's loan application forms. If a client completes the application, the finance company decides whether to lend the client money and on what terms. The finance company disburses the loan funds directly to the client, but the finance company provides the lawyer with a "portal" through which he or she can learn whether the client applied for a loan, and when and in what amount loan funds were disbursed to the client. To participate in these programs, the lawyer pays a fee to the finance company of several hundred dollars either as a one-time registration fee or as a monthly subscription fee.[6] Again, any loan to a client is non-recourse with respect to the lawyer.

Fifth, a finance company offers a "same as cash" funding program for a lawyer's fees or retainer in which the company provides the physical equipment necessary to carry out the mechanics of the arrangement on-site in the lawyer's office. To initiate the process at the lawyer's office, the client swipes an item of personal financial identification through an identifying device provided to the lawyer by the finance company. The finance company also provides the lawyer with an imaging machine that scans the client's personal check to facilitate the finance company's collection of periodic loan repayments directly from the client's checking account. The finance company then may qualify the client for a loan at a wide range of interest rates depending on the finance company's determination of the risk of non-payment and the length of the repayment period. If the client qualifies, the lawyer provides the client with the loan documents and the finance company pays the lawyer directly. The finance company has no recourse against the lawyer if the client defaults.[7]

Sixth, but similarly, a lawyer may associate with a financial brokerage company that helps clients obtain legal fee financing. The broker is not a

---

6. N.Y. State Bar Ass'n, Comm. on Prof'l Ethics Op. 1108 (2016), www.nysba.org [hereinafter N.Y. Ethics Op. 1108] (explaining this arrangement, and identifying factors the lawyer should consider).

7. Utah State Bar, Ethics Advisory Opinion Comm. Op. 13-05 (2013), 2013 WL 7393113, at *1 (explaining this arrangement and addressing the conflicts and other issues the lawyer should consider).

lender; it locates banks willing to finance the client's legal fees. The broker charges the lawyer an initial setup fee and a monthly fee to create and maintain a webpage that facilitates the brokerage function. The lawyer also pays a "merchant fee" on the amount of the financed legal fee. More particularly, the broker provides interested clients with loan applications to submit to banks. Approved clients receive offers from competing banks, and are free to pick the offer that works best for them, or to decline all offers. If the client accepts an offer, the lending bank pays the loan amount to the client. The client then pays the lawyer's fee in accordance with their fee agreement.[8] Once again the loan is non-recourse insofar as the lawyer is concerned.

As explained below, fee financing arrangements of the types described here are ethically permissible provided that the lawyer complies with Model Rules of Professional Conduct 1.2(c), 1.4(b), 1.5(a) and (b), 1.6, 1.7(a)(2), and 1.9(a).[9]

II. Analysis

First, a lawyer who is willing to allow a client to finance the lawyer's fee must under Model Rule 1.4(b) explain the arrangement to the client to the extent reasonably necessary to permit the client to make informed decisions about the representation. Depending on the facts, this may include explaining (1) the lawyer's relationship with the finance company or broker, including any fees paid by the lawyer to the company or broker, the payments received by the lawyer, and whether the company or broker is also a client of the lawyer; (2) how the lawyer's fee will be paid by the finance company or bank where the finance company or bank disburses funds directly to the lawyer, or how the client is expected to pay the lawyer's fee where the finance company or bank disburses the loan funds to the client; (3) that the finance company will inform the lawyer when it makes a loan to the client and disburses funds to the client, as in the third scenario outlined above; (4) the costs and benefits of the transaction to the client; (5) the terms of the arrangement between the finance company or broker and the client as known or understood by the lawyer; (6) alternative payment options for the client; (7) any payment terms that the lawyer intends to impose if the finance company disburses the loan proceeds to the client rather than to the lawyer; (8) whether the lawyer will charge a higher fee than he or she would charge otherwise because of the financing arrangement,

8. 2018 N.C. State Bar Formal Op. 4 (2018), 2018 WL 2215870, at *1 [hereinafter N.C. Ethics Op. 4] (describing this arrangement and identifying factors the lawyer should consider).

9. Model Rules of Prof'l Conduct (2018) [hereinafter Model Rules]. The Committee expresses no opinion on whether such arrangements may violate consumer protection or usury laws. Should they do so, a lawyer who facilitates the arrangements may risk violating Model Rules 1.2(d), 4.1(a), 8.4(b), and 8.4(d).

as perhaps to recoup any financing or other fee the lawyer must pay to the finance company or broker;[10] (9) the lawyer's obligation to maintain the confidentiality of client information with respect to the finance company, broker, or bank; (10) that paying the lawyer through fee financing may affect the rights and remedies the client might have to obtain the repayment or return of those funds or the forgiveness or reduction of the client's debt in a dispute arising out of the lawyer's performance; and (11) any other factor that the lawyer knows or reasonably should know to be material to the financing of the representation.

A lawyer may not want to advise a client about the costs and benefits of financing the lawyer's fee or the terms of any such agreement or transaction. For example, the lawyer may view those conversations as more suitably held between the client and representatives of the finance company or broker, or between the client and the client's family or other advisors. If so, and given the possibility that a client might believe that the lawyer is exercising professional judgment in recommending the finance company or broker, or that the lawyer has evaluated the loan terms and believes them to be suitable for the client, the lawyer must limit the scope of the representation in accordance with Model Rule 1.2(c).[11]

The lawyer may wish to advise the client that the finance company, broker, or bank will not direct or regulate the lawyer's professional judgment in representing the client in accordance with Model Rule 5.4(c).[12] Admittedly, Model Rule 5.4(c) does not apply to any of the scenarios under consideration because the finance company, broker, or bank is not paying the lawyer—the client is paying the lawyer with borrowed funds.[13] Furthermore, unlike litiga-

10. A lawyer always has a duty to communicate to the client "the basis or rate of the fee and expenses for which the client will be responsible" unless the lawyer "will charge a regularly represented client on the same basis or rate." Model Rules R. 1.5(b) (2018).

11. *See* Model Rules R. 1.2(c) (2018) ("A lawyer may limit the scope of the representation if the limitation is reasonable under the circumstances and the client gives informed consent."); *see also* N.Y. Ethics Op. 1108, *supra* note 6 (endorsing the lawyer's limitation of the representation under Rule 1.2(c) where a potential client might believe that the lawyer is exercising professional judgment in recommending financing, recommending a particular financier, or has evaluated the loan terms).

12. *See* Model Rules R. 5.4(c) (2018) ("A lawyer shall not permit a person who recommends, employs, or pays the lawyer to direct or regulate the lawyer's professional judgment in rendering such legal services.").

13. Model Rule 1.8(f) does not apply because the client is paying the lawyer with the client's own funds; this is not a situation where someone other than the client is paying the lawyer to represent the client. The fact that the client has borrowed the funds used to pay the lawyer does not change the fact that the funds belong to the client. *See id.* (stating that a lawyer "shall not accept compensation for representing a client from one other than the client" unless three conditions are met). *But see* N.Y. Ethics Op. 1108, *supra* note 6 (noting that "For all practical purposes, the lawyer is accepting fees 'from one other than the client' (the lender). . . . [A]lthough the funds are not paid directly to the lawyer, the lender informs the

tion funding or financing, a legal fee lender in the scenarios described above has no direct financial interest in the outcome of the matter, and therefore no incentive to attempt to influence the lawyer's advice, strategy, or tactics. Accordingly, the lawyer generally has no obligation to inform the client of the professional independence that Model Rule 5.4(c) assures in appropriate cases. Even so, because the loaned funds are tied to the representation and because an unsophisticated client may view the finance company, broker, or lending bank as "paying" the lawyer, a lawyer may see value in assuring the client of the lawyer's obligation to exercise independent professional judgment in representing the client regardless of the source of the funds used to pay the lawyer.

Second, any fee that the lawyer charges the client must be reasonable.[14] If the lawyer increases the fee for the representation above what the lawyer normally charges for a similar matter to account for any finance fee or subscription the lawyer must pay to the finance company or broker, the fee charged to the client must still be reasonable.[15] Furthermore, the lawyer must inform the client that the lawyer will be charging the client a higher fee to account for the finance or subscription fee that the lawyer must pay to the finance company or broker.[16]

Third, if a lawyer accepts loan proceeds to pay a flat fee, the lawyer must deposit those funds in the lawyer's trust account or operating account and treat them as unearned or earned just as the jurisdiction provides for the payment of flat fees generally.[17] If either the client or the lawyer terminates the representation before the lawyer fully earns the flat fee, the lawyer must refund the unearned funds to the client. The failure to do so would result in the lawyer collecting an unreasonable fee in violation of Model Rule 1.5(a).

Fourth, while a lawyer may refer a client to a finance company or broker, the lawyer may not reveal information regarding the client's representa-

---

lawyer when the funds are disbursed, presumably to help ensure that the lawyer gets paid. When the lender gives the lawyer information about a disbursement, that information is something 'of value' that triggers Rule 1.8(f).")

14. Model Rules R. 1.5(a) (2018) (stating that a lawyer "shall not make an agreement for, charge, or collect an unreasonable fee or an unreasonable amount for expenses").

15. In some jurisdictions, a lawyer may be prohibited from charging a higher fee because the fee is being financed. *See, e.g.*, Fla. Rules of Prof'l Conduct 4-1.5(h) (2015) ("A lawyer or law firm may accept payment under a credit plan. No higher fee shall be charged and no additional charge shall be imposed by reason of a lawyer's or law firm's participation in a credit plan.").

16. Model Rules R. 1.4(b) (2018).

17. Some jurisdictions permit lawyers to treat flat fees as earned upon receipt and therefore not entrusted. In those jurisdictions, lawyers who elect to treat flat fees as earned upon receipt must deposit them in their operating accounts to avoid commingling allegations. Other jurisdictions hold that because flat fees are merely advance fee payments, they must be held in trust until earned through the lawyer's performance of the agreed services.

tion to the company, broker, or lending bank except as permitted under Rules 1.6(a) or (b).

Fifth, in referring a client to a finance company or broker, a lawyer must be alert to the possibility of a material limitation conflict of interest under Model Rule 1.7(a)(2).[18] Arguably the greatest risk is that the lawyer will recommend the finance company or broker to the client even though fee financing is not in the client's interests because the client's arrangement of financing best assures payment or timely payment of the lawyer's fee. A conflict of interest might also exist if the finance company or broker is also a client of the lawyer. A lawyer may avoid a conflict in the first instance by not recommending fee financing to the client. As the North Carolina State Bar has explained, "[a] lawyer does not put his own financial interests ahead of those of his client by providing payment options to a client who requires financial assistance in paying the lawyer's fees. However, given the lawyer's self interest in being paid in full for his services, the lawyer may not recommend one payment option over another."[19] In either instance, the client may give informed consent to the representation notwithstanding any material limitation conflict provided that the Model Rule 1.7(b) requirements are satisfied.[20]

Sixth, if the lawyer previously represented the finance company, broker, or lender in connection with loans to clients of other lawyers and is representing his or her current client in obtaining fee financing from the finance company, broker, or lender, the lawyer must consider whether the current client's interests are materially adverse to the former client's interests. If they are, the lawyer must obtain the former client's informed consent to the representation at hand and confirm it in writing.[21]

As noted earlier, some finance companies charge a lawyer a financing or subscription fee. For example, if a finance company loans a client $10,000 to pay a lawyer's flat fee, the company may deduct a 5% financing fee from the loan proceeds paid to the lawyer, such that the lawyer receives $9,500 for his or her services rather than the full $10,000. Such terms do not constitute fee sharing in violation of Model Rule 5.4(a)[22] because the financing or sub-

---

18. *See* Model Rules R. 1.7(a)(2) (2018) (stating that a concurrent conflict of interest exists if "there is a significant risk that the representation of one or more clients will be limited by the lawyer's responsibilities to another client, a former client or a third person or by a personal interest of the lawyer").

19. N.C. Ethics Op. 4, *supra* note 8, at *1.

20. *See, e.g.*, Or. Ethics Op. 2005-133, *supra* note 5, at *3 (noting the risk that the lawyer might encourage a client to enter into a financing plan to assure the payment of fees or to avoid the expense of collecting fees even if the plan was not necessarily in the client's best interests, but stating that the client could give informed consent to the representation notwithstanding the Rule 1.7(a)(2) material limitation conflict).

21. Model Rules R. 1.9(a) (2018).

22. *Id. See also* Model Rules R. 5.4(a) (2018) (stating that a lawyer or law firm "shall not share legal fees with a nonlawyer" except in circumstances not pertinent here).

scription fee is basically an administrative fee that is deducted from the payment to the lawyer.[23] This is akin to a merchant fee that credit card companies charge.[24] It is settled that lawyers' payment of credit card merchant fees does not constitute impermissible fee-sharing.[25] Additionally, the prohibition on fee-sharing is intended to protect a lawyer's "professional independence of judgment."[26] As previously explained, a legal fee financier has no direct financial interest in the outcome of the matter, and thus no incentive to influence the lawyer's professional judgment. In short, this is not a situation to which the Model Rule 5.4(a) prohibition on fee-sharing is meant to apply.

Finally, although not among the fee financing scenarios of which the Committee has been made aware, it is conceivable that a lawyer might acquire an ownership or other financial interest in a finance company or brokerage, or wish to form such a business. If a lawyer did so and referred a client to that entity, the lawyer would be entering into a business transaction with the client or would be acquiring a security or pecuniary interest adverse to the client, or both. In those situations, the lawyer would need to comply with Model Rule 1.8(a). Compliance with Rule 1.8(a) would require the lawyer to (1) ensure that the terms and transaction are fair and reasonable to the client, and fully disclose and transmit the terms and an explanation of the transaction to the client in a manner that the client could reasonably understand; (2) advise the client of the desirability of seeking independent legal advice regarding the transaction and afford the client a reasonable opportunity to do so; and (3) obtain the client's informed written consent to the transaction's essential terms and the lawyer's role in the transaction, including whether the lawyer is representing the client in the transaction.

---

23. *See* Pa. Bar Ass'n, Comm. on Legal Ethics & Prof'l Responsibility Op. 94-30 (1994), 1994 WL 928021, at *1–2 (discussing a fee financing service in which the amounts charged to the lawyer were for the collection of fees rather than for legal services rendered); Sup. Ct. of Tex., Prof'l Ethics Comm. Op. 481, 1994 WL 848496, at *1 (stating that "the retention by the finance corporation of a reasonable portion of the amount borrowed by the client is properly viewed as finance arrangement rather than a fee-splitting arrangement").

24. *See* Fla. Ethics Op. 16-2, *supra* note 3, 2016 WL 8648795, at *2 (reasoning that legal fee financing is not impermissible fee sharing because it is a form of credit plan and Florida ethics rules permit lawyers to accept payments through credit plans, which include credit cards); Or. Ethics Op. 2005-133, *supra* note 5, at *3 (describing a fee financing plan in which the finance company deducts a 10% service fee from every payment to the lawyer as analogous to the client's use of a credit card to pay legal fees).

25. *See, e.g.*, 2010 N.C. State Bar Formal Op. 4 (2010), 2010 WL 4730432, at *3 (discussing fee sharing under Rule 5.4(a) in connection with a barter exchange and stating that "[t]he use of credit cards to pay for legal services has long been allowed, although credit card banks routinely charge a 'discount fee' that is a percentage of the legal fee charged to the credit card"); Phila. Bar Ass'n, Prof'l Guidance Comm. Op. 00-10 (2000), 2000 WL 33173001, at *1 (stating that "allowing clients to use credit cards to pay legal fees and expenses does not constitute a violation of the Rules of Professional Conduct").

26. Model Rules R. 5.4 cmt. 1 (2018).

III. Conclusion

Lawyers may participate in the fee financing arrangements described in Part I of this opinion provided they comply with Model Rules 1.2(c), 1.4(b), 1.5(a), 1.6, 1.7(a)(2), and 1.9(a). They may further acquire an interest in or form a finance company or brokerage and thereafter refer clients to that entity provided that they comply with Model Rule 1.8(a).

AMERICAN BAR ASSOCIATION
STANDING COMMITTEE ON ETHICS AND PROFESSIONAL RESPONSIBILITY

Formal Opinion 485 **February 14, 2019**

Judges Performing Same-Sex Marriages

A judge for whom performing marriages is a mandatory obligation of judicial office may not decline to perform marriages of same-sex couples. A judge for whom performing marriages is a discretionary judicial function may not decline to perform marriages of same-sex couples if the judge agrees to perform opposite-sex marriages. A judge's refusal to perform same-sex marriages while performing opposite-sex marriages calls into question the judge's integrity and impartiality and reflects bias and prejudice in violation of Rules 1.1, 2.2, 2.3(A), and 2.3(B) of the Model Code of Judicial Conduct. In a jurisdiction in which a judge is not obligated to perform marriages but has the discretion to do so, a judge may refuse to perform marriages for members of the public. A judge who declines to perform marriages for members of the public may still perform marriages for family and friends. If a judge chooses to perform marriages for family and friends, however, the judge may not decline to perform same-sex marriages for family and friends.

Introduction

The Committee has been asked whether a judge subject to the Model Code of Judicial Conduct[1] may perform marriages of opposite-sex couples but refuse to perform marriages for same-sex couples. The Committee concludes that such a refusal violates the Model Code. A judge for whom performing marriages is a discretionary function may, however, decline to perform any marriages for members of the public. A judge who declines to perform any marriages for members of the public may still perform marriages for family and friends. If a judge chooses to perform marriages for family and friends, though, the judge may not decline to perform same-sex marriages for family and friends.

Background

The laws of all fifty states and the District of Columbia authorize one or more categories of judicial officers to perform marriages. This opinion cov-

1. Model Code of Judicial Conduct (2011) [hereinafter Model Code].

ers judges for whom performing marriages is either a mandatory obligation of judicial office or a discretionary function.[2] The conclusions stated here are based solely on the Model Code.

The Model Code

Canon I of the Model Code articulates the bedrock principle that "[a] judge shall uphold and promote the independence, integrity, and impartiality of the judiciary, and shall avoid impropriety and the appearance of impropriety."[3] Rule 1.1 provides that "[a] judge shall comply with the law, including the Code of Judicial Conduct."[4] Accordingly, a judge must "act at all times in a manner that promotes public confidence in the independence, integrity, and impartiality of the judiciary, and shall avoid impropriety and the appearance of impropriety."[5] The term "impartiality" as used in this context means "the absence of bias or prejudice in favor of, or against, particular parties or classes of parties."[6]

Canon II expresses another fundamental principle: "A judge shall perform the duties of judicial office impartially, competently, and diligently."[7] Although a judge's performance of a marriage typically is a discretionary function rather than a mandatory function, it is nonetheless a duty of judicial office within the meaning of the Model Code.[8] Correspondingly, Model

2. A judge, within the meaning of [the Model] Code, is anyone who is authorized to perform judicial functions, including an officer such as a justice of the peace, magistrate, court commissioner, special master, referee, or member of the administrative law judiciary." *Id.* at Application I(B).

3. *Id.* at Canon I.

4. *Id.* at R. 1.1. The Model Code defines the term "law" to include constitutional provisions, court rules, decisional law, and statutes. *Id.* Terminology.

5. *Id.* at R. 1.2.

6. *Id.* at Terminology.

7. *Id.* at Canon II.

8. *See, e.g., In re* Day, 413 P.3d 907, 950 (Or. 2018) (concluding that the act of solemnizing marriages, once a judge has chosen to do so, qualifies as a judicial duty within the meaning of judicial ethics rules), *cert. denied*, 139

S. Ct. 324 (2018); Ariz. Sup. Ct., Judicial Ethics Advisory Comm. Op. 15-01, 2015 WL 1530659, at *1 (2015) ("Although the performance of a marriage by a judge is a 'discretionary function' rather than a mandatory function . . . it is based on statutory authority granted by the legislature. Because of this specific grant of authority . . . the performance of a marriage by a judicial officer is performance of a 'judicial duty' as contemplated by the Code [of Judicial Conduct]."); Sup. Ct. of Ohio, Bd. of Prof'l Conduct Adv. Op. 15-001, 2015 WL 4875137, at *1 (2015) ("When a judge performs a civil marriage ceremony . . . the judge is performing a judicial duty and is thus required to follow the Code of Judicial Conduct in the performance of that duty."); Wis. Sup. Ct., Judicial Conduct Advisory Comm. Op. No. 15-1, 2015 WL 5928528, at *2 (2015) (discussing judges' discretionary functions in connection with the performance of marriages); Elizabeth A. Flaherty, *Impartiality in Solemnizing Marriages*, JUDICIAL CONDUCT BD. OF PA. NEWSLETTER, Summer 2014, at 18, 25 ("When a judge chooses to conduct a wedding ceremony, s/he acts in an official judicial capacity, authorized by statute.").

Rule 2.2 requires a judge to "uphold and apply the law" and to "perform all duties of judicial office fairly and impartially."[9] Although judges come to the bench with different backgrounds and personal views or philosophies, judges "must interpret and apply the law, without regard to whether the judge approves or disapproves of the law" or principle or rule in question.[10] Model Rule 2.3(A) mandates that judges perform the duties of judicial office without bias or prejudice.[11]

Most importantly for present purposes, Model Rule 2.3(B) prohibits a judge who is performing judicial duties from manifesting bias or prejudice based on people's sex, gender, sexual orientation, or marital status.[12] A judge who manifests such bias or prejudice threatens to undermine public confidence in the judiciary and to bring it into disrepute.[13] Indeed, because impartiality and unbiased decision-making and conduct are critical to our justice system and to the public's faith in the judiciary, the Model Code emphasizes in several places that judges must avoid even conduct that may be *perceived* as biased or prejudiced.[14]

State Judicial Ethics Opinions

Several states have analyzed judges' obligations to perform same-sex marriages. In a leading opinion, the Supreme Court of Ohio Board of Professional Conduct was asked by judges and a judicial association on behalf of its members (1) whether a judge who is authorized to perform marriages may refuse to marry same-sex couples on personal, moral, or religious grounds, but still marry opposite-sex couples; and (2) whether a judge may decline to perform all marriages to avoid marrying same-sex couples.[15] Relying on the oath of office to which all Ohio judges swear, and provisions of the Ohio Code of Judicial Conduct, which track the Model Code, the Board concluded that "[a] judge who performs civil marriages may not refuse to perform same-sex marriages while continuing to perform opposite-sex marriages, based upon his or her personal, moral, and religious beliefs."[16] The

---

9. Model Code R. 2.2, *supra* note 1.

10. *Id.* at cmt. [2].

11. *Id.* at R. 2.3(A).

12. *See id.* at R. 2.3(B) (prohibiting bias, prejudice, or harassment "based upon attributes including but not limited to race, sex, gender, religion, national origin, ethnicity, disability, age, sexual orientation, marital status, socioeconomic status, or political affiliation").

13. *Id.* at cmt. [1].

14. *See, e.g., id.* at Preamble cmt. [2] ("Judges should maintain the dignity of judicial office at all times, and avoid both impropriety and the *appearance of impropriety* in their professional and personal lives.") (emphasis added); *Id.* at R. 1.2 cmt. [3] ("Conduct that compromises or *appears to compromise the independence, integrity, and impartiality of a judge* undermines public confidence in the judiciary. . . . (emphasis added)).

15. Sup. Ct. of Ohio, Bd. of Prof'l Conduct Advisory Op. 15-001, 2015 WL 4875137, at *1 (2015).

16. *Id.* at *5.

Board further concluded that "[a] judge who takes the position that he or she will discontinue performing all marriages in order to avoid marrying same-sex couples based on his or her personal, moral, or religious beliefs may be interpreted as manifesting an improper bias or prejudice toward a particular class."[17] Thus, Ohio judges may not decline to perform all marriages to avoid marrying same-sex couples on personal, moral, or religious grounds.[18] Other authorities have disagreed on this final point, however, and have held that judges may decline to perform all marriages without manifesting bias or prejudice toward same-sex couples.[19]

The Arizona Supreme Court Judicial Ethics Advisory Committee concluded that judges may not (1) distinguish between same-sex and opposite-sex couples when deciding whether to perform marriage ceremonies; (2) decline to perform same-sex marriage ceremonies even if the judge refers would-be spouses to other courts or individuals; (3) decline to perform same-sex marriages if they perform other marriages in court facilities; or (4) decline to perform same-sex marriages even if they conduct all opposite-sex weddings outside of court facilities.[20] These principles hold true even if a judge's decision not to conduct same-sex marriages reflects the judge's sincerely-held religious beliefs.[21]

Because performing marriages is a discretionary function, an Arizona judge may choose to perform no marriages.[22] An Arizona judge may also choose to perform marriages exclusively for family and friends without violating judicial conduct rules because the judge's practice is unrelated to the celebrants' sexual orientation.[23] If judges opt to perform marriages only for friends and relatives, however, they cannot ethically refuse to perform same-sex marriages for friends and relatives.[24] To do so would violate Arizona Rule of Judicial Conduct 2.3(B), which prohibits judges who are performing judicial duties from manifesting bias or prejudice based on sexual orientation.[25]

The Nebraska Judicial Ethics Committee reached essentially the same conclusion. In Opinion 15-1, the Nebraska Committee held that judges may not refuse to perform same-sex marriages notwithstanding their personal

---

17. *Id.*

18. *Id.* at *1, *5.

19. *See, e.g.*, Wis. Sup. Ct., Judicial Conduct Advisory Comm. Op. 15-1, 2015 WL 5928528, at *1 (2015) (stating that judicial officers may not decline to officiate at same-sex weddings because of their religious or personal beliefs, but that judicial officers may decline to perform marriages at all, regardless of whether the parties seeking to be married are of the same or opposite genders, because officiating at weddings is a discretionary duty).

20. Ariz. Sup. Ct., Judicial Ethics Advisory Comm. Op. 15-01, 2015 WL 1530659, at *1 (2015).

21. *Id.*

22. *Id.*

23. *Id.* at *2.

24. *Id.* (citing Rule 2.3(B)).

25. *Id.*

or sincerely-held religious beliefs that marriage is limited to the union of one man and one woman.[26] Nor may a judge refuse to perform a same-sex wedding if he or she refers the couple to a judge who is willing to perform same-sex marriages because the refusal to perform the ceremony manifests bias or prejudice based on the couple's sexual orientation notwithstanding the referral.[27] A judge may choose to avoid such personal or religious conflicts by refusing to perform marriages altogether.[28] Judges may also choose to perform marriages exclusively for close friends and relatives, but if they do so, they may not refuse to perform same-sex marriages for close friends and relatives.[29]

Analysis

The public is entitled to expect that judges will perform their activities and duties fairly, impartially, and free from bias and prejudice.[30] Further, while actual impartiality is necessary, it is not sufficient; the public must also *perceive* judges to be impartial.[31]

If state law authorizes or obligates a judge to perform marriages, a judge's refusal to perform same-sex marriages while agreeing to perform marriages for opposite-sex couples is improper under Rules 1.1, 2.2, 2.3(A), and 2.3(B) Model Code. This conclusion would have been true in any state that recognized same-sex marriages before the Supreme Court decided *Obergefell v. Hodges*,[32] but it is broadly correct now. In *Obergefell*, the Supreme Court held that the Fourteenth Amendment to the U.S. Constitution prohibits states from refusing to license marriages between individuals of the same sex. As the Court explained, the U.S. Constitution "does not permit the State to bar same-sex couples from marriage on the same terms as accorded to couples of the opposite sex."[33] The Court further determined that "there is no

---

26. Neb. Judicial Ethics Comm. Op. 15-1, at 2 (2015), *available at* https://supremecourt.nebraska.gov/sites/default/ files/ethics-opinions/Judicial/15-1_0.pdf.

27. *Id.*

28. *Id.*

29. *Id.*

30. *See generally* Liteky v. United States, 510 U.S. 540, 558 (1994) (Kennedy, J., concurring) (noting that judicial impartiality in both fact and appearance is "one of the very objects of law"); Alexander v. Primerica Holdings, 10 F.3d 155, 162 (3d Cir. 1993) (noting the importance of "'the public's confidence in the judiciary, which may be irreparably harmed if a case is allowed to proceed before a judge who appears to be tainted'") (citations omitted); United States v. CBS, 497 F.2d 107, 109 (5th Cir. 1974) (observing that "the protection of the integrity and dignity of the judicial process from any hint or appearance of bias is the palladium of our judicial system").

31. *See* Caperton v. A.T. Massey Coal Co., 556 U.S. 868, 888–89 (2009).

32. 135 S. Ct. 2584 (2015).

33. *Id.* at 2607; *see also id.* at 2604–2605 (stating that "the right to marry is a fundamental right inherent in the liberty of the person, and under the Due Process and Equal Protection Clauses of the Fourteenth Amendment couples of the same-sex may not be deprived of that right and that liberty").

lawful basis for a State to refuse to recognize a lawful same-sex marriage performed in another State on the ground of its same-sex character."[34]

Model Rule 1.1 obligates judges to comply with the law. *Obergefell* makes clear that the U.S. Constitution prohibits state officials from engaging in discrimination and bias toward gays and lesbians in decisions related to same-sex marriage; in short, the decision establishes law with which judges must comply. Model Rule 2.2 requires judges to "uphold and apply [this] law," and further directs that judges "perform all duties of judicial office fairly and impartially."[35] As noted earlier, the term "impartiality" as used in this context means "the absence of bias or prejudice in favor of, or against, particular parties or classes of parties."[36]

Furthermore, Model Rule 2.3(A) specifically requires judges to perform their duties free from bias and prejudice. Model Rule 2.3(B) prohibits a judge who is performing judicial duties from manifesting bias or prejudice based on sex, gender, sexual orientation, or marital status. Indeed, we are aware of no state judicial ethics opinion concluding that similar judicial code provisions permit judges who perform marriage ceremonies for opposite sex couples to refuse to perform marriage ceremonies for same-sex couples.

A judge may choose to perform no marriages, or to perform marriages exclusively for family and friends. If judges opt to perform marriages only for friends and relatives, however, they cannot refuse to perform same-sex marriages for friends and relatives. Again, to refuse to perform same-sex marriages for friends and relatives while performing marriages of opposite-sex friends and relatives would violate Model Rules 2.2, 2.3(A), and 2.3(B). The fact that the judge's conduct affects a smaller group of people—that is, friends and family versus the public at large—does not change the judge's ethical obligations.

34. *Id.* at 2607–2608. We recognize that a judge's refusal to perform a same-sex marriage may be based on the judge's sincerely-held beliefs regarding the concept of marriage. As the Supreme Court noted in *Obergefell*, "[m]any who deem same-sex marriage to be wrong reach that conclusion based on decent and honorable religious or philosophical principles, and neither they nor their beliefs are disparaged here." *Id.* at 2602. We also recognize, as the Supreme Court observed in *Masterpiece Cakeshop, Ltd. v. Colorado Civil Rights Comm'n*, 138 S. Ct. 1719 (2018), that the First Amendment ensures that people receive proper protection as they seek to live according to the principles of their religious faith. *Id.* at 1727. *Masterpiece Cakeshop* also underscored the fundamental importance of impartiality on the part of all officials vested by the state with adjudicative authority. *Id.* at 1721 (noting that biased comments and differential treatment on the part of a state agency "cast doubt on the fairness and impartiality of the Commission's adjudication"). But as noted earlier and reiterated here, this opinion addresses the obligations of judicial officers under the Model Code.

35. MODEL CODE R. 2.2, *supra* note 1.

36. *Id.* at Terminology.

Our conclusions are reinforced by the Oregon Supreme Court's decision in *In re Day*.[37] The respondent in that case, Judge Vance Day, was appointed to the Oregon trial court bench in 2011 and re-elected in 2012. He made himself available to solemnize marriages upon becoming a judge in 2011.

After an Oregon federal judge invalidated Oregon's constitutional ban on same-sex marriage in 2014, Day's judicial assistant and clerk asked him about possibly performing weddings going forward given Day's religious belief that marriage should be confined to a man and a woman.[38] Judge Day "instructed [his clerk and judicial assistant] that, when his chambers received any marriage request, [they] should obtain" personal gender information available in the Oregon Judicial Information Network (OJIN)—which they had never done before—to try to determine whether the request involved a same-sex couple.[39] If it did, they were to inform the couple that the judge was not available on the desired date or otherwise notify him, so that he could decide how to proceed.[40] If the request came from an opposite-sex couple, however, his judicial assistant and clerk were to schedule the wedding.[41] On one occasion Day's judicial assistant checked OJIN and determined that the requesters might be a same-sex couple. Day had a genuine scheduling conflict, so the judicial assistant truthfully told the couple that the judge was unavailable. Day stopped performing marriages soon thereafter.

The Oregon Commission on Judicial Fitness and Disability charged Day with violating Rule 3.3(B) of the Oregon Code of Judicial Conduct, which provides: "A judge shall not, in the performance of judicial duties, by words or conduct, manifest bias or prejudice . . . against parties, witnesses, lawyers, or others based on attributes including but not limited to, sex, gender identity, race, national origin, ethnicity, religion, sexual orientation, marital status, disability, age, socioeconomic status, or political affiliation and shall not permit court staff, court officials, or others subject to the judge's direction and control to do so."[42] The *In re Day* court easily concluded that the act of solemnizing marriages, once a judge has chosen to do so, constitutes a judicial duty

37. 413 P.3d 907 (Or. 2018), *cert. denied*, 139 S. Ct. 324 (2018); *see also In re* Neely, 390 P.3d 728, 753 (Wyo. 2017) ("Judge Neely must perform her judicial functions, including performing marriages, with impartiality. She must either commit to performing marriages regardless of the couple's sexual orientation, or cease performing all marriage ceremonies. This does not mean . . . that no judge can now turn down any request to perform a marriage. What it means is that no judge can turn down a request to perform a marriage for reasons that undermine the integrity of the judiciary by demonstrating a lack of independence and impartiality."), *cert. denied*, 138 S. Ct. 639 (2018).

38. *In re Day*, 413 P.3d at 921, 949.

39. *Id.* at 921–22, 949.

40. *Id.* at 922, 949.

41. *Id.*

42. *Id.* at 950 (quoting Oregon Code of Judicial Conduct R. 3.3(B) (2013)).

under Oregon Rule 3.3(B).[43] That led the court to the question of whether Day had manifested bias or prejudice against same-sex couples. Day argued that he had not done so because he never actually refused to marry any same-sex couple as a result of his short-lived screening process.[44] According to Day, Oregon Rule 3.3(B) could not authorize punishment "for discrimination that did not occur against unknown parties."[45]

The *In re Day* court reasoned that to "manifest" bias or prejudice, "the act in question must be undertaken such that it is obvious to others" or "must be capable of perception."[46] To be sure, Day's screening process was not displayed or made known in a manner that was capable of perception by anyone outside his chambers. But that factor did not resolve the issue because his "chosen course of action—motivated by his intention to marry only opposite-sex couples—was evident to his staff."[47] His instructions to his staff in implementing his plan to avoid marrying same-sex couples "indisputably communicated to his staff his intention to treat same-sex couples who requested a marriage officiant differently from opposite-sex couples."[48] Furthermore, he instructed his staff to implement "that differential treatment, which included providing inaccurate information to same-sex couples. Those actions 'manifest[ed]' prejudice in the performance of judicial duties, within the meaning of [Oregon] Rule 3.3(B)."[49]

Next, Day contended that because no same-sex couple was denied the opportunity to marry by virtue of his screening process, he did not discriminate or manifest prejudice "against" any such couple as required for a violation of Oregon Rule 3.3(B).[50] While it was true that he never actually refused to marry a same-sex couple, the *In re Day* court nevertheless concluded that Day's conduct manifested prejudice against others within the meaning of the rule.

> We reiterate that, in prohibiting a judge from manifesting prejudice against court participants or others based on personal attributes, [Oregon] Rule 3.3(B) seeks to prevent judicial actions that impair the fairness of a proceeding or prompt an unfavorable view of the judiciary Most commonly, problematic conduct likely would involve a judge's overt and prejudicial treatment of a particular person involved in a proceeding before the court—such as a litigant, juror, witness, or lawyer. . . . However, a judge could manifest prejudice against others based on personal attributes in a more general way that still

43. *Id.*
44. *Id.* at 951.
45. *Id.*
46. *Id.*
47. *Id.* at 952.
48. *Id.*
49. *Id.*
50. *Id.*

> could affect perceptions of fairness or prompt an unfavorable view of the judiciary. . . . Given the fundamental objective of [Oregon] Rule 3.3(B)—ensuring the public's trust in an impartial and fair judiciary—we conclude that that rule is not limited to a manifestation of prejudice against an identified, particular person. Rather, it may encompass an expression of bias against an identifiable group, based on personal characteristics, in the performance of judicial duties.[51]

Day crafted a screening process that was intended to ensure that he married only opposite- sex couples. The screening process demonstrated to his staff that, in exercising his judicial duty to solemnize marriages, he would not treat all couples fairly. That conduct, in turn, manifested prejudice against same-sex couples based on their sexual orientation in violation of Oregon Rule 3.3(B).[52]

Conclusion

A judge for whom performing marriages is either a mandatory part of his or her official duties or an optional exercise of judicial authority violates the Model Code of Judicial Conduct by refusing to perform marriages for same-sex couples while agreeing to perform marriages of opposite-sex couples. In a jurisdiction where a judge is not obligated to perform marriages, the judge may decline to perform all marriages for members of the public. A judge who chooses not to perform any marriages for the public may still perform marriages for family and friends, so long as the judge does not discriminate between same-sex and opposite-sex couples when performing marriages for family and friends.

---

51. *Id.* at 952–53 (citations omitted).

52. *Id.* at 953. Although the Court found that Day violated Rule 3.3(B), it did not consider this violation in calculating the three-year suspension it imposed, explaining that "[i]n light of the other, notably serious misconduct that the commission has proved by clear and convincing evidence, we conclude that—whether respondent's constitutional challenges are meritorious or not—our ultimate conclusion to impose a lengthy, three-year suspension remains the same." *Id.* at 954.

AMERICAN BAR ASSOCIATION
STANDING COMMITTEE ON ETHICS AND PROFESSIONAL RESPONSIBILITY

Formal Opinion 486 **May 9, 2019**

Obligations of Prosecutors in Negotiating Plea Bargains for Misdemeanor Offenses

Model Rules 1.1, 1.3, 3.8(a), (b), and (c), 4.1, 4.3, 5.1, 5.3, and 8.4(a), (c) and (d) impose obligations on prosecutors when entering into plea bargains with persons accused of misdemeanors. These obligations include the duty to ensure that each charge incident to a plea has an adequate foundation in fact and law, to ensure that the accused is informed of the right to counsel and the procedure for securing counsel, to avoid plea negotiations that jeopardize the accused's ability to secure counsel, and, irrespective of whether an unrepresented accused has invoked the right to counsel, to avoid offering pleas on terms that knowingly misrepresent the consequences of acceptance or otherwise pressure or improperly induce acceptance on the part of the accused.[1]

I. Introduction

This opinion addresses a prosecutor's obligations under Model Rules 1.1, 1.3, 3.8(a), (b), and (c), 4.1, 4.3, 5.1, 5.3, and 8.4(a), (c), and (d) when negotiating with an unrepresented individual who is or may be entitled to counsel at the time the prosecutor initiates the plea bargaining process for a misdemeanor charge. The opinion also addresses a prosecutor's duties when plea bargaining with an unrepresented accused on a misdemeanor charge irrespective of whether the accused has invoked the right to counsel. These ethical obligations exist independently of any constitutional or statutory obligations prosecutors may have to an accused.

Part I emphasizes the unique role that prosecutors play in the administration of justice and highlights (i) the expansion of misdemeanor criminal enforcement and (ii) the displacement of trial by plea bargaining. Part II identifies evidence of practices that have developed in some jurisdictions to

---

1. This opinion is based on the ABA Model Rules of Professional Conduct as amended by the ABA House of Delegates through August 2018. The laws, court rules, regulations, rules of professional conduct and opinions promulgated in individual jurisdictions are controlling.

manage misdemeanor pleas. Part III turns to Model Rule 3.8, addressing first the need for guidance and then examining the text and scope of Rules 3.8(a)-(c) and related rules as they apply to misdemeanor plea bargaining. Part IV identifies the specific obligations of a prosecutor under Rules 3.8(b) and (c) with respect to the accused's right to counsel. Part V interprets Rules 4.1, 4.3, and 8.4 as they apply to negotiation and entry of plea bargains.

A. The Special Role of Prosecutors

The professional integrity of prosecutors is essential to the administration of criminal justice.[2] Their special role is reflected in a distinctive standard of professional responsibility. Under the Model Rules, a prosecutor "has the responsibility of a minister of justice and not simply that of an advocate."[3] Canon 5 of the 1908 American Bar Association Canons of Professional Ethics stated that "[t]he primary duty of a lawyer engaged in public prosecution is not to convict, but to see that justice is done."[4] The ABA Model Code of Professional Responsibility also emphasized a categorical difference between the responsibility of a public prosecutor and "that of the usual advocate."[5] A prosecutor's duty

> is to seek justice, not merely to convict. This special duty exists because: (1) the prosecutor represents the sovereign and therefore should use restraint in the discretionary exercise of governmental powers, such as in the selection of cases to prosecute; (2) during trial the prosecutor is not only an advocate but he may also make deci-

---

2. *See* John Jay Douglass, National College of District Attorneys, Ethical Issues In Prosecution 36 (1988) ("The first, best, and most effective shield against injustice for an individual accused, or society in general, must be found not in the persons of defense counsel, trial judge, or appellate jurist, but in the integrity of the prosecutor.") (quoting former prosecutor Carol Corrigan, Commentary, *Prosecutorial Ethics*, 13 HASTINGS CONST. L.Q. 537, 537 (1986)).

3. Model Rules of Prof'l Conduct R. 3.8 cmt. [1]. *See also* ABA Comm. on Ethics & Prof'l Responsibility, Formal Op. 454 at 3 n.10 (2009) (a prosecutor's interest "in a criminal prosecution is not that it shall win a case, but that justice shall be done") (quoting Berger v. United States, 295 U.S. 78, 88 (1935)); ABA Comm. on Ethics & Prof'l Responsibility, Formal Op. 467 at 1 (2014) (same).

4. Specific references to the American prosecutor as a minister of justice date to the nineteenth century. *See, e.g.*, People v. Davis, 18 N.W. 362, 363 (Mich. 1884) (the prosecutor is a "sworn minister of justice, whose duty it was, while endeavoring to bring the guilty to punishment, to take care that the innocent should be protected"); Hurd v. People, 25 Mich. 405, 416 (1872) ("The prosecuting officer represents the public interest, which can never be promoted by the conviction of the innocent. His object like that of the court, should be simply justice; and he has no right to sacrifice this to any pride of professional success."), *superseded on other grounds by statute*, 1986 Mich. Pub. Acts 114, *as stated in* People v. Koonce, 648 N.W.2d 153, 155-56 (Mich. 2002).

5. Model Code of Prof'l Responsibility EC 7-13 (1980).

> sions normally made by an individual client, and those affecting the public interest should be fair to all; and (3) in our system of criminal justice the accused is to be given the benefit of all reasonable doubts.[6]

As this Committee has emphasized in prior opinions, there are "many excellent prosecutors who scrupulously follow or exceed the mandates of the Rules of Professional Conduct."[7] This opinion focuses on the distinctive challenges and obligations of prosecutors when negotiating pleas in misdemeanor cases.

B. Background on Misdemeanor Enforcement

Misdemeanors make up approximately 80 percent of state criminal dockets.[8] The number of misdemeanor prosecutions is estimated to have doubled since 1972.[9] The expansion has had a "concentrated impact on communities of color."[10] Most misdemeanor arrests result in charges – declination rates

---

6. *Id.*

7. ABA Comm. on Ethics & Prof'l Responsibility, Formal Op. 14-467 at 6 (2014) (on the supervisory and managerial responsibilities of prosecutors); *id.* at 1 ("We believe that most prosecutors know and follow the rules of professional conduct. Indeed, the laudable efforts of such prosecutors have provided good examples" for this and other opinions of the Committee.).

8. *See* Ben Kempinen, *The Ethics of Prosecutor Contact with the Unrepresented Defendant*, 19 Geo. J. Legal Ethics 1147, 1148 n.3 (2006) (citing Wisconsin data showing that in 2002, 79 percent of criminal cases filed in the state were for "criminal traffic or misdemeanor" offenses); Robert C. LaFountain et al., Examining the Work of State Courts: An Analysis of 2008 State Court Caseloads 47 (2010) (listing data from study of 11 state dockets). A more recent study estimates that "there are three times as many misdemeanor cases as felony cases filed nationally each year." Megan Stevenson & Sandra Mayson, *The Scale of Misdemeanor Justice*, 98 B.U. L. Rev. 731, 764 (2017).

Although there is variation in the exact classification of low-level offenses across state and federal jurisdictions, in this opinion we use the term "misdemeanor" in its generic sense to refer to any criminal offense less serious than a felony according to the law of the relevant jurisdiction.

9. *See* Robert C. Boruchowitz et al., Minor Crimes, Massive Waste: The Terrible Toll of America's Broken Misdemeanor Courts 11 (2009) ("Most people who go to court in the United States go to misdemeanor courts," describing growth of misdemeanor prosecutions since 1972); Alexandra Natapoff, *Misdemeanors*, *in* 1 Reforming Criminal Justice 71 (Erik Luna, ed. 2017) ("Most criminal convictions in this country are misdemeanors, and most Americans experience criminal justice through the petty offense process."). *But see* Stevenson & Mayson, *supra* note 8, at 747, 764 (estimating a seventeen percent decline in state misdemeanor filings over the last decade while reporting that the total number of misdemeanor cases remains substantial: 13.2 million in 2016).

10. *See* Issa Kohler-Hausmann, Misdemeanorland: Criminal Courts and Social Control in an Age of Broken Windows Policing 51 & fig.1.10 (2018) (an empirical study of New York City courts, describing data showing that "the dramatic expansion of misdemeanor arrests has been hyperconcentrated on . . . black, and . . . Latino individuals"); Stevenson & Mayson, *supra* note 8, at 737 (finding a "profound . . . remarkably constant" racial disparity in the misdemeanor arrest rate over the last thirty-seven years); Civil Rights Div., U.S. Dep't of Justice, Investigation of the Baltimore City Police Department 55-56 (2016) (reporting data showing that while African Americans make up 63 percent of

are low in many states, sometimes as low as 3 or 4 percent.[11] And "the vast majority of defendants plead guilty" at their initial appearance.[12] The result is a significant increase in the pre-trial dockets of state and local courts, and daunting legal and administrative burdens for both judges and prosecutors.[13] Collateral consequences for misdemeanor convictions have also expanded.[14] A misdemeanor conviction can lead to denial of employment, expulsion from school, deportation, denial of a professional license, and loss of eligibility for a wide range of public services including food assistance, public housing, health care, and federal student loans.[15]

To realize the legitimate law enforcement objectives of plea bargaining, a practice that has become "an essential component of the administration of

---

the population of Baltimore, for "misdemeanor street offense[s], unconnected to a more serious charge" between 2010 and 2015, they comprised 91 percent of trespassing charges, 91 percent of failure to obey charges, 88 percent of hindering charges, 84 percent of disorderly conduct charges, and 90 percent of people charged with resisting arrest where no other charge supported the resisting charge); Sean Webby, *Policing in San Jose: Strict Enforcement of "Conduct Crimes," Are Latinos Targeted?*, THE MERCURY NEWS (Apr. 4, 2009), https://www.mercurynews.com/2009/04/04/policing-in-san-jose-strict-enforcement-of- conduct-crimes-are-latinos-targeted/ (reporting that 70 percent of arrests for disturbing the peace, 57 percent of charges for resisting arrest, and 57 percent of arrests for public drunkenness were of Latinos, even though this group comprises less than a third of San Jose residents).

11. *See* Natapoff, *supra* note 9, at 78.

12. *Id.; see also* BORUCHOWITZ ET AL., *supra* note 9, at 8 ("In New York City in 2000, almost 70 percent of misdemeanor cases were disposed of at the first appearance—most through a guilty plea."); *Protecting the Constitutional Right to Counsel for Indigents Charged with Misdemeanors: Hearing Before the S. Comm. on the Judiciary*, 114th Cong. (2015) [hereinafter *Hearing*] (statement of Prof. Erica J. Hashimoto at 3), https://www.judiciary.senate.gov/imo/media/doc/05-13-15%20Hashimoto%20Testimony.pdf.

13. Hearing times in some jurisdictions run as short as three minutes. *See* ALISA SMITH ET AL., NAT'L ASS'N OF CRIMINAL DEF. LAWYERS, RUSH YO JUDGMENT: HOW SOUTH CAROLINA'S SUMMARY COURTS FAIL TO PROTECT CONSTITUTIONAL RIGHTS 19 (2017) (reporting that in South Carolina courts the hearings for misdemeanors and other minor crimes average 3.29 minutes and just two minutes long if a few outlier cases are excluded); ALISA SMITH & SEAN MADDAN, NAT'L ASS'N OF CRIMINAL DEF. LAWYERS, THREE-MINUTE JUSTICE: HASTE AND WASTE IN FLORIDA'S MISDEMEANOR COURTS 14-15 (2011); BORUCHOWITZ ET AL., *supra* note 9, at 32

14. *See National Inventory of the Collateral Consequences of Conviction*, JUSTICE CENTER, COUNCIL OF STATE GOVERNMENTS; JAMES B. JACOBS, THE ETERNAL CRIMINAL RECORD 225-300 (2015); Michael Pinard, *Collateral Consequences of Criminal Convictions: Confronting Issues of Race and Dignity*, 85 N.Y.U. L. REV. 457, 489-94 (2010); BORUCHOWITZ ET AL., *supra* note 9, at 12-13 (listing collateral consequences); People v. Suazo, 118 N.E.3d 168, 178 (N.Y. 2018) (requiring a jury trial where a misdemeanor conviction carries the potential penalty of deportation; "even if deportation is technically collateral, it is undoubtedly a severe statutory penalty that flows from the federal government as the result of a state criminal conviction"). A misdemeanor conviction can also result in sentence enhancements should the person reoffend. *See* Nichols v. United States, 511 U.S. 738, 746-48 (1994) (upholding use of misdemeanor DUI conviction to add 25 months to a subsequent felony drug sentence).

15. *See* sources gathered *supra* note 14.

justice,"[16] there must be "fairness in securing agreement between an accused and a prosecutor."[17] This is particularly so in the misdemeanor setting where, as the Supreme Court has warned, "the volume of . . . cases, far greater in number than felony prosecutions, may create an obsession for speedy dispositions, regardless of the fairness of the result."[18] Observance of the special obligations of prosecutors under the Rules of Professional Conduct is critical to achieving fair guilty pleas.

II. Evidence of Plea Bargaining Practices in Misdemeanor Cases

Notwithstanding the commitment of most prosecutors to high professional standards, there is evidence that in misdemeanor cases where the accused is or may be legally entitled to counsel, methods of negotiating plea bargains have been used in some jurisdictions that are inconsistent with the duties set forth in the Rules of Professional Conduct. As the report of a comprehensive five-year study chaired by a distinguished group of former prosecutors and judges summarized, "[w]hether because of a desire to move cases through the court system, a desire to keep indigent defense costs down, or ignorance, pervasive and serious problems exist in misdemeanor courts across the country because counsel is oftentimes either not provided, or provided late, to those who are lawfully eligible to be represented."[19] Methods of negotiating pleas documented in this report and other studies include:

(i) requiring or encouraging plea negotiation with a prosecutor before the right to counsel has been raised;[20]

---

16. Santobello v. New York, 404 U.S. 257, 260 (1971); *see also id.* at 261 (the plea bargain "leads to prompt and largely final disposition of most criminal cases[,] . . . and, by shortening the time between charge and disposition, it enhances whatever may be the rehabilitative prospects of the guilty"). Counting both misdemeanors and felonies, "[n]inety-seven percent of federal convictions and ninety-four percent of state convictions are the result of guilty pleas." Missouri v. Frye, 566 U.S. 134, 143 (2012); *see also* Lafler v. Cooper, 566 U.S. 156, 170 (2012) ("[C]riminal justice today is for the most part a system of pleas, not a system of trials.").

17. *Santobello*, 404 U.S. at 261.

18. Argersinger v. Hamlin, 407 U.S. 25, 34 (1972) (citation omitted).

19. NAT'L RIGHT TO COUNSEL COMM., CONSTITUTION PROJECT, JUSTICE DENIED: AMERICA'S CONTINUING NEGLECT OF OUR CONSTITUTIONAL RIGHT TO COUNSEL 85 (2009) [hereinafter JUSTICE DENIED]. The Committee added that "when counsel is not provided, all too often, the defendant's waiver of legal representation is inadequate under Supreme Court precedents. As a result, there is a shocking disconnect between the system of justice envisioned by the Supreme Court's right-to-counsel decisions and what actually occurs in many of this nation's courts." *Id.* (citation omitted). The Committee's co-chairs included a former director of the Federal Bureau of Investigations, a former state attorney general, a former district attorney and chair of the National District Attorney's Association, two former United States Attorneys, and a former state district and state supreme court judge.

20. *See* Thomas B. Harvey et al., *Right to Counsel in Misdemeanor Prosecutions After Alabama v. Shelton*, 29 CRIM. JUST. POL'Y REV. 688, 699 (2018) (reporting from court observations

(ii) using delay or the prospect of a harsher sentence to dissuade the accused from invoking the right to counsel;[21]

(iii) gathering arrestees into court *en masse* and instructing them, prior to any advice regarding the right to counsel or other rights, that they must tell the clerk of the court how they intend to plead;[22]

(iv) using forms to obtain waivers of the right to counsel and other rights either as a condition of negotiating a plea or following a

---

in St. Louis, Missouri "that mention of a defendant's right to counsel occurred after the defendant, prosecutor, and judge have discussed sentencing and have decided that the defendant will enter a formal guilty plea. . . . [P]roceedings usually lasted only a few minutes."); STEPHEN F. HANLON ET AL., SECTION ON CIVIL RIGHTS AND SOCIAL JUSTICE, AMERICAN BAR ASS'N, DENIAL OF THE RIGHT TO COUNSEL IN MISDEMEANOR CASES: COURT WATCHING IN NASHVILLE, TENNESSEE 8-9 (2017); SIXTH AMENDMENT CTR., ACTUAL DENIAL OF COUNSEL IN MISDEMEANOR COURTS 6 (2015) [hereinafter ACTUAL DENIAL]; SIXTH AMENDMENT CTR., THE CRUCIBLE OF ADVERSARIAL TESTING: ACCESS TO COUNSEL IN DELAWARE'S CRIMINAL COURTS 29-33 (2014); JUSTICE DENIED, *supra* note 19, at 89 ("In several courts, the Committee's investigators found that defendants were encouraged to negotiate with prosecutors without the assistance of counsel, and in one court they were required to do so."); *see also* BORUCHOWITZ ET AL., *supra* note 9, at 9, 16-17.

This opinion addresses only the ethical obligations of prosecutors, including obligations under Rules 5.1, 5.3, and 8.4(a) toward lawyers and non-lawyers directed or supervised by the prosecutor. The opinion does not address the obligations of courts and court staff. While the Committee recognizes that courts and court staff are involved in some of the practices discussed in this opinion, prosecutors have independent and specific obligations in these circumstances, as discussed in this opinion.

21. *See* STANDING COMMITTEE ON LEGAL AID AND INDIGENT DEFENDANTS, AM. BAR ASS'N, *GIDEON'S* BROKEN PROMISE: AMERICA'S CONTINUING QUEST FOR EQUAL JUSTICE 25 (2004) [hereinafter *GIDEON'S* BROKEN PROMISE] (describing Rhode Island judge who "told the defendant that by requesting a lawyer, the defendant likely would receive three years of jail time instead" of six months, and California judges who told defendants "If you plead guilty today, you'll go home. If you want an attorney, you'll stay in jail for two more days" and noting that the judicial encouragement of waivers of fundamental rights is "especially acute" with regard to juvenile defendants); *see also* JUSTICE DENIED, *supra* note 19, at 85-86, 87 (noting that in Mississippi "[m]onths may pass before counsel is appointed, causing many people charged with non-violent offenses to serve more time in pretrial custody than warranted for the offenses themselves") (citations omitted); *see also id.* at 85-86, 89; BORUCHOWITZ ET AL., *supra* note 9, at 18-19.

22. *See* SMITH ET AL., *supra* note 13, at 8 (reporting from court observation in Richland County that defendants in a "packed courtroom" were told in an address that took less than two minutes that "everyone needed to form a line and come to the front of the room to tell the clerk how they intended to handle their case today. . . . No mention was made of the right to counsel. . . . Over the next hour or so, the defendants formed a line and the clerk worked through the [cases]. This process, though technically in open court, was a secret to observers who were present—whatever conversations the clerk had with those facing charges were not on the record and were inaudible to those in the seating area.").

negotiation absent proper confirmation that the defendant understands the forms and the rights being waived;[23]

(v) permitting police officers involved in the investigation of a crime or arrest to act as prosecutors and negotiate pleas;[24]

(vi) advising defendants of the right to counsel but failing to provide any procedure for asserting or validly waiving that right before requiring plea negotiation with a prosecutor;[25] and

---

23. *See* Harvey et al., *supra* note 20, at 700 (describing process of signing waivers after judge accepted uncounseled guilty plea); BORUCHOWITZ ET AL, *supra* note 9, at 16 (describing forms presented with instructions simply to sign); *GIDEON'S* BROKEN PROMISE, *supra* note 21, at 25 (reporting witness testimony that "in many Georgia courts, the clerk provides defendants with a complicated form that, if signed, serves as a waiver of counsel and guilty plea. Defendants are told that their case will not be called unless they sign the form.").

Forms are sometimes used after displaying a video describing the right to counsel and other important rights. *See* ACTUAL DENIAL, *supra* note 20, at 15-16 n.17 (describing use of video recordings to advise defendants of rights); SMITH & MADDAN, *supra* note 13, at 15, 23 tbl.8 (describing use of video advisements and written forms). However, in some jurisdictions no effort is made to ensure that all the defendants gathered in the screening area have seen the full video or understand its contents (e.g., a video may begin before some defendants arrive or end after others have been called to appear or have to step out of court). *See* ACTUAL DENIAL, *supra* note 20, at 15- 16 n.17; SMITH ET AL., *supra* note 13, at 8.

24. SMITH ET AL, *supra* note 13, at 19 (In South Carolina's minor crimes courts, police officers "were the majority of prosecutors in all counties, and nearly the sole prosecutor of defendants in [four]. . . . [T]hey negotiated directly with the defendants who they accused of violating the law. . . . Defendants were almost three times more likely to enter a plea of guilty or no contest when confronted by a police-officer-prosecutor. . . ."). *See also* State ex rel McLeod v. Seaborn, 244 S.E.2d 317, 319 (S.C. 1978) (holding that practice of arresting officers acting as prosecutors in certain misdemeanor cases does not constitute unauthorized practice of law); State v. Messervy, 187 S.E.2d 524, 525 (S.C. 1972) (noting that this practice in the state's magistrates courts has "been followed under a ruling of the attorney general since 1958"). For evidence of the practice in another jurisdiction, see State v. Aberizk, 345 A.2d 407 (N.H. 1975) (dismissing challenge of misdemeanor defendant to arresting officer serving as both prosecutor and witness). *Cf.* N.J. Supreme Court Advisory Comm. on Prof'l Ethics, Op. 672 *Conflict of Interest: Municipal Police Officer Serving as Municipal Prosecutor*, (1993), 1993 WL 137686, at *1 ("[T]he specter of an appearance of impropriety so permeates this situation as to preclude the dual service."); Ohio Bd. of Comm'rs on Grievances and Discipline, Advisory Op. No. 89-23 (1989), 1989 WL 535028, at *1-2 (advising that an impermissible conflict of interest arises from county prosecutor serving simultaneously as city police officer within same county if "one position is a check on, or subordinate to the other," if the officer acting as a prosecutor is "aware of the possibility of being called as a witness in the same case," or if there would otherwise be an "appearance of impropriety").

25. *See* *GIDEON'S* BROKEN PROMISE, *supra* note 21, at 24-25 (describing observation of Georgia court "mass arraignment of defendants charged with jailable misdemeanors during which the judge informed defendants of their rights and then left the bench. Afterwards, three prosecutors told defendants to line up and follow them one by one into a private room. When the judge reentered the courtroom, each defendant approached with the prosecutor, who informed the judge that the defendant intended to waive counsel and plead guilty to the charges.") (citations omitted).

(vii) failing to inform indigent defendants of the procedure for requesting a waiver of court application fees associated with assignment of a state subsidized defense lawyer.[26]

A prosecutor's use or endorsement of practices such as these would violate the Model Rules of Professional Conduct, as discussed in Parts III through V below.

III. The Prosecutor's Responsibilities Under Model Rule 3.8 and Related Rules

A. The Need for Guidance

Model Rules 3.8(a), (b), and (c) provide the foundation for analysis. Yet more than thirty years after their adoption by the American Bar Association there is still relatively little interpretive authority.[27] We address each of these

26. *See* Actual Denial, *supra* note 20, at 6 (noting that a county in Michigan charges $240 for all misdemeanor representation, a practice that contributes to 95% of defendants waiving counsel and 50% "pleading guilty at first appearance"); Boruchowitz et al., *supra* note 9, at 19 (describing pressure to waive right to counsel arising from the amount of application fees in New Jersey, South Carolina, and Washington).

27. Rule 3.8(d) is discussed in detail in an earlier opinion of this Committee, *see* ABA Comm. on Ethics & Prof'l Responsibility, Formal Op. 454 (2009). However, as the Illinois State Bar Association has summarized, "[t]here is a dearth of legal opinions, not only in Illinois but in other states, on prosecutors seeking to obtain a waiver of an important pretrial right from a pro se defendant." Ill. State Bar Ass'n, Advisory Op. 14-02, 2014 WL 2434672, at *2 (2014); *see id.* at *3 (concluding nonetheless that "a prosecutor may convey a plea offer to a pro se defendant prior to a court proceeding, regardless of who initiates the contact" as long as the prosecutor does "not recommend the plea or otherwise force, threaten or coerce the person to waive any important pretrial right," and the prosecutor "clearly identif[ies] that he or she is not disinterested, clarif[ies] any misconception the person may have about the prosecutor's role and advise[s] the person about the right to secure counsel."). *See also* Pa. Bar Ass'n Comm. on Legal Ethics and Prof'l Responsibility, Formal Op. 2014-500, 2014 WL 10383870, at *7 (2014) (concluding that prosecutor may not condition guilty plea and eligibility for favorable deferred adjudication program on defendant's waiver of right to discovery because practice violates Rule 3.8(d), constitutes a "coercive practice" in violation of Rules 8.4(a) and (d) and "abdicat[es] his responsibility as a minister of justice by not according the defendant procedural justice"; explaining that "[a] *pro se* defendant would have little or no understanding of the importance of his procedural right of discovery; and even if he had some understanding, the prosecution threat of facing increased penalties, including incarceration, if he does not accept [the program] and its conditions, negates any voluntary waiver of such procedural rights"); *see also* Va. State Bar Legal Ethics Advisory Op. 1876, 2015 WL 4977834, at *4-6 (2015) (identifying duty of prosecutor who knows defendant is a noncitizen to include reference to immigration consequences in the plea or request the court to include such consequences in the plea colloquy under the state version of Rule 3.8(b), which prohibits "knowingly tak[ing] advantage of an unrepresented defendant"; prohibiting a prosecutor from offering legal advice under Rule 4.3 to an unrepresented non-citizen defendant). Wisconsin amended its rules for prosecutors in the wake of United States v. Acosta, 111 F.Supp. 2d 1082, 1092-97 (E.D. Wis. 2000), *aff'd sub nom.* United States

sections of Rule 3.8 and its relationship to other provisions of the Rules of Professional Conduct below. At the outset, however, we note that faithful interpretation of the special responsibilities of a prosecutor under the Model Rules demands sensitivity to the higher calling of the role.[28] In some respects a prosecutor's duties exceed the requirements of statutory and constitutional law.[29]

B. Model Rule 3.8(a) and the Duty to Ascertain the Existence of Probable Cause to Charge

Rule 3.8(a) prohibits the prosecution of "a charge that the prosecutor knows is not supported by probable cause." The provision avoids undue interference with the exercise of prosecutorial discretion.[30] As Comment [1] emphasizes, however, the prosecutor has a "specific obligation [] to see that the defendant is accorded procedural justice [and] that guilt is decided upon the basis of sufficient evidence."[31] Read together with the duty of competence under Rule 1.1, the duty of diligence under Rule 1.3, and the prohibition on conduct "prejudicial to the administration of justice" in Rule 8.4(d), it is axiomatic that a prosecutor must actually exercise informed discretion with respect to the selection and prosecution of each charge. Thus, a prosecutor may not negotiate pleas without first making an independent assessment of the relevant facts and law for each charge.[32] While it is common for prosecutors

---

v. Olson, 450 F.3d 655, 681-82 (7th Cir. 2006). *See* WIS. SUP. CT. R. 20:3.8 (creating, inter alia, affirmative duty to inform an unrepresented person of the prosecutor's "role and interest in the matter" and of the person's right to counsel; specifying terms upon which prosecutor may negotiate a plea bargain with an unrepresented person); *see also* Wis. Bar Ass'n, Formal Op. E-09-02, slip op. at 3-4 (2009).

28. *See In re* Swarts, 30 P.3d 1011, 1031 (Kan. 2001) ("A prosecutor is a servant of the law and a representative of the people of Kansas. When one undertakes the responsibility of prosecution we must view his or her conduct by an enhanced standard.") (internal quotation marks and citation omitted).

29. *See, e.g.*, ABA Comm. on Ethics & Prof'l Responsibility, Formal Op. 454 at 4 (2009) ("Courts as well as commentators have recognized that the ethical obligation [of a prosecutor under Rule 3.8(d)] is more demanding than the constitutional obligation."); *see also* ABA/BNA Lawyer's Manual on Prof'l Conduct, *Prosecutors* 61:601 (ABA/BNA 2019) ("Model Rule 3.8 goes beyond what constitutional guarantees require of prosecutors on the subject of pretrial responsibilities to the unrepresented accused.").

30. *See also* Model Code of Prof'l Responsibility DR 7-103(A) (1980).

31. Model Rules of Prof'l Conduct R. 3.8 cmt. [1].

32. *See* Model Rules of Prof'l Conduct R. 1.1 cmt. [5] ("Competent handling of a particular matter includes inquiry into and analysis of the factual and legal elements of the problem, and use of methods and procedures meeting the standards of competent practitioners."). *See also* Criminal Justice Standards for the Prosecution Function 3-5.6(c) (Am. Bar Ass'n 2015) ("The prosecutor should not enter into a disposition agreement before having information sufficient to assess the defendant's actual culpability."); *id.* at 3-5.6(g) ("A prosecutor should not agree to a guilty plea if the prosecutor reasonably believes that sufficient admissible evidence to support conviction beyond reasonable doubt would be lacking if the matter went to trial.").

to make a careful assessment of evidence compiled incident to a decision to offer a plea, in some jurisdictions the volume of misdemeanor cases and their relatively lower stakes may dispose a prosecutor to rely uncritically on a police report or citation and a criminal background check.[33] Unless the prosecutor has reasonable confidence in the thoroughness of the fact finding and the evenhandedness of the judgment of other law enforcement officers who prepare the supporting documents and investigation, reliance on them is likely to be misplaced and the very discretion the Rule is designed to protect may be abused.

If a prosecutor's workload is too heavy to permit the independent assessment of each charge as required by Rule 3.8(a) and the supervision of other state actors and their work product relevant to each case as required by Rules 5.1(b) and (c) and 5.3(b) and (c), the prosecutor may not be able to provide the competent representation required by Rule 1.1, nor act with the diligence required by Rule 1.3. A supervising prosecutor is responsible, under Rules 5.1(a), 5.3(a), and 8.4(a), for establishing policies, practices, and methods of monitoring prosecutors and non-lawyers that give "reasonable assurance" of compliance with prosecutors' ethical obligations, including the obligation to be diligent and perform competent work.[34] In the words of Comment [2] to

---

33. *See* State v. Young, 863 N.W.2d 249, 253 (Iowa 2015) ("Given the pressures of docket management, there is a risk that the ability of the system to function efficiently and at low cost, rather than the reliability of fact-finding, will shape judicial outcomes. . . . [T]he risk of an inaccurate verdict in uncounseled misdemeanor cases is higher than in most felony prosecutions."); *see also* Kohler-Hausmann, *supra* note 10, at 131 (noting from lengthy New York City court observations and interviews with district attorneys, judges, and public defenders that "arraignment plea offers are based largely on prosecutorial practice and policy, and only minimally on factual or legal investigation"); *id.* at 125, 133, 138 (same). Evidence that misdemeanor convictions are not always tied to factual guilt can be found in studies going back to the 1950s. *See id.* at 62. On increases in misdemeanor dockets over the last three decades, see *id.* at 110, 111 fig 3.1, 119.

34. On the prosecutor's managerial and supervisory responsibilities, see ABA Comm. on Ethics & Prof'l Responsibility, Formal Op. 467 (2014). *See also* Model Rules of Prof'l Conduct R. 3.8 cmt. [6] ("Like other lawyers, prosecutors are subject to Rules 5.1 and 5.3, which relate to responsibilities regarding lawyers and nonlawyers who work for or are associated with the lawyer's office."); N.Y. State Bar Ass'n Comm. on Prof'l Ethics Op. No. 2, 2018 WL 3019993, at *2 (discussing prosecutor's post-conviction duties regarding potential wrongful conviction, "[t]he Rules apply not only to individual prosecutors but also to their offices."); *id.* at *2 n.3 (referencing both state analogue to Model Rule 3.8 cmt. [6] and Rule 5.1(a)); Or. State Bar Ass'n Bd. of Governors, *Trial Publicity*, Formal Op. 2007-179, 2007 WL 7261223, at *8 (2007) (a prosecutor's level of responsibility under state analogues to Model Rule 5.1 and 5.3 "depends on the level of the prosecutor's authority over the investigator" with whom she works); *id.* *8 n.8 (describing circumstances under state analogue to Model Rule 5.1 in which a supervising prosecutor would be responsible for impermissible pre-trial publicity). *See also* Model Rules of Prof'l Conduct R. 8.4(a) & R. 8.4 cmt. [1] (2019) ("Lawyers are subject to discipline when they . . . knowingly assist or induce another to [violate or attempt to violate the Rules of Professional Conduct] or do so through the acts of another, as when they request or instruct an agent to do so on the lawyer's behalf.").

Rule 1.3, a lawyer's workload "must be controlled so that each matter can be handled competently."

In Formal Opinion 441, the Committee addressed the ethical obligations of lawyers representing indigent criminal defendants when caseloads interfere with competent and diligent representation.[35] The same analysis applies to prosecutors. If workloads interfere with competent and diligent representation, appropriate remedial steps must be taken by the prosecutor and/or the supervising attorney to whom the prosecutor reports by, for example, reassigning cases or limiting other duties.[36]

C. Model Rule 3.8(b) and the Right to Counsel

Rule 3.8(b) requires the prosecutor to "make reasonable efforts to assure that the accused has been advised of the right to, and the procedure for obtaining, counsel and has been given reasonable opportunity to obtain counsel." This opinion does not address constitutional issues, but our analysis of a prosecutor's responsibilities under Rule 3.8(b) is aided by identifying circumstances in which the right to counsel applies. In a series of cases beginning with *Argersinger v. Hamlin,* the Supreme Court has held that the Sixth Amendment right to state subsidized counsel applies to misdemeanors if the punishment includes either actual imprisonment or a suspended sentence that may result in imprisonment.[37] Federal courts are divided over the test to determine when the Sixth Amendment right to state subsidized counsel attaches,[38] but there is no doubt that it can attach as early as an ini-

---

35. *See* ABA Comm. on Ethics & Prof'l Responsibility, Formal Op. 441 at 1, 7 (2006) ("[L]awyer supervisors must, working closely with the lawyers they supervise, monitor the workload of the supervised lawyers to ensure that the workloads do not exceed a level that may be competently handled by the individual lawyers"; possible ameliorative measures might include, for example, reassigning cases to others, refusing new cases, or reassigning non- representational work to others).

36. *Id.* at 1, 7.

37. *See* Argersinger v. Hamlin, 407 U.S. 25, 37 (1972) (extending right to counsel to misdemeanors and petty offenses involving imprisonment); *see also* Alabama v. Shelton, 535 U.S. 654, 658 (2002) ("a suspended sentence that may 'end up in the actual deprivation of a person's liberty' may not be imposed unless the defendant was accorded 'the guiding hand of counsel' in the prosecution of the crime charged") (quoting *Argersinger*, 407 U.S. at 40); Scott v. Illinois, 440 U.S. 367, 373-74 (1979) (clarifying that the Sixth Amendment right to counsel does not apply where state law provides both for fines and imprisonment, and a defendant is sentenced only to a fine).

38. Compare Turner v. United States, 885 F.3d 949, 953 (6th Cir. 2018) (en banc) (holding that Sixth Amendment right to counsel attaches "only at or after the time that adversary judicial proceedings have been initiated" and therefore does not extend to pre-indictment plea negotiations) (quoting United States v. Gouveia, 467 U.S. 180, 187 (1984)), *with* United States v. Larkin, 978 F.2d 964 (7th Cir. 1992) (holding that although Sixth Amendment right presumptively attaches only at or after the initiation of adversary judicial criminal proceedings . . . . [a] defendant may rebut this presumption by demonstrating that . . . the government had crossed the constitutionally significant divide from fact-finder to adversary" at an earlier stage) (internal quotations and citations omitted).

tial appearance,[39] that plea bargaining is a "critical phase" of the representation during which the assistance of counsel is important to ensure fair and accurate outcomes,[40] and that the Sixth Amendment protects against interference with the right to counsel whether counsel is subsidized by the state, appointed, or independently retained.[41] As importantly, a right to state subsidized counsel in misdemeanor cases may exist in circumstances not covered by the U.S. Constitution.[42] An accused person also has a constitutional right to proceed *without* the assistance of counsel, but the waiver of such assistance must be knowing, voluntary, and intelligent.[43]

---

39. *See* Brewer v. Williams, 430 U.S. 387, 398 (1977).

40. *See* Padilla v. Kentucky, 559 U.S. 356, 373 (2010) ("[W]e have long recognized that the negotiation of a plea bargain is a critical phase of litigation for purposes of the Sixth Amendment right to effective assistance of counsel"); Missouri v. Frye, 566 U.S. 134, 143-44 (2012). The right may attach even before a prosecutor decides formally to proceed with charges. *See* Rothgery v. Gillespie Cty., Tex., 554 U.S. 191, 207-08 (2008) (rejecting claim that the Sixth Amendment right to counsel attaches only after a prosecutor has formally decided to prosecute; the government's commitment is "sufficiently concrete" once an accusation is "filed with a judicial officer" by the police incident to arrest and incarceration, triggering an initial appearance). The key for attachment of the Sixth Amendment right is initiation of "adversary judicial proceedings." *Gouveia*, 467 U.S. at 187.

41. *See* Johnson v. Zerbst, 304 U.S. 458, 460, 469 (1938) (holding right to counsel violated where defendant allegedly invoked right in discussion with prosecutor and jailer but was not permitted by either to contact a lawyer and was tried and convicted); Powell v. Alabama, 287 U.S. 45, 58 (1932) (gathering state cases finding violation of right to counsel where accelerated pre-trial and trial process compromised appointed counsel's preparation of defense); *In re* Motz, 136 N.E.2d 430, 433 (Ohio Ct. App. 1955) (right to counsel violated where court refused a continuance to permit counsel retained by defendant to prepare, counsel withdrew, court refused to appoint new counsel, and defendant forced to trial pro se). Although we do not address how Rule 3.8 applies to the right to counsel in custodial interrogations, we note that the Fifth Amendment right to counsel can apply to misdemeanor defendants. *See* Miranda v. Arizona, 384 U.S. 436, 469-70 (1966); *cf. infra* notes 45 & 47.

42. State law frequently guarantees a right to subsidized counsel in circumstances in which the federal constitution does not. *See* State v. Young, 863 N.W.2d 249, 272 (Iowa 2015) (citing 2009 study showing that a majority of states provide a right to subsidized counsel broader than the Sixth Amendment "actual imprisonment" standard); DeWolfe v. Richmond, 76 A.3d 1019, 1031 (Md. 2013) (state constitutional right to due process requires right to state subsidized counsel at initial appearance). *See also Pretrial Right to Counsel*, National Conference of State Legislatures, http://www.ncsl.org/research/civil-and-criminal-justice/pretrial-right-to-counsel.aspx (offering 50 state survey of state constitutional and statutory provisions establishing right to counsel) (last visited Apr. 30, 2019).

43. *See* Faretta v. California, 422 U.S. 806, 835 (1975); *see also* Godinez v. Moran, 509 U.S. 389, 390 (1993) ("[W]hen a defendant seeks to waive his right to counsel, a determination that he is competent to stand trial is not enough; the waiver must also be intelligent and voluntary before it can be accepted."). "[T]he law ordinarily considers a waiver knowing, intelligent, and sufficiently aware if the defendant fully understands the nature of the right and how it would likely apply *in general* in the circumstances—even though the defendant may not know the *specific detailed* consequences of invoking it." United States v. Ruiz, 536 U.S. 622, 629 (2002) (emphasis in original). Whether a waiver is knowing, intelligent and voluntary is a question of law on which we do not opine.

The first draft of the Model Rules addressed the accused's right to counsel, enjoining a prosecutor to "advise the defendant of the right to counsel and provide assistance in obtaining counsel."[44] The language of the current rule is more precise in several respects. First, rather than simply enjoin the prosecutor to "provide assistance," it specifies that the lynchpin to assistance is ensuring (i) that the accused is advised of the procedure for obtaining counsel and (ii) that the nature and timing of prosecution does not interfere with this procedure. Second, it replaces the restrictive term of art "defendant" with the more flexible term "accused," thus clarifying that the assistance obligations of the Rule apply before the filing of an indictment. Third, the shift to passive voice makes the prosecutor responsible for ensuring that the accused is aware of the state's procedure for obtaining counsel and has adequate time and access to the necessary administrative assistance to invoke it, irrespective of whether another state actor (e.g., the judge, the court clerk, the public defender office) is legally charged with providing counsel, making indigence determinations, or soliciting and recording waivers of the right. Fourth, the modifier "reasonable" in "reasonable efforts" clarifies that a prosecutor is not required to suffer undue delay or otherwise compromise legitimate law enforcement objectives in order to meet the obligations of the Rule. The prosecutor is therefore charged with specific responsibilities to ensure that those who are or may be entitled to counsel are afforded the information and reasonable time necessary to retain a lawyer.[45]

D. Model Rule 3.8(c) and the Duty Not to Seek Waivers of Important Pretrial Rights

Rule 3.8(c) provides that a prosecutor "shall not seek to obtain from an unrepresented accused a waiver of important pretrial rights, such as the right to a preliminary hearing." As with Rule 3.8(b), there is no direct analogue to this provision in the 1908 Canons or the 1969 Code. The first draft of the Model Rules provided that a prosecutor "shall not induce an unrepresented defendant to surrender important procedural rights, such as the right to a preliminary hearing."[46] The Rule as adopted is broader for several reasons. First, it prohibits seeking a waiver from an unrepresented "accused" and is therefore not limited to someone who is formally a "defendant." Second, "inducement" implies efforts to persuade, whereas "seek to obtain" reaches even a bare request. Finally, the replacement of "procedural rights" with

---

44. Model Rules of Prof'l Conduct R. 3.10(b) (Discussion Draft 1980).

45. Although the Rule applies broadly to the right to counsel, this opinion is limited to its application in the context of misdemeanor plea bargaining. For guidance on the right to counsel under the Fifth Amendment in custodial interrogation, see ABA/BNA Lawyer's Manual on Prof'l Conduct, *Prosecutors* 61:616 (ABA/BNA 2019) (citing Criminal Justice Standards for the Prosecution Function 3-2.7, 3-3.2, 3-3.6 (Am. Bar Ass'n 1992)).

46. Model Rules of Prof'l Conduct R. 3.10(c) (Discussion Draft 1980).

"pretrial rights" broadens the scope of the Rule by extending its application to all "important" rights (whether classified as substantive or procedural) and by explicitly targeting the pretrial stage—a particularly delicate phase of prosecution where judges exercise minimal or only intermittent supervision, the leverage of a prosecutor is extraordinary, and the risks and consequences of improper waiver by an unrepresented accused person are correspondingly acute.[47] As the Comment makes clear, the Rule does not apply to individuals who have elected to proceed pro se "with the approval of the tribunal," or to "the lawful questioning of an uncharged suspect who has knowingly waived the rights to counsel and silence."[48]

IV. Duties Arising from the Accused's Right to Counsel

As discussed in Parts III.C through III.D above, Model Rules 3.8(b) and (c) provide that the "prosecutor in a criminal case shall:

> (b) make reasonable efforts to assure that the accused has been advised of the right to, and the procedure for obtaining, counsel and has been given reasonable opportunity to obtain counsel;
>
> (c) not seek to obtain from an unrepresented accused a waiver of important pretrial rights, such as the right to a preliminary hearing."[49]

---

47. The example of a preliminary hearing indicates, as the Comment notes, that in jurisdictions where waiver can lead to the loss of a chance to challenge probable cause or use the preliminary hearing to ascertain relevant facts about the prosecution's case, prosecutors should not seek to deprive defendants of those opportunities. *See* MODEL RULES OF PROF'L CONDUCT R. 3.8 cmt. [2]. The contemporaneous ABA Standards of Criminal Justice, Prosecution Function, noted these features of the preliminary hearing in some jurisdictions. *See* CRIMINAL JUSTICE STANDARDS FOR THE PROSECUTION, Standard 3-5.1 (AM. BAR ASS'N 1980). But in its general reference to "important pretrial rights" the Rule as adopted plainly sweeps beyond that illustration. *See* ABA/BNA LAWYER'S MANUAL ON PROF'L CONDUCT 61:617 ("the phrase is broad enough to cover pretrial rights grounded on federal or state constitutions, statutes, or case law"). As the Comment emphasizes, "prosecutors should not seek to obtain waivers of preliminary hearings *or other important pretrial rights* from unrepresented accused persons." MODEL RULES OF PROF'L CONDUCT R. 3.8 cmt. [2] (emphasis added). *See also* ABA/BNA LAWYER'S MANUAL ON PROF'L CONDUCT 61:617 (ABA/BNA 2019) ("Rule 3.8(c) precludes prosecutors from seeking a waiver of important pretrial rights from an unrepresented accused, even when this conduct maybe permissible as a matter of constitutional law."). The Rule's reference to other "important pretrial rights" is particularly relevant to misdemeanor plea bargaining because there is often no requirement of a preliminary hearing or grand jury to provide an external check on prosecutors in misdemeanor cases and there are many important pretrial rights (among them not only the right to counsel but the right to disclosure of exculpatory evidence, the right to inspect evidence, and other discovery rights). This opinion addresses the right to counsel.

48. MODEL RULES OF PROF'L CONDUCT R. 3.8 cmt. [2].

49. MODEL RULES OF PROF'L CONDUCT R. 3.8 (b) & (c).

Rule 3.8(b) and (c) are of central importance to misdemeanor prosecutions because many people accused of misdemeanors are issued citations and notices to appear rather than arrested and brought in for questioning. Alternatively, they may be questioned in the field by police, arrested, and, particularly for the indigent, held if they cannot make bail. In these circumstances, they functionally become "unrepresented accused" persons either upon receipt of a citation and notice to appear, or as a consequence of an arrest. And yet, this early in the proceedings they may not be aware of their right to state subsidized counsel, the process for exercising it, or the fact that they have the right to retain a lawyer not paid for by the state. As importantly, a prosecutor may control whether the right to state subsidized counsel attaches because the Sixth Amendment right to counsel may hinge on the classification of the underlying offense and the prosecutor's decision about what kind of plea to offer.[50] Under these circumstances, a prosecutor must scrupulously conform to Rules 3.8(b) and (c), as well as Rule 4.3, which prohibits giving legal advice to an unrepresented person whose interests in defending herself may conflict with the prosecutor's interest in securing a conviction.[51] A prosecutor must also take steps to be reasonably sure that the conduct of her subordinates and agents is "'compatible with the professional obligations of the [prosecutor].'"[52]

Accordingly, if the charge associated with a plea offer triggers the right to counsel under *Argersinger* or where the circumstances of the offense, arrest, or initial appearance otherwise indicate that the accused has or may have a right to counsel under state or federal law, the prosecutor may not make a plea offer or seek a waiver of the right to counsel before complying with Rule 3.8(b). The prosecutor must make reasonable efforts to assure that the accused has been advised of the right to counsel and the procedure for obtaining counsel, and has been given a reasonable opportunity to exercise that right and obtain counsel. If the prosecutor delegates authority to or otherwise relies upon police officers or other state actors to discuss waivers of rights in misdemeanor cases, pursuant to Rules 5.1(b) and (c), 5.3(b) and (c), and 8.4(a), the prosecutor is responsible for ensuring that Rules 3.8 and 4.3 are not violated during those discussions. As noted earlier in this opinion, under Rules 5.1(a) and 5.3(a) a supervising prosecutor is responsible for es-

50. A plea offer of release for time served, for instance, triggers *Argersinger* because it is a sentence of actual imprisonment. Of course, state law, federal statutes, and the requirements of due process may create a legal right to subsidized counsel even though the Sixth Amendment does not. *See* note 42 *supra*. And the unrepresented accused has a core Sixth Amendment right to retain counsel at her own expense unless she elects to proceed pro se on terms approved by the court or by the laws and rules of the jurisdiction.

51. For a prosecutor's duties under Rule 4.3 when negotiating pleas in misdemeanor cases, see Part V *infra*.

52. ABA Comm. on Ethics & Prof'l Responsibility, Formal Op. 467 at 3 (2014) (quoting Rule 5.3(b)).

tablishing policies, practices, and methods of monitoring that give "reasonable assurance" of compliance with prosecutors' ethical obligations.

Moreover, under Rule 3.8(b) and (c), a prosecutor may not pressure, advise, or induce acceptance of a plea or waiver of the right to counsel after an unrepresented accused has been informed of the right to counsel and is deciding whether to invoke or has initiated the process to invoke that right.[53] Even asking an unrepresented accused if she wishes to waive the right to counsel or accept a plea is improper if it is clear from the circumstances that the accused does not understand the consequences of acceding to the request. This is so because legal advice may be necessary to clarify any such misunderstanding, and, consistent with Rules 3.8(b), 3.8(c), and as required by Rule 4.3, a prosecutor is precluded from offering legal advice other than to seek counsel.

On the other hand, if the accused has independently elected to proceed pro se on terms approved by the court or by the laws and rules of the jurisdiction, the prosecutor may negotiate a plea, but any negotiations must comply with the Rules discussed in Part V below.

V. Duties When Plea Bargaining with an Unrepresented Accused

Irrespective of whether an unrepresented accused has invoked the right to counsel, Model Rules 4.1, 4.3 and 8.4(c) constrain a prosecutor's conduct when negotiating a plea bargain with, e.g., (i) persons who are ineligible under state and federal law for state subsidized defense counsel and cannot afford or otherwise cannot secure private counsel, (ii) those who elect to proceed pro se even though they are eligible for subsidized counsel or could retain private counsel, and (iii) those who have invoked the right to counsel but are still in the process of securing counsel or deciding whether to do so.

Rule 4.1 prohibits a lawyer from knowingly making "a false statement of material fact or law to a third person." The rule "was intended to incorporate the law of misrepresentation by recognizing that the failure to disclose can amount to a misrepresentation in some circumstances. . . ."[54] Comment [1] emphasizes that misrepresentations can "occur by partially true but misleading statements or omissions that are the equivalent of false statements."[55] Rule 4.3 states that "[i]n dealing on behalf of a client with a person who is not represented by counsel" a lawyer "shall not give legal advice to an unrepre-

---

53. This is so whether the unrepresented accused intends to pursue counsel subsidized by the state or retain counsel at the accused's expense.

54. CTR. FOR PROF'L RESPONSIBILITY, AM. BAR ASS'N, A LEGISLATIVE HISTORY OF THE DEVELOPMENT OF THE ABA MODEL RULES, 1982-2005, at 522 (2006) [hereinafter LEGISLATIVE HISTORY] (discussion at February 1983 Midyear Meeting). Rules 4.1 and 8.4(c) also apply when the accused has retained counsel, as does Rule 4.2.

55. The comment was amended in 2002 according to the recommendations of the Ethics 2000 Commission. The amendment explicitly expanded emphasis on misrepresentation by omission, substituting the current language for the prior, more vague, reference to misrepresentation by "failure to act." *See id.* at 527-28.

sented person, other than the advice to secure counsel, if the lawyer knows or reasonably should know that the interests of such a person are or have a reasonable possibility of being in conflict with the interests of the client."[56] Finally, Rule 8.4(c) prohibits a lawyer from engaging "in conduct involving dishonesty, fraud, deceit or misrepresentation."[57]

In the context of plea negotiations, these rules circumscribe the terms on which a prosecutor may deal with an unrepresented accused. An unrepresented accused, particularly one who lacks experience with the intricacies of the criminal justice system, is in an acutely vulnerable position.[58] The accused faces the vast array of resources at the prosecutor's disposal as well as the prosecutor's legal expertise at a moment in which, even in misdemeanor cases, substantial liberty interests and financial security are in jeopardy.[59] Moreover, once a prosecutor has committed to pursue a misdemeanor charge in plea negotiations, the interests of the prosecutor and the unrepresented accused are adverse, so the prosecutor must take particular care to avoid giving the impression that she is "disinterested" and to correct any misunderstanding regarding the prosecutor's role in the matter. From the moment of arrest there is already, within the meaning of Rule 4.3, "a reasonable possibility of . . . conflict with the interests of" the unrepresented accused. Accordingly, a prosecutor is prohibited by Rule 4.3 from offering legal advice regarding the substance of the plea, the process of its negotiation and entry, or the consequences incident to conviction.[60] As discussed below, however, a prosecutor can and sometimes must disclose material information regarding the substance of the plea, the process of its negotiation and entry, and known consequences of a conviction to an unrepresented person.

Comment [2] to Rule 4.3 states that a lawyer is not generally prohibited from "settling a dispute with an unrepresented person," but a plea bargain

---

56. Amendments approved in 2002 on the recommendation of the Ethics 2000 Commission elevated the prohibition on giving advice from the comments to the rule in response to reports that "in negotiations between lawyers and unrepresented parties, the giving of legal advice (often misleading or overreaching) is not uncommon." *Id.* at 550. The Commission recognized that "although the line may be difficult to draw, it is important to discourage lawyers from overreaching in their negotiations with unrepresented persons." *Id.* at 549-50. On the law of misrepresentation by omission, see Restatement (Second) of Torts § 551 (Am. Law Inst. 1977).

57. Comment [1] to Rule 4.1 states that for "dishonest conduct that does not amount to a false statement or for misrepresentations by a lawyer other than in the course of representing a client, see Rule 8.4."

58. Comment [2] to Rule 4.3 emphasizes that "[w]hether a lawyer is giving impermissible advice may depend on the experience and the sophistication of the unrepresented person, as well as the setting in which the behavior and comments occur."

59. *See* Part IB *supra*.

60. *See* Ill. State Bar Ass'n, Advisory Op. No. 02, 2014 WL 2434672, at *3 ("It would be a violation of Rule 4.3 . . . should the communication [with a person who has elected to proceed pro se] give value to the plea offer or in any way advise the pro se defendant ('It is a good offer' or 'Take the deal.').").

is no ordinary arms-length transaction or settlement agreement. The stakes are often significantly higher than in civil matters and the terms must meet specific constitutional standards designed to ensure that the accused's acceptance is "voluntary, knowing, and intelligent."[61] Thus while a prosecutor may negotiate a plea bargain with a pro se litigant, the prosecutor's duties under Rules 4.1 and 8.4(c) are heightened in this setting. Assertions regarding the terms of a plea violate these rules if the prosecutor knows they are materially underinclusive. For example, statements regarding the value of a plea offer, particularly those which omit known collateral consequences of accepting a plea or the legal relevance of a plea to enhancement of a sentence in any subsequent case, can constitute prohibited misrepresentations under Rule 4.1 or deceptive conduct under Rule 8.4(c).[62] Thus, where a prosecutor knows from the charge selected, the accused's record, or any other information that certain collateral consequences or sentence enhancements apply to a plea on that charge, statements like the following would constitute prohibited misrepresentations:

> "Take this plea for time served and you are done, you can go home now."
>
> "This is a suspended sentence, so as long as you comply with its terms, you avoid jail time with this plea."
>
> "You only serve three months on this plea, that's the sentence."

A prosecutor will rarely know all of the potentially relevant collateral consequences of accepting a plea or the exact nature of any subsequent sentence enhancement. However, if the prosecutor knows the consequences of a plea—either generic consequences or consequences that are particular to the accused—the prosecutor must disclose them during the plea negotiation.[63]

Finally, a prosecutor's duties under these rules do not end once a plea has been accepted. If a prosecutor learns during the plea colloquy with the court or other interactions that the unrepresented accused's acceptance of a plea or waiver of the right to counsel is not in fact voluntary, knowing, and

---

61. *See* Part IIIB *supra.*

62. Furthermore, in the context of plea negotiations, violation of either rule is conduct prejudicial to the administration of justice under Rule 8.4(d).

63. Given the delicacy of balancing the need to disclose material information to avoid either misrepresentation or deception, on the one hand, and the prohibition on legal advice, on the other, the best practice is to carefully record and preserve plea negotiations with an unrepresented accused. *See* CRIMINAL JUSTICE STANDARDS FOR THE PROSECUTION FUNCTION 3-5.6(b) (AM. BAR ASS'N 2015) (encouraging record keeping where defendant waives right to counsel and proceeds pro se). Additional guidance is provided in the NAT'L PROSECUTION STANDARDS §§ 2-7.2, 2-7.4 and 2-7.5 (3d ed. 2009).

intelligent, or if the plea colloquy conducted by the court is inadequate to ascertain whether the plea or waiver of the right to counsel is in fact voluntary, knowing, and intelligent, the prosecutor is obliged to intervene. The prosecutor cannot, consistent with her role as a minister of justice under Rule 3.8 and the duty to avoid conduct prejudicial to the administration of justice under Rule 8.4(d), knowingly permit an unconstitutional plea to be entered by an unrepresented accused.[64]

VI. Conclusion

Under Model Rules 1.1, 1.3, 3.8(a), and 8.4(a) and (d), prosecutors have a duty to ensure that charges underlying a plea offer in misdemeanor cases have sufficient evidentiary and legal foundation. Under Model Rules 1.1, 5.1, 5.3, and 8.4(a) prosecutors must take appropriate steps to make reasonably sure that the work of their subordinates and agents is compatible with their professional obligations. Under Model Rule 3.8(b) prosecutors must make reasonable efforts to assure that unrepresented accused persons are informed of the right to counsel and the process for securing counsel, and must avoid conduct that interferes with that process. After an unrepresented accused has been informed of the right to counsel and is deciding whether to invoke that right or is in the process of attempting to secure counsel, a prosecutor may not, under Model Rules 3.8(b) and (c), pressure, advise, or induce acceptance of a plea or waiver of the right to counsel. Finally, irrespective of whether an unrepresented accused has invoked the right to counsel, a prosecutor must, under Model Rules 4.1, 4.3 and 8.4(c) and (d), avoid offering, negotiating, and entering pleas on terms that knowingly misrepresent the consequences of acceptance, or otherwise improperly pressure, advise, or induce acceptance on the part of the unrepresented accused.

64. *See also* ABA Comm. on Ethics & Prof'l Responsibility, Formal Op. 454 (2009).

AMERICAN BAR ASSOCIATION
STANDING COMMITTEE ON ETHICS AND PROFESSIONAL RESPONSIBILITY
321 N. Clark Street, Chicago, Illinois 60654-4714 Telephone (312) 988-5328
CHAIR: Barbara S. Gillers, New York, NY
■ John M. Barkett, Miami, FL ■ Robert Hirshon, Ann Arbor, MI ■ Thomas B. Mason, Washington, DC
■ Michael H. Rubin, Baton Rouge, LA ■ Douglas R. Richmond, Chicago, IL
■ Lynda Shely, Scottsdale, AZ ■ Norman W. Spaulding, Stanford, CA
■ Elizabeth Clark Tarbert, Tallahassee, FL ■ Lisa D. Taylor, Parsippany, NJ

CENTER FOR PROFESSIONAL RESPONSIBILITY

AMERICAN BAR ASSOCIATION

STANDING COMMITTEE ON ETHICS AND PROFESSIONAL RESPONSIBILITY

Formal Opinion 487 **June 18, 2019**

Fee Division with Client's Prior Counsel

In a contingent fee matter, when a counsel (successor counsel) from one firm replaces a counsel (predecessor counsel) from another firm as counsel for the client, Rules 1.5(b) and (c) require that the successor counsel notify the client, in writing, that a portion of any contingent fee earned may be paid to the predecessor counsel. The successor counsel may not be able to state at the beginning of the representation the specific amount or percentage of a recovery, if any, that may be owed to the predecessor counsel unless the amount or percentage has been agreed by the client and both predecessor and successor counsels. The successor counsel is not bound by the requirements of Rule 1.5(e), either at the time of engagement or upon a recovery, because Rule 1.5(e) addresses situations where two lawyers are working on a case together, not situations where one lawyer is replacing another. Upon a monetary recovery, the successor counsel may only disburse a portion of the overall attorney's fee to the predecessor counsel with client consent or pursuant to an order of a tribunal of competent jurisdiction. If there is a dispute as to the amount due to the predecessor counsel under Rule 1.15(e) the disputed amount may have to remain in a client trust account until the matter is resolved. If successor counsel negotiates with predecessor counsel on the client's behalf, successor counsel must explain to the client the potential conflict of interest in the dual roles pursuant to Rule 1.7, where successor counsel has a personal interest in the amount predecessor counsel may receive or in the timing of the release of funds held pursuant to Rule 1.15(e).[1]

I. Introduction

A client has the right to terminate a lawyer's services at any time[2] but when the client terminates the services of a contingent fee counsel, without

1 This opinion is based on the ABA Model Rules of Professional Conduct as amended by the ABA House of Delegates through August 2018. The laws, court rules, regulations, rules of professional conduct and opinions promulgated in individual jurisdictions are controlling.

2 Model Rules of Prof'l Conduct R. 1.16 cmt. 4 (2018) [hereinafter Model Rules]; Restatement (Third) of the Law Governing Lawyers § 32(1) (2000) [hereinafter Restatement].

cause, prior to the occurrence of the contingency on which the parties' agreement is based, the counsel may be entitled to a fee for services performed before discharge under *quantum meruit* or, in some jurisdictions, pursuant to a so-called "conversion clause" or "termination clause" in the contingent fee agreement. This opinion addresses the successor counsel's obligations under the Model Rules of Professional Conduct after taking over the case when there is a monetary recovery. A counsel who subsequently takes over the case (the successor counsel) must advise the client, in writing, of the predecessor counsel's potential claim on a recovery.[3]

II. Analysis

A. The Successor Counsel's Obligation to Advise the Client that the Predecessor Counsel May Make a Claim Against Any Recovery

Just as in any contingent fee matter, the successor counsel must comply with both Model Rule 1.5(b) in describing the rate or basis of the fee and with Model Rule 1.5(c)'s requirement that the written fee agreement include the method of determining the fee. Paragraphs (b) and (c) of Rule 1.5 provide:

> (b) The scope of the representation and the basis or rate of the fee and expenses for which the client will be responsible shall be communicated to the client, preferably in writing, before or within a reasonable time after commencing the representation, except when the lawyer will charge a regularly represented client on the same basis or rate. Any changes in the basis or rate of the fee or expenses shall also be communicated to the client.
>
> (c) A fee may be contingent on the outcome of the matter for which the service is rendered, except in a matter in which a contingent fee is prohibited by paragraph (d) or other law. A contingent fee agreement shall be in a writing signed by the client and shall state the method by which the fee is to be determined, including the percentage or percentages that shall accrue to the lawyer in the event of settlement, trial or appeal; litigation and other expenses to be deducted from the recovery; and whether such expenses are to be deducted before or after the contingent fee is calculated. The agreement must

3 This opinion applies where the client terminates a lawyer without cause and hires a new lawyer to replace that lawyer to handle a contingent fee matter. The opinion does not apply when a client terminates a lawyer with cause, or the lawyer withdraws without cause. In such situations, a lawyer may forfeit some or all of her fee. RESTATEMENT § 37 (2000); David Hricik, *Dear Lawyer: If you decide it's not economical to represent me, you can fire me as your contingent fee client, but I agree I will still owe you a fee*, 64 MERCER L. REV. 363 (2012-2013).

> clearly notify the client of any expenses for which the client will be liable whether or not the client is the prevailing party. Upon conclusion of a contingent fee matter, the lawyer shall provide the client with a written statement stating the outcome of the matter and, if there is a recovery, showing the remittance to the client and the method of its determination.

Although Rules 1.5(b) and 1.5(c) do not specifically address obligations when one counsel replaces another, both rules are designed to ensure that the client has a clear understanding of the total legal fee, how it is to be computed, when it is to be paid, and by whom. "[A]n understanding as to fees . . . must be promptly established."[4] A contingent fee agreement that fails to mention that some portion of the fee may be due to or claimed by the first counsel in circumstances addressed by this opinion is inconsistent with these requirements of Rule 1.5(b) and (c).[5] To avoid client confusion, making the disclosure in the fee agreement itself is the better practice, but this disclosure may be made in a separate document associated with the contingent fee agreement and provided to the client at the same time.

Assume, for example, that a client retains a lawyer in a matter and enters into a written fee agreement in which the lawyer is entitled to one-third of any recovery. The client then decides to terminate the lawyer, without cause, and hires new counsel. The successor counsel takes the matter on the same terms as the predecessor counsel (one-third of any recovery) but the successor counsel's written fee agreement is silent on whether that one-third is in addition to or in lieu of the one-third specified in the predecessor counsel's fee agreement, and no such disclosure is made in a separate document provided to the client. In these circumstances, the client may not know whether the client must pay one or both lawyers or the amount of the fees owed. The client may be aware of the right to terminate a lawyer's representation at any

---

4 Model Rules R. 1.5 cmt. 2.

5 ABA Comm. on Ethics & Prof'l Responsibility, Formal Op. 94-389, at 4 (1994) (explaining that "the nature (and details) of the compensation arrangement should be fully discussed by the lawyer and client before any final agreement is reached."); Joyce v. Elliott, 857 P.2d 549, 552 (Colo. App. 1993) (stating that "one of the principal purposes of the rules respecting contingency fee agreements is to assure that a client is fully advised at the time such agreement is executed of all of the financial obligations that such client is assuming by the establishment of the attorney-client relationship."); Shaw v. Manufacturers Hanover Trust Co., 499 N.E.2d 864, 866 (N.Y. 1986) ("The importance of an attorney's clear agreement with a client as to the essential terms of representation cannot be overstated. The client should be fully informed of all of the relevant facts and the basis of the fee charges, especially in contingent fee arrangements[.]"); *In re* Davenport, 522 S.W.3d 452, 458 (Tex. 2017) ("The goal of an attorney-client fee agreement is to ensure that the client is informed of its terms. . . . whether the lawyer was reasonably clear is determined from the client's perspective.") (footnotes omitted).

time but may not be aware that termination does not necessarily extinguish an obligation to pay prior counsel for the value of the work performed – the *quantum meruit* claim – or in some cases a termination amount specified in the predecessor counsel's fee agreement. If the predecessor counsel was not terminated for cause, that lawyer may be entitled to payment for the fair value contributed to the case before being terminated.[6] Under those circumstances, "a contingency client should be advised by the successor attorney of the existence and effect of the discharged attorney's claim for fees on the occurrence of the contingency as part of the terms and conditions of the employment by the successor attorney."[7]

Where a client hires successor counsel to handle an existing contingency fee matter, it does not pose an unreasonable burden on the successor counsel to advise the client that the predecessor counsel may have a claim to a portion of the legal fee if there is a recovery. In many instances, precision on this issue may be difficult as successor counsel may need to review the predecessor counsel's fee agreement and assess its enforceability. Similarly, successor counsel may not be fully familiar with the nature and extent of the prior lawyer's work on the matter. Successor counsel also will not know the amount of the recovery, if any, at the beginning of the representation. Nevertheless, Rules 1.5(b) and (c) mandate that successor counsel provide written notice that a portion of the fee may be claimed by the predecessor counsel.

Successor counsel must address with the client whether the client risks paying twice: one contingent fee to the predecessor counsel and another to the successor counsel. A client cannot be exposed to more than one contingent fee when switching attorneys, given that under the Rule 1.5(a) factors, each counsel did not perform all of the services required to achieve the result. Thus, neither the predecessor nor the successor counsel ordinarily would be entitled to a full contingent fee.

B. Rule 1.5(e) Fee Division Provisions Do Not Apply

There is some authority concluding that successor counsel replacing a client's prior counsel must comply with Rule 1.5(e);[8] however, this Rule is de-

6 *See generally* Restatement § 40 cmts. b & c (2000) (On discharge, a lawyer may be entitled to the fair value of the lawyer's services. Determination of fair value takes into account the proportion of work performed by the discharged lawyer, and the value of work contributed. The determination also may consider a contract amount prorated for work actually performed.).

7 San Francisco Bar Ass'n, Ethics Comm., Advisory Op. 1989-1 (1989).

8 These authorities focus on client consent to a fee division. *See, e.g.*, Statewide Grievance Comm. v. Dixon, 772 A.2d 160, 164-65 (Conn. App. Ct. 2001) (concluding that the lawyer violated Rule 1.5(e) by failing to inform the client of payment made from recovery to prior lawyer in a different firm); Conn. Bar Ass'n, Comm. on Prof'l Ethics Op. 01-10, 2001 WL 34004971, at *1 (2001) (involving a new lawyer replacing the original lawyer because of conflict). None discuss other provisions of the rule, for example, how "joint responsibility" works. As dis-

signed to regulate fee-sharing between lawyers in different firms who handle a case simultaneously. Comment 7 to Rule 1.5 underscores this reading. It states:

> A division of fee is a single billing to a client covering the fee of two or more lawyers who are not in the same firm. *A division of fee facilitates association of more than one lawyer in a matter in which neither alone could serve the client as well,* and most often is used when the fee is contingent and the division is between a referring lawyer and a trial specialist. Paragraph (e) permits the lawyers to divide a fee either on the basis of the proportion of services they render or if each lawyer assumes responsibility for the representation as a whole. In addition, the client must agree to the arrangement, including the share that each lawyer is to receive, and the agreement must be confirmed in writing. Contingent fee agreements must be in a writing signed by the client and must otherwise comply with paragraph (c) of this Rule. Joint responsibility for the representation entails financial and ethical responsibility for the representation as if the lawyers were associated in a partnership. A lawyer should only refer a matter to a lawyer whom the referring lawyer reasonably believes is competent to handle the matter. See Rule 1.1. (Emphasis added.)

Comment 7 thus clarifies that Rule 1.5(e) is limited to situations where two or more lawyers are working on a case simultaneously – not sequentially. Accordingly, Rule 1.5(e) was not meant to apply to the situation where one lawyer's services are terminated and the client retains a second lawyer to complete the matter.

Under Rule 1.5(e), fees must either be divided in proportion to the work performed or in some other specified division where both lawyers assume "joint responsibility" for the matter. Fee-sharing in proportion to the work performed by lawyers concurrently representing a client is similar to the *quantum meruit* analysis that is frequently used post-hoc to divide contingent fees between successive law firms. What differs where predecessor and successor counsel are involved in such fee issues before a recovery has been obtained is that the underlying case and the client's rights to discharge her lawyer may be adversely affected if the client is required to enter into a fee-sharing agreement under Rule 1.5(e). Requiring the predecessor and successor counsel and the client to agree on a proportional fee division may hinder the client's right to terminate a counsel by making the process of finding a replacement more difficult and protracted. A simple fee negotiation between the client and successor counsel would turn into a three-way debate.

---

cussed above, we agree that client consent to a payment by the successor lawyer to the predecessor lawyer is necessary, but reach that conclusion without reliance on Rule 1.5(e).

The other approach under Rule 1.5(e) to divide a fee among lawyers concurrently representing a client requires that all counsel assume "joint responsibility" for the related matter. Such responsibility entails financial and ethical responsibility for the representation as if the counsel were associated in a partnership.[9] A referring counsel is allowed to receive a greater portion of the fee than the counsel's own efforts would otherwise merit through the acceptance of joint responsibility.[10] When a client discharges a lawyer and hires a new one, there is no "referring counsel" and there is no simultaneous representation of the client. Joint responsibility in practice does not exist because predecessor counsel has been replaced. To require "joint responsibility" under Rule 1.5(e) in these situations as a pre-condition of paying the predecessor counsel's fee claim is not realistic and ultimately burdens the client's ability to discharge the first lawyer and find replacement counsel. If the successor counsel would be responsible for the errors or omissions of a discharged predecessor, he or she would at best be reluctant to accept the engagement.

C. Client Agreement on the Eventual Fee Allocation Between the Discharged Counsel and the Current Counsel and Conflict of Interest Waiver

Because the client approval requirement is explicit in Rule 1.5(e), some authorities have used it as the vehicle to mandate client consent to fee divisions in consecutive representations even though Rule 1.5(e) is limited to joint representations. Rule 1.5(a), however, alone supports the conclusion that client consent is required to divide the fee at the end of the case.

Rule 1.5(a) requires that any fee be reasonable, including the total fees of predecessor and successor counsel, and client consent is required for all disbursements, including all fees payable to predecessor and successor counsel.

A client always has the right to challenge the total fee charged or the separate fee claimed by the predecessor counsel. The successor counsel may not disburse fees claimed by that counsel absent the client's consent. Otherwise, the client's right to challenge the fee as unreasonable would be impaired, if not extinguished. Of course, there may be circumstances where client consent may be inferred. For example, consent may be inferred where successor counsel has repeatedly provided notice of a proposed payment to predecessor counsel and the client has not responded.[11]

9 Model Rules R. 1.5 cmt. 7; N.Y. Cnty. Lawyers' Ass'n, Comm. on Prof'l Ethics Op. 715, 1996 WL 592658, at *4 & n.2 (1996).

10 Model Rules R. 1.5(e)(1).

11 The fee must, of course, be within the total fee as authorized by the client in the successor lawyer's fee agreement. The successor lawyer must also have a reasonable basis to conclude that the client has received the communications and is not suffering from any mental or physical disorder that prevents the client from considering the successor lawyer's communications.

D. Role of Successor Counsel with Respect to Predecessor Counsel's Claim for a Share of the Fee

The role of the successor counsel in the process of addressing the predecessor counsel's claim for a share of the fee may vary. The successor counsel's work may include an assessment of the legitimacy of the predecessor counsel's fee claim to properly advise the client on the client's share of any recovery and the amount of funds, if any, that successor counsel must hold in trust under Rule 1.15. If the initial scope of successor counsel's representation of the client simply leaves the matter to be decided by the predecessor counsel and the client, the successor counsel should so indicate in the engagement agreement. But if the successor counsel offers to represent the client in the *client's* dispute (as opposed to the successor counsel's dispute) with the predecessor counsel, such scope of representation should be reflected either in the initial fee agreement or in a new or revised fee agreement. Typically, where successor counsel is negotiating on behalf of a client with predecessor counsel, successor counsel should review with the client the nature and extent of the predecessor counsel's entitlement to a fee, including whether the predecessor counsel has forfeited the right to a fee, in whole or in part.

Successor counsel's compensation for representing the client in the client's dispute with predecessor counsel must be reasonable, which in this context means, at a minimum, that the successor counsel cannot charge the client for work that only increases the successor counsel's share of the contingent fee and does not increase the client's recovery. Successor counsel must also obtain the client's informed consent to any conflict of interest that exists due to successor counsel's dual roles as counsel for the client *and* a party interested in a portion of the proceeds.

In many situations, the fees paid to predecessor and successor counsel may not affect the client's recovery. In these instances, successor counsel may obtain the client's consent to any fee split that does not alter the client's recovery. The client can, after consultation and adequate disclosure, decide that the matter should be worked out between counsel without further need for consent or consultation with the client. The client's consent should be informed and successor counsel may need to raise the possibility of protracted proceedings that could burden a client who may have nothing to gain and may be indifferent about the outcome.[12] Where the client is indifferent as to

12 Most disputes between lawyers about a fee will likely involve the client as a witness. The disputes may also involve disclosure of the client's confidential information under Rule 1.6. In many such circumstances, the client may wish simply to move on and not be involved in any dispute between her lawyers. In addition, where recoveries are obtained through settlement, many settlement agreements impose confidentiality obligations on the client as to the settlement terms. In adjudicating a fee dispute with predecessor counsel, the successor lawyer must take steps to ensure that any confidentiality term of a settlement is respected.

the fee allocation between the two counsel, both counsel must, in adjudicating their own dispute over their respective shares of the contingent fee, take adequate steps to protect client confidentiality under Rule 1.6, as well as any confidentiality provisions in any underlying settlement agreement.

The predecessor counsel may also seek client consent to a share of the fee. If the successor counsel represents the client in the fee dispute, then the predecessor counsel may not communicate about the fee directly with the former client without successor counsel's consent under Rule 4.2.

E. The Successor Counsel's Obligations with Respect to the Funds

Where a disagreement persists between the predecessor counsel and the client, or predecessor counsel and successor counsel, about the amount of the predecessor counsel's fees from the proceeds obtained by the successor counsel, the successor counsel must comply with Rule 1.15 and substantive law in notifying predecessor counsel of the receipt of the funds and in deciding how to handle the funds. In many jurisdictions, a counsel terminated without cause has the right to payment based on *quantum meruit*. If the client asserts that client terminated the predecessor counsel for cause, that counsel may not have any right to proceeds from the recovery.[13] If there is a dispute as to whether some or all of those funds should be paid to the predecessor counsel by the client but there is a claim to the proceeds by that counsel, the successor counsel must hold the disputed portion of the funds in a client trust account pursuant to Rule 1.15(e).[14]

III. Conclusion

Where a client has engaged successor counsel in a contingent fee matter to replace predecessor counsel, successor counsel must inform the client in writing that predecessor counsel may have a claim against the contingent fee. Successor counsel is not, however, bound by the fee-division procedures set forth in Model Rule 1.5(e) because such procedures are designed to address

---

13 Determination of what constitutes terminating a lawyer's services "for cause" or a lawyer withdrawing from a representation *without* "just cause" vary by state, but some examples of situations where a lawyer had justifiable cause to withdraw and may be entitled to a *quantum meruit* fee are: obligation to withdraw due to unforeseen conflict of interest (Smith & Burnetti, P.A. v. Faulk, 677 So. 2d 404 (Fla. Dist. Ct. App. 1996)); unanticipated costs and expenses of litigation (Smith v. R.J. Reynolds Tobacco Co., 630 A.2d 820 (N.J. Super. Ct. App. Div. 1993)); client refused to comply with discovery obligations (Ashford v. Interstate Trucking Corp. of America, Inc., 524 N.W.2d 500 (Minn. Ct. App. 1994)).

14 The statements in this section are general in nature and do not address substantive law issues that may vary from state to state regarding charging or retaining liens. The rights and claims of the predecessor lawyer may depend on whether the client terminated the lawyer for cause or without cause, whether the lawyer withdrew with or without cause, or whether the lawyer has an effective lien. These substantive law issues are not addressed in this Opinion.

situations where two lawyers from different firms handle a case concurrently. Upon a recovery, successor counsel must obtain the client's agreement before dividing any fee with predecessor counsel. In resolving any dispute, particularly a dispute solely between counsel, both successor and predecessor counsel remain bound by their confidentiality obligations to the client and any further confidentiality obligations undertaken by the client in a settlement of the underlying matter. In handling funds that are in dispute, the successor lawyer must follow the requirements of Model Rule 1.15.

AMERICAN BAR ASSOCIATION
STANDING COMMITTEE ON ETHICS AND PROFESSIONAL RESPONSIBILITY

Formal Opinion 488 **September 5, 2019**

Judges' Social or Close Personal Relationships with Lawyers or Parties as Grounds for Disqualification or Disclosure

Rule 2.11 of the Model Code of Judicial Conduct identifies situations in which judges must disqualify themselves in proceedings because their impartiality might reasonably be questioned—including cases implicating some familial and personal relationships—but it is silent with respect to obligations imposed by other relationships. This opinion identifies three categories of relationships between judges and lawyers or parties to assist judges in evaluating ethical obligations those relationships may create under Rule 2.11: (1) acquaintanceships; (2) friendships; and (3) close personal relationships. In short, judges need not disqualify themselves if a lawyer or party is an acquaintance, nor must they disclose acquaintanceships to the other lawyers or parties. Whether judges must disqualify themselves when a party or lawyer is a friend or shares a close personal relationship with the judge or should instead take the lesser step of disclosing the friendship or close personal relationship to the other lawyers and parties, depends on the circumstances. Judges' disqualification in any of these situations may be waived in accordance and compliance with Rule 2.11(C) of the Model Code.[1]

I. Introduction

The Committee has been asked to address judges' obligation to disqualify[2] themselves in proceedings in which they have social or close personal relationships with the lawyers or parties other than a spousal, domestic partner, or other close family relationship. Rule 2.11 of the Model Code of Judi-

1 This opinion is based on the Model Code of Judicial Conduct as amended by the House of Delegates through February 2019. Individual jurisdictions' court rules, laws, opinions, and rules of professional conduct control. The Committee expresses no opinion on the applicable law or constitutional interpretation in a particular jurisdiction.

2 The terms "recuse" and "disqualify" are often used interchangeably in judicial ethics. *See* Model Code of Judicial Conduct R. 2.11 cmt. 1 (2011) [hereinafter Model Code] (noting the varying usage between jurisdictions). We have chosen to use "disqualify" because that is the term used in the Model Code of Judicial Conduct.

cial Conduct ("Model Code") lists situations in which judges must disqualify themselves in proceedings because their impartiality might reasonably be questioned—including cases implicating some specific family and personal relationships—but the rule provides no guidance with respect to the types of relationships addressed in this opinion.[3]

Public confidence in the administration of justice demands that judges perform their duties impartially, and free from bias and prejudice. Furthermore, while actual impartiality is necessary, the public must also perceive judges to be impartial. The Model Code therefore requires judges to avoid even the appearance of impropriety in performing their duties.[4] As part of this obligation, judges must consider the actual and perceived effects of their relationships with lawyers and parties who appear before them on the other participants in proceedings.[5] If a judge's relationship with a lawyer or party would cause the judge's impartiality to reasonably be questioned, the judge must disqualify himself or herself from the proceeding.[6] Whether a judge's relationship with a lawyer or party may cause the judge's impartiality to reasonably be questioned and thus require disqualification is (a) evaluated against an objective reasonable person standard;[7] and (b) depends on the facts of the case.[8] Judges are presumed to be impartial.[9] Hence, judicial disqualification is the exception rather than the rule.

Judges are ordinarily in the best position to assess whether their impartiality might reasonably be questioned when lawyers or parties with whom they have relationships outside of those identified in Rule 2.11(A) appear before them.[10] After all, relationships vary widely and are unique to the individuals involved. Furthermore, a variety of factors may affect judges' decisions whether to disqualify themselves in proceedings. For example, in smaller communities and relatively sparsely-populated judicial districts,

3 *See* Model Code R. 2.11(A) (listing relationships where a judge's impartiality might reasonable be questioned, including where (1) the judge has "a personal bias or prejudice" toward a lawyer or party; (2) the judge's spouse, domestic partner, or a person within the third degree of relationship to the judge or the judge's spouse or domestic partner is a party or a lawyer in the proceeding; or (3) such person has more than a de minimis interest in the matter or is likely to be a material witness).

4 Model Code R. 1.2.

5 *See* Model Code R. 2.4(B) (stating that a judge shall not permit family or social interests or relationships to influence the judge's judicial conduct or judgment).

6 Model Code R. 2.11(A).

7 Mondy v. Magnolia Advanced Materials, Inc., 815 S.E.2d 70, 75 (Ga. 2018); State v. Payne, 488 S.W.3d 161, 166 (Mo. Ct. App. 2016); Thompson v. Millard Pub. Sch. Dist. No. 17, 921 N.W.2d 589, 594 (Neb. 2019).

8 N.Y. Advisory Comm. on Judicial Ethics Op. 11-125, 2011 WL 8333125, at *1 (2011) [hereinafter N.Y. Jud. Adv. Op. 11-125].

9 Isom v. State, 563 S.W.3d 533, 546 (Ark. 2018); L.G. v. S.L., 88 N.E.3d 1069, 1073 (Ind. 2018); State v. Nixon, 254 So.3d 1228, 1235 (La. Ct. App. 2018); *Thompson*, 921 N.W.2d at 594.

10 N.Y. Jud. Adv. Op. 11-125, *supra* note 8, at *2.

judges may have social and personal contacts with lawyers and parties that are unavoidable. In that circumstance, too strict a disqualification standard would be impractical to enforce and would potentially disrupt the administration of justice. In other situations, the relationship between the judge and a party or lawyer may have changed over time or may have ended sufficiently far in the past that it is not a current concern when viewed objectively. Finally, judges must avoid disqualifying themselves too quickly or too often lest litigants be encouraged to use disqualification motions as a means of judge-shopping, or other judges in the same court or judicial circuit or district become overburdened.

Recognizing that relationships vary widely, potentially change over time, and are unique to the people involved, this opinion provides general guidance to judges who must determine whether their relationships with lawyers or parties require their disqualification from proceedings, whether the lesser remedy of disclosing the relationship to the other parties and lawyers involved in the proceedings is initially sufficient, or whether neither disqualification nor disclosure is required. This opinion identifies three categories of relationships between judges and lawyers or parties to assist judges in determining what, if any, ethical obligations Rule 2.11 imposes: (1) acquaintanceships; (2) friendships;[11] and (3) close personal relationships. Judges need not disqualify themselves in proceedings in which they are acquainted with a lawyer or party. Whether judges must disqualify themselves when they are friends with a party or lawyer or share a close personal relationship with a lawyer or party or should instead disclose the friendship or close personal relationship to the other lawyers and parties, depends on the nature of the friendship or close personal relationship in question. The ultimate decision of whether to disqualify is committed to the judge's sound discretion.

II. Analysis

Rule 2.11(A) of the Model Code provides that judges must disqualify themselves in proceedings in which their impartiality might reasonably be questioned and identifies related situations. Perhaps most obviously, under Rule 2.11(A)(1), judges must disqualify themselves when they have a personal bias or prejudice concerning a party or a party's lawyer, or personal

11 Social media, which is simply a form of communication, uses terminology that is distinct from that used in this opinion. Interaction on social media does not itself indicate the type of relationships participants have with one another either generally or for purposes of this opinion. For example, Facebook uses the term "friend," but that is simply a title employed in that context. A judge could have Facebook "friends" or other social media contacts who are acquaintances, friends, or in some sort of close personal relationship with the judge. The proper characterization of a person's relationship with a judge depends on the definitions and examples used in this opinion.

knowledge of facts that are in dispute in the proceeding. The parties may not waive a judge's disqualification based on personal bias or prejudice.[12]

Beyond matters in which the judge's alleged or perceived personal bias or prejudice is at issue, Rule 2.11(A) identifies situations in which a judge's personal relationships may call into question the judge's impartiality. Under Rule 2.11(A)(2), these include proceedings in which the judge knows that the judge, the judge's spouse or domestic partner, or a person within the third degree of relationship to either of them, or the spouse or domestic partner of such a person (a) is a party to the proceeding, or is a party's officer, director, general partner, or managing member; (b) is acting as a lawyer in the proceeding; (c) has more than a de minimis interest that could be affected by the proceeding; or (d) is likely to be a material witness in the proceeding. Under Rule 2.11(A)(4), a judge may further be required to disqualify himself or herself if a party, the party's lawyer, or that lawyer's law firm has made aggregate contributions to the judge's election or retention campaign within a specified number of years that exceed a specified amount or an amount that is reasonable and appropriate for an individual or entity. But, while Rule 2.11(A) mandates judges' disqualification in these situations, Rule 2.11(C) provides that a judge may disclose on the record the basis of the judge's disqualification and may ask the parties and their lawyers whether they waive disqualification. If the parties and lawyers agree that the judge should not be disqualified, the judge may participate in the proceeding.[13]

Apart from the personal relationships identified in Rule 2.11(A), a judge may have relationships with other categories of people that, depending on the facts, might reasonably call into question the judge's impartiality. These include acquaintances, friends, and people with whom the judge shares a close personal relationship.

A. Acquaintances

A judge and lawyer should be considered acquaintances when their interactions outside of court are coincidental or relatively superficial, such as being members of the same place of worship, professional or civic organization, or the like.[14] For example, the judge and the lawyer might both attend bar association or other professional meetings; they may have represented co-parties in litigation before the judge ascended to the bench; they may meet each other at school or other events involving their children or spouses; they may see each other when socializing with mutual friends; they may belong to the same country club or gym; they may patronize the same businesses and periodically encounter one another there; they may live in the same area or

12 Model Code R. 2.11(C).

13 Disqualification may not be waived where the judge harbors a personal bias or prejudice toward a party or a party's lawyer. *See* Model Code R. 2.11(A)(1) & (C).

14 N.Y. Jud. Adv. Op. 11-125, *supra* note 8, at *2.

neighborhood and run into one another at neighborhood or area events, or at homeowners' meetings; or they might attend the same religious services. Generally, neither the judge nor the lawyer seeks contact with the other, but they greet each other amicably and are cordial when their lives intersect.[15]

A judge and party should be considered acquaintances in the same circumstances in which a judge and lawyer would be so characterized. Additionally, a judge and party may be characterized as acquaintances where the party owns or operates a business that the judge patronizes on the same terms as any other person.

Evaluated from the standpoint of a reasonable person fully informed of the facts,[16] a judge's acquaintance with a lawyer or party, standing alone, is not a reasonable basis for questioning the judge's impartiality.[17] A judge therefore has no obligation to disclose his or her acquaintance with a lawyer or party to other lawyers or parties in a proceeding. A judge may, of course, disclose the acquaintanceship if the judge so chooses.

B. Friendships

In contrast to simply being acquainted, a judge and a party or lawyer may be friends. "Friendship" implies a degree of affinity greater than being acquainted with a person; indeed, the term connotes some degree of mutual affection. Yet, not all friendships are the same; some may be professional, while others may be social. Some friends are closer than others. For example, a judge and lawyer who once practiced law together may periodically meet for a meal when their busy schedules permit, or, if they live in different cities, try to meet when one is in the other's hometown. Or, a judge and lawyer who were law school classmates or were colleagues years before may stay in touch through occasional calls or correspondence, but not regularly see one another. On the other hand, a judge and lawyer may exchange gifts at holidays and special occasions; regularly socialize together; regularly communicate and coordinate activities because their children are close friends and routinely spend time at each other's homes; vacation together with their families; share a mentor-protégé relationship developed while colleagues before the judge was appointed or elected to the bench; share confidences and intimate details of their lives; or, for various reasons, be so close as to consider the other an extended family member.

---

15 *Id.*

16 *See* State v. Mouelle, 922 N.W.2d 706, 713 (Minn. 2019) ("In deciding whether disqualification is required, the relevant question is 'whether a reasonable examiner, with full knowledge of the facts and circumstances, would question the judge's impartiality.'" (quoting *In re* Jacobs, 802 N.W.2d 748, 753 (Minn. 2011)).

17 N.Y. Jud. Adv. Op. 11-125, *supra* note 8, 2011 WL 8333125, at *2; Va. Judicial Ethics Advisory Comm. Op. 01-08, 2001 WL 36352802, at *1, *2 (2001).

Certainly, not all friendships require judges' disqualification,[18] as the Seventh Circuit explained over thirty years ago:

> In today's legal culture friendships among judges and lawyers are common. They are more than common; they are desirable. A judge need not cut himself off from the rest of the legal community. Social as well as official communications among judges and lawyers may improve the quality of legal decisions. Social interactions also make service on the bench, quite isolated as a rule, more tolerable to judges. Many well-qualified people would hesitate to become judges if they knew that wearing the robe meant either discharging one's friends or risking disqualification in substantial numbers of cases. Many courts therefore have held that a judge need not disqualify himself just because a friend—even a close friend—appears as a lawyer.[19]

Judicial ethics authorities agree that judges need not disqualify themselves in many cases in which a party or lawyer is a friend.[20]

There may be situations, however, in which the judge's friendship with a lawyer or party is so tight that the judge's impartiality might reasonably be questioned. Whether a friendship between a judge and a lawyer or party reaches that point and consequently requires the judge's disqualification in

18 *See, e.g., In re* Complaint of Judicial Misconduct, 816 F.3d 1266, 1268 (9th Cir. 2016) (stating that "friendship between a judge and a lawyer, or other participant in a trial, without more, does not require recusal"); Schupper v. People, 157 P.3d 516, 520 (Colo. 2007) (reasoning that friendship between a judge and a lawyer is not a per se basis for disqualification; rather, a reviewing court should "look for those situations where the friendship is so close or unusual that a question of partiality might reasonably be raised"); *In re* Disqualification of Park, 28 N.E.3d 56, 58 (Ohio 2014) ("[T]he existence of a friendship between a judge and an attorney appearing before her, without more, does not automatically mandate the judge's disqualification . . . ."); *In re* Disqualification of Lynch, 985 N.E.2d 491, 493 (Ohio 2012) ("The reasonable person would conclude that the oaths and obligations of a judge are not so meaningless as to be overcome merely by friendship with a party's counsel."); State v. Cannon, 254 S.W.3d 287, 308 (Tenn. 2008) ("The mere existence of a friendship between a judge and an attorney is not sufficient, standing alone, to mandate recusal.").

19 United States v. Murphy, 768 F.2d 1518, 1537 (7th Cir. 1985).

20 U.S. Judicial Conf., Comm. on Codes of Conduct Advisory Op. No. 11, 2009 WL 8484525, at *1 (2009); Ariz. Supreme Ct., Judicial Ethics Advisory Comm. Op. 90-8, 1990 WL 709830, at *1 (1990) [hereinafter Ariz. Jud. Adv. Op. No. 11]; N.Y. Jud. Adv. Op. 11-125, *supra* note 8, 2011 WL 8333125, at *2. *But see* Fla. Supreme Ct., Judicial Ethics Advisory Comm. Op. No. 2012-37, 2012 WL 663576, at *1 (2012) (stating that a judge "must recuse from any cases in which the judge's [close personal] friend appears as a party, witness or representative" of the bank where the friend was employed).

the proceeding is essentially a question of degree.[21] The answer depends on the facts of the case.[22]

A judge should disclose to the other lawyers and parties in the proceeding information about a friendship with a lawyer or party "that the judge believes the parties or their lawyers might reasonably consider relevant to a possible motion for disqualification, even if the judge believes there is no basis for disqualification."[23] If, after disclosure, a party objects to the judge's participation in the proceeding, the judge has the discretion to either continue to preside over the proceeding or to disqualify himself or herself. The judge should put the reasons for the judge's decision to remain on the case or to disqualify himself or herself on the record.

C. Close Personal Relationships

A judge may have a personal relationship with a lawyer or party that goes beyond or is different from common concepts of friendship, but which does not implicate Rule 2.11(A)(2). For example, the judge may be romantically involved with a lawyer or party, the judge may desire a romantic relationship with a lawyer or party or be actively pursuing one, the judge and a lawyer or party may be divorced but remain amicable, the judge and a lawyer or party may be divorced but communicate frequently and see one another regularly because they share custody of children, or a judge might be the godparent of a lawyer's or party's child or vice versa.

A judge must disqualify himself or herself when the judge has a romantic relationship with a lawyer or party in the proceeding, or desires or is pursuing such a relationship. As the New Mexico Supreme Court has observed, "the rationale for requiring recusal in cases involving family members also applies when a close or intimate relationship [between a judge and a lawyer appearing before the judge] exists because, under such circumstances, the judge's impartiality is questionable."[24] A judge should disclose other intimate

---

21 *See Schupper*, 157 P.3d at 520 (explaining that friendship between a judge and a lawyer is not an automatic basis for disqualification; rather, a reviewing court should "look for those situations where the friendship is so close or unusual that a question of partiality might reasonably be raised"); Ariz. Jud. Adv. Op. No. 11, *supra* note 20, at *1 (suggesting that in weighing disqualification where a lawyer who is a friend appears in the judge's court, the judge should consider as one factor "the closeness of the friendship"); Charles G. Geyh et al., Judicial Conduct and Ethics § 4.07[4], at 4-27 (5th ed. 2013) ("Whether disqualification is required when a friend appears as a party to a suit before a judge depends on how close the personal . . . relationship is between the judge and the party.").

22 N.Y. Jud. Adv. Op. 11-125, *supra* note 8, at *1.

23 *See* Model Code R. 2.11 cmt. [5] ("A judge should disclose on the record information that the judge believes the parties or their lawyers might reasonably consider relevant to a possible motion for disqualification, even if the judge believes there is no basis for disqualification.").

24 *In re* Schwartz, 255 P.3d 299, 304 (N.M. 2011).

or close personal relationships with a lawyer or party to the other lawyers and parties in the proceeding even if the judge believes that he or she can be impartial.[25] If, after disclosure, a party objects to the judge's participation in the proceeding, the judge has the discretion to either continue to preside over the proceeding or to disqualify himself or herself. The judge should put the reasons for the judge's decision to remain on the case or to disqualify himself or herself on the record.

D. Waiver

In accordance and compliance with Rule 2.11(C), a judge subject to disqualification based on a friendship or close personal relationship with a lawyer or party may disclose on the record the basis for the judge's disqualification and may ask the parties and their lawyers to consider whether to waive disqualification.[26] If the parties and lawyers agree that the judge should not be disqualified, the judge may participate in the proceeding. The agreement that the judge may participate in the proceeding must be put on the record of the proceeding.

III. Conclusion

Judges must decide whether to disqualify themselves in proceedings in which they have relationships with the lawyers or parties short of spousal, domestic partner, or other close familial relationships. This opinion identifies three categories of relationships between judges and lawyers or parties to assist judges in determining what, if any, ethical obligations those relationships create under Rule 2.11: (1) acquaintances; (2) friendships; and (3) close personal relationships. In summary, judges need not disqualify themselves if a lawyer or party is an acquaintance, nor must they disclose acquaintanceships to the other lawyers or parties. Whether judges must disqualify themselves when a party or lawyer is a friend or shares a close personal relationship with the judge or should instead take the lesser step of disclosing the friendship or close personal relationship to the other lawyers and parties, depends on the circumstances. Judges' disqualification in any of these situations may be waived in accordance and compliance with Rule 2.11(C) of the Model Code.

---

25 *See* Model Code R. 2.11 cmt. [5]. A judge who prefers to keep such a relationship private may disqualify himself or herself from the proceeding.

26 Disqualification may not be waived if the judge has a personal bias or prejudice concerning a party or a party's lawyer. Model Code R. 2.11(C).

AMERICAN BAR ASSOCIATION

STANDING COMMITTEE ON ETHICS AND PROFESSIONAL RESPONSIBILITY

Formal Opinion 489 **December 4, 2019**

Obligations Related to Notice When Lawyers Change Firms

Lawyers have the right to leave a firm and practice at another firm. Likewise, clients have the right to switch lawyers or law firms, subject to approval of a tribunal, when applicable (and conflicts of interest). The ethics rules do not allow non-competition clauses in partnership, member, shareholder, or employment agreements. Lawyers and law firm management have ethical obligations to assure the orderly transition of client matters when lawyers notify a firm they intend to move to a new firm. Firms may require some period of advance notice of an intended departure. The period of time should be the minimum necessary, under the circumstances, for clients to make decisions about who will represent them, assemble files, adjust staffing at the firm if the firm is to continue as counsel on matters previously handled by the departing attorney, and secure firm property in the departing lawyer's possession. Firm notification requirements, however, cannot be so rigid that they restrict or interfere with a client's choice of counsel or the client's choice of when to transition a matter. Firms also cannot restrict a lawyer's ability to represent a client competently during such notification periods by restricting the lawyer's access to firm resources necessary to represent the clients during the notification period. The departing lawyer may be required, pre- or post-departure, to assist the firm in assembling files, transitioning matters that remain with the firm, or in the billings of pre-departure matters.[1]

I. Introduction

As succinctly noted in ABA Op. 09-455, "Many lawyers change law firm associations during their careers." That opinion addressed the need to disclose to new firms information about clients of a departing lawyer in order to perform a conflict of interest analysis before the departing lawyer joins the new firm. This opinion discusses the ethical obligations of both a departing

1 This opinion is based on the ABA Model Rules of Professional Conduct as amended by the ABA House of Delegates through August 2019. The laws, court rules, regulations, rules of professional conduct, and opinions promulgated in individual jurisdictions are controlling.

lawyer and their former firm in protecting client interests during the lawyer's transition. Such ethical obligations include providing the firm with sufficient notice of the intended departure for the firm and departing lawyer to notify clients, work together to ensure that the transition of files as directed by clients is orderly and timely, return firm property, update remaining firm staff/lawyers, and organize files that clients authorize to remain with the firm.[2] A departing lawyer's and law firm's agreement to cooperate in these matters post-departure is relevant in determining whether notice provided by such lawyer to the firm is consistent with these obligations and with Rule 5.6(a) as further discussed below. Ideally the firm will have written policies to provide guidance to lawyers about the procedures the firm anticipates following when a lawyer leaves the firm. This affords everyone some uniform expectations about working together to facilitate transitioning clients.

Firm partnership/shareholder/member/employment agreements cannot impose a notification period that would unreasonably delay the diligent representation of the client or unnecessarily interfere with a lawyer's departure beyond the time necessary to address transition issues, particularly where the departing lawyer has agreed to cooperate post-departure in such matters. Nor may a firm penalize a client who wants to go with a departing lawyer by withholding firm resources the lawyer needs to continue to represent the client prior to departure. Departing lawyers also have a duty, pre- or post-departure to cooperate with the firm they are leaving to assist in the organization and updating of client files for clients remaining with the firm, including docketing of deadlines, updating lawyers at the firm who will take over the file and the like, and similarly to cooperate reasonably in billing. A departing partner may be required to return or account for firm property, such as intellectual property, proprietary information, and hardware/phones/computers, and to allow firm data to be deleted from all devices retained by the departing attorney, unless the data is part of the client files transitioning with the departing lawyer.[3]

2 *See* ABA Comm. on Ethics & Prof'l Responsibility, Formal Op. 99-414 (1999) at n. 1 (clients should be given the option to stay with a firm, go with a departing attorney, or choose another firm altogether).

3 *See* State Bar of Ariz., Formal Op. 10-02 (2010) ("When a lawyer's employment with a firm is terminated, both the firm and the departing lawyer have ethical obligations to notify affected clients, avoid prejudice to those clients, and share information as necessary to facilitate continued representation and avoid conflicts. These ethical obligations can best be satisfied through cooperation and planning for any departure.").

II. Analysis

A. The Lawyer's Obligation to Represent Clients Diligently

Lawyers must represent clients competently and diligently. Rule 1.3 provides:

> A lawyer shall act with reasonable diligence and promptness in representing a client.

Rule 3.2 similarly requires:

> A lawyer shall make reasonable efforts to expedite litigation consistent with the interests of the client.

In addition to the duty to represent clients diligently, lawyers have an obligation to communicate relevant information to clients in a timely manner, according to Rule 1.4. This would include promptly notifying a client if a lawyer is changing law firm affiliations.[4] Law firms may not restrict a lawyer's prompt notification of clients, once the law firm has been notified or otherwise learns of the lawyer's intended departure. As noted in ABA Op. 99-414, "informing the client of the lawyer's departure in a timely manner is critical to allowing the client to decide who will represent him."[5] While the departing lawyer and the firm each may unilaterally inform clients of the lawyer's impending departure at or around the same time that the lawyer provides notice to the firm, the firm and departing lawyer should attempt to agree on a joint communication to firm clients with whom the departing lawyer has had significant contact, giving the clients the option of remaining with the firm, going with the departing attorney, or choosing another attorney.[6] In the event that a firm and departing lawyer cannot promptly agree on the terms of a joint letter, a law firm cannot prohibit the departing lawyer from soliciting firm clients.[7]

Some states, such as Florida and Virginia, have a specific Rule of Professional Conduct regarding such situations. For instance, Florida Rule of Professional Conduct 4-5.8(c)(1) provides:

---

4 *See* D.C. Bar Op. 273 (1997) (A lawyer has an obligation under Rule 1.4 to notify a client "sufficiently in advance of the departure to give the client adequate opportunity to consider whether it wants to continue representation by the departing lawyer and, if not, to make other representation arrangements.").

5 *See* ABA Comm. on Ethics & Prof'l Responsibility, Formal Op. 99-414, *supra* note 2, at 2.

6 *Id.* at n. 2 & 5; State Bar of Ariz., Formal Op. 99-14 (1999).

7 *See* Ill. State Bar Ass'n, Advisory Op. 91-12 (1991); Iowa Bd. of Prof'l Ethics Op. 89-48 (1990); State Bar of Mich., Inf. Op. RI-86 (1991); Tex. Comm. on Prof'l Ethics Op. 422 (1985); Va. State Bar, Legal Ethics Op. 1403 (1991); Wash. State Bar Ass'n, Advisory Op. 2118 (2006); Restatement of the Law Third, The Law Governing Lawyers § 9(3)(a) (2000).

> *Lawyers Leaving Law Firms.* Absent a specific agreement otherwise, a lawyer who is leaving a law firm may not unilaterally contact those clients of the law firm for purposes of notifying them about the anticipated departure or to solicit representation of the clients unless the lawyer has approached an authorized representative of the law firm and attempted to negotiate a joint communication to the clients concerning the lawyer leaving the law firm and bona fide negotiations have been unsuccessful.

Under the Model Rules, departing lawyers need not wait to inform clients of the fact of their impending departure, provided that the firm is informed contemporaneously. Law firm management and lawyers remaining at the firm may also contact clients to inform them of the lawyer's impending departure. The preferred next step is for the departing lawyer and the firm to agree upon a joint communication sent to the clients requesting that the clients elect who will continue representing them.

Departing lawyers should communicate with all clients with whom the departing lawyer has had significant client contact that the lawyer intends to change firms. "Significant client contact" would include a client identifying the departing lawyer, by name, as one of the attorneys representing the client.[8] A departing attorney would not have "significant client contact," for instance, if the lawyer prepared one research memo on a client matter for another attorney in the firm but never spoke with the client or discussed legal issues with the client. Similarly, remaining members of the firm may communicate with these clients, offering for the client to be represented by the firm, another firm, or the departing lawyer. Neither the departing lawyer nor the firm may engage in false or misleading statements to clients.[9]

B. Clients Determine Who Will Represent Them

Clients are not property. Law firms and lawyers may not divide up clients when a law firm dissolves or a lawyer transitions to another firm. Subject to conflicts of interest considerations, clients decide who will represent them going forward when a lawyer changes firm affiliation.[10] Where the departing lawyer has principal or material responsibility in a matter, firms should not assign new lawyers to a client's matter, pre-departure, displacing

8 *See* State Bar of Ariz., Formal Op. 99-14 (1999), *see also* RESTATEMENT, *supra* note 7, at § 9(3)(a)(i) (limiting solicitation by departing lawyer to "firm clients on whose matters the lawyer is actively and substantially working").

9 *See, e.g.*, Va. Rules of Prof'l Conduct R. 5.8; MODEL RULES OF PROF'L CONDUCT R. 7.1.

10 *See* ABA Comm. on Ethics & Prof'l Responsibility, Formal Op. 99-414, *supra* note 2; *see also* Heller Ehrman LLP v. Davis Wright Tremaine LLP, 411 P.3d 548, 555 (Cal. 2018) (noting "the client's right to terminate counsel at any time, with or without cause" and that "[t]he client always owns the matter") (citations omitted).

the departing lawyer, absent client direction or exigent circumstances arising from a lawyer's immediate departure from the firm and imminent deadlines needing to be addressed for the client. Thus, clients must be notified promptly of a lawyer's decision to change firms so that the client may decide whether to go with the departing lawyer or stay with the existing firm and have new counsel at the firm assigned.

C. Firm and Departing Lawyer Obligations for Orderly Transitions

Law firm management also has obligations to establish reasonable procedures and policies to assure the ethical transition of client matters when lawyers elect to change firms.

Rule 5.1 provides:

> (a) A partner in a law firm, and a lawyer who individually or together with other lawyers possesses comparable managerial authority in a law firm, shall make reasonable efforts to ensure that the firm has in effect measures giving reasonable assurance that all lawyers in the firm conform to the Rules of Professional Conduct.

Firms may require that departing lawyers notify firm management contemporaneously with the departing lawyer communicating with clients, employees of the firm, or others about the anticipated departure so that the firm and departing lawyer may work together to assure a professional transition of the client matters. The orderly transition of a client matter may require the firm to assess if it has the capacity and expertise to offer to continue to represent the clients. If a departing lawyer is the only lawyer at the firm with the expertise to represent a client on a specific matter, the firm should not offer to continue to represent the client unless the firm has the ability to retain other lawyers with similar expertise.[11]

The firm and departing lawyer must coordinate to assure that all electronic and paper records for client matters are organized and up to date so that the files may be transferred to the new firm or to new counsel at the existing firm, depending upon the clients' choices. A departing lawyer who does not continue to represent a client nevertheless has the obligation to take "steps to the extent reasonably practicable to protect a client's interests."[12] This duty includes the departing lawyer updating files and lawyers at the firm who take over the representation, when possible. If exigent circumstances cause a lawyer's immediate departure from the firm, either voluntarily or involuntarily, relevant clients of that lawyer still must be notified of

---

11 *See* Model Rules of Prof'l Conduct R. 1.1.

12 *Id.* at R. 1.16(d).

the departure and the firm should provide the lawyer with a list of their current and former clients for conflict-checking purposes. The departed lawyer and firm should endeavor to coordinate after the departure, if necessary, to protect client interests.

Firm management should establish policies and procedures to protect the confidentiality of client information from inadvertent disclosure or misuse.[13] The duty of confidentiality requires that departing attorneys return and/or delete all client confidential information in their possession, unless the client is transferring with the departing attorney. The exception to this requirement is for a departing lawyer to retain names and contact information for clients for whom the departing lawyer worked while at the firm, in order to determine conflicts of interests at the departing lawyer's new firm and comply with other applicable ethical or legal requirements. Rule 1.6(b)(7) provides that a lawyer may disclose confidential information "to detect and resolve conflicts of interest arising from the lawyer's change of employment or from changes in the composition or ownership of a firm, but only if the revealed information would not compromise the attorney-client privilege or otherwise prejudice the client." Firms should have policies that require the deletion or return of all electronic and paper client data in a departing lawyer's possession, including on a departing lawyer's personal electronic devices, if the clients are remaining with the firm. Personal electronic devices may include, for instance, cell phones, laptop computers, tablets, home computers, jump drives, discs, cloud storage, and hard drives.

D. Reasonable Notice Periods Cannot Restrict Client's Choice of Counsel or the Right of Lawyers to Change Firms

Model Rule 5.6 prohibits restraints on a client's choice of counsel. The Rule provides:

> A lawyer shall not participate in offering or making:
>
> (a) a partnership, shareholders, operating, employment, or other similar type of agreement that restricts the right of a lawyer to practice after termination of the relationship, except an agreement concerning benefits upon retirement . . .

Firms have an ethical obligation to assure that client matters transition smoothly and therefore, firm partnership/shareholder/member/employment agreements may request a reasonable notification period, necessary to assure that files are organized or updated, and staffing is adjusted to meet client needs. In practice, these notification periods cannot be fixed or rigidly

13 *Id.* at R. 1.6(c).

applied without regard to client direction, or used to coerce or punish a lawyer for electing to leave the firm, nor may they serve to unreasonably delay the diligent representation of a client. If they would affect a client's choice of counsel or serve as a financial disincentive to a competitive departure, the notification period may violate Rule 5.6. A lawyer who wishes to depart may not be held to a pre-established notice period particularly where, for example, the files are updated, client elections have been received, and the departing lawyer has agreed to cooperate post-departure in final billing. In addition, a lawyer who does not seek to represent firm clients in the future should not be held to a pre-established notice period because client elections have not been received.

Case law interpreting Rule 5.6 supports the conclusion that lawyers cannot be held to a fixed notice period and required to work at a firm through the termination of that period. Financial disincentives to a competitive departure have routinely been struck down by the courts and criticized in ethics opinions. In *Cohen v. Lord, Day & Lord*, 550 N.E.2d 410, 411 (N.Y. 1989), the Court of Appeals of New York held that any provision that imposes a "significant monetary penalty" on an attorney who remains in private practice is the functional equivalent of a restriction on the practice of law, even though there is no express prohibition on competitive activities imposed on the withdrawing partner.[14] Courts routinely refuse to enforce provisions in partnership agreements or the like that restrict the right of a lawyer to practice law by means of financial disincentives to competitive departures. "[C]ourts will not enforce contract terms that violate public policy . . . the foundation for Rule 5.6 rests on considerations of public policy, and it would be inimical to public policy to give effect" to provisions inconsistent with the rule.[15]

---

14 *See* Pettingell v. Morrison, Mahoney & Miller, 687 N.E.2d 1237, 1238 (Mass. 1997) (reduction in payments based on the net worth of the firm); Whiteside v. Griffis & Griffis, P.C., 902 S.W.2d 739, 741 (Tex. App. 1995) (same); Jacob v. Norris McLaughlin & Marcus, 607 A.2d 142, 146 (N.J. 1992) (reduced payments based on annual draws); Gray v. Martin, 663 P.2d 1285 (Or. Ct. App. 1983) (reduced share of future firm profits).

15 Dowd & Dowd, Ltd. v. Gleason, 693 N.E.2d 358, 370 (Ill. 1998); *see also* Stevens v. Rooks Pitts and Poust, 682 N.E.2d 1125, 1130 (Ill. App. Ct. 1997) ("courts have overwhelmingly refused to enforce provisions in partnership agreements which restrict the practice of law through financial disincentives to the withdrawing attorney"); *Pettingell*, 687 N.E.2d at 1239 ("[t]he strong majority rule . . . is that a court will not give effect to an agreement that greatly penalizes a lawyer for competing with a former law firm"); Pierce v. Hand, Arendall, Bedsole, Greaves & Johnston, 678 So.2d 765, 767 (Ala. 1996); *Gray*, 663 P.2d at 1290. *But see* Howard v. Babcock, 863 P.2d 150 (Cal. 1993). The Supreme Court of California reviewed a partnership agreement which provided that departing partners who competed in the Los Angeles area in the field of insurance defense during the year following their departure forfeited their entitlement to withdrawal benefits other than their capital accounts. The court upheld the forfeiture provision: "[a]n agreement that assesses a reasonable cost against a partner who chooses to compete with his or her former partners does not restrict the practice of law." *Id.* at 156. The *Babcock* decision has been rejected by courts outside of California

There is no meaningful distinction for the purposes of Rule 5.6 between an agreement provision that imposes a financial disincentive to a competitive departure irrespective of the pre-departure notice requirements and a provision that imposes a financial disincentive for the failure to comply with a fixed, pre-established notice period that extends beyond the time necessary, generally or in a particular case, to ensure an appropriate transition, as discussed above. "Although 'reasonable' notice provisions may be justified to ensure clients are protected when firm lawyers depart, what is 'reasonable' in any given circumstances can turn on whether it is truly the client's interest that is being protected or simply a thinly disguised restriction on the right to practice in violation of RPC 5.6(a)."[16] Moreover, to the extent that a firm routinely waives the full notice requirement, enforcement in a particular instance is problematic when used to penalize a lawyer who leaves to compete with the firm.[17]

E. Access to Firm Resources During Transition Period

After the firm knows that a lawyer intends to depart but such lawyer has not yet, in fact, left the firm, the lawyer must have access to adequate firm resources needed to competently represent the client during any interim period. For instance, the lawyer cannot be required to work from home or remotely, be deprived of appropriate and necessary assistance from support staff or other lawyers necessary to represent the clients competently, including access to research and drafting tools that the firm generally makes available to lawyers. A lawyer cannot be precluded from using associates or other lawyers, previously assigned to a client matter or otherwise normally available to lawyers at the firm to represent firm clients competently and diligently during the pre-departure period.

---

that have considered it. *Pettingell*, 687 N.E.2d at 1239 ("[c]ourts have not been attracted to the contrary view expressed in *Howard v. Babcock*"); *see also Stevens*, 682 N.E.2d at 1130–33; Zeldes, Needle & Cooper v. Shrader, 1997 WL 644908, at *6 n.6 (Conn. Super. Ct. 1997); *Whiteside*, 902 S.W.2d at 744 ("[w]e are unwilling to follow this distinctly minority position and abandon the concept of client choice that we believe remains the premise underlying DR 2-108"); Restatement, *supra* note 7, at § 13 RN to cmt. b. ("Only in California . . . are restrictive covenants in law-firm agreements enforced"); *but see* Capozzi v. Latasha & Capozzi, P.C., 797 A.2d 314, 320-322 (Pa. Sup. Ct. 2002) (holding that forfeiture for competition provisions were enforceable but striking down the clause at issue as unreasonable).

16 Mark J. Fucile, *Moving On: Duties Beyond the RPCs When Changing Law Firms*, Or. St. B. Bull. (June 2013); *see also* Borteck v. Riker, Danzig, Scherer, Hyland & Perretti LLP, 179 N.J.246, 260–261 (N.J. 2004) ("firms must guard against provisions that unreasonably delay an attorney's orderly transition from one firm to another").

17 *See* Angela Morris, *Are Law Firms Invoking Obscure Contractual Clauses to Delay Lateral Moves? Or Does It Just Seem That Way?*, ABA J., Apr. 1, 2019.

Similarly, firms cannot prohibit or restrict access to email, voicemail, files, and electronic court filing systems where such systems are necessary for the departing attorney to represent clients competently and diligently during the notice period. Once the lawyer has left the firm, the firm should set automatic email responses and voicemail messages for the departed lawyer's email and telephones, to provide notice of the lawyer's departure, and offer an alternative contact at the firm for inquiries. A supervising lawyer at the firm should review the departed lawyer's firm emails, voicemails, and paper mail in accordance with client directions and promptly forward communications to the departed lawyer for all clients continuing to be represented by that lawyer.

F. New Matters Coming in During Transition Period

During the notification period the lawyer and firm should determine how any new matters or new clients coming into the departing attorney will be treated—as a new client (or matter) of the existing firm or the new firm. To avoid client confusion and disputes, the firm and departing lawyer should discuss and clarify how new client matters will be addressed at the time that the departing lawyer notifies the firm of the impending departure.

G. Conclusion

Lawyers have the right to leave a firm and practice at another firm. Likewise, clients have the right to switch lawyers or law firms, subject to the approval of a tribunal, when applicable (and conflicts of interest). The ethics rules do not allow non-competition clauses in partnership or employment agreements. Lawyers and law firm management have ethical obligations to assure the orderly transition of client matters when lawyers notify a firm they intend to move to a new firm. Firms may require some period of advance notice of an intended departure to provide sufficient time to notify clients to select who will represent them, assemble files, adjust staffing at the firm if the firm is to continue as counsel on matters previously handled by the departing attorney, and secure firm property in the departing lawyer's possession. Firm notification requirements, however, cannot be fixed or pre-determined in every instance, cannot restrict or interfere with a client's choice of counsel, and cannot hinder or unreasonably delay the diligent representation of a client. Firms also cannot restrict a lawyer's ability to represent a client competently during any pre-departure notification periods by restricting the lawyer's access to firm resources necessary to represent the clients during the notification period. Firms should not displace departing lawyers before departure by assigning new lawyers to a client's matter, absent client direction or exigent circumstances requiring protection of clients' interests. A firm's reliance on a fixed notice period set forth in an agreement either to attempt to require the lawyer to stay at the firm for that period or to impose a financial penalty for an early departure must be justified by particular circumstances related to the orderly transition of client matters and must account for the departing lawyer's offer to cooperate post-departure in these and other matters. Otherwise, a firm's imposition of a fixed notice period may be inconsistent with Rule 5.6(a).

Abstaining: Hon. Goodwin Liu.

AMERICAN BAR ASSOCIATION
STANDING COMMITTEE ON ETHICS AND PROFESSIONAL RESPONSIBILITY

Formal Opinion 490 **March 24, 2020**

Ethical Obligations of Judges in Collecting Legal Financial Obligations and Other Debts

Summary
This opinion addresses the ethical requirement of judges under the Model Code of Judicial Conduct, Rules 1.1 and 2.6, to undertake a meaningful inquiry into a litigant's ability to pay court fines, fees, restitution, other charges, bail, or civil debt before using incarceration as punishment for failure to pay, as inducement to pay or appear, or as a method of purging a financial obligation whenever state or federal law so provides. Meaningful inquiry is also required by Rules 1.2, 2.2, and 2.5 as a fundamental element of procedural justice necessary to maintain the integrity, impartiality, and fairness of the administration of justice and the public's faith in it. According to the same Rules, a judge may not set, impose, or collect legal financial obligations under circumstances that give the judge an improper incentive either to multiply legal financial obligations or to fail to inquire into a litigant's ability to pay. The opinion also discusses innovative guidance on best practices for making ability to pay inquiries, including model bench cards, methods of notice, and techniques for efficiently eliciting relevant financial information from litigants.[1]

I. Introduction
Local, municipal, state, and federal trial court judges do essential work administering justice day in and day out with the utmost integrity, fairness, and dedication. It has long been said that "[f]our things belong to a judge; to hear courteously; to answer wisely; to consider soberly and to decide impartially."[2] Every day, in courtrooms all around the country, trial judges display these and other qualities essential to the administration of justice.

---

1. This opinion is based on the Model Code of Judicial Conduct as amended by the House of Delegates through February 2019. Individual jurisdictions' court rules, laws, opinions, and rules of judicial conduct control. The Committee expresses no opinion on the applicable law or constitutional interpretation in a particular jurisdiction.

2. Leon R. Yankwich, *The Art of Being A Judge*, 105 U. Penn. L. Rev. 374, 385 (1957) (quoting Socrates).

They do so both on and off the bench and despite managing heavy dockets, shrinking budgets, and other constraints.

This opinion is addressed to one important area of procedural justice in which the high standard consistently set by so many judges has not been met in some jurisdictions. There is evidence that judges in some jurisdictions have repeatedly failed to inquire into litigants' ability to pay financial obligations prior to incarceration for nonpayment. Inquiry into a litigant's ability to pay before resorting to incarceration—either as punishment for failure to pay, as a means of purging or inducing payment of a financial obligation (whether civil or criminal), or as leverage to demand bail in amounts unconnected to public safety—is a core ethical obligation of the judiciary. Failure to inquire in the circumstances described in this opinion can violate not only settled law requiring such inquiry, and thus violate Rules 1.1 and 2.6 of the Model Code of Judicial Conduct, (MCJC) but also Rules 1.2, 2.2, and 2.5. The duty to inquire is foundational not just to the constitutional rights of litigants but to the integrity of the judicial process and public confidence in it.[3]

In Section II this opinion describes specific evidence of failures to make legally required inquiries into litigants' ability to pay, as well as the background budget constraints, expansion of court fines, fees, and other legal financial obligations, and the standards relating to judicial discipline. In Section III the opinion analyzes the standards for discipline and presents innovative guidance on best practices for making ability-to-pay inquiries developed by judges and flagship organizations such as the National Center for State Courts and the Conference of State Court Administrators.

II. Background

The U.S. Department of Justice investigation of Ferguson, Missouri, found in 2015 that the city's "municipal court does not act as a neutral arbiter of the law or a check on unlawful police conduct. Instead, the court primarily uses its judicial authority as the means to compel the payment of fines and fees that advance the City's financial interests."[4] The Report concluded that the court's method of collecting legal financial obligations violated the Due Process and the Equal Protection Clauses of the Fourteenth Amendment,

---

3. *See* ABA Standards for Criminal Justice Special Functions of the Trial Judge 6-1.1(a) (Am. Bar Ass'n 3d ed. 2000) ("The trial judge has the responsibility for safeguarding both the rights of the accused and the interests of the public in the administration of criminal justice."); *see also* Model Code of Judicial Conduct pmbl.¶ 1 (Am. Bar Ass'n 2011) ("Inherent in all the Rules contained in this Code are the precepts that judges, individually and collectively, must respect and honor the judicial office as a public trust and strive to maintain and enhance confidence in the legal system.").

4. Civil Rights Div., U.S. Dep't of Justice, Investigation of the Ferguson Police Department 3 (2015).

"impose[d] unnecessary harm, overwhelmingly on African-American individuals, and [ran] counter to public safety."[5]

Ferguson is a particularly egregious example, unrepresentative of the integrity and care regularly shown by fair and dedicated judges in local, municipal, state, and federal courts. But there is evidence that problems with debt collection procedures extend to other jurisdictions. The problems include:

- Threatening to incarcerate or incarcerating individuals for failure to pay legal financial obligations without inquiry into their ability to pay;[6]
- Ordering individuals to pay legal financial obligations with disability benefits, welfare benefits, or money borrowed from family members as a condition of avoiding incarceration and without inquiring into ability to pay;[7]
- Making payment of legal financial obligations a condition of probation and subsequently failing to determine ability to pay before revoking probation for failure to pay either the underlying legal fi-

5. *Id.* at 3, 57-58; *see also* Fant v. City of Ferguson, 107 F. Supp. 3d 1016, 1030–32 (E.D. Mo. 2015), *amended by* Fant v. City of Ferguson, No. 4:15-CV-00253-AGF, 2015 WL 4232917, at *3–4 (E.D. Mo. July 13, 2015); Alicia Bannon et al., Brennan Ctr. for Justice, Criminal Justice Debt: A Barrier to Reentry 4 (2010) (describing racially disproportionate effects of fines, fees, and other charges).

6. *See* West v. City of Santa Fe, No. 3:16-CV-00309, 2018 WL 5276264, at *1 (S.D. Tex. Sept. 19, 2018) (denying defendants' motion to dismiss complaint alleging *Bearden* violations), adopting report and recommendation of Magistrate Judge, West v. City of Santa Fe, 2018 WL 4047115, at *10 (S.D. Tex. Aug. 16, 2018)]; Brown v. Lexington Cty., No. 3:17-cv-1426-MBS, 2018 WL 1556189, at *2–3,*14–15 (D.S.C. Mar. 29, 2018) (plaintiffs alleged incarceration for failing to pay legal financial obligations occurred without inquiry into ability to pay; denying defendants' motion for summary judgment on ground that there are genuine issues of material fact on judicial immunity claims); Cain v. City of New Orleans, 281 F. Supp. 3d 624, 632–33, 647–52 (E.D. La. 2017) ("There is no evidence that the Judges now consider, or have ever considered, ability to pay before imprisoning indigent criminal defendants for failure to pay" unless "the issue is brought to their attention."), *aff'd sub nom.*, Cain v. White, 937 F.3d 446, 448 (5th Cir. 2019); Doe v. Angelina Cty., 733 F. Supp 245, 253–54 (E.D. Tex. 1990); *see also* Campbell Robertson, *Missouri City to Pay $4.7 Million to Settle Suit Over Jail Practices*, N.Y. Times (July 15, 2016), https://www.nytimes.com/2016/07/16/us/missouri-city-to-pay-4-7-million-to-settle-suit-over-jailing-practices.html (describing settlement of suit against City of Jennings for practices similar to those in Ferguson); *id.* ("Many of the 90 cities around [St. Louis County] were generating substantial proportions of their revenues by aggressively charging fines and fees for violations as minor as broken taillights. Warrants were issued for those who could not or did not pay, and jail time for unpaid traffic tickets was routine."); *id.* (noting the suit's allegation that many of those jailed were "poor and black").

7. *See* Joseph Shapiro, *Supreme Court Ruling Not Enough to Prevent Debtors Prisons*, NPR (May 21, 2014, 5:01 AM), https://www.npr.org/2014/05/21/313118629/supreme-court-ruling-not-enough-to-prevent-debtors-prisons (noting that even when inquiry into ability to pay occurs it is frequently informal and subjective).

nancial obligations or new obligations associated with the costs of administering probation;[8]

- Linking warrants, bonds, and arrest for accused persons, probationers, and others not already serving a prison sentence, in ways that either result in incarceration without inquiry into ability to pay the bond, or result in payment under threat of incarceration;[9]
- Using the contempt power to collect unpaid civil debt by jailing or threatening to jail individuals without inquiry into their ability to pay, or using the contempt power to punish failure to appear at judgment debtor examinations by incarceration where bail on the warrant for contempt of court is set without inquiry into ability to pay and bail is automatically applied to satisfy the civil judgment.[10]
- Maintaining an improper pecuniary interest in the setting, imposition, or enforcement of legal financial obligations, or outsourcing these functions to private entities that have an improper pecuniary interest.[11]

---

8. *See Cain*, 281 F. Supp. 3d at 629–31; Human Rights Watch, Profiting from Probation: America's "Offender-Funded" Probation Industry 1–5 (2014) [hereinafter Profiting from Probation].

9. *See* O'Donnell v. Harris Cty., 892 F.3d 147, 152 (5th Cir. 2018) (affirming preliminary injunction granted by the district court on claim that county bail policies violated due process); McNeil v. Cmty. Prob. Services, LLC, No. 1:18-cv-00033, 2019 WL 633012, at *2-7, 16 (M.D. Tenn. Feb. 14, 2019) (granting preliminary injunction against issuing arrest warrants with secured bail amounts set without inquiry into ability of misdemeanor probationers' ability to pay as a condition of avoiding jail pending probation revocation hearing), *aff'd*, 945 F.3d 991 (6th Cir. 2019); Rodriguez v. Providence Cmty. Corrs., Inc., 155 F. Supp. 3d 758 (M.D. Tenn. 2015) (granting preliminary injunction against issuing arrest warrants with secured bail amounts absent inquiry into a probationers' ability to pay when only alleged probation violation was nonpayment); Jones v. City of Clanton, No. 2:15cv34-MHT, 2015 WL 5387219, at *2 (M.D. Ala. Sept. 14, 2015) (same); *cf.* Walker v. City of Calhoun, 901 F.3d 1245, 1266 (11th Cir. 2018) (concluding that a forty-eight-hour hearing requirement for bail hearings for accused persons is presumptively constitutional).

10. *See* Turner v. Rogers, 564 U.S. 431 (2011) (vacating judgment of civil contempt and remanding for an ability to pay inquiry); *see also* ACLU, A Pound of Flesh: The Criminalization of Private Debt 6 (2018) (noting that forty-four states allow judges to issue arrest warrants for contempt for failure to appear at post-judgment proceedings or failing to otherwise provide financial information); *id.* ("Judges sometimes set bail at the exact amount of the judgment. And the bail money is often turned over to the debt collector or creditor as payment against the judgment.").

11. *See* Caliste v. Cantrell, 937 F.3d 525, 530–31 (5th Cir. 2019) (setting bond without inquiry into ability to pay where court generates significant revenue from bonds for salaries of court staff violates due process); *Cain*, 281 F. Supp. 3d at 655–56 (concluding that an unconstitutional conflict of interest arises when a court's "funding structure puts the Judges in the difficult position of not having sufficient funds to staff their offices unless they impose and collect sufficient fines and fees from a largely indigent population of criminal defendants"); *id.*("[T]he Judges' practice of failing to inquire into ability to pay is itself indicative of their conflict of interest."); Profiting from Probation, *supra* note 8, at 1-7.

In addition to the cases and materials cited in notes 6–10 and this note other cases have resulted in judgments, injunctive relief, or settlement agreements requiring compli-

The Committee recognizes that courts across the country have faced *severe* budget crises over the last few decades as a result of recessions and cuts in traditional sources of state and local funding.[12] To address these significant deficits, many courts have increased legal fines, fees, and other charges.[13] Over the same period, misdemeanor enforcement grew and a movement to require criminal defendants to pay restitution and other costs of administering the criminal justice system expanded (including costs related to appointment of counsel, bail, probation, and jury trial).[14] Furthermore, in some jurisdictions, elements of the administration of criminal justice have been outsourced to private contractors whose compensation may be linked to fines, fees, and other charges assessed against defendants. Overall, the effect is that a person can incur substantial legal financial obligations for conviction of a petty or juvenile offense or even a non-criminal code violation.[15]

---

ance with *Bearden*. *See* Edwards v. Cofield, No. 3:17-CV-321-WKW, 2017 WL 2255775 (M.D. Ala. May 18, 2017); Bell v. City of Jackson, No. 3:15-cv-00732-TSL-RHW, 2016 WL 6405833 (S.D. Miss. June 20, 2016); Kennedy v. City of Biloxi, No. 1:15cv348-HSO-JCG, 2016 WL 4425862 (S.D. Miss. Mar. 7, 2016); Snow v. Lambert, No. 15-567-SDD-RLB, 2015 WL 5071981 (M.D. La. Aug. 27, 2015); Pierce v. City of Velda City, No. 4:15-cv-570-HEA, 2015 WL 10013006 (E.D. Mo. June 3, 2015); Powell v. City of St. Ann, No. 4:15-cv-00840 (E.D. Mo. May 27, 2015); Edwards v. Red Hills Cmty. Prob., No. 1:15-cv-00067-LJA (M.D. Ga. Apr. 10, 2015); Jenkins v. City of Jennings, No. 4:15-cv-00252 (E.D. Mo. Feb. 8, 2015); Burks v. Scott Cty., No 3:14-cv-00745-HTW-LRA (S.D. Miss. Sept. 23, 2014); Fuentes v. Benton Cty., No. 15-2-02976-1 (Sup. Ct. Wash. Yakima Cty. Oct. 6, 2015).

12. John T. Matthias & Laura Klaversma, Nat'l Ctr. For State Courts, Current Practices in Collecting Fines and Fees in State Courts: A Handbook of Collection Issues and Solutions 3, 8 (2d ed. 2009) [hereinafter NCSC Handbook] (describing fiscal crises).

13. *See* Alexes Harris et al., *Drawing Blood from Stones: Legal Debt and Social Inequality in the Contemporary United States*, 115 Am. J. Soc. 1753, 1769 fig. 1 (2010); Bannon et al., *supra* note 5, at 7.

14. In the area of bail, for instance, see Press Release, U.S. Dep't of Justice, Fact Sheet on White House and Justice Dep't Convening — A Cycle of Incarceration: Prison, Debt and Bail Practices (Dec. 3, 2015) (The "rising use of bail payments has contributed to a 60 percent increase in the number of un-convicted inmates in jails between 1996 and 2014 . . . . [I]n New York City in 2010, nearly 80 percent of arrestees failed to make bail at arraignment for bail amounts less than $500."). On changes in misdemeanor enforcement, see Alexandra Natapoff, Punishment Without Crime: How Our Massive Misdemeanor System Traps the Innocent and Makes America More Unequal (2018).

15. *See* State v. Blazina, 344 P.3d 680, 683–84 (Wash. 2015) (en banc) (summarizing data); Claire Greenberg et al., *The Growing and Broad Nature of Legal Financial Obligations: Evidence from Alabama Court Records*, 48 Conn. L. Rev. 1079 (2016); ACLU of Wash. & Columbia Legal Services, Modern-Day Debtors' Prisons: The Ways Court-Imposed Debts Punish People for Being Poor (2014); Juleyka Lantigua-Williams, *How Prison Debt Ensnares Offenders*, The Atlantic (June 2, 2016), https://www.theatlantic.com/politics/archive/2016/06/how-prison-debt-ensnares-offenders/484826/; Monica Llorente, *Criminalizing Poverty Through Fines, Fees, and Costs*, Am. Bar Ass'n (Oct. 3, 2016), https://www.americanbar.org/groups/litigation/committees/childrens-rights/articles/2016/criminalizing-poverty-fines-fees-costs/ (describing a range of legal financial obligations associated with juvenile cases and adult criminal cases; reporting that Illinois charges a fifteen

Enforcement policies for legal financial obligations have shifted as well. The traditional view that judicial independence and impartiality demand restraint in the collection of legal financial obligations[16] gave way over the last three decades to more vigorous collection policies adopted on the view that prompt collection is necessary to "encourage[] personal responsibility by those assessed," to "maintain [the] credibility" and "authority" of courts in the eyes of the public and litigants, and to "increase[] revenue" in the face of "[t]ight operating budgets."[17] These are important state interests as long as the person who faces legal financial obligations is not indigent or otherwise unable to pay. In endorsing this shift in enforcement policy a decade ago, the National Center for State Courts ("NCSC") Handbook admonished that courts should still "pay attention to defendants' perceptions of procedural fairness . . . ."[18] The Handbook added that serving warrants and incarcerating people is not only "expensive ... [t]he defendant often fails once again to appear or pay, and the process starts over . . . ."[19] Incarceration for failure to pay legal financial obligations should therefore be "a last resort."[20]

III. Analysis

The key MCJC Rules that apply to procedural justice are Rule 1.1 ("a judge shall comply with the law); Rule 1.2 ("a judge shall act at all times in a manner that promotes public confidence in the independence, integrity and impartiality of the judiciary"); Rule 2.2 ("a judge shall uphold the law and shall perform all duties of judicial office fairly and impartially"); Rule 2.5 ("a judge shall perform judicial and administrative duties, competently and diligently" and "shall cooperate with other judges and court officials in the administration of court business"); and Rule 2.6 (a judge shall "accord every person who has a legal interest in a proceeding, or that person's lawyer, the right to be heard according to law"). These rules make clear that "[c]onduct that compromises or appears to compromise the independence, integrity, and impartiality of a judge undermines public confidence in the judiciary."[21]

---

percent penalty on unpaid balances and a thirty percent collection fee); Joseph Shapiro, *As Court Fees Rise, the Poor Are Paying the Price*, NPR (May 19, 2014, 4:02 PM), https://www.npr.org/2014/05/19/312158516/increasing-court-fees-punish-the-poor (noting an increase in court fees over time in forty-eight states); *State-by-State Court Fees*, NPR (May 19, 2014, 4:02 PM), https://www.npr.org/2014/05/19/312455680/state-by-state-court-fees (survey of the types of legal financial obligations imposed in each state); NATAPOFF, *supra* note 14, at 125–26.

16. *See* NCSC HANDBOOK, *supra* note 12, at 20.

17. *Id.* at 3, 6, 12.

18. *Id.* at 1.

19. *Id.* at 31.

20. *Id.*

21. MODEL CODE OF JUDICIAL CONDUCT R. 1.2 cmt. 3 (AM. BAR ASS'N 2011).

Judges must also "seek the necessary docket time, court staff, expertise, and resources to discharge all adjudicative and administrative responsibilities."[22]

As discussed below, the right to procedural justice addressed in this opinion derives from several sources: state and federal constitutional guarantees of due process of law, statutory prescriptions, and a judge's ethical responsibility to ensure the integrity and fairness of proceedings before the judge.

The Committee recognizes and concurs that "[i]mposing discipline upon a judge for an incorrect legal ruling is an extremely sensitive issue because of the potential impact on judicial independence."[23] For this reason, ordinary legal errors that can be corrected on appeal are not generally subject to discipline. However, "egregious legal error, legal error motivated by bad faith, or a continuing pattern of legal error may well violate several provisions of the Code of Judicial Conduct."[24] A "pattern of repeated legal error obviously is more serious than an isolated instance," and there is consensus among courts and disciplinary bodies "that legal error is egregious when judges deny individuals their basic or fundamental procedural rights."[25] Significantly, for present purposes, in contexts where the *pro se* status of litigants or the relatively modest amount of the money owed makes appeal unlikely or too costly, discipline is one of the only methods to ensure that violations of fundamental rights are prevented.[26]

A. The Right to an Inquiry into Ability to Pay

This Committee does not opine on questions of substantive law, but in interpreting the model rules of judicial conduct that apply to procedural justice we observe the distinctive significance of the right to be heard prior to facing incarceration for failure to pay.[27] As the Supreme Court held decades ago in *Bearden v. Georgia*, a defendant cannot be incarcerated for failure to

---

22. *Id.* R. 2.5 cmt. 2.

23. Charles Geyh et al., Judicial Conduct and Ethics § 2.02, 2-5 (5th ed. 2013).

24. *Id.* at 2-7; *see also* State v. Blazina, 344 P.3d 680, 682–84 (Wash. 2015) (describing barriers to appeal of legal financial obligations).

25. Geyh, *supra* note 23, at 2-8; *see also In re* Aucoin, 767 So. 2d 30 (La. 2000) (trying defendants immediately after arraignment merited public censure); *In re* Scott, 386 N.E.2d 218, 222 (Mass. 1979) (denying counsel to juveniles and invoking nonexistent law merited prohibition on criminal and juvenile sittings); *In re* McGee, 452 N.E.2d 1258, 1259 (N.Y. 1983) (coercing guilty pleas merited removal).

26. *See In re* Piraino, Determination, 2014 WL 3889892, at *6 (N.Y. Comm'n Jud. Conduct, July 30, 2014) ("We reject respondent's argument that such sentencing errors are properly addressed by an appellate court, not in a disciplinary setting. Since most of the overpayments in this case involved relatively small amounts, it is unrealistic to expect that the defendants would expend the resources necessary to pursue an appellate remedy.").

27. Model Code of Judicial Conduct pmbl. ¶5 ("The Rules . . . are rules of reason that should be applied consistent with constitutional requirements, statutes, other court rules, and decisional law, and with due regard for all relevant circumstances.").

pay absent an opportunity to be heard on the question whether the failure to pay is "willful," whether "bona fide" efforts have been made to acquire the resources to pay, and whether there are alternatives to incarceration that would meet the state's interests.[28] As long as a defendant's failure to pay is due to genuine financial incapacity, alternatives to incarceration must be explored.[29] More recently, the Supreme Court extended the *Bearden* framework for inquiry into ability to pay to contempt proceedings in *civil* debt collection cases that rely on incarceration to induce payment.[30] Finally, some states have adopted an ability-to-pay requirement via their state's constitutional guarantee of due process of law, by statute, or both.[31]

Thus although the outer limits of *Bearden* may vary from jurisdiction to jurisdiction,[32] the fundamental right to be heard on one's ability to pay rests

---

28. Bearden v. Georgia, 461 U.S. 660, 668–69 (1983) (revocation of probation of defendant required to pay fine and restitution was unconstitutional absent inquiry into ability to pay).

29. *Id.* at 668–69 ("[I]t is fundamentally unfair to revoke probation automatically without considering whether adequate alternative methods of punishing the defendant are available").

30. *See* Turner v. Rogers, 564 U.S. 431, 435 (2011) (holding that while there is no per se right to counsel in civil contempt proceedings leading to incarceration for failure to pay child support, "the State must nonetheless have in place alternative procedures that ensure a fundamentally fair determination of the critical incarceration-related question, whether the supporting parent is able to comply with the support order"); *id.* at 435 (citing Moseley v. Mosier, 306 S.E.2d 624, 626 (S.C. 1983) for the state's rule that a parent unable to make the required payments is not in contempt under *Bearden*). Neither *Bearden* nor *Turner* addresses a judge's discretion to waive a legal financial obligation under either state or federal law, though that discretion sometimes exists. This opinion does not address waiver of legal financial obligations. *See also* Timbs v. Indiana, 139 S.Ct. 682 (2019) (holding excessive fines clause of the Eight Amendment applies to the states).

31. *See, e.g.*, Del Valle v. State, 80 So. 3d 999, 1005–06, 1012 (Fla. 2011); State v. Blazina, 344 P.3d 680, 685 (Wash. 2015) (en banc); Arthur W. Pepin, Conference of State Court Administrators, The End of Debtors' Prisons: Effective Court Policies for Successful Compliance with Legal Financial Obligations 19, n.97 (2015–2016) (citing Ohio Admin. Code, § 5120:1-1-02(K); Va. Code Annot., § 19.2-305 (2012)).

32. Some jurisdictions, for instance, have (a) distinguished bail for arrestees who could be charged with crimes from bail on arrest in post-judgment contexts, *see* Walker v. City of Calhoun, 901 F.3d 1245, 1266 (11th Cir. 2018) (holding that forty-eight-hour period of detention before conducting a hearing on indigency, probable cause, and bail for arrestees who may be charged with criminal offenses is consistent with due process principles of *Bearden*); (b) upheld the constitutionality of probation revocation hearings where the willfulness determination required by *Bearden* is not explicitly made by the trial court, but is implicit in record evidence, *see* State v. Brady, 300 P.3d 778, 780–81 (Utah Ct. App. 2013); (c) placed the burden of proving that failure to pay was not willful and that bona fide efforts have been made on the probationer once failure to pay has been established at a hearing, *see* Winbush v. State, 433 P.3d 1275, 1278 (Okla. Crim. App. 2018) (gathering other authorities); and (d) declined to apply *Bearden* to plea bargains in which the defendant specifically agreed to pay restitution in exchange for a reduced sentence under circumstances suggesting bad faith, *see* State v. Nordahl, 680 N.W.2d 247, 252 (N.D. 2004) (relying on U.S. v. Mitchell, 51 M.J. 490 (C.A.A.F. 1999)); *see also* U.S. v. Johnson, 767 F. Supp. 243, 248 (N.D. Ala. 1991) (*Bearden* does

upon a clearly established principle for the fair administration of justice[33]—one that resonates with the abolition of debtor's prisons for private debts in the 19th century.[34] The Supreme Court of Maine stated the principle in a judicial discipline case decided shortly after *Bearden*:

> The most basic right of citizens in this country is to be at liberty in society. That right is so essential to our way of life that it may only be taken away by the courts following carefully prescribed procedures.[35]

Procedural regularity in this setting is essential. Failure to adopt and consistently follow "carefully prescribed procedures" in proceedings that could result in incarceration for failure to pay strikes at the very roots of the fair and impartial administration of justice and poses a direct threat to public faith in the legitimacy of the judicial process. As the Georgia Supreme Court observed in a disciplinary case involving other serious procedural irregularities at the trial level, trial judges "*are* the judicial system"[36] for many litigants.

> [T]heir initial, possibly only, contact of any serious nature with our judicial system occurs in the [local state court]. These individuals' experiences may constitute the sole basis for their personal impression of our judicial system, and for their respect, or lack thereof, for the judiciary of this State. ... *Nowhere is the community more sensitive to the regularities, or irregularities, of judicial conduct than at the local level.* ... The state court judge plays a crucial role in achieving even-

---

not apply to plea-bargained probation terms); Wright v. State, 610 So. 2d 1187, 1189 (Ala. Crim. App. 1992) (same); Dickey v. State, 570 S.E. 2d 634, 636 (Ga. Ct. App. 2002) (same); Gamble v. Commonwealth, 293 S.W.3d 406, 411–12 (Ky. Ct. App. 2009) (same); Commonwealth v. Payne, 602 N.E.2d 594, 597 (Mass. App. Ct. 1992). *But see* Dirico v. State, 728 So. 2d 763, 767 (Fla. Dist. Ct. App. 1999) (plea bargain that included waiver of defense of inability to pay invalid); State v. Myles, 882 So. 2d 1254, 1257 (La. Ct. App. 2004) (holding *Bearden* applies to plea bargained probation terms).

33. *Bearden* relied on a series of earlier cases in which the Supreme Court held that a prison term cannot be imposed or extended beyond the statutory maximum term of imprisonment merely for failure to pay a fine, and that the right to appeal cannot be denied merely for inability to pay a fee for a trial transcript. *See* Tate v. Short, 401 U.S. 395 (1971); Williams v. Illinois, 399 U.S. 235 (1970); Griffin v. Illinois, 351 U.S. 12 (1956).

34. On the efforts to abolish debtors' prison for private debts in the 19th century, see Bruce H. Mann, Republic of Debtors: Bankruptcy in the Age of American Independence (2002).

35. *In re* Benoit, 487 A.2d 1158, 1165 (Me. 1985); *see also* Foucha v. Louisiana, 504 U.S. 71, 80 (1992) ("Freedom from bodily restraint has always been at the core of the liberty protected by the Due Process Clause . . . .").

36. *In re* Inquiry Concerning a Judge, 462 S.E.2d 728, 733 (Ga. 1995).

handed and just results, particularly because litigants of widely disparate backgrounds, resources and abilities are involved.[37]

Procedural irregularity regarding incarceration for failure to pay is, therefore, a serious breach of a judge's Rule 1.1 duty "to comply with the law."[38] Indeed, discipline has been imposed for procedural irregularity of this kind for decades as a violation of clearly established law, and, in at least one jurisdiction, years before *Bearden* was decided.[39]

B. The Integrity and Fairness of the Judicial Process, Public Confidence in the Judiciary, and Inquiry into a Litigant's Ability to Pay

Procedural irregularity regarding incarceration for failure to pay directly implicates other fundamental rule of law values—values the courts are bound by other provisions of the MCJC to protect. Without meaningful inquiry into a litigant's ability to pay, public confidence in the independence, integrity, and impartiality of the judiciary is not "promoted" within the meaning of Rule 1.2. It is compromised. This is particularly true in circumstances where the court, the municipal government, or private contractors seek financial gain through incarceration or the threat of it, and there is no genuine public safety justification supporting incarceration.[40] The fairness and impartiality required by Rules 1.2 and 2.2 are compromised by bail requirements and collection methods that affect low income litigants while litigants of means can simply pay to avoid incarceration. Procedural irregularity

---

37. *Id.* at 733 (emphasis added); *see In re* Bailey, 541 So. 2d 1036, 1039 (Miss. 1989) ("[M] ost of our citizens have their primary, if not their only, direct contact with the law through the office of the justice court judge."); *see also In re* Restaino, 890 N.E.2d 224, 230 (N.Y. 2008) (when "tools of judicial administration are abused as punitive instruments to deprive a person of his or her liberty—a right of the most fundamental order—such conduct is inexcusable and does violence to the court's integrity and the inviolable public trust").

38. *See also* Model Code of Judicial Conduct R. 2.6(A) (Am. Bar Ass'n 2011) (duty to "accord to every person who has a legal interest in a proceeding, or that person's lawyer, the right to be heard according to law"). See also discussion in the text, *supra*, at p. 6.

39. *See In re* Aucoin, 767 So.2d 30 (La. 2000) (public censure); *In re* Benoit, 487 A.2d 1158 (Me. 1985) (censure and suspension); *In re* Roberts, 689 N.E.2d 911 (N.Y. 1997) (removal); *In re* Skinner, 690 N.E.2d 484 (N.Y. 1997) (censure); *In re* Hammel, 668 N.E.2d 390 (N.Y. 1996) (removal); *In re* Nichols, Determination, (N.Y. Com'n Jud. Conduct, Nov. 19, 2001) (admonition); *In re* Bartie, 138 S.W.3d 81 (Tex. 2004) (removal); *see also In re* Scott, 386 N.E.2d 218, 227 (Mass. 1979) (barred from criminal and juvenile sittings for a year).

40. The Conference of State Court Administrators has warned that "funding courts through fines and fees that flow to the local town or county that pays court staff and judges creates at least the perception that judicial independence is diminished." Pepin, *supra* note 31, at 9 (quoting earlier report); *see infra*, note 46.

in the use of a court's contempt power also directly compromises the fairness and impartiality required by these Rules.[41]

Significantly, the Comments to Rule 2.2 invite courts to show particular solicitude to those who cannot afford counsel in order to ensure that they have "the opportunity to have their matters fairly heard" by making "reasonable accommodations."[42] Incarcerating *pro se* litigants for failure to pay legal financial obligations without inquiring into their ability to pay directly undermines their opportunity to be heard on issues as to which they may most need accommodation. Finally, to the extent that courts do not have "carefully prescribed procedures" in place to prevent incarceration for failure to pay and do not provide training to judges, court staff, prosecutors, and public defenders on proper procedures, the competent and diligent performance of "judicial and administrative duties" as well as the "cooperat[ion] with other judges and court officials in the administration of court business" required by Rule 2.5 is compromised.[43]

Accordingly, a judge's uncertainty regarding whether inquiry into a litigant's ability to pay in a particular circumstance is necessary under binding precedent should be resolved in favor of making the inquiry.[44] And where a

41. *See* Comm'n on Judicial Performance v. Willard, 788 So. 2d 736 (Miss. 2001) (removing judge for, among other things, misuse of contempt process to collect civil debt); *In re* Pizzi, 617 A.2d 663 (N.J. 1993) (mem.) (reprimand of judge who failed to give defendant notice of a contempt charge and sentenced defendant without receiving evidence); *In re* Hammel, 668 N.E.2d 390, 391 (N.Y. 1996) (removing judge who failed to follow procedures for summary contempt and incarcerated defendants without inquiry into ability to pay legal financial obligations); Public Admonition of Kennedy (Tex. Com. Jud. Conduct, July 12, 1996) (admonishing judge for using arrest warrant incident to contempt in order to enforce civil judgment). Setting bail after arrest for allegedly contumacious failure to appear at a civil post-judgment debtor examination in the amount dedicated to satisfaction of the judgment deprives the defendant of both the opportunity to be heard on whether her failure to appear is in fact punishable as contempt and whether she has the means to satisfy the judgment. *See supra* note 10. Procedural irregularity in entering an underlying default judgment can also result in discipline. *See In re* Landry, 789 So. 2d 1271 (La. 2001).

42. Model Code of Judicial Conduct R. 2.2, cmt. [4].

43. *In re* Benoit, 487 A.2d 1158, 1165 (Me. 1985) (emphasizing the importance of "carefully prescribed procedures"). The above referenced Rules protecting the integrity and fairness of the judicial process along with public confidence in the administration of justice warrant particular attention in the handful of jurisdictions that expressly limit the circumstances in which discipline can be imposed for legal error under Rules 1.1 and 2.6. *See* Cynthia Gray, *The Line Between Judicial Error and Judicial Misconduct: Balancing Judicial Independence and Accountability*, 32 Hofstra L. Rev. 1245, 1278–79 (2004) (describing relevant limitations in these jurisdictions).

44. *See In re* Aucoin, 767 So. 2d 30, 31–33 (La. 2000) (judge censured for "grossly negligent disregard for procedural due process" for using "instanter trial" procedure seventeen times after appellate court had reversed a conviction on instanter trial; discipline appropriate even though judge understood the reversal to concern whether he was required to allow defendants to obtain evidence and call witnesses at instanter trials, *not* whether the trials themselves violated due process, and even though judge's conduct followed "long-

litigant is unrepresented or the matter is civil, doubts about ability to pay, the willfulness of a litigant's failure to pay, the bona fide efforts of the litigant to secure the means to pay, and the viability of alternatives to incarceration, should generally be resolved against incarceration in the absence of circumstances indicating that the litigant poses a threat to public safety. Whatever the status of the litigant, inquiry into ability to pay should be grounded in objective financial data to the extent such information can reasonably be ascertained.[45] Judges must also avoid conflicts of interest that arise from setting, imposing, or enforcing legal financial obligations to fund the court on terms that give judges a direct incentive either to increase these obligations or to avoid inquiring into ability to pay.[46]

To comply with these obligations, courts should adopt policies, practices, and procedures to efficiently and accurately determine a litigant's ability to pay, to divide administrative tasks to guard against even the appearance of impropriety in the setting and enforcement of legal financial obligations, and to provide training to judges, court staff, prosecutors, and defense attorneys. Innovative options and comprehensive guidance on how to design and implement these policies, practices, and procedures may be found in materials recently published by the Conference of State Court Administrators, the National Center for State Courts, and other organizations.[47] Ways to ensure

---

standing" practice in that district); *id.* (although "not an excuse for respondent's failure to recognize the constitutional infirmity in the procedure," judge's misapprehension and the fact that he was following local practice "mitigate to some extent against a finding of willful misconduct"); *cf. In re* Gremillion, 204 So. 3d 183, 194 (La. 2016) (discipline is warranted for legal error where a ruling is "made contrary to clear and determined law about which there is no confusion or question as to its interpretation and . . . [the error is] egregious, made in bad faith, or made as part of a pattern or practice of legal error") (quoting *In re* Quirk, 705 So.2d 172, 180–81 (La. 1997)).

45. *See* Turner v. Rogers, 564 U.S. 431, 447–48 (2011); Commonwealth v. Henry, 55 N.E.3d 943, 953 (Mass. 2016) ("In determining the defendant's ability to pay, the judge must consider the financial resources of the defendant, including income and net assets, and the defendant's financial obligations, including the amount necessary to meet minimum basic human needs such as food, shelter, and clothing for the defendant and his or her dependents.").

46. *See In re* Storie, 574 S.W.2d 369 (Mo. 1978) (en banc) (judge suspended for personally administering a law "library fund" from charges assessed in guilty pleas where funds were spent on law books, wages, court furnishings, and court maintenance); *see also* Brown v. Vance, 637 F.2d 272 (5th Cir. 1981); Brucker v. City of Doraville, 391 F. Supp. 3d 1207 (N.D. Ga. 2019); Augustus v. Roemer, 771 F. Supp. 1458, 1473 (E.D. La. 1991).

47. *See* Harvard Law School Criminal Justice Policy Program, Confronting Criminal Justice Debt: A Guide for Policy Reform (2016); National Center for State Courts, Missouri Municipal Courts: Best Practice Recommendations (2015); Roopal Patel & Meghna Philip, Brennan Ctr. for Justice, Criminal Justice Debt: A Toolkit for Action (2012), https://www.brennancenter.org/sites/default/files/2019-08/Report_Criminal%20Justice%20Debt.pdf; Arthur Pepin, Conference of State Court Administrators, Four Essential Elements Required to Deliver Justice in Limited Jurisdiction Courts in the 21st Century (2013–2014); Roopal Patel & Meghna Philip, *A*

observance of basic procedural safeguards include, for example, (i) using a "bench card" that provides judges and other staff relevant instructions on ability-to-pay inquiries, including a workable definition of indigence and alternatives to incarceration,[48] (ii) providing advance notice to litigants of their ability-to-pay hearing and emphasizing that financial means will be "a critical issue" covered at the hearing, (iii) distributing a form "to elicit relevant financial information," and (iv) providing a meaningful opportunity to address questions about the litigant's "financial status" at the hearing.[49]

IV. Conclusion

The liberty interests protected by the duty to inquire into ability to pay prior to incarceration for failure to pay are fundamental to litigants and to the rule of law itself. Courts have an ethical duty not only to comply with the law insofar as it requires inquiry into ability to pay but to protect the integrity, fairness, and impartiality of the judicial process by ensuring that compliance is robust and consistent with legitimate state interests in public safety. See Rules 1.1, 1.2, 2.2, 2.5, and 2.6. Courts should therefore adopt carefully prescribed procedures to prevent incarceration where a litigant lacks the resources to pay legal financial obligations or private civil debts.

Abstaining: Hon. Goodwin Liu.

Legislative Model for Dismantling Debtors' Prisons, BRENNAN CTR. FOR JUSTICE (Aug. 7, 2012), https://www.brennancenter.org/our-work/analysis-opinion/legislative-model-dismantling-debtors-prisons (describing Illinois statute); PEPIN, *supra* note 31.

48. The Task Force on Fines, Fees and Bail Practices of the Conference of Chief Justices, a joint effort of the Conference of State Court Administrators, the State Justice Institute, the Bureau of Justice Assistance, and the National Center for State Courts, has published a model "bench card." *See* NATIONAL TASK FORCE ON FINES, FEES AND BAIL PRACTICES, LAWFUL COLLECTION OF LEGAL FINANCIAL OBLIGATIONS (2017), https://www.ncsc.org/~/media/Images/Topics/Fines%20Fees/BenchCard_FINAL_Feb2_2017.ashx.

49. *See Turner*, 564 U.S. at 447–48.

AMERICAN BAR ASSOCIATION
STANDING COMMITTEE ON ETHICS AND PROFESSIONAL RESPONSIBILITY

Formal Opinion 491 **April 29, 2020**

Obligations Under Rule 1.2(d) to Avoid Counseling or Assisting in a Crime or Fraud in Non-Litigation Settings

Model Rule 1.2(d) prohibits a lawyer from advising or assisting a client in conduct the lawyer "knows" is criminal or fraudulent. That knowledge may be inferred from the circumstances, including a lawyer's willful blindness to or conscious avoidance of facts. Accordingly, where facts known to the lawyer establish a high probability that a client seeks to use the lawyer's services for criminal or fraudulent activity, the lawyer has a duty to inquire further to avoid advising or assisting such activity. Even if information learned in the course of a preliminary interview or during a representation is insufficient to establish "knowledge" under Rule 1.2(d), other rules may require the lawyer to inquire further in order to help the client avoid crime or fraud, to avoid professional misconduct, and to advance the client's legitimate interests. These include the duties of competence, diligence, communication, and honesty under Rules 1.1, 1.3, 1.4, 1.13, 1.16, and 8.4. If the client or prospective client refuses to provide information necessary to assess the legality of the proposed transaction, the lawyer must ordinarily decline the representation or withdraw under Rule 1.16. A lawyer's reasonable evaluation after inquiry and based on information reasonably available at the time does not violate the rules. This opinion does not address the application of these rules in the representation of a client or prospective client who requests legal services in connection with litigation.[1]

1. This opinion is based on the ABA Model Rules of Professional Conduct as amended by the ABA House of Delegates through August 2019. The laws, court rules, regulations, rules of professional conduct, and opinions promulgated in individual jurisdictions are controlling.

I. Introduction

In the wake of media reports,[2] disciplinary proceedings,[3] criminal prosecutions,[4] and reports on international counter-terrorism enforcement and efforts to combat money-laundering, the legal profession has become increasingly alert to the risk that a client or prospective client[5] might try to retain a lawyer for a transaction or other non-litigation matter that could be legitimate but which further inquiry would reveal to be criminal or fraudulent.[6] For example, a client might seek legal assistance for a series of purchases and sales of properties that will be used to launder money. Or a client might propose an all-cash deal in large amounts and ask that the proceeds be deposited in a bank located in a jurisdiction where transactions of this kind are commonly used to conceal terrorist financing or other illegal activities.[7] On the other hand, further inquiry may dispel the lawyer's concerns.

This opinion addresses a lawyer's obligation to inquire when faced with a client who may be seeking to use the lawyer's services in a transaction to commit a crime or fraud. Ascertaining whether a client seeks to use the lawyer's services for prohibited ends can be delicate. Clients are generally entitled to be believed rather than doubted, and in some contexts investigations can be both costly and time-consuming. At the same time, clients ben-

2. *See* Debra Cassens Weiss, *Group Goes Undercover at 13 Law Firms to Show How U.S. Laws Facilitate Anonymous Investment*, A.B.A. J. (Feb. 1, 2016), https://www.abajournal.com/news/article/group_goes_undercover_at_13_law_firms_to_show_how_us_laws_facilitate; *see also* Louise Story & Stephanie Saul, *Stream of Foreign Wealth Flows to Elite New York Real Estate*, N.Y. Times (Feb. 7, 2015), https://www.nytimes.com/2015/02/08/nyregion/stream-of-foreign-wealth-flows-to-time-warner-condos.html.

3. *In re* Albrecht, 42 P.3d 887, 898–900 (Or. 2002) (disbarment for assisting client in money laundering).

4. *See, e.g.*, United States v. Farrell, 921 F.3d 116 (4th Cir. 2019) (affirming conviction for money laundering); United States v. Blair, 661 F.3d 755 (4th Cir. 2011) (same); Laura Ende, *Escrow, Money Laundering Cases Draw Attention to the Perils of Handling Client Money*, State Bar of Cal. (Feb. 2017), http://www.calbarjournal.com/February2017/TopHeadlines/TH1.aspx (lawyer sentenced "to five years in prison after being convicted of felonies related to a money laundering scheme").

5. "Client" refers hereinafter to "client and prospective client" unless otherwise indicated.

6. Hereinafter, "transaction" refers both to transactions and other non-litigation matters unless otherwise indicated. This opinion does not address the application of rules triggering a duty to inquire where a client requests legal services in connection with litigation. ABA Comm. on Ethics & Prof'l Responsibility, Informal Op. 1470 (1981), discusses how a lawyer *not* involved in the past misconduct of a client should handle the circumstance of a proposed transaction arising from or relating to the past misconduct.

7. *See* Am. Bar Ass'n Task Force on Gatekeeper Regulation and the Profession, Voluntary Good Practices Guidance for Lawyers to Detect and Combat Money Laundering and Terrorist Financing 15–16 (2010) [hereinafter Good Practices Guidance] (describing institutions, such as the United Nations, the World Bank, the International Monetary Fund, and the U.S. Department of State, believed to be "credible sources" for information regarding risks in different jurisdictions); *id.* at 24 (noting the "higher risk situation" when a client offers to pay in cash).

efit greatly from having informed assistance of counsel. A lawyer's obligation to inquire when faced with circumstances addressed in this opinion is well-grounded in authority interpreting Rule 1.2(d) and in the rules on competence, diligence, communication, honesty, and withdrawal.

As set forth in Section II of this opinion, a lawyer who has knowledge of facts that create a high probability that a client is seeking the lawyer's services in a transaction to further criminal or fraudulent activity has a duty to inquire further to avoid assisting that activity under Rule 1.2(d). Failure to make a reasonable inquiry is willful blindness punishable under the actual knowledge standard of the Rule. Whether the facts known to the lawyer require further inquiry will depend on the circumstances. As discussed in Section III, even where Rule 1.2(d) does not require further inquiry, other Rules may. These Rules include the duty of competence under Rule 1.1, the duty of diligence under Rule 1.3, the duty of communication under Rule 1.4, the duty to protect the best interests of an organizational client under Rule 1.13, the duties of honesty and integrity under Rules 8.4(b) and (c), and the duty to withdraw under Rule 1.16(a). Further inquiry under these Rules serves important ends. It ensures that the lawyer is in a position to provide the informed advice and assistance to which the client is entitled, that the representation will not result in professional misconduct, and that the representation will not involve counseling or assisting a crime or fraud. Section IV addresses a lawyer's obligations in responding to a client who either agrees or does not agree to provide information necessary to satisfy the duty to inquire. Finally, Section V examines hypothetical scenarios in which the duty to inquire would be triggered, as well as instances in which it would not.

II. The Duty to Inquire Under Rule 1.2(d)

Rule 1.2(d) states that a lawyer "shall not counsel a client to engage, or assist a client, in conduct that the lawyer knows is criminal or fraudulent." A duty to inquire to avoid knowingly counseling or assisting a crime or fraud may arise under this Rule in two ways. First, Rule 1.0(f) states that to "know[]" means to have "actual knowledge of the fact in question." When facts already known to the lawyer are so strong as to constitute "actual knowledge" of criminal or fraudulent activity, the lawyer must "consult with the client regarding the limitations on the lawyer's conduct."[8] This consultation will ordinarily include inquiry into whether there is some misapprehension regarding the relevant facts. If there is no misunderstanding and the client persists, the lawyer must withdraw.[9]

---

8. MODEL RULES OF PROF'L CONDUCT R. 1.2 cmt. [13] [hereinafter MODEL RULES].

9. *See* MODEL RULES R. 1.16(a)(1); Section IV, *infra*. Rule 1.2(d) nevertheless permits a lawyer to "discuss the legal consequences of any proposed course of conduct with a client and may counsel or assist a client to make a good faith effort to determine the validity, scope, meaning or application of the law."

In *In re Blatt*,[10] for example, the New Jersey Supreme Court disciplined a lawyer for participation in a real estate transaction where "*[o]n their face* the [transaction] documents suggest[ed] impropriety if not outright illegality."[11] Addressing the lawyer's duties, the court wrote:

> A lawyer may not follow the directions of a client without first satisfying himself that the latter is seeking a legitimate and proper goal and intends to employ legal means to attain it. . . . The propriety of any proposed course of action must be initially considered by the attorney, and it may be thereafter pursued only if the lawyer is completely satisfied that it involves no ethical compromise. . . . [The lawyer's] duty, upon being requested to draft the aforementioned agreements, was to learn all the details of the proposed transaction. Only then, upon being satisfied that he had indeed learned all the facts, and that his client's proposed course of conduct was proper, would he have been at liberty to pursue the matter further.[12]

Additionally, if facts before the lawyer indicate a high probability that a client seeks to use the lawyer's services for criminal or fraudulent activity, a lawyer's conscious, deliberate failure to inquire amounts to knowing assistance of criminal or fraudulent conduct. Rule 1.0(f) refers to "actual knowledge" and provides that "[a] person's knowledge may be inferred from circumstances." Substantial authority confirms that a lawyer may not ignore the obvious.[13]

The obligation to inquire is well established in ethics opinions. Nearly forty years ago, prior to the adoption of the Model Rules, ABA Informal Opinion 1470 (1981) declared that "a lawyer should not undertake represen-

---

10. 324 A.2d 15 (N.J. 1974).

11. *Id.* at 18 (emphasis added).

12. *Id.* at 18–19; *see also In re* Evans, 759 N.E.2d 1064 (Ind. 2001) (mem.) (three-year suspension for filing fraudulent federal tax returns knowingly misrepresenting sale proceeds from real estate transaction); *In re* Harlow, 2004 WL 5215045, at *2 (Mass. State Bar Disciplinary Bd. 2004) (suspending lawyer for violation of 1.2(d) for assisting client in knowing manipulation of state licensing agency's escrow account requirements); State *ex rel.* Counsel for Discipline of Nebraska Supreme Court v. Mills, 671 N.W.2d 765 (Neb. 2003) (two-year suspension for participating in illegal scheme to avoid estate taxes by knowingly backdating and preparing false documents); *accord* N.C. State Bar, Formal Op. 12, 2001 WL 1949450 (2001).

13. In the words of Charles Wolfram, "as in the criminal law, a lawyer's studied ignorance of a readily ascertainable fact by consciously avoiding it is the functional equivalent of knowledge of the fact. . . . As a lawyer, one may not avoid the bright light of a clear fact by averting one's eyes or turning one's back." Charles W. Wolfram, Modern Legal Ethics 696 (1986); *see also* Ellen J. Bennett & Helen W. Gunnarsson, Annotated Model Rules of Professional Conduct 47 (9th ed. 2019) ("[a] lawyer's assistance in unlawful conduct is not excused by a failure to inquire into the client's objectives"); *id.* (gathering cases).

tation in disregard of facts *suggesting* that the representation might aid the client in perpetrating a fraud or otherwise committing a crime . . . . A lawyer cannot escape responsibility by avoiding inquiry. A lawyer must be satisfied, on the facts before him and readily available to him, that he can perform the requested services without abetting fraudulent or criminal conduct . . . ."[14]

Relying on ABA Informal Opinion 1470, the Legal Ethics Committee of the Indiana State Bar Association concluded in 2001 that "[a] lawyer should not undertake representation without making further inquiry if the facts presented by a prospective client suggest that the representation might aid the client in perpetrating a fraud or otherwise committing a crime."[15] The opinion reasoned that an attorney asked to create a "new" sole power of attorney for a prospective client on behalf of her wealthy grandfather in matters concerning his estate has a duty to inquire further. The opinion emphasized the possibility that the granddaughter could fraudulently use the power of attorney to benefit herself rather than serve the interests of her grandfather, whom the attorney had not consulted, the possibility that the grandfather would not wish to grant sole power of attorney to his granddaughter, and the possibility that the grandfather might lack the capacity to consent to such an arrangement (made likely by the fact that the lawyer's paralegal observed the grandfather's deteriorated condition). Thus, although it is possible that the granddaughter's representation of the facts was accurate and therefore consistent with Rule 1.2(d), "the fact that a proposed client in drafting a power of attorney was the agent and not a frail principal should have suggested to [the lawyer] the possibility that the client's real objective might be fraud. [The lawyer] then *had an ethical responsibility to find out whether the proposal was above-board* before performing the services. By failing to make further inquiry, [the lawyer] violated Rule 1.2."[16]

Similarly, New York City Ethics Opinion 2018-4 concluded that lawyers must inquire when "retained to assist an individual client in a transaction that appears to the lawyer to be suspicious."[17] The opinion explains that "[i]n general, assisting in a suspicious transaction is not competent where a reasonable lawyer prompted by serious doubts would have refrained from providing assistance or would have investigated to allay suspicions before rendering or continuing to render legal assistance. . . . What constitutes a

14. ABA Comm. on Ethics & Prof'l Responsibility, Informal Op. 1470 (1981) (emphasis added) (interpreting the analogous ABA Model Code provision 7-102(A)(7), which provides that a lawyer must not "[c]ounsel or assist his client in conduct that the lawyer knows to be illegal or fraudulent").

15. Ind. State Bar Ass'n Comm. on Legal Ethics, Op. 2, at 4 (2001).

16. *Id.* at 4 (emphasis added). The Opinion reaches the same conclusion if the grandfather is considered to be the true client. *Id.* at 6–7. *Accord* N.C. State Bar Ass'n, Formal Op. 7 (2003).

17. N.Y.C. Bar Ass'n Comm. on Prof'l Ethics, Formal Op. 2018-4, at 2 (2018); *see also* Conn. Bar Ass'n Standing Comm. on Prof'l Ethics, Informal Op. 91-22 (1991).

suspicion sufficient to trigger inquiry will depend on the circumstances."[18] Failure to inquire may constitute "conscious avoidance" when, for example, "the lawyer is aware of serious questions about the legality of the transaction and renders assistance without considering readily available facts that would have confirmed the wrongfulness of the transaction."[19]

Courts imposing discipline are generally in accord. When a lawyer deliberately or consciously avoids knowledge that a client is or may be using the lawyer's services to further a crime or fraud, discipline is imposed.[20] Some courts have applied the even broader standard set out in Comment [13] to Rule 1.2, which requires a lawyer to consult with the client when the lawyer "comes to know or *reasonably should know* that [the] client expects assistance not permitted by the Rules of Professional Conduct . . . ." (Emphasis added.) For example, in *In re Dobson*,[21] the South Carolina Supreme Court identified facts showing that the lawyer "knew" or "*should have known*" that he was furthering a client's illegal scheme, and added, "[w]e also find that respondent *deliberately evaded* knowledge of facts which tended to implicate him in a fraudulent scheme. This Court will not countenance the conscious avoidance of one's ethical duties as an attorney."[22]

---

18. N.Y.C Bar Ass'n Comm. on Prof'l Ethics, Formal Op. 2018-4, at 3 (2018).

19. *Id.* Hypotheticals in Section V of this opinion, *infra*, identify circumstances that should prompt further inquiry.

20. *See In re* Bloom, 745 P.2d 61 (Cal. 1987) (affirming disbarment of lawyer who assisted client in sale and transport of explosives to Libya; categorically rejecting lawyer's defense that he believed in good faith that transaction was authorized by national security officials); *In re* Albrecht, 42 P.3d 887, 898–99 (Or. 2002) ("suspicious nature" of transactions, combined with other facts, support inference that lawyer must have known his participation in scheme constituted money laundering; upholding disbarment for knowingly assisting crime or fraud and rejecting defense that lawyer was "an unwitting dupe to a talented con man"); *see also* Ellen Bennett & Helen Gunnarsson, Annotated Model Rules of Professional Conduct 47 (9th ed.) ("[a] lawyer's assistance in unlawful conduct is not excused by a failure to inquire into the client's objectives"). *But see* Iowa Supreme Court Att'y Disciplinary Bd. v. Ouderkirk, 845 N.W. 2d 31, 45–48 (Iowa 2014) (declining to infer knowledge of client's fraud despite what disciplinary counsel argued were "highly suspicious" circumstances where sophisticated, longstanding client who typically relied on the lawyer exclusively to prepare final paperwork deceived the lawyer about a fraudulent transfer to avoid creditors).

21. 427 S.E.2d 166 (S.C. 1993).

22. *Id.* at 427 (emphasis added); *see also* Florida Bar v. Brown, 790 So.2d 1081, 1088 (Fla. 2001) (suspension for soliciting illegal campaign contributions from employees and others for political candidates viewed as favorable to business interests of major client of firm; lawyer "should have known" conduct was criminal or fraudulent under Florida version of Rule 1.2(d) which expressly incorporates this standard); *In re* Siegel, 471 N.Y.S. 2d 591, 592 (N.Y. App. Div. 1984) (attorney "knew *or should have known* that at the very least, his conduct was a breach of trust, if not illegal") (emphasis added). Other jurisdictions have rejected a negligence standard for Rule 1.2(d). *See In re* Tocco, 984 P.2d 539, 543 (Ariz. 1999) (en banc) (declining to read a should have known standard into Arizona Rule 1.2(d); "While actual knowledge can be proven by circumstantial evidence, a mere showing that the attorney reasonably *should have known* her conduct was in violation of the rules, without more, is insuf-

Criminal cases treat deliberate ignorance or willful blindness as equivalent to actual knowledge.[23] As the Supreme Court recently summarized:

> The doctrine of willful blindness is well established in criminal law. Many criminal statutes require proof that a defendant acted knowingly or willfully, and courts applying the doctrine of willful blindness hold that defendants cannot escape the reach of these statutes by deliberately shielding themselves from clear evidence of critical facts that are strongly suggested by the circumstances. . . . [The Model Penal Code defines] "knowledge of the existence of a particular fact" to include a situation in which "a person is aware of a *high probability* of [the fact's] existence, unless he actually believes that it does not exist." Our Court has used the Code's definition as a guide . . . [a]nd every Court of Appeals—with the possible exception of the District of Columbia Circuit—has fully embraced willful blindness, applying the doctrine to a wide range of criminal statutes.[24]

A lawyer may accordingly face criminal charges or civil liability, in addition to bar discipline, for deliberately or consciously avoiding knowledge that a client is or may be using the lawyer's services to further a crime or fraud.[25] To prevent these outcomes, a lawyer must inquire further when the

---

ficient."); *accord* Iowa Supreme Court Bd. of Prof'l Ethics and Conduct v. Jones, 606 N.W.2d 5, 7–8 (Iowa 2000).

The Committee acknowledges the tension between the "actual knowledge" standard of Model Rule 1.2(d), on the one hand, and those authorities applying a reasonably should know standard. This opinion concludes only that the standard of actual knowledge set out in the text of Model Rules 1.2(d) and 1.0(f) is met by appropriate evidence of willful blindness. When the Model Rules intend a lower threshold of scienter, such as "reasonably should know," the text generally makes this explicit. *See, e.g.*, Model Rules R. 2.3(b), 2.4(b), 4.3.

23. United States v. Ramsey, 785 F.2d 184, 189 (7th Cir. 1986) ("[A]ctual knowledge and deliberate avoidance of knowledge are the same thing.").

24. Global-Tech Appliances, Inc. v. SEB USA, 563 U.S. 754, 767 (2011) (emphasis added) (citations omitted) (applying willful blindness standard to statute prohibiting knowing inducement of patent infringement).

25. *See* United States v. Cavin, 39 F.3d 1299, 1310 (5th Cir. 1994) (upholding deliberate ignorance jury instruction in prosecution of a lawyer); United States v. Scott, 37 F.3d 1564, 1578 (10th Cir. 1994) (affirming use of deliberate ignorance instruction against an attorney convicted of conspiracy to defraud the IRS); Wyle v. R.J. Reynolds Indus., Inc., 709 F.2d 585, 590 (9th Cir. 1983) (upholding deliberate ignorance finding against law firm in antitrust suit because firm was aware of high probability that client made illegal payments and failed to investigate); United States v. Benjamin, 328 F.2d 854, 862 (2d Cir. 1964) (a lawyer may be held liable in a securities fraud suit if the lawyer has "deliberately closed his eyes to the facts he had a duty to see"); Harrell v. Crystal, 611 N.E. 2d 908, 914 (Ohio Ct. App. 1992) (affirming finding of liability in malpractice action for lawyer's failure to investigate sham tax shelters); Pa. Bar Ass'n Comm. on Legal Ethics & Prof'l Responsibility, Informal Op. 2003-104 (2003) (where facts suggested property transfer to client from relative was to con-

facts before the lawyer create a high probability that a client seeks to use the lawyer's services for criminal or fraudulent activity.[26]

III. The Duty To Inquire Under Other Rules

Rule 1.2(d) is not the only source of a lawyer's duty to inquire. A lawyer may be obliged to inquire further in order to meet duties of competence, diligence, communication, honesty, and withdrawal under Rules 1.1, 1.3, 1.4, 1.13, 1.16, and 8.4. The kinds of facts and circumstances that would trigger a duty to inquire under these rules include, for example, (i) the identity of the client, (ii) the lawyer's familiarity with the client, (iii) the nature of the matter (particularly whether such matters are frequently associated with criminal or fraudulent activity), (iv) the relevant jurisdictions (especially whether any jurisdiction is classified as high risk by credible sources), (v) the likelihood and gravity of harm associated with the proposed activity, (vi) the nature and depth of the lawyer's expertise in the relevant field of practice, (vii) other facts going to the reasonableness of reposing trust in the client,[27] and (viii)

---

ceal assets from creditors, lawyer handling sale of property to a third party "must evaluate whether the transfer of realty to your client was 'fraudulent'" under state law); *cf.* RESTATEMENT (THIRD) OF THE LAW GOVERNING LAWYERS § 94, Reporter's Note, cmt. g. at 17 (AM. LAW INST. 2000) ("the preferable rule is that proof of a lawyer's conscious disregard of facts is relevant evidence which, together with other evidence bearing on the question, may warrant a finding of actual knowledge").

26. As the authorities and analysis in this Section make clear, the duty to inquire under Model Rule 1.2(d) is tied to the circumstances and the lawyer's state of knowledge. It is *not* a freestanding, blanket obligation to scrutinize every client for illicit ends irrespective of the nature of the specific matter and the attorney-client relationship. *See* United States v. Sarantos, 455 F.2d 877, 881 (2d Cir. 1972) ("Construing 'knowingly' in a criminal statute to include willful blindness . . . is no radical concept in the law," but the standard does not mean that an attorney has a general duty to "investigate 'the truth of his client's assertions' or risk going to jail"; upholding criminal conviction of lawyer who actively aided in immigration related marriage fraud); Pa. Bar Ass'n Comm. on Legal Ethics & Prof'l Responsibility, Informal Op. 2001-26 ("*Generally*, a lawyer has no obligation to inquire or otherwise uncover facts that are not necessary to enable the lawyer to fulfill his or her obligations with respect to the representation"; warning nevertheless that Rule 1.2(d) applies to filing of worker's compensation claims and leaving attorney to determine relevance of client's fatal condition to client's specific claim) (emphasis added). However, the Committee rejects the view that the actual knowledge standard of Rule 1.2(d) relieves the lawyer of a duty to inquire further where the lawyer is aware of facts creating a high probability that the representation would further a crime or fraud. *Cf.* RESTATEMENT (THIRD) OF THE LAW GOVERNING LAWYERS § 94 cmt. g. at 11 ("Under the actual knowledge standard . . . a lawyer is not required to make a particular kind of investigation in order to ascertain more clearly what the facts are, although it will often be prudent for the lawyer to do so."); *id.* § 51 cmt. h., ill. 6 at 366; George M. Cohen, *The State of Lawyer Knowledge Under the Model Rules of Professional Conduct*, 3 AM. U. BUS. L. REV. 115, 116 (2014) (discussing association of willful blindness with recklessness, without citing to *Global-Tech Appliances*, and analyzing assumption that "the actual knowledge standard aims to exclude a duty to inquire").

27. For facts that can undermine the reasonableness of reposing trust, see the discussion of "risk categories" provided by the GOOD PRACTICES GUIDANCE, *supra* note 7, at 15–36.

any other factors traditionally associated with providing competent representation in the field.

First, Rule 8.4(b) makes it professional misconduct for a lawyer to "commit a criminal act that reflects adversely on the lawyer's honesty, trustworthiness or fitness as a lawyer in other respects." Rule 8.4(c) makes it professional misconduct for a lawyer to "engage in conduct involving dishonesty, fraud, deceit or misrepresentation." Providing legal services could violate Rules 8.4(b) and (c) where the relevant law on criminal or fraudulent conduct defines the lawyer's state of mind as culpable even without proof of actual knowledge.[28] In such a situation, the lawyer must conduct further investigation to protect the client, advance the client's legitimate interests, and prevent the crime or fraud.

Second, and more broadly, the lawyer's duty of competence, diligence, and communication under Rules 1.1, 1.3, and 1.4 may require the lawyer, prior to advising or assisting in a course of action, to develop sufficient knowledge of the facts and the law to understand the client's objectives, identify means to meet the client's lawful interests, to probe further, and, if necessary, persuade the client not to pursue conduct that could lead to criminal liability or liability for fraud. Comment [5] of Rule 1.1 states that "[c]ompetent handling of a particular matter requires inquiry into and analysis of the factual and legal elements of the problem."[29] The duty of diligence under Rule 1.3 requires that a lawyer ascertain the relevant facts and law in a timely and appropriately thorough manner.[30] Rule 1.4(a)(5), which requires consultation with the client regarding "any relevant limitation on the lawyer's conduct" arising from the client's expectation of assistance that is not permitted by the Rules of Professional Conduct or other law, may require investigation of the relevant facts and law. Rule 1.4(b) requires the lawyer to give the client explanations sufficient to enable the client to make informed decisions about the representation.

---

28. *See In re* Berman, 769 P.2d 984, 989 (Cal. 1989) (en banc) (holding, in disciplinary proceeding for aiding a money laundering scheme, that attorney's "*belief* that the financial statements contained false information reflects sufficient indicia of fraudulent intent to constitute moral turpitude"). The same conduct would require the lawyer's withdrawal under Rule 1.16(a)(1).

29. *See also* Iowa Supreme Court Att'y Disciplinary Bd. v. Wright, 840 N.W.2d 295, 301 (Iowa 2013) (failure to conduct even preliminary research on overseas internet scam violates Rule 1.1); *In re* Winkel, 577 N.W.2d 9 (Wis. 1998) (failure to obtain information on trust funds of clients' business prior to surrendering clients' assets to bank). *See also* RESTATEMENT (THIRD) OF THE LAW GOVERNING LAWYERS § 52 cmt. c at 377 ("[A] lawyer must perform tasks reasonably appropriate to the representation, including, where appropriate, inquiry into the facts.").

30. *See In re* Konnor, 694 N.W. 2d 376 (Wis. 2005) (failure to investigate concern that rents owed to estate were being misappropriated).

Rule 1.13 imposes a duty to inquire in entity representations. Rule 1.13(a) provides that a lawyer "employed or retained by the organization represents the organization acting through its duly authorized constituents." Determining the interests of the organization will often require further inquiry to clarify any ambiguity about who has authority and what the organization's priorities are. Under Rule 1.13(b), once the lawyer learns of action, omission, or planned activity on the part of an "officer, employee, or other person associated with the organization . . . that is a violation of a legal obligation to the organization, and that is likely to result in substantial injury to the organization, then the lawyer shall proceed as is reasonably necessary in the best interests of the organization." Even if the underlying facts regarding the violation or potential violation are already well established and require no additional inquiry, determining what is "reasonably necessary" and in the "best interest of the organization" will commonly involve additional communication and investigation.[31]

Recent ABA guidance and opinions support this approach. Concern that individuals might use the services of U.S. lawyers for money-laundering and terrorist financing prompted the ABA House of Delegates to adopt in 2010 the *ABA Voluntary Good Practices Guidance for Lawyers to Detect and Combat Money Laundering and Terrorist Financing* ("Good Practices Guidance"). The Good Practices Guidance advocates a "risk-based approach" to avoid assisting in money laundering or terrorist financing, according to guidelines developed by the Financial Action Task Force on Money Laundering ("FATF").[32] Recommended measures include "examining the nature of the legal work involved, and where the [client's] business is taking place."[33]

31. *See* Model Rules R. 1.13 cmts. [3] & [4]. Rule 1.13(b) was added after a series of high profile financial accounting scandals in the early 2000s. Am. Bar Ass'n Task Force on Corporate Responsibility (2003), *reprinted in* 59 Bus. Law. 145, 166–70 (2003). Other law may also create a duty to inquire. The Sarbanes-Oxley Act of 2002 creates a duty for the "chief legal officer" to conduct an "appropriate" investigation in response to another lawyer's report of "evidence of a material violation" by the company. 17 C.F.R. § 205.3(b)(2) (2012); *see also In re* Kern, 816 S.E. 2d 574 (S.C. 2018) (discussing obligations of securities lawyers); U.S. Dep't of Justice, Principles of Federal Prosecution of Business Organizations § 9-28.720 (quality of internal investigation can affect eligibility for "cooperation credit"); Cohen, *supra* note 26, at 129–30 (discussing obligations of securities lawyers).

32. *See* Good Practices Guidance, *supra* note 7, at 2. A "risk-based approach" is generally "intended to ensure that measures to prevent or mitigate money laundering and terrorist financing are commensurate with the risks identified . . . [H]igher risk areas should be subject to enhanced procedures, such as enhanced client due diligence ("CDD") . . . ." *Id.* at 8. The report continues: "This paper [identifies] the risk categories and offer[s] voluntary good practices designed to assist lawyers in detecting money laundering while satisfying their professional obligations." *Id.*

33. ABA Standing Comm. on Ethics & Prof'l Responsibility, Formal Op. 463, at 2 (2013) (summarizing Good Practices Guidance).

ABA Formal Opinion 463 addresses efforts to require U.S. lawyers to perform "gatekeeping" duties to protect the international financing system from criminal activity arising out of worldwide money-laundering and terrorist financing activities. Observing that "the Rules do not mandate that a lawyer perform a 'gatekeeper' role," especially in regards to "mandatory reporting" to public authorities "of suspicion about a client," Opinion 463 nevertheless identifies the Good Practices Guidance as a resource "consistent with the Model Rules" and with Informal Opinion 1470.[34] It also reinforces the duty to investigate in appropriate circumstances. Specifically, Opinion 463 states that "[i]t would be prudent for lawyers to undertake Client Due Diligence ("CDD") in appropriate circumstances to avoid facilitating illegal activity or being drawn unwittingly into a criminal activity. . . . *[P]ursuant to a lawyer's ethical obligation to act competently, a duty to inquire further may also arise.* An appropriate assessment of the client and the client's objectives, and the means for obtaining those objectives, are *essential prerequisites* for accepting a new matter or continuing a representation as new facts unfold."[35]

A lawyer's reasonable judgment under the circumstances presented, especially the information known and reasonably available to the lawyer at the time, does not violate the rules. Nor should a lawyer be subject to discipline because a course of action, objectively reasonable at the time it was chosen, turned out to be wrong with hindsight.[36]

---

34. *Id.*

35. *Id.* at 2–3 (emphasis added); *see also id.* at 2 n.10 ("The Good Practices Guidance encourages all lawyers to perform basic CDD by (1) identifying and verifying the identity of each client; (2) identifying and verifying the identity of any 'beneficial owner' of the client, defined as the natural person(s) with ultimate control of a client, when such an analysis is warranted from a risk-based standpoint; and (3) obtaining enough information to understand a client's circumstances, business, and objectives.").

36. In numerous contexts of evaluating attorney conduct, courts and regulators have warned against hindsight bias. *See* Woodruff v. Tomlin, 616 F.2d 924, 930 (6th Cir. 1980) ("[E]very losing litigant would be able to sue his attorney if he could find another attorney who was willing to second guess the decisions of the first attorney with the advantage of hindsight."); *In re* Claussen, 14 P.3d 586, 593–94 (Or. 2000) (en banc) (declining to discipline lawyer who aided client in converting insurance policy to cash while client's bankruptcy petition was pending; lawyer did not know client would abscond with money and cannot be judged by a standard of "clairvoyance" that reflects the knowledge of "hindsight"); N.Y.C. Bar Ass'n Comm. on Prof'l Ethics, Formal Op. 2018-4 (2018) ("Under the knowledge standard of Rule 1.2(d), a lawyer is not deemed to 'know' facts, or the significance of facts, that become evident only with the benefit of hindsight."); N.Y.C. Bar Ass'n Comm. on Prof'l Ethics, Formal Op. 2005-05 (2005) (in handling of "'thrust upon' concurrent client conflicts a lawyer who does balance the relevant considerations in good faith should not be subject to discipline for getting it wrong in hindsight"); Pa. Bar Ass'n Comm. on Legal Ethics & Prof'l Responsibility, Formal Op. 2001-100 (2001) (the propriety of accepting stock as payment of legal fees for a start-up "should be made based on the information available at the time of the transaction and not with the benefit of hindsight").

IV. Other Obligations Incident to the Duty to Inquire

If the client refuses to provide information or asks the lawyer not to evaluate the legality of a transaction the lawyer should explain to the client that the lawyer cannot undertake the representation unless an appropriate inquiry is made. If the client does not agree to provide information, then the lawyer must decline the representation or withdraw.[37] If the client agrees, but then temporizes and fails to provide the requested information, or provides incomplete information, the lawyer must remonstrate with the client. If that fails to rectify the information deficit, the lawyer must withdraw. Indeed, proceeding in a transaction without the requested information may, depending on the circumstances, be evidence of the lawyer's willful blindness under Rule 1.2(d).[38] If the client agrees, provides additional information, and the lawyer concludes that the requested services would amount to assisting in a crime or fraud, the lawyer must either discuss the matter further with the client, decline the representation, or seek to withdraw under Rule 1.16(a).[39]

In general, a lawyer should not assume that a client will be unresponsive to remonstration. However, if the client insists on proceeding with the proposed course of action despite the lawyer's remonstration, the lawyer must decline the representation or withdraw.[40] The lawyer may have discretion to disclose information relating to the representation under Model Rule 1.6(b)(1)-(3).[41]

If the lawyer needs information from sources other than the prospective client and can obtain that information without disclosing information protected by Rules 1.6 and 1.18, the information should be sought. If the lawyer needs to disclose protected information in order to analyze the transaction,

37. As discussed below, under Rule 1.2(c) a lawyer cannot assent to an unreasonable limitation on the representation even if the client seeks or insists upon such a limitation and offers consent.

38. *See also* N.Y.C. Bar Ass'n Comm. on Prof'l Ethics, Formal Op. 2018-4 at 5 ("[A] client's refusal to authorize and assist in an inquiry into the lawfulness of the client's proposed conduct will ordinarily constitute an additional, and very significant, 'red flag.'").

39. Model Rules R. 1.2 cmt. [13] ("If a lawyer comes to know or reasonably should know that a client expects assistance not permitted by the Rules of Professional Conduct or other law . . . the lawyer must consult with the client regarding the limitations on the lawyer's conduct.").

40. *See also* N.Y.C. Bar Ass'n Comm. on Prof'l Ethics, Formal Op. 2018-4 at 6 ("If it becomes clear during a lawyer's representation that the client has failed to take necessary corrective action, and the lawyer's continued representation would assist client conduct that is illegal or fraudulent, Rule 1.16(b)(1) mandates that the lawyer withdraw from representation."). For a discussion of the obligation to withdraw upon learning that a lawyer's services have been used to further a fraud, see ABA Standing Comm. on Ethics and Prof'l Responsibility, Formal Op. 92-366 (1992).

41. N.Y.C. Bar Ass'n Comm. on Prof'l Ethics, Formal Op. 2018-4 at 6.

the lawyer must seek the client's informed consent in advance.[42] If the client will not consent or the lawyer believes that seeking consent will lead to criminal or fraudulent activity, the lawyer must decline the representation or withdraw.[43]

If an inquiry would result in expenses that the client refuses to pay, the lawyer may choose to conduct the inquiry without payment or to decline or discontinue the representation.

Overall, as long as the lawyer conducts a reasonable inquiry, it is ordinarily proper to credit an otherwise trustworthy client where information gathered from other sources fails to resolve the issue, even if some doubt remains.[44] This conclusion may be reasonable in a variety of circumstances. For example, the lawyer may have represented the client in many other matters. The lawyer may know the client personally, professionally, or socially. The business arrangements and other individuals or parties involved in the transaction may be familiar to the lawyer.

Finally, Rule 1.2(c) permits a lawyer to "limit the scope of [a] representation if the limitation is reasonable under the circumstances and the client gives informed consent." Permitted scope limitations include, for example, that the client has limited but lawful objectives for the representation, or that certain available means to accomplish the client's objectives are too costly for the client or repugnant to the lawyer.[45] Any limitation, however, must "accord with the Rules of Professional Conduct and other law," including the lawyer's duty to provide competent representation.[46] In the circumstances addressed by this opinion, a lawyer may not agree to exclude inquiry into the legality of the transaction.

V. Hypotheticals

The following hypotheticals are intended to clarify when circumstances might require further inquiry because of risk factors known to the lawyer.

---

42. Model Rules R. 1.0(e) ("'Informed consent' denotes the agreement by a person to a proposed course of conduct after the lawyer has communicated adequate information and explanation about the material risks of and reasonably available alternatives to the proposed course of conduct.").

43. Model Rules R. 1.16(c)(2).

44. *See* N.Y.C. Bar Ass'n Comm. on Prof'l Ethics, Formal Op. 2018-4 at 5.

45. *See* Model Rules R. 1.2 cmt. [6] ("A limited representation may be appropriate because the client has limited objectives for the representation. In addition, the terms upon which representation is undertaken may exclude specific means that might otherwise be used to accomplish the client's objectives. Such limitations may exclude actions that the client thinks are too costly or that the lawyer regards as repugnant or imprudent.")

46. *See id.* cmt. [7] ("an agreement for a limited representation does not exempt a lawyer from the duty to provide competent representation"); *id.* cmt. [8] ("All agreements concerning a lawyer's representation of a client must accord with the Rules of Professional Conduct and other law.").

Some are drawn from the Good Practices Guidance, an important resource for transactional lawyers detailing how to conduct proper due diligence as well as how to identify and address risk factors in the most common scenarios in which a lawyer's assistance might be sought in criminal or fraudulent transactions.[47]

Further inquiry would be required in the first two examples because the combination of risk factors known to the lawyer creates a high probability that the client is engaged in criminal or fraudulent activity.

#1: A prospective client has significant business connections and interests abroad. The client has received substantial payments from sources other than his employer. The client holds these funds outside the US and wants to bring them into the US through a transaction that minimizes US tax liability. The client says: (i) he is "employed" outside the US but will not say how; (ii) the money is in a "foreign bank" in the name of a foreign corporation but the client will not identify the bank or the corporation; (iii) he has not disclosed the payments to his employer or any governmental authority or to anyone else; and (iv) he has not included the amounts in his US income tax returns.[48]

#2: A prospective client tells a lawyer he is an agent for a minister or other government official from a "high risk" jurisdiction[49] who wishes to remain anonymous and would like to purchase an expensive property in the United States. The property would be owned through corporations that have undisclosed beneficial owners. The prospective client says that large amounts of money will be involved in the purchase but is vague about the source of the funds, or the funds appear to come from "questionable" sources.[50]

If, on the same facts as #2, the client assures the lawyer that information will be provided but does not follow through, the lawyer must either withdraw or again discuss with the client the need for the information to continue

---

47. The analysis of the hypotheticals that follows draws on the Good Practices Guidance but should not be read to support the conclusion that any isolated risk factor identified in the Good Practices Guidance necessarily creates a duty to inquire in all matters in which it may be present. The question is whether a reasonable lawyer under the specific circumstances would be obliged to conduct further inquiry. The Committee further cautions that circumstances that render a specific jurisdiction or other factor "high risk" can change. On the one hand, if new circumstances presenting a greater risk arise the lawyer should take appropriate action, and may need to seek advice on what, if any, action is required. On the other hand, new circumstances may support acceptance or continuation of the representation by showing that, upon inquiry, the high-risk designation is inaccurate or inapplicable to the matter.

48. This hypothetical is drawn from ABA Comm. on Ethics & Prof'l Responsibility, Informal Opinion 1470, which concludes that a lawyer must conduct further inquiry.

49. For information about "high risk" jurisdictions, see Good Practices Guidance, *supra* note 7, at 15–16.

50. This hypothetical is based on *In re* Jankoff, 81 N.Y.S.3d 733, 734 (N.Y. App. Div. 2018) (public censure imposed on stipulated facts), and *In re* Koplik, 90 N.Y.S.3d 187 (N.Y. App. Div. 2019) (same).

in the representation, seek an explanation for the delay, and withdraw if the explanation the client offers is unsatisfactory. If the information provided is incomplete — e.g., information that leaves the identity of the actual funding sources opaque — the lawyer must follow the same course: withdraw or again discuss with the client the need for the information to continue in the representation, seek an explanation for the delay, and withdraw if the explanation offered is unsatisfactory.[51]

In examples #3 through #5 below, the duty to inquire depends on contextual factors, most significantly, the lawyer's familiarity with the client and the jurisdiction.

#3: A general practitioner in rural North Dakota receives a call from a long-term client asking her to form a limited liability company for the purpose of buying a ranch.[52]

#4: The general practitioner in rural North Dakota receives a call from a new and unknown prospective client saying that the client just won several million dollars in Las Vegas and needs the lawyer to form a limited liability company to buy a ranch.[53]

#5: A prospective client in New York City asks a general practitioner in a mid-size town in rural Georgia to provide legal services for the acquisition of several farms in rural Georgia. The prospective client tells the lawyer that he has made a lot of money in hedge funds and now wants to diversify his investments by purchasing these farms but says he doesn't want his purchases to cause a wave of land speculation and artificially inflate local prices. He wants to wire money into the law firm's trust account over time for the purchases. He asks the lawyer to create a series of LLCs to make strategic (and apparently unrelated) acquisitions.[54]

VI. Conclusion

Model Rule 1.2(d) prohibits a lawyer from advising or assisting a client in a transaction or other non-litigation matter the lawyer "knows" is criminal or fraudulent. That knowledge may be inferred from the circumstances, including a lawyer's willful blindness or conscious disregard of available facts. Accordingly, where there is a high probability that a client seeks to use the lawyer's services for criminal or fraudulent activity, the lawyer must in-

---

51. *See supra*, Section IV.

52. This hypothetical is drawn from Good Practices Guidance, *supra* note 7, at 8, and should not require further inquiry regarding the legitimacy of the transaction assuming prior matters have not involved abuse of the attorney-client relationship on the part of the client. It is likely, of course, that some inquiry into other details will be necessary to handle the transaction competently.

53. This hypothetical is drawn from Good Practices Guidance, *supra* note 7, at 8, and requires further inquiry.

54. This hypothetical is drawn from American Law Institute, Anti-Money Laundering Rules and Other Ethics Issues 450-51 (2017) and requires further inquiry.

quire further to avoid advising or assisting such activity. Even if information learned in the course of a preliminary interview or during a representation is insufficient to establish "knowledge" under Rule 1.2(d), other rules may require further inquiry to help the client avoid crime or fraud, to advance the client's legitimate interests, and to avoid professional misconduct. These include the duties of competence, diligence, communication, and honesty under Rules 1.1, 1.3, 1.4, 1.13, 1.16, and 8.4. If the client or prospective client refuses to provide information necessary to assess the legality of the proposed transaction, the lawyer must ordinarily decline the representation or withdraw under Rule 1.16. A lawyer's reasonable evaluation after that inquiry based on information reasonably available at the time does not violate the rules.

AMERICAN BAR ASSOCIATION

STANDING COMMITTEE ON ETHICS AND PROFESSIONAL RESPONSIBILITY

Formal Opinion 492 **June 9, 2020**

Obligations to Prospective Clients: Confidentiality, Conflicts and "Significantly Harmful" Information

A prospective client is a person who consults a lawyer about the possibility of forming a client-lawyer relationship. Model Rule 1.18 governs whether the consultation limits the lawyer or the lawyer's firm from accepting a new client whose interests are materially adverse to the prospective client in a matter that is the same or substantially related to the subject of the consultation, even when no client-lawyer relationship results from the consultation. Under Model Rule 1.18 a lawyer is prohibited from accepting a new matter if the lawyer received information from the prospective client that could be significantly harmful to the prior prospective client in the new matter. Whether information learned by the lawyer could be significantly harmful is a fact-based inquiry depending on a variety of circumstances including the length of the consultation and the nature of the topics discussed. The inquiry does not require the prior prospective client to reveal confidential information. Further, even if the lawyer learned information that could be significantly harmful to the prior prospective client in the new matter, the lawyer's firm can accept the new matter if the lawyer is screened from the new matter or the prospective client provides informed consent, as set forth in Model Rule 1.18(d)(1) and (2).[1]

I. Introduction

Prospective clients often consult with a lawyer in anticipation of forming a client-lawyer relationship. These consultations give clients and lawyers an opportunity to get to know one another, to ascertain whether they will like working together, and to discuss preliminary matters like conflicts, fee arrangements, and the client's legal needs. During these consultations it is likely that the prospective client will reveal information necessary for each to decide whether to proceed. Some of that information could create a con-

1. This opinion is based on the ABA Model Rules of Professional Conduct as amended by the ABA House of Delegates through August 2019. The laws, court rules, regulations, rules of professional conduct and opinions promulgated in individual jurisdictions are controlling.

flict of interest that would prevent the lawyer from undertaking a future representation.

This opinion provides guidance on the types of information that could give rise to such disqualifying conflicts, what the prospective client should be asked to demonstrate in support of a claim that the lawyer has a conflict of interest in a subsequent matter, what precautions the lawyer and the lawyer's firm might take to avoid receiving disqualifying information during an initial consultation with a prospective client, and how to minimize the consequences of receiving such information.[2]

Prior to 2002, the Model Rules did not address obligations owed to individuals who consulted with a lawyer but never established a client-lawyer relationship with the lawyer.[3] In 2002, as part of the Ethics 2000 amendments, the ABA adopted Model Rule 1.18, which establishes a lawyer's obligations to a "prospective client."[4] Earlier, the ABA had provided guidance on ethical obligations to prospective clients in Formal Opinion 90-398 (1990).[5]

II. Analysis

A. Who is a "Prospective Client"?

Under Model Rule 1.18(a), a "prospective client" is "[a] person who consults with a lawyer about the possibility of forming a client-lawyer relationship with respect to a matter."[6] Comment [2] to Model Rule 1.18 explains:

> A person becomes a prospective client by consulting with a lawyer about the possibility of forming a client-lawyer relationship with re-

---

2. Unless otherwise indicated, "prospective client" (sometimes referred to in case law as a "former prospective client") refers to an individual who has consulted with the lawyer about the possibility of forming a client-lawyer relationship with respect to a matter, but no client-lawyer relationship is subsequently established.

3. *See, e.g.*, Art Garwin, A Legislative History: The Development of the ABA Model Rules of Professional Conduct, 1982-2013 (2013).

4. *Id.* at 397-406. The only change to Rule 1.18 after 2002 was made in 2012, when the word "consults" was substituted for "discusses" in Rule 1.18(a) and in the Comments. This was not intended as a substantive change. The amendment clarified that communications that could constitute a "discussion" or a "consultation" could be written, oral or electronic. *See* Model Rules of Prof'l Conduct R. 1.18 cmt. [2] (2019) [hereinafter Model Rules]; Ellen J. Bennett & Helen W. Gunnarsson, Annotated Model Rules of Professional Conduct 309 (9th ed. 2019).

5. *See* ABA Comm. on Ethics & Prof'l Responsibility, Formal Op. 90-358 (1990) ("Information imparted to a lawyer by a would-be client seeking legal representation is protected from revelation or use under Model Rule 1.6 even though the lawyer does not undertake representation of or perform legal work for the would-be client.").

6. Model Rules R. 1.18 (2019). As discussed below a client-lawyer relationship may be formed during the consultation. The lawyer should take the precautions discussed in this opinion to avoid that result if that is not the lawyer's intention.

> spect to a matter. Whether communications, including written, oral, or electronic communications, constitute a consultation depends on the circumstances. For example, a consultation is likely to have occurred if a lawyer, either in person or through the lawyer's advertising in any medium, specifically requests or invites the submission of information about a potential representation without clear and reasonably understandable warnings and cautionary statements that limit the lawyer's obligations, and a person provides information in response.[7]

Comment [2] clarifies, however, that not every contact between a lawyer and an individual regarding legal services makes that individual a "prospective client:"

> [A] consultation does not occur if a person provides information to a lawyer in response to advertising that merely describes the lawyer's education, experience, areas of practice, and contact information, or provides legal information of general interest. Such a person communicates information unilaterally to a lawyer, without any reasonable expectation that the lawyer is willing to discuss the possibility of forming a client-lawyer relationship, and is thus not a "prospective client." Moreover, a person who communicates with a lawyer for the purpose of disqualifying the lawyer is not a "prospective client."[8]

Thus, a person who communicates information unilaterally to a lawyer after reviewing the lawyer's website or other advertising describing the lawyer's education and experience does not *for that reason alone* become a "prospective client" within the meaning of Model Rule 1.18.[9] Additionally, as the

---

7. Model Rules R. 1.18(b) cmt. [2].

8. *Id.*

9. *See* ABA Comm. on Ethics & Prof'l Responsibility, Formal Op. 10-457 (2010) ("not all initial communications from persons who wish to be prospective clients" result in such status); Ariz. State Bar, Advisory Op. 02-04 (2002) (no duty of confidentiality owed to person who unilaterally sends unsolicited information to a lawyer); Fla. Bar, Advisory Op. 07-3 (2009) (a person seeking legal services who sends information unilaterally to a lawyer has no reasonable expectation of confidentiality regarding that information); San Diego County Bar Ass'n, Advisory Op. 2006-1 (2006) (no duty of confidentiality owed to someone who sends information to a lawyer after obtaining the email address of the lawyer from a state bar website); Va. State Bar Op. 1842 (2008) (lawyer has no duty of confidentiality to person who unilaterally transmits unsolicited information in voice mail or email); Wis. State Bar Prof'l Ethics Comm., Formal Op. EF-11-03 (2011) (person seeking representation who sends unsolicited confidential information through email to a lawyer does not thereby establish a client-lawyer relationship or a duty of confidentiality).

last sentence of Comment [2] notes, if the person consulting with the lawyer does not have a reasonable intent to retain the lawyer, but instead is merely attempting to disqualify the lawyer from representing anyone else in the matter, the person is not a "prospective client."[10]

B. The Obligation to Protect Confidential Information

Model Rule 1.18(b) imposes a duty of confidentiality with respect to information learned during a consultation, even when no client-lawyer relationship ensues. It provides:

> Even when no client-lawyer relationship ensues, a lawyer who has learned information from a prospective client shall not use or reveal that information, except as Rule 1.9 would permit with respect to information of a former client."[11]

This duty includes protecting all information learned during the consultation, unless the lawyer has the informed consent of the prospective client to condition the consultation on the lawyer *not* maintaining the confidentiality of the information communicated. As stated by Comment [5] to Model Rule 1.18, "[a] lawyer may condition a consultation with a prospective client on the person's informed consent that no information disclosed during the consultation will prohibit the lawyer from representing a different client in the matter."[12] Model Rule 1.0(e) defines "informed consent."[13]

---

10. Bernacki v. Bernacki, 1 N.Y.S.3d 761, 764 (Sup. Ct. 2015) (husband in a divorce sent an email to his wife titled "Attorneys Which [sic] Whom I Have Sought Legal Advice" and then listed "twelve of the most experienced matrimonial attorneys in the county," each of whom the husband asserted "would conflict themselves out" or be subject to disqualification); RESTATEMENT OF THE LAW (THIRD), THE LAW GOVERNING LAWYERS § 15 cmt. c [hereinafter RESTATEMENT THIRD] ("a tribunal may consider whether the prospective client disclosed confidential information to the lawyer for the purpose of preventing the lawyer or the lawyer's firm from representing an adverse party rather than in a good faith endeavor to determine whether to retain the lawyer").

11. MODEL RULES R. 1.18(b). *See also* N.Y.C. Bar Ass'n Comm. on Prof'l Ethics, Formal Op. 2013-1 (2013) (discussing the scope of protected information under Rule 1.18(b)); D.C. Bar Op. 374 (2018) (information from prospective client is protected from disclosure to the same extent as client information is protected by D.C. Rule 1.6)); RESTATEMENT THIRD, *supra* note 10, § 59 cmt. c (2000) ("Information acquired during the representation or before or after the representation is confidential so long as it is not generally known . . . and relates to the representation. Such information, for example, might be acquired by the lawyer in considering whether to undertake a representation.").

12. MODEL RULES R. 1.18 cmt. [5].

13. MODEL RULES R. 1.0(e).

C. Disqualifying Conflicts Based on the Acquisition of "Significantly Harmful" Information

Model Rule 1.18(c) provides for potential disqualification arising out of the consultation:

> A lawyer subject to paragraph (b) shall not represent a client with interests materially adverse to those of a prospective client in the same or a substantially related matter *if the lawyer received information from the prospective client that could be significantly harmful to that person in the matter* . . . .[14]

The phrase "significantly harmful" qualifies the lawyer's duties toward prospective clients where no client-lawyer relationship is established and distinguishes these duties from duties owed to clients. Comment [1] explains:

> Prospective clients, like clients, may disclose information to a lawyer, place documents or other property in the lawyer's custody, or rely on the lawyer's advice. A lawyer's consultations with a prospective client usually are limited in time and depth and leave both the prospective client and the lawyer free (and sometimes required) to proceed no further. Hence, *prospective clients should receive some but not all of the protection afforded clients.*[15]

The notion that "prospective clients" receive "some but not all of the protections afforded clients" can be illustrated by comparing the application of Model Rule 1.9 with Model Rule 1.18 with respect to possible conflicts of interests. Under Model Rule 1.9, "[a] lawyer who has formerly represented a client in a matter shall not thereafter represent another person in the same or substantially related matter in which that person's interest are materially adverse to the interests of the former client" unless certain conditions are met.[16] As Comment [3] to Model Rule 1.9 explains, for former clients the question is whether confidential information *could have been* shared, not whether confi-

14. Model Rules R. 1.18(c) (emphasis added).

15. Model Rules R. 1.18 cmt. [1] (emphasis added). *See also* Wis. State Bar Prof'l Ethics Comm., Formal Op. EI-10-03 (2011) (the "more lenient standard [in Rule 1.18] reflects the attenuated relationship with prospective clients"); N.Y.C. Bar Ass'n Comm. on Prof'l Ethics, Formal Op. 2013-1, *supra* note 11 ("The 'significantly harmful' test makes the [Rule 1.18(c)] restriction less exacting than the corresponding restriction on representations that are materially adverse to a former client."). A person and a lawyer may, of course, have as many consultations and discussions as they mutually find beneficial in order to determine whether to enter into a client-lawyer relationship. In such circumstances, however, the lawyer is more likely to receive information that could be "significantly harmful" in a later representation adverse to the prospective client.

16. Model Rules R. 1.9(a).

dences were in fact shared, regardless of the harmful quality of the information. The Comment reads, in part,

> A former client is not required to reveal the confidential information learned by the lawyer in order to establish a substantial risk that the lawyer has confidential information to use in a subsequent matter. A conclusion about the possession of such information may be based on the nature of the services the lawyer provided the former client and the information that would in ordinary practice be learned by a lawyer providing such services.[17]

A former client need not reveal confidential information to satisfy the "substantial relationship" test. "Matters are 'substantially related' for purposes of [Model Rule 1.9] if they involve the same transaction or legal dispute or *if there otherwise is a substantial risk* that confidential factual information as would normally have been obtained in the prior representation would materially advance the client's position in the subsequent matter."[18] As described by Judge Posner in in *Analytica v. NPD Research*:

> [A] lawyer may not represent an adversary of his former client if the subject matter of the two representations is "substantially related," which means: if the lawyer *could have obtained confidential information* in the first representation that would have been relevant in the second. It is irrelevant whether he actually obtained such information and used it against his former client . . . .[19]

Model Rule 1.18 is different than Model Rule 1.9 because it imposes the additional requirement, not found in Model Rule 1.9, that the prospective client have communicated information that "could be significantly harmful" in a subsequent matter. As a result, the mere fact that a prospective client consulted with a lawyer in a substantially related matter is not sufficient, alone, to disqualify the lawyer from a later matter.[20] Nor is it sufficient to conclude

17. Model Rules R. 1.9 cmt. [3]. *See also* N.Y.C. Bar Ass'n Comm. on Prof'l Ethics, Formal Op. 2013-1, *supra* note 11, at 5 ("Under Rule 1.9(a), the bar against adverse representation is automatic; if the relevant parties' interests are materially adverse and the matters are the same or substantially related, the bar applies whether or not the lawyer received any information, harmful or otherwise from the former client.") (footnote omitted); Analytica Inc. v. NPD Research, 708 F.2d 1263, 1267 (7th Cir. 1983) ("If the 'substantial relationship' test applies . . . it is not appropriate for the court to inquire into whether actual confidences were disclosed [by the former client].").

18. Model Rules R. 1.9 cmt. [3] (emphasis added) .

19. *Analytica, Inc.*, 708 F.2d at 1266 (emphasis added).

20. Bernacki v. Bernacki, 1 N.Y.S.3d 761, 764 (Sup. Ct. 2015) (prospective client's "reference to the information as 'confidential' without more is insufficient"); Restatement Third,

that a conflict exists merely because a prospective client volunteers information to a lawyer because, as noted above, the unilateral transmission of information to a lawyer does not create a Model Rule 1.18 duty, nor will Model Rule 1.18 protect someone who contacts a lawyer with the intent to disqualify the lawyer from representing other parties in the matter.[21]

With respect to what must be shown to establish that a person is entitled to the protections of Model Rule 1.18, evidence beyond the mere fact of a consultation is generally required.[22] The fact that the prospective client must come forward with some evidence concerning the contents of the consultation with the lawyer does not mean, however, that the prospective client must disclose confidential information or detail the substance of the discussions. The cases and other authorities support the conclusion that only certain disclosures are required, for example, the date, duration and manner of communication (*i.e.*, in person, email, over the phone, etc.), and a summary description of the topics discussed.[23]

With respect to the "significantly harmful" test, information disclosed by the person invoking the protection of Model Rule 1.18 need not demonstrate that the harm is certain to occur in order to demonstrate a conflict. Instead, the Model Rule addresses information that "could be significantly harmful,"

---

supra note 10, § 15, cmt. c (after a consultation with a prospective client, "a lawyer is not always prohibited from representing a client with interests adverse to those of the prospective client in the same or a substantially related matter").

21. *See* Model Rules R. 1.18 cmt. [2]. *See also supra* note 9 (collecting opinions).

22. *See* Thomson v. Duker, 346 S.W.3d 390, 396 (Mo. Ct. App. 2011) (Rule 1.18 requires "at least some disclosure, either by the objecting prospective client or by the lawyer, of the scope of information discussed" during the consultation) (cites omitted); Restatement Third, *supra* note 10, § 15(c) (the prospective client "bears the burden of persuading the tribunal that the lawyer received information "that could be significantly harmful to the prospective client in the matter"); *but see* ABA Comm. on Ethics & Prof'l Responsibility, Formal Op. 10-457, *supra* note 9 (a lawyer's website that "specifically encourages a website visitor to submit a personal inquiry about a proposed representation on a conveniently provided electronic form" may be deemed to invite the submission of confidential information and therefore provide information to the lawyer that could be "significantly harmful" to the prospective client in a subsequent adverse representation).

23. The format could be similar to what is known as a "privilege log," submitted to a court in connection with a claim of privilege. The information which is the subject of the privilege claim is not disclosed. Rather information sufficient to establish the claim of privilege is ordinarily all that is required. Federal Rule of Civil Procedure 26(b)(5) (requiring that privilege logs "describe the nature of the documents, communications, or tangible things not produced or disclosed --- and do so in a manner that, without revealing information itself privileged or protected will enable other parties to assess the claim [of privilege or other protection]." In appropriate instances, protected information can be disclosed to courts *in camera*. *See* O Builders Associates, Inc. v. Yuna Corp. of N.J., 19 A.3d 966, 978 (N.J. 2011) ("the parties may protect the confidentiality of their information by, among other means, requesting that the record be subject to a protective order . . . and the movant may further request that the application be considered *in camera*") (cites omitted); Keith v. Keith, 140 So.3d 1202, 1211-1212 (La. Ct. App. 2014) (discussing the use of *in camera* proceedings in Rule 1.18 decisions).

a standard that "focuses on the *potential* use of the information."[24] Post-hoc promises by the lawyer not to use the information do not change the standard from one of potential use or harm to a standard that requires actual use or harm.[25]

Information that is typically viewed as "significantly harmful" includes, for instance, "views on various settlement issues including price and timing"; "personal accounts of each relevant event [and the prospective client's] strategic thinking concerning how to manage the situation"; an "18-minute phone call" with a "prospective client-plaintiff [during which a firm] "had 'outlined potential claims'" against defendant and "'discussed specifics as to amount of money needed to settle the case'"; and a presentation by a corporation seeking to bring an action of "the underlying facts and legal theories about its proposed lawsuit."[26] Other recognized categories of significantly harmful information include: "sensitive personal information" in a divorce case; "premature possession of the prospective client's financial information"; knowledge of "settlement position"; a "prospective client's personal thoughts and impressions regarding the facts of the case and possible litigation strategies,"[27] and "the possible terms and structure of a proposed bid" by one corporation to acquire another.[28]

The Restatement also offers helpful guidance. Section 15(2) of the Restatement provides for disqualification of a lawyer who, in discussing "the possibility of . . . forming a client-lawyer relationship" received "from the prospective client confidential information that could be significantly harmful to the prospective client" in a matter."[29] Further, in the words of the North Dakota Supreme Court:

> Information may be "significantly harmful" if it is sensitive or privileged information that the lawyer would not have received in the ordinary course of due diligence; or if it is information that has long-term significance or continuing relevance to the matter, such as motives, litigation strategies or potential weakness. "Significantly harmful" may also be the premature possession of information that could have a substantial impact on settlement proposals and trial

---

24. N.Y.C. Bar Ass'n Comm. on Prof'l Ethics, Formal Op. 2013-1, *supra* note 11, at 5 (emphasis in original).

25. *Id.*

26. *Id.* at 8, note 9 (cites omitted).

27. Wis. State Bar Prof'l Ethics Comm., Formal Op. EI-10-03, *supra* note 15, at 4-5 (cites omitted).

28. *See* N.Y.C. Bar Ass'n Comm. on Prof'l Ethics, Formal Op. 2013-1, *supra* note 11, at 7 (discussion of "Scenario 3").

29. Restatement Third, *supra* note 10, § 15 (2000). The language "information that could be significantly harmful to that person" in Rule 1.18(c) tracks the Restatement's language.

strategy; the personal thoughts and impression about the facts of the case; or information that is extensive, critical, or of significant use.[30]

As an illustration, the Restatement discusses an initial meeting between a lawyer and a prospective client seeking a divorce. The prospective client and the lawyer have an hour-long conversation in which they discuss the prospective client's "reasons for seeking a divorce and the nature and extent of his and Spouse's property interests." The prospective client decides not to retain the lawyer because "the suggested fee [is] too high." Thereafter, the spouse seeks to hire the lawyer. The Restatement concludes that the lawyer received "significantly harmful information" from the prospective client and cannot represent the opposing spouse.[31]

On the other hand, and as the New Jersey Supreme Court explained in *O Builders & Associates v. Yuna Corp*, "significantly harmful" information under Rule 1.18 "cannot be simply detrimental in general to the former prospective client, but the harm suffered must be prejudicial in fact to the former prospective client within the confines of the specific matter in which disqualification is sought, a determination that is exquisitely fact-sensitive and -specific."[32]

So, for example, information that causes embarrassment or inconvenience "does not seem to be '*significant*'" while information relating to "[c] ivil or criminal liability would seem to easily qualify."[33] Specific instances in which information was deemed *not* to be "significantly harmful" include: a lawyer who "avoided learning the details of the case in half-hour consultation"; a brief consultation that occurred ten years earlier and concerned a "tenuously related matter"; and a one-day "'beauty contest'" consultation where the prospective client's in-house lawyer "regulated disclosures and

30. Kuntz v. Disciplinary Bd. of Supreme Court of North Dakota, 869 N.W.2d 117, 125 (N.D. 2015) (comparing duties under North Dakota Rule 1.18 with duties under North Dakota Rule 1.9, which are analogous to the corresponding Model Rules) (cites omitted). *See also In re* Carpenter, 863 N.W.2d 223 (N.D. 2015) ([a] lawyer can also violate Rule 1.18(b) if the lawyer misuses information gathered in connection with a consultation with a prospective client; discipline imposed for using information about owners of mineral rights learned as part of a consultation with a prospective client for the benefit of a subsequent client in a substantially related matter).

31. Restatement Third, *supra* note 10, § 15(2), at 142 (2000). *See also* Sturdivant v. Sturdivant, 241 S.W.3d. 740, 742 (Ark. 2006) (prospective client provided "significantly harmful information" when he told divorce attorney "everything he knew regarding the children and his concerns about his former wife"). *See also* Wis. State Bar Prof'l Ethics Comm., Formal Op. EI-10-03, *supra* note 15, at 4-5 (collecting cases); N.Y.C. Bar Ass'n Comm. on Prof'l Ethics, Formal Op. 2013-1, *supra* note 11, at note 9 (collecting cases).

32. O Builders Associates, Inc. v. Yuna Corp. of N.J., 19 A.3d 966, 978 (N.J. 2011) (cites omitted). *See also Kuntz*, 869 N.W.2d at 125.

33. John M. Burman, *Waiving a Conflict of Interest and Revoking That Waiver Part III – Conflicts Involving Prospective and Former Clients*, 34 Wyo. Law. 45, note 53 (2011) (emphasis added).

there was no showing that confidential information disclosed could be detrimental to client."[34]

Context is important. In *Marriage of Perry*, for instance, the court concluded that information had been disclosed during the consultation but did not disqualify the lawyer pursuant to Montana's Rule 1.18 because the prospective client "did not establish that any information [she disclosed to the challenged counsel] in telephone calls several years earlier could have any impact on the proceeding, particularly since [the challenged counsel] "was not associated as counsel until three years into the proceeding, by which time substantially more information had been disclosed."[35] Further, information that may be on its face "significantly harmful," may not be such if the court determines that it was generally known by the parties.[36]

D. Limiting Information During an Initial Consultation and Avoiding Imputation of Conflicts.

In order to avoid receiving "significantly harmful information" from a prospective client, lawyers should warn prospective clients against disclosing detailed information. Comment [4] to Model Rule 1.18 states that a lawyer "should limit the initial consultation [with a prospective client] to only such information as reasonably appears necessary" for the purpose of "considering whether or not to undertake a new matter."[37] This caution, however, is not intended to discourage lawyers from engaging in a thorough discussion with prospective clients in order to ascertain whether the lawyer wants to take on the representation. It is simply a reminder that the more information learned in a consultation, the more likely that the lawyer may be precluded from representing other parties in a substantially related matter. Comment [5] provides that a lawyer "may condition a consultation with a prospective client on the person's informed consent that no information disclosed during the consultation will prohibit the lawyer from representing a different client in the matter."[38] If an agreement between the lawyer and the prospective cli-

34. Restatement Third, *supra* note 10, § 15 cmt. c, Reporters Note (cites omitted).

35. *Marriage of Perry*, 293 P.3d 170, 176 (Mont. 2013) *but see* Wis. State Bar Prof'l Ethics Comm., Formal Op. EI-10-03, *supra* note 15 ("the fact that information may be discoverable at some point in current or future litigation, does not by itself mean that the information should not be considered significantly harmful. [It] may be a factor in the analysis, but is not . . . determinative.").

36. Mayers v. Stone Castle Partners, 1 N.Y.S.3d 58, 62 (1st Dept. 2015) (information not significantly harmful because it was generally known, the adversary was aware of some of the details of the relevant transaction, and the motion to disqualify opposing counsel was made "a year into the litigation").

37. Model Rules R. 1.18 cmt. [4].

38. Model Rules R. 1.18 cmt. [5]. With prospective clients who are inexperienced in legal matters, the burden will be on the lawyer to demonstrate that the discussions conformed to the agreed limitations or that the prospective client provided informed consent to the use of the information provided during the consultation. How the lawyer meets this

ent "*expressly so provides*, the prospective client may also consent to the lawyer's subsequent use of information received from the prospective client."[39] This may include, for example, an explicit caution on a website intake link saying that sending information to the firm will not create a client-lawyer relationship and the information may not be kept privileged or confidential.

Once a lawyer receives confidential information from a prospective client that disqualifies the lawyer from future adverse representations imputation of the conflict to other lawyers in a firm may be avoided through screening, in some circumstances. Model Rule 1.18(d) reads:

> When the lawyer has received disqualifying information as defined in paragraph (c), representation is permissible if: (1) both the affected client and the prospective client have given informed consent, confirmed in writing; *or:* (2) the lawyer who received the information took reasonable measures to avoid exposure to more disqualifying information than was reasonably necessary to determine whether to represent the prospective client; and (i) the disqualified lawyer is timely screened from any participation in the matter and is apportioned no part of the fee therefrom; and (ii) written notice is promptly given to the prospective client.[40]

---

burden depends on the circumstances. N.Y.C. Bar Ass'n Comm. on Prof'l Ethics, Formal Op. 2013-1, *supra* note 11 ("the adequacy [of the lawyer's explanation and disclosure] will depend on the relevant facts, particularly the sophistication of the consenting party and [the party's] familiarity with the retention of legal representation and conflict waivers. For example, if the prospective client is an organization that frequently retains lawyers, particularly one with in-house legal advisors, it may need to be told little more than that the law firm would be free to use or reveal information received in the consultation or to represent others with materially adverse interests in the same or any related matter . . . in the event the organization does not retain the firm.").

39. Model Rules R. 1.18 cmt. [5] (emphasis added). *See also* N.Y.C. Bar Ass'n Comm. on Prof'l Ethics, Formal Op. 2013-1, *supra* note 11, at 5 (noting that the consent must be informed and confirmed in writing and recommending other steps to ensure the effectiveness of the waiver); Model Rules R. 1.0 cmt. [6] (discussing how adequacy of disclosure and explanation by the lawyer may depend on the sophistication of the client); Wis. State Bar Prof'l Ethics Comm., Formal Op. EI-10-03, *supra* note 15, at 6 (discussing how to avoid later disqualification through informed consent of the prospective client).

40. Model Rules R. 1.18(d) (emphasis added). For the requirements of informed consent see Model Rule 1.0(e) and Comments [6] and [7] to Rule 1.0. Informed consent under Rule 1.18 may occur in different contexts. "Informed consent" may be obtained at the outset of a consultation containing a condition that any information provided by the prospective client "will not be disqualifying," as set forth in Comment [5] to Model Rule 1.18. "Informed consent" may also allow a lawyer who has received "significantly harmful" information from a prospective client to represent an adverse party pursuant to Model Rule 1.18(d) above. In the former scenario, providing adequate disclosure at the outset of a consultation with a prospective client poses challenges for the lawyer who may not know much about the prospective client's matter and may know even less about the opposing party's potential claims.

E. Resolving Disputes Related to "Significantly Harmful" Information

Finally, when the basic facts are contested, courts or disciplinary authorities may benefit from reviewing documents and/or holding a hearing to assess the facts and, if necessary, determine the credibility of the lawyer and of the person invoking Model Rule 1.18.[41] However, evidentiary hearings may not be necessary and, when conducted, should avoid forcing the prospective client to reveal confidential information.[42]

IV. Conclusion

A lawyer who receives information that "could be significantly harmful" from a prospective client and then represents a client in the same or a substantially related matter where that client's interests are materially adverse to those of the prospective client violates Model Rule 1.18(c) unless the conflict is waived by the prospective client. Whether information that "could be significantly harmful" has been disclosed by a prospective client is a fact-specific inquiry and determined on a case-by-case basis. The test focuses on the potential harm in the new matter. The prospective client must provide some details about the time, manner and duration of communications with the lawyer and also some description of the topics discussed, but need not disclose the contents of the discussion or confidential information. Whether information conveyed is "significantly harmful" in the subsequent matter will depend on, for example, the duration of the discussion, the topics discussed, whether the lawyer reviewed documents, and whether the information conveyed is known by other parties, as well as the relationship between the information and the issues in the subsequent matter.

---

41. *See, e.g.*, Marriage of Perry, 293 P.3d 170, 176-77 (Mont. 2013) (trial court held an evidentiary hearing and examined notes taken by the lawyer concerning the communications with the prospective client before ruling on whether "significantly harmful information" had been disclosed).

42. *See* Richman v. Eighth Judicial Dist. Court, No. 60676, 2013 WL 3357115 at *6 (Nev. May 31, 2013) (trial court did not abuse its discretion by ruling on affidavits and documents without an evidentiary hearing).

AMERICAN BAR ASSOCIATION
STANDING COMMITTEE ON ETHICS AND PROFESSIONAL RESPONSIBILITY

Formal Opinion 493 **July 15, 2020**

Model Rule 8.4(g): Purpose, Scope, and Application

This opinion offers guidance on the purpose, scope, and application of Model Rule 8.4(g). The Rule prohibits a lawyer from engaging in conduct related to the practice of law that the lawyer knows or reasonably should know is harassment or discrimination on the basis of various categories, including race, sex, religion, national origin, and sexual orientation. Whether conduct violates the Rule must be assessed using a standard of objective reasonableness, and only conduct that is found harmful will be grounds for discipline. [1]

Rule 8.4(g) covers conduct related to the practice of law that occurs outside the representation of a client or beyond the confines of a courtroom. In addition, it is not restricted to conduct that is severe or pervasive, a standard utilized in the employment context. However, and as this opinion explains, conduct that violates paragraph (g) will often be intentional and typically targeted at a particular individual or group of individuals, such as directing a racist or sexist epithet towards others or engaging in unwelcome, nonconsensual physical conduct of a sexual nature.

The Rule does not prevent a lawyer from freely expressing opinions and ideas on matters of public concern, nor does it limit a lawyer's speech or conduct in settings unrelated to the practice of law. The fact that others may personally disagree with or be offended by a lawyer's expression does not establish a violation. The Model Rules are rules of reason, and whether conduct violates Rule 8.4(g) must necessarily be judged, in context, from an objectively reasonable perspective.

Besides being advocates and counselors, lawyers also serve a broader public role. Lawyers "should further the public's understanding of and confidence in the rule of law and the justice system because legal institutions in a constitutional democracy depend on popular participation and support to maintain their authority."[2] *Discriminatory and harassing conduct, when engaged in by lawyers in connection with the practice of law, engenders skepticism and distrust of those charged with ensuring*

1. This opinion is based on the ABA Model Rules of Professional Conduct as amended by the ABA House of Delegates through August 2019. The laws, court rules, regulations, rules of professional conduct, and opinions promulgated in individual jurisdictions are controlling.

2. Model Rules of Prof'l Conduct Scope [14] (2019) [hereinafter Model Rules].

justice and fairness. Enforcement of Rule 8.4(g) is therefore critical to maintaining the public's confidence in the impartiality of the legal system and its trust in the legal profession as a whole.[3]

I. Introduction

In August 2016, the ABA House of Delegates adopted Model Rule 8.4(g).[4] The Rule prohibits a lawyer from "engag[ing] in conduct that the lawyer knows or reasonably should know is harassment or discrimination on the basis of race, sex, religion, national origin, ethnicity, disability, age, sexual orientation, gender identity, marital status or socioeconomic status in conduct related to the practice of law."[5] Adoption of paragraph (g) followed years of study and debate within the ABA. This opinion offers guidance on the Rule's purpose, scope, and application.

The conduct addressed by Rule 8.4(g) harms the legal system and the administration of justice. As one court emphasized in sanctioning a male lawyer for disparagingly referring to his female adversary as "babe" and making other derogatory, sexual comments during a deposition,

> [The lawyer's] behavior . . . was a crass attempt to gain an unfair advantage through the use of demeaning language, a blatant example of "sexual [deposition] tactics." . . . "These actions . . . have no place in our system of justice and when attorneys engage in such actions they do not merely reflect on their own lack of professionalism but they disgrace the entire legal profession and the system of justice that provides a stage for such oppressive actors."[6]

---

3. As explained in this opinion, events in the legal profession and in the broader community influenced the development of Rule 8.4(g) and demonstrated the necessity for its adoption. The police-involved killing of George Floyd and the unprecedented social awareness generated by it and other similar tragedies have brought the subject of racial justice to the forefront, further underscoring the importance of Rule 8.4(g) and this opinion.

4. *See Annual Meeting 2016: ABA Amends Model Rules to Add Anti-Discrimination, Anti-Harassment Provision* (Aug. 8, 2016),

https://www.americanbar.org/groups/professional_responsibility/committees_commissions/ethicsandprofessionalresponsibility/ (summarizing events at the House of Delegates meeting). The provision was adopted by voice vote, with no one speaking in opposition. *See* Stephen Gillers, *A Rule to Forbid Bias and Harassment in Law Practice: A Guide for State Courts Considering Model Rule 8.4(g)*, 30 Geo. J. Legal Ethics 195, 197 (2017).

5. Model Rules R. 8.4(g).

6. Mullaney v. Aude, 730 A.2d 759, 767 (Md. Ct. Spec. App. 1999) (quoting trial judge in the case); *see also* Principe v. Assay Partners, 586 N.Y.S.2d 182, 185 (Sup. Ct. 1992) ("[D]iscriminatory conduct on the part of an attorney is inherently and palpably adverse to the goals of justice and the legal profession. . . . 'The continued existence of a free and democratic society depends upon recognition of the concept that justice is based upon the rule of law grounded in respect for the dignity of the individual. . . . Law so grounded makes justice possible, for only through such law does the dignity of the individual attain respect

Comment [3] to the prior version of Rule 8.4 explained that some of the same behavior subjected a lawyer to discipline when the behavior was prejudicial to the administration of justice.[7] Other rules prohibit similar conduct in contexts related to the representation of a client.[8] Rule 8.4(g) is

---

and protection. . . .' While the conduct here falls under the heading of sexist, the same principle applies to any professional discriminatory conduct involving any of the variations to which human beings are subject, whether it be religion, sexual orientation, physical condition, race, nationality or any other difference.") (quoting Preamble to the Code of Professional Responsibility)); Cruz-Aponte v. Caribbean Petroleum Corp., 123 F. Supp. 3d 276, 280 (D.P.R. 2015) ("When an attorney engages in discriminatory behavior, it reflects not only on the attorney's lack of professionalism, but also tarnishes the image of the entire legal profession and disgraces our system of justice."); *In re* Thomsen, 837 N.E.2d 1011, 1012 (Ind. 2005) ("Interjecting race into proceedings where it is not relevant is offensive, unprofessional and tarnishes the image of the profession as a whole."); *In re* Charges of Unprofessional Conduct, 597 N.W.2d 563, 568 (Minn. 1999) (maintaining that "it is especially troubling" when a lawyer engages in "race-based misconduct" and, if not addressed, "undermines confidence in our system of justice").

On June 4, 2020, the Washington Supreme Court issued an open letter regarding the issues raised by the George Floyd situation, forcefully embracing the cause of racial justice: "We call on every member of our legal community to reflect on this moment and ask ourselves how we may work together to eradicate racism. . . . We go by the title of "Justice" and we reaffirm our deepest level of commitment to achieving justice by ending racism. We urge you to join us in these efforts. This is our moral imperative." Supreme Court of Washington, *Open Letter to the Judiciary and the Legal Community* (June 4, 2020), https://www.courts.wa.gov/content/publicUpload/Supreme%20Court%20News/Judiciary%20Legal%20Community%20SIGNED%20060420.pdf.

7. Model Rules R. 8.4(d) cmt. [3] (1998). In particular, the Comment stated:

> A lawyer who, in the course of representing a client, knowingly manifests by words or conduct, bias or prejudice based upon race, sex, religion, national origin, disability, age, sexual orientation or socioeconomic status, violates paragraph (d) *when such actions are prejudicial to the administration of justice.* Legitimate advocacy respecting the foregoing factors does not violate paragraph (d). A trial judge's finding that peremptory challenges were exercised on a discriminatory basis does not alone establish a violation of this rule.

Id. (emphasis added).

8. *See, e.g.*, Model Rules R. 3.5(d) (prohibits "conduct intended to disrupt a tribunal"); Model Rules R. 4.4(a) (prohibits using "means that have no substantial purpose other than to embarrass, delay, or burden a third person" when "representing a client").

The Model Code of Judicial Conduct has long contained a provision prohibiting judges from engaging in this sort of discriminatory and harassing conduct and requiring that judges ensure that lawyers appearing before them adhere to the same restrictions. Model Code of Judicial Conduct R. 2.3 (2011). The pertinent portion of the Rule provides:

> (B) A judge shall not, in the performance of judicial duties, by words or conduct manifest bias or prejudice, or engage in harassment, including but not limited to bias, prejudice, or harassment based upon race, sex, gender, religion, national origin, eth-

more expansive, also forbidding harassment and discrimination in practice-related settings beyond the courtroom and in contexts that may not be connected to a specific client representation.[9] Such breadth was necessitated by evidence that sexual harassment, in particular, occurs outside of court-related and representational situations—for example, in non-litigation matters or at law firm social events or bar association functions.[10]

> nicity, disability, age, sexual orientation, marital status, socioeconomic status, or political affiliation, and shall not permit court staff, court officials, or others subject to the judge's direction and control to do so.
>
> (C) A judge shall require lawyers in proceedings before the court to refrain from manifesting bias or prejudice, or engaging in harassment, based upon attributes including but not limited to race, sex, gender, religion, national origin, ethnicity, disability, age, sexual orientation, marital status, socioeconomic status, or political affiliation, against parties, witnesses, lawyers, or others.

MODEL RULES R. 2.3(B) & (C); *see also* Gillers, *supra* note 4, at 209-11 (discussing adoption of CJC Rule 2.3 and its relationship to Model Rule 8.4(g)). In addition, in 2015, the ABA revised its *Standards for Criminal Justice: Prosecutorial Function and Defense Function* to add anti-bias provisions for both prosecutors and defense counsel. For example, the Defense Function standard provides:

> (a) Defense counsel should not manifest or exercise, by words or conduct, bias or prejudice based upon race, sex, religion, national origin, disability, age, sexual orientation, gender identity, or socioeconomic status. Defense counsel should strive to eliminate implicit biases, and act to mitigate any improper bias or prejudice when credibly informed that it exists within the scope of defense counsel's authority.
>
> (b) Defense counsel should be proactive in efforts to detect, investigate, and eliminate improper biases, with particular attention to historically persistent biases like race, in *all of counsel's work*. A public defense office should regularly assess the potential for biased or unfairly disparate impacts of its policies on communities within the defense office's jurisdiction, and eliminate those impacts that cannot be properly justified.

CRIMINAL JUSTICE STANDARDS FOR THE DEFENSE FUNCTION, Std. 4-1.6 (4th ed. 2017) (emphasis added). *See also* CRIMINAL JUSTICE STANDARDS FOR THE PROSECUTION FUNCTION, Std. 3-1.6 (4th ed. 2017) (setting forth the same standard for prosecutors).

9. Some jurisdictions have limited their antidiscrimination and anti-harassment rules to conduct related to the representation of a client. *See, e.g.*, COLO. RULES OF PROF'L CONDUCT R. 8.4(g) (2020) (conduct "in the representation of a client"); MASS. RULES OF PROF'L CONDUCT R. 3.4(i) (2020) (conduct "in appearing in a professional capacity before a tribunal"); MO. RULES OF PROF'L CONDUCT R. 4-8.4(g) (2020) (conduct "in representing a client"); NEB. RULES OF PROF'L CONDUCT § 3-508.4(d) (2020) (conduct when "a lawyer is employed in a professional capacity").

10. *See generally* Wendy N. Hess, *Addressing Sexual Harassment in the Legal Profession: The Opportunity to Use Model Rule 8.4(g) to Protect Women from Harassment*, 96 U. DET. MERCY L. REV. 579 (2019). *See also* STANDING COMMITTEE ON ETHICS & PROF'L RESPONSIBILITY, ET AL., REPORT TO THE HOUSE OF DELEGATES ON REVISED RESOLUTION 109, at 10 (Aug. 2016); *infra* note 31 and accompanying text; *Standing Committee on Ethics and Professional Responsibility*

Furthermore, Rule 8.4(g) prohibits conduct that is not covered by other law, such as federal proscriptions on discrimination and harassment in the workplace.[11] Although conduct that violates Title VII of the Civil Rights Act of 1964 would necessarily violate paragraph (g),[12] the reverse may not be true. For example, a single instance of a lawyer making a derogatory sexual comment directed towards another individual in connection with the practice of law would likely not be severe or pervasive enough to violate Title VII, but would violate Rule 8.4(g).[13] The isolated nature of the conduct, however, could be a mitigating factor in the disciplinary process.[14]

Rule 8.4(g) does not regulate conduct unconnected to the practice of law, as do some other rules of professional conduct.[15] Nevertheless, it does im-

---

Hearing on Model Rule 8.4(*g*), at 39, 61-62 (Feb. 2016) (Wendy Lazar testifying that "so much sexual harassment and bullying against women actually takes place on the way home from an event or in a limo traveling on the way back from a long day of litigation"; former ABA president Laura Bellows testifying about anecdotal evidence of sexual harassment, such as, at a "Christmas party"), https://www.americanbar.org/content/dam/aba/administrative/professional_responsibility/aba_model_rule%208_4_comments/february_2016_public_hearing_transcript.pdf.

11. *See* Title VII of the Civil Rights Act of 1964, 42 U.S.C. § 2000 *et seq.* (2019). *See also* Bostock v. Clayton County, 590 U.S. ___ (2020) (recognizing that discrimination and harassment based on sexual orientation and gender identity are prohibited by Title VII as components of "sex," one of the protected categories listed in the statute). Sexual orientation and gender identity are expressly included among Model Rule 8.4(g)'s categories.

12. *See* Model Rules R. 8.4(g) cmt. [3] (noting that "[t]he substantive law of antidiscrimination and anti-harassment statutes and case law may guide application of paragraph (g)").

13. *See* Harris v. Forklift Systems, Inc., 510 U.S. 17, 21 (1993) ("Conduct that is not severe or pervasive enough to create an objectively hostile or abusive work environment—an environment that a reasonable person would find hostile or abusive—is beyond Title VII's purview."); Saxton v. American Tel. & Tel. Co., 10 F.3d 526, 533 (7th Cir. 1993) (observing that "'relatively isolated' instances of non-severe misconduct will not support a hostile environment claim") (quoting Weiss v. Coca-Cola Bottling Co. of Chicago, 990 F.2d 333, 337 (7th Cir. 1993); Martinelli v. Bancroft Chophouse, LLC, 357 F. Supp. 3d 95, 102 (D. Mass. 2019) (finding that "[a] single, isolated incident of harassment . . . is ordinarily insufficient to establish a claim for hostile work environment unless the incident was particularly egregious and the employee must demonstrate how his or her ability to work was negatively affected").

14. Whether discipline is imposed for any particular violation of Rule 8.4(g) will depend on a variety of factors, including, for example: (1) severity of the violation; (2) prior record of discipline or lack thereof; (3) level of cooperation with disciplinary counsel; (4) character or reputation; and (5) whether or not remorse is expressed. For a full discussion of factors that influence the imposition of discipline imposed, see Annotated ABA Standards for Imposing Lawyer Sanctions (2d ed. 2019).

15. The most noteworthy example is Rule 8.4(c). Indeed, the misconduct addressed in that rule—dishonesty, fraud, deceit, and misrepresentation—has traditionally been viewed as unacceptable by the legal profession, whether it occurs in the courtroom or on the street. Other Model Rules that subject lawyers to discipline for conduct not necessarily connected with the practice of law include Model Rules 8.2.(a) (prohibiting statements by lawyers about judges or other legal officials known to be false or in reckless disregard as to their truth), and 8.4(b) (misconduct for a lawyer to commit a criminal act that reflects adversely on the lawyer's honesty, trustworthiness, or fitness). *See also* Rebecca Aviel, *Rule 8.4(g) and*

pose a higher standard on lawyers than that expected of the general public.[16] As the Preamble to the Model Rules states, "A lawyer, as a member of the legal profession, is a representative of clients, an officer of the legal system and a public citizen having special responsibility for the quality of justice."[17] Harassment and discrimination damage the public's confidence in the legal system and its trust in the profession.

Section II of this opinion elaborates further on the scope of Rule 8.4(g) and explains in more detail how it safeguards the integrity of the legal system and the profession. Section III contains hypotheticals that illustrate the Rule's application.

II. Analysis

Rule 8.4(g) provides:

> It is professional misconduct for a lawyer to . . . engage in conduct that the lawyer knows or reasonably should know is harassment or discrimination on the basis of race, sex, religion, national origin, ethnicity, disability, age, sexual orientation, gender identity, marital status or socioeconomic status in conduct related to the practice of law. This paragraph does not limit the ability of a lawyer to accept, decline or withdraw from a representation in accordance with Rule 1.16. This paragraph does not preclude legitimate advice or advocacy consistent with these Rules.[18]

Comment [3] to Rule 8.4(g) addresses the meaning of "discrimination" and "harassment" and emphasizes that such conduct "undermine[s] confidence in the legal profession and the legal system."[19] It defines "discrimina-

---

the First Amendment: Distinguishing Between Discrimination and Free Speech, 31 GEO. J. LEGAL ETHICS 31, 67 (2018) (noting that "the bar readily considers conduct completely unconnected to the practice of law when such conduct is either deceptive or otherwise reflective on fitness, with some jurisdictions requiring and others omitting the element that the conduct in question be criminal").

16. *See, e.g.*, MODEL RULES R. 3.6(a) ("A lawyer who is participating or has participated in the investigation or litigation of a matter shall not make an extrajudicial statement that the lawyer knows or reasonably should know will be disseminated by means of public communication and will have a substantial likelihood of materially prejudicing an adjudicative proceeding in the matter."); MODEL RULES R. 4.1(a) ("In the course of representing a client a lawyer shall not knowingly make a false statement of material fact or law to a third person . . .."); MODEL RULES R. 8.4(c) ("It is professional misconduct for a lawyer to engage in conduct involving dishonesty, fraud, deceit or misrepresentation . . .."). *See also* Hess, *supra* note 10, at 596 ("Rather than having lawyers escape accountability for their sexually harassing conduct that might not meet Title VII's high bar, the legal profession can instead take the opportunity to hold itself to a higher standard of professionalism.").

17. MODEL RULES Preamble [1].

18. MODEL RULES R. 8.4(g).

19. *Id.* cmt. [3].

tion" to include "harmful verbal or physical conduct that manifests bias or prejudice towards others."[20] Harassment includes "derogatory or demeaning verbal or physical conduct."[21] "Sexual harassment" is more specifically described as "unwelcome sexual advances, requests for sexual favors, and other unwelcome verbal or physical conduct of a sexual nature."[22] The Comment also indicates that "[t]he substantive law of antidiscrimination and anti-harassment statutes and case law may guide application of paragraph (g)."[23]

The existence of the requisite harm is assessed using a standard of objective reasonableness. In addition, a lawyer need only know or reasonably should know that the conduct in question constitutes discrimination or harassment.[24] Even so, the most common violations will likely involve conduct that is intentionally discriminatory or harassing.

Comment [4] identifies the scope of "conduct related to the practice of law," listing such activities as: "representing clients; interacting with witnesses, coworkers, court personnel, lawyers and others while engaged in the practice of law; operating or managing a law firm or law practice; and participating in bar association, business or social activities in connection with the practice of law."[25]

Comment [5] describes specific circumstances that do not violate paragraph (g). For example, a judge's determination that a lawyer has utilized peremptory challenges in a discriminatory manner, alone, will not subject the lawyer to discipline.[26] Furthermore, limiting one's practice to providing representation to underserved populations, consistent with the rules of professional conduct and other law, will not constitute a violation.[27]

---

20. *Id.*

21. *Id.*

22. *Id. See also* Model Code of Judicial Conduct R. 2.3 cmt. [4] (noting that "[s]exual harassment includes but is not limited to sexual advances, requests for sexual favors, and other verbal or physical conduct of a sexual nature that is unwelcome").

23. Model Rules R. 8.4(g) cmt. [3].

24. "Knows" and "reasonably should know" are defined terms in the Model Rules. *See* Model Rules R. 1.0(f) & (j).

25. Model Rules R. 8.4 cmt. [4].

26. *See id.* cmt. [5].

27. *See id.* The balance of the Comment notes some additional actions that will not violate Rule 8.4(g):

> A lawyer may charge and collect reasonable fees and expenses for a representation. . . . Lawyers also should be mindful of their professional obligations under Rule 6.1 to provide legal services to those who are unable to pay, and their obligation under Rule 6.2 not to avoid appointments from a tribunal except for good cause. . . . A lawyer's representation of a client does not constitute an endorsement by the lawyer of the client's views or activities.

Id. (citations omitted).

Finally, Rule 8.4(g) specifically excludes from its scope "[l]egitimate advice or advocacy consistent with these Rules." Thus, the Rule covers only conduct for which there is no reasonable justification. Common usage and Rule 8.4(g)'s Comments reinforce this point by elucidating the type of harassing or discriminatory conduct that is disciplinable.

A. "Harassment"

Harassment is a term of common meaning and usage under the Model Rules.[28] It refers to conduct that is aggressively invasive, pressuring, or intimidating.[29] Rule 8.4(g) addresses harassment in relation to the practice of law that targets others on the basis of their membership in one or more of the identified categories.[30]

Preventing sexual harassment is a particular objective of Rule 8.4(g).[31] As Comment [3] makes clear, sexual harassment encompasses "unwelcome sexual advances, requests for sexual favors, and other unwelcome verbal or physical conduct of a sexual nature."[32] This type of behavior falls squarely within the broader, plain meaning of harassment and is consistent with the term's application throughout the Model Rules.

Model Rule 3.5(c)(3), for example, prohibits lawyers from communicating with jurors or prospective jurors following their discharge if "the communication involves misrepresentation, coercion, duress or *harassment*."[33]

---

28. *See, e.g.*, MODEL RULES R. 3.5(c)(3) & 7.3(c)(2) (both discussed in the text). *See also* MODEL RULES Preamble [5] ("A lawyer should use the law's procedures only for legitimate purposes and not to harass or intimidate others.").

29. *See, e.g.*, NEW OXFORD AMERICAN DICTIONARY 790 (3d ed. 2010) (defining "harassment" as "aggressive pressure or intimidation"); MERRIAM-WEBSTER DICTIONARY (defining "harass" as meaning "to annoy persistently"; "to create an unpleasant or hostile situation for, especially by uninvited and unwelcome verbal or physical conduct"), https://www.merriam-webster.com/dictionary/harass (last visited June 23, 2020).

30. Consistent with the guiding principle that the Model Rules are rules of reason and "should be interpreted with reference to the purposes of legal representation and of the law itself," the term "harassment" in Rule 8.4(g) must be construed and applied in a reasonable manner. *See* MODEL RULES Scope [14].

31. *See* Gillers, *supra* note 4, at 200 (noting that decisions and surveys cited overwhelmingly "disclose that the targets [of bias and harassment] are predominantly women"); Hess, *supra* note 10, at 582 (noting conservatively that an estimated "25% of women in the legal workplace have reported unwanted sexual harassment"); Chuck Lundberg, *#MeToo in the Law Firm*, BENCH & BAR MINN., Vol. 75, No. 3, at 16, 17 (Mar. 2018) (noting that in speaking to many male and female "bar leaders, judges, present and former ethics partners and managing partners at large law firms," the author learned from the men that they had observed or heard about a "broad spectrum of workplace conduct" of a sexual nature, including "some pretty egregious sexual misconduct"; as for the women with whom the author spoke, "[t]o a person, they were able to relate multiple instances of such behaviors—in law firms, law schools, court chambers, and other legal workplaces").

32. MODEL RULES R. 8.4(g) cmt. [3].

33. MODEL RULES R. 3.5(c)(3) (emphasis added).

Here, the term "harassment," as in Rule 8.4(g), refers to conduct that is aggressively invasive, pressuring, or intimidating, including that which is reasonably perceived to be demeaning or derogatory, as demonstrated in *In re Panetta.*[34] In *Panetta,* the respondent was disciplined for sending an email to another lawyer who had served as the jury foreperson in a trial the respondent had lost several years earlier. The message was insulting, badgering, and threatening. Its subject line read, "ALL THESE YEARS LATER I WILL NEVER FORGET . . . THE LIAR" and went on to state, among other things: "After numerous multi-million dollar verdicts and success beyond anything you will attain in your lifetime, I will never forget you: the bloated Jury [Foreperson] that I couldn't get rid of and that misled and hijacked my jury." He ended the message with "Well you should get attacked you A-hole. Good Luck in Hell."[35] The court easily found that this conduct was intended to harass the former jury foreperson and adversely reflected on the respondent's fitness as a lawyer.[36]

Model Rule 7.3(c)(2) also prohibits "harassment." It forbids "solicitation that involves coercion, duress or *harassment.*"[37] As with other uses of "harassment" in the Model Rules, a rational reading of the term includes badgering or invasive behavior, as well as conduct that is demeaning or derogatory. Similarly, Model Rule 4.4(a) subjects lawyers to discipline for using "means that have no substantial purpose other than to embarrass, delay, or burden a third person."[38] While it does not expressly use the word "harassment," the conduct prohibited is clearly of the same sort that comes within that word's definition.

B. "Discrimination"

Discrimination "includes harmful verbal or physical conduct that manifests bias or prejudice towards others."[39] Bias or prejudice can be exhibited in any number of ways, some overlapping with conduct that also constitutes harassment. Use of a racist or sexist epithet with the intent to disparage an individual or group of individuals demonstrates bias or prejudice.

For example, in *In re McCarthy,*[40] a lawyer was suspended for a minimum of thirty days for sending an email message that was deeply offensive and

34. 127 A.D.3d 99 (N.Y. 2d Dept. 2015).

35. *Id.* at 101.

36. *Id.* at 102. *See also* Pa. Bar Ass'n Legal Ethics & Prof'l Responsibility Comm., Advisory Op. 91-52 (1991) (finding that it was permissible for a lawyer's paralegal to conduct post-trial interviews of jurors, provided that no intimidation or pressure was used).

37. Model Rules R. 7.3(c)(2) (emphasis added).

38. Model Rules R. 4.4(a).

39. Model Rules R. 8.4(g), cmt. [3] (emphasis added). In addition, "[t]he substantive law of antidiscrimination and anti-harassment statutes and case law" may serve as a guide in applying paragraph (g). *Id.*

40. 938 N.E.2d 698 (Ind. 2010).

undoubtedly evinced racial bias. In connection with a real estate title dispute, the secretary of the seller's agent sent a message to the lawyer demanding that he take certain action. The lawyer responded, by stating, among other things, that "I am here to tell you that I am neither you [sic] or [your boss's] n****r."[41] The Indiana Supreme Court found that such remarks "serve only to fester wounds caused by past discrimination and encourage future intolerance."[42] Similarly, the same court found that a lawyer engaged in conduct manifesting bias or prejudice in relation to a personal bankruptcy proceeding by distributing flyers that referred to other counsel in the matter as "'bloodsucking shylocks' who were part of a 'heavily Jewish [sic] . . . reorganization cartel.'"[43]

As many courts have emphasized, such behavior is unacceptable generally but especially when engaged in by members of the bar. In *In re Charges of Unprofessional Conduct*,[44] for instance, the Minnesota Supreme Court expressed this general judicial perspective: "When any individual engages in race-based misconduct it undermines the ideals of society founded on the belief that all people are created equal. When the person who engages in this misconduct is an officer of the court, the misconduct is especially troubling."[45] Rule 8.4(g) embodies this principle.

C. Rule 8.4(g) and the First Amendment

The Committee does not address constitutional issues, but analysis of Rule 8.4(g), as with our analysis of other rules, is aided by constitutional context.[46] For Rule 8.4(g), two important constitutional principles guide and constrain its application. First, an ethical duty that can result in discipline must

---

41. *Id.*

42. *Id.* (quoting *In re* Thomsen, 837 N.E.2d 1011, 1012 (Ind. 2005)).

43. *In re* Dempsey, 986 N.E.2d 816 (Ind. 2013). *See also In re* Thomsen, 837 N.E.2d 1011 (Ind. 2005) (publicly reprimanding lawyer for filing a petition in a divorce action arguing that couple's children were put in "harm's way" by wife's association with an African-American man); *In re* Charges of Unprofessional Conduct, 597 N.W.2d 563 (Minn. 1999) (prosecutor disciplined for filing motion seeking to prohibit defendant's counsel from including a lawyer of color as part of the defense team "for the sole purpose of playing upon the emotions of the jury"); People v. Sharpe, 781 P.2d 659, 660, 661 (1989) (prosecutor disciplined for exhibiting racial prejudice against Latinos by stating, in reference to two Latino defendants, that he did not "believe either one of those chili-eating bastards").

44. 597 N.W.2d 563 (Minn. 1999).

45. *Id.* at 567-68.

46. *See, e.g.*, ABA Comm. on Ethics & Prof'l Responsibility, Formal Op. 490 (2020) (discussing ability-to-pay inquiries required by the due process and equal protection clauses, as interpreted in *Bearden v. Georgia*, 461 U.S. 669 (1983) and its progeny); ABA Comm. on Ethics & Prof'l Responsibility, Formal Op. 486, at 9 (2019) (discussing Sixth Amendment Right to Counsel rooted "[i]n a series of cases beginning with Argersinger v. Hamlin," 407 U.S. 25 (1972)); ABA Comm. on Ethics & Prof'l Responsibility, Formal Op. 09-454 (2009) (discussing obligations based on Brady v. Maryland, 373 U.S. 83 (1963)).

be sufficiently clear to give notice of the conduct that is required or forbidden. Second, the rule must not be overbroad such that it sweeps within its prohibition conduct that the law protects. Identifying the proper balance between freedom of speech or religion and laws against discrimination or harassment is not a new problem, however. The scope of Rule 8.4(g) is no more or less reducible to a precise verbal formula than any number of regulations of lawyer speech or workplace speech that have been upheld and applied by courts.[47]

Courts have consistently upheld professional conduct rules similar to Rule 8.4(g) against First Amendment challenge. For example, in addressing the constitutional authority of a court of appeals to discipline a lawyer for "conduct unbecoming a member of the bar of the court," the Supreme Court observed that a lawyer's court-granted license "requires members of the bar to conduct themselves in a manner compatible with the role of courts in the administration of justice."[48] More recently, the Kentucky Supreme Court echoed this message in an opinion concerning Rule 8.2(a), which generally prohibits a lawyer from making a false or reckless statement concerning the qualifications or integrity of a judicial or other legal official, stating that regulation of lawyer speech "is appropriate in order to maintain the public confidence and credibility of the judiciary and as a condition of '[t]he license granted by the court.'"[49]

Rule 8.4(d)'s prohibition of conduct that is prejudicial to the administration of justice has likewise withstood constitutional challenges based on vagueness and overbreadth arguments, with one court observing that: "The language of a rule setting guidelines for members of the bar need not meet

47. For a discussion of workplace speech limitations upheld against a First Amendment challenge, see Aviel, *supra* note 15, at 48-50. For a discussion of lawyers' speech and Rule 8.4(g), see Robert N. Weiner, *"Nothing to See Here": Model Rule of Professional Conduct 8.4(g) and the First Amendment*, 41 Harv. J.L. & Public Policy 125 (2018). *See also infra* note 49.

48. *In re Snyder*, 472 U.S. 634, 644-45 (1985).

49. Ky. Bar Ass'n v. Blum, 404 S.W.3d 841, 855 (Ky. 2013) (*quoting In re* Snyder) (observing that while a lawyer does not surrender First Amendment rights in exchange for a law license, once admitted, "he must temper his criticisms in accordance with professional standards of conduct") (quoting *In re* Sandlin, 12 F.3d 861, 866 (9th Cir. 1993)). There are also other Model Rules that curtail attorney speech but are uniformly understood as proper regulatory measures, including, for example, the following: Rule 1.6 (generally prohibiting disclosure of "information relating to the representation of a client"); Rule 3.5(d) (prohibiting a lawyer from "engag[ing] in conduct intended to disrupt a tribunal"); Rule 3.6 (restricting a lawyer's ability to comment publicly about an investigation or litigation matter in which the lawyer is participating or has participated when the lawyer knows or reasonably should know that the comments "have a substantial likelihood of materially prejudicing an adjudicative proceeding"); Rule 4.1 (prohibiting a lawyer from "knowingly mak[ing] a false statement of material fact or law to a third person"); and Rule 7.1 (limiting communications about a lawyer or a lawyer's services to those that are truthful and not otherwise misleading).

the precise standards of clarity that might be required of rules of conduct for laymen."[50] Similarly, in rejecting a vagueness challenge to the prohibition against conduct prejudicial to the administration of justice, the Fifth Circuit stated:

> The traditional test for vagueness in regulatory prohibitions is whether "they are set out in terms that the ordinary person exercising ordinary common sense can sufficiently understand and comply with, without sacrifice to the public interest." . . . The particular context in which a regulation is promulgated therefore is all important. . . . *The regulation at issue herein only applies to lawyers, who are professionals and have the benefit of guidance provided by case law, court rules and the "lore of the profession."*[51]

There is wide and longstanding acceptance of these principles, given lawyers' status as members of the bar. For example, in upholding the constitutionality of DR 1-102(A)(6), which prohibited a lawyer from engaging "in any other conduct that adversely reflects on [the lawyer's] fitness to practice law," the New York Court of Appeals noted: "As far back as 1856, the Supreme Court acknowledged that 'it is difficult if not impossible, to enumerate and define, with legal precision, every offense for which an attorney or counsellor ought to be removed'. . .. Broad standards governing professional conduct are permissible and indeed often necessary."[52]

Furthermore, the fact that it is possible to construe a rule's language to reach conduct protected by the First Amendment is not fatal to its application to unprotected conduct. As observed by Justice Scalia in *Virginia v. Hicks*:

> [T]here comes a point at which the chilling effect of an overbroad law, significant though it may be, cannot justify prohibiting all enforcement of that law—particularly a law that reflects "legitimate state interests in maintaining comprehensive controls over harmful, constitutionally unprotected conduct". . . . For there are substantial social costs *created* by the overbreadth doctrine when it blocks appli-

50. *In re* Keiler, 380 A.2d 119, 126 (D.C. 1977), *overruled on other grounds, by In re* Hutchinson, 534 A.2d 919 (D.C. 1987) (upholding against a vagueness challenge DR 1-102(A)(5), Rule 8.4(d)'s predecessor).

51. Howell v. State Bar of Texas, 843 F.2d 205, 208 (5th Cir. 1988) (emphasis added); *see also* Attorney Grievance Comm'n of Maryland v. Korotki, 569 A.2d 1224, 1235 (1990) (observing that a professional conduct rule for lawyers need not "meet the standards of clarity that might be required for rules governing the conduct of laypersons") (citations omitted).

52. *In re* Holtzman, 577 N.E.2d 30, 33 (N.Y. 1991) (quoting *Ex Parte* Secombe, 60 U.S. [19 How.] 9, 14 (1857) (citing *In re* Charges of Unprofessional Conduct Against N.P., 361 N.W.2d 386, 395 (Minn. 1985), appeal dismissed, 474 U.S. 976 (1985)); *see also In re* Knutson, 405 N.W.2d 234, 238 (Minn. 1987).

> cation of a law to constitutionally unprotected speech, or especially to constitutionally unprotected conduct. To ensure that these costs do not swallow the social benefits of declaring a law "overbroad," we have insisted that a law's application to protected speech be "substantial," not only in an absolute sense, but also relative to the scope of the law's plainly legitimate applications . . . before applying the "strong medicine" of overbreadth invalidation.[53]

Rule 8.4(g) promotes a well-established state interest by prohibiting conduct that reflects adversely on the profession and diminishes the public's confidence in the legal system and its trust in lawyers.[54]

Numerous judicial opinions confirm the significance and legitimacy of a state's regulatory interest in this area. For instance, the Minnesota Supreme Court has noted that "racially-biased actions" engaged in by lawyers "not only undermine confidence in our system of justice, but also erode the very foundation upon which justice is based."[55] Similarly, in affirming the public reprimand of a lawyer who made racially disparaging accusations in a court filing, the Indiana Supreme Court stressed that "[i]nterjecting race into proceedings where it is not relevant is offensive, unprofessional and tarnishes the image of the profession as a whole."[56] The New Jersey Supreme Court expressed the same opinion in *Matter of Vincenti*, observing that:

> Any kind of conduct or verbal oppression or intimidation that projects offensive and invidious discriminatory distinctions, be it based on race or color, . . . or . . . on gender, or ethnic or national background or handicap, is especially offensive. In the context of either the practice of law or the administration of justice, prejudice both to the standing of this profession and the administration of justice will be virtually conclusive if intimidation, abuse, harassment, or threats focus or dwell on invidious discriminatory distinctions.[57]

Rule 8.4(g) protects specific categories of victims from identified harm, and a violation can only take place when the offending conduct engaged in is

---

53. 539 U.S. 113, 119-20 (2003) (emphasis in original) (citations omitted); *see also* Howell v. State Bar of Texas, 843 F.2d 205, 208 (5th Cir. 1988) ("Assuming for the argument that [the rule prohibiting conduct prejudicial to the administration of justice] might be considered vague in some hypothetical, peripheral application, this does not, as this Court [has] observed, . . . warrant throwing the baby out with the bathwater. To invalidate the regulation in toto, . . . we would have to hold that it is impermissibly vague in all of its applications.") (citations omitted).

54. *See supra* note 6 and accompanying text.

55. *In re* Charges of Unprofessional Conduct, 597 N.W.2d 563, 568 (Minn. 1999).

56. *In re* Thomsen, 837 N.E.2d 1011, 1012 (Ind. 2005).

57. 554 A.2d 470, 474 (N.J. 1989).

"related to the practice of law" and the lawyer knows or reasonably should know that it constitutes harassment or discrimination.

Using these various interpretative principles and applying them in an objectively reasonable manner, a lawyer would clearly violate Rule 8.4(g) by directing a hostile racial, ethnic, or gender-based epithet toward another individual, in circumstances related to the practice of law. For example, in a case referenced earlier, under Indiana's version of Rule 8.4(g), a lawyer received a three-year suspension for distributing flyers in relation to personal litigation depicting his adversaries as "slumlords," calling their counsel "bloodsucking shylocks," and making various derogatory remarks about Jews generally.[58] Another Indiana lawyer representing a husband in a custody dispute violated that state's version of Rule 8.4(g) by filing a petition in which he alleged that the wife associated herself "in the presence of a black male, and such association [caused] and [placed] the children in harm's way."[59] Similarly, a Colorado lawyer was disciplined for disparagingly referring to a female judge as a "c**t" in the course of negotiating a plea deal with prosecutors.[60]

Each of these examples would likewise violate Model Rule 8.4(g), even if the conduct occurred outside of a court-related setting. It need only take place in a context related to the practice of law, as Comment [4] explains.

III. Application of Rule 8.4(g) to Hypotheticals

To further illustrate the scope and application of Rule 8.4(g), this section discusses several representative situations.

(1) A religious organization challenges on First Amendment grounds a local ordinance that requires all schools to provide gender-neutral restroom and locker room facilities.[61] Would a lawyer who accepted representation of the organization violate Rule 8.4(g)?

No. This situation does not involve the type of conduct covered by Rule 8.4(g). The blackletter text underscores this by explaining that the "paragraph does not limit the ability of a lawyer to *accept*, decline or withdraw from a representation in accordance with Rule 1.16."[62] In addition, the provision's next sentence further emphasizes that it "does not preclude legitimate advice or advocacy consistent with these Rules." Though individuals may disagree with

58. *In re* Dempsey, 986 N.E.2d 816, 817 (Ind. 2013) (court specifically found that "none of these violations are based on any communication that falls within Respondent's broad constitutional right to freedom of speech and expression").

59. *Thomsen*, 837 N.E.2d at 1012.

60. People v. Gilbert, 2011 WL 10PDJ067, *10-11 (Colo. O.P.D.J. Jan. 14, 2011).

61. *Cf.* Texas Att'y Gen. Op. KP-0123 (Dec. 20, 2016).

62. Model Rules R. 8.4(g) (emphasis added).

the position the lawyer in the hypothetical would be defending, that would not affect the legitimacy of the representation.

(2) A lawyer participating as a speaker at a CLE program on affirmative action in higher education expresses the view that rather than using a race-conscious process in admitting African-American students to highly-ranked colleges and universities, those students would be better off attending lower-ranked schools where they would be more likely to excel. Would the lawyer's remarks violate Rule 8.4(g)?

No. While a CLE program would fall within Comment [3]'s description of what constitutes "conduct related to the practice of law," the viewpoint expressed by the lawyer would not violate Rule 8.4(g). Specifically, the lawyer's remarks, without more, would not constitute "conduct that the lawyer knows or reasonably should know is harassment or discrimination on the basis of . . . race." A general point of view, even a controversial one, cannot reasonably be understood as harassment or discrimination contemplated by Rule 8.4(g). The fact that others may find a lawyer's expression of social or political views to be inaccurate, offensive, or upsetting is not the type of "harm" required for a violation.

(3) A lawyer is a member of a religious legal organization, which advocates, on religious grounds, for the ability of private employers to terminate or refuse to employ individuals based on their sexual orientation or gender identity.[63] Will the lawyer's membership in this legal organization constitute a violation of Rule 8.4(g)?

No. As with the prior hypothetical, Rule 8.4(g) does not forbid a lawyer's expression of his or her political or social views, whether through membership in an organization or through oral or written commentary. Furthermore, to the extent that such conduct takes the form of pure advocacy it would not qualify as sufficiently "harmful" or targeted. Moreover, even though the Supreme Court has now recognized that discrimination based on sexual orientation and gender identity violates Title VII,[64] it is not a violation of Rule 8.4(g) to express the view that the decision is wrong.

(4) A lawyer serving as an adjunct professor supervising a law student in a law school clinic made repeated comments about the student's appearance and also made unwelcome, nonconsensual physical contact of a sexual nature with the student. Would this conduct violate Rule 8.4(g)?

Yes. This is an obvious violation and demonstrates the importance of making the scope of the provision broad enough to en-

63. *See Cf.* Texas Att'y Gen. Op. KP-0123 (Dec. 20, 2016).

64. *See* Bostock v. Clayton County, 590 U.S.__ (2020); *see also supra* note 11.

compass conduct that may not necessarily fall directly within the context of the representation of a client.[65]

(5) A partner and a senior associate in a law firm have been tasked with organizing an orientation program for newly-hired associates to familiarize them with firm policies and procedures. During a planning session, the partner remarked that: "Rule #1 should be never trust a Muslim lawyer. Rule #2 should be never represent a Muslim client. But, of course, we are not allowed to speak the truth around here." Do the partner's remarks violate Rule 8.4(g)?

Yes. Even if one assumes that the associate was not Muslim, the comments violate Rule 8.4(g).[66] **The partner's remarks are discriminatory in so far as they are harmful and manifest bias and prejudice against Muslims. Furthermore, the partner surely knew or reasonably should have known this. In addition, the fact that the comments may not have been directed at a specific individual would not insulate the lawyer from discipline; though, in many instances, the offending conduct will be targeted towards someone who falls within a protected category. Because the remarks were made within the law firm setting, they were "related to the practice of law." Moreover, given the supervisory-subordinate nature of the partner's relationship to the associate, the remarks may influence how similarly-situated firm lawyers treat clients, opposing counsel, and others at the firm who are Muslim.**

IV. Conclusion

Model Rule 8.4(g) prohibits a lawyer from engaging in conduct related to the practice of law that the lawyer knows or reasonably should know is harassing or discriminatory. Whether conduct violates the Rule must be assessed using a standard of objective reasonableness, and only conduct that is found harmful will be grounds for discipline.

Rule 8.4(g) covers conduct that occurs outside the representation of a client or beyond the confines of a courtroom. In addition, it is not restricted to conduct that is severe or pervasive, a standard utilized in the employment context. However, and as this opinion explains, conduct that violates paragraph (g) will often be intentional and typically targeted at a particular individual or group of individuals, such as directing a racist or sexist epithet

---

65. *See In re* Griffith, 838 N.W.2d 792 (Minn. 2013) (lawyer suspended for ninety days and required to petition for reinstatement for engaging in unwelcome verbal and physical sexual advances towards a student the lawyer was supervising in a law school clinic); *see also id.* at 793-96 (Lillenhaug, J., dissenting) (maintaining that more severe discipline was warranted in light of the egregious nature of the misconduct).

66. *Cf. In re* McCarthy, 938 N.E.2d 698 (Ind. 2010); *see also supra* text accompanying notes 40-42.

towards others or engaging in unwelcome, nonconsensual physical conduct of a sexual nature.

The Rule does not prevent a lawyer from freely expressing opinions and ideas on matters of public concern, nor does it limit in any way a lawyer's speech or conduct in settings unrelated to the practice of law. The fact that others may personally disagree with or be offended by a lawyer's expression does not establish a violation. The Model Rules are rules of reason, and whether conduct violates Rule 8.4(g) must necessarily be judged, in context, from an objectively reasonable perspective.

Besides being advocates and counselors, lawyers also serve a broader public role. Lawyers "should further the public's understanding of and confidence in the rule of law and the justice system because legal institutions in a constitutional democracy depend on popular participation and support to maintain their authority."[67] Discriminatory and harassing conduct, when engaged in by lawyers in connection with the practice of law, engenders skepticism and distrust of those charged with ensuring justice and fairness. Enforcement of Rule 8.4(g) is therefore critical to maintaining the public's confidence in the impartiality of the legal system and its trust in the legal profession as a whole.

Abstaining: Hon. Goodwin Liu.

---

67. Model Rules Preamble [6].

AMERICAN BAR ASSOCIATION
STANDING COMMITTEE ON ETHICS AND PROFESSIONAL RESPONSIBILITY

Formal Opinion 494 **July 29, 2020**

Conflicts Arising Out of a Lawyer's Personal Relationship with Opposing Counsel

Model Rule 1.7(a)(2) prohibits a lawyer from representing a client without informed consent if there is a significant risk that the representation of the client will be materially limited by a personal interest of the lawyer. A personal interest conflict may arise out of a lawyer's relationship with opposing counsel. Lawyers must examine the nature of the relationship to determine if it creates a Rule 1.7(a)(2) conflict and, if so, whether the lawyer reasonably believes the lawyer will be able to provide competent and diligent representation to each affected client who must then give informed consent, confirmed in writing.

To assist lawyers in applying Rule 1.7(a)(2), this opinion identifies three categories of personal relationships that might affect a lawyer's representation of a client: (i) intimate relationships, (ii) friendships, and (iii) acquaintances. Intimate relationships with opposing counsel involve, e.g. cohabiting, engagement to, or an exclusive intimate relationship. These relationships must be disclosed to clients, and the lawyers ordinarily may not represent opposing clients in the matter, unless each client gives informed consent confirmed in writing. Because friendships exist in a wide variety of contexts, friendships need to be examined carefully. Close friendships with opposing counsel should be disclosed to clients, and, where required as described in this opinion, their informed consent obtained. By contrast, some friendships and most relationships that fall into the category of acquaintances need not be disclosed, nor must clients' informed consent be obtained. Regardless of whether disclosure is required, however, the lawyer may choose to disclose the relationship to maintain good client relations.[1]

I. Introduction

The ABA Model Rules of Professional Conduct address conflicts arising when lawyers "closely related by blood or marriage" represent "different cli-

1. This opinion is based on the ABA Model Rules of Professional Conduct as amended by the ABA House of Delegates through August 2020. The laws, court rules, regulations, rules of professional conduct, and opinions promulgated in individual jurisdictions are controlling.

ents in the same matter or in substantially related matters." This guidance appears in Comment [11] to Model Rule 1.7, which reads:

> When lawyers representing different clients in the same matter or in substantially related matters are closely related by blood or marriage, there may be a significant risk that client confidences will be revealed and that the lawyer's family relationship will interfere with both loyalty and independent professional judgment. . . . . [A] lawyer related to another lawyer, e.g., *as parent, child, sibling or spouse*, ordinarily may not represent a client in a matter where that lawyer is representing another party, unless each client gives informed consent. . . .[2]

The Model Rules do not address other types of personal relationships with opposing counsel.[3] But these other personal relationships may also cre-

2. Model Rules of Prof'l Conduct R. 1.7 cmt. 11 (2020) (emphasis added) [hereinafter Model Rules].

3. By contrast, there is significant authority, from the ABA and elsewhere, addressing business relationships with opposing counsel. For opinions on a lawyer's obligations when negotiating or seeking employment with the opposing firm. *See, e.g.*, ABA Comm. on Ethics & Prof'l Responsibility Formal Op. 96-400 (1996); N.C. State Bar Formal Op. 3 (2016); D.C. Bar Op. 367 (2014); N.Y.C. Bar Ass'n Comm. on Prof'l Ethics, Formal Op. 1991-1 (1991); Pa. Bar Ass'n Legal Ethics & Prof'l Responsibility Comm. Advisory Op. 2007-300 (2007); Ky. Bar Ass'n Formal Op. E-399 (1998). There is also significant authority addressing a lawyer's obligations when the lawyer represents or has represented opposing counsel in an unrelated matter. *See, e.g.*, ABA Comm. on Ethics & Prof'l Responsibility Formal Op. 97-406 (1997) ("lawyers cannot simultaneously have a lawyer-client relationship and represent third party clients whose interest are adverse if a reasonable lawyer would conclude that his relationship as a lawyer for or client of opposing counsel may materially limit and would adversely affect the lawyer's representation of his 'third-party' client"; opinion discusses when disclosure and consent will permit the representation; "imputation analysis differs for the representing lawyer and the represented lawyer"); Utah State Bar Ethics Advisory Comm. Op. 14-05 (2014) (both affected clients may consent to conflict caused by one's lawyer representing opposing counsel in unrelated malpractice or discipline case); Conn. Bar Ass'n Informal Op. 2012-10 (2012) (personal injury lawyer and insurance defense counsel who are opponents in many cases and one represents the other in unrelated litigation must determine if the representation would materially limit the representation of each lawyer's clients and, if so, must obtain the affected clients' informed consent, confirmed in writing); Me. Prof'l Ethics Comm'n Opinion 205 (2011) (lawyer who is representing opposing counsel in an unrelated matter must determine if there is a significant risk of materially limiting his ability to represent either client and may seek informed consent to continued representation of each client if the lawyer reasonably believes the lawyer can give competent diligent representation to each); N.J. Advisory Comm. on Prof'l Ethics Op. 679 (1995) (conflict of interest caused by lawyer's representation of opposing counsel in unrelated matter may be waived with informed consent); Iowa State Bar Ass'n Ethics & Practice Guidelines Comm. Advisory Op. 92-28 (1993) (lawyer may represent a frequent opposing counsel in an unrelated matter); N.Y. State Bar Ass'n Comm. on Prof'l Ethics Op. 579 (1987) (lawyer may represent opposing counsel in unrelated litigation with client's informed consent if no effect on their independent professional judgment); Ill. State Bar Ass'n Advisory Op. 724 (1981) (no conflict for opposing counsel where one previously represented the other).

ate conflicts of interest. Because changing living patterns suggest that more people are living in households and arrangements that do not correspond to traditional categories,[4] this opinion offers guidance on conflicts that may arise from personal relationships with opposing counsel that fall within the Rules but are not specifically addressed by the Comments. In explaining these obligations, this opinion relies heavily on ABA Formal Opinion 488, issued in September 2019, which addresses judges' personal relationships with lawyers or parties that may require disqualification or disclosure."[5]

Section II below sets out the framework for analysis and identifies three categories of potential relationships between opposing counsel, drawing on the analysis in ABA Formal Opinion 488. The categories here are: (i) "intimate relationships," (ii) "friendships," and (iii) "acquaintances."[6] This opinion explains the relevant considerations in these circumstances.

II. Analysis

Model Rule 1.7(a)(2) provides that in the absence of informed consent confirmed in writing a lawyer may not represent a client if "there is a significant risk that the representation of one or more clients will be materially limited by the lawyer's responsibilities to another client, a former client or a third person or by a personal interest of the lawyer." Comment [11] explains that when opposing counsel are related by blood or marriage "there may be a significant risk that client confidences will be revealed and that the lawyer's family relationship will interfere with both loyalty and independent professional judgment."[7] The Committee concludes that these risks also arise when there are close personal or intimate relationships between lawyers who rep-

4. For example, according to U.S. Census Bureau data from November 2018, "[t]he median age at first marriage in the United States has continued to rise in recent years." The number of young adults living with an unmarried partner has also increased. For example, "[a]mong young adults 18 to 24, cohabitation is now more prevalent than living with a spouse." *See* U.S. Census Bureau Releases 2018 Families and Living Arrangements Tables, https://www.census.gov/newsroom/press-releases/2018/families.html (Nov. 14, 2018).

5. ABA Comm. on Ethics & Prof'l Responsibility Formal Op. 488 (2019) [hereinafter ABA Formal Op. 488].

6. *See id.* at 1, 2, 4-6. Some different considerations affect judicial disclosure and disqualification, e.g. judges must appear to be impartial as well as be impartial in fact, but the categories and considerations set forth in Formal Opinion 488 are useful for lawyers when analyzing their personal relationships with opposing counsel, as described in this opinion.

7. By contrast, some jurisdiction's rules explicitly address the types of personal relationships discussed in this opinion. *See, e.g.*, Cal. Rules of Prof'l Conduct R. 1.7(c)(2) (2018) (addressing "intimate personal relationship"); Iowa Rules of Prof'l Conduct R. 1.8(i) (2012) (including cohabiting lawyers and lawyers in any "romantic capacity"); Or. Rules of Prof'l Conduct R. 1.7 (2020) (including "domestic partner"); Va. Rules of Prof'l Conduct R. 1.8(i) (2020) (including a lawyer "intimately involved with another lawyer"); Wash. Rules of Prof'l Conduct R. 1.8(k)(1) (2015) (including "intimate relationship with another lawyer"); and W. Va. Rules of Prof'l Conduct R. 1.7 cmt. [11] addressing "sharing living quarters with another lawyer").

resent opposing clients. How lawyers should analyze these relationships for purposes of Rule 1.7(a)(2) is discussed below in Sections A, B, and C. There are general principles, however, that apply to all of them.

First, not all personal relationships with opposing counsel create a conflict that would require client informed consent or even disclosure. Some relationships with opposing counsel are so casual that they would not affect a lawyer's independent professional judgment. For other relationships, a lawyer's duty of communication under Rule 1.4 might obligate the lawyer to disclose a relationship, even if the lawyer believes that the relationship would not create a conflict under Rule 1.7. For still other relationships, a conflict based on personal relationships with opposing counsel exists and may be waived if the lawyer "reasonably believes that the lawyer will be able to provide competent and diligent representation to [the client]" and the lawyer obtains the affected client's informed consent, confirmed in writing.[8]

The reasonableness of the lawyer's belief will depend on the circumstances. "Reasonable" is defined in Model Rule 1.0(h).[9] For instance, a lawyer's independent judgment is likely to be materially limited if due to the personal relationship with opposing counsel the lawyer would refrain from filing a well-founded motion for sanctions against opposing counsel. In that circumstance, the conflict may not be waivable. In addition, if the lawyer's personal relationship is one that is not known to others and the lawyer is therefore hesitant to disclose it to the client, the lawyer may not be in a position to seek the client's informed consent. For example, if the personal relationship with opposing counsel is an affair that the lawyer wishes to keep secret, the lawyer may be unable to comply with the rule's requirements of disclosure and informed consent. In that situation the lawyer is unlikely to be able to commence or continue the client-lawyer relationship.

Second, in determining whether a personal interest conflict exists, the lawyer should consider the lawyer's role in the matter. A lawyer who is sole or lead counsel in a matter is more likely to have a disqualifying conflict than

---

8. Model Rules R. 1.7(b)(1). If a lawyer believes that informed consent of a client due to the lawyer's relationship with opposing counsel is required, the lawyer should confer with opposing counsel. If opposing counsel disagrees that informed consent is required, the lawyer should consider whether the issue should be raised with the court if the matter is in litigation, and whether the lawyer has an obligation pursuant to Model Rule 8.3(a) to report opposing counsel. Model Rule 8.3(a) reads: "A lawyer who knows that another lawyer has committed a violation of the Rules of Professional Conduct that raises a substantial question as to that lawyer's honesty, trustworthiness or fitness as a lawyer in other respects, shall inform the appropriate professional authority."

9. Model Rule 1.0(h) reads: "'Reasonable' or 'reasonably' when used in relation to conduct by a lawyer denotes the conduct of a reasonably prudent and competent lawyer." *See also* Model Rule 1.0(i) which reads: "'Reasonable belief' or 'reasonably believes' when used in reference to a lawyer denotes that the lawyer believes the matter in question and that the circumstances are such that the belief is reasonable."

a lawyer who has a subordinate or tangential role, such as researching discrete issues or drafting sections of papers to be filed, where that lawyer has little or no direct decision-making authority in the matter and minimal contact with the opposing counsel.[10]

Third, even when the lawyer has obtained informed consent confirmed in writing from the affected client, the lawyer must not reveal information relating to the representation unless permitted by one of the exceptions in Model Rule 1.6(b). Additionally, such a lawyer must take reasonable measures to assure that no confidential information is inadvertently disclosed to the opposing counsel with whom the lawyer has the personal relationship.[11] Inadvertent disclosure could occur, for example, if papers relating to the representation are left in view or telephone conversations are overheard.

Fourth, if a lawyer undertakes representation in which the lawyer has a personal relationship with opposing counsel and later determines that the lawyer will no longer be able to provide competent and diligent representation to the client because of the personal relationship, the lawyer must withdraw from the representation.[12]

Finally, personal interest conflicts ordinarily are not imputed. As Rule 1.10(a)(1) provides:

> While lawyers are associated in a firm, none of them shall knowingly represent a client when any one of them practicing alone would be prohibited from doing so by Rules 1.7 or 1.9, unless (1) the prohibition is based on a personal interest of the disqualified lawyer and does not present a significant risk of materially limiting the representation of the client by the remaining lawyers in the firm.

For close family relationships, Rule 1.7, cmt. [11] explains: "[t]he disqualification arising from a close family relationship is personal and ordinarily is not imputed to members of firms with whom the lawyers are associated."[13] Similarly, a conflict arising when a lawyer seeks employment with an oppos-

---

10. Subordinate lawyers may have to consult with supervisory lawyers in order to withdraw or move to withdraw. A subordinate lawyer, or any other lawyer who is not lead counsel, should disclose the relationship to a supervisor and seek advice on how to proceed in the circumstances, consistent with this opinion. *See also* Model Rules R. 5.1 & 5.2.

11. *See* Model Rule R. 1.6(c): "A lawyer shall make reasonable efforts to prevent the inadvertent or unauthorized disclosure of, or unauthorized access to, information relating to the representation of a client." *See also* Model Rule R. 1.6 cmt. [18].

12. *See, e.g.*, Model Rule R. 1.16(a), which provides in relevant part, "[a] lawyer shall not represent a client or, where representation has commenced, shall withdraw from the representation of a client if: (1) the representation will result in violation of the Rules of Professional Conduct . . . ". This obligation to withdraw may arise if a personal relationship develops during the course of a representation.

13. Model Rule R. 1.7 cmt. [11].

ing law firm is not ordinarily imputed.[14] The Committee concludes, as have other ethics committees, that conflicts arising out of the types of personal relationships discussed in this opinion also are not ordinarily imputed under Rule 1.10.[15] Imputation would be appropriate, for example, when other lawyers at either firm also have personal relationships with the opposing counsel or where the personal relationships involve managing partners. In such circumstances, the broader ties to the opposing counsel's firm may influence the lawyer's independent judgment.

A. Intimate Relationships

Lawyers who cohabit in an intimate relationship should be treated similarly to married couples for conflicts purposes. The same is true for couples who are engaged to be married or in exclusive intimate relationships. These lawyers must disclose the relationship to their respective clients and ordinarily may not represent the clients in the matter, unless each client gives informed consent confirmed in writing, assuming the lawyers reasonably believe that they will be able to provide competent and diligent representation to each client.[16]

---

14. ABA Comm. on Ethics & Prof'l Responsibility Formal Op. 96-400, at 8 (1996). For situations where the negotiating lawyer's conflict might be imputed, *see id.* at note 12. *See also* D.C. Bar Ethics Op. 367 (2014).

15. *See, e.g.*, State Bar of Ariz. Advisory Op. 01-12 (2001) (finding that a conflict created by "romantic relationship" between a public defender and a police officer is not imputed to the entire public defender's office); State Bar of Mich. Op. R-3 (1989) (regarding lawyer spouses (or their firms) representing opposing clients; no imputation unless the lawyer spouses or the lawyers litigating the cases have a personal interest in the outcome of the litigation); N.C. State Bar Formal Op. 2019-3 (2019) (stating that where there is an "ongoing" and "sexually intimate relationship" between a public defender and a prosecutor there is no imputation "so long as the conflict 'does not present a significant risk of materially limiting the representation of the client by the remaining lawyers in the firm [or office]'").

16. Comment [11] to Rule 1.7 provides in relevant part: "[A] lawyer related to another lawyer, e.g. as parent, child, sibling *or spouse, ordinarily* may not represent a client in a matter where that lawyer is representing another party, unless each client gives informed consent." (Emphasis added.) Opinions from several jurisdictions agree that intimate and cohabiting relationships should be treated like spousal ones. *See, e.g.*, State Bar of Ariz. Advisory Op. 01-10 (2001) (stating that attorney in Legal Defender's Office who is cohabiting with an attorney in the County Attorney's Office may work opposite each other on the same case only if: (i) both attorneys believe that the representation will not be materially limited by their relationship and (ii) both obtain informed consent by the clients; "[t]he conflict created by the cohabiting relationship is not imputed to other members of the offices"); State Bar of Mich. Op. R-3 (1989) (finding cohabiting lawyers must follow the same rule as lawyer spouses; they may not represent clients who are adverse unless the clients are informed of the relationship and give their consent to the representation; dating lawyers representing adverse parties also have obligations: they should "disclose the relationship to the clients if their relationship is sufficiently close that it could raise questions in the minds of the clients as to whether their interests would be zealously served"; "[l]awyers should err on the side of caution and should disclose such relationships or decline representation . . . if there is any possibility that the clients would consider the existence of the lawyers' dating relationship to be detrimental to the

Opposing counsel who are in some type of intimate relationship, but are not exclusive, engaged to be married or cohabiting, must carefully consider whether the relationship creates a significant risk that the representation of either client will be materially limited by the lawyers' personal relationships.[17] The prudent course would be to disclose to the affected clients and obtain their informed consent.[18]

---

lawyer-client relationship."); N.C. State Bar Formal Op. 2019-3 (2019) (noting that assistant district attorney and criminal defense lawyer in an intimate relationship may not be adversaries in a case unless they disclose the relationship to and obtain written informed consent from the affected clients and the appropriate governmental official).

Failure to disclose intimate relationships and secure adequate consents can result in discipline, disqualification or other significant consequences. A conviction may be reversed. *See* People v. Jackson, 213 Cal. Rptr. 521, 522 (3d Dist. Ct. App. 1985) (reversing conviction; defense counsel failed to inform defendant of his "dating" relationship with the prosecutor; the two "appeared as counsel in directly adverse roles representing defendant and the People respectively at the preliminary examination, at the pretrial settlement conferences, and at trial"); Commonwealth v. Stote, 922 N.E.2d 768, 778 (Mass. 2010) (Marshall, C.J.) (denying reversal after evidentiary hearing, and noting, "[w]e remind members of the bar of their professional obligation under rule 1.7(b) [analogous to M.R. 1.7(a)(2) and (b)(1)&(4)] to disclose to their clients any intimate personal relationship that might impair their ability to provide untrammeled and unimpaired assistance of counsel."). Fees may be forfeited. *See* DeBolt v. Parker, 560 A.2d 1323 (N.J. 1988) (finding lawyer spouses represented adverse interests; fees allowed but only after finding adequate disclosure and consent under then NJ RPC 1.8(i): "[a] lawyer related to another lawyer as parent child, sibling or spouse shall not represent a client in a representation directly adverse to a person who the lawyer knows is represented by the other lawyer except upon consent by the client after consultation regarding the relationship").

17. *See, e.g.*, State Bar of Mich. Op. R-3 (1989) (opposing counsel who are dating but not cohabiting or engaged must determine whether the relationship is sufficiently close to require disclosure to and informed consent of affected clients); N.Y. State Bar Ass'n Comm. on Prof'l Ethics Op. 660 (1993) ("a couple who date frequently" may not appear opposite one another in a criminal case; "a dating relationship between adversaries is inconsistent with the independence of professional judgement required by [the New York Rules]"; "whether other lawyers [in defense counsel's firm] will be disqualified depends on the facts and circumstances"). *See also* ABA Formal Op. 488, *supra* note 5, at 6-7 (discussing judges' close personal relationships).

18. This opinion does not address personal relationships involving previous marriages or cohabitations, engagements, and exclusive dating arrangements that have ended. Adversaries in such situations, however, must also determine pursuant to Rule 1.7(a)(2) whether there is "a significant risk that the representation of one or more clients will be materially limited" by the lawyer's prior relationship with opposing counsel and act accordingly. *See also* ABA Formal Opinion 488, *supra* note 5, at 6 (stating that "close personal relationships" include "an amicable divorce" and being a "godparent" of a lawyer's or party's child). This opinion also does not address when an existing relationship between opposing counsel ends during the course of the representation. The lawyer whose relationship ends while the representation continues must analyze whether the lawyer's new circumstances create a significant risk that the representation of the client will be materially limited by the change in the relationship and, if so, whether the lawyer must disclose the new circumstances to the affected client and obtain the client's informed consent to continued representation. A factor to be considered would be whether the breakup is amicable or hostile.

B. Friendships

Friendships may be the most difficult category to navigate. On the one hand, an adversary may be a dear and longtime friend or someone with whom the lawyer regularly socializes. On the other hand, an adversary may be considered a "friend" even though contact is occasional, brief, or superficial. As noted in ABA Formal Opinion 488:

> 'Friendship' implies a degree of affinity greater than being acquainted with a person . . . the term connotes some degree of mutual affection. Yet, not all friendships are the same; some may be professional, while others may be social. Some friends are closer than others.[19]

Close friendships with opposing counsel should be disclosed to each affected client and, when circumstances require as described further below, their informed consent obtained. ABA Formal Opinion 488 provides guidance here, too. The following are indicia of friendships that would require disclosure and, ordinarily, informed consent:

> [Lawyers who] exchange gifts at holidays and special occasions; regularly socialize together; regularly communicate and coordinate activities because their children are close friends and routinely spend time at each other's homes; vacation together with their families; share a mentor-protégé relationship developed while colleagues . . . [or] share confidences and intimate details of their lives.[20]

By contrast, friendships that might require disclosure to the affected clients but will not ordinarily require consent from clients include lawyers who "once practiced law together [and] may periodically meet for a meal when their busy schedules permit or, if they live in different cities, try to meet when one is in the other's hometown."[21] Similarly, adversaries who "were law school classmates or were colleagues years before [and] may stay in touch through occasional calls or correspondence, but not regularly see one another"[22] will typically not require the consent of affected clients and may not even require disclosure. Whether either consent or disclosure is required depends on the lawyer's considered judgment as to whether Model Rule 1.7(a)(2) applies and,

---

19. ABA Formal Op. 488, *supra* note 5, at 4. In addition, as noted in footnote 11 of Formal Opinion 488, "[s]ocial media, which is simply a form of communication, uses terminology that is distinct from that used in this opinion. Interaction on social media does not itself indicate the type of relationships participants have with one another either generally or for purposes of this opinion. . . . The proper characterization of a person's relationship with an opposing counsel depends on the definitions and examples used in this opinion."

20. ABA Formal Op. 488, *supra* note 5, at 4.

21. *Id.*

22. *Id.*

if so, whether the lawyer reasonably believes the lawyer can competently and diligently carry out the representation notwithstanding the conflict.

In sum, opposing lawyers who are friends are not *for that reason* alone prohibited from representing adverse clients. The analysis turns on the closeness of the friendship. If there is a significant risk that the representation of one or more clients will be materially limited by a lawyer's relationships, the lawyers must disclose the relationship to each affected client and obtain that client's informed consent, confirmed in writing, assuming the lawyers reasonably believe they will be able to provide competent and diligent representation to each affected client. If the lawyers cannot do so, one or both of the lawyers must decline or withdraw from the affected representations, consistent with Model Rule 1.16.

C. Acquaintances

Acquaintances are relationships that do not carry the familiarity, affinity or attachment of friendships. Lawyers, like judges, "should be considered acquaintances when their interactions . . . are coincidental or relatively superficial, such as being members of the same place of worship, professional or civil organizations, or the like."[23] Lawyers who are "acquaintances" may see each other at such gatherings, even frequently, without feeling a close personal bond. They might regularly meet at bar association or other business events, present continuing education programs together, or serve on bar association committees or boards together where their relationships may be collegial but not necessarily fall into the category of a "friend" that could materially limit the lawyer's independent professional judgment on behalf of a client. Similarly, lawyers who regularly see each other at civic or social events but do not make any particular effort to seek each other's company do not have the type of close personal friendship requiring disclosure and informed consent. Again, as described in ABA Formal Opinion 488, the following without more do not create a close personal relationship:

> [Lawyers] might both attend bar association or other professional meetings; they may have represented co-parties in litigation. . .; they may meet each other at school or other events involving their children or spouses; they may see each other when socializing with mutual friends; they may belong to the same country club or gym; they may patronize the same businesses and periodically encounter one another there; they may live in the same area or neighborhood and run into one another at neighborhood or area events, or at homeowners' meetings; or they might attend the same religious services. . . . Generally, neither . . . seeks contact with the other, but they greet each other amicably and are cordial when their lives intersect.[24]

23. *Id.* at 4.
24. *Id.*

Lawyers who are acquaintances of opposing counsel need not disclose the relationship to clients, although the lawyer may choose to do so. Disclosure may be advisable to maintain good client relations. It may be helpful to inform a client that the lawyer has a professional connection with opposing counsel and then explain how that will not materially limit the lawyer's objectivity but may, in fact, assist in the representation because the lawyers can work collegially.

III. Conclusion

A lawyer's personal relationship with opposing counsel may create a conflict under Model Rule 1.7(a)(2). Lawyers must examine the nature of the relationship to determine if there is a significant risk that lawyer's representation of the client will be materially limited by the lawyer's personal relationship and, if so, whether the lawyer reasonably believes the lawyer will be able to provide competent and diligent representation to each affected client and each affected, who must then give informed consent, confirmed in writing.

Using the guidelines in this opinion, lawyers should evaluate whether the relationship is a close personal or intimate relationship, a friendship, or the adversary is merely an acquaintance. Cohabiting, intimate and similar relationships with opposing counsel must be disclosed, and the lawyers ordinarily may not represent clients in the matter, unless each client gives informed consent confirmed in writing. Because friendships exist in a wide variety of contexts, friendships need to be examined closely. Close friendships with opposing counsel should be disclosed to clients and, where appropriate, as discussed in Part IIB, their informed consent, confirmed in writing, obtained. By contrast, some friendships and most relationships that fall into the category of acquaintances need not be disclosed, nor is clients' informed consent required. Regardless of whether disclosure is mandated, however, the lawyer may choose to disclose the relationship. Disclosure may even be advisable to maintain good client relations.

AMERICAN BAR ASSOCIATION
STANDING COMMITTEE ON ETHICS AND PROFESSIONAL RESPONSIBILITY

Formal Opinion 495 **December 16, 2020**

Lawyers Working Remotely

Summary

Lawyers may remotely practice the law of the jurisdictions in which they are licensed while physically present in a jurisdiction in which they are not admitted if the local jurisdiction has not determined that the conduct is the unlicensed or unauthorized practice of law and if they do not hold themselves out as being licensed to practice in the local jurisdiction, do not advertise or otherwise hold out as having an office in the local jurisdiction, and do not provide or offer to provide legal services in the local jurisdiction. This practice may include the law of their licensing jurisdiction or other law as permitted by ABA Model Rule 5.5(c) or (d), including, for instance, temporary practice involving other states' or federal laws. Having local contact information on websites, letterhead, business cards, advertising, or the like would improperly establish a local office or local presence under the ABA Model Rules.[1]

Introduction

Lawyers, like others, have more frequently been working remotely: practicing law mainly through electronic means. Technology has made it possible for a lawyer to practice virtually in a jurisdiction where the lawyer is licensed, providing legal services to residents of that jurisdiction, even though the lawyer may be physically located in a different jurisdiction where the lawyer is not licensed. A lawyer's residence may not be the same jurisdiction where a lawyer is licensed. Thus, some lawyers have either chosen or been forced to remotely carry on their practice of the law of the jurisdiction or jurisdictions in which they are licensed while being physically present in a jurisdiction in which they are not licensed to practice. Lawyers may ethically engage in practicing law as authorized by their licensing jurisdiction(s)

1. This opinion is based on the ABA Model Rules of Professional Conduct as amended by the ABA House of Delegates through August 2020. The laws, court rules, regulations, rules of professional conduct, and opinions promulgated in individual jurisdictions are controlling.

while being physically present in a jurisdiction in which they are not admitted under specific circumstances enumerated in this opinion.

Analysis

ABA Model Rule 5.5(a) prohibits lawyers from engaging in the unauthorized practice of law: "[a] lawyer shall not practice law in a jurisdiction in violation of the regulation of the legal profession in that jurisdiction, or assist another in doing so" unless authorized by the rules or law to do so. It is not this Committee's purview to determine matters of law; thus, this Committee will not opine whether working remotely by practicing the law of one's licensing jurisdiction in a particular jurisdiction where one is not licensed constitutes the unauthorized practice of law under the law of that jurisdiction. If a particular jurisdiction has made the determination, by statute, rule, case law, or opinion, that a lawyer working remotely while physically located in that jurisdiction constitutes the unauthorized or unlicensed practice of law, then Model Rule 5.5(a) also would prohibit the lawyer from doing so.

Absent such a determination, this Committee's opinion is that a lawyer may practice law pursuant to the jurisdiction(s) in which the lawyer is licensed (the "licensing jurisdiction") even from a physical location where the lawyer is not licensed (the "local jurisdiction") under specific parameters. Authorization in the licensing jurisdiction can be by licensure of the highest court of a state or a federal court. For purposes of this opinion, practice of the licensing jurisdiction law may include the law of the licensing jurisdiction and other law as permitted by ABA Model Rule 5.5(c) or (d), including, for instance, temporary practice involving other states' or federal laws. In other words, the lawyer may practice from home (or other remote location) whatever law(s) the lawyer is authorized to practice by the lawyer's licensing jurisdiction, as they would from their office in the licensing jurisdiction. As recognized by Rule 5.5(d)(2), a federal agency may also authorize lawyers to appear before it in any U.S. jurisdiction. The rules are considered rules of reason and their purpose must be examined to determine their meaning. Comment [2] indicates the purpose of the rule: "limiting the practice of law to members of the bar protects the public against rendition of legal services by unqualified persons." A local jurisdiction has no real interest in prohibiting a lawyer from practicing the law of a jurisdiction in which that lawyer is licensed and therefore qualified to represent clients in that jurisdiction. A local jurisdiction, however, does have an interest in ensuring lawyers practicing in its jurisdiction are competent to do so.

Model Rule 5.5(b)(1) prohibits a lawyer from "establish[ing] an office or other systematic and continuous presence in [the] jurisdiction [in which the lawyer is not licensed] for the practice of law." Words in the rules, unless otherwise defined, are given their ordinary meaning. "Establish" means "to found, institute, build, or bring into being on a firm or stable basis."[2] A local office is not "established" within the meaning of the rule by the lawyer working in the local jurisdiction if the lawyer does not hold out to the public an address in the local jurisdiction as an office and a local jurisdiction address does not appear on letterhead, business cards, websites, or other indicia of a lawyer's presence.[3] Likewise it does not "establish" a systematic and continuous presence in the jurisdiction for the practice of law since the lawyer is neither practicing the law of the local jurisdiction nor holding out the availability to do so. The lawyer's physical presence in the local jurisdiction is incidental; it is not for the practice of law. Conversely, a lawyer who includes a local jurisdiction address on websites, letterhead, business cards, or advertising may be said to have established an office or a systematic and continuous presence in the local jurisdiction for the practice of law.

Subparagraph (b)(2) prohibits a lawyer from "hold[ing] out to the public or otherwise represent[ing] that the lawyer is admitted to practice law in [the] jurisdiction" in which the lawyer is not admitted to practice. A lawyer practicing remotely from a local jurisdiction may not state or imply that the lawyer is licensed to practice law in the local jurisdiction. Again, information provided on websites, letterhead, business cards, or advertising would be indicia of whether a lawyer is "holding out" as practicing law in the local jurisdiction. If the lawyer's website, letterhead, business cards, advertising, and the like clearly indicate the lawyer's jurisdictional limitations, do not provide an address in the local jurisdiction, and do not offer to provide legal services in the local jurisdiction, the lawyer has not "held out" as prohibited by the rule.

A handful of state opinions that have addressed the issue agree. Maine Ethics Opinion 189 (2005) finds:

> Where the lawyer's practice is located in another state and where the lawyer is working on office matters from afar, we would conclude that the lawyer is not engaged in the unauthorized practice of law. We would reach the same conclusion with respect to a lawyer who

---

2. DICTIONARY.COM, https://www.dictionary.com/browse/establish?s=t (last visited Dec. 14, 2020).

3. To avoid confusion of clients and others who might presume the lawyer is regularly present at a physical address in the licensing jurisdiction, the lawyer might include a notation in each publication of the address such as "by appointment only" or "for mail delivery."

> lived in Maine and worked out of his or her home for the benefit of a law firm and clients located in some other jurisdiction. In neither case has the lawyer established a professional office in Maine, established some other systematic and continuous presence in Maine, held himself or herself out to the public as admitted in Maine, or even provided legal services in Maine where the lawyer is working for the benefit of a non-Maine client on a matter focused in a jurisdiction other than Maine.

Similarly, Utah Ethics Opinion 19-03 (2019) states: "what interest does the Utah State Bar have in regulating an out-of-state lawyer's practice for out-of-state clients simply because he has a private home in Utah? And the answer is the same—none."

In addition to the above, Model Rule 5.5(c)(4) provides that lawyers admitted to practice in another United States jurisdiction and not disbarred or suspended from practice in any jurisdiction may provide legal services on a temporary basis in the local jurisdiction that arise out of or reasonably relate to the lawyer's practice in a jurisdiction where the lawyer is admitted to practice. Comment [6] notes that there is no single definition for what is temporary and that it may include services that are provided on a recurring basis or for an extended period of time. For example, in a pandemic that results in safety measures—regardless of whether the safety measures are governmentally mandated—that include physical closure or limited use of law offices, lawyers may temporarily be working remotely. How long that temporary period lasts could vary significantly based on the need to address the pandemic. And Model Rule 5.5(d)(2) permits a lawyer admitted in another jurisdiction to provide legal services in the local jurisdiction that they are authorized to provide by federal or other law or rule to provide. A lawyer may be subject to discipline in the local jurisdiction, as well as the licensing jurisdiction, by providing services in the local jurisdiction under Model Rule 8.5(a).

Conclusion

The purpose of Model Rule 5.5 is to protect the public from unlicensed and unqualified practitioners of law. That purpose is not served by prohibiting a lawyer from practicing the law of a jurisdiction in which the lawyer is licensed, for clients with matters in that jurisdiction, if the lawyer is for all intents and purposes invisible *as a lawyer* to a local jurisdiction where the lawyer is physically located, but not licensed. The Committee's opinion is that, in the absence of a local jurisdiction's finding that the activity constitutes the unauthorized practice of law, a lawyer may practice the law authorized by the lawyer's licensing jurisdiction for clients of that jurisdiction, while physically located in a jurisdiction where the lawyer is not licensed if the lawyer does not hold out the lawyer's presence or availability to perform legal services in the local jurisdiction or actually provide legal services for matters subject to the local jurisdiction, unless otherwise authorized.

AMERICAN BAR ASSOCIATION
STANDING COMMITTEE ON ETHICS AND PROFESSIONAL RESPONSIBILITY

Formal Opinion 496 **January 13, 2021**

Responding to Online Criticism

Lawyers are regularly targets of online criticism and negative reviews. Model Rule of Professional Conduct 1.6(a) prohibits lawyers from disclosing information relating to any client's representation or information that could reasonably lead to the discovery of confidential information by another. A negative online review, alone, does not meet the requirements of permissible disclosure in self-defense under Model Rule 1.6(b)(5) and, even if it did, an online response that discloses information relating to a client's representation or that would lead to discovery of confidential information would exceed any disclosure permitted under the Rule. As a best practice, lawyers should consider not responding to a negative post or review, because doing so may draw more attention to it and invite further response from an already unhappy critic. Lawyers may request that the website or search engine host remove the information. Lawyers who choose to respond online must not disclose information that relates to a client matter, or that could reasonably lead to the discovery of confidential information by another, in the response. Lawyers may post an invitation to contact the lawyer privately to resolve the matter. Another permissible online response would be to indicate that professional considerations preclude a response.[1]

I. Introduction

Lawyers regularly are the target of online (and offline) criticism. Clients, opposing parties, and others are increasingly taking to the internet to express their opinions of lawyers they have encountered. Lawyers are left in the quandary of determining whether and how they ethically may respond when the opinions posted are unflattering, and the facts presented are inaccurate or even completely untrue. This opinion addresses a lawyer's ethical obligations in responding to negative online reviews.

1. This opinion is based on the ABA Model Rules of Professional Conduct as amended by the ABA House of Delegates through August 2020. The laws, court rules, regulations, rules of professional conduct, and opinions promulgated in individual jurisdictions are controlling.

II. Analysis

The main ethical concern regarding any response a lawyer may make to an online review is maintaining confidentiality of client information. The scope of the attorney-client privilege, as opposed to confidentiality, is a legal question that this Committee will not address in this opinion. As this Committee itself concluded in ABA Formal Ethics Opinion 480 (2018), lawyers cannot blog about information relating to clients' representation without client consent, even if they only use information in the public record, because that information is still confidential. ABA Model Rule of Professional Conduct 1.6 prohibits a lawyer's voluntary disclosure of *any* information that relates to a client's representation, whatever its source, without the client's informed consent, implied authorization to disclose,[2] or application of an exception to the general rule. Model Rule 1.6 states:

> (a) A lawyer shall not reveal information relating to the representation of a client unless the client gives informed consent, the disclosure is impliedly authorized in order to carry out the representation or the disclosure is permitted by paragraph (b).
>
> (b) A lawyer may reveal information relating to the representation of a client to the extent the lawyer reasonably believes necessary:
>
> (1) to prevent reasonably certain death or substantial bodily harm;
>
> (2) to prevent the client from committing a crime or fraud that is reasonably certain to result in substantial injury to the financial interests or property of another and in furtherance of which the client has used or is using the lawyer's services;
>
> (3) to prevent, mitigate or rectify substantial injury to the financial interests or property of another that is reasonably certain to result or has resulted from the client's commission of a crime or fraud in furtherance of which the client has used the lawyer's services;
>
> (4) to secure legal advice about the lawyer's compliance with these Rules;

2. Comment [5] of Rule 1.6 states "Except to the extent that the client's instructions or special circumstances limit that authority, a lawyer is impliedly authorized to make disclosures about a client when appropriate in carrying out the representation." A client or former client's negative online comments do not create "implied authorization" for the lawyer to disclose confidential information in response to the online criticism because that is not required to carry out the representation.

> (5) to establish a claim or defense on behalf of the lawyer in a controversy between the lawyer and the client, to establish a defense to a criminal charge or civil claim against the lawyer based upon conduct in which the client was involved, or to respond to allegations in any proceeding concerning the lawyer's representation of the client;
>
> (6) to comply with other law or a court order; or
>
> (7) to detect and resolve conflicts of interest arising from the lawyer's change of employment or from changes in the composition or ownership of a firm, but only if the revealed information would not compromise the attorney-client privilege or otherwise prejudice the client.

Only subparagraph (b)(5) is implicated here, and there are three exceptions bundled into that provision, the first two of which are clearly inapplicable to online criticism. First, online criticism is not a "proceeding," in any sense of that word, to allow disclosure under the exception "to respond to allegations in any proceeding concerning the lawyer's representation of the client."[3] Second, responding *online* is not necessary "to establish a defense to a criminal charge or civil claim against the lawyer based upon conduct in which the client was involved." A lawyer may respond directly to a person making such a claim, if necessary, to defend against a criminal charge or civil claim, but making public statements online to defend such a claim is not a permissible response. Thus, the remaining question is whether online criticism rises to the level of a controversy between a lawyer and client and, if so, whether responding online to the criticism is reasonably necessary to defend against it.

The Committee concludes that, alone, a negative online review, because of its informal nature, is not a "controversy between the lawyer and the client" within the meaning of Rule 1.6(b)(5), and therefore does not allow disclosure of confidential information relating to a client's matter.[4] As stated in

---

3. Definition of "proceeding" from NOLO'S PLAIN-ENGLISH LAW DICTIONARY, https://www.nolo.com/dictionary (last visited Jan. 4, 2021):

> 1) The ordinary process of a lawsuit or criminal prosecution, from the first filing to the final decision. 2) A procedure through which one seeks redress from a court or agency. 3) A filing, hearing, or other step that is part of a larger action. 4) A particular matter that arises and is dealt with in a bankruptcy case.

4. *See also* Louima v. City of New York, No. 98 CV 5083 (SJ), 2004 WL 2359943 (E.D.N.Y. Oct. 5, 2004), *aff'd sub nom.* Roper-Simpson v. Scheck, 163 F. App'x 70 (2d Cir. 2006) ("mere press reports regarding an attorney's conduct do not justify disclosure of a client's confidences and secrets even if the reports are false and the accusations are unfounded"); Lawyer Disciplinary Bd. v. Farber, 488 S.E.2d 460, 462 (1997) (lawyer's disclosure of confidential information in motion to withdraw inappropriate); ABA Comm. on Ethics & Prof'l Respon-

New York State Bar Association Ethics Opinion 1032 (2014), "[u]nflattering but less formal comments on the skills of lawyers, whether in hallway chatter, a newspaper account, or a website, are an inevitable incident of the practice of a public profession, and may even contribute to the body of knowledge available about lawyers for prospective clients seeking legal advice."

The Committee further concludes that, even if an online posting rose to the level of a controversy between lawyer and client, a public response is not reasonably necessary or contemplated by Rule 1.6(b) in order for the lawyer to establish a claim or defense on behalf of the lawyer in a controversy between the lawyer and the client. Comment [16] to Rule 1.6 supports this reading explaining, "Paragraph (b) permits disclosure only to the extent the lawyer reasonably believes the disclosure is necessary to accomplish one of the purposes stated."

There are a number of state ethics opinions that have analyzed this issue.[5] The majority reach the conclusion that, even if the online posting was

---

sibility, Formal Op. 476 (2016) (ABA Model Rule of Professional Conduct 1.6(b)(5) allows lawyer to disclose only such confidential information as is reasonably necessary for the court to make an informed decision on a motion to withdraw); Or. State Bar Formal Op. 2011-85 (2011) (lawyer may not disclose confidential information in motion to withdraw as "[n]either a disagreement between Lawyer and Client about how the client's matter should be handled nor the client's failure to pay fees when due" are considered a controversy triggering the self-defense exception).

5. *See, e.g.*, Los Angeles County Bar Ass'n Prof'l Responsibility & Ethics Comm. Formal Op. 525 (2012) (lawyer may respond to online criticism only if the lawyer discloses no confidential information, the response does not harm the client, and the response is "proportionate and restrained"); Mo. Bar Informal Op. 2018-08 (2018) (negative online review by former client does not create sufficient controversy to permit lawyer to disclose confidential information in response and any response may not disclose confidential information but may acknowledge the lawyer's professional obligations); N.J. Advisory Comm. on Prof'l Ethics Op. 738 (2020) (in response to negative online review by client, a lawyer may state that the lawyer disagrees with the facts in the review but may not disclose information that relates to the representation except information that is "generally known" based on New Jersey's rule which permits disclosure of "generally known" information); Bar Ass'n of Nassau County Comm. on Prof'l Ethics Op. 2016-01 (2016) ("A lawyer may not disclose a former client's confidential information solely to respond to criticism of the lawyer posted on the Internet or a website by a relative of the former client or by the former client himself"); N.Y. State Bar Ass'n Comm. on Prof'l Ethics Op. 1032 (2014) (lawyer may not disclose confidential information just to respond to online criticism by the client on a rating site because the "self-defense" exception to confidentiality does not apply to informal criticism where there is no actual or threatened proceeding against the lawyer); Pa. Bar Ass'n Legal Ethics & Prof'l Responsibility Comm. Op. 2014-200 (2014) (lawyer may not give detailed response to online criticism of the lawyer by a client because the self-defense exception is not triggered by a negative online review and may choose to ignore the online criticism); State Bar of Tex. Prof'l Ethics Comm. Op. 662 (2016) (lawyer may not respond to client's negative internet review if the response discloses confidential information, but may "post a proportional and restrained response that does not reveal any confidential information or otherwise violate the Texas Disciplinary Rules of Professional Conduct"); W. Va. Ethics Comm. Advisory Op.

made by a client, the posting of criticism does not rise to the level of a controversy that would allow a lawyer to disclose confidential information in responding. The Committee notes that Colorado Ethics Opinion 136 (2019) specifically finds that *if* the online criticism rises to the level of a controversy between lawyer and client, the lawyer may ethically disclose limited information, yet urges caution in responding. This Committee disagrees with the Colorado opinion, to the extent it concludes that lawyers may disclose a limited amount of confidential information in a public response; a public posting that discloses confidential information goes beyond a direct response to the accuser allowed by Rule 1.6 and its explanatory Comments. District of Columbia Ethics Opinion 370 (2016) permits disclosure of confidential information in responding to online criticism but is based on a rule that is significantly different than ABA Model Rule 1.6.[6] In addition to the ethics opinions addressing the issue, there are also disciplinary cases in which lawyers have been sanctioned for disclosing confidential information online.[7]

2015-02 (2015) (lawyer may respond to positive or negative online reviews, but may not disclose confidential client information while doing so, even in response to a review); San Francisco Ethics Comm. Op. 2014-1 (2014) (lawyer may respond to online review by client if matter has concluded and the lawyer discloses no confidential information in the response; if the client's matter is ongoing, lawyer may not be able to respond at all).

6. D.C. Bar Op. 370 (2016) concludes that a lawyer may disclose confidential information in responding to any specific allegations in a former client's negative online review, but is based on D.C. Rule 1.6, which states: "A lawyer may use or reveal client confidences or secrets: (3) to the extent reasonably necessary to establish a defense to a criminal charge, disciplinary charge, or civil claim, formally instituted against the lawyer, based upon conduct in which the client was involved, or *to the extent reasonably necessary to respond to specific allegations by the client concerning the lawyer's representation of the client*" [emphasis added]. State Bar of Ariz. Formal Op. 93-02 (1993) does not address online criticism but concludes that a lawyer may agree to an interview and disclose confidential information to defend against accusations by a former client that the lawyer was incompetent and involved in a conspiracy against the client made to the author of a proposed book, even though there are no pending or imminent legal proceedings.

7. Illinois Disciplinary Board v. Peshek, No. M.R. 23794 (Ill. May 18, 2010) (assistant public defender suspended for 60 days for blogging about her clients' cases, on a website which was open to the public, including providing confidential information, some of which was detrimental to clients and some of which indicated that the lawyer may have knowingly failed to prevent a client from making misrepresentation to the court); Reciprocal discipline of 60-day suspension by Wisconsin in *In re* Peshek, 798 N.W.2d 879 (2011); People v. Isaac, No. 15PDJ099, 2016 WL 6124510 (Colo. O.P.D.J. Sept. 22, 2016) (lawyer suspended 6 months for responding to online reviews of former clients; lawyer revealed criminal charges made against clients, revealed that client wrote check that bounced, and revealed that client committed other unrelated felonies); *In re* Quillinan, 20 DB Rptr. 288 (2006) (Oregon disciplinary board approved a stipulation for discipline for 90-day suspension for lawyer who sent an e-mail disclosing to members of the Oregon State Bar's workers' compensation listserve personal and medical information about a client whom she named, indicating the client wanted a new lawyer); *In re* Skinner, 740 S.E.2d 171 (Ga. 2013) (Supreme Court of Georgia rejected a petition for voluntary discipline seeking a public reprimand for lawyer's viola-

III. Best Practices

The Committee therefore offers the following best practices to lawyers who are the subject of negative online reviews.

A lawyer may request that the host of the website or search engine remove the post. This may be particularly effective if the post was made by someone other than a client. If the post was made by someone pretending to be a client, but who is not, the lawyer may inform the host of the website or search engine of that fact. In making a request to remove the post, unless the client consents to disclosure, the lawyer may not disclose any information that relates to a client's representation or that could reasonably lead to the discovery of confidential information by another,[8] but may state that the post is not accurate or that the lawyer has not represented the poster if that is the case.

Lawyers should give serious consideration to not responding to negative online reviews in all situations.[9] Any response frequently will engender further responses from the original poster. Frequently, the more activity any individual post receives, the higher the post appears in search results online. As a practical matter, no response may cause the post to move down in search result rankings and eventually disappear into the ether. Further exchanges between the lawyer and the original poster could have the opposite effect.

Lawyers may respond with a request to take the conversation offline and to attempt to satisfy the person, if applicable. For example, a lawyer might

---

tion of the confidentiality rule by disclosing confidential client information on the internet in response to client's negative reviews of lawyer, citing lack of information about the violation in the record and presumably feeling the public reprimand too lenient as it cited to the 60-day suspension in *Peshek* and 90-day suspension in *Quillinan* above); *In re* David J. Steele, No. 49S00-1509-DI-527 (Ind. 2015) (Among other violations, Indiana lawyer disbarred for, by his own description, "actively manipulate[ing his] Avvo reviews by monetarily incentivizing positive reviews, and punishing clients who wr[o]te negative reviews by publicly exposing confidential information about them" and including numerous false statements in the responses to the negative reviews); *In re* Tsamis, Commission No. 2013PR00095 (Ill. 2014) (public reprimand for lawyer who disclosed confidential information beyond that necessary to defend herself on Avvo in response to a client's negative reviews of the lawyer on Avvo: "I dislike it very much when my clients lose, but I cannot invent positive facts for clients when they are not there. I feel badly for him, but his own actions in beating up a female co-worker are what caused the consequences he is now so upset about"); *People v. Underhill*, 15PDJ040 (Colo. 2015) (lawyer suspended eighteen months for responding to multiple clients' online criticism by posting confidential and sensitive information about the clients).

8. Model Rules of Prof'l Conduct R. 1.6, cmt. [4] reads, in part, "Paragraph (a) . . . also applies to disclosures by a lawyer that do not in themselves reveal protected information but could reasonably lead to the discovery of such information by a third person."

9. *The Economist Explains What Is the Streisand Effect?*, The Economist (Apr. 16, 2013), https://www.economist.com/the-economist-explains/2013/04/15/what-is-the-streisand-effect. The social phenomenon known as the Barbara Streisand effect recognizes that efforts to suppress a piece of online information may actually call more attention to its existence.

post in response to a former client (or individual posting on behalf of a former client), "Please contact me by telephone so that we can discuss your concerns." A lawyer whose unhappy former client accepts such a request may offer to refund or reduce the lawyer's fees in the matter. As a practical matter, this approach is not effective unless the lawyer has the intent and ability to try to satisfy the person's concerns. A lawyer who makes such a post but does nothing to attempt to assuage the person's concerns risks additional negative posts.

If the poster is not a client or former client, the lawyer may respond simply by stating that the person posting is not a client or former client, as the lawyer owes no ethical duties to the person posting in that circumstance. However, a lawyer must use caution in responding to posts from nonclients. If the negative commentary is by a former opposing party or opposing counsel, or a former client's friend or family member, and relates to an actual representation, the lawyer may not disclose any information relating to the client or former client's representation without the client or former client's informed consent. Even a general disclaimer that the events are not accurately portrayed may reveal that the lawyer was involved in the events mentioned, which could disclose confidential client information. The lawyer is free to seek informed consent of the client or former client to respond, particularly where responding might be in the client or former client's best interests. In doing so, it would be prudent to discuss the proposed content of the response with the client or former client.

If the criticism is by a client or former client, the lawyer may, but is not required to, respond directly to the client or former client. The lawyer may wish to consult with counsel before responding. The lawyer may not respond online, however.

An additional permissible response, including to a negative post by a client or former client, would be to acknowledge that the lawyer's professional obligations do not permit the lawyer to respond. A sample response is: "Professional obligations do not allow me to respond as I would wish." The above examples do not attempt to provide every possible response that a lawyer would be permitted to make, but instead provide a framework of analysis that may be of assistance to lawyers faced with this issue.

IV. Conclusion

Lawyers are frequent targets of online criticism and negative reviews. ABA Model Rule of Professional Conduct 1.6(a) prohibits lawyers from disclosing information relating to any client's representation or information that could reasonably lead to the discovery of confidential information by another. A negative online review, alone, does not meet the requirements for permissible disclosure under Model Rule 1.6(b)(5) and, even if it did, an online response would exceed any disclosure permitted under the Rule.

Lawyers who are the subject of online criticism may request that the website or search engine host remove the information but may not disclose information relating to any client's representation, or information that could reasonably lead to the discovery of confidential information by others. Lawyers should consider ignoring a negative post or review because responding may draw more attention to it and invite further response from an already unhappy critic. Lawyers who choose to respond online must not disclose information that relates to a client matter or that could reasonably lead to the discovery of confidential information by others. Lawyers may post an invitation to contact the lawyer privately to resolve the matter. Another permissible response would be to indicate that professional considerations preclude a response. A lawyer may respond directly to a client or former client who has posted criticism of the lawyer online but must not disclose information relating to that client's representation online.

AMERICAN BAR ASSOCIATION
STANDING COMMITTEE ON ETHICS AND PROFESSIONAL RESPONSIBILITY

FORMAL OPINION 497 **February 10, 2021**

Conflicts Involving Materially Adverse Interests

Rules 1.9(a) and 1.18(c) address conflicts involving representing a current client with interests that are "materially adverse" to the interests of a former client or prospective client on the same or a substantially related matter.[1] *But neither Rule specifies when the interests of a current client are "materially adverse" to those of a former client or prospective client. Some materially adverse situations are typically clear, such as, negotiating or litigating against a former or prospective client on the same or a substantially related matter, attacking the work done for a former client on behalf of a current client, or, in many but not all instances, cross-examining a former or prospective client.*[2] *Where a former client is not a party to a current matter, such as proceedings where the lawyer is attacking her prior work for the former client, the adverseness must be assessed to determine if it is material. General economic or financial adverseness alone does not constitute material adverseness.*

Introduction

ABA Model Rule of Professional Conduct 1.9(a) addresses conflicts between current clients and former clients of a lawyer. It reads:

> (a) A lawyer who has formerly represented a client in a matter shall not thereafter represent another person in the same or a substantially related matter in which that person's interests are materially adverse to the interests of the former client unless the former client gives informed consent, confirmed in writing.

(Emphasis added).

Model Rule 1.18 addresses prospective clients and its paragraph (c) similarly requires analysis when a lawyer subsequently represents another

1. This opinion is based on the ABA Model Rules of Professional Conduct as amended by the ABA House of Delegates through August 2020. The laws, court rules, regulations, rules of professional conduct, and opinions promulgated in individual jurisdictions are controlling.

2. Typically, the lawyer does not perform legal work for a prospective client, and therefore it is unlikely the lawyer would "attack" work done for a prospective client.

person with "interests materially adverse to those of the prospective client." Rule 1.18(c) provides:

> (c) A lawyer subject to paragraph (b) shall not represent a client *with interests materially adverse to those of a prospective client* in the same or a substantially related matter if the lawyer received information from the prospective client that could be significantly harmful to that person in the matter, except as provided in paragraph (d). If a lawyer is disqualified from representation under this paragraph, no lawyer in a firm with which that lawyer is associated may knowingly undertake or continue representation in such a matter, except as provided in paragraph (d).

(Emphasis added). This Opinion addresses how to construe the language "interests [that] are materially adverse to the interests of the former client" in Rule 1.9(a) and similar language used in Rule 1.18(c).

I. The Origins of the "Materially Adverse" Standard

The language "interests [that] are materially adverse to the interests of the former client" has roots in Canon 6 of the ABA's 1908 Canons of Ethics. Canon 6 prohibited, in relevant part, "the subsequent acceptance of retainers or employments from others in matters adversely affecting any interest of the client with respect to which confidence has been reposed."

Under the ABA Model Code of Professional Responsibility, "there was no direct corollary to" Model Rule 1.9(a). [3] Instead, "former client conflicts were sometimes treated under Canon 9 of the Code under the appearance of impropriety standard."[4] The current language was crafted by the 1977 Commission on the Evaluation of Professional Standards, frequently referred to as the Kutak Commission. Initial ideas appear in the Commission's January 1980 and May 1981 Reports, but the current formulation was not proposed until the August 1982 draft, with non-substantive wording changes made in advance of final adoption of Rule 1.9 in August 1983.[5] Rule 1.18 was adopted

3. Peter Geraghty, *Ethics Tip—August 2017*, A.B.A. (Aug. 1, 2017). https://www.americanbar.org/groups/professional_responsibility/services/ethicssearch/ethicstipaugust2017/.

4. *Id.*

5. The January 1980 and May 1981 drafts proposed that lawyers be prohibited from representing clients in the same or substantially related matters where the interest of the client "is adverse in any material respect to the interest of the former client." *See, e.g.*, A.B.A. Comm'n on Evaluation of Professional Standards Discussion Draft, https://www.americanbar.org/content/dam/aba/administrative/professional_responsibility/kutak_1-80.pdf (Jan. 30, 1980); A.B.A. Comm'n on Evaluation of Professional Standards Proposed Final Draft https://www.americanbar.org/content/dam/aba/administrative/professional_responsibility/kutak_5-81.pdf (May 30, 1981); A.B.A. Comm'n on Evaluation of Professional Standards Report to the House of Delegates, https://www.americanbar.org/content/dam/aba/administrative/professional_responsibility/kutak_8-82.pdf (last visited Jan. 26, 2021). *See*

in 2002 and appears simply to have borrowed the language "materially adverse to those [the interests] of the former client" from Rule 1.9(a).

As adopted in 1983, Comment [1] to Rule 1.9 stated that "[t]he principles in Rule 1.7 determine whether the interests of the present and former client are adverse."[6] Citing this language, ABA Formal Op. 99-415 (1999) concluded that "a lawyer must look to Rule 1.7 to determine . . . whether the interests of the parties are materially adverse."

Rule 1.7 prohibits the representation of interests that are "directly" as opposed to "materially" adverse. As a result, ABA Op. 99-415 concluded that "only direct adverseness of interest meets the threshold of 'material adverseness' sufficient to trigger the prohibitions established in Rule 1.9."[7] However, as part of the Ethics 2000 revisions to the Rules, Comment [1] to Rule 1.9 was changed. The sentence relied upon in ABA Op. 99-415 in Comment [1] to Rule 1.9—that Rule 1.7 governed the issue of adverseness—was deleted, without specific explanation.[8]

II. Subsequent Interpretation of the Language "Materially Adverse to the Interests of the Former Client" in Rule 1.9

Subsequent to the Ethics 2000 amendments, courts, regulatory authorities, and ethics scholars have interpreted the meaning of "material adverseness" in Rule 1.9. These authorities have generally concluded that "material adverseness" includes, but is not limited to, matters where the lawyer is directly adverse on the same or a substantially related matter. While material adverseness is present when a current client and former client are directly adverse, material adverseness also can be present where direct adverseness is not.

---

also A Legislative History: The Development of the ABA Model Rules of Professional Conduct, 1982 – 2013, 901 (Art Garwin ed. 2013) [hereinafter A Legislative History] (Rules as adopted).

6. A Legislative History, *supra* note 5, at 901.

7. ABA Comm. on Ethics & Prof'l Responsibility, Formal Op. 99-415 (1999).

8. The minutes of the Commission's December 12, 1998, meeting note that one member observed: "that the organization and content of the comment to Rule 1.9 should be revised." He noted the illogical organization of the comment, the irrelevance of some comments (e.g., Comments [4] and [5] regarding legal history), the use of the term 'material adversity' with no explanation, and the incomplete definition of 'substantial relationship'. *See* Commission on Evaluation of the Rules of Professional Conduct (Ethics 2000), *Meeting Minutes Friday Dec. 11 & Saturday Dec. 12, 1998*, A.B.A. (last visited Jan. 26, 2021), https://www.americanbar.org/groups/professional_responsibility/policy/ethics_2000_commission/121198mtg/. The next reference to Rule 1.9's Comment [1] by the Ethics 2000 Commission was in the Minutes from the May 7, 2000 meeting: "A member noted that two stricken sentences in Comment [1] were relied on in a recent ethics opinion, 99-415. The Commission felt that no action was necessary in response." But there was no explanation about why the two sentences (including the reference to "direct adversity") were stricken. *See* Commission on Evaluation of the Rules of Professional Conduct (Ethics 2000), *Meeting Minutes Friday May 5 – Sunday May 7, 2000*, A.B.A. (last visited Jan 26, 2021), https://www.americanbar.org/groups/professional_responsibility/policy/ethics_2000_commission/050500mtg/.

However, "material adverseness" does not reach situations in which the representation of a current client is simply harmful to a former client's economic or financial interests, without some specific tangible direct harm. In *Gillette Co. v. Provost,* the court concluded that "[w]ith respect to the 'material adverse' prong of Rule 1.9, representation of one client is not 'adverse' to the interests of another client, for the purposes of lawyers' ethical obligations, merely because the two clients compete economically."[9] As noted in New York State Bar Association Ethic Opinion 1103, "[j]ust as competing economic interests do not create [a Rule 1.7 conflict] so they do not create a 'material adverse' interest within the meaning of Rule 1.9(a)."[10] Thus, a lawyer does not have a Rule 1.9 conflict solely because the lawyer previously represented a competitor of a current client whose economic interests are adverse to the current client. Material adverseness, referred to by the *Gillette* court, "requires a conflict as to the legal right and duties of the clients, not merely conflicting or competing economic interests."[11]

As the Court of Appeals for the Eighth Circuit explained in *Zerger & Mauer LLP v. City of Greenwood*:

> Generally, whether a former client and current client have materially adverse interests is not a difficult question, as the situation usually involves a new client suing a former client. However, the question is more complicated when a former client, "although not directly involved in the [current] litigation may be affected by it in some manner. When such is the case . . . a fact-specific analysis is required in order to evaluate 'the degree to which the current representation may actually be harmful to the former client.' This analysis focuses on 'whether the current representation may cause legal, financial, or other identifiable detriment to the former client.'"[12]

---

9. Gillette Co. v. Provost, 2016 WL 2610677 (Mass. Feb. 11, 2019).

10. N.Y. State Bar Ass'n Comm. on Prof'l Ethics Op. 1103 (2016).

11. *See Gillette Co.*, 2016 WL 2610677, at *3.

12. Zerger & Mauer LLP v. City of Greenwood, 751 F.3d 928, 933 (8th Cir. 2014) (internal citations omitted). *See, e.g.*, Plotts v. Chester Cycles LLC, 2016 WL 614023 *7-8 (D. Ariz. Feb. 16, 2016) (stating that "[w]hile the existence of possible personal liability [as to a former client] would establish material adversity [in a substantially related matter], the non-existence of personal liability does not necessarily dictate a different result."). In *Plotts*, an adverse financial impact on an entity in which the former client had an ownership interest and that had been the subject of the prior representation constituted material adverseness. *See also, In re* Carpenter, 863 N.W. 2d 223 (N.D. 2015). In *Carpenter*, an individual met with a lawyer about representation in a matter adverse to the Christian Science Church of Boston. Through extensive research, the prospective client had discovered that the mineral rights to 300 acres of North Dakota land had been left by a decedent to the Church and hoped for a fee or other compensation from the Church for bringing the information to its attention. The individual briefed the attorney on his research and conclusions. The attorney, after declining to represent the individual, promptly took the information that he had been given and contacted the Church, offering to represent it with respect to the mineral rights. The lawyer's representation

Such detriment has it limits, otherwise the concept of materiality would have no meaning. Further, in the absence of direct adverseness, generalized financial harm or a claimed detriment that is not accompanied by demonstrable harm to the former or prospective client's interests does not constitute "material adverseness."

The following are types of situations where "material adverseness" may be found.

A. Suing or Negotiating Against a Former Client

Suing a former client or defending a new client against a claim by a former client (*i.e.*, being on the opposite side of the "v" from former client) on the same or on a substantially related matter is a classic example of representing interests that are directly adverse and therefore "materially adverse" to the interests of a former client.[13] In assessing whether a lawyer has represented parties on both sides of the "v," the analysis of who or what the lawyer at issue formerly represented may be important.[14] In addition, being across the table, so to speak, from a former client and negotiating against that former client in transactional matters typically constitutes "material adverseness."[15]

B. Attacking Lawyer's Own Prior Work

Another type of "material adverseness" exists when a lawyer attempts to attack her own prior work.[16] For example, one court held that a lawyer cannot

---

of the Church was found to be "materially adverse" to the prospective client's interests. Carpenter was found to have violated Rule 1.18 and was suspended for 90 days.

13. *See, e.g.*, Persichette v. Owners Insurance Co., 462 P.3d 581, 585-86 (Colo. 2020) (law firm representing plaintiff in lawsuit against former client was "materially adverse" to the interests of such former client); Anderson & Anderson LLP v. North American Foreign Trading Corp., 3 N.Y.S.3d 284 (Sup. Ct. 2014) ("direct adversity in litigation meets the definition of 'materially adverse interests.'"); Jordan v. Philadelphia Housing Authority, 337 F. Supp. 2d 666, 672 (E.D. Pa. 2004) ("There is no situation more 'materially adverse' than where a lawyer's former client is in a suit against lawyer's current client . . ."); Disciplinary Counsel v. Broyles, 49 N.E.3d 1238 (Ohio 2015) (lawyer disciplined for representing bank at a default hearing in a foreclosure case and then seeking to vacate the default on behalf of the property owners).

14. Delso v. Trustees for the Retirement Plan for Hourly Employees of Merck, 2007 WL 766349 *10-11(D. N.J. Mar. 6, 2007) (finding no past attorney-client relationship between current lawyer for plaintiff and the defendant); *see also* Pa. Bar Ass'n Legal Ethics & Prof'l Responsibility Comm. Op. 2005-61 (2005) (concluding that there was likely no conflict as law firm represented seller, not corporation being sold).

15. Sylvia Stevens, *Conflicts Part II: Former Client Conflicts*, OR. STATE BAR BULLETIN (Dec. 2009) ("Where the current and former clients are opposing parties in litigation or in a transaction, the adversity of their interests is obvious."), https://www.osbar.org/publications/bulletin/09dec/barcounsel.html.

16. Franklin v. Callum, 146 N.H. 779, 782-83 (2001) (plaintiff's lawyer disqualified because case "may require her to interpret" an agreement drafted by one of her partners for a non-party to the litigation). Typically, the lawyer does not perform legal work for a prospective client, so it is unlikely the lawyer could "attack" work done for such a client.

challenge a patent that the lawyer previously obtained for a former client.[17] Another court found that a lawyer may not challenge a real estate restrictive covenant for a new client that the lawyer previously drafted for the prior seller of the land.[18] When a lawyer represents a current client challenging the lawyer's own prior work done for a former client on the same or a substantially related matter, the situation creates a materially adverse conflict.

Even when lawyers are not directly attacking their own prior work, but instead seeking to undermine that work or the result achieved for a former client, material adverseness may exist. These situations, however, do not lend themselves to a "bright line" test of when there is and is not material adverseness. An examination of the facts in three cases provides guidance as to what circumstances may constitute material adverseness.

In *Zerger & Mauer*,[19] the City of Greenwood prosecuted and settled a nuisance claim against Martin Marietta involving the latter's truck traffic to a local quarry. As part of the settlement, the City could designate the specific route that Martin Marietta's trucks took on the way to the quarry. The law firm of Zerger & Mauer represented the City in this litigation. Thereafter, Zerger & Mauer brought a private nuisance action against Martin Marietta on behalf of various individuals with property interests along the route designated by the City for Martin Marietta's traffic to the quarry. The City was not a part of the private nuisance action but sought to disqualify Zerger & Mauer from representing the private plaintiffs in that case. The court disqualified the firm, finding that it was "advocate[ing] a position that contradicts a term in [the City's] settlement."[20] The court also found that Zerger & Mauer's current clients "have an interest in . . . disrupting Martin's use of the [City's] designated route" and "there is a very real possibility that other routes will come into play."[21] The City also "may demand that its former counsel not advocate positions that pose the serious threat of once again embroiling [it] in protracted litigation."[22] The court upheld the lower court's finding that the interests of the City and the private plaintiffs "remain[ed] materially adverse."[23]

---

17 Sun Studs, Inc. v. Applied Theory Associates, 772 F.2d 1557, 1566-68 (Fed. Cir. 1985); Nasdaq, Inc. v. Miami International Holdings, 2018 WL 6171819 *4-6 (D. N.J. Nov. 26, 2018) (failure to disqualify law firm "would allow the same law firm that argued for the patentability of Nasdaq's inventions to represent parties adverse to Nasdaq in this suit who are arguing those very same patents are invalid.") (internal quotations omitted).

18. North Carolina Bar Association v. Sossomon, 197 N.C. App. 261, 266-67, 676 S.E.2d 910 (2009) (lawyer who previously represented seller of land in drafting of restrictive covenant disciplined for, in part, violation of Rule 1.9 for materially adverse representation on the very same matter by attempting to negotiate a waiver of the restrictive covenant from the former client for a new client, without getting a waiver of the conflict of interest or even disclosing that he was representing the other party).

19. 751 F.3d 928 (8th Cir. 2014).

20. *Id.* at 934.

21. *Id.*

22. *Id.*

23. *Id.*

National Medical Enterprises, Inc. v. Godfrey,[24] is another example of circumstances in which a non-party, non-witness former client nevertheless had materially adverse interests to a lawyer's current client.[25] In this case, a lawyer represented a former hospital administrator for National Medical Enterprises (NME). NME was accused of mistreating patients and defrauding insurers in a criminal investigation and parallel civil actions. The former client (the hospital administrator) had denied any wrongdoing, had not been charged with any crime, and had been dismissed from dozens of civil actions. About seventeen months after the lawyer and his firm withdrew from the representation of the former client, the lawyer's firm brought an action against NME on behalf of some ninety former patients making the same types of allegations of physical and mental abuse at various NME facilities, including facilities under the administrative responsibility of the former client. The claims brought against NME did not include any allegations of misconduct by the former client. The lawyer for the former client was screened from the action against NME. The appellate court, reversing the district court, found the requisite adverseness to exist and ordered NME's law firm disqualified citing the risk of renewed allegations or inquiries into the former client's conduct as a result of the new action.[26]

Not every situation involving adverseness constitutes material adverseness. There is a threshold below which adverseness is not material. In *Simpson Performance Products, Inc. v. Robert W. Horn, PC.*,[27] for instance, seat belt manufacturer Simpson Performance Products (SSP) hired lawyer Horn to investigate and evaluate and the possibility of a lawsuit by SPP against NASCAR when NASCAR alleged that SSP's defective product was partially responsible for the death of Dale Earnhardt at the NASCAR Daytona 500 in 2001. To preserve a good relationship with NASCAR, SSP decided not to bring suit to challenge NASCAR's allegations that SSP's product was at fault. Thereafter, however, the retired founder of the company hired lawyer Horn to represent the founder in a suit against NASCAR on his own. When SSP refused to pay Horn, he sued SSP for unpaid fees. In response, SSP alleged that Horn violated Rule 1.9(a). The court found no material adverseness existed because the record demonstrated that the manufacturer's relationship with NASCAR had not been adversely affected by the founder's lawsuit—the

24. 924 S.W.2d 123 (Tex. 1996)

25. It is not entirely clear from the court's opinion whether the former client would be a witness in the proceedings at issue, but the court's analysis of material adverseness does not rely on potential testimony of the former client or cross-examination by the client's former law firm.

26. *See also* Ill. State Bar Ass'n Comm. on Prof'l Conduct Advisory Op. 16-03 (2016) (representation of a second spouse in child support proceedings was "materially adverse to the interests" of the first spouse, a former client previously represented by lawyer, because recovery for current client could reduce husband's ability to pay support to former client).

27. 92 P.3d 283, 287-89 (Wyo. 2004).

very reason SSP declined to sue NASCAR—and that the "company is doing just fine."[28]

C. Examining a Former Client

Rule 1.9(c)(1) prohibits using information from a former client "to the disadvantage of the former client." If a lawyer must use information relating to the former representation to the disadvantage of a former client to competently examine the former client, the lawyer has a conflict, unless that information has become "generally known."[29] However, even if a lawyer ethically can use the information or does not need to use information, the lawyer still may have a conflict of interest in examining a former client under Rule 1.9(a) if the former client's interests are "materially adverse" to the current client *and* the current matter is substantially related to the prior matter. Courts have sometimes found "material adverseness" when the lawyer proposes to examine a former client, where no information from the prior representation will be used.[30]

In ABA Opinion 92-367, this Committee considered the question of whether examining a current client in another client's matter created a conflict under ABA Model Rule 1.7. Discussing adverseness, the Opinion stated

28. Comment [1] to Wyoming Rule 1.9 contained the sentence adopting Rule 1.7's "directly adverse" provision as the standard for the term "materially adverse" in Rule 1.9 that had been deleted from the Model Rules in 2002. The Court's analysis of "materially adverse" does not appear to hinge on that comment and the discussion in *Simpson* of the materially adverse issue has been noted by one commentator as unusual in its "care and precision." FREIVOGEL ON CONFLICTS, FORMER CLIENT, PART I, *available at* http://www.freivogelonconflicts.com/formerclientparti.html (last visited Jan. 27, 2021).

29. *See* Supreme Ct. of Ohio Bd. of Comm'rs on Grievances & Discipline, Advisory Op. 2013-4 (2013) (lawyer may impeach former client with criminal conviction only if conviction is "generally known" under Rule 1.9(c)); Utah State Bar Ethics Advisory Opinion Comm. Op. 02-06 (2002) (permitting lawyer to cross examine former client if matters are not substantially related and lawyer does not disclose or use information from former client to such client's disadvantage); Ill. State Bar Ass'n Comm. on Prof'l Conduct Advisory Op. 05-01 (2006) (same). *See* ABA Comm. on Ethics & Prof'l Responsibility, Formal Op. 479 (2017) for an explanation about what information is "generally known."

30. In Illaraza v. Hovensa LLC, 2012 WL 1154446 *6-10 (D. V.I. Mar. 31, 2012), the plaintiffs' lawyer was disqualified from representing plaintiffs in action against their employer and others for wrongful discharge and defamation stemming from an incident in which plaintiffs and another employee-manager were prosecuted for grand larceny for stealing employer's property. The charges against the two plaintiffs were dismissed, but the third individual pled guilty to possession of stolen property. The plaintiffs' lawyer had represented the employee-manager in his criminal case. In the wrongful discharge and defamation action, the plaintiffs contended in their summary judgement submission that the employee-manager defamed them. The court found that this constituted "material adverseness" that could not be alleviated by various promises by the plaintiffs' lawyer not to use confidential information against the former client, employee-manager. The court rejected the lawyer's offer not to cross examine her former client on any topics in which the lawyer had confidential information.

that "[i]t should be emphasized that the degree of adverseness of interest involved . . . will depend on the particular circumstances in which the question arises." In order to avoid this conflict, the current client could retain separate counsel from a different firm just for the cross-examination and screen the conflicted lawyer from the examination.[31] Similarly in the former client examination situation a lawyer may avoid the potential conflict altogether by having the current client retain separate counsel to examine the former client, and screen the lawyer with the conflict from participating in the examination of the former client or sharing with separate counsel any information from the prior representation.[32]

III. Waiver of Materially Adverse Conflicts

If a reasonable lawyer reviewing the situation would conclude that the representation of a current client is "materially adverse" to a former client, the lawyer may still represent the current client, even if the current and prior matters are "substantially related,"[33] provided the lawyer obtains the informed consent of the former client (or prospective client), to waive the potential conflict of interest and that consent is confirmed in writing.[34] Thus, even if a lawyer is hired to sue a former client on behalf of a current client, or negotiate against a former client, or take the deposition of a former client on a substantially related matter, the lawyer may ask for the former client's informed consent to waive the conflict and permit the lawyer's representation of the current client. Informed consent to waive a conflict under Rule 1.9(a) will not, however, waive the lawyer's obligation to maintain the confidentiality of all information learned during the prior representation. To allow the use or disclosure of information protected by Rule 1.6, the former client also must provide informed consent pursuant to Rule 1.6(a).

Similarly, if a lawyer seeks to represent a current client in a matter that is materially adverse to a prior prospective client in the same or substantially related matter on which that prospective client consulted the lawyer, and the lawyer has received "significantly harmful" information from the prior pro-

---

31. ABA Comm. on Ethics & Prof'l Responsibility, Formal Op. 92-367 (1992).

32. *See* N.Y. City Bar Ass'n Formal Ethics Op. 2017-6 (suggesting that lawyer may associate with separate counsel to subpoena a current client).

33. Model Rules of Prof'l Conduct R. 1.9, cmt. [3] (2020). "Matters are 'substantially related' for purposes of this Rule if they involve the same transaction or legal dispute or if there otherwise is a substantial risk that confidential factual information as would normally have been obtained in the prior representation would materially advance the client's position in the subsequent matter."

34. Informed consent may also need to be obtained from the lawyer's current client if there is a "significant risk" that the lawyer's representation of such client "will be materially limited" by the lawyer's responsibilities to the former client. Model Rules of Prof'l Conduct R. 1.7(a)(2).

spective client,[35] Rule 1.18(d)(1) permits representation of the current client if the current client and the prospective client give informed consent, confirmed in writing. Alternatively, the firm of the lawyer who received the "significantly harmful" information from the prospective client can represent the current client if the information-receiving lawyer is screened from the current representation and is apportioned no part of the fee from the representation and written notice is promptly provided to the prospective client pursuant to Rule 1.18(d)(2).[36]

IV. Conclusion

"Material adverseness" under Rule 1.9(a) and Rule 1.18(c) exists where a lawyer is negotiating or litigating against a former or prospective client or attacking the work done for the former client on behalf of a current client in the same or a substantially related matter.[37] It also exists in many but not all instances, where a lawyer is cross-examining a former or prospective client. "Material adverseness" may exist when the former client is not a party or a witness in the current matter if the former client can identify some specific material legal, financial, or other identifiable concrete detriment that would be caused by the current representation. However, neither generalized financial harm nor a claimed detriment that is not accompanied by demonstrable and material harm or risk of such harm to the former or prospective client's interests suffices.

---

35. *See* ABA Comm. on Ethics & Prof'l Responsibility, Formal Op. 492 (2020) for a discussion of "significantly harmful information."

36. In addition, the information-receiving lawyer must have taken "reasonable measures to avoid exposure to more disqualifying information than was reasonably necessary to determine whether to represent the prospective client." MODEL RULES OF PROF'L CONDUCT R. 1.18(d)(2).

37. Typically, the lawyer does not perform legal work for a prospective client and therefore there are unlikely to be situations where the lawyer "attacks" work done for such a client.

AMERICAN BAR ASSOCIATION

STANDING COMMITTEE ON ETHICS AND PROFESSIONAL RESPONSIBILITY

Formal Opinion 498 **March 10, 2021**

Virtual Practice

The ABA Model Rules of Professional Conduct permit virtual practice, which is technologically enabled law practice beyond the traditional brick-and-mortar law firm.[1] *When practicing virtually, lawyers must particularly consider ethical duties regarding competence, diligence, and communication, especially when using technology. In compliance with the duty of confidentiality, lawyers must make reasonable efforts to prevent inadvertent or unauthorized disclosures of information relating to the representation and take reasonable precautions when transmitting such information. Additionally, the duty of supervision requires that lawyers make reasonable efforts to ensure compliance by subordinate lawyers and nonlawyer assistants with the Rules of Professional Conduct, specifically regarding virtual practice policies.*

I. Introduction

As lawyers increasingly use technology to practice virtually, they must remain cognizant of their ethical responsibilities. While the ABA Model Rules of Professional Conduct permit virtual practice, the Rules provide some minimum requirements and some of the Comments suggest best practices for virtual practice, particularly in the areas of competence, confidentiality, and supervision. These requirements and best practices are discussed in this opinion, although this opinion does not address every ethical issue arising in the virtual practice context.[2]

---

1. This opinion is based on the ABA Model Rules of Professional Conduct as amended by the ABA House of Delegates through August 2020. The laws, court rules, regulations, rules of professional conduct, and opinions promulgated in individual jurisdictions are controlling.

2. Interstate virtual practice, for instance, also implicates Model Rule of Professional Conduct 5.5: Unauthorized Practice of Law; Multijurisdictional Practice of Law, which is not addressed by this opinion. *See* ABA Comm. on Ethics & Prof'l Responsibility, Formal Op. 495 (2020), stating that "[l]awyers may remotely practice the law of the jurisdictions in which they are licensed while physically present in a jurisdiction in which they are not admitted if the local jurisdiction has not determined that the conduct is the unlicensed or unauthorized practice of law and if they do not hold themselves out as being licensed to practice in the local jurisdiction, do not advertise or otherwise hold out as having an office in the local jurisdiction, and do not provide or offer to provide legal services in the local jurisdiction."

II. Virtual Practice: Commonly Implicated Model Rules

This opinion defines and addresses virtual practice broadly, as technologically enabled law practice beyond the traditional brick-and-mortar law firm.[3] A lawyer's virtual practice often occurs when a lawyer at home or on-the-go is working from a location outside the office, but a lawyer's practice may be entirely virtual because there is no requirement in the Model Rules that a lawyer have a brick-and-mortar office. Virtual practice began years ago but has accelerated recently, both because of enhanced technology (and enhanced technology usage by both clients and lawyers) and increased need. Although the ethics rules apply to both traditional and virtual law practice,[4] virtual practice commonly implicates the key ethics rules discussed below.

A. Commonly Implicated Model Rules of Professional Conduct

1. Competence, Diligence, and Communication

Model Rules 1.1, 1.3, and 1.4 address lawyers' core ethical duties of competence, diligence, and communication with their clients. Comment [8] to Model Rule 1.1 explains, "To maintain the requisite knowledge and skill [to be competent], a lawyer should keep abreast of changes in the law and its practice, *including the benefits and risks associated with relevant technology*, engage in continuing study and education and comply with all continuing legal education requirements to which the lawyer is subject." (*Emphasis added*). Comment [1] to Rule 1.3 makes clear that lawyers must also "pursue a matter on behalf of a client despite opposition, obstruction or personal inconvenience to the lawyer, and take whatever lawful and ethical measures are required to vindicate a client's cause or endeavor." Whether interacting face-to-face or through technology, lawyers must "reasonably consult with the client about the means by which the client's objectives are to be accomplished; . . . keep the client reasonably informed about the status of the matter; [and] promptly comply with reasonable requests for information. . . ."[5] Thus, lawyers should have plans in place to ensure responsibilities regarding

3. *See generally* Model Rules of Professional Conduct R. 1.0(c), defining a "firm" or "law firm" to be "a lawyer or lawyers in a partnership, professional corporation, sole proprietorship or other association authorized to practice law; or lawyers employed in a legal services organization on the legal department of a corporation or other organization." Further guidance on what constitutes a firm is provided in Comments [2], [3], and [4] to Rule 1.0.

4. For example, if a jurisdiction prohibits substantive communications with certain witnesses during court-related proceedings, a lawyer may not engage in such communications either face-to-face or virtually (e.g., during a trial or deposition conducted via videoconferencing). *See, e.g.*, Model Rules of Prof'l Conduct R. 3.4(c) (prohibiting lawyers from violating court rules and making no exception to the rule for virtual proceedings). Likewise, lying or stealing is no more appropriate online than it is face-to-face. *See, e.g.*, Model Rules of Prof'l Conduct R. 1.15; Model Rules of Prof'l Conduct R. 8.4(b)-(c).

5. Model Rules of Prof'l Conduct R. 1.4(a)(2) – (4).

competence, diligence, and communication are being fulfilled when practicing virtually.[6]

2. Confidentiality

Under Rule 1.6 lawyers also have a duty of confidentiality to all clients and therefore "shall not reveal information relating to the representation of a client" (absent a specific exception, informed consent, or implied authorization). A necessary corollary of this duty is that lawyers must at least "make reasonable efforts to prevent the inadvertent or unauthorized disclosure of, or unauthorized access to, information relating to the representation of a client."[7] The following non-exhaustive list of factors may guide the lawyer's determination of reasonable efforts to safeguard confidential information: "the sensitivity of the information, the likelihood of disclosure if additional safeguards are not employed, the cost of employing additional safeguards, the difficulty of implementing the safeguards, and the extent to which the safeguards adversely affect the lawyer's ability to represent clients (e.g., by making a device or important piece of software excessively difficult to use)."[8] As ABA Formal Op. 477R notes, lawyers must employ a "fact-based analysis" to these "nonexclusive factors to guide lawyers in making a 'reasonable efforts' determination."

Similarly, lawyers must take reasonable precautions when transmitting communications that contain information related to a client's representation.[9] At all times, but especially when practicing virtually, lawyers must fully consider and implement reasonable measures to safeguard confidential information and take reasonable precautions when transmitting such information. This responsibility "does not require that the lawyer use special security measures if the method of communication affords a reasonable expectation of privacy."[10] However, depending on the circumstances, lawyers may need to take special precautions.[11] Factors to consider to assist the lawyer in de-

---

6. Lawyers unexpectedly thrust into practicing virtually must have a business continuation plan to keep clients apprised of their matters and to keep moving those matters forward competently and diligently. ABA Comm. on Ethics & Prof'l Responsibility, Formal Op. 482 (2018) (discussing ethical obligations related to disasters). Though virtual practice is common, if for any reason a lawyer cannot fulfill the lawyer's duties of competence, diligence, and other ethical duties to a client, the lawyer must withdraw from the matter. Model Rules of Prof'l Conduct R. 1.16. During and following the termination or withdrawal process, the "lawyer shall take steps to the extent reasonably practicable to protect a client's interests, such as giving reasonable notice to the client, allowing time for employment of other counsel, surrendering papers and property to which the client is entitled and refunding any advance payment of fee or expense that has not been earned or incurred." Model Rules of Prof'l Conduct R. 1.16(d).

7. Model Rules of Prof'l Conduct R. 1.6(c).

8. Model Rules of Prof'l Conduct R. 1.6 cmt. [18].

9. Model Rules of Prof'l Conduct R. 1.6 cmt. [19].

10. *Id.*

11. The opinion cautions, however, that "a lawyer may be required to take special security precautions to protect against the inadvertent or unauthorized disclosure of client informa-

termining the reasonableness of the "expectation of confidentiality include the sensitivity of the information and the extent to which the privacy of the communication is protected by law or by a confidentiality agreement."[12] As ABA Formal Op. 477R summarizes, "[a] lawyer generally may transmit information relating to the representation of a client over the Internet without violating the Model Rules of Professional Conduct where the lawyer has undertaken reasonable efforts to prevent inadvertent or unauthorized access."

3. Supervision

Lawyers with managerial authority have ethical obligations to establish policies and procedures to ensure compliance with the ethics rules, and supervisory lawyers have a duty to make reasonable efforts to ensure that subordinate lawyers and nonlawyer assistants comply with the applicable Rules of Professional Conduct.[13] Practicing virtually does not change or diminish this obligation. "A lawyer must give such assistants appropriate instruction and supervision concerning the ethical aspects of their employment, particularly regarding the obligation not to disclose information relating to representation of the client, and should be responsible for their work product."[14] Moreover, a lawyer must "act competently to safeguard information relating to the representation of a client against unauthorized access by third parties and against inadvertent or unauthorized disclosure by the lawyer *or other persons who are participating in the representation of the client or who are subject to the lawyer's supervision*."[15] The duty to supervise nonlawyers extends to those both within and outside of the law firm.[16]

---

tion when required by an agreement with the client or by law, or when the nature of the information requires a higher degree of security." ABA Comm. on Ethics & Prof'l Responsibility, Formal Op. 477R (2017).

12. Model Rules of Prof'l Conduct R. 1.6 cmt. [19].

13. Model Rules of Prof'l Conduct R. 5.1 & 5.3. *See, e.g.*, ABA Comm. on Ethics & Prof'l Responsibility, Formal Op. 467 (2014) (discussing managerial and supervisory obligations in the context of prosecutorial offices). *See also* ABA Comm. on Ethics & Prof'l Responsibility, Formal Op. 483 n.6 (2018) (describing the organizational structures of firms as pertaining to supervision).

14. Model Rules of Prof'l Conduct R. 5.3 cmt. [2].

15. Model Rules of Prof'l Conduct R. 1.6 cmt. [18] (emphasis added).

16. As noted in Comment [3] to Model Rule 5.3:

> When using such services outside the firm, a lawyer must make reasonable efforts to ensure that the services are provided in a manner that is compatible with the lawyer's professional obligations. The extent of this obligation will depend upon the circumstances, including the education, experience and reputation of the nonlawyer; the nature of the services involved; the terms of any arrangements concerning the protection of client information; and the legal and ethical environments of the jurisdictions in which the services will be performed, particularly with regard to confidentiality. See also Rules 1.1 (competence), 1.2 (allocation of authority), 1.4 (communication with client), 1.6 (confidentiality), 5.4(a) (professional independence of the lawyer), and 5.5(a) (unauthorized practice of law).

B. Particular Virtual Practice Technologies and Considerations

Guided by the rules highlighted above, lawyers practicing virtually need to assess whether their technology, other assistance, and work environment are consistent with their ethical obligations. In light of current technological options, certain available protections and considerations apply to a wide array of devices and services. As ABA Formal Op. 477R noted, a "lawyer has a variety of options to safeguard communications including, for example, using secure internet access methods to communicate, access and store client information (such as through secure Wi-Fi, the use of a Virtual Private Network, or another secure internet portal), using unique complex passwords, changed periodically, implementing firewalls and anti-Malware/Anti-Spyware/Antivirus software on all devices upon which client confidential information is transmitted or stored, and applying all necessary security patches and updates to operational and communications software." Furthermore, "[o]ther available tools include encryption of data that is physically stored on a device and multi-factor authentication to access firm systems." To apply and expand on these protections and considerations, we address some common virtual practice issues below.

1. Hard/Software Systems

Lawyers should ensure that they have carefully reviewed the terms of service applicable to their hardware devices and software systems to assess whether confidentiality is protected.[17] To protect confidential information from unauthorized access, lawyers should be diligent in installing any security-related updates and using strong passwords, antivirus software, and encryption. When connecting over Wi-Fi, lawyers should ensure that the routers are secure and should consider using virtual private networks (VPNs). Finally, as technology inevitably evolves, lawyers should periodically assess whether their existing systems are adequate to protect confidential information.

2. Accessing Client Files and Data

Lawyers practicing virtually (even on short notice) must have reliable access to client contact information and client records. If the access to such "files is provided through a cloud service, the lawyer should (i) choose a reputable company, and (ii) take reasonable steps to ensure that the confidentiality of client information is preserved, and that the information is readily accessible to the lawyer."[18] Lawyers must ensure that data is regularly backed

17. For example, terms and conditions of service may include provisions for data-soaking software systems that collect, track, and use information. Such systems might purport to own the information, reserve the right to sell or transfer the information to third parties, or otherwise use the information contrary to lawyers' duty of confidentiality.

18. ABA Comm. on Ethics & Prof'l Responsibility, Formal Op. 482 (2018).

up and that secure access to the backup data is readily available in the event of a data loss. In anticipation of data being lost or hacked, lawyers should have a data breach policy and a plan to communicate losses or breaches to the impacted clients.[19]

3. Virtual Meeting Platforms and Videoconferencing

Lawyers should review the terms of service (and any updates to those terms) to ensure that using the virtual meeting or videoconferencing platform is consistent with the lawyer's ethical obligations. Access to accounts and meetings should be only through strong passwords, and the lawyer should explore whether the platform offers higher tiers of security for businesses/enterprises (over the free or consumer platform variants). Likewise, any recordings or transcripts should be secured. If the platform will be recording conversations with the client, it is inadvisable to do so without client consent, but lawyers should consult the professional conduct rules, ethics opinions, and laws of the applicable jurisdiction.[20] Lastly, any client-related meetings or information should not be overheard or seen by others in the household, office, or other remote location, or by other third parties who are not assisting with the representation,[21] to avoid jeopardizing the attorney-client privilege and violating the ethical duty of confidentiality.

---

19. *See, e.g.*, ABA Comm. on Ethics & Prof'l Responsibility, Formal Op. 483 (2018) ("Even lawyers who, (i) under Model Rule 1.6(c), make 'reasonable efforts to prevent the . . . unauthorized disclosure of, or unauthorized access to, information relating to the representation of a client,' (ii) under Model Rule 1.1, stay abreast of changes in technology, and (iii) under Model Rules 5.1 and 5.3, properly supervise other lawyers and third-party electronic-information storage vendors, may suffer a data breach. When they do, they have a duty to notify clients of the data breach under Model Rule 1.4 in sufficient detail to keep clients 'reasonably informed' and with an explanation 'to the extent necessary to permit the client to make informed decisions regarding the representation.'").

20. *See, e.g.*, ABA Comm. on Ethics & Prof'l Responsibility, Formal Op. 01-422 (2001).

21. Pennsylvania recently highlighted the following best practices for videoconferencing security:

- Do not make meetings public;
- Require a meeting password or use other features that control the admittance of guests;
- Do not share a link to a teleconference on an unrestricted publicly available social media post;
- Provide the meeting link directly to specific people;
- Manage screensharing options. For example, many of these services allow the host to change screensharing to "Host Only;"
- Ensure users are using the updated version of remote access/meeting applications.

Pennsylvania Bar Ass'n Comm. on Legal Ethics & Prof'l Responsibility, Formal Op. 2020-300 (2020) (citing an FBI press release warning of teleconference and online classroom hacking).

4. Virtual Document and Data Exchange Platforms

In addition to the protocols noted above (e.g., reviewing the terms of service and any updates to those terms), lawyers' virtual document and data exchange platforms should ensure that documents and data are being appropriately archived for later retrieval and that the service or platform is and remains secure. For example, if the lawyer is transmitting information over email, the lawyer should consider whether the information is and needs to be encrypted (both in transit and in storage).[22]

5. Smart Speakers, Virtual Assistants, and Other Listening-Enabled Devices

Unless the technology is assisting the lawyer's law practice, the lawyer should disable the listening capability of devices or services such as smart speakers, virtual assistants, and other listening-enabled devices while communicating about client matters. Otherwise, the lawyer is exposing the client's and other sensitive information to unnecessary and unauthorized third parties and increasing the risk of hacking.

6. Supervision

The virtually practicing managerial lawyer must adopt and tailor policies and practices to ensure that all members of the firm and any internal or external assistants operate in accordance with the lawyer's ethical obligations of supervision.[23] Comment [2] to Model Rule 5.1 notes that "[s]uch policies and procedures include those designed to detect and resolve conflicts of interest, identify dates by which actions must be taken in pending matters, account for client funds and property and ensure that inexperienced lawyers are properly supervised."

---

22. *See, e.g.*, ABA Comm. on Ethics & Prof'l Responsibility, Formal Op. 477R (2017) (noting that "it is not always reasonable to rely on the use of unencrypted email").

23. As ABA Formal Op. 477R noted:

> In the context of electronic communications, lawyers must establish policies and procedures, and periodically train employees, subordinates and others assisting in the delivery of legal services, in the use of reasonably secure methods of electronic communications with clients. Lawyers also must instruct and supervise on reasonable measures for access to and storage of those communications. Once processes are established, supervising lawyers must follow up to ensure these policies are being implemented and partners and lawyers with comparable managerial authority must periodically reassess and update these policies. This is no different than the other obligations for supervision of office practices and procedures to protect client information.

a. Subordinates/Assistants

The lawyer must ensure that law firm tasks are being completed in a timely, competent, and secure manner.[24] This duty requires regular interaction and communication with, for example, associates, legal assistants, and paralegals. Routine communication and other interaction are also advisable to discern the health and wellness of the lawyer's team members.[25]

One particularly important subject to supervise is the firm's bring-your-own-device (BYOD) policy. If lawyers or nonlawyer assistants will be using their own devices to access, transmit, or store client-related information, the policy must ensure that security is tight (e.g., strong passwords to the device and to any routers, access through VPN, updates installed, training on phishing attempts), that any lost or stolen device may be remotely wiped, that client-related information cannot be accessed by, for example, staff members' family or others, and that client-related information will be adequately and safely archived and available for later retrieval.[26]

Similarly, all client-related information, such as files or documents, must not be visible to others by, for example, implementing a "clean desk" (and "clean screen") policy to secure documents and data when not in use. As noted above in the discussion of videoconferencing, client-related information also should not be visible or audible to others when the lawyer or nonlawyer is on a videoconference or call. In sum, all law firm employees and lawyers who have access to client information must receive appropriate over-

---

24. The New York County Lawyers Association Ethics Committee recently described some aspects to include in the firm's practices and policies:

- Monitoring appropriate use of firm networks for work purposes.
- Tightening off-site work procedures to ensure that the increase in worksites does not similarly increase the entry points for a data breach.
- Monitoring adherence to firm cybersecurity procedures (e.g., not processing or transmitting work across insecure networks, and appropriate storage of client data and work product).
- Ensuring that working at home has not significantly increased the likelihood of an inadvertent disclosure through misdirection of a transmission, possibly because the lawyer or nonlawyer was distracted by a child, spouse, parent or someone working on repair or maintenance of the home.
- Ensuring that sufficiently frequent "live" remote sessions occur between supervising attorneys and supervised attorneys to achieve effective supervision as described in [New York Rule of Professional Conduct] 5.1(c).

N.Y. County Lawyers Ass'n Comm. on Prof'l Ethics, Formal Op. 754-2020 (2020).

25. *See* ABA Model Regulatory Objectives for the Provision of Legal Services para. I (2016).

26. For example, a lawyer has an obligation to return the client's file when the client requests or when the representation ends. *See, e.g.*, Model Rules of Prof'l Conduct R. 1.16(d). This important obligation cannot be fully discharged if important documents and data are located in staff members' personal computers or houses and are not indexed or readily retrievable by the lawyer.

sight and training on the ethical obligations to maintain the confidentiality of such information, including when working virtually.

b. Vendors and Other Assistance

Lawyers will understandably want and may need to rely on information technology professionals, outside support staff (e.g., administrative assistants, paralegals, investigators), and vendors. The lawyer must ensure that all of these individuals or services comply with the lawyer's obligation of confidentiality and other ethical duties. When appropriate, lawyers should consider use of a confidentiality agreement,[27] and should ensure that all client-related information is secure, indexed, and readily retrievable.

7. Possible Limitations of Virtual Practice

Virtual practice and technology have limits. For example, lawyers practicing virtually must make sure that trust accounting rules, which vary significantly across states, are followed.[28] The lawyer must still be able, to the extent the circumstances require, to write and deposit checks, make electronic transfers, and maintain full trust-accounting records while practicing virtually. Likewise, even in otherwise virtual practices, lawyers still need to make and maintain a plan to process the paper mail, to docket correspondence and communications, and to direct or redirect clients, prospective clients, or other important individuals who might attempt to contact the lawyer at the lawyer's current or previous brick-and-mortar office. If a lawyer will not be available at a physical office address, there should be signage (and/or online instructions) that the lawyer is available by appointment only and/or that the posted address is for mail deliveries only. Finally, although e-filing systems have lessened this concern, litigators must still be able to file and receive pleadings and other court documents.

---

27. *See, e.g.*, Mo. Bar Informal Advisory Op. 20070008 & 20050068.

28. *See* Model Rules of Prof'l Conduct R. 1.15; *See, e.g.*, ABA Comm. on Ethics & Prof'l Responsibility, Formal Op. 482 (2018) ("Lawyers also must take reasonable steps in the event of a disaster to ensure access to funds the lawyer is holding in trust. A lawyer's obligations with respect to these funds will vary depending on the circumstances. Even before a disaster, all lawyers should consider (i) providing for another trusted signatory on trust accounts in the event of the lawyer's unexpected death, incapacity, or prolonged unavailability and (ii) depending on the circumstances and jurisdiction, designating a successor lawyer to wind up the lawyer's practice.").

III. Conclusion

The ABA Model Rules of Professional Conduct permit lawyers to conduct practice virtually, but those doing so must fully consider and comply with their applicable ethical responsibilities, including technological competence, diligence, communication, confidentiality, and supervision.

AMERICAN BAR ASSOCIATION
STANDING COMMITTEE ON ETHICS AND PROFESSIONAL RESPONSIBILITY

Formal Opinion 499 **September 8, 2021**

Passive Investment in Alternative Business Structures

A lawyer may passively invest in a law firm that includes nonlawyer owners ("Alternative Business Structures" or "ABS") operating in a jurisdiction that permits ABS entities, even if the lawyer is admitted to practice law in a jurisdiction that does not authorize nonlawyer ownership of law firms.[1] *To avoid transgressing Model Rule 5.4 or other Model Rules and to avoid imputation of conflicts under Model Rule 1.10, a passively investing lawyer must not practice law through the ABS or be held out as a lawyer associated with the ABS and cannot have access to information protected by Model Rule 1.6 without the ABS client's informed consent or compliance with an applicable exception to Rule 1.6 adopted by the ABS jurisdiction. The fact that a conflict might arise in the future between the investing lawyer's practice and the ABS's work for its clients does not mean that the lawyer cannot make a passive investment in the ABS. If, however, at the time of the investment the lawyer's investment would create a personal interest conflict under Model Rule 1.7(a)(2), the lawyer must refrain from the investment or appropriately address the conflict under Model Rule 1.7(b).*

Introduction

ABA Model Rule of Professional Conduct 5.4 features a number of prohibitions designed to preserve the professional independence of lawyers. In general, the Rule prohibits a lawyer or law firm from sharing legal fees with a nonlawyer, forming a partnership with a nonlawyer (if any of the activities of the partnership consist of the practice of law), and practicing in a business structure in which a nonlawyer owns any interest in the business or serves as a corporate director or officer.

Model Rule 5.4 or its close equivalent has been adopted in nearly every U.S. jurisdiction; to date only Arizona, the District of Columbia, and Utah have modified their jurisdiction's Rule 5.4 to permit business structures that

1. This opinion is based on the ABA Model Rules of Professional Conduct as amended by the ABA House of Delegates through August 2020. The laws, court rules, regulations, rules of professional conduct, and opinions promulgated in individual jurisdictions are controlling.

allow nonlawyer ownership of law firms and the sharing of legal fees with nonlawyers.[2] Since 1991, the District of Columbia's version of Rule 5.4 has, in circumstances defined in and limited by that rule, permitted individual nonlawyer partners in law firms, as long as such nonlawyers are providing professional services that assist the firm in delivering legal services. The District of Columbia does not permit passive investment in law firms. In 2020 the Utah Supreme Court launched a two-year pilot legal-regulatory "sandbox" project whereby Court-approved entities may include nonlawyer owners in firms that provide legal services.[3] In 2021 Arizona eliminated Rule 5.4 altogether, substituting a system in which Arizona law firms that include nonlawyer owners or investors may be certified by the Arizona Supreme Court as "alternative business structures" ("ABS"). Given these changes, the question raised is whether a lawyer admitted to practice law in a jurisdiction adhering to Model Rule 5.4 (i.e., a jurisdiction that strictly prohibits nonlawyer ownership of law firms) (hereinafter "Model Rule Lawyer") may acquire a "passive" investment interest in an ABS?[4]

For purposes of this opinion, a "passive" investment interest means that a lawyer contributes money to an ABS with the goal of receiving a monetary return on that investment. Passive investment does not include scenarios in which the investing lawyer practices law through the ABS, manages or holds a position of corporate or managerial authority in the ABS, or is otherwise involved in the daily operations of the ABS.

Further, passive investment, as used in this Opinion, means that the investing lawyer does not have access to information protected by Model Rule 1.6 without the ABS client's informed consent.

Under these circumstances, a Model Rule Lawyer who makes a passive investment in an ABS does not violate Model Rule 5.4. However, in some circumstances the Model Rule Lawyer may have a conflict of interest, arising from the Model Rule Lawyer's own practice. The conflict might arise at the time the investment is made or thereafter. The potential for a conflict does not prohibit a Model Rule Lawyer from making the passive investment, but it does require the Model Rule Lawyer to address a conflict that later materializes. If, however, at the time of the investment the Model Rules Lawyer's investment would create a personal interest conflict under Model Rule 1.7(a)

---

2. In 2015 the Washington State Supreme Court authorized Limited License Legal Technicians to share fees and form business structures with lawyers. *See* WASH. R. OF PROF'L CONDUCT R. 5.9 (Business Structures Involving LLLT and Lawyer Ownership). The United States Patent and Trademark Office permits patent agents to be partners in a law firm practicing before the Office. 37 C.F.R. § 11.1 (definition of practitioner); 37 C.F.R. § 11.504.

3. In May 2021, the Utah Supreme Court extended the term of the Utah legal-regulatory sandbox to seven years.

4. This Opinion only addresses "passive investment" in an ABS and is not, at this time, evaluating other scenarios involving a Model Rule lawyer practicing in an ABS.

(2), the Model Rule Lawyer must refrain from the investment or appropriately address the conflict pursuant to Model Rule 1.7(b).

Analysis

A. A Lawyer May Have Business Interests Separate from the Practice of Law

In general, a lawyer may own a business or an investment interest that is separate from and unrelated to the lawyer's practice of law. For instance, a lawyer may have an ownership interest in a restaurant, be a partner in a consulting business, invest in a mutual fund, or buy stock in a publicly traded company (collectively "unrelated personal investments").

An unrelated personal investment does not intrinsically implicate the Model Rules, except to the extent that the lawyer's activities vis-à-vis the investment present a conflict of interest under Model Rule 1.7 or 1.8. For example, if a lawyer were to ask a client to invest in the lawyer's separate business or offer to refer ancillary business services to a client, the lawyer would need to comply with the disclosure and writing requirements in Model Rule 1.8(a).[5]

Similarly, the Rules do not prohibit a lawyer from making unrelated personal investments, albeit in some circumstances the Rules require the client's informed consent. When the lawyer invests in an entity that is a client or accepts an interest in a client's business as a fee, the lawyer must comply with Rule 1.8(a).[6] And if a lawyer owns a significant investment interest in a business that is an adversary of the lawyer's client, that interest could materially limit the lawyer's representation as discussed in Part C, below.

B. Choice of Law Considerations

If a Model Rule Lawyer is a passive investor in an entity operating in a jurisdiction that permits investment in an ABS, there is a choice-of-law question about which jurisdiction's ethics rules apply to the Model Rule Lawyer's passive-investment conduct: the rules of the Model Rule jurisdiction or the rules of the ABS-friendly jurisdiction. Model Rule 8.5(b) resolves the conflict of laws that arises when a lawyer is potentially subject to more than one set of rules of professional conduct that impose different obligations.

---

5. *See* ABA Comm. on Ethics & Prof'l Responsibility, Formal Op. 484 (2018) (offering litigation funding services to a client when the lawyer has a financial interest in the offered services requires informed consent). *See also* Model Rules of Prof'l Conduct R. 1.7, cmt. [10] (a lawyer may not allow related business interests to affect representation, for example, by referring clients to an enterprise in which the lawyer has an undisclosed financial interest); Model Rules of Prof'l Conduct R. 5.7, cmt. [5] (noting that when a client-lawyer relationship exists with a person who is referred by a lawyer to a separate law-related service entity controlled by the lawyer, the lawyer must comply with Rule 1.8(a)).

6. *See* Model Rules of Prof'l Conduct R. 1.8, cmt. [1].

Under Model Rule 8.5(b)(1), the rules to be applied depend on whether the conduct relates to a matter pending before a tribunal, in which case the rules of the jurisdiction in which the tribunal sits apply. In other circumstances, the applicable rules are those of the jurisdiction in which the lawyer's conduct occurred, unless the predominant effect of that conduct is in another jurisdiction.[7]

In the Committee's view, the conflict-of-law issue in the passive investment context is resolved by applying the law of the jurisdiction in which the ABS is authorized to operate because under Rule 8.5(b)(2), the predominant effect of a Model Rule Lawyer's *passive* investment in an ABS would be in the jurisdiction(s) where the ABS would be permitted. That conclusion follows from the fact that the investment is passive and is made in order to fund the activities of an ABS in a jurisdiction that permits such entities.[8] Assuming the Model Rule Lawyer's investment is genuinely passive, the lawyer cannot be deemed to be practicing law in the ABS-permissive jurisdiction, just as a lawyer who is an investor in a mutual fund that includes widget company stock in its portfolio is not deemed to be making widgets. Accordingly, when the Model Rule Lawyer is passively investing, the only relevant "conduct" and the only meaningful "effect" of that conduct occurs in the ABS-permissive jurisdiction. As to that conduct, the Model Rule Lawyer's passive investment does not violate the rules of professional conduct of the ABS-permissive jurisdiction.

This outcome is, from a policy standpoint, consistent with this Committee's earlier opinion on cross-border fee dividing between lawyers. In ABA Formal Opinion 464 (2013), the issue was whether a lawyer in a Model Rules jurisdiction could serve as co-counsel in a matter and divide legal fees with a Washington, D.C. lawyer who practiced in a firm that included a non-lawyer partner as permitted under the District of Columbia's Rule 5.4(b). The Committee concluded that such a fee division did not violate the Model Rules because the lawyer would be dividing a legal fee only with "another lawyer," and a lawyer may divide legal fees with a lawyer admitted in another jurisdiction. In the Committee's view, the possibility that the District of Columbia firm might eventually "share" some fraction of that firm's portion of the fee with a nonlawyer because a portion of it becomes part of that firm's over-

7. *See* Model Rules of Prof'l Conduct R. 8.5(b)(2).

8. *Cf.* NY State Bar Ass'n Comm. on Prof'l Ethics Op. 1093 (2016) (predominant effect of New York-admitted lawyer practicing in England was in the latter jurisdiction). The analysis does not change if the passive investment funds, in whole or in part, litigation before a tribunal. In order for Rule 8.5(b)(1) to apply, instead of Rule 8.5(b)(2), the conduct at issue must be before a tribunal. A lawyer making a passive investment in an ABS-firm is not engaged in "conduct in connection with a matter pending before a tribunal." *See* Model Rules of Prof'l Conduct R. 8.5 cmt. [4] (conduct by litigating lawyer "in anticipation of a proceeding not yet pending before a tribunal" is governed by Rule 8.5(b)(2).)

all revenues was not a basis upon which to expose the lawyer in the Model Rules jurisdiction to discipline. Just as the Committee previously concluded that a Model Rule Lawyer can jointly represent a client and ethically divide a fee with a lawyer practicing in a firm whose structure is not permitted by Model Rule 5.4 but allowed by the local jurisdiction's rules, so too the Committee concludes that a Model Rule Lawyer's passive investment in such a firm is likewise allowed where ABS's are permitted by a jurisdiction's rules.

C. Conflict of Interest Risks Presented by Passive Investment

A passive investment in an ABS, without more, does not mean that the Model Rule Lawyer is practicing law through the ABS. To avoid any appearance of practicing law through the ABS, the investing Model Rule Lawyer must ensure that the ABS does not identify the Model Rule Lawyer as a lawyer or hold out the Model Rule Lawyer as a lawyer associated with the ABS.

A passive investment does not create an "of counsel" relationship where conflicts are imputed to other lawyers. Nothing about a passive investment necessarily creates the "close, regular and personal relationship" characteristic of "of counsel" arrangements.[9]

As a result, the mere fact of a passive investment by a Model Rules Lawyer in an ABS does not require imputation of conflicts under Model Rule 1.10 between the Model Rule Lawyer (or that lawyer's firm) and the ABS.

However, even if a Model Rule Lawyer is only a passive investor with no other relationship to the ABS, that Model Rule Lawyer still must consider the possibility of the concurrent conflicts of interest that could arise from the Model Rule Lawyer's representation of clients in the Model Rule jurisdiction.

For example, a Model Rule 1.7(a)(2) concurrent conflict of interest based on the Model Rule Lawyer's personal interest in the investment in the ABS would likely exist if, when the Model Rule Lawyer made the investment the Model Rule Lawyer also represented a client whose interests were adverse to a client of the ABS. Such a conflict would exist if the Model Rule Lawyer were to act as an advocate against a client of the ABS or represent a business in a transactional matter requiring negotiation with a client of the ABS. In these situations, among others, the Model Rule Lawyer's investment interest in the ABS could "create a significant risk" that the Model Rule Lawyer's representation of the client would be "materially limited" by the lawyer's investment interest in the ABS.[10]

In most circumstances, such a conflict will only preclude the investing Model Rule Lawyer from representing the client, because personal interest conflicts are generally not imputed to other lawyers in the same firm unless

9. *See* ABA Comm. on Ethics & Prof'l Responsibility, Formal Ops. 90-357 & 94-388.

10. *See* ABA Model Rules of Prof'l Conduct R. 1.7, cmt. [10] (a "lawyer's own interests should not be permitted to have an adverse effect on representation of a client").

those interests create a significant risk of materially limiting the representation of a client by the remaining lawyers in the Model Rule Lawyer's firm.[11]

The fact that a conflict might arise in the future between the Model Rule Lawyer's practice and the ABS firm's work for its clients does not mean that the Model Rule Lawyer cannot make a passive investment in the ABS. If, however, the Model Rule Lawyer's investment in an ABS will create a conflict of interest at the time of the investment, the Model Rule Lawyer would need to refrain from the investment unless the conflict can be resolved appropriately under Model Rule 1.7(b).[12]

D. ABS Client Confidential Information

While it is hard to assess what information might be requested by investors or potential ABS investors, it is unrealistic to assume that there will be no investor requests for information about the ABS operations or revenue. The issue of disclosure of confidential information by an ABS is a developing area of the law and beyond the scope of this opinion; when investing in an ABS, the Model Rule Lawyer should exercise due care to avoid exposure to confidential client information held by the ABS or other associations that could result in a determination that the Model Rule Lawyer is part of the ABS "firm."

Conclusion

A lawyer admitted to practice law in a Model Rule jurisdiction may make a passive investment in a law firm that includes nonlawyer owners operating in a jurisdiction that permits such investments provided that the investing lawyer does not practice law through the ABS, is not held out as a lawyer associated with the ABS, and has no access to information protected by Model Rule 1.6 without the ABS clients' informed consent or compliance with an applicable exception to Rule 1.6 adopted by the ABS jurisdiction. With these limitations, such "passive investment" does not run afoul of Model Rule 5.4 nor does it, without more, result in the imputation of the ABS's client conflicts of interest to the investing Model Rule Lawyer under Model Rule 1.10. The fact that a conflict might arise in the future between the Model Rule Lawyer's practice and the ABS firm's work for its clients does not mean that the Model Rule Lawyer cannot make a passive investment in the ABS. If, however, at the time of the investment the Model Rules Lawyer's

11. ABA Model Rules of Prof'l Conduct R. 1.10(a)(1).

12. The potential inability of the Model Rule Lawyer to redeem or liquidate her investment at any time may create difficulties in resolving conflicts that arise post-investment. The Model Rule Lawyer may not be able to withdraw from the passive investment at any time, absent simply giving up the interest, and that leaves informed consent from the Model Rule Lawyer's client or withdrawal from the representation of that client as the only options.

investment would create a personal interest conflict under Model Rule 1.7(a)(2), the Model Rule Lawyer must refrain from the investment or appropriately address the conflict pursuant to Model Rule 1.7(b).

Abstaining: Norman W. Spaulding

AMERICAN BAR ASSOCIATION

STANDING COMMITTEE ON ETHICS AND PROFESSIONAL RESPONSIBILITY

Formal Opinion 500 **October 6, 2021**

Language Access in the Client-Lawyer Relationship

Communication between a lawyer and a client is necessary for the client to participate effectively in the representation and is a fundamental component of nearly every client-lawyer relationship.[1] *When a client's ability to receive information from or convey information to a lawyer is impeded because the lawyer and the client do not share a common language, or owing to a client's non-cognitive physical condition, such as a hearing, speech, or vision disability, the duties of communication under Model Rule 1.4 and competence under Model Rule 1.1 are undiminished. In that situation, a lawyer may be obligated to take measures appropriate to the client's circumstances to ensure that those duties are capably discharged. When reasonably necessary, a lawyer should arrange for communications to take place through an impartial interpreter or translator*[2] *capable of comprehending and accurately explaining*

---

1. This opinion is based on the ABA Model Rules of Professional Conduct as amended by the ABA House of Delegates through August 2020. The laws, court rules, regulations, rules of professional conduct, and opinions promulgated in individual jurisdictions are controlling.

2. For purposes of this opinion, an interpreter is a person who converts "speech from a source language into a target language" while a translator "works with the written word." *Translator vs. Interpreter: What's the Difference*, AMERICAN TRANSLATORS ASSOCIATION (last visited Sept. 23, 2021), https://www.atanet.org/client-assistance/translator-vs-interpreter/. The Committee recognizes that there are existing and emerging technologies that in some circumstances may enable a lawyer and client to partially or fully address language access issues. For example, closed captioning, live transcription, screen readers, refreshable braille displays, and speech recognition software, are examples of the assistive technologies that may address access issues for some individuals with a non-cognitive physical condition, such as a hearing, speech, or vision disability. *See Assistive Devices for People with Hearing, Voice, Speech or Language Disorders*, NATIONAL INSTITUTE ON DEAFNESS AND OTHER COMMUNICATION DISORDERS, https://www.nidcd.nih.gov/health/assistive-devices-people-hearing-voice-speech-or-language-disorders (last visited Sept. 23, 2021). Electronic text and voice translation software and devices, including text-to-text, text-to-speech, and speech-to-speech translators such as telecommunications relay service (TRI) (free—dial 7-1-1), video relay service (VRS) (free—subscriber based) and video remote interpreting (VRI) (fee based), have the capacity to translate from one language to another in close to real time. Brian Heater, *Interpreter, Google's real-time translator, comes to mobile*, TECH CRUNCH (Dec. 12, 2019, 9:00 AM), https://techcrunch.com/2019/12/12/interpreter-googles-real-time-translator-comes-to-mobile/. Depending on

the legal concepts involved, and who will assent to and abide by the lawyer's duty of confidentiality. The lawyer also should use other assistive or language-translation technologies, when necessary. In addition, particularly when there are language considerations affecting the reciprocal exchange of information, a lawyer must ensure that the client understands the legal significance of translated or interpreted communications and that the lawyer understands the client's communications, bearing in mind potential differences in cultural and social assumptions that might impact meaning.

I. Introduction

As the population of the United States continues to become ever more diverse and multicultural, communication issues stemming from language differences, as well as physical disabilities, are increasing.[3] Between 1990 and 2013, the population of persons having limited English proficiency grew 80 percent, from nearly 14 million to 25.1 million.[4] The adoption of the Americans with Disabilities Act in 1990, coupled with ongoing advocacy by and on behalf of persons with disabilities, has led to the profession's growing awareness that clients seeking representation may not be able to hear, speak, or read without accommodation.[5] For these reasons, with increasing frequency

---

the circumstances, use of such technologies in lieu of or in addition to the engagement of a human interpreter or translator may be appropriate and sufficient to satisfy the ethical obligations of communication and competence. Owing to the rapid evolution of these technologies and the variability of client needs in the context of language access, an analysis of whether and when a technology will address a particular language-access quandary is beyond the scope of this opinion. The Committee notes that the availability of assistive and translation technologies is another example of the ever-increasing impact of technology on the practice of law and underscores the duty of lawyers to develop an understanding of relevant technology. Model Rules of Prof'l Conduct R. 1.1 cmt. [8] ("To maintain the requisite knowledge and skill, a lawyer should keep abreast of changes in the law and its practice, including the benefits and risks associated with relevant technology . . . .").

3. In 2013, approximately 61.6 million individuals, foreign and U.S. born, spoke a language other than English at home. While the majority of these individuals also spoke English with native fluency or very well, about 41 percent (25.1 million) were considered as having Limited English Proficiency (LEP), which is defined as speaking English "less than very well." Jie Zong & Jeanne Batalova, *The Limited English Proficient Population in the United States in 2013*, Migration Policy Institute (July 8, 2015) [hereinafter *Limited English Proficient Population*], https://www.migrationpolicy.org/article/limited-english-proficient-population-united-states-2013. 2019 data from the U.S. Census bureau estimates that 22% of households in the U.S. speak a language other than English in the home. U.S. Census Bureau Selected Social Characteristics in the United States (2019), https://data.census.gov/cedsci/table?d=ACS%201-Year%20Estimates%20Data%20Profiles&tid=ACSDP1Y2019.DP02&hidePreview=false.

4. *See Limited English Proficient Population*, *supra* note 3.

5. *See generally* Alex B. Long, *Reasonable Accommodation As Professional Responsibility, Reasonable Accommodation as Professionalism*, 47 U.C. Davis L. Rev. 1753 (2014) (evaluating ethical and professional obligations to reasonably accommodate disabilities).

lawyers are called upon to communicate with clients who do not speak the lawyer's native language or speak the lawyer's language with limited proficiency, or for whom the conventional written or spoken word is not an accessible form of communication.[6]

The foundational rules of competence (Rule 1.1) and communication (Rule 1.4) in the ABA Model Rules of Professional Conduct establish a baseline for a lawyer's duties when there is a barrier to communication because the lawyer and the client do not share a common language, or when a client is a person with a non-cognitive physical condition that affects how the lawyer communicates with a client, such as a hearing or speech disability.[7] This baseline prescribes that when a lawyer and client cannot communicate with reasonable efficacy, the lawyer must take steps to engage the services of a qualified and impartial interpreter and/or employ an appropriate assistive or language-translation device to ensure that the client has sufficient information to intelligently participate in decisions relating to the representation and that the lawyer is procuring adequate information from the client to meet the standards of competent practice.[8]

This opinion analyzes the duties of Rules 1.1, 1.4, and 5.3 in the context of language access and explains in more detail (1) the lawyer's obligation to evaluate the need for a translator or interpreter or interpretive device, (2) the appropriate qualifications for a person or service providing translation or

---

6. For an excellent discussion of issues facing lawyers due to the changing demographics of the United States population and the increase of language diversity, see Muneer I. Ahmad, *Interpreting Communities, Lawyering Across Language Difficulties*, 54 U.C.L.A. L. Rev. 999 (2007).

7. Some mental conditions may affect the traditional client-lawyer relationship or the lawyer's customary means of delivering legal services in other ways. For example, a client may suffer from a diminished mental capacity or a non-sensory cognitive condition. The legal obligation to accommodate a client's mental disability and the ethical duties applicable to representing clients with diminished capacity are addressed in Model Rule 1.14 and beyond the scope of this opinion.

8. In addition to the ethical duties analyzed in this opinion, law firms and other legal organizations may be legally required to provide and pay for auxiliary aids and services in order to provide a client with reasonable accommodation under the ADA. Law offices are explicitly included in the definition of public accommodations under Title III of the ADA, 42 U.S.C. § 12181(7)(f), and as a general rule, ADA Title III entities cannot pass along the costs of auxiliary aids and services to the person with the disability. *See* 28 C.F.R. § 36.301(c). Although particulars of a lawyer's duties under the ADA are beyond the scope of this opinion, a lawyer, law firm, and legal organization should be aware of the legal risks and responsibilities related to ADA compliance. *See generally* Elana Nightingale Dawson, *Lawyers' Responsibilities Under Title III of the ADA: Ensuring Communication Access for the Deaf and Hard of Hearing*, 45 Val. U. L. Rev. 1143 (2011); Janine Robben, *You Are Us What Every Lawyer Needs to Know About Representing Disabled Clients*, Or. St. B. Bull. 19 (Feb./Mar. 2008); National Ass'n of the Deaf Law Center, *Attorneys, Deaf Clients, and the Americans with Disabilities Act*, W. Va. Law. 30 (Jan. 2004); Jo Anne Simon, *The Use of Interpreters for the Deaf and the Legal Community's Obligation to Comply with the A.D.A.*, 8 J.L. & Health 155 (1994).

interpretive services, and (3) a lawyer's supervisory duties when engaging or directing a translator or interpreter. The opinion also provides additional guidance on the advisability of maintaining awareness of potential differences in cultural and social assumptions, particularly those based on national origin or ethnicity, which may affect the way in which legal advice is sought or understood.[9]

II. Analysis

Lawyers must communicate with clients in a manner that is reasonably understandable to those clients. This is a central tenet of the duties applicable to the client-lawyer relationship under the Model Rules of Professional Conduct. In 1983, the ABA Commission on Evaluation of Professional Standards (commonly known as the Kutak Commission) recommended the adoption of Model Rule 1.4, codifying the importance of communication with clients so that clients know what is happening on their matters and can participate intelligently in the representation.[10]

The duty of communication under current Model Rule 1.4 includes a number of communicative components, including duties: (1) to promptly inform the client of information when the client's informed consent is re-

---

9. The role of interpreters for parties and witnesses is well established in U.S. criminal, civil, and administrative justice systems, and use of interpreters for individuals with limited English proficiency in adjudicative proceedings may be required by the Constitution, a statute, or a court rule. United States ex rel. Negron v. New York, 434 F.2d 386, 390–91 (2d Cir. 1970) (defendant's Sixth Amendment rights violated when interpreter not appointed); U.S. Court Interpreters Act, 28 U.S.C. § 1827 (right to an interpreter applied to all "judicial proceedings," including pretrial hearings in federal district court); EXEC. ORDER NO. 13166, IMPROVING ACCESS TO SERVICES FOR PERSONS WITH LIMITED ENGLISH PROFICIENCY DEPARTMENT OF JUSTICE ENFORCEMENT OF TITLE VI OF THE CIVIL RIGHTS ACT OF 1964, NATIONAL ORIGIN DISCRIMINATION AGAINST PERSONS WITH LIMITED ENGLISH PROFICIENCY (2000), *available at* https://www.justice.gov/sites/default/files/crt/legacy/2010/12/14/eolep.pdf. "While the Court Interpreters Act provides a singular guideline for use in the federal courts, there is much greater variation among state interpreter laws. Some states mirror the federal scheme, requiring the appointment of an interpreter upon a judicial determination that a defendant cannot comprehend the proceedings. Other states afford even more discretion to judicial officers." Kate O. Rahel, *Why the Sixth Amendment Right to Counsel Includes an Out-of-Court Interpreter*, 99 IOWA L. REV. 2299 (2014).

10. ART GARWIN, A LEGISLATIVE HISTORY: THE DEVELOPMENT OF THE ABA MODEL RULES OF PROFESSIONAL CONDUCT, 1982-2013, 72 (2013). There was no direct counterpart to Rule 1.4 in the predecessor Model Code of Professional Responsibility, but because a lawyer's failure to communicate was a frequent source of disciplinary complaints, the Commission believed it was important to clarify the obligation to keep a client reasonable informed. *Id.* The black letter of Model Rule 1.4 has been amended only once since its adoption in 1983—in 2002 as part of Ethics 2000 amendments. The Ethics 2000 Commission explained that Rule 1.4(a) was amended to "specifically identify five different aspects of the duty to communicate." *Id.* at 77.

quired; (2) to "reasonably consult" with the client about the representation; (3) to "keep the client reasonably informed" about the status of a matter; (4) to promptly comply with "reasonable requests for information"; and (5) to "consult with" the client on relevant limitations on the lawyer's ability to provide legal assistance.[11] Additionally it is incumbent on the lawyer to ensure that the client has sufficient information to participate intelligently in the client-lawyer relationship, to "explain a matter to the extent reasonably necessary to permit the client to make informed decisions regarding the representation."[12]

Reasonably understandable client-lawyer communication is not only necessary to enable the client to make informed decisions; it is also an element of the lawyer's obligation to provide the client with competent representation under Model Rule 1.1.[13] If a lawyer does not communicate with a client in a mutually understood language, it is doubtful that the lawyer is exercising the thoroughness and preparation necessary to provide the client with competent representation.[14]

In short, communication between a lawyer and a client is both the means by which a client is provided with the advice and explanations needed to make informed decisions and the vehicle through which the lawyer obtains information required to address the client's legal matter appropriately.

---

11. Model Rules of Prof'l Conduct R. 1.4(a).

12. Model Rules of Prof'l Conduct R. 1.4(b) & cmt. [5]. *See* N.H. Bar Ass'n Ethics Comm., Advisory Op. 2009-10/02 (2010) (obligations of Rule 1.4 "require that the attorney and the client be able to exchange information and understand one another").

13. Model Rules of Prof'l Conduct R. 1.1 cmt. [5] ("Competent handling of a matter includes inquiry into and analysis of the factual and legal elements of the problem . . .."). *See* N.H. Bar Ass'n Ethics Comm., Advisory Op. 2009-10/02 (2010) (noting that attorney's obligation to provide competent representation to clients requires that the attorney gather sufficient facts regarding the client's problem from the client and that the attorney develop a strategy, in consultation with the client, for solving the legal problems of the client); State Bar of Cal., Formal Op. 1984-77 (1984) (sensitivity to a non-English or limited English-speaking client's communication barriers in explaining their legal problem and in understanding legal advice provided is an important aspect of competence); Alex B. Long, *Reasonable Accommodation As Professional Responsibility, Reasonable Accommodation As Professionalism*, 47 U.C. Davis L. Rev. 1753, 1760 (2014) ("Competent representation lies at the heart of every lawyer's professional obligation to clients. Law firms should view the reasonable accommodation requirement as a means of complying with this obligation.").

14. *See* N.Y. City Bar Formal Op. 1995-12 (1996) (noting that adequate preparation requires that a lawyer gather information material to the client's claims or defenses: "The lawyer's inability, because of a language barrier, to understand fully what the client is telling him or her may unnecessarily impede the lawyer's ability to gather the information from the client needed to familiarize the lawyer with the circumstances of the case.").

In general, the information that must be provided when discharging the duty to explain a matter reasonably is "that appropriate for a client who is a *comprehending* and responsible adult."[15] The Model Rule 1.1 and 1.4 obligations do not change when a client's ability to receive information from or convey information to a lawyer is impeded because the lawyer and the client do not share a common language, or when a client is a person with a non-cognitive physical condition, such as a hearing, speech, or vision disability.[16]

If communications issues are such that the client cannot adequately comprehend the lawyer's advice and other communications, and thus, cannot participate intelligently in the representation, or the lawyer is unable to ascertain the information needed to competently assist the client, the lawyer must take measures to establish a reasonably effective mode of communication. Ordinarily, this will require engagement of a qualified impartial interpreter or translator (or, in some situations, the use of an appropriate assistive or language-translation device) so that the lawyer and client can reasonably understand one another to a degree that is compatible with the lawyer's professional obligations.[17]

---

15. Model Rules of Prof'l Conduct R. 1.4 cmt. [6] (emphasis added). Comment [6] addresses the impracticability of this standard when the client is a child or suffers from diminished capacity. Duties arising from representation of a client with diminished capacity are governed by Model Rule 1.14. *See generally* ABA Comm. on Ethics & Prof'l Responsibility, Formal Op. 96-404 (Client Under a Disability) (1996). This opinion does not address the manifold ethics issues that arise when representing a client with diminished capacity, except to the extent that there are language, speech, hearing, or visual considerations also affecting the reciprocal exchange of information between lawyer and client.

16. *See* State Bar of Ariz. Op. 97-05 (1997) (presence of interpreters to facilitate communication between lawyers and clients who do not share a common language furthers the purposes of Rule 1.4); Utah Ethics Advisory Op. Comm., No. 96-06 (1996) ("A language barrier does not reduce the attorney's duty to communicate adequately with the client, as required by Rule 1.4."); N.Y. City Bar Formal Op. 1995-12 (1996) (Rule 1.4 obligation applies to client with whom the only means of effective communication is through a sign language interpreter).

17. *See* N.Y. City Bar Formal Op. 1995-12 (1996) (a language barrier may make the use of an interpreter "the only practical way that a free-flowing dialogue can be maintained with the client, and the only means by which the lawyer can actually and substantially assist the client"); N.H. Bar Ass'n Ethics Comm., Advisory Op. 2009-10/02 (2010) ("When the attorney cannot communicate directly and fluently with the client in a language that the client can understand—whether the inability to engage in a direct communication is because the attorney and the client do not speak the same language, or because either the client or attorney is deaf or hearing impaired—the attorney must make use of the services of a qualified, impartial interpreter"); Utah Ethics Advisory Op. Comm., No. 96-06 (1996) ("If the attorney cannot communicate fluently in the client's own language, the attorney should communicate through an interpreter skilled in the client's particular language or dialect.").

A. Evaluating Whether an Interpreter or Translator Is Required

Once a lawyer determines that there is a language-access issue affecting the ability to communicate sufficiently with a client, the lawyer must evaluate whether engagement of an interpreter, translator, and/or the use of other assistive or language-translation technologies is needed to satisfy the lawyer's professional obligations.[18] This is true regardless of whether the language-access issue is attributable to limited language proficiency or a non-cognitive disability.[19]

Ordinarily, the mode of communication to be used during a representation is a matter to be decided between the lawyer and the client,[20] and, in the case of language-access issues, consultation with the client is appropriate if possible. A lawyer may not, however, passively leave the decision to the client or thrust the responsibility to make arrangements for interpretation or translation entirely upon the client.[21] Once it is reasonably apparent that, without an interpreter, translator, or an appropriate assistive or language-translation device, there cannot be a reliably understandable reciprocal exchange of information between the lawyer and the client, the lawyer must take steps to help the client understand the need for and purpose of an interpreter or translator, and, when reasonably necessary, take steps to secure such services.[22]

In this as in other contexts requiring client-lawyer communication, it is the lawyer's affirmative responsibility[23] to ensure the client understands

18. *See* N.Y. City Bar Formal Op. 1995-12 (1996) ("When the need for an interpreter is apparent or it is reasonable to conclude that an interpreter is required for effective communication, failure to take steps with the client to secure an interpreter may be a breach of the duty to represent the client competently.").

19. *See* N.H. Bar Ass'n Ethics Comm., Advisory Op. 2009-10/02 (2010); N.Y. City Bar Formal Op. 1995-12 (1996).

20. Model Rules of Prof'l Conduct R. 1.2(a) (a lawyer shall consult with the client as to the means by which the objectives of the representation are to be pursued).

21. Attorney Grievance Comm'n v. Aita, 181 A. 3d 774 (Md. 2016) (lawyer failed to fulfill obligation to enable client to make informed decision by sending a letter in English to client who did not read or write in English and telling client to get letter translated); N.Y. City Bar Formal Op. 1995-12 (1996) ("once the lawyer agrees to represent a client with whom effective and meaningful direct communications can only be maintained through an interpreter, the need for qualified interpreter services cannot be ignored").

22. *See* State Bar of Cal., Formal Op. 1984-77 (1984) (though client may have selected the lawyer knowing that direct communication may be limited, or even not possible, this does not reduce the lawyer's duty to communicate adequately).

23. The ADA generally obligates the lawyer to bear the cost of procuring such services when they are necessary to accommodate a disability. *See* note 5, *supra*. In other language-access situations, lawyers should confer with the prospective client about the expense of providing needed language access and address the issue of responsibility for that expense in the initial fee agreement. *See* Model Rules of Prof'l Conduct R. 1.5(a) & (b) & cmt. 2 (prohibiting unreasonable amounts for expenses and requiring the basis for expenses for which the client will be responsible be communicated to the client; noting desirability of furnishing client with a writing that states "to what extent the client will be responsible for any costs, expenses or disbursements").

the lawyer's communications and that the lawyer understands the client's communications.[24] In situations where there is doubt about the efficacy of client-lawyer communication, that doubt should be resolved in favor of engagement of an interpreter, translator, or an appropriate assistive or language-translation device.[25] Furthermore even in situations when an interpreter is used to facilitate spoken communication between a lawyer and a client, it may also be necessary to secure the translation of specific written documents to satisfy the duties of communication and competence in a particular case.[26]

B. Qualifications of a Person Providing Translation or Interpretive Services

In general, an individual engaged to facilitate communication between a lawyer and a client must be qualified to serve as an interpreter or translator in the language or mode required, familiar with and able to explain the law and legal concepts in that language or mode, and free of any personal or other potentially conflicting interest that would create a risk of bias or prevent the individual from providing detached and impartial interpretive or translation services.

In assessing the qualifications of a prospective interpreter or translator, a lawyer should verify that the individual is skilled in the particular language or dialect required. In addition, the lawyer should confirm that the individual has the expertise needed to comprehend the legal concepts/terminology

---

24. *See* State Bar of Cal., Formal Op. 1984-77 (1984) ("On any matter which requires client understanding, the attorney must take all reasonable steps to insure that the client comprehends the legal concepts involved and the advice given, irrespective of the mode of communication used, so that the client is in a position to make an informed decision.").

25. Even if a client speaks *some* English in informal contexts, an interpreter may be needed to ensure that the client understands the legal concepts involved in client-lawyer communications. *See In re* Welke, 131 N.E.3d 161, 163 (Ind. 2019) (respondent violated Rule 1.4 by failing to hire an interpreter to communicate with client with "extremely poor English language skills"; court rejected respondent's argument, based on testimony of a kitchen supervisor at the client's workplace, that the "client may have had a marginally better English-language proficiency than other evidence indicated" on grounds that communicating with a supervisor of a kitchen staff and communicating about legal matters are very different things); Attorney Grievance Comm'n of Maryland v. Landeo, 132 A.3d 196, 215 (Md. 2016) (in representing an immigration client who could speak English but preferred Spanish, lawyer failed to comply with Rule 1.4 obligations by sending client documents and letters about her Abused Spouse Petition and Adjustment of Status without explaining process to client).

26. State Bar of Cal., Formal Op. 1984-77 (1984) (providing as examples a contingent fee agreement, a general release of claims, or a written consent to a conflict of interest).

at issue so that the legal advice being provided is communicated accurately in a language or format accessible to the client.[27]

In most situations, the verification of a prospective interpreter's or translator's level of skill and capacity to convey legal concepts is best achieved through engagement of the services of an outside professional to assist the lawyer in the delivery of legal services.[28] Depending on the circumstances, alternative arrangements may suffice.[29] For example, a lawyer may look to a multilingual lawyer or nonlawyer staff member within the firm to facilitate communication with a client. If a nonprofessional interpreter is contemplated, however, the lawyer should proceed cautiously in light of the reduced ability to assess the nonprofessional's level of proficiency and the concomitant increased risk of inaccuracies in interpretation or translation.[30]

In some instances, a client's friend or a family member may function as a viable interpreter or translator.[31] But particular care must be taken when using a client's relatives or friends because of the substantial risk that an individual in a close relationship with the client may be biased by a personal interest in the outcome of the representation.[32] In such situations, a lawyer must exercise appropriate diligence to guard against the risk that the lay-

27. *See* N.H. Bar Ass'n Ethics Comm., Advisory Op. 2009-10/02 (2010).

28. A lawyer should be able to verify a prospective translator's or interpreter's professional qualifications in the same manner used when engaging the services of an expert, i.e., by evaluating the individual's training, experience, certifications, and professional standing. *See* N.Y. City Bar Formal Op. 1995-12 (1996) (noting "obvious benefits to communicating through professionals, who have formal training in languages, experience with legal terminology and concepts, and skill" and who provide greater assurance of accuracy in translation because often they belong to professional associations that adhere to professional and ethical standards); N.H. Bar Ass'n Ethics Comm., Advisory Op. 2009-10/02 (2010).

29. "The Rules of Professional Conduct are rules of reason. They should be interpreted with reference to the purposes of legal representation and the law itself." Model Rules of Prof'l Conduct Preamble, Scope [14].

30. N.Y. City Bar Formal Op. 1995-12 (1996). The mere fact that the person selected is bilingual is insufficient to establish compliance with the lawyer's ethical duties. The person must have a reasonable degree of competence and fitness to serve as an interpreter or translator. *See In re* Welke, 131 N.E.3d 161, 163 (Ind. 2019) (failure to hire appropriate interpreter violated Rule 1.4(b) when lawyer "brought an untrained and unpaid woman who needed community service credit for her own criminal conviction to serves as an interpreter, and through that woman . . . attempted to [discuss client's case]").

31. *See* Attorney Grievance Comm'n of Maryland v. Ibebuchi, 241 A.3d 870, 881 (Md. 2020) (holding respondent did not violate Rule 1.4(b) "in connection with the language barrier issue" with Spanish-speaking client where client relied on a friend to interpret at every client meeting because client "trusted" friend).

32. *See* N.H. Bar Ass'n Ethics Comm., Advisory Op. 2009-10/02 (2010) (using relatives or friends of clients as interpreters carries substantial risks).

interpreter is distorting or altering communications in a way that skews the information provided to the lawyer or the advice given to the client.[33] Lacking accountability to the lawyer or firm derived from an employment or other contractual relationship, relatives and friends of the client may also be less reliable in providing interpretation or translation services when needed.[34]

Finally, if obtaining necessary services would place an unreasonable financial burden on the lawyer or the client[35] or if necessary services are unavailable, the lawyer should ordinarily decline or withdraw from the representation[36] or associate with a lawyer or law firm that can appropriately address the language-access issue,[37] such as a multilingual lawyer. In an emergency situation where the need for legal action is exigent—for example, if a client or potential client is subject to an expedited removal action in an immigration proceeding—and the lawyer reasonably believes that necessary interpretive services cannot obtained expeditiously, a lawyer should take steps to prevent immediate and irreparable harm to the client.[38]

---

33. *See* Utah Ethics Advisory Op. Comm., No. 96-06 (1996) (lawyer must be "cautious in insuring [*sic*] that the attorney and client are communicating with each other through the interpreter, rather than the interpreter giving legal advice independent of the attorney"). N.H. Bar Ass'n Ethics Comm., Advisory Op. 2009-10/02 (2010) (lawyer "should watch for cues that indicate that the interpreter is speaking for the client or filtering the attorney's statements rather than impartially conveying the communications"). In these situations, it would be prudent for the lawyer to consult with the client about the risks and benefits of using a family member as an interpreter or translator. *See* Model Rules of Prof'l Conduct R. 1.2, cmt. 1 ("With respect to the means by which the client's objectives are to be pursued, the lawyer shall consult with the client as required by Rule 1.4(a)(2) . . . ."). The Committee recognizes the potential circularity of this dilemma, which further suggests that use of the client's friends or family members to solve a language access problem is ethically fraught.

34. *Cf. In re* Howe, 843 N.W.2d 325, 331 (N.D. 2014) (rejecting lawyer's defense that he "tried to communicate the date, but confusion persisted because the [client's] daughter was not there to translate," and holding that "[r]easonable efforts to ensure the client is informed of the status of the matter include assuring the [clients] understood their hearing was rescheduled despite their daughter not being available to translate").

35. Model Rules of Prof'l Conduct R. 1.16(b)(6) (authorizing withdrawal if representation "will result in an unreasonable financial burden on the lawyer").

36. Model Rules of Prof'l Conduct R. 1.16(a)(1).

37. Model Rules of Prof'l Conduct R. 1.1 cmt. [2] ("Competent representation can also be provided through the association of a lawyer of established competence in the field in question.").

38. *See, e.g.*, Model Rules of Prof'l Conduct R. 1.14 cmt. [9] (authorizing lawyer to take emergency legal action on behalf of person with seriously diminished capacity where person's health, safety, or a financial interest is threatened with imminent and irreparable harm, even though person is unable to establish a client-lawyer relationship or to make or express considered judgments about matter, but only to extent reasonably necessary to maintain status quo or otherwise avoid imminent and irreparable harm).

C. Supervisory Duties When Engaging or Directing the Work of a Translator or Interpreter

Model Rule 5.3 governs a lawyer's responsibilities for nonlawyers employed, retained by, or associated with a lawyer. In general, a lawyer is responsible to ensure that the conduct of a nonlawyer service provider is compatible with the professional obligations of the lawyer.[39] This principle applies with equal force to individuals serving as interpreters or translators to facilitate communications within the client-lawyer relationship, i.e., the lawyer must make reasonable efforts to ensure that the interpretive or translation services are provided in a manner that is compatible with the lawyer's ethical obligations, particularly the Rule 1.6 duty of confidentiality.[40]

In this regard, the terms of any arrangement between the lawyer and the interpreter or translator should address the protection of client information, and when retaining or directing the work of an interpreter or translator, the lawyer should communicate directions appropriate under the circumstances to give reasonable assurance that the interpreter or translator understands the lawyer's ethical duty of confidentiality and agrees to abide by it.[41]

D. Guidance Regarding Social and Cultural Differences

In addressing language access issues within the client-lawyer relationship, the duty of competence requires close attention to social and cultural differences that can affect a client's understanding of legal advice, legal concepts, and other aspects of the representation.[42] When a lawyer and a client do not share a common language, there may be other significant cultural differences bearing on the representation including, but not limited to, ethnicity, religion, and national origin.[43] The client may view the representation and choices it entails through the lens of cultural and social perspectives that are not shared by or familiar to the lawyer. Beyond language differences, the ability to understand, effectively communicate, gather information, and attribute meaning from behavior and expressions are all affected by cultural

---

39. Model Rules of Prof'l Conduct R. 5.3 cmt. [1].

40. N.H. Bar Ass'n Ethics Comm., Advisory Op. 2009-10/02 (2010) ("Attorneys representing clients through interpreters should ensure that the interpreter has a clear understanding of the obligation to keep the client's communications confidential.") (citing Utah Ethics Advisory Op. Comm., No. 96-06 (1996)).

41. *See* Model Rules of Prof'l Conduct R. 5.3 cmt. [3].

42. *See* Utah Ethics Advisory Op. Comm., No. 96-06 (1996); *see also* Flowers v. Bd. of Prof'l Responsibility, 314 S.W.3d 882, 889 (Tenn. 2010) (imposing discipline, court found clients were "vulnerable victims" because they did not speak or write English and did not often have "a solid understanding of the broader culture").

43. For an overview of the impact of implicit cultural bias on the delivery of legal services, see Debra Chopp, *Addressing Cultural Bias in the Legal Profession*, 41 N.Y.U. Rev. Law & Social Change 367 (2017).

experiences.[44] Competently mediating these differences to achieve the ends of the representation for the client requires: (i) identifying these differences; (ii) seeking to understand them and how they bear upon the representation; (iii) paying attention to implicit bias and other cognitive biases that can distort understanding; (iv) adapting the framing of questions to help elicit information relating to the representation in context-sensitive ways; (v) explaining the matter in multiple ways to promote better client insight and comprehension; (vi) "allow[ing] for additional time for client meetings and ask[ing] confirming questions to assure that information is being exchanged accurately and completely";[45] and (vii) conducting additional research or drawing upon the expertise of others when that is necessary to ensure effective communication and mutual understanding.[46]

A lawyer should not assume that a translator has this deeper cultural expertise merely because the translator is adept with the client's language. Awareness of, and ability to understand, issues of culture and disability that might affect communication techniques and influence client objectives is inextricably intertwined with providing effective legal advice to a client. Communication is a two-way street. To convey information about the representation in a meaningful way, it is essential that the lawyer understands the client and the client understands the lawyer. Client-lawyer communication is not merely a translation of words but a determination by the lawyer that the client understands the relevant law and legal, institutional, and social contexts of the communication.

III. Conclusion

A lawyer's fundamental obligations of communication and competence are not diminished when a client's ability to receive information from or convey information to a lawyer is impeded because the lawyer and the client do not share a common language, or owing to a client's non-cognitive physical condition, such as a hearing, speech, or vision disability. Under such circumstances, a lawyer may be obligated to take measures appropriate to the client's situation to ensure that those duties are properly discharged. When reasonably necessary, a lawyer should arrange for communications to take place through an impartial interpreter or translator capable of comprehending and accurately explaining the legal concepts involved, and who will assent to and abide by the lawyer's duty of confidentiality. In addition, particularly when there are language considerations

44. *See* Susan Bryant, *The Five Habits: Building Cross-Cultural Competence in Lawyers*, CUNY School of Law (2001) [hereinafter *The Five Habits*], *available at* https://academicworks.cuny.edu/cgi/viewcontent.cgi?article=1257&context=cl_pubs.

45. N.H. Bar Ass'n Ethics Comm., Advisory Op. 2009-10/02 (2010).

46. *The Five Habits*, *supra* note 44.

affecting the reciprocal exchange of information, a lawyer must ensure that the client understands the legal significance of translated or interpreted communications and that the lawyer understands the client's communications, bearing in mind potential differences in cultural and social assumptions that might impact meaning.

AMERICAN BAR ASSOCIATION
STANDING COMMITTEE ON ETHICS AND PROFESSIONAL RESPONSIBILITY

Formal Opinion 501 **April 13, 2022**
Solicitation

ABA Model Rule of Professional Conduct 7.3(a), amended in 2018, contains a narrowed definition of what constitutes a "solicitation." Rule 7.3(b) delineates the type of solicitation that is expressly prohibited. Rules 8.4(a) and 5.3 extend a lawyer's responsibility for solicitation prohibitions not only to actions carried out by the lawyer directly but also to the acts of persons employed by, retained by, or associated with the lawyer under certain circumstances.

Rule 5.3(b) requires lawyer supervisors to make reasonable efforts to ensure that all persons employed, retained, or associated with the lawyer are trained to comply with the Rules of Professional Conduct, including Rule 7.3(b)'s prohibition. Partners and lawyers possessing comparable managerial authority in a law firm must make reasonable efforts to ensure that the firm has training that reasonably assures that nonlawyer employees' conduct is compatible with the professional obligations of lawyers. Under Rule 5.3(c), a lawyer will be responsible for the conduct of another if the lawyer orders or with specific knowledge of the conduct ratifies it, or if the lawyer is a manager or supervisor and knows of the conduct at a time when its consequences can be avoided or mitigated but fails to take reasonable remedial action.

Rule 8.4(a) makes it professional misconduct for a lawyer to "knowingly assist or induce another," to violate the Rules or knowingly do so through the acts of another. Failing to train a person employed, retained, or associated with the lawyer on Rule 7.3's restrictions may violate Rules 5.3(a), 5.3(b), and 8.4(a).

Many legal consumers obtain information about lawyers from acquaintances and other professionals. The Model Rules of Professional Conduct are rules of reason. Recommendations or referrals by third parties who are not employed, retained, or similarly associated with the lawyer and whose communications are not directed to make specific statements to particular potential clients on behalf of a lawyer do not generally constitute "solicitation" under Rule 7.3.

Introduction

In 2018, the American Bar Association adopted amendments to ABA Model Rule of Professional Conduct 7.3, defining solicitation in the text of the rule and creating new exceptions to the general prohibition against live, person-to-person solicitation of legal services where a significant motive is "pecuniary gain."[1] The definition of solicitation under the current amended version of Model Rule 7.3 is:

> a communication initiated by or on behalf of a lawyer or law firm that is directed to a specific person the lawyer knows or reasonably should know needs legal services in a particular matter and that offers to provide, or reasonably can be understood as offering to provide, legal services for that matter.[2]

The ABA also amended the prohibition on solicitation to clarify that it applies only to "live person-to-person contact."[3] The reason for restricting such in-person face-to-face, live telephone, or other real-time communications between a lawyer and potential client is set forth in Comment [2] to Rule 7.3:

> A potential for overreaching exists when a lawyer, seeking pecuniary gain, solicits a person known to be in need of legal services. This form of contact subjects a person to the private importuning of the trained advocate in a direct interpersonal encounter. The person, who may already feel overwhelmed by the circumstances giving rise to the need for legal services, may find it difficult to fully evaluate all available alternatives with reasoned judgment and appropriate self-interest in the face of the lawyer's presence and insistence upon an immediate response. The situation is fraught with the possibility of undue influence, intimidation, and overreaching.

---

1. This opinion is based on the ABA Model Rules of Professional Conduct as amended by the ABA House of Delegates through August 2020. The laws, court rules, regulations, rules of professional conduct, and opinions promulgated in individual jurisdictions are controlling. This opinion addresses solely the ABA Model Rules. Lawyers should consult the rules, opinions, and cases of the jurisdiction(s) in which they are practicing. Some states have not adopted or have modified the ABA Model Rule and their definition of solicitation may differ. *See, e.g.*, Fla. Bar R. 4-7.18(a), which prohibits any in-person or telephone solicitation with a significant motive of pecuniary gain of any person with whom the lawyer has no prior family or professional relationship, regardless of whether the lawyer knows the person needs legal services.

2. Model Rules of Prof'l Conduct R. 7.3(a). Both "knows" and "reasonably should know" are defined terms in Rule 1.0 of the Model Rules. Knows means "denotes actual knowledge of the fact in question. A person's knowledge may be inferred from circumstances." Reasonably should know means "that a lawyer of reasonable prudence and competence would ascertain the matter in question."

3. Model Rules of Prof'l Conduct R. 7.3(b).

In addition to the other changes, the 2018 amendments broadened the exceptions to prohibited solicitation, and the Rule in paragraph (b) now permits solicitation by live person-to-person contact if the person contacted is a:

(1) lawyer;

(2) person who has a family, close personal, or prior business or professional relationship with the lawyer or law firm; or

(3) person who routinely uses for business purposes the type of legal services offered by the lawyer.

The Rule prohibits live person-to-person solicitation even when otherwise allowed if the person has made clear that the person does not want to be solicited by the lawyer or if "the solicitation involves coercion, duress or harassment" under paragraphs (c)(1) and (2).

However, the prohibition does not preclude any communication "authorized by law or ordered by a court or other tribunal,"[4] nor does it prohibit a lawyer from being part of a group or prepaid legal service plan owned by someone other than the lawyer that enlists new members or sells subscriptions via live person-to-person contact where it is not known the persons need the services covered by the plan.[5] The latter exception also existed in the pre-2018 version of Rule 7.3.

Despite the 2018 clarifications, ambiguity remains concerning a lawyer's ethical responsibility for the lawyer's actions and for the actions of others who engage in live, person-to-person solicitation with specific individuals. The scope of "others" who might solicit on behalf of a lawyer could include, for instance, current employees of the lawyer, marketing firms hired by the lawyer, existing clients, former clients, friends and family of the lawyer, or even professional colleagues such as bankers, real estate agents, and accountants. Traditionally, lawyers often have obtained new clients because the firm's existing clients tell their friends, business colleagues, or family members about positive lawyer-client experiences.[6] Many of these communications do not fall within the Rule 7.3 definition of "solicitation."

When analyzing the actions of others and whether the lawyer is responsible for those actions, Rule 8.4 and Rule 5.3 are relevant. Rule 8.4(a) provides that it is professional misconduct for a lawyer to "violate or attempt to vio-

---

4. Model Rules of Prof'l Conduct R. 7.3(d).

5. Model Rules of Prof'l Conduct R. 7.3(e).

6. *See, e.g.*, *2019 Clio Legal Trends Report*, Clio (2019), https://www.clio.com/resources/legal-trends/2019-report/ (noting that thirty-two percent of consumers surveyed sought lawyer referrals from friends and family and sixteen percent sought referrals from a lawyer).

late the Rules of Professional Conduct, knowingly assist or induce another to do so, or do so through the acts of another." In other words, a lawyer cannot do through another person that which the lawyer could not do directly. Rule 8.4(a) does not impose responsibility on a lawyer who has no knowledge of someone else's actions. For culpability the lawyer must "knowingly assist or induce another," or knowingly do so through the acts of another, which means, for the purpose of solicitation, the lawyer must knowingly permit, ask, direct, or encourage someone to solicit on the lawyer's behalf.

The Committee interprets Rule 8.4(a) as subjecting a lawyer to discipline for the conduct of another only if the lawyer knows of the other person's conduct and in some way requests or authorizes the conduct. This reading is consistent with agency principles. It would be manifestly unfair and illogical to hold a lawyer responsible for another's actions that the lawyer does not even know about. This reading is consistent with both *The Restatement of Law Governing Lawyers* § 5, *Professional Discipline,* and Hazard, Hodes & Jarvis, *The Law of Lawyering* § 69.05, 4th ed.

Model Rule 5.3 addresses a lawyer's responsibilities regarding nonlawyer assistance by persons employed or retained by or associated with the lawyer. Model Rule 5.3(b) requires lawyers with direct supervisory authority over a nonlawyer whom the lawyer employs, retains, or is associated with (collectively referred to as "employees" in this opinion for ease of reading) to make reasonable efforts to ensure that the nonlawyer's conduct is compatible with the professional obligations of the lawyer. Lawyers who are managers of firms[7] must ensure that the firm "has in effect measures giving reasonable assurances that the nonlawyer's conduct is compatible with the professional obligations of the lawyer."[8] A lawyer is responsible for ethics violations of an employee, according to Rule 5.3(c), but only if:

> (1) the lawyer orders or, with the knowledge of the specific conduct, ratifies the conduct involved; or
>
> (2) the lawyer is a partner or has comparable managerial authority in the law firm in which the person is employed, or has direct supervisory authority over the person, and knows of the conduct at a time when its consequences can be avoided or mitigated but fails to take reasonable remedial action.

Thus if a lawyer knows of specific unethical conduct by an employee and either directed that conduct, ratifies the conduct after the fact, or fails to take reasonable remedial measures after the fact, the lawyer violates Rule 5.3(c), among other rules.

---

7. Model Rules of Prof'l Conduct R. 1.0(c) (definition of a "firm").
8. Model Rules of Prof'l Conduct R 5.3(a).

Under Rule 5.3, a lawyer with supervisory responsibility over the nonlawyer employees must discuss ethical rules with these employees to ensure that they understand the limitations on their conduct imposed by the fact of their employment with the law firm. Just as a supervisory lawyer must explain the ethical duty of confidentiality to employees, the supervisory lawyer must likewise explain the requirements of Rule 7.3 to refrain from improper solicitation on behalf of the lawyer. However, what constitutes a prohibited "solicitation" on behalf of the lawyer versus merely making a recommendation about the lawyer can be complicated.

This opinion examines various solicitation scenarios, some of which involve employees and agents of lawyers, in light of the 2018 amendments to Model Rule 7.3, and provides guidance for lawyers in determining what activities are permissible.

Hypothetical 1

A lawyer obtains a list from the local sheriff of persons arrested within the last week, calls them on the telephone, and offers to provide general legal services. None of the arrestees are lawyers. The lawyer also does not personally or professionally know, nor is lawyer related to, any of the arrestees. Does the conduct violate Rule 7.3?

Answer: Yes. The conduct is prohibited solicitation under Rule 7.3(b). The communication was initiated by the lawyer. It was directed to specific persons whom the lawyer knows or reasonably should know need legal services in a particular matter. The communication offers to provide, or reasonably can be understood as offering to provide, legal services. The offer to provide "general legal services" reasonably can be understood by a prospective client as offering to provide legal services for a particular matter of which the lawyer has knowledge, i.e., the arrest. The communication by telephone was live and person-to-person, falling within the ambit of the Rule[9] and was made for the lawyer's pecuniary gain. None of the exceptions in Rule 7.3(b) are applicable. Therefore, the lawyer's conduct is prohibited solicitation.

Hypothetical 2

A lawyer with direct supervison over a law firm's marketing department hires a professional lead generator to obtain client leads. The lawyer signs an agreement with the lead generator to pay a flat monthly fee for leads in mass tort cases. The agreement includes no information on how the lead generator obtains leads, nor does the lawyer provide any direction or limitation on how the lead generator does so.

The lead generator pays its employees to "lurk" in online chat rooms set up for family members and survivors of aviation disasters, medical device and drug product liability matters, and other possible mass torts. The lead

9. Model Rules of Prof'l Conduct R. 7.3 cmt. [2].

generator also pays its employees to research the family members and survivors and telephone those persons to inform them of the lawyer's experience and availability in mass tort cases. The lead generator also asks these same persons if they would like to be represented in their cases.

The lawyer receives a report from the lead generator with a list of 10 new clients and says to the lead generator, "I don't know what you are doing, and I don't care! Keep 'em coming!" The lead generator responds, "We just call the people who are online discussing accidents." The lawyer does not inquire further, signs the clients sent by the lead generator, and continues to use the lead generator. Does the conduct violate any rules?

Answer: Yes. The telephone calls were initiated by the lead generator on behalf of the lawyer based on the contractual relationship between the lawyer and the lead generator. The telephone calls were directed to specific persons who the lawyer knows needed legal services in a particular matter. The lead generator's communications offered to provide, or reasonably could be understood as offering to provide, legal services for the matter.

The communications were live and person-to-person and made for the lawyer's pecuniary gain. Therefore, the communications were prohibited solicitations and did not qualify for any of the exceptions under Rule 7.3(b). The lawyer learned that the lead generator offered to provide legal services on the lawyer's behalf, using impermissible direct telephone solicitation, and still accepted the client leads. The lawyer therefore is responsible for the lead generator's conduct under Rules 7.3(b) and 8.4(a) when the lawyer accepted the clients, knowing they were obtained in contravention of Rule 7.3.

The lawyer, with direct supervison over the lead generator, has made no effort to ensure that the lead generator, specifically hired to generate clients, understood and would conform its actions to be compatible with the lawyer's professional obligations. By failing to train the lead generator concerning the limitations on direct solicitation contained in Rule 7.3, the lawyer violated Rule 5.3(b), and by accepting the leads, knowing they were generated through prohibited solicitiation, the lawyer ratified the conduct of which he had knowledge and violated Rule 5.3(c).[10] If the lawyer also was a partner or a lawyer with comparable managerial authority in the firm, Rule 5.3(a) would require the lawyer to "make reasonable efforts to ensure that the firm has in effect measures giving reasonable assurance that the person's conduct is compatible with the professional obligations of the lawyer."

Hypothetical 3

A paralegal at a law firm works as a paramedic on weekends. As part of the paralegal's employment agreement with the firm, the paralegal lists

10. The Committee notes that in Formal Op. 491 this Committee found a lawyer to have "knowledge" when the lawyer consciously, deliberately failed to inquire into the facts of a matter.

the paramedic work as outside employment. To explain away any perceived conflict, the paralegal maintains that "not only does the outside employment not conflict with law firm work, but *it also contributes by bringing in new firm business.*"

No lawyer at the law firm apprised the paralegal of any prohibitions or limitations on soliciting firm business. The paralegal hands the law firm's business cards to injured people transported by the ambulance from accident scenes and states that the firm handles accident cases and is available to help them. When the firm agrees to represent new clients, the firm requests that the new clients list where they heard about the firm. Several new clients state they received business cards from the paralegal during the paralegal's paramedic work.

After being told by the paralegal of how the law firm's cards were being distributed, the paralegal's direct supervisory lawyer congratulated the paralegal on bringing in new business and promised a bonus as a reward. Does the conduct violate any Rules?

Answer: The conduct is a prohibited solicitation under Rule 7.3(b). The paralegal initiated live person-to-person contact, on behalf of the law firm employer, with injured persons being transported from an accident scene whom the paralegal knew had a specific need for legal services. Further, the law firm ratified this solicitation by knowing how the clients were solicited and still accepting clients from the paralegal's solicitation. The paralegal's communications were for the pecuniary gain of the law firm, and the injured persons could reasonably have understood the communications as offering legal services.

None of the exceptions to the prohibition on live person-to-person solicitation in Rule 7.3(b) are present—employment as a paramedic is not the type of existing business or professional relationship that permits live, person-to-person solicitation.

No lawyer at the firm made any effort to train or ensure that the paralegal's conduct comported with the professional obligations of a lawyer. In fact, the paralegal's supervisory lawyer has knowledge of the specific conduct and has ratified the conduct by speaking of it approvingly and suggesting the paralegal would receive a bonus for bringing in new clients. Therefore the supervisory lawyer has violated Rules 5.3(b) and (c).

Because no partner or managing lawyer has in place measures giving reasonable assurances that nonlawyers' conduct is compatible with the professional obligations of the lawyer, they have violated Rule 5.3(a).[11]

Again, lawyers have an obligation to train employees of a law firm on the ethical obligations of the lawyers so that the nonlawyer employees' conduct comports with those ethical obligations. All employees of a law firm need training on such ethics topics as confidentiality, conflicts of interest,

11. For a full discussion of Rule 5.3 and the duties of partners, managers, and supervisory lawyers working with nonlawyer assistance, see ABA Comm. on Ethics & Prof'l Responsibility, Formal Op. 467 (2014).

communication requirements, diligence, avoiding the unauthorized practice of law, *and* refraining from impermissible "solicitation," among other things.

Because the supervisory lawyer has knowledge of the paralegal's actions, the supervisory lawyer also has violated Rule 8.4(a) by knowingly violating Rule 7.3 through the acts of another.[12]

Hypothetical 4

A lawyer asks a personal friend and colleague who is a banker to provide the lawyer's name and contact information to any banking customer or employee that the banker thinks might need an estate plan. Does the lawyer violate any Rules?

Answer: The conduct does not violate Rule 7.3 because the actions are not solicitation as defined by paragraph (a). The lawyer did not target a specific person the lawyer knew or reasonably should have known was in need of legal services in a particular matter, nor communicate or direct communications with that person. The lawyer has no authority over the banker's conduct, does not control either the content of any communication the banker makes nor even whether any communication occurs at all. The banker's communication with bank customers should not reasonably be construed as an offer to provide legal services, because the banker is not authorized to make that offer on behalf of the lawyer. The communication, if one occurs at all, is a recommendation, the type of "word-of-mouth" referral that is permissible under Rule 7.3. Moreover, because the lawyer is not directing what the banker should say and the banker's customers are not speaking directly to the lawyer, the lawyer's request to the banker is permissible.[13]

12. This opinion only addresses application of the ABA Model Rules to these scenarios. Lawyers also should be cognizant of any statutes or other law addressing solicitation. Solicitation can be barred or limited by law as well as rule. *See, e.g.*, 49 U.S.C. §1136(g)(2) (banning solicitation of victims or family members of air carrier accidents occurring in the U.S. by lawyers or their employees, agents, or representatives within 45 days of the accident); Fla. Stat. §877.02 (barring solicitation on behalf of lawyers by certain persons including a person "in any capacity attached to any hospital, sanitarium, police department, wrecker service or garage, prison or court, or for a person authorized to furnish bail bonds, investigators, photographers, insurance or public adjusters").

13. *See* Model Rules of Prof'l Conduct R. 7.3 cmt. [7] ("This Rule does not prohibit a lawyer from contacting representatives of organizations or groups that may be interested in establishing a group or prepaid legal plan for their members, insureds, beneficiaries or other third parties for the purpose of informing such entities of the availability of and details concerning the plan or arrangement which the lawyer or lawyer's firm is willing to offer. This form of communication is not directed to people who are seeking legal services for themselves. Rather, it is usually addressed to an individual acting in a fiduciary capacity seeking a supplier of legal services for others who may, if they choose, become prospective clients of the lawyer. Under these circumstances, the activity which the lawyer undertakes in communicating with such representatives and the type of information transmitted to the individual are functionally similar to and serve the same purpose as advertising permitted under Rule 7.2.").

Similarly lawyers who build their practices based on referrals by satisfied clients may suggest to clients that if they are happy with the lawyer's services, the clients should give the lawyer a favorable review online and let their friends and family know about the lawyer. Such satisfied client recommendations to the public or directly to the client's friends and family are permissible.

The Rule's concern about a potential client feeling pressured by live, person-to-person contact by a lawyer is not present where the banker's customers or the former clients' acquaintances receive information about the lawyer's services.

Many legal consumers obtain information about lawyers from acquaintances and/or other professionals such as bankers, accountants, and real estate agents.[14] The Rules of Professional Conduct are "rules of reason."[15] Recommendations or referrals by third parties who are not employees of a lawyer and whose communications are not directed to make specific statements to particular potential clients on behalf of a lawyer do not constitute "solicitations" under Rule 7.3. To suggest that Rule 7.3 prohibits a lawyer's colleagues in other professions or satisfied clients from providing information about a lawyer's services to other people is not realistic or consistent with the purpose of the Rule.

Conclusion

The current version of Model Rule 7.3(a) contains a narrowed definition of what constitutes a "solicitation." It is a "communication initiated by or on behalf of a lawyer that is directed to a specific person" that is known, or reasonably should be known, to be in need of "legal services in a particular matter *and* that offers to provide, or can reasonably be understood as offering to provide, legal services for that matter."

Rule 7.3(b) delineates the type of solicitation that is expressly prohibited—"live person-to-person contact when a significant motive for the lawyer's doing so is the lawyer's or law firm's pecuniary gain"—unless the potential client is one of the noted exceptions to that prohibition.

The prohibition applies not only to actions carried out by a lawyer directly but also to persons employed by, retained by, or associated with the lawyer under certain circumstances.

Lawyers with supervisory responsibility have a duty to supervise and train all persons employed, retained, or associated with the lawyer to ensure compliance with the Rules of Professional Conduct, including Rule 7.3(b)'s prohibition. Partners and lawyers possessing comparable managerial authority in a law firm must make reasonable efforts to ensure that the firm has

---

14. *See 2019 Clio Legal Trends Report*, *supra* note 6 (showing that nine percent of consumers surveyed found lawyer referrals from other professionals).

15. Model Rules of Prof'l Conduct, Preamble [14].

training that reasonably assures that nonlawyer employees' conduct is compatible with the professional obligations of lawyers. This includes training employees to refrain from impermissible solicitation of potential clients on a lawyer's behalf.

Under Rule 5.3, a lawyer will be responsible for the conduct of another if the lawyer orders, or with specific knowledge of the conduct ratifies it, or if the lawyer is a manager or supervisor and knows of the conduct at a time when its consequences can be avoided or mitigated but fails to take reasonable remedial action.

Under Rule 8.4(a) a lawyer must not "knowingly assist or induce another," to violate the rules or knowingly do so through the acts of another, which means, for the purpose of solicitation, that the lawyer must not knowingly permit, ask, direct, or encourage someone to engage in impermissible solicitation on the lawyer's behalf.

Satisfied clients or third parties not employed by the lawyer may share with others their opinions and recommendations about the lawyer. The lawyer may even request such appropriate communications by clients and others. Such satisfied client recommendations to the public or directly to the client's friends and family are permissible.

AMERICAN BAR ASSOCIATION
STANDING COMMITTEE ON ETHICS AND PROFESSIONAL RESPONSIBILITY

Formal Opinion 502 **September 28, 2022**

Communication with a Represented Person by a Pro Se Lawyer

Under Model Rule 4.2,[1] if a person is represented in a matter, lawyers for others in the matter may not communicate with that represented person about the subject of the representation but instead must communicate about the matter through the person's lawyer, unless the communication is authorized by law or court order or consented to by the person's lawyer.

When a lawyer is self-representing, i.e., pro se, that lawyer may wish to communicate directly with another represented person about the subject of the representation and may believe that, because they are not representing another in the matter, the prohibition of Model Rule 4.2 does not apply. In fact, both the language of the Rule and its established purposes support the conclusion that the Rule applies to a pro se lawyer because pro se individuals represent themselves and lawyers are no exception to this principle.

Accordingly, unless the pro se lawyer has the consent of the represented person's lawyer or is authorized by law or court order to communicate directly with the other represented person about the subject of the representation, such communication is prohibited. In this context, if direct pro se lawyer-to-represented person communication about the subject of the representation is desired, the pro se lawyer and counsel for the represented person should reach advance agreement on the permissibility and scope of any direct communications.

I. Introduction

Model Rule 4.2, Communication with Person Represented by Counsel, is commonly known as the "no-contact" or "anticontact" rule.[2] It has been part of the ABA Model Rules of Professional Conduct since their 1983 inception

1. This opinion is based on the ABA Model Rules of Professional Conduct as amended by the ABA House of Delegates through 2022. The laws, court rules, regulations, rules of professional conduct, and opinions promulgated in individual jurisdictions are controlling.

2. ELLEN J. BENNETT & HELEN W. GUNNARSON, ANNOTATED MODEL RULES OF PROFESSIONAL CONDUCT 454 (9th ed. 2019).

in largely its present form.[3] The rule is "universally followed" in American jurisdictions.[4] It provides as follows:

> In representing a client, a lawyer shall not communicate about the subject of the representation with a person the lawyer knows to be represented by another lawyer in the matter, unless the lawyer has the consent of the other lawyer or is authorized to do so by law or court order.

Viewed broadly, the rule requires that a lawyer's communications about a legal matter be routed through a represented person's lawyer; direct communication with the represented person about the subject of the representation is prohibited unless the lawyer has the consent of the represented person's lawyer or is authorized to engage in the communication by law or a court order. The rule "contributes to the proper functioning of the legal system" by preventing lawyers from overreaching, from interfering in other lawyers' relationships with their clients, and from eliciting protected information via "uncounselled disclosure."[5]

---

3. In 1995, an amendment proposed by the ABA Standing Committee on Ethics and Professional Responsibility changed the term "party" to "person" in the text of the rule and revised the Comment. In 2002, amendments proposed by the ABA Ethics 2000 Commission added a reference to "court order" in the text of the rule and revised the Comment. *See* Art Garwin, A Legislative History: The Development of the ABA Model Rules of Professional Conduct, 1982-2013, 558-66 (2013). Model Rule 4.2 can be traced back to Canon 9 of the 1908 ABA Canons of Professional Ethics, which stated that "[a] lawyer should not in any way communicate upon the subject of controversy with a party represented by counsel; much less should he undertake to negotiate or compromise the matter with him, but should deal only with his counsel." The concept carried forward into the 1969 ABA Model Code of Professional Responsibility, DR 7-104(A)(1), which provided that a lawyer should not "communicate . . . on the subject of the representation with a party he knows to be represented by a lawyer in that matter unless he has the prior consent of the lawyer representing such other party or is authorized by law to do so." *See* ABA Comm. on Ethics & Prof'l Responsibility, Formal Op. 95-396, at 3-4 (1995) (recounting long history of anti-contact rule); Geoffrey C. Hazard, Jr. & Dana Remus Irwin, *Toward A Revised 4.2 No-Contact Rule*, 60 Hastings L.J. 797, 799 (2009).

4. Restatement (Third) of the Law Governing Lawyers §99 cmt. b (2000) [hereinafter Restatement Third].

5. Model Rules of Prof'l Conduct R. 4.2 cmt. [1]; ABA Comm. on Ethics & Prof'l Responsibility, Formal Op. 95-396 (1995) ("the anti-contact rules provide protection of the represented person against overreaching by adverse counsel, safeguard the client-lawyer relationship from interference by adverse counsel, and reduce the likelihood that clients will disclose privileged or other information that might harm their interests"). *See also* Restatement Third, *supra* note 4 (purpose is to "protect against overreaching and deception of nonclients," protect "the relationship between the represented nonclient and that person's lawyer" and "assure [] the confidentiality of the nonclient's communications with the lawyer").

When a lawyer engages in self-representation in a legal matter in which that lawyer is personally involved, in other words, when a lawyer is acting pro se,[6] application of Model Rule 4.2 is less straightforward. Such a lawyer might not appear to be "representing a client" in the matter because the lawyer is acting solely on the lawyer's own behalf, i.e., "without a lawyer."[7] Moreover, the commentary to Rule 4.2 specifically states that "Parties to a matter may communicate directly with each other . . . ."[8] However, a pro se lawyer *is* representing a client. Pro se individuals represent themselves and lawyers are no exception to this principle.[9]

This opinion analyzes applicability of Model Rule 4.2 and the rationale for the anticontact rule in the context of a lawyer engaged in self-representation. The opinion also provides guidance on the advisability in these situations of reaching advance agreement on the permissibility and scope of any direct pro se lawyer-to-represented person communications.[10]

II. Analysis

Although the general prohibition of Model Rule 4.2 is ubiquitous in U.S. jurisdictions, as applied to pro se lawyers the scope of the rule is less clear.[11] Interpretation of the Rule in this circumstance involves consideration of both its plain language and policy purposes.

The language in the Rule that is primarily at issue in this analysis is its first clause: "*In representing a client*, a lawyer shall not . . . ."[12] The key evils in-

---

6. Pro se is defined as "For oneself; on one's own behalf; without a lawyer." Black's Law Dictionary (11th ed. 2019); *see also* definition of propria persona as "In his own person." *Id.*

7. Carl A. Pierce, *Variations on A Basic Theme: Revisiting the ABA's Revision of Model Rule 4.2 (Part II)*, 70 Tenn. L. Rev. 321, 325 (2003) ("On its face, the reference in the Rule to a lawyer 'representing a client' can be read to suggest a negative inference that it does not apply to communication by a lawyer who is acting pro se, or is represented by another lawyer, in a matter in which she is interested.").

8. Model Rules of Prof'l Conduct R. 4.2 cmt. [4].

9. *See* Ronald D. Rotunda & John S. Dzienkowski, Legal Ethics – The Lawyer's Deskbook on Professional Responsibility § 4.2-5 (2021-2022 ed.) ("when a lawyer represents himself pro se, Rule 4.2 can be interpreted to prohibit the lawyer-party from communicating directly with an opposing represented party"); *In re* Haley, 156 Wash. 2d 324, 338, 126 P.3d 1262, 1269 (2006) ("we hold that a lawyer acting pro se is 'representing a client' for purposes of RPC 4.2(a)").

10. This opinion does not address the related question of applicability of Rule 4.2 when a lawyer is represented by another lawyer and the represented lawyer wishes to communicate with another represented person about the matter.

11. Samuel J. Levine, *The Law and the "Spirit of the Law,"* 2015 Prof. Law. 1, 17 (2015) (noting the Model Rules do not expressly address a case in which a lawyer is proceeding as a pro se party to a matter) [hereinafter *Spirit of the Law*]; Margaret Raymond, *Professional Responsibility for the Pro Se Attorney*, 1 St. Mary's J. Legal Mal. & Ethics 2, 37 (2011) (issue of whether a lawyer who is pro se is constrained by the no-contact rule when the opposing party is represented by counsel was not explicitly addressed in Model Rule 4.2).

12. Model Rules of Prof'l Conduct R. 4.2 (emphasis added).

tended to be managed by Model Rule 4.2 are (1) overreaching and deception; (2) interference with the integrity of the client-lawyer relationship; and (3) elicitation of uncounselled disclosures, including inappropriate acquisition of confidential lawyer-client communications.[13] In the context of pro se lawyers, balanced against these policy goals is the principle that, as a general proposition, parties to a matter may communicate directly with each other.[14]

Yet, both the language of the Model Rule and its purpose lead to the conclusion that the no-contact rule applies to pro se lawyers. Pro se lawyers represent themselves as "a client," and direct pro se lawyer-to-represented person communication in such circumstances can result in a substantial risk of overreaching, disruption of the represented person's client-lawyer relationship, and acquisition of uncounselled disclosures. That risk outweighs the sometimes-salutary benefit of direct communication. That said, it is important to remember that Model Rule 4.2 applies only when a communication is "about the subject of the representation," i.e., the Rule is matter specific, and a lawyer may speak with another represented person about matters that do not constitute the subject of the representation. *See* Model Rules R. 4.2, cmt. [4] ("This Rule does not prohibit communication with a represented person, or an employee or agent of such a person, concerning matters outside the representation.").[15]

A. Model Rule 4.2 and Pro Se Lawyers

Application of the Rule 4.2 anticontact principle to pro se lawyers is a well-documented ethical dilemma. There are decades worth of disciplinary

---

13. *See* Model Rules of Prof'l Conduct R. 4.2 cmt. [1]; Restatement Third, *supra* note 4.

14. Model Rules of Prof'l Conduct R. 4.2 cmt. [4]. *See also* ABA Comm. on Ethics & Prof'l Responsibility, Formal Op. 92-362 (1992) (noting that Rule 4.2's prohibition on the lawyer does not purport to govern communications by the lawyer's client and observing that in some circumstances a lawyer is obligated to explain to the client the freedom to communicate with an opposing party).

15. Note, however, that perspectives can differ in this context about whether a lawyer's effort to communicate with a represented person is beyond the scope of the rule. *See In re* Steele, 181 N.E.3d 976 (Ind. 2022) (rejecting respondent's contention that an email was not "about the subject of the representation" but rather "spoke only of matters involving friendship," a contention that was belied both by the language of the email itself, which thrice explicitly requested that the adverse party bypass their lawyer, and by the context in which it was sent, after two weeks of unsuccessful discussions with opposing counsel and the filing of a lawsuit).

cases,[16] civil cases,[17] and ethics opinions[18] concluding that a lawyer acting in a pro se capacity may not communicate directly with a represented adversary or other represented person about the subject of the representation without the consent of that person's lawyer, unless the communication is authorized by law or court order.[19] These authorities reason that a pro se lawyer is "representing a client" for purposes of Model Rule 4.2, and that the policy underlying the prohibition makes it clear that such communications are "ripe with potential for overreaching and exploitation,"[20] and that "the integrity of the relationship between the represented person and counsel is not entitled to less protection merely because the lawyer is appearing pro se."[21]

Viewed in this light, it is not possible for a pro se lawyer to "take off the lawyer hat" and navigate around Rule 4.2 by communicating solely as a client. Consequently, the proposition, set forth in Comment [4] to Model Rule 4.2, that "[p]arties to a matter may communicate directly with each other"[22] does not apply to pro se lawyers. This proposition recognizes that, in general,

---

16. *In re* Steele, 181 N.E.3d 976 (Ind. 2022); The Florida Bar v. Faro, Report of Referee, Florida Bar File 2014-70, 913 (11J) (July 24, 2017), *available at* https://lsg.floridabar.org/dasset/DIVADM/ME/MPDisAct.nsf/DISACTVIEW/68D12AE245D19BFB852582AA000A78F3/$FILE/_461.PDF, aff'd as modified, Case No. SC16-1408, 2018 WL 4691179 (Fla. Sept. 28, 2018); *In re* Hodge, 407 P.3d 613 (Kan. 2017); Medina County Bar Association v. Cameron, 958 N.E.2d 138 (Ohio 2011); *In re* Lucas,789 N.W.2d 73 (N.D. 2010); *In re* Haley, 126 P.3d 1262 (Wash. 2006); *In re* Schaefer, 25 P.3d 191 (Nev. 2001); Vickery v. Comm'n for Lawyer Discipline, 5 S.W.3d 241 (Tex. Ct. App. 1999); Office of Disciplinary Counsel v. Donnell, 684 N.E.2d 36 (Ohio 1997); Runsvold v. Idaho State Bar, 925 P.2d 1118 (Idaho 1996); *In re* Smith, 861 P.2d 1013 (Or. 1993) (application to corporate representation); *In re* Segall, 509 N.E.2d 988 (Ill. 1987) (application to corporate representation).

17. Fichelson v. Skorupa, 13 Mass. L. Rptr. 458 (Mass. Super. Ct. July 31, 2001) (citing Annotated Model Rules of Professional Conduct (4th ed.)); Sandstrom v. Sandstrom, 880 P.2d 103 (Wyo. 1993).

18. Ala. State Bar Op. RO-85-52 (1985); Alaska Bar Ass'n Op. 95-7 (1995); D.C. Bar Op. 258 (1995); Haw. Disciplinary Bd. Op. 44 (2003); Mass. Bar Ass'n Op. 97-1 (1997); State Bar of Mich. Op. CI-1206 (1988); State Bar of Nev. Standing Comm. On Ethics & Prof 'l Responsibility, Formal Op. 8 (1987); N.Y. City Bar, Formal Op. 2011-01 (2011); Va. State Bar Op. 1527 (1993) (application to corporate representation); Va. State Bar Op. 1890 (2020).

19. Oregon has adopted a modified version of Model Rule 4.2 to address this issue. Or. Rules of Prof'l Conduct R. 4.2 ("In representing a client or the lawyer's own interests, a lawyer shall not communicate or cause another to communicate on the subject of the representation with a person the lawyer knows to be represented by a lawyer on that subject . . . .").

20. The Florida Bar v. Faro, Report of Referee, Florida Bar File 2014-70, 913 (11J), at 10 (July 24, 2017), https://lsg.floridabar.org/dasset/DIVADM/ME/MPDisAct.nsf/DISACTVIEW/68D12AE245D19BFB852582AA000A78F3/$FILE/_461.PDF, aff'd as modified, Case No. SC16-1408, 2018 WL 4691179 (Fla. Sept. 28, 2018).

21. *In re* Schaefer, 25 P.3d 191, 199 (Nev. 2001).

22. Model Rules of Prof'l Conduct R. 4.2 cmt. [4]; ABA Comm. on Ethics & Prof'l Responsibility, Formal Op. 11-461 (2011) ("Even though parties to a matter are represented by counsel, they have the right to communicate directly with each other.").

the rules of professional conduct establish limits on lawyer behavior, not that of their clients.[23]

The first clause of Model Rule 4.2—"*In representing a client,* a lawyer shall not . . . ."[24]—may be seen as creating an ambiguity as applied to lawyers representing themselves. The conclusion of many jurisdictions is more persuasive and consistent with the purposes of Model Rule 4.2.[25] A pro se lawyer is self-representing, i.e., "representing a client" for purposes of Model Rule 4.2. The risk in this situation of overreaching, disruption of the represented person's client-lawyer relationship, and acquisition of uncounselled disclosures, is acute, outweighing the potential benefit of direct client-to-client communication.[26] Accordingly, unless a pro se lawyer has the consent of the other

---

23. ABA Comm. on Ethics & Prof'l Responsibility, Formal Op. 92-362 (1992) (noting that Model Rule 4.2's prohibition on the lawyer does not purport to govern communications by the lawyer's client); RONALD D. ROTUNDA & JOHN S. DZIENKOWSKI, LEGAL ETHICS – THE LAWYER'S DESKBOOK ON PROFESSIONAL RESPONSIBILITY § 4.2-5 (2021-2022 ed.) ("The rule governs lawyer, not their clients . . . ."). It is well established, however, that a lawyer cannot direct client-to-client communication as a way of evading Model Rule 4.2's prohibition. *See* ABA Comm. on Ethics & Prof'l Responsibility, Formal Op. 11-461 (2011) (when advising a client about direct client-to-client communication, the line between permissible advice and impermissible assistance "must be drawn on the basis of whether the lawyer's assistance is an attempt to circumvent the basic purpose of Rule 4.2"). In the pro se lawyer situation, it is not feasible to parse the distinction between a lawyer acting as a lawyer and a lawyer acting as a client.

24. MODEL RULES OF PROF'L CONDUCT R. 4.2 (emphasis added).

25. *See, e.g.*, Md. Bar Ass'n Ethics Comm., *Can Pro Se Lawyer Speak with A Represented Party over the Objection of the Party's Lawyer?*, MD. B.J., Sept./Oct. 2006, at 57, 59 ("We believe the opinions that prohibit a lawyer from having contact with a represented party opponent to be the most persuasive."). We recognize that a handful of authorities, including the Restatement of the Law Governing Lawyers, have come to a different conclusion. *See* RESTATEMENT THIRD, *supra* note 4, cmt. e, at 73 ("[a] lawyer representing his or her own interests pro se may communicate with an opposing represented non-client on the same basis as any other principals."). The Reporter's Note, however, recognizes that "The position of the ABA ethics committee is probably contrary to that in the Section and Comment . . . ." *Id.* Reporter's Note on Illustration 3 (citing ABA Comm. on Ethics & Prof'l Responsibility, Informal Op. 982 (1967)). *See also In re* Benson, 275 Kan. 913, 918, 69 P.3d 544, 548 (2003); Texas Ethics Comm'n Advisory Op. 653 (Jan. 2016); Cal. Rules of Prof'l Conduct R. 4.2, cmt. 3 ("The rule also does not prohibit a lawyer who is a party to a legal matter from communicating on his or her own behalf with a represented person* in that matter."). *Cf.* N.Y. Rules of Prof'l Conduct R. 4.2(c) ("A lawyer who is acting pro se or is represented by counsel in a matter is subject to paragraph (a), but may communicate with a represented person, unless otherwise prohibited by law and unless the represented person is not legally competent, provided the lawyer or the lawyer's counsel gives reasonable advance notice to the represented person's counsel that such communications will be taking place.").

26. *See generally Spirit of the Law, supra* note 11 ("The methodologies courts have employed to expand the scope of the no-contact rule to include pro se lawyers exemplify the potential relevance of a spirt of the law approach for the interpretation of ethics codes."). Recognizing the significance of Rule 4.2's underlying public policy, an Illinois appellate court upheld application of Rule 4.2 to a non-lawyer pro se plaintiff in a civil case. *See* Ze-

represented person's lawyer or is authorized by law or court order to communicate directly with the other represented person about the subject of the representation, such communication is prohibited.[27]

B. Obtaining Consent for Client-to-Client Communication

In certain situations, otherwise prohibited client-to-client communications involving a pro se lawyer may be beneficial.[28] If a pro se lawyer wishes in good faith to communicate with another represented person about the subject of the representation, that lawyer should contact the represented person's counsel and seek to obtain consent, providing an opportunity for that lawyer to object, consent, or consent by agreement to conditions under which such communications are to take place. If a lawyer receives such a request from a pro se lawyer, it is prudent to discuss with the client in advance the advisability of such communication, along with the risks and benefits of such communication.[29] In some circumstances it may be appropriate to advise the client not to communicate with the pro se lawyer.

Although a lawyer's decision to consent to a pro se lawyer's communication with the lawyer's client is within the lawyer's discretion and will depend on the circumstances, there are certain situations in which direct communication between a pro se lawyer and the represented person are likely necessary or appropriate such that consenting to the communication makes sense.

Conversely, consenting to a communication where the pro se lawyer appears to be overreaching for a strategic advantage—such as seeking the communication for a concession to an extension of time to produce documents, renegotiating terms of an agreed-upon contract, or calling to elicit disclosures—is not advisable.

---

mater v. Village of Waterman, 157 N.E.3d 1069, 1074 (Ill. App. 2020) ("Protecting defendant under these circumstances also furthered public policy regarding the confidential and fiduciary nature of the attorney-client relationship.").

27. This conclusion is consistent with this Committee's 1967 analysis of Canon 9 of the former Canons of Professional Ethics. *See* ABA Comm. on Ethics & Prof'l Responsibility, Informal Op. 982 (1967) (attorney who is a defendant in a case may not settle the case directly with the plaintiff who is represented by counsel without the knowledge of the plaintiff's counsel).

28. *See* Att'y Grievance Comm'n of Maryland v. Trye, 444 Md. 201, 221, 118 A.3d 980, 991 (2015) (noting that "direct communication between the principals—leaving the lawyers out of the room—is sometimes the path to settlement of a dispute").

29. *See* ABA Comm. on Ethics & Prof'l Responsibility, Formal Op. 92-362 (1992) (in some circumstances a lawyer is obligated to explain to the client the freedom to communicate with an opposing party).

Advance agreements between counsel for the represented person and the pro se lawyer are important to avoid disputes about compliance and ensure no disruption of Model Rule 4.2's protections. Thus, the agreement should be clear about the scope of any direct pro se lawyer-to-represented person communications. It would be prudent to memorialize the agreement in writing.

III. Conclusion

Under Model Rule 4.2, in representing a client, a lawyer may not communicate with a person the lawyer knows is represented by counsel about the subject of the representation, unless that person's counsel has consented to the communication, or the communication is authorized by law or court order. When a lawyer is participating in a matter pro se, that lawyer is engaged in self-representation and is therefore subject to Model Rule 4.2's prohibition.

Dissent

I must respectfully dissent from the conclusion of the well-written majority opinion because I cannot agree that "both the language of the Model Rule and its purpose lead to the conclusion that the no-contact rule applies to pro se lawyers." While the *purpose* of the rule would clearly be served by extending it to self-represented lawyers, its language clearly prohibits such application. Again, Model Rule 4.2 states:

> *In representing a client,* a lawyer shall not communicate about the subject of the representation with a person the lawyer knows to be represented by another lawyer in the matter, unless the lawyer has the consent of the other lawyer or is authorized to do so by law or court order. [Emphasis added.]

Our majority opinion thoughtfully and candidly discusses the split of authority interpreting the rule. It is not uncommon for ethics committees to weigh in when there is such a split. But it is, I hope, unusual for a committee to nullify plain language through interpretation, especially when the committee has jurisdiction to propose rule amendments.

The interpretation of our majority opinion and the ethics and discipline opinions cited therein depend upon the conclusion that, "A pro se lawyer is self-representing, i.e., 'representing a client' for purposes of Model Rule 4.2." Majority Opinion, at p. 5. This logic provides the rationale for cases holding that the rule applies to pro se lawyers.[1] The number of opinions following

1. *See, e.g., In re* Haley, 126 P.3d 1262 (Wash. 2006) (forthrightly summarizing authorities and all of the reasons one might think the rule means what it says, but noting that jurisdictions considering the question "have generally concluded that the policies underlying

this approach is not convincing if the analysis is not persuasive; error compounded is still error.

Applying Rule 4.2 to pro se lawyers is supported by compelling policy arguments. It is not the result I object to, it is the mode of rule construction that I cannot endorse. Self-representation is simply not "representing a client," nor will an average or even sophisticated reader of these words equate the two situations. See *In re Haley*, 126 P.3d 1262, 1267, 1272 (Wash. 2006) (majority and concurring opinions referencing definitions and authorities). Rather, this is an "ingenious bit of legal fiction." *Haley*, at p. 1272 (Sanders, J., concurring). Further, this approach to construing the rule's language renders the phrase "in representing a client" surplusage, contrary to a basic canon of construction.[2]

It is also simply wrong to perpetuate language that *was* clear but has been made misleading by opinions effectively reading that language out of the rule. When an attorney consults the rule, it is highly unlikely that the phrase "in representing a client" will be considered to include self-representation. If the attorney goes further and consults Comment [4], the Comment will assure the attorney that, "Parties to a matter may communicate directly with each other." Given this apparent clarity, what will tip off the attorney that further research is required? The lesson here must be that nothing is clear. Clear text cannot be relied upon but may only be understood by reading ethics opinions and discipline decisions. Does the text mean what it actually says, as it does in Connecticut, Kansas, and Texas?[3] Or, does it mean what we wish it said, as several other states have declared?

---

the rule are better served by extending the restriction to lawyers acting pro se"). *See also* Runsvold v. Idaho State Bar, 129 Idaho 419, 421, 925 P.2d 1118, 1120 (1996) ("We thus construe the phrase of Rule 4.2, 'in representing a client' to include the situation in which an attorney is acting pro se because this interpretation better effectuates the purpose of Rule 4.2.").

2. *See* "Surplusage canon," BLACK'S LAW DICTIONARY (11th ed. 2019) ("if possible, every word and every provision in a legal instrument is to be given effect"), citing ANTONIN SCALIA & BRYAN A. GARNER, READING LAW: THE INTERPRETATION OF LEGAL TEXTS 174 (2012) ("it is no more the court's function to revise by subtraction than by addition").

3. *See* Pinsky v. Statewide Grievance Comm., 216 Conn. 228, 236, 578 A.2d 1075, 1079 (1990) ("plaintiff's letter was a communication between litigants and that the plaintiff had a right to make such a communication because he was not representing a client"); *In re* Benson, 275 Kan. 913, 918, 69 P.3d 544, 548 (2003) ("violation of KRPC 4.2 was not shown to have occurred, as the rule applies only to acts done '[i]n representing a client.'"); and Texas Comm. on Prof'l Ethics Op. 653 (2016) ("Under the Texas Disciplinary Rules of Professional Conduct, a lawyer who is a party in a legal matter but who does not represent any other party in the matter may communicate concerning the matter directly with a represented adverse party without the consent of the adverse party's lawyer.").

Model Rule 4.2's plain language making it applicable only to lawyers who represent clients has also been recognized by the Restatement,[4] cases applying the rule prospectively because to do otherwise would amount to a deprivation of due process,[5] and by courts modifying the Model Rule to make it expressly applicable to pro se lawyers.[6]

Thoughtful commentators have identified the problems with Model Rule 4.2's language and inconsistent interpretations, and have recommended fixing the rule rather than straining to achieve its purposes when lawyers represent themselves.[7] By leaving this rule in place, we are also leaving in place a trap. The rule should be amended to achieve the result advocated for in the majority opinion.

Mark Armitage
Robinjit Eagleson

---

4. Restatement (Third) of the Law Governing Lawyers §99(1)(b), and cmt. (e) thereto ("A lawyer representing his or her own interests pro se may communicate with an opposing represented nonclient on the same basis as other principals").

5. *See, e.g., In re* Discipline of Shaeffer, 25 P.3d 191, 199-202 (Nev. 2001), and *In re* Disciplinary Proceeding Against Haley, 156 Wash. 2d 324, 1267-69; 126 P.3d 1262 (2006).

6. *See, e.g.,* Or. Rules of Prof'l Conduct R. 4.2: "In representing a client *or the lawyer's own interests,* a lawyer shall not communicate . . ." (emphasis added).

7. *See, e.g.,* Carl A. Pierce, *Variations on A Basic Theme: Revisiting the ABA's Revision of Model Rule 4.2 (Part II),* 70 Tenn. L. Rev. 321, 324-329 (2003) (tracing the Ethics 2000 Commission's failure to address the problem pointed out by the author and others and recommending that states adopt a rule with language clearly prohibiting contact by pro se lawyers); Margaret Raymond, *Professional Responsibility for the Pro Se Attorney,* 1 St. Mary's J. Legal Mal. & Ethics 2, 38 (2011) (recognizing the split, asserting that the rule does not answer the question and consulting the purpose should be done, but stating: "It would, of course, be optimal for rule drafters to consider explicitly whether particular rules apply to pro se lawyers."); and Geoffrey C. Hazard, Jr. & Dana Remus Irwin, *Toward A Revised 4.2 No-Contact Rule,* 60 Hastings L.J. 797, 831 (2009) (also recognizing this mess and concluding: "We therefore propose changing the text of the Rule from 'In representing a client, a lawyer shall not . . . .' to 'A lawyer participating in a matter shall not . . . .'").

AMERICAN BAR ASSOCIATION
STANDING COMMITTEE ON ETHICS AND PROFESSIONAL RESPONSIBILITY

Formal Opinion 503 **November 2, 2022**

"Reply All" in Electronic Communications

In the absence of special circumstances, lawyers who copy their clients on an electronic communication sent to counsel representing another person in the matter impliedly consent to receiving counsel's "reply all" to the communication. Thus, unless that result is intended, lawyers should not copy their clients on electronic communications to such counsel; instead, lawyers should separately forward these communications to their clients. Alternatively, lawyers may communicate in advance to receiving counsel that they do not consent to receiving counsel replying all, which would override the presumption of implied consent.

I. Introduction

Lawyers now commonly use electronic communications like email and text messaging in their law practice.[1] Subject to handling, security, and maintenance considerations beyond this opinion's scope,[2] the Model Rules permit these forms of electronic communication. This permissible communication extends to communications with counsel representing another person in the matter.

Under Rule 4.2 of the ABA Model Rules of Professional Conduct, in representing a client, a lawyer may not "communicate" about the subject of the representation with a represented person absent the consent of that person's lawyer, unless the law or court order authorizes the communication.[3]

---

1. This opinion is based on the ABA Model Rules of Professional Conduct as amended by the ABA House of Delegates through August 2022. The laws, court rules, regulations, rules of professional conduct, and opinions promulgated in individual jurisdictions are controlling.

2. *See, e.g.*, ABA Comm. on Ethics & Prof'l Responsibility, Formal Op. 498 (2021) (discussing ethical considerations in virtual law practice); ABA Comm. on Ethics & Prof'l Responsibility, Formal Op. 483 (2018) (discussing lawyers' obligations in response to data breaches); ABA Comm. on Ethics & Prof'l Responsibility, Formal Op. 477R (2017) (discussing reasonable security precautions when communicating through email).

3. The authorized-by-law exception is not the focus of this opinion.

When a lawyer ("sending lawyer") copies the lawyer's client on an electronic communication to counsel representing another person in the matter ("receiving counsel"), the sending lawyer creates a group communication.[4] This group communication raises questions under the "no contact" rule because of the possibility that the receiving counsel will reply all, which of course will be delivered to the sending lawyer's client. This opinion addresses the question of whether sending lawyers, by copying their clients on electronic communications to receiving counsel, *impliedly* consent to the receiving counsel's "reply all" response.

Several states have answered this question in the negative, concluding that sending lawyers have *not* impliedly consented to the reply all communication with their clients. Although these states conclude that consent may not be implied solely because the sending lawyer copied the client on the email to receiving counsel, they also generally concede that consent may be implied from a variety of circumstances beyond simply having copied the client on a particular email.[5] This variety of circumstances, however, muddies the interpretation of the Rule, making it difficult for receiving counsel to discern the proper course of action or leaving room for disputes.

II. Copying a Client on Emails and Texts Is Implied Consent to a Reply All Response

We conclude that given the nature of the lawyer-initiated group electronic communication, a sending lawyer impliedly consents to receiving counsel's "reply all" response that includes the sending lawyer's client, subject to certain exceptions discussed below. Several reasons support this conclusion, and we think that this interpretation will provide a brighter and fairer line for lawyers who send and receive group emails or text messages.

---

4. Throughout this opinion, the lawyer who sends the electronic communication is referred to as the "sending lawyer." The lawyer who represents another person in the matter and who receives the communication on which the sending lawyer's client is copied is referred to as the "receiving counsel."

5. *See, e.g.*, Wa. State Bar Ass'n Advisory Op. 202201 (2022); S.C. Bar Advisory Op. 18-04 (2018). For a list of the factors bearing on implied consent, *see* Cal. Standing Comm. on Prof'l Responsibility & Conduct Formal Op. 2011-181 ("Such facts and circumstances may include the following: whether the communication is within the presence of the other attorney; prior course of conduct; the nature of the matter; how the communication is initiated and by whom; the formality of the communication; the extent to which the communication might interfere with the attorney-client relationship; whether there exists a common interest or joint defense privilege between the parties; whether the other attorney will have a reasonable opportunity to counsel the represented party with regard to the communication contemporaneously or immediately following such communication; and the instructions of the represented party's attorney.").

First, Model Rule 4.2 permits lawyers to communicate about the subject of the representation with a represented person with the "consent" of that person's lawyer. Consent for purposes of Rule 4.2 may be implied; it need not be express.[6] Similar to adding the client to a videoconference or telephone call with another counsel or inviting the client to an in-person meeting with another counsel, a sending lawyer who includes the client on electronic communications to receiving counsel generally impliedly consents to receiving counsel "replying all" to that communication.[7] The sending lawyer has chosen to give receiving counsel the impression that replying to all copied on the email or text is permissible and perhaps even encouraged. Thus, this situation is not one in which the receiving counsel is overreaching or attempting to pry into confidential lawyer-client communications, the prevention of which are the primary purposes behind Model Rule 4.2.[8]

This conclusion also flows from the inclusive nature and norms of the group electronic communications at issue. It has become quite common to reply all to emails. In fact, "reply all" is the default setting in certain email platforms. The sending lawyer should be aware of this context,[9] and if the sending lawyer nonetheless chooses to copy the client, the sending lawyer is essentially inviting a reply all response. To be sure, the sending lawyer's implied consent should not be stretched past the point of reason.[10] Unless otherwise explicitly agreed, the consent covers only the specific topics in the initial

---

6. *See* RESTATEMENT (THIRD) OF THE LAW GOVERNING LAWYERS § 99 cmt. j (2000) ("[A] lawyer . . . may communicate with a represented nonclient when that person's lawyer has consented to or acquiesced in the communication. An opposing lawyer may acquiesce, for example, by being present at a meeting and observing the communication. Similarly, consent may be implied rather than express, such as where such direct contact occurs routinely as a matter of custom, unless the opposing lawyer affirmatively protests.").

7. *See, e.g.*, N.J. Advisory Comm. on Prof'l Ethics Op. 739 (2021) ("While under RPC 4.2 it would be improper for another lawyer to initiate communication directly with a client without consent, by email or otherwise, nevertheless when the client's own lawyer affirmatively includes the client in an email thread by inserting the client's email address in the 'to' or 'cc' field, we think the natural assumption by others is that the lawyer intends and consents to the client receiving subsequent communications in that thread."); *see also* Va. Legal Ethics Op. 1897 (2022) ("A lawyer who includes their client in the "to" or "cc" field of an email has given implied consent to a reply-all response by opposing counsel."); N.Y.C. Bar Formal Ethics Op. 2022-3 (similar).

8. Model Rules of Prof'l Conduct R. 4.2 cmt. [1].

9. *See* Model Rules of Prof'l Conduct R. 1.1, cmt. [8] ("To maintain the requisite level of knowledge and skill, a lawyer should keep abreast of the changes in law and its practice, including the benefits and risks of relevant technology[.]").

10. *Cf.* Model Rules of Prof'l Conduct, Scope [14] ("The Rules of Professional Conduct are rules of reason. They should be interpreted with reference to the purposes of legal representation and of the law itself.").

email; the receiving counsel cannot reasonably infer that such email opens the door to copy the sending lawyer's client on unrelated topics.[11]

Second, we think that placing the burden on the initiator—the sending lawyer—is the fairest and most efficient allocation of any burdens. The sending lawyer should be responsible for the decision to include the sending lawyer's client in the electronic communication, rather than placing the onus on the receiving counsel to determine whether the sending lawyer has consented to a communication with the sending lawyer's client. Moreover, in a group email or text with an extensive list of recipients, the receiving counsel may not realize that one of the recipients is the sending lawyer's client.[12] We see no reason to shift the burden to the receiving counsel, when the sending lawyer decided to include the client on the group communication in the first instance.

Furthermore, resolving the issue is simpler for the sending lawyer. If the sending lawyer would like to avoid implying consent when copying the client on the electronic communication, the sending lawyer should separately forward the email or text to the client. Indeed, we think this practice is generally the better one. By copying their clients on emails and texts to receiving counsel, sending lawyers risk an imprudent reply all from their clients. Email and text messaging replies are often generated quickly, and the client may reply hastily with sensitive or compromising information.[13] Thus, the better practice is not to copy the client on an email or text to receiving counsel; instead, the lawyer generally should separately forward any pertinent emails or texts to the client.[14]

III. The Presumption of Implied Consent to Reply All Communications Is Not Absolute

The presumption of implied consent to reply all communications may be overcome. We highlight several common examples to guide lawyers.

11. *See also* Va. Legal Ethics Op. 1897 (2022) ("The reply must not exceed the scope of the email to which the lawyer is responding . . . as the sending lawyer's choice to use 'cc' does not authorize the receiving lawyer to communicate beyond what is reasonably necessary to respond to the initial email."); N.Y.C. Bar Ethics Op. 2022-3 ("Where an attorney sends an email copying their client, such communication gives implied consent for other counsel to reply all on the same subject within a reasonable time thereafter.").

12. *See* N.J. Advisory Comm. on Prof'l Ethics Op. 739 (2021) ("[M]any emails have numerous recipients and it is not always clear that a represented client is among the names in the 'to' and 'cc' lines. The client's email address may not reflect the client's name, making it difficult to ascertain the client's identity. Rather than burdening the replying lawyer with the task of parsing through the group email's recipients, the initiating lawyer who does not consent to a response to the client should bear the burden of omitting the client from the group email or blind copying the client.").

13. *See, e.g.*, N.Y.C. Bar Ethics Op. 2022-3 (discussing the lawyer competence and client risk issues arising when lawyers copy their clients on emails to opposing counsel).

14. A separate forward is safer than "bcc'ing" the client because in certain email systems, the client's reply all to that email would still reach the receiving counsel.

First, an express oral or written remark informing receiving counsel that the sending lawyer does not consent to a reply all communication would override the presumption of implied consent. Thus, lawyers who do not wish for their client to receive a "reply all" communication should communicate that fact in advance to receiving counsel, preferably in writing.[15] This communication should be prominent; lawyers who simply insert this preference in a long list of boilerplate disclaimers in their email signature area run the risk of the receiving counsel missing it. Although such disclaimers are better than nothing, a more effective approach would be to inform the receiving counsel—at the beginning of the email or in an earlier, separate communication—that including the client in the communication does not signify consent (or as noted above, not copy the client at all).

Second, the presumption applies only to emails or similar group electronic communications, such as text messaging, which the lawyer initiates. It does not apply to other forms of communication, such as a traditional letter printed on paper and mailed. Implied consent relies on the circumstances, including the group nature and other norms of the electronic communications at issue. For paper communications, a different set of norms currently exists. There is no prevailing custom indicating that by copying a client on a traditional paper letter, the sending lawyer has impliedly consented to the receiving counsel sending a copy of the responsive letter to the sending lawyer's client. Accordingly, receiving counsel generally should not infer consent and reply to the letter with a copy to the sending lawyer's client simply because the sending lawyer copied that lawyer's client on a traditional paper letter. The sending lawyer, as a matter of prudence, should consider forwarding the letter separately, instead of copying the client, but failing to do so does not itself provide implied consent to the receiving counsel to copy the sending lawyer's client on a responsive letter. In sum, although Model Rule 4.2 applies equally to electronic and paper communications, only in group emails or text messages does copying the client convey implied consent for the receiving counsel to reply all to the communication.

Finally, although the act of "replying all" is generally permitted under Model Rule 4.2, other Model Rules restrict the content of that reply.[16]

15. As in many other areas of professional responsibility and the law generally, written communications are advisable because they create an accurate record and help to prevent misunderstandings. Moreover, to avoid implied consent, an oral statement of course would need to be made in advance of the email communication at issue.

16. *See, e.g.,* Model Rules of Prof'l Conduct R. 4.4(a) cmt. [1] (prohibiting "unwarranted intrusions into privileged relationships, such as the client-lawyer relationship"); Model Rules of Prof'l Conduct R. 4.4(b) cmt. [2] ("If a lawyer knows or reasonably should know that [an email] was sent inadvertently, then this Rule requires the lawyer to promptly notify the sender in order to permit that person to take protective measures."); Model Rules of Prof'l Conduct R. 8.4(c) (prohibiting counsel from making misrepresentations).

IV. Conclusion

Absent special circumstances, lawyers who copy their clients on emails or other forms of electronic communication to counsel representing another person in the matter impliedly consent to a "reply all" response from the receiving counsel. Accordingly, the reply all communication would not violate Model Rule 4.2. Lawyers who would like to avoid consenting to such communication should forward the email or text to the client separately or inform the receiving counsel in advance that including the client on the electronic communication does not constitute consent to a reply all communication.

AMERICAN BAR ASSOCIATION

STANDING COMMITTEE ON ETHICS AND PROFESSIONAL RESPONSIBILITY

Formal Opinion 504 **March 1, 2023**

Choice of Law

When a lawyer practices the law of more than one jurisdiction, choice-of-law questions arise concerning which jurisdiction's ethics rules the lawyer must follow. Model Rule 8.5 provides that when a lawyer's conduct is in connection with a matter pending before a tribunal, the lawyer must comply with the ethics rules of the jurisdiction in which the tribunal sits, unless otherwise provided. For all other conduct, including conduct in anticipation of litigation not yet filed, a lawyer must comply with the ethics rules of the jurisdiction in which the lawyer's conduct occurs. However, if the predominant effect of the lawyer's conduct is in a different jurisdiction, then the lawyer must comply with the ethics rules of that jurisdiction.

Introduction

Lawyers frequently are admitted to practice law or are authorized to practice the law of more than one jurisdiction. When jurisdictions have differing ethical requirements, the lawyer must determine which jurisdiction's ethics rules govern the lawyer's actions in the representation.[1] This Formal Opinion addresses several scenarios applying ABA Model Rule of Professional Conduct 8.5, Disciplinary Authority; Choice of Law, to determine which jurisdiction's rules govern the situation, including: 1) fee agreements; 2) law firm ownership; 3) reporting professional misconduct; 4) confidentiality duties; and 5) screening lawyers who leave one firm to join another (referred to as "lateral" lawyers).

ABA Model Rule of Professional Conduct 8.5, Disciplinary Authority; Choice of Law—An Overview

Pursuant to ABA Model Rule of Professional Conduct 8.5(a), lawyers are subject to the disciplinary authority of the jurisdiction(s) in which they are

1. This opinion is based on the ABA Model Rules of Professional Conduct as amended by the ABA House of Delegates through February 2023. The laws, court rules, regulations, rules of professional conduct, and opinions promulgated in individual jurisdictions are controlling.

licensed regardless of where their conduct occurred. Lawyers also are subject to the disciplinary authority of the jurisdiction(s) in which they are offering to provide or are providing legal services regardless of whether they are admitted to practice or licensed by that jurisdiction. For example, lawyers practicing pursuant to a jurisdiction's in-house counsel rule, or pro hac vice rule, or providing legal services temporarily pursuant to Model Rule 5.5, are all subject to the disciplinary authority of the jurisdiction in which they are providing legal services. Finally, a lawyer "may be subject to the disciplinary authority of *both this jurisdiction and another jurisdiction for the same conduct.*"[2]

ABA Model Rule of Professional Conduct 8.5(b) determines which jurisdiction's ethics rules apply to a lawyer's conduct. In answering the choice of law question, Rule 8.5(b) addresses litigation matters and non-litigation matters differently.

For litigation matters, Rule 8.5(b)(1) provides: "In any exercise of the disciplinary authority of this jurisdiction, the rules of professional conduct to be applied shall be as follows: (1) for conduct in connection with a matter pending before a tribunal, the rules of the jurisdiction in which the tribunal sits, unless the rules of the tribunal provide otherwise[.]"

For "any other conduct," Rule 8.5(b)(2) explains that the ethics rules of the jurisdiction where the lawyer's conduct occurred will govern unless the "predominant effect" of that conduct is in a different jurisdiction, in which case, the "rules of that jurisdiction shall be applied to the conduct."

For litigation matters, a key question is what does Rule 8.5(b)(1)'s phrase "in connection with a matter pending before a tribunal" mean? Does it apply to the fee agreement entered into before the matter is filed in court or to the ownership structure of a law firm in a different jurisdiction than the tribunal?

Another key question is what does Rule 8.5(b)(2)'s phrase "any other conduct" mean? Does it apply to transactional matters and/or conduct that is *not* involving a tribunal—such as the fee agreement or conduct occurring before a case is filed?

Comment [4] is instructive, explaining that the phrase "any other conduct" includes "all other conduct, including conduct in anticipation of a proceeding not yet pending before a tribunal."

Rule 8.5(b)(2) provides a safe harbor for a lawyer's "predominant effect" determination: "A lawyer shall not be subject to discipline if the lawyer's conduct conforms to the rules of a jurisdiction in which the lawyer reasonably believes the predominant effect of the lawyer's conduct will occur." This safe harbor from disciplinary action is not without limits. The lawyer's belief about the jurisdiction of the predominant effect of the lawyer's conduct must be a reasonable belief. Reasonable belief is a defined term and "denotes

2. Model Rules of Prof'l Conduct R. 8.5(a) (emphasis added).

that the lawyer believes the matter in question and that the circumstances are such that the belief is reasonable."[3]

Although Rule 8.5 does not provide lawyers guidance on what factors the lawyer should consider when determining where the predominant effect of the lawyer's conduct occurs, the Committee believes lawyers should look to the following factors:

- the client's location, residence, and/or principal place of business;
- where the transaction may occur;
- which jurisdiction's substantive law applies to the transaction;
- the location of the lawyer's principal office;
- where the lawyer is admitted;
- the location of the opposing party and other relevant third parties (residence and/or principal place of business);[4] and
- the jurisdiction with the greatest interest in the lawyer's conduct.[5]

When a choice of law question concerning the applicable conflict of interest rules arises and a regulatory authority must determine whether the lawyer's belief—that a specific jurisdiction's rules applied because the predominant effect of that lawyer's conduct occurred in that jurisdiction—was reasonable, then a written agreement between the lawyer and client that explains a particular jurisdiction's conflict of interest rules will apply may be considered, at least if certain requirements are satisfied.

Specifically, the ABA added to the last sentence of Comment [5] to Rule 8.5 in 2013 to address this concept:

> [5] When a lawyer's conduct involves significant contacts with more than one jurisdiction, it may not be clear whether the predominant effect of the lawyer's conduct will occur in a jurisdiction other than the one in which the conduct occurred. So long as the lawyer's conduct conforms to the rules of a jurisdiction in which the lawyer reasonably believes the predominant effect will occur, the lawyer shall not be subject to discipline under this Rule. *With respect to conflicts of interest, in determining a lawyer's reasonable belief under paragraph (b)(2), a written agreement between the lawyer and client that reasonably speci-*

3. Model Rules of Prof'l Conduct R. 1.0(i).

4. *See, e.g.*, N.Y. State Bar Ass'n Comm. on Prof'l Ethics Op. 1027 (2014) (noting that factors for determining "predominant effect" may include where client resides, where funds will be deposited, where the services will be performed, and where the business will operate).

5. For example, conduct permitted in one jurisdiction that has little or no relationship to the client and legal matter may be the subject of discipline if the conduct is prohibited in another jurisdiction that has a greater nexus with the matter.

fies a particular jurisdiction as within the scope of that paragraph may be considered if the agreement was obtained with the client's informed consent confirmed in the agreement. (emphasis added)[6]

To offer guidance to lawyers on these important choice-of-law principles, the following scenarios illustrate how Rule 8.5 applies when a lawyer may be subject to more than one jurisdiction's ethics rules.

Scenario 1: Fee Agreements

Lawyer is admitted in State X and enters into a client-lawyer relationship with Client who resides in State X. Lawyer will work from Lawyer's office in State X on Client's matter. Litigation is to be filed in State Y. In drafting the terms of the fee agreement,[7] should Lawyer adhere to the Rules of Professional Conduct of State X or State Y?

---

6. Ethics 20/20 Commission Report and Resolution 107D that recommended adding the last sentence to this Comment explained "[l]awyers and clients can resolve some of the unavoidable uncertainties of Rule 8.5(b)(2) in the same way choice of law issues are resolved in other contexts: through choice of law agreements ... They may also be useful to disciplinary authorities who are asked to consider whether a lawyer's determination of the applicable jurisdiction's conflict of interest rule was 'reasonable' ... These kinds of agreements are analogous to waivers of future conflicts, which are already authorized in Comment [22] of Rule 1.7, and will have a similar effect.". *See* Ethics 20/20 Commission Report and Resolution 107D (2013), *available at* 20121112_ethics_20_20_choice_of_rule_resolution_and_report_final.pdf (americanbar.org).

The Ethics 20/20 Commission specifically limited any contractual authorization between lawyers and clients to conflicts of interest considerations. *See* Resolution and Report 107D (2013) at p.3. A lawyer and client cannot contract around Rule 8.5(b)(1)'s choice of law conclusion for conduct "in connection with a matter pending before a tribunal." The report noted that "[d]espite the advantages of these agreements, the Commission concluded that they should be subject to several limitations. First, such agreements should only be used in the context of conflicts of interest; they should not be used to specify the rules of a jurisdiction on other issues, such as the duty of confidentiality. The Commission did not want to authorize parties to contract around rules intended to protect adverse parties or tribunals. To ensure the limited use of the agreements, the proposed Comment language begins with the phrase 'With respect to conflicts of interest...'" This "essentially permits a lawyer and client to enter into a choice-of-law agreement regarding the applicable conflict-of-interest rules, although the agreement is not binding on a court or disciplinary authority." ABA Annotated Model Rules of Professional Conduct 748 (2019).

7. "Principles of substantive law external to these Rules determine whether a client-lawyer relationship exists." Model Rules of Professional Conduct, Scope [17]. Once the client-lawyer relationship is formed, Rule 1.5(b) states that the scope of representation and how fees and costs will be charged "shall be communicated to the client, preferably in writing, [. . .]". Many jurisdictions' versions of Rule 1.5(b) require written fee agreements for all representations. Rule 1.5(c) and (e) require specific written disclosures for contingent fee agreements and situations where lawyers in different firms will be sharing a fee.

As noted above, Rule 8.5(b)(1) will apply the rules of the jurisdiction of the tribunal for conduct "in connection with a matter pending before a tribunal" but Comment [4] to the Rule expressly recognizes:

> [. . .] As to all other conduct, including conduct in anticipation of a proceeding not yet pending before a tribunal, paragraph (b)(2) provides that a lawyer shall be subject to the rules of the jurisdiction in which the lawyer's conduct occurred, or, if the predominant effect of the conduct is in another jurisdiction, the rules of that jurisdiction shall be applied to the conduct.[. . .]

Securing a fee agreement is "conduct in anticipation of a proceeding not yet pending before a tribunal" and, therefore, Rule 8.5(b)(2) applies. Applying the factors set forth above to determine the jurisdiction in which the "predominant effect" of the lawyer's conduct occurs, a lawyer admitted in State X, who is hired to represent a resident of State X, may reasonably conclude that State X's rules apply to the terms of the fee agreement both because the Lawyer's conduct, executing the fee agreement and accepting the representation, and the predominant effect of the agreement to represent the Client take place in State X.[8]

The agreement is signed in State X, where Lawyer's office is located, where Lawyer is admitted to practice, where Lawyer will research and prepare for the matter (even if done virtually), and where Client resides. Therefore, State X's version of Rule 1.5 would apply to the fee agreement including whether the fee agreement must be in writing, whether it must be signed by a client if it is a contingent fee agreement, and whether the fee may be divided with lawyers in different firms who assume joint responsibility.

Certainly, from a client protection perspective, the jurisdiction where the lawyer is licensed and/or the jurisdiction where the client resides has a significant interest in requiring certain provisions in the fee agreement, and therefore, application of that jurisdiction's version of Rule 1.5 is most appropriate.[9]

---

8. This Opinion is limited to analyzing which jurisdiction's rules of professional conduct apply to a fee agreement and does not opine on which state's substantive contract laws would apply.

9. The Committee recognizes that Mass. Bar Ass'n Op. 12-02 (2012) comes to a different conclusion as to which state's rules apply in a dispute over a fee agreement. Massachusetts' version of Rule 8.5 is different than the ABA Model Rule and the issue presented involved the reasonableness of the fee charged in litigation, not the formation of the agreement. The Committee's position is consistent with Bernick v. Frost, 510 A.2d 56 (N.J. 1986), construing contract law to find that New Jersey—the state in which the lawyer was licensed, and the client lived—was the appropriate venue for a dispute between a lawyer and client over the engagement agreement for a matter litigated in New York. *But see In re* Schiller, 808 S.E.2d

To avoid ambiguity, a lawyer may want to identify in the fee agreement the lawyer's belief as to which jurisdiction's rules of professional conduct will apply to the fee agreement. That fee agreement may list the factors considered by the lawyer in reasonably concluding where the lawyer's conduct will occur and where the predominant effect of the fee agreement will occur.[10]

Of course, there must be some reasonable relationship between the jurisdiction whose rules of professional conduct are selected to govern the fee agreement and where the lawyer is admitted to practice, as well as the other factors listed above.[11] It would not be reasonable for a lawyer to conclude that the applicable ethics rules would be those of a jurisdiction in which the lawyer is not admitted to practice or a jurisdiction for which there is no reasonable basis to find the "predominant effect" of the lawyer's conduct occurred.

The ethics rules that apply to fee agreements between lawyers and clients may include not just Rule 1.5 but also the ethics rules regulating what the lawyer may then do with those fees such as rules governing with whom the lawyer may share or divide a legal fee.[12]

This hypothetical demonstrates the relevance of the final sentence of Model Rule 8.5(b)(2): "A lawyer shall not be subject to discipline if the lawyer's conduct conforms to the rules of a jurisdiction in which the lawyer reasonably believes the predominant effect of the lawyer's conduct will occur." Thus, a lawyer who reasonably believes that the predominant effect of the fee agreement will be in a specific jurisdiction should not be subject to discipline, even if the scope of representation contemplates filing a case for the client in a different jurisdiction.

Scenario 2: Law Firm Ownership

State A permits Lawyer to have nonlawyer partners in the law firm, while State B follows Model Rule 5.4, which does not permit nonlawyer partners in law firms. Lawyer is admitted to practice law only in State A and has a law firm formed in State A with a nonlawyer partner. Lawyer seeks to appear in a case *pro hac vice* pending before a tribunal in State B. Will State B's Rules of Professional Conduct prohibit Lawyer from sharing the fees earned on the

---

378 (S.C. 2017) applying rules of professional conduct of North Carolina, the state in which litigation was filed, to South Carolina licensed lawyer fee agreement.

10. In addition to Rule 1.5 applying to fee agreements, Rules 1.15 and 5.4 also may be relevant.

11. *See In re Wyatt*, 159 N.H. 285 (2009) (lawyer cannot use another state's rules as defense to disciplinary charges where lawyer was not licensed or admitted pro hac vice).

12. For instance, a lawyer admitted in jurisdiction X and practicing law in jurisdiction X will have the fee agreement enforced and interpreted by the Rules of Professional Conduct in jurisdiction X, which might, for instance, permit paying referral fees or permit jurisdiction X lawyers to have nonlawyer partners. Compare MODEL RULES OF PROF'L CONDUCT R. 5.4 with Ariz. Rule 1.5 Cmt [9].

case pending before State B tribunal with Lawyer's nonlawyer partners?[13] Can one jurisdiction in essence reach into a law firm in another jurisdiction and find that jurisdiction's permissible firm structure to be unethical and subject lawyers from another jurisdiction to discipline?

When a lawyer seeks to appear before a tribunal by *pro hac vice* admission the lawyer agrees to be bound by the rules of the tribunal, and Rule 8.5(b)(1) provides that the ethics rules of that tribunal apply to "conduct in connection with a matter pending before a tribunal." Under the ABA Model Rules on Pro Hac Vice Admission, the tribunal has the discretion to admit the out-of-state lawyer and Rule 1.D.3 provides:

> [. . .] An application ordinarily should be granted unless the court or agency finds reason to believe that such admission:
>
> a. may be detrimental to the prompt, fair and efficient administration of justice,
>
> b. may be detrimental to legitimate interests of parties to the proceedings other than the client(s) the applicant proposes to represent,
>
> c. one or more of the clients the applicant proposes to represent may be at risk of receiving inadequate representation and cannot adequately appreciate that risk, or
>
> d. the applicant has engaged in such frequent appearances as to constitute regular practice in this state.

Thus, the Model Rule on Pro Hac Vice Admission defaults to permitting admission unless there is some fact to suggest the admission would be detrimental to the administration of justice, or competent representation of the client is an issue, or the lawyer is too frequently appearing in the court. There is nothing in the Model Rules on Pro Hac Vice Admission that says the tribunal should inquire into the Lawyer's business model particularly when it is permitted by the Lawyer's home licensing jurisdiction. Nor is there any indication that the business model permitted in the Lawyer's home jurisdic-

13. There is no ethical concern for Lawyer's local counsel who is admitted to practice law only in State B in sharing fees with Lawyer under a co-counsel agreement so long as local counsel is in a separate firm and not part of Lawyer's State A law firm. ABA Comm. on Ethics & Prof'l Responsibility, Formal Op. 464 (2013); *See also* N.Y. City Bar Formal Op. 2020-1 (2020) (finding that New York lawyer may share fees with Arizona lawyer who has separate firm from New York lawyer and Arizona firm has nonlawyer owners); Fla. Bar Op. 17-1 (2017); Phila. Bar Ass'n Op. 2010-7 (2010).

tion would be detrimental to the "prompt, fair and efficient administration of justice."

Even so, a Lawyer admitted pro hac vice agrees to be bound by the ethics rules of the tribunal and Rule 8.5(b)(1) provides that the Rules of Professional Conduct of that tribunal apply to "conduct in connection with a matter pending before a tribunal [. . .]".[14] Certainly, the tribunal's ethics rules with respect to the Lawyer's conduct in representing the client in the proceeding, in dealing with the tribunal, and dealing with the opposing party and counsel will be governed by tribunal's Rules of Professional Conduct. Model Rule 8.5(b) expressly chooses the tribunal's ethics rules regarding the lawyer's "conduct in connection with a matter pending before a tribunal"—suggesting that the tribunal has a relevant interest in assuring the Lawyer's conduct *in that tribunal's matter* complies with the tribunal's Rules.

But does Model Rule 8.5 make the Lawyer who is licensed in State A—which allows nonlawyer partners in firms—subject to discipline for having nonlawyer partners when the Lawyer is admitted pro have vice to represent a client in a matter pending in a tribunal, in State B which does not allow nonlawyer partners?

The Lawyer's law firm is in State A, where the Lawyer is admitted to practice and has an office, and that firm structure is not "conduct in connection with a matter pending before a tribunal." The firm is not located in State B—the partnership conduct is occurring in State A, not State B where the tribunal sits.

Therefore, Rule 8.5(b)(2), not (b)(1), governs which ethics rules regulate the structure of the firm. Lawyer's conduct—establishing a firm structure—and the "predominant effect" of Lawyer's partnership with a nonlawyer is in State A, not State B. Thus, even if the Lawyer is admitted before a tribunal in State B, pro hac vice, Lawyer's law firm ownership in State A is governed by State A's ethics rules and not State B's.

Scenario 3: Reporting Professional Misconduct

Lawyer is admitted to practice law in States A and B, with Lawyer's office located in State B. Client residing in State A hires Lawyer to complete litigation in State A. Prior counsel on this matter forged the Client's signature on a document that was filed with the tribunal, which has prejudiced the rights of Client going forward in this matter.

State A requires Lawyer to report professional misconduct of another lawyer to State A's disciplinary authority even if doing so requires Lawyer to disclose information relating to the representation without the consent of

14. As noted above, if the tribunal does not have a rule designating the rules of professional conduct that apply to a lawyer appearing before the tribunal, the applicable rules will be those of the jurisdiction where the tribunal sits.

the client. State B follows Model Rule 8.3, which requires Lawyer to report professional misconduct of another lawyer, but if Lawyer would have to reveal information relating to the representation in making such a report, the Lawyer only may report the misconduct if Client provides informed consent to make the disclosure.

Which State's version of Rule 8.3 governs Lawyer's reporting obligations? State A or State B?

Because Lawyer is representing a State A client and Lawyer's work for Client is in connection with a matter pending before a State A tribunal, Rule 8.5(b)(1) would require Lawyer to follow the Rules of State A and report prior counsel in accordance with State A's version of Rule 8.3. Even though Lawyer's office is in State B, and even if prior counsel of the Client was admitted only in State B, or even if the *Client* was only a resident of State B, State A's version of Rule 8.3 applies because the matter is pending before the tribunal in State A and Lawyer's conduct—reporting prior counsel—is conduct in connection with a matter pending before a tribunal in State A.

Scenario 4: Confidentiality Duties

Lawyer is licensed in State A and State B, and practices from an office in State A. State A is a Model Rules state and Model Rule 1.6, Confidentiality of Information, permits, but does not require, a lawyer to disclose information relating to the representation to the extent the lawyer reasonably believes necessary "to prevent reasonably certain death or substantial bodily harm."[15] State B's confidentiality rule requires a lawyer to reveal such information, using the term "must reveal," client confidential information to prevent death or substantial bodily harm to another person.

Lawyer is representing a Client/Buyer, who resides in State B, in a transactional matter to purchase residential real estate in State A from Seller in State A. The matter is not before a tribunal. The transaction has become contentious because Buyer and Seller are having a difficult time coming to terms on the agreement. Buyer and Seller have been engaging in negotiations on the transaction at Buyer's place of business in State B. At a recent meeting, Client/Buyer privately made a specific threat to Lawyer to gravely physically harm the Seller at their next meeting if Seller refuses to accept Buyer's terms. Lawyer reasonably believes that the Client will carry out the threat. Is Lawyer required to disclose the threat by Client/Buyer to Seller?

Rule 8.5(b)(2) will determine which jurisdiction's version of Rule 1.6 applies to the situation because the matter is not before a tribunal. Paragraph (b)(2) tells Lawyer to look to the "rules of the jurisdiction in which the law-

15. Model Rules of Prof'l Conduct R. 1.6(b)(1).

yer's conduct occurred, or, if the predominant effect of the conduct is in a different jurisdiction, the rules of that jurisdiction."

Although the Lawyer's conduct, informing the Seller of the Client/Buyer's threat, could take place from any number of locations, the Committee believes that the predominant effect of Lawyer's conduct is in State B. In assessing where the predominant effect of Lawyer's conduct occurs, a lawyer should consider where the client is located, where the client's actions might occur, which jurisdiction's substantive law would be applied to the client's actions and where the lawyer is admitted. In this scenario both State A and State B are involved because the Client/Buyer is residing in State B, but the Seller and transaction are in State A. However, the threatened harm would most likely occur in State B because Client/Buyer made a specific threat to Lawyer to harm the Seller at their next meeting and prior meetings have been held in State B at Client/Buyer's place of business.

The Lawyer may reasonably conclude that the predominant effect for the matter involving the Client's/Buyer's threat is in State B due to the Client's location and the location where the threat is specified to occur. Therefore, State B's version of Rule 1.6 will applicable and Lawyer must disclose the Client's threat.

Scenario 5: Screening for Laterals Lawyers

A law firm with multiple U.S. offices would like to hire a Lawyer A who is currently associated with another firm. Lawyer A is licensed in State A and would practice law from the firm's office in State A. The firm's hiring of Lawyer A would impute a former client conflict of interest to another lawyer at the firm, Lawyer B. Lawyer B is licensed in State B and practices law from the firm's office in State B.

As prescribed in Model Rule 1.10(a)(2), State A allows the law firm to screen Lawyer A without obtaining the consent of the affected clients (Lawyer A's soon-to-be former client and Lawyer B's current client). State B, however, does not follow Model Rule 1.10(a)(2) and would impute Lawyer A's conflict to Lawyer B unless Lawyer A's soon-to-be former client and Lawyer B's current client gives informed consent, confirmed in writing. To prevent imputing Lawyer A's conflict to Lawyer B, may the law firm screen Lawyer A without obtaining the consent of the affected clients?

This is a common scenario where the hiring law firm wants to hire a lawyer who is practicing at a different firm, commonly called a "lateral hire," but the lateral is currently working on a client matter adverse to a client of a lawyer at the hiring firm. The hiring firm wants to avoid imputation of the new lawyer's conflicts to the hiring firm. Most states have adopted a screening rule similar to Model Rule 1.10(a)(2), which permits the screening of a lateral irrespective of the lateral's level of involvement with the soon-to-be former client's matter. Some states have adopted rules where the availability of screening depends on the lateral's level of knowledge or participation in the soon-to-be-former client's matter. Other states do not permit screening to avoid the imputed conflict, and therefore require the hiring firm to obtain the informed consent of the affected clients.

The choice of law analysis for screening laterals will initially pivot on whether the imputed conflict of interest affects a pending lawsuit or a transactional matter. If the conflict that would be imputed from Lawyer A to Lawyer B concerns litigation filed in State B, then State B's screening rules would govern unless the tribunal's rules provide otherwise.[16] Similarly, if the imputed conflict arises in a matter that Lawyer B is litigating before a tribunal located in State C, then State C's screening rules would govern unless the tribunal's rules provide otherwise.[17]

The analysis is more complicated if the conflict that would be imputed from Lawyer A to Lawyer B involves a transactional matter. The location of Lawyer B's conduct—handling a potentially conflicted representation from the law firm's office in State B—is but one consideration.

Under this non-litigation scenario, Lawyer B's client and the client on the opposite side of the transaction—Lawyer A's soon-to-be former client—will shoulder any harm associated with the imputed conflict. Considering the factors referenced above to assess where the "predominant effect" will be, if the affected parties to the transaction have their principal places of business or reside in State A, then the predominant effect of the imputed conflict will be in State A even though Lawyer B practices from an office in State B.[18] State B's screening rules would apply if both parties to the transaction are in State B.

When the parties to the potentially conflicted transaction are in different states, additional factors such as the location of the subject of the transaction (e.g., the location of real property, business operations, or services to be performed), the substantive law governing the transaction, and the location of deposited funds may point the predominant effect to one state over another. For instance, if Lawyer B's client resides in State B and is purchasing real estate located in State B (which means State B's law would govern the transaction), then the predominant effect of Lawyer B's conduct remains in State B even if the selling client (Lawyer A's soon-to-be former client) is in State A and the selling client will deposit the transaction's funds in a bank account in State A.

In non-litigated matters with significant contacts to more than one state, it may be unclear where the predominant effect of Lawyer's B representation will occur. For those situations, it would be prudent for Lawyer B to follow the more restrictive rule in State B (which is also the location of Lawyer B's

16. Model Rules of Prof'l Conduct R. 8.5(b)(1).
17. *Id.*
18. Model Rules of Prof'l Conduct R. 8.5(b)(2).

conduct and Lawyer B's state of licensure) and obtain the informed consent of each affected client, confirmed in writing. Lawyer B, however, will not be subject to professional discipline for violations of Model Rules 1.9 and 1.10 so long as Lawyer B acts in accordance with the rules of the jurisdiction in which Lawyer B reasonably believes the predominant effect of Lawyer B's representation will occur.[19]

Conclusion

Model Rule 8.5 provides guidance for determining which jurisdiction's rules of professional conduct apply to a lawyer's conduct. When a lawyer's conduct is in connection with a matter pending before a tribunal, the lawyer must comply with the ethics rules of the jurisdiction in which the tribunal sits, unless otherwise provided. For all other conduct, including conduct in anticipation of litigation not yet filed and conduct not involving litigation, a lawyer must comply with the ethics rules of the jurisdiction where the lawyer's conduct occurs or, if different, where the predominant effect of the lawyer's conduct occurs. Factors to assess where that "predominant effect" occurs may include the client's location, where a transaction occurs, which jurisdiction's substantive law applies to the transaction, the location of the lawyer's principal office, where the lawyer is admitted, the location of the opposing party, and the jurisdiction with the greatest interest in the lawyer's conduct. A lawyer will not be subject to discipline if the lawyer's conduct conforms to the rules of a jurisdiction in which the lawyer reasonably believes the predominant effect of the lawyer's conduct will occur.

19. Model Rules of Prof'l Conduct R. 8.5(b)(2). Another alternative when the predominant effect is uncertain is for a lawyer and client to agree that the lawyer's representation will be governed by a particular state's conflicts of interest rules. Model Rules of Prof'l Conduct R. 8.5 cmt. [5]. The specified state must have a reasonable relationship to the client representation.

AMERICAN BAR ASSOCIATION
STANDING COMMITTEE ON ETHICS AND PROFESSIONAL RESPONSIBILITY

Formal Opinion 505 **May 3, 2023**

Fees Paid in Advance for Contemplated Services

Under the Model Rules of Professional Conduct, a fee paid to a lawyer in advance for services to be rendered in the future must be placed in a client trust account and may be withdrawn only as earned by the performance of the contemplated services. This protects client funds and promotes client access to legal services in the event the representation terminates before all contemplated services have been rendered. All fees must be reasonable, and unearned fees must be returned to the client. Therefore, it is not accurate to label a fee "nonrefundable" before it actually has been earned, and labels do not dictate whether a fee has been earned.

This opinion examines a lawyer's obligations under the ABA Model Rules of Professional Conduct with respect to fees paid in advance for legal work to be performed by the lawyer in the future.[1] In particular, this opinion seeks to clarify the proper handling and disposition of fees paid in advance for legal work to be performed in the future, including where the lawyer must deposit and maintain the funds and when the lawyer may treat them as earned. The opinion also explains when a lawyer must refund all or a portion of fees paid in advance and discusses whether such a payment may be, or can even be labeled, "nonrefundable." The answers are derived from the application of several Model Rules, including: 1.5(a), 1.5(b), 1.15(a), 1.15(c), 1.15(d), and 1.16(d).

Fees for services may be paid after completion of the services, of course. However, for certain matters, many lawyers request or require that funds in a certain amount be paid to the lawyer at the outset of the representation to secure payment for the lawyer's later work. Under the Model Rules such fees must be placed in a Rule 1.15-compliant trust account, to be disbursed to the

1. This opinion is based on the American Bar Association Model Rules of Professional Conduct as amended by the ABA House of Delegates through August 2022. The laws, court rules, regulations, rules of professional conduct, and opinions promulgated in individual jurisdictions are controlling. This is especially noteworthy for this opinion as jurisdictions have adopted substantially different rules relating to the management of client property including fees paid in advance for legal work to be performed in the future.

lawyer only after the fee has been earned. This is to protect the client from the risk that the lawyer may not be able to refund the prepaid fee in the event the representation terminates before the contemplated work is completed. The Model Rules protect the lawyer from the risk of nonpayment by allowing advance fees to be received and protect the client by requiring that the funds are kept safe and separate from the funds of the lawyer or firm.

I. Terminology

As a preliminary matter, it is useful to define terms commonly used to label certain client-lawyer fee arrangements: advances, retainers, flat or fixed fees, and "nonrefundable" or "earned-on-receipt" fees.

A. Advances v. Retainers

Fees paid by a client to a lawyer in advance for legal work to be performed by the lawyer in the future are sometimes referred to as an "advance fee," an "advanced fee," an "advance fee payment," an "advance fee deposit," a "fee advance," or simply an "advance." Advances are also sometimes called "special retainers," "security retainers," or simply "prepaid fees." To be consistent and clear, this opinion will use the term "advance" when discussing fees paid to the lawyer for legal work to be performed in the future.

When a client pays an advance to a lawyer, the lawyer takes possession—but not ownership—of the funds to secure payment for the services the lawyer will render to the client in the future.

This opinion will also refer to the term "retainer" fee. Neither the term "retainer" nor "retainer fee" is found in the Model Rules of Professional Conduct. Regrettably, many lawyers use the term loosely to mean any sum of money paid to the lawyer at or near the commencement of representation.[2] Whereas an advance is a deposit of money with the lawyer to pay for services to be rendered in the future, there is another type of payment that is not for services. Rather, "[t]he purpose of [a retainer] is to assure the client that the lawyer will be contractually on call to handle the client's legal matters."[3] This type of agreement and payment is variously referred to as a "general retainer," "classic retainer," "true retainer," "availability retainer," or an "engagement retainer."[4] Because all of these terms mean the same thing, this

2. There is widespread agreement that the word "retainer" has been used so inconsistently that is has practically lost all definable meaning. Black's Law Dictionary (11th ed. 2019) ("Over the years, lawyers have used the term 'retainer' in so many conflicting senses that it should be banished from the legal vocabulary.") (quoting Mortimer D. Schwartz & Richard C. Wydick, Problems in Legal Ethics 100, 101 (2d ed. 1988)).

3. Charles W. Wolfram, Modern Legal Ethics 506 (West 1986).

4. Some jurisdictions have commendably sought to define terms and draw distinctions in their court rules. *See* Ariz. Rules of Prof'l Conduct R. 1.5 cmt. [7] ("The 'true' or 'classic' retainer is a fee paid . . . merely to insure the lawyer's availability to represent the client and to preclude the lawyer from taking adverse representation. What is often called a retainer

opinion will use the term "general retainer" to refer to this arrangement.[5] A general retainer is paid—and deemed earned—upon the promise of availability to represent a client, whether or not services are actually needed or requested by the client.[6] Thus, a general retainer has been conceptualized as a form of an option contract.[7] In other words, hourly time is not billed against a general retainer and a general retainer is not a flat fee for a specific amount of the lawyer's time—it is solely to reserve the lawyer's availability. An important result of these related features is that the money paid by the client in connection with a general retainer should not be placed in a trust account since it is considered earned upon the commencement of the contract.[8]

---

but is in fact merely an advance fee deposit involves a security deposit to insure the payment of fees when they are subsequently earned, either on a flat fee or hourly fee basis. A flat fee is a fee of a set amount for performance of agreed work, which may or may not be paid in advance but is not deemed earned until the work is performed. . . ."). *See also* Fla. State Bar R. 4-1.5(e)(2) (defining "retainer," "flat fee," and "advance fee") and Iowa R. Civ. P. 45.8-10 (defining "general retainer," "special retainer, and "flat fee").

5. It is sometimes said that retainers come in two varieties: "general retainers" and "special retainers." A special retainer is simply an advance going by another, unfortunately misleading, name. *See* Lester Brickman & Lawrence A. Cunningham, *Nonrefundable Retainers Revisited*, 72 N.C. L. Rev. 1, 5-6 (1993) ("A special retainer is an agreement between lawyer and client in which the client agrees to pay the lawyer a specified fee in exchange for specified services to be rendered. The fee may be calculated on an hourly, percentage or other basis and may be payable either in advance or as billed.") (footnotes omitted). The Committee is of the opinion that a special retainer is the same thing as an "advance." To be consistent and clear, this opinion will use the term "advance" when referring to such arrangements, although some of the cited sources and authorities may use the term "special retainer."

6. "Because the general retainer is not a payment for the performance of services, but rather is compensation for the lawyer's promise of availability, the fee is earned by the lawyer at the time the retainer is paid and thus should not be deposited into a client trust account. The general retainer is not an advance deposit against future legal services, which instead would be separately calculated and charged should the lawyer actually be called upon by the client to perform the legal services in the future." Gregory C. Sisk, *Duties to Effectively Represent the Client*, § 4-4.4(b) (A Retainer for Lawyer Availability), *in* Legal Ethics, Professional Responsibility, and the Legal Profession (West 2016).

7. Lester Brickman, *The Advance Payment Dilemma: Should Payments be Deposited to the Client Trust Account or to the General Office Account*, 10 Cardozo L Rev. 647, 649 n.13 (1989). *See also In re* O'Farrell, 942 N.E.2d 799, 803 (Ind. 2011).

8. This opinion does not attempt to exhaustively discuss general retainers. Though they can and do have legitimate uses, for years they have been criticized, disfavored, and narrowly construed based on contract law, public policy, and contemporary ethics principles. *See, e.g.*, Charles J. McClain, Jr., *The Strange Concept of the Legal Retaining Fee*, 8 J. Legal Prof. 123 (1983) (common law of retainers "rests on rather shaky conceptual foundations" full of "inconsistencies and contradictions" and "contributing yet another irritant to the already strained relations between the legal profession and the public at large"); Pamela S. Kunen, *No Leg to Stand on: The General Retainer Exception to the Ban on Nonrefundable Retainers Must Fall*, 17 Cardozo L. Rev. 719 (1996) (discussing "historical and descriptive misconceptions" and arguing that, in many instances, such retainers generate the fiduciary obligations attending other lawyer-client fee agreements); and Joseph M. Perillo, *The Law of Lawyers' Contracts Is Different*, 67 Fordham L. Rev. 443, 449-453 (1998).

Some authorities treat the term "general retainer" or "true retainer," etc., as synonymous with "nonrefundable." This is not correct. A general retainer may, by custom, be considered earned when paid, but this does not mean that it is forever exempt from scrutiny under the Rules. It may be determined to be an unreasonable fee, or even unearned if the lawyer does not make himself or herself available. For example, if a company retains a lawyer to handle a hostile takeover bid should one arise and the lawyer does not, in fact, accept the engagement, then the fee, which may have been paid many months earlier and treated as the lawyer's own property, may be determined to be unreasonable and/or unearned and therefore the subject of an order requiring it to be returned, refunded, or repaid to the client. Other circumstances requiring refund might include the death, disability, suspension, or disbarment of the lawyer. Like all fees, a general retainer must be reasonable under the circumstances.[9]

General retainers "are quite rare,"[10] and have "largely disappeared from the modern practice of law."[11] However, attempts to cast what is actually an advance payment of fees for services to be performed later as a general retainer are very much present today. Given the rarity and unusual nature of a general retainer, and the fact that very few clients would actually need or benefit from one, the nature of the fee and lawyer's obligations and client's benefits under such an agreement must be explained clearly and in detail, including the fact that fees for legal services performed will be charged in addition to the general retainer,[12] and use of the term should be restricted to its traditional definition.

This opinion focuses on advance fees paid by individual clients, usually for a single legal matter (or related matters) that will not recur on a regular basis. Examples include a divorce, defense of criminal charges, and discharge from employment or other civil matters not handled on a contingent fee basis. However, some clients may need legal services of a certain type on a repeat basis and may contract for such services. For example, the client and lawyer may enter into a renewable one-year agreement providing for a monthly payment to handle any or all collections arising out of one or more of the client's businesses. Some lawyers and clients may use the term "retainer" or "general retainer" to refer to such an arrangement. Such arrangements may be perfectly appropriate although they may not meet the definition of a general retainer even if "availability" is said to be a part of the arrangement. Perhaps the arrangement may best be understood as a fixed fee agreement, except that instead of handling one matter for a set fee no matter

9. Model Rules of Prof'l Conduct R. 1.5(a); Restatement (Third) of the Law Governing Lawyers § 34 (2001) [hereinafter Restatement].

10. Douglas R. Richmond, *Understanding Retainers and Flat Fees*, 34 J. Legal Prof. 113, 116 (2009). *See also In re* O'Farrell, 942 N.E.2d at 804 n.5.

11. Provanzano v. Nat'l Auto Credit, Inc., 10 F. Supp. 2d 44, 51 (D. Mass. 1998).

12. Model Rules of Prof'l Conduct R. 1.5(b); RESTATEMENT, *supra* note 9, § 38.

what services end up being required, the lawyer is handling several matters (subject to whatever limitations the parties place on the number, type, geography, etc., of the matters).[13]

B. Flat or Fixed Fees

Some lawyers prefer to charge their clients a flat or fixed fee for discrete legal services they provide. Examples include closing the purchase of a single-family home, incorporating a small business, drafting a will, or providing a defined, limited-scope service, such as drafting a motion. A flat fee is one that "embraces all work to be done, whether it be relatively simple and of short duration, or complex and protracted."[14]

If a flat or fixed fee is paid by the client in advance of the lawyer performing the legal work, the fees are an advance. Use of the term "flat fee" or "fixed fee" does not transform the arrangement into a fee that is "earned when paid." "Flat" or "fixed" does not even mean that the fee must be paid at the commencement of the representation, although most lawyers who do not have an existing relationship with a client may want to ensure payment and may, therefore, ask for the fee to be paid in advance before committing to the representation. If they do, as will be emphasized below, then that fee must be placed in a Rule 1.15-compliant trust account, to be disbursed to the lawyer only after the fee has been earned.

Several courts and ethics opinions endorse the option of dividing the representation into segments such that certain portions of a flat fee advance are considered earned before completion of all the contemplated work.[15]

---

13. As we have noted, courts scrutinize purported general retainers to ensure that the lawyer is not attempting to circumvent the ethics rules requiring refund of unearned fees upon termination of the representation. The same is true with what are sometimes called "hybrid" fees or retainers. Such a fee is "a putative general retainer that is denominated as both for availability and for services," and it is likely to be considered by courts to be "fully refundable to the extent not earned by services rendered." Lester Brickman & Lawrence A. Cunningham, *Nonrefundable Retainers: A Response to Critics of the Absolute Ban*, 64 U. Cin. L. Rev. 11, 22 (1995). *See also*

N.Y. City Bar Formal Op. 2015-2 (Nonrefundable Monthly Fee in a Retainer Agreement) (2015), *citing* Agusta & Ross v. Trancamp Contracting Corp., 193 Misc.2d 781, 785-86 (N.Y. Civ. Ct. 2002) for the proposition that "enforcement of a hybrid retainer 'should be subject to close scrutiny, governed by a rebuttable presumption that any moneys retained by counsel are for services, rather than availability.'"

14. ABA Comm. on Ethics and Professional Responsibility, Informal Op. 1389 (1977).

15. *See, e.g.*, New Hampshire Bar Assoc. Ethics Committee Practical Ethics Article, *Practical Suggestions for Flat Fees or Minimum Fees in Criminal Cases* (Jan. 17, 2008). *See also In re* Mance, 980 A.2d 1196, 1202, 1204-1205 (D.C. 2009), *citing* Alec Rothrock, *The Forgotten Flat Fee; Whose Money is it and Where Should it be Deposited?*, 1 Fla. Costal L.J. 293, 323 (1999) for the proposition that some opinions "allow the lawyer to withdraw fees according to milestones 'based upon passage of time, the completion of certain tasks, or any other basis mutually agreed upon between the lawyer and client.'"

Some jurisdictions have codified this approach in their rules.[16] Thus, if agreed to, the lawyer may remove such earned portions of a flat fee advance from trust prior to the completion of the full scope of the legal services to be performed as certain "milestones" or stages of the representation are reached or completed. This approach allows the lawyer to be paid in part before the end of the representation and provides some assistance in determining the refund amount in case of early termination. Of course, "extreme 'front-loading' of payment milestones in the context of the anticipated length and complexity of the representation" may not be reasonable.[17]

C. So Called "Nonrefundable" and "Earned Upon Receipt" Fees

Some lawyers use labels like "nonrefundable retainer," "nonrefundable fee," or "earned on receipt" in the body or title of a fee agreement. These are not actual types of fees. And use of these descriptors does not, in and of itself, make a fee arrangement a general retainer. In fact, these terms are most often used in an attempt to make an advance fee nonrefundable.

The Model Rules of Professional Conduct do not allow a lawyer to sidestep the ethical obligation to safeguard client funds with an act of legerdemain: characterizing an advance as "nonrefundable" and/or "earned upon receipt." This approach does not withstand even superficial scrutiny. A lawyer may not charge an unreasonable fee. See Model Rule 1.5(a) ("A lawyer shall not make an agreement for, charge, or collect an unreasonable fee or an unreasonable amount for expenses."). Comment [4] to Rule 1.5 provides this additional guidance: "A lawyer may require advance payment of a fee, but is obliged to return any unearned portion. See Rule 1.16(d)." See also, Model Rule 1.15(c) and others discussed in connection with Hypothetical 1 below. Therefore, under the Model Rules, an advance fee paid by a client to a lawyer for legal services to be provided in the future cannot be nonrefundable. Any unearned portion must be returned to the client. Labeling a fee paid in advance for work to be done in the future as "earned upon receipt" or "nonrefundable" does not make it so.[18]

---

16. *See, e.g.*, Colo. Rules of Prof'l Conduct R. 1.5(h) (defining a flat fee, explaining proper handling, setting forth required contents of the agreement, and appending an authorized form agreement).

17. *In re* Mance, *supra* note 15.

18. *See, e.g.*, *In re* O'Farrell, 942 N.E.2d 799, 803 (Ind. 2011) ("Regardless of the term used to describe a client's initial payment, its type is determined by its purpose, i.e., what it is intended to purchase."); Mo. Sup. Ct. Advisory Comm. Formal Op. 128 (Amended 2018) (labels not conclusive); *In re* Wintroub, 277 Neb. 787, 801; 765 N.W.2d 482 (2009) (citing cases from several jurisdictions for the proposition that "a lawyer may not retain an unearned fee, even if the fee agreement clearly provides that the fee is nonrefundable"); Iowa Sup. Ct. Att'y Disciplinary Bd. v. Turner, 918 N.W.2d 130, 147 (Iowa 2018) (simply labeling payment of advance fees as "nonrefundable" does not relieve attorney from obligation to deposit them into trust accounts).

Hypothetical scenarios illustrating these concepts and applying the Model Rules are discussed in Section IV below.

II. Model Rule of Professional Conduct 1.15: The Anti-commingling Rule and the Need to Protect Client Funds, Including Advances

Rules of professional conduct exist for the protection of the public. That purpose is well served when the rules are designed and enforced to prevent concrete financial harm to clients. The anti-commingling principle, embodied in Rule 1.15, is a longstanding and effective component in the client protection arsenal. This is why, since their inception in 1908, the American Bar Association's model codes and rules of ethics have prohibited lawyers from commingling their property (including funds) with the property of clients and third parties.[19]

Under the general anti-commingling rule, Model Rule 1.15(a), client property, which includes unearned fees paid in advance, must be held in an account separate from the lawyer's own property.[20] In 2002, Model Rule 1.15 was amended to address specifically the issue of advance fees in a new paragraph (c): "A lawyer shall deposit into a client trust account legal fees and expenses that have been paid in advance, to be withdrawn by the lawyer only as fees are earned or expenses incurred." Therefore, advances must be placed into a lawyer's trust account until those fees are earned.

The Commission on Evaluation of the Rules of Professional Conduct ("Ethics 2000 Commission"), which recommended the addition of this paragraph, did so in response to reports "that the single largest class of claims made to client protection funds is for the taking of unearned fees."[21] Accord-

---

19. *See* ABA Canons of Professional Ethics, Canon 11 (1908); ABA Model Code of Prof'l Responsibility, DR 9-102 (1969); ABA Model Rules of Prof'l Conduct R. 1.15 (1983, revised 2002). One treatise explains the nature and breadth of this key obligation:

> One of the core fiduciary duties of a lawyer is to safeguard the property that the lawyer receives from the client or from other sources but that belongs to the client or third persons. Property received from a client may include funds to be applied to a transaction, a payment in satisfaction of a judgment or settlement, an advance deposit against lawyer's fees, valuable documents to be analyzed, or property of evidentiary value. Under Rule 1.15(a) of the Model Rules of Professional Conduct, "[a] lawyer shall hold property of clients or third persons that is in a lawyer's possession in connection with a representation separate from the lawyer's own property." The lawyer therefore must keep the property in a secure location and segregate those assets from the lawyer's own property. Gregory C. Sisk, Duties to Effectively Represent the Client, § 4-5.6 (The Duty to Safeguard Client Funds and Property), in Legal Ethics, Professional Responsibility, and the Legal Profession (West Academic Publishing, 2016).

20. *In re* Kendall, 804 N.E.2d 1152, 1161 (Ind. 2004). Also, Rule 1.15(a)'s predecessor was applied to advance fees. Iowa Sup. Ct. Bd. of Prof'l Ethics & Conduct v. Frerichs, 671 N.W.2d 470, 477 (Iowa 2003) (failure to place advance fee in a trust account violated DR 9-102(A)).

21. A Legislative History: The Development of the ABA Model Rules of Professional Conduct, 1982–2005 342 (ABA 2006).

ingly, paragraph (c) "provides needed practical guidance to lawyers on how to handle advance deposits of fees and expenses."[22] Stated simply, under the Model Rules advance fees must be placed in a Rule 1.15-compliant trust account, to be disbursed to the lawyer only after the fee has been earned.

Some jurisdictions have authorized lawyers to treat advances as the lawyer's property upon payment, so long as the client signs a fee agreement designating the sum as "nonrefundable" or "earned on receipt" or some other variation on this theme.[23] This approach departs from the safekeeping policy of the Model Rules described herein and creates unnecessary risks for the client.[24]

---

22. *Id.*

23. *See, e.g.*, Or. Rules of Prof'l Conduct R. 1.5(c)(3). That jurisdiction's version of Rule 1.15(c) contains an exception to the anti-commingling rule for advance fees when "the fee is denominated as 'earned on receipt,' 'nonrefundable' or similar terms and complies with Rule 1.5(c)(3)." Or. Rules of Prof'l Conduct R. 1.15-1(c). A considerable minority of U.S. jurisdictions have authorized this variant approach to advances by rule, ethics opinion, or judicial decree. *See, e.g.*, State Bar of Ariz. Op. 99-02 (1999) (non-refundable, earned-upon-receipt fee is ethical if reasonable under Rule 1.5 and client is fully informed about and expressly agrees to such a fee, preferably in writing; such a fee does not go into a lawyer's trust account); Fla. Rules of Prof'l Conduct R. 4-1.5(e)(2)(B) and Comment (nonrefundable flat fee is the property of the lawyer and should not be held in trust); Wash. State Rules of Prof'l Conduct R. 1.5(f)(2) (if agreed to in advance in a writing signed by the client, a flat fee is the lawyer's property on receipt and shall not be deposited into a trust account); and N.Y. St. Bar. Assn. Comm. Prof'l Ethics Op. 816 (2007) (reaffirming 1985 opinion concluding that "fees paid to a lawyer in advance of services rendered are not necessarily client funds and need not be deposited in client trust account"). Such jurisdictions typically provide, via rule or otherwise, that advance fees must be refunded if unreasonable or work remains to be done even if language to the contrary is used and the funds have been taken by the lawyer pursuant to a rule and/or agreement.

24. See *In re* Long, 368 Or. 452, 455–56, 474-75, 491 P.3d 783, 788–89, 798-99 (2021), cert. denied 142 S. Ct. 2685 (2022), in which the court candidly discussed the rule and its fallout:

> Respondent's limited financial resources also led to his extensive use of fee agreements that allowed him to access advance fees before completing the promised services. . . . The [Oregon] Rules of Professional Conduct allow for alternative fee agreements, under which advance fees become the lawyer's property at the time the fees are received—that is, before the lawyer has performed the promised services. RPC 1.5(c)(3). In those instances, the advance fees are not placed in the lawyer's trust account and are sometimes referred to as "earned on receipt." Fees may be "earned on receipt" only pursuant to a written fee agreement disclosing that "the funds will not be deposited into the lawyer trust account" and that "the client may discharge the lawyer at any time and in that event may be entitled to a refund of all or part of the fee if the services for which the fee was paid are not completed." *Id.* [¶] According to respondent, because he frequently had pressing personal and business costs, he would not have been able to operate his legal practice if he could access a client›s fees only after he completed the promised services. . . . [¶] Although respondent's handling of those advance fees did not itself violate a Rule of Professional Conduct, it nevertheless left respondent's clients vulnerable. "Earned on receipt" fee agreements shift the risk of loss to the client. If the client relationship ends before the lawyer has performed the services needed to keep the advance fees, then the lawyer is required to return the fees for the uncompleted work. If the lawyer has already spent the advance fees and has no other financial resources upon which to draw, then the

III. Model Rule of Professional Conduct 1.16: Declining or Terminating Representation

Model Rule 1.16(d) requires that, upon termination of representation, a lawyer shall refund "any advance payment of fee or expense that has not been earned or incurred." This Rule, and Rule 1.15, work in tandem to achieve the regulatory objective of protection of the public from financial harm caused by inattentive or unscrupulous lawyers.[25]

Advances are unearned because they are payment today for work to be performed in the future. They were unearned upon receipt and remain unearned until the work is performed. The Model Rules mandate that advances belong to the client, must be preserved until they are actually earned, and must be refunded if the representation terminates before the fees are earned.

As a practical matter it may be somewhat more difficult to determine what has been earned and what is unearned when a representation ends before completion of the contemplated services when the client pays a flat or fixed fee instead of an hourly rate. However, courts routinely apportion the services completed and sum earned when a representation terminates before a lawyer has completed all of the contemplated work.[26]

> lawyer may be unable to provide the client with the required refund. [¶] That is what happened to many of respondent's clients. . . . [¶] Respondent's misconduct caused extensive injuries, which were not merely financial. Many of respondent's clients had limited financial means and needed their advance fees returned before they could afford to hire new lawyers. When respondent failed to return those advance fees, some clients simply went without legal representation.

25. Nothing tarnishes the profession's reputation like a lawyer who takes an advance fee for legal services to be performed in the future, does not complete the work contemplated by the fee arrangement, and does not refund the money, perhaps because he or she cannot. Once the money has been spent by the lawyer, it may never be recovered by the client (or by the client protection fund which may have reimbursed the client). Even if a civil judgment or disciplinary order of restitution is entered it may do little good if the lawyer is impecunious, judgment-proof, or bankrupt. Discipline in that case may offer a measure of public protection through deterrence, but it does not recompense the client. That client's access to justice may also be impeded. The client may be unable to pay another advance fee and may, therefore, be unrepresented if legal aid or pro bono assistance is unavailable. Model Rules 1.15 and 1.16 exist to protect a client from these consequences.

26. *See, e.g.*, *In re* O'Farrell, 942 N.E.2d 799, 808 (Ind. 2011) (quantum meruit available upon client termination of flat fee agreement). *Cf.* Plunkett & Cooney, PC v. Capitol Bancorp Ltd, 212 Mich. App. 325, 331; 536 N.W.2d 886 (1995) (discharged lawyer with fixed-fee agreement entitled to compensation for services rendered calculated by percentage of services required under contract, unless lawyer and client have agreed to other terms for valuing work completed).

IV. Hypothetical Scenarios Involving Client Payments at the Commencement of a Specific Representation.

Hypothetical 1 ("Nonrefundable Retainer")

A lawyer is consulted by a client seeking to terminate her marriage. The lawyer informs the client that the lawyer requires a $6,000 "retainer" to cover the filing of a divorce complaint, preparing a motion to enjoin the transfer of assets and a possible motion for a protective order, attending hearings relative to those motions, and any negotiations or related work until the lawyer expends 20 hours. The client was also informed that additional "retainers" may be required to complete the matter, and that the retainers will be credited toward payment for the lawyer's services at the reasonable rate of $300 per hour. The lawyer's fee agreement states, in pertinent part:

> Client agrees to pay Lawyer a nonrefundable retainer fee of $6,000. Client understands that no portion of this fee shall be refunded or returned to Client for any reason.
>
> Client further agrees that should Lawyer expend more than 20 hours on Client's matter, Client shall pay additional retainers as requested by Lawyer which shall be applied to Lawyer's billing for this matter at a rate of $300 per hour and to any costs or expenses incurred in the representation.

Three weeks after signing the agreement and paying the $6,000, Client notified Lawyer that she wanted to reconcile with her husband and asked for an itemization of Lawyer's time and expenses and a refund of any unearned fees. Lawyer had filed the complaint, but it had not been served. Lawyer had also prepared but had not filed a motion to enjoin the transfer of certain assets. Lawyer had spent 5.5 hours on the file and $150 to file the complaint, but responded to the Client that no refund was due because the $6,000 was a nonrefundable fee.

Question: Does Lawyer owe Client a refund for any of the $6,000 paid to Lawyer and are any rule violations established by this scenario?

Answer: Yes, Lawyer owes Client a refund. First, the $6,000 paid by Client to the Lawyer are fees paid in advance not a general retainer. Under this agreement, Lawyer is rendering legal services at the rate of $300 per hour. This is true from the outset as is established by simply reading the portion of the agreement quoted above and performing some simple math. The $6,000 entitles Client to 20 hours of Lawyer's work on the matter.

Second, lawyer was required to have placed the $6,000 of advanced fees into the Lawyer's client trust account. Model Rule 1.15(c) provides that: "A lawyer shall deposit into a client trust account legal fees and expenses that have been paid in advance, to be withdrawn by Lawyer only as fees are earned or expenses incurred." The so-called nonrefundable fee here is an advance payment of fees that may only be withdrawn from the client trust account as earned by Lawyer. The facts of this hypothetical are silent as to whether Lawyer placed the $6,000 in the trust, operating, or personal account and as to whether it was spent in whole or in part. Lawyers may be disciplined for treating advance fees as their own property before the fees are earned, i.e., before the contemplated legal services are rendered.[27] Commingling and perhaps misappropriation may have occurred here if Lawyer deposited the $6,000 into an account other than a client trust account and spent it.

In this scenario, assuming that the legal work performed was appropriate and useful, Lawyer has earned $1,650.00 in legal fees. Lawyer also spent $150 for the expense of filing the complaint. Failure to return the balance of $4,200 is a violation of Model Rule 1.16(d) (upon termination of representation, a lawyer shall refund any advance payment of fee or expense that has not been earned or incurred). Comment [4] to Rule 1.16(d) explains the fundamental legal principle underlying this requirement: "A client has a right to discharge a lawyer at any time, with or without cause, subject to liability for payment for the lawyer's services." Lawyer's failure to provide an accounting for the fees paid in advance also constitutes a violation of Rule 1.15(d).

Model Rule 1.5(a) provides: "A lawyer shall not make an agreement for, charge, or collect an unreasonable fee or an unreasonable amount for expenses." Comment [4] to Rule 1.5 states: "A lawyer may require advance payment of a fee, but is obliged to return any unearned portion. See Rule 1.16(d)." Thus, keeping the balance ($4,200) violates Rule 1.5(a) on these facts. Because Rule 1.5 precludes a lawyer from agreeing to an unreasonable fee, it is also violated by the Lawyer's inclusion of the following provision in the fee agreement: "Client agrees to pay Lawyer a nonrefundable fee of $6,000. Client understands that no portion of this fee shall be refunded or returned to Client for any reason."[28]

---

27. "A lawyer misappropriates client funds in violation of DR 1–102(A)(3), (4), (5), and (6)DR 1–102(A)(3), (4), (5), and (6) when special retainers and flat fees paid in advance are treated as money belonging to the lawyer and not maintained in a trust account until the fee has been earned." Iowa Sup. Ct. Bd. of Pro. Ethics & Conduct v. Frerichs, 671 N.W.2d 470, 475 (Iowa 2003). *See also In re* Fazande, 290 So. 3d 178, 185 (La. 2020) (lawyer violated Rule 1.15(c) by failing to deposit into his client trust account advance fees and costs).

28. *In re* Kendall, 804 N.E.2d 1152, 1160 (Ind. 2004) ("We hold that the assertion in a lawyer fee agreement that such advance payment is nonrefundable violates the requirement of Prof. Cond. R. 1.5(a) that a lawyer's fee 'shall be reasonable.'"). *See also* N.Y. City Bar Ass'n Formal Opinion 1991-3 (in light of reasonableness requirement, duty to refund unearned fees, and client's "essentially absolute" right to discharge counsel, "a lawyer may

Finally, because a lawyer may, in fact, be required to refund an advance payment of fees in various situations, characterizing such an advance as "nonrefundable" may also amount to a violation of Rule 1.4 (communication) and Rule 8.4(c) (misrepresentation) as the mischaracterization of the funds may have a chilling effect on a client seeking a refund of unearned fees upon termination of the representation.[29]

Lawyer and the fee agreement use the words "retainer" and "fee" interchangeably. In this hypothetical it appears that the word "retainer" is used incorrectly to refer to the advance payment of legal fees at the initiation of a matter, or, really, at any time during the representation as is suggested by the agreement's provision that additional "retainers" may be required.

Hypothetical 2 (Purported General Retainer)

The facts are the same as in Hypothetical 1, except that the lawyer's standard fee agreement states, in pertinent part:

> Client agrees to pay Lawyer a non-refundable engagement fee of $6,000 which shall be deemed earned upon receipt by Lawyer. This engagement fee is for the purpose of retaining Lawyer and assuring the availability of Lawyer in this matter. Client understands that no portion of the engagement fee shall be refunded or returned to Client for any reason.
>
> Client further agrees that should Lawyer expend more than 20 hours, Client shall pay upon request an additional retainer in an amount determined by Lawyer which shall be applied to Lawyer's billing for this matter at a rate of $300 per hour and to any costs or expenses incurred in the representation.

Again, the facts are the same: Lawyer spent 5.5 hours and a filing fee for the complaint, and Client reconciles and seeks a refund. Lawyer declines to refund any portion of the fee, claiming it is nonrefundable.

---

not properly denominate or characterize a fee as 'nonrefundable' or otherwise use words that could reasonably be expected to convey to the client the understanding that a fee paid before the services are performed will not be subject to refund or adjustment under any possible circumstance").

29. *See, e.g., In re* Sather, 3 P.3d 403, 415 (Colo. 2000) (knowing use of misleading language, i.e., describing flat advance fee as "nonrefundable," violated Colo. RPC 8.4(c)) and Ala. State Bar Op. RO-93-21 (1993) ("Any indication by the lawyer that the fee is non-refundable is inaccurate and inherently misleading and would violate Rule 1.4(b) Communication; Rule 1.5(b) Fees; and Rule 8.4(c) Misrepresentation."). *See also* Mo. Sup. Ct. Advisory Comm. Formal Op. 128 (Amended 2018) (in various situations "the description of the fee as 'nonrefundable' is misleading").

Question: Does Lawyer owe Client a refund for any of the $6,000 paid to Lawyer and are any rule violations established by this scenario?

Answer: Yes. The answer and analysis for Hypothetical 1 apply here as well. The only difference ("retainer" and "engagement fee" language) makes no difference at all. The fee arrangement still has the same basic structure and, for the reasons discussed above, the $6,000 is clearly an advance payment for the future performance of legal services, not an actual "retainer" because the lawyer contemplates billing time against the advance.[30] Accordingly, the $6,000 must be held in trust until earned and any unearned portion properly refunded to the client.

Under the Model Rules, there are no magic words that a lawyer can use to change what is actually an advance payment for fees into a general retainer: "an attorney cannot treat a fee as 'earned' simply by labeling the fee 'earned on receipt' or referring to the fee as an 'engagement retainer.'"[31] Notwithstanding the use of the terms "engagement fee," "retainer," and "availability," the fee in Hypothetical 2 is still not a general retainer fee and is, therefore, not deemed earned on receipt. The purpose of the fee dictates its character and treatment irrespective of labels or terminology used.

Courts examine the transaction and agreement very carefully to ensure that the purported general retainer is not an attempt to charge and retain unearned advance fees.[32] Accordingly, a lawyer claiming to have a general retainer must be prepared to demonstrate a valuable benefit to the client and/or an actual detriment to the lawyer.[33] It is easy to recite that the lawyer is prioritizing the client's work, turning away other work, keeping up on the relevant law, etc. However, it must be shown that such things were not only

30. *Cf. In re* Lais, No. 91-O-08572, 1998 WL 391171, at *14-15 (Cal. Bar Ct. July 10, 1998) (characterization as "'fixed, non-refundable retaining fee' paid 'for the purpose of assuring the availability of [respondent] in this matter'" was "not determinative" and the fee was not a "true" (general) retainer, but actually payment for the first 10 hours of lawyer's services).

31. *In re* Sather, 3 P.3d 403, 412 (Colo. 2000). *See also* note 18, *supra*.

32. Richmond, *supra* note 10, at 116: "As a practical matter, general retainers are rare. . . . The types of representations that justify or require general retainers are also scarce. Courts hearing fee related controversies are therefore properly skeptical of general retainer claims." *See also* RESTATEMENT, *supra* note 9, § 34 ("Engagement-retainer fees agreed to by clients not so experienced should be more closely scrutinized to ensure that they are no greater than is reasonable and that the engagement-retainer fee is not being used to evade the rules requiring a lawyer to return unearned fees.")

33. Att'y Grievance Comm'n of Maryland v. Stinson, 428 Md. 147, 183-185, 50 A.3d 1222, 1244-1245 (2012) (purported engagement fee for "willingness and availability" to represent client not a true general retainer where no benefit to client or detriment to lawyer established and lawyer "produced no useable work").

actually done, but that they were necessary for the representation and not part of the lawyer's basic responsibilities.[34]

Hypothetical 3 (Flat Fee)

A client seeks to hire a lawyer for representation in a criminal matter. The fee agreement provides: "Client shall pay Lawyer the sum of $15,000 for representation in the matter of State v Client, and that no part of the flat fee shall be refunded for any reason. Client understands that the flat fee is the agreed upon amount due Lawyer regardless of the time expended on the matter or how it is resolved." Client signed the agreement and paid the full $15,000. Lawyer deposited the $15,000 into his firm's operating account. Lawyer reviewed the police report, left a message for the prosecutor and law enforcement officer, appeared on behalf of the defendant at the arraignment, and filed an appearance with the court. A few weeks after the arraignment, Client discharged Lawyer and requested an accounting and partial refund. Lawyer refused, stating that the flat fee was earned when it was paid.

As we noted above, flat fees paid in advance of performing the work are subject to Rule 1.15(c) and the other rules set forth in the analyses in Hypotheticals 1 and 2. In other words, the foregoing rules regarding safekeeping, refundability, and reasonableness apply.

Flat fees are not general retainers and must not be treated as such. That the price set for the representation is not based on hours worked but is instead based on the completion of certain described services does not mean that the fee must be considered earned on receipt or nonrefundable when there is work yet to be done. Of course, if the flat fee is paid *after* the work is completed, the funds are earned and are not deposited into the trust account.

V. Conclusion

The Model Rules protect a client's right to terminate the fiduciary relationship with a lawyer and have the money to which the client is entitled available to obtain successor counsel if desired. Rule 1.15 requires that fees paid in advance must be held in a trust account until the services for which the fees will be paid are actually rendered, thereby allocating various risks to lawyer and client. The lawyer does not have to bear the risk of nonpayment after the work is completed; Rule 1.15 provides a process for withdrawal of earned fees and even for disputes, should they arise. And the client does not

34. *See Stinson*, 50 A.3d at 1243 (benefits offered to the client in exchange for the nonrefundable fee were "nothing more than the ethical obligation imposed on all lawyers when they agree to provide legal services to a client. . . . A lawyer who agrees to perform legal services also necessarily agrees to be available to perform those services."), *citing* Lester Brickman & Lawrence A. Cunningham, *Nonrefundable Retainers Revisited*, 72 N.C. L. Rev. 1, 24 (1993), and Iowa Sup. Ct. Bd. of Pro. Ethics & Conduct v. Frerichs, 671 N.W.2d 470, 477 (Iowa 2003).

have to bear the risk that the funds will be spent, attached by the lawyer's creditors, or otherwise dissipated before the legal work is performed due to a lawyer's unwillingness or inability to do so.

Other ethics opinions and resources discuss good billing practices and fee agreement drafting tips. However, we offer the following suggestions in relation to the matters addressed in this opinion. Use plain language. Thus, instead of "retainer" say "advance" and explain that it is a "deposit for fees."[35] Explain that the sum deposited will be applied to the balance owed for work on the matter, and how and when this will happen. For example, the fee agreement could provide that on a monthly basis the client will be invoiced for the time expended by the lawyer and state when the sum reflected in the invoice will be withdrawn from the trust account. When the arrangement is for hourly billing, explain that if the deposit exceeds the final billing any balance will be remitted to the client. If the advance fee is fixed and the representation may continue for some time or involve several stages, consider dividing the representation into reasonable segments and providing for withdrawal of a reasonable portion of the deposited fee as the representation progresses and the fee becomes partially earned.[36] Finally, it may be wise to recognize the reality that many relationships do not last and include a provision explaining what will happen if the representation is terminated before the matter is completed.[37]

---

35. Geoffrey C. Hazard, Jr., Peter R. Jarvis, Trisha Thompson & W. William Hodes, The Law of Lawyering §9.07 (4th ed. 2022-2 Supp. 2014). Of course, the applicable Rules of Professional Conduct must be consulted, and it may be prudent or required to use certain terms. However, accurately translating legal terms of art is not only helpful to the client but also assists with interpretation and enforcement. So, if the term "advance" or "special retainer" is used in the applicable rules, the lawyer will want to use it in the fee agreement. However, consider also adding an explanation that it is functionally a deposit to cover fees for work in the future.

36. *See supra* notes 15 & 16.

37. Again, see Colo. R. Prof'l Conduct R. 1.5(h) and accompanying flat fee form providing helpful language for dividing a representation into increments and explaining a method of calculating the fees the lawyer has earned should the representation terminate prior to completion of the tasks or events specified in the agreement.

AMERICAN BAR ASSOCIATION

STANDING COMMITTEE ON ETHICS AND PROFESSIONAL RESPONSIBILITY

Formal Opinion 506 **June 7, 2023**

Responsibilities Regarding Nonlawyer Assistants

A lawyer may train and supervise a nonlawyer to assist with prospective client intake tasks including obtaining initial information about the matter, performing an initial conflict check, determining whether the assistance sought is in an area of law germane to the lawyer's practice, assisting with answering general questions about the fee agreement or process of representation, and obtaining the prospective client's signature on the fee agreement provided that the prospective client always is offered an opportunity to communicate with the lawyer including to discuss the fee agreement and scope of representation. Because Model Rule 5.5 prohibits lawyers from assisting in the unauthorized practice of law, whether a nonlawyer may answer a prospective client's specific question depends on the question presented. If the prospective client asks about what legal services the client should obtain from the lawyer, wants to negotiate the fees or expenses, or asks for interpretation of the engagement agreement, the lawyer is required to respond to ensure that the non-lawyer does not engage in the unauthorized practice of law and that accurate information is provided to the prospective client so that the prospective client can make an informed decision about whether to enter into the representation.[1]

I. Introduction

Nonlawyers[2] provide tremendous client and lawyer support for law firms. This Formal Opinion addresses a lawyer's ethical obligations when

1. This opinion is based on the ABA Model Rules of Professional Conduct as amended by the ABA House of Delegates through February 2023. The laws, court rules and opinions, regulations, and rules of professional conduct, promulgated in individual jurisdictions are controlling.

2. The term "nonlawyer" is used in this Opinion, consistent with the term as used in Rule 5.3, to include all law firm employees, agents, contractors, and vendors who are not licensed lawyers (or otherwise authorized to practice law) but work under the supervision of a licensed lawyer including, for instance, paralegals, legal assistants, case managers, firm administrators, intake staff, and clerks. This term does *not* refer to professionals who are licensed by a jurisdiction to provide legal services in that jurisdiction, such as Arizona Legal Paraprofessionals, Utah Regulatory Sandbox participants, Minnesota Legal Paraprofessional Pilot Project, New York Court Navigators, or Washington Limited License Legal Technicians.

the lawyer delegates to a nonlawyer specific prospective client-intake tasks. Lawyers may train and supervise nonlawyers to assist with initial client intake tasks if the lawyers have met their obligations for management and supervision of the nonlawyers pursuant to ABA Model Rule of Professional Conduct 5.3 and prospective clients are given the opportunity to consult with the lawyers to discuss the matter.[3]

II. Analysis

A. Rule 5.3 Responsibilities Regarding Nonlawyer Assistants ABA Model Rule of Professional Conduct 5.3 addresses a lawyer's responsibilities regarding nonlawyer assistants.[4] Rule 5.3(a) provides that lawyers who are partners or managers in a firm must ensure that the firm has policies that assure a nonlawyer's conduct is "compatible" with the professional obligations of the lawyer. Paragraph (b) of the Rule requires that lawyers who directly supervise nonlawyer assistants must "make reasonable efforts to ensure that the person's conduct is compatible with the professional obligations of the lawyer." Comment [2] notes, "A lawyer must give such assistants appropriate instruction and supervision concerning the ethical aspects of their employment. . . ."[5]

A lawyer's delegation of prospective client intake tasks to a nonlawyer or the lawyer's use of technology to assist with the initial intake of clients provides significant benefits and increased efficiency to lawyers. For example, nonprofit legal services organizations frequently train, supervise, and rely on nonlawyers to perform initial screening of prospective clients to determine whether there are conflicts of interest and whether the prospective clients are requesting services that fall within the organization's practice areas. Similarly, for-profit law firms have offered limited scope online legal services that provide website intake questions, a menu of available limited scope legal document completion services (such as simple powers of attorney, LLC formation, property deed transfers, and name changes), a conflict checking algorithm, and then "click-to-accept-terms" engagement agreements.[6] Delegating initial client intake to nonlawyers also is common in mass

3. Because this Committee does not opine on substantive legal questions, this Formal Opinion assumes that the assistance provided by the nonlawyer does not violate applicable unauthorized practice of law regulations or statutes. Different jurisdictions may have different views on what constitutes the practice of law.

4. Model Rules of Prof'l Conduct R. 5.3, cmt. [2] "Lawyers generally employ assistants in their practice, including secretaries, investigators, law student interns, and paraprofessionals. Such assistants, whether employees or independent contractors, act for the lawyer in rendition of the lawyer's professional services."

5. For an extensive analysis of Rule 5.3, see ABA Comm. on Ethics & Prof'l Responsibility, Formal Op. 467 (2014).

6. *See* ABA Comm. on Ethics & Prof'l Responsibility, Formal Op. 10-457 & Model Rules of Prof'l Conduct R. 1.18, cmt. [2] for guidance regarding lawyer websites and when an individual becomes a prospective client.

tort and class action practices. There, trained intake personnel may check for conflicts of interest, collect basic information from prospective plaintiffs or class members for lawyers to ascertain their eligibility to make a claim, and explain how fees and costs are charged in such cases. If the prospective client meets the eligibility criteria and specifics set forth by the lawyers, then the intake personnel send the prospective clients the standard fee agreement for consideration.

While the benefits of using nonlawyer assistants are many, without proper policies, training, and supervision in place, this delegation could lead to ethical violations and unfortunate consequences for clients and lawyers.[7] The practice must be "carefully and astutely managed."[8]

B. Establishing the Client-Lawyer Relationship

When a prospective client contacts a lawyer for help in solving a legal matter, the lawyer and the prospective client discuss the scope of representation including the client's objectives for the representation and the actions the lawyer will take to achieve the client's goal.[9] Rule 1.5(b) requires a lawyer to communicate to the client the "scope of the representation and the basis or rate of the fee and expenses for which the client will be responsible ... preferably in writing, before or within a reasonable time after commencing the representation, except when the lawyer will charge a regularly represented client on the same basis or rate."[10] Essentially, the client must know what the client bargained for.[11]

Rule 1.4(b) mandates that a lawyer communicate with clients and provide the clients, to the extent reasonably necessary, with explanations that allow the clients to make informed decisions regarding their representation. Some of the communication duties set forth in Rules 1.5(b) and 1.4(b) also apply in the context of explaining fee agreements to prospective clients. We note that Rule 1.4(b) does not expressly apply to prospective clients. Indeed, some of Rule 1.4(a)'s requirements—such as providing updates, consulting about means being employed to address objectives, and responding

---

7. See *In re* Phillips, 226 Ariz. 112, 244 P.3d 549 (2010) (setting forth guidelines for use of nonlawyers in intake process, including applicability of Rule 5.3 and prohibiting nonlawyers from having clients sign engagement agreements without attorney involvement); *In re* Pinkins, 213 B.R. 818 (Bankr. E.D. Mich. 1997) (relying, in part, on State Bar of Mich. Informal Op. RI-128 (1992), superseded by RI-349).

8. State Bar of Mich. Informal Op. RI-349 (2010).

9. Model Rules of Prof'l Conduct R. 1.2(a).

10. Though the Model Rule states this obligation in the passive context, jurisdictions have interpreted the obligation to communicate this information to be a lawyer's obligation. *See, e.g.*, *In re* Freeman, 835 N.E.2d 494, 498 (Ind. 2005). That interpretation logically flows from the conclusion that the Model Rules govern the conduct of lawyers.

11. Geoffrey C. Hazard, W. William Hodes & Peter R. Jarvis, The Law of Lawyering § 9.02, 9-8 (4th ed. 2002); Model Rules of Prof'l Conduct R. 1.5(b) ("requires" discussion of fees).

promptly to requests for information regarding a representation—would not make sense in that context. But it would seem imprudent to wait until after engagement for a lawyer to "explain a matter to the extent reasonably necessary to permit the client to make informed decisions regarding the representation" as required by Rule 1.4(b). ABA Formal Opinion 02-425 (2002) applied Rule 1.4(b) to lawyers who "ask prospective clients to execute retainer agreements that include provisions mandating the use of arbitration to resolve fee disputes and malpractice claims." This interpretation has been extended to explaining "certain implications of the joint representation" by at least one ethics committee.[12] Therefore, we apply Rule 1.4(b) to lawyers when they communicate with both current and prospective clients.

A lawyer may develop policies, train, and supervise a nonlawyer so that the lawyer may delegate to the nonlawyer client intake tasks assuming those tasks do not constitute the practice of law in the applicable jurisdiction. For example, a lawyer may delegate to the nonlawyer obtaining initial information about the matter,[13] performing an initial conflict check,[14] determining whether the assistance sought is in an area of law germane to the lawyer's practice,[15] answering general questions about the fee agreement or process of representation, and even obtaining the prospective client's signature on the fee agreement as long as the prospective client is offered an opportunity to communicate with the lawyer to discuss the matter.

While many client-intake tasks lawyers perform may be delegable with proper policies in place, training, and supervision, lawyers who delegate do not relinquish their responsibilities under the Model Rules. Once the attorney-client relationship is formed, lawyers still have the responsibility to reasonably consult with the client regarding the client's objectives and how to achieve them.[16] Lawyers also have the responsibility to "promptly comply with reasonable requests for information" and consult with clients who

12. N.Y.C. Bar Ass'n Comm. on Prof'l Ethics, Formal Op. 2017-7 (2017).

13. Nonlawyers can be trained to obtain the names of all relevant parties, the date(s) of the incident(s) involved, and the nature of the legal matter.

14. Nonlawyers can be trained to run conflict checks with the firm's systems and to filter for not just parties, but witnesses, opposing counsel, vendors, and other individuals who may create a potential conflict of interest for the firm. However, when a relevant or closely related name comes up in the conflict checking process, the lawyer must be the one to review the similarities and make the final determination of whether or not a conflict exists and whether any such conflict or not it is a waivable conflict.

15. Where the lawyer's services would involve a single transaction, such as helping companies register their corporation filing documents with the state, with the appropriate training, a nonlawyer would likely be able to explain the type of services provided for a set fee. Allowing a nonlawyer to answer general questions related to the lawyer's services in such a situation would not require them to provide independent legal advice. However, the nonlawyer must be trained to recognize when the client's questions venture from discussing general services.

16. Model Rules of Prof'l Conduct R. 1.2(a) & 1.4(a)(2).

have engaged them regarding limits on the lawyers' conduct given applicable laws and ethical duties.[17] And, Rules 1.2, 1.4, and 1.5(b) require a lawyer to communicate with clients about fees, the scope of representation, and any limitations thereon.

Whether a nonlawyer may answer a prospective client's *specific question* depends on the question presented and what would be considered to be the practice of law in the jurisdiction. That is important because Model Rule 5.5(a) prohibits lawyers from assisting others in practicing law in a jurisdiction in violation of the regulation of the legal profession in that jurisdiction. As Comment [2] notes, the definition of the practice of law is established by law and varies from one jurisdiction to another. Lawyers should understand how it is defined in their jurisdiction and take care that the supervised nonlawyers understand that definition and how it limits what nonlawyers may do. For example, whether a nonlawyer may answer a question relating to fee or cost calculation or how payments can be made may depend on whether the question requires the application of law to the facts of the case, as opposed to a question that merely asks about a firm procedural matter. When the question presented would require the application of law to facts, a nonlawyer also may convey a client question to the lawyer, have the lawyer determine the answer to the question, and then relay the lawyer's answer to the client, again, depending on the complexity of the question posed. The lawyer will be responsible for determining if the inquiry is best answered by the lawyer communicating directly with the client, so the lawyer can gather more information to make an informed recommendation.

Nonlawyers may provide general information about how the firm charges legal fees, such as explaining that fees are charged hourly, or on a contingency basis, or the matter is billed at a fixed rate. Or, if the question merely relates to how payments can be processed or other administrative matters, then the nonlawyer may provide information to answer the inquiry. However, if the prospective client asks about what legal services the client should obtain from the lawyer to address the client's objectives, wants to negotiate the fees or expenses, or asks for an interpretation of the rights and responsibilities set forth in the engagement agreement, Model Rules 1.4(b), 1.5, and 5.5[18] require the lawyer to respond. Ultimately, the scope of what the nonlawyers may do in this context will depend on whether the services in question constitute the practice of law in the jurisdiction where they are being provided.[19] Because Model Rule 5.5(a) precludes lawyers from assist-

17. Model Rules of Prof'l Conduct R. 1.2 & 1.4(a)(4), (a)(5).

18. Once the prospective client becomes a client, then Rules 1.2 and 1.4(a) would also be implicated.

19. Indeed, the question of which jurisdiction's definition of the practice of law should be applied may be subject to a legal analysis. *See* ABA Comm. on Ethics & Prof'l Responsibility, Formal Op. 504 (2023).

ing others in engaging in the unauthorized practice of law, and Model Rule 5.3(b) requires lawyers to reasonably ensure the supervised nonlawyers conduct themselves compatibly with the lawyer's professional obligations, the lawyers are responsible for making sure this line is not crossed.

As noted above, delegation of prospective client intake must be carefully and astutely managed. What appears to be a simple question about how long the lawyer will spend on the matter, may actually be a question about the representation itself and cannot be accurately answered without the lawyer's personal knowledge and expertise.[20] Therefore, a lawyer must provide nonlawyers who are performing client-intake tasks with policies, training, and supervision regarding which questions the nonlawyer may answer, how to respond to those questions, and which questions should be presented to the lawyer.

Conclusion

Nonlawyers provide significant client and lawyer support for law firms. A lawyer may train and supervise a nonlawyer to assist during prospective client intake screening by obtaining initial information about the matter, performing an initial conflict check, determining whether the assistance sought is in an area of law germane to the lawyer's practice, assisting with answering general questions about the fee agreement or process of representation, and even by obtaining the prospective client's signature on the fee agreement provided that these tasks do not constitute the practice of law in the applicable jurisdiction and that the prospective client always is offered an opportunity to discuss the fee agreement and scope of representation with the lawyer.

---

20. The Law of Lawyering, *supra* note 11, at §9.04; *see also* ABA Model Guidelines for Utilization of Paralegal Services, Guideline 3(b), at 9, *available at* https://www.americanbar.org/content/dam/aba/administrative/paralegals/aba-model-guidelines-for-utilization-of-paralegal-services-2021-web.pdf ("Many state guidelines prohibit paralegals from "setting fees" or "accepting cases. . . . NALA Ethics Canon 3 states that a paralegal must not establish attorney-client relationships or set fees.").

AMERICAN BAR ASSOCIATION

STANDING COMMITTEE ON ETHICS AND PROFESSIONAL RESPONSIBILITY

Formal Opinion 507 **July 12, 2023**

Office Sharing Arrangements with Other Lawyers

It is generally permissible for lawyers to participate in office sharing arrangements with other lawyers under the ABA Model Rules of Professional Conduct. At the same time, office sharing lawyers should appreciate that such arrangements will require them to take appropriate measures to comply with their ethical duties concerning the confidentiality of information, conflicts of interest, supervision of non-lawyers, and communications about their services. The nature and extent of any additional safeguards will necessarily depend on the circumstances of each arrangement.

I. Introduction[1]

Office sharing among lawyers comes in many forms—lawyers with separate law practices sharing office space, support staff, and equipment; law firms renting unused office space to unaffiliated lawyers; or even lawyers sharing an office suite, receptionist, and conference room as part of a virtual law practice or on a temporary basis. Lawyers participating in these arrangements must take appropriate steps to secure client information and clearly communicate the nature of the relationship to the public and their clients.[2] In addition, there are potential conflicts of interest issues that office sharing lawyers must appreciate, including imputed conflicts for lawyers "associated in a firm," representing clients with adverse interests, and consultations be-

1. This opinion is based on the ABA Model Rules of Professional Conduct as amended by the ABA House of Delegates through February 2023. The laws, court rules and opinions, regulations, and rules of professional conduct, promulgated in individual jurisdictions are controlling.

2. Compliance with the obligations imposed by the Model Rules of Professional Conduct, as discussed in this opinion, depends on a lawyer's role, level of authority, and responsibility in the law firm's operations. ABA Comm. on Ethics & Prof'l Responsibility, Formal Op. 483, at n. 6 (2018). *See generally* ABA Comm. on Ethics & Prof'l Responsibility, Formal Op. 467 (2014). *See* MODEL RULES OF PROF'L CONDUCT R. 5.1 (2022) (Responsibilities of Partners, Managers, and Supervisory Lawyers); MODEL RULES OF PROF'L CONDUCT R. 5.2 (Responsibilities of a Subordinate Lawyer); and MODEL RULES OF PROF'L CONDUCT R. 5.3 (Responsibilities Regarding Nonlawyer Assistance).

tween lawyers. This opinion addresses some minimum ethical requirements and suggested practices arising in the office sharing context, particularly in the areas of confidentiality, conflicts of interest, supervision, and communications concerning a lawyer's services.

II. Discussion

A. Protecting Client Information

Confidentiality is central to the practice of law.[3] Maintaining the confidentiality of client information is therefore imperative for lawyers in an office sharing arrangement.[4] The mere sharing of office space does not automatically equate with the disclosure of client information.[5] The physical arrangement of the shared office space, however, must not expose client information to other office-sharing lawyers and their staff. Everyone should also avoid discussing cases in or near common areas, which could lead to the disclosure of client information.[6]

Depending on the specific circumstances of the office sharing arrangement, lawyers may need to consider additional confidentiality safeguards. This could include separate lobby or waiting areas; refraining from leaving client files out on workspaces, conference rooms, or kitchen tables; installing privacy screens on computer monitors and locking down computers when not actively in use; clean desk policies; and regular training and reminders to staff of the need to keep all client information confidential.[7] Office sharing lawyers can also restrict access to client-related information by securing

---

3. *See* Model Rules of Prof'l Conduct R. 1.6(a) (providing that "[a] lawyer shall not reveal information relating to the representation of a client unless the client gives informed consent, the disclosure is impliedly authorized in order to carry out the representation or the disclosure is permitted by paragraph (b)").

4. State Bar of Cal. Comm. on Prof'l Responsibility & Conduct Op. 1997-150, 1997 WL 240818, at *3–4 (1997); Conn. Bar Ass'n Prof'l Ethics Comm. 2014-04, 2014 WL 12823983, at *1 (2014); D.C. Bar Ass'n Op. 303, at 1 (2001) [hereinafter D.C. Bar Op.]; La. State Bar Ass'n Rules of Prof'l Conduct Comm. Op. 07-RPCC-013, at 1 (2007); Mich. State Bar Comm. on Prof'l & Judicial Ethics Op. RI-249, 1996 WL 381521, at *2 (1996) [hereinafter Mich. State Bar Op. RI-249]; Mo. Bar Informal Op. 950169, at 1 (1995); N.J. Sup. Ct. Advisory Comm. on Prof'l Ethics Op. 498, 1982 WL 117856, at *1 (1982); Ohio Bd. of Prof'l Conduct Advisory Op. 2022-11, 2022 WL 10219976 (2022); Ohio Bd. of Prof'l Conduct Advisory Op. 2017-05, 2022 WL 10219976, at *1 (2017).

5. Ill. St. Bar Ass'n Comm. on Prof'l Ethics Advisory Op. 85-14, 1986 WL 378934, at *4 (1986).

6. State Bar of Cal. Comm. on Prof'l Responsibility & Conduct Op. 1997-150, 1997 WL 240818, at *3–4 (1997); Colo. Bar Ass'n Ethics Comm. Op. 89, at 5 (2018); Mich. State Bar, Comm. on Prof'l & Judicial Ethics Op. RI-313, 1999 WL 406884, at *1 (1999); N.Y. State Bar Ass'n Comm. on Prof'l Ethics Op. 794, 2006 WL 1386607, at *4 (2006).

7. *See, e.g.*, ABA Comm. on Ethics & Prof'l Responsibility, Formal Op. 498, at 3–7 (2021) [hereinafter ABA Formal Op. 498] (discussing technologies and related strategies to protect the confidentiality of client information in a virtual practice).

physical client files in locked cabinets or offices and using separate telephone lines and computer systems.[8] Lawyers, however, may overcome confidentiality concerns with shared telephone and computer systems with appropriate security measures, staff training, and client disclosures.[9]

Lawyers in an office sharing arrangement may decide to share support staff, such as receptionists, administrative assistants, and paralegals. In these situations, maintaining the confidentiality of client information is tested. Instructing all lawyers and employees, and particularly shared employees, on their confidentiality obligations and the office procedures in place to guard sensitive client documents and communications are examples of reasonable measures to protect client confidentiality.[10] Of course, appropriate supervision of shared personnel is also required under Model Rule 5.3.[11]

B. Clear Communication About the Relationship

Lawyers who share offices but do not practice together as a law firm must take appropriate steps to clearly communicate the nature of their relationship to the public and to their clients.

Model Rule 7.1 prohibits any "false or misleading communication about the lawyer or the lawyer's services."[12] Comment [7] to the Rule further ex-

---

8. Colo. Bar Ass'n Ethics Comm. Op. 89, *supra* note 6, at 4–7; Ind. State Bar Ass'n Legal Ethics Comm. Op. 8, at 2–3 (1985); D.C. Bar Op. 303, *supra* note 4, at 1; Mo. Bar Informal Op. 980220, at 1 (1998); N.Y. State Bar Ass'n Comm. on Prof'l Ethics Op., 2012 WL 6087183, at *1–2 (2012); Ohio Bd. of Prof'l Conduct Advisory Op. 91-9, 1991 WL 717479, at *2 (1991); Va. State Bar Legal Ethics Comm. Op. 754, 1986 WL 1180470, at *1 (1986).

9. Colo. Bar Ass'n Ethics Comm. Op. 89, *supra* note 6, at 1, 5; D.C. Bar Op. 303, *supra* note 8, at 1; Mo. Bar Informal Op. 970192 (1997); Ohio Bd. of Prof'l Conduct Advisory Op. 92-13, 1992 WL 739420, at *3 (1992); Or. St. Bar Ass'n Op. 2005-50, 2005 WL 5679639, at *1 (2005). *See also* ABA Formal Op. 498, *supra* note 7, at 3–5 (discussing virtual practice technologies and other security measures to safeguard client information); Ohio Bd. of Prof'l Conduct Adv. Op. 2022-11, 2022 WL 10219976, at *2 (2022) (recommending that computers connected to a shared network "be secured by individual credentials and other security measures to prevent lawyers or staff from accessing the data and files on a network belonging to others").

10. State Bar of Cal. Comm. on Prof'l Responsibility & Conduct Op. 1997-150, *supra* note 4, at *3–4; D.C. Bar Op. 303, *supra* note 4, at 1; Mich. State Bar Op. RI-249, *supra* note 4, at *2; Mo. Bar Informal Op. 950169, *supra* note 4, at 1; Neb. Jud. Ethics Comm. Op. 89-2, 1989 WL 1803035, at *4 (1989); Ohio Bd. of Prof'l Conduct Advisory Op. 2022-11, *supra* note 4, at *3. *But see* Utah State Bar Advisory Op. 125, 1994 WL 631269, at *2 (1994) (finding it "difficult to see how it would be possible for shared secretarial arrangements not to put confidential information at risk").

11. Model Rule 5.3 addresses both partner and supervisor responsibilities for ensuring that nonlawyer assistants' behavior is compatible with lawyers' professional obligations. Model Rules of Prof'l Conduct R. 5.3. *See* ABA Comm. on Ethics & Prof'l Responsibility, Formal Op. 498, at 3–4 (examining lawyers' supervisory obligations for nonlawyer assistants in a virtual practice); Ohio Bd. of Prof'l Conduct Advisory Op. 2022-11, *supra* note 4, at *3 (discussing the sharing of nonlawyer staff).

12. Model Rules of Prof'l Conduct R. 7.1.

plains that lawyers "may not imply or hold themselves out as practicing together in one firm when they are not a firm, as defined in Rule 1.0(c), because to do so would be false and misleading."[13] Accordingly, office-sharing lawyers must ensure that the public is not misled about the nature of their relationship, such as confusion about whether the lawyers are part of a law firm, partnership, or professional corporation when no such affiliation exists.[14]

Lawyers in an office sharing arrangement should use separate business cards, letterhead, and directory listings, as well as office signs, firm names, and advertisements that describe their distinct practices and do not suggest a close association between professionals operating within the same space.[15] It is desirable for lawyers sharing office space to have separate telephone lines, but a receptionist may answer a common telephone line with a generic salutation such as "Law Offices" to avoid implying that the lawyers are practicing together in the same firm.[16]

It may not be possible to have separate signage where a law firm subleases excess space to unaffiliated lawyers or to lawyers with whom the firm works on a matter-by-matter basis, or where lawyers work in rented temporary space such as WeWork or Regus™ offices. Nevertheless, unaffiliated lawyers sharing space must take reasonable measures to ensure that clients are not confused about their associations with the other lawyers practicing in the immediate area. Office sharing lawyers must understand the need to clarify for their clients these distinct professional relationships. Any communications to the public should also signal that the law practices are not affiliated with one another, other than in their resource-sharing arrangement.[17]

---

13. *Id.* at cmt. 7. *See also* Model Rules of Prof'l Conduct R. 1.0(c) (defining "firm" or "law firm" as "a lawyer or lawyers in a law partnership, professional corporation, sole proprietorship or other association authorized to practice law; or lawyers employed in a legal services organization or the legal department of a corporation or other organization").

14. Model Rules of Prof'l Conduct R. 1.4 & 7.1; State Bar of Cal. Comm. on Prof'l Responsibility & Conduct Op. 1997-150, *supra* note 4, at *1; Colo. Bar Ass'n Ethics Comm. Op. 89, *supra* note 6, at 2; D.C. Eth. Op. 303, *supra* note 4, at 1.

15. State Bar of Cal. Comm. on Prof'l Responsibility & Conduct Op. 1997-150, *supra* note 4, at *1; Colo. Bar Ass'n Ethics Comm. Op. 89, *supra* note 6, at 6; Conn. Bar Ass'n Prof'l Ethics Comm. Op. 97-9, 1997 WL 700580, at *2 (1997); D.C. Eth. Op. 303, at 1; Mich. State Bar Op. RI-249, *supra* note 4, at * 3; Mo. Bar Informal Adv. Op. 980220, *supra* note 8, at 1; N.Y. City Bar Ass'n Prof'l Ethics Comm. Advisory Op. 680, 1990 WL 677022, at *1 (1990); Ohio Bd. of Comm'rs on Grievances & Discipline Advisory Op. 89-36, 1989 WL 535040, at *2 (1989); Va. State Bar Legal Ethics Comm. Op. 874, 1987 WL 1379105, at *1 (1987).

16. State Bar of Ariz. Op. 01-09 (2001); Conn. Bar Ass'n Prof'l Ethics Comm. Op. 97-9, *supra* note 15, at *2; D.C. Bar Op. 303, at 1; Mich. Eth. Op. RI-249, 1996 WL 381521, at *3; Ohio Adv. Op. 95-1, 1995 WL 813784, at *4 (Ohio Bd. of Comm'rs on Grievances & Discipline 1995); Wash. Adv. Op. 1304, at 1 (Wash. State Bar, Comm on Prof'l Ethics 1989).

17. Conn. Eth. Op. 2014-04, 2014 WL 12823983, at *1; D.C. Bar. Op. 303, *supra* note 4, at 1; Mich. State Bar Op. RI-249, *supra* note 4, at *2; Mo. Bar Informal Op. 950169, *supra* note 4, at 1.

C. Conflicts of Interest Considerations

Lawyers in shared office arrangements should pay particular attention to (1) avoiding the imputation of conflicts of interest, (2) taking on potential new matters that are adverse to clients represented by other office sharing lawyers, and (3) consulting with fellow office sharing lawyers.

1. Imputation of Conflicts

Model Rule 1.10(a) imputes conflicts of interest to all lawyers "associated in a firm."[18] Thus, imputation of a lawyer's conflict of interest to other lawyers in an office-sharing arrangement will pivot on whether the lawyers are, or appear to the public or their clients as, "associated in a firm."[19]

Under the Model Rules, office sharing lawyers are not automatically treated as a single law firm for conflicts of interest purposes.[20] This determination will depend on the facts and circumstances of each arrangement.[21] Office sharing lawyers who do not protect the confidentiality of their respective clients, regularly consult with each other on matters, share staff who have access to client information, mislead the public about their identity and services, or otherwise fail to keep their practices separate, are more likely to be treated as "associated in a firm" for conflict imputation purposes.[22]

---

18. Model Rules of Prof'l Conduct R. 1.10(a).

19. Model Rules of Prof'l Conduct R. 1.10(a) & cmt. 1; Colo. Bar Ass'n Ethics Comm. Op. 89, *supra* note 6, at 1; Mich. State Bar Op. RI-249, *supra* note 4, at *5.

20. Mich. State Bar Op. RI-249, *supra* note 4, at *1; N.Y. State Bar Ass'n Comm. on Prof'l Ethics Op. 794, *supra* note 6, at *1 (2011); *see* Model Rules of Prof'l Conduct R. 1.0(c) & cmt. 2 (stating that "two practitioners who share office space and occasionally consult or assist each other ordinarily would not be regarded as constituting a firm," but "if they present themselves to the public in a way that suggests that they are a firm or conduct themselves as a firm, they should be regarded as a firm" under the Model Rules).

21. *See* ABA Comm. on Ethics & Prof'l Responsibility, Formal Op. 88-356, at 2–4 (1988) (explaining that whether a temporary lawyer should be treated as "associated in a firm" for conflicts imputation purposes requires "a functional analysis of the facts and circumstances involved in the relationship," with a particular focus on the temporary lawyer's access to information relating to the representation of other firm clients).

22. *In re* Sexson, 613 N.E.2d 841, 843 (Ind. 1993); Model Rules of Prof'l Conduct R. 1.0(c) & cmt. 2; Ariz. State Bar Comm. on the Rules of Prof'l Conduct Op. 01-09, at 1 (2001); Colo. Bar Ass'n Ethics Comm. Op. 89, *supra* note 6, at 1, 4; D.C. Bar Op. 303, *supra* note 4, at 1; Ky. Bar Ass'n Ethics Comm. Op. E-418, at 4 (2001); Ind. State Bar Ass'n Legal Ethics Comm. Op. 8, *supra* note 8, at 3; La. State Bar Ass'n Rules of Prof'l Conduct Comm. Op. 07-RPCC-013, *supra* note 4, at 3; Mo. Bar Informal Op. 950169, *supra* note 4, at 1; N.Y. State Bar Ass'n Comm. on Prof'l Ethics Op. 794, *supra* note 6, at *4; N.Y. City Bar Ass'n Prof'l Ethics Comm. Advisory Op. 680, *supra* note 15, at *2; Ohio Bd. of Prof'l Conduct Advisory Op. 2022-11, *supra* note 4, at *2; S.C. Bar Ethics Advisory Comm. Op. 08-11, 2008 WL 8089795, at *2 (2008); Utah State Bar Advisory Op. 125, *supra* note 10, at *2; Vt. Bar Ass'n Prof'l Responsibility Comm. Op. 79-22, at 1 (1979).

2. Representing Clients with Adverse Interests

Where lawyers in an office sharing arrangement properly shield the confidentiality of their respective clients and do not hold themselves out to the public as members of the same firm, it may be permissible under the Model Rules to represent clients with adverse interests—even in the same lawsuit or transaction.[23] Although this determination will ultimately turn on specifics of the office sharing arrangement and the nature of the proposed representations, Model Rules 1.4 and 1.7 may obligate lawyers to disclose the details of the office sharing arrangement to their respective clients, including their efforts to maintain confidentiality, and to obtain each clients' informed consent, confirmed in writing.[24]

In addition, any staff shared by the lawyers should not possess or otherwise have access to information from both adverse clients.[25] Implementing an adequate ethical screen between shared staff members can be an effective measure in this regard, and to avoid the sharing of client information more generally.[26]

Notwithstanding the ability of office sharing lawyers to represent clients with adverse interests, some state ethics opinions understandably advise

---

23. ABA Comm. on Ethics & Prof'l Responsibility, Informal Op. 1486, at 1 (1982) [hereinafter ABA Informal Op. 1486] (lawyers who share space and represent adverse interests in pending lawsuits should explain fully the relationship to, and obtain the consent of, clients to continue to represent adverse interests).; Md. State Bar Ass'n Op. 1987-43, at 1 (1987); Mo. Bar Informal Adv. Op. 970192, *supra* note 9, at 1; N.J. Sup. Ct. Advisory Comm. on Prof'l Ethics Op. 515, 1983 WL 106225, at *1–2 (1983); Ohio Bd. of Prof'l Conduct Advisory Op. 89-005, 1989 WL 535010, at *1 (1989); Or. St. Bar Ass'n Op. 2005-50, *supra* note 9, at *1; S.C. Bar Ethics Advisory Comm. Op. 08-11, *supra* note 22, at *2 (2008); S.C. Bar Ethics Advisory Comm. Op. 91-37, 1992 WL 810417, at *1–2 (1992); Vt. Bar Ass'n Prof'l Responsibility Comm. Op. 80-15, at 1–2 (1980); Va. State Bar Legal Ethics Comm. Op. 943, 1987 WL 1378998, at *1 (1987); Va. State Bar Legal Ethics Comm. Op. 799, 1986 WL 1180507, at *1 (1986); Wash. State Bar Comm. on Prof'l Ethics Op. 1793, at 1 (1997); Wash. State Bar Comm. on Prof'l Ethics Op. 1559, at 1 (1994).

24. ABA Informal Op. 1486, *supra* note 23, at 1; Colo. Bar Ass'n Ethics Comm. Op. 89, *supra* note 6, at 4; Md. Eth. Op. 1987-43, at 1; Mich. Eth. Op. RI-249, 1996 WL 381521, at *3; N.J. Eth. Op. 515, 1983 WL 106225, at *1–2; Ohio Adv. Op. 89-005, 1989 WL 535010, at *2 (Ohio Bd. of Comm'rs on Grievances & Discipline 1989); S.C. Bar Ethics Advisory Comm. Op. 91-37, *supra* note 23, at *1–2; Vt. Bar Ass'n Prof'l Responsibility Comm. Op. 80-15, *supra* note 23, at 1–2; Va. State Bar Legal Ethics Comm. Op. 943, *supra* note 23, at *1; Wash. State Bar Comm. on Prof'l Ethics Op. 1793, *supra* note 23, at 1.

25. Ky. Bar Ass'n Ethics Comm. Op. E-406, at 3 (1998); Me. Bd. of Overseers of the Bar Prof'l Ethics Comm'n Op. 41, at 1 (2019); Or. St. Bar Ass'n Op. 2005-50, *supra* note 9, at *1; S.C. Bar Ethics Advisory Comm. Op. 91-37, *supra* note 23, at *1–2. The Committee does not believe it is possible for lawyers in an office sharing arrangement to maintain this kind of separation when representing clients with adverse interests if the lawyers together share only one staff member.

26. *See generally* Cal. Lawyers Ass'n Ethics Comm. Formal Op. 2021-1 (2021) (discussing elements of effective ethical screens).

lawyers to avoid these situations entirely.[27] Potential pitfalls range from inadvertent disclosures of client information in a shared office to opposing parties coincidentally scheduling meetings at the same time. Before entering an office sharing arrangement, it is prudent for a lawyer to examine the nature of the other lawyers' practices to determine whether conflicts of interest are likely to arise.[28]

3. Consultations Between Office Sharing Lawyers

It is natural for lawyers in office sharing arrangements to informally consult one another about their respective client matters. Merely engaging in informal consultations from time to time, however, does not result in the lawyers being "associated in a firm" under Model Rule 1.10(a).[29] At the same time, lawyers who occasionally consult with other lawyers in shared office arrangements should not disclose "client information that may reveal the identity of a client or privileged information."[30] Lawyers may instead discuss issues using hypothetical facts. As comment [4] to Model Rule 1.6 explains, "[a] lawyer's use of a hypothetical to discuss issues relating to the representation is permissible so long as there is no reasonable likelihood that the listener will be able to ascertain the identity of the client or the situation involved."[31]

Consultations between office sharing lawyers can also trigger unanticipated conflicts of interest, restricting a consulted lawyer's ability to represent a current or future client under Model Rule 1.7(a)(2).[32] For instance, if Lawyer A and Lawyer B share office space, and Lawyer A divulges client information to Lawyer B during an informal consultation to help Lawyer A prepare a case for trial, then Lawyer B may assume a responsibility not to use or reveal the information, which could materially limit Lawyer B's ability to represent a current or future client.[33] This situation parallels the confidentiality

---

27. Colo. Bar Ass'n Ethics Comm. Op. 89, *supra* note 6, at 3; S.C. Bar Ethics Advisory Comm. Op. 08-11, *supra* note 22, at *2; Va. State Bar Legal Ethics Comm. Op. 943, *supra* note 23, at *1; *see also* ABA Comm. on Ethics & Prof'l Responsibility, Informal Op. 1474, at 1 (1982) (concluding that "representation of opposing sides by lawyers working in the same military office and sharing common secretarial and filing facilities should be avoided").

28. Colo. Bar Ass'n Ethics Comm. Op. 89, *supra* note 6, at 3.

29. Ohio Bd. of Prof'l Conduct Advisory Op. 2022-11, *supra* note 4, at *1.

30. *Id.*

31. Model Rules of Prof'l Conduct R. 1.6 cmt. 4.

32. Model Rules of Prof'l Conduct R. 1.7(a)(2); ABA Comm. on Ethics & Prof'l Responsibility, Formal Op. 98-411, at 7 (1998) [hereinafter ABA Formal Op. 98-411].

33. Model Rules of Prof'l Conduct R. 1.7(a)(2); ABA Formal Op. 98-411, at 9. *See also* Liebnow v. Boston Enterprises, 296 P.3d 108, 115 (Colo. 2013) (citing ABA Formal Op. 98-411, at 7) (concluding that where "one lawyer has consulted another lawyer and has revealed confidential information about her case, including her theory of the case and trial strategy, that could materially limit the consulted attorney's ability to represent the opposing party . . . due to the consulted attorney's potential responsibility to keep the information confidential").

duties that lawyers owe to prospective clients under Model Rule 1.18 and the conflicts problems that can surface if a lawyer receives too much information from a prospective client during an initial consultation.[34]

To prevent these issues, Lawyer B can conduct a standard conflict check prior to any informal consultation or collaboration with Lawyer A.[35]

III. Conclusion

The ABA Model Rules of Professional Conduct permit lawyers to participate in office sharing arrangements, but those doing so must fully consider and comply with their applicable ethical responsibilities, including confidentiality, conflicts of interest, supervision, and communications concerning a lawyer's services.

---

34. Model Rules of Prof'l Conduct R. 1.18. *See also* ABA Comm. on Ethics & Prof'l Responsibility, Formal Op. 492 (2020) (discussing lawyers' obligations to prospective clients and the conflicts issues that can surface if lawyers receive "significantly harmful" information from a prospective client).

35. *See generally* Conn. Bar Ass'n Prof'l Ethics Comm. Op. 98-11, 1998 WL 993681, at *1–2 (1998).

AMERICAN BAR ASSOCIATION
STANDING COMMITTEE ON ETHICS AND PROFESSIONAL RESPONSIBILITY

Formal Opinion 508 **August 5, 2023**

The Ethics of Witness Preparation

A lawyer's role in preparing a witness to testify and providing testimonial guidance is not only an accepted professional function; it is considered an essential tactical component of a lawyer's advocacy in a matter in which a client or witness will provide testimony. Under the Model Rules of Professional Conduct1 governing the client-lawyer relationship and a lawyer's duties as an advisor, the failure adequately to prepare a witness would in many situations be classified as an ethical violation. But, in some witness-preparation situations, a lawyer clearly steps over the line of what is ethically permissible. Counseling a witness to give false testimony or assisting a witness in offering false testimony, for example, is a violation of at least Model Rule 3.4(b). The task of delineating what is necessary and proper and what is ethically prohibited during witness preparation has become more urgent with the advent of commonly used remote technologies, some of which can be used to surreptitiously "coach" witnesses in new and ethically problematic ways.

Introduction

> **Jack McCall:** Well, I'm a hard case for you, counselor. And no mistake, everyone in there saw me shoot him.
>
> **Lawyer:** If you'll let me set our strategy, I don't think we'll dispute what people saw.
>
> **Jack:** Now, I guess you're here to break me out.
>
> (*Lawyer chuckles*)
>
> **Lawyer:** Son, did James Butler Hickok ever kill a -- relative of yours?

---

1. This opinion is based on the ABA Model Rules of Professional Conduct as amended by the ABA House of Delegates through 2023. The laws, court rules, regulations, rules of professional conduct, and opinions promulgated in individual jurisdictions are controlling.

Jack: James Butler Hickok?

Lawyer: Wild Bill Hickok. Did he ever kill a brother of yours or—or the like?

Jack: A brother?

Lawyer: I'm asking you if what happened in that saloon was vengeance, for the death of a family member? Possibly a brother in Abilene. Or the like.

Jack: (*Jack smirks, cocks head pensively*) A brother in Abilene . . . .

(*Lawyer smiles, pats Jack twice on the knee, and exits*).[2]

Preparing a witness or a client to testify in advance of a deposition or adjudicative proceeding—or in some situations providing a client or witness with midstream guidance during the testimonial process – is such a familiar component of a lawyer's trial-advocacy repertoire that it needs little introduction or explanation. Many would condemn a lawyer's failure to prepare a client or witness.[3] Failure to do so competently and diligently can constitute an ethics violation.[4]

But, in some witness-preparation situations, a lawyer clearly steps over the line of what is ethically permissible. Certain categories of lawyer activity are firmly established as unethically interfering with the integrity of the justice system and unethically obstructing another party's access to evidence. Among the rules applicable to such conduct are Rule 1.2 (Scope of Representation and Allocation of Authority between Client and Lawyer), Rule 3.3 (Candor Toward

2. The Trial of Jack McCall, Deadwood, season 1, episode 5 (Home Box Office, Inc. 2010).

3. William Hodes, *The Professional Duty to Horseshed Witnesses Zealously Within the Bounds of the Law*, 30 Texas Tech. L. Rev. 1343 (1999) ("Journey not far enough, and a lawyer deserves sanction for failing to carry out the most basic duties encompassed by the client-lawyer relationship.") (footnote omitted); Roberta K. Flowers, *Witness Preparation: Regulation of the Profession's Dirty Little Secret*, 38 Hastings Const. L.Q. 1007, 1009 (2011) ("Witness preparation is considered by most criminal attorneys—prosecutors and criminal defense attorneys alike—to be an essential part of trial advocacy.") (footnote omitted); Adam Liptak, *Crossing a Fine Line on Witness Coaching*, N.Y. Times (Mar. 16, 2006) ("[L]awyers often spend hours preparing witnesses to testify, a practice that is not only accepted but also generally considered necessary. Lawyers have been punished for incompetent representation for failing to interview and prepare witnesses.").

4. *See* Model Rules of Prof'l Conduct R. 1.1 (Competence) & cmt. [5]; Model Rules of Prof'l Conduct R. 1.3 (Diligence).

the Tribunal), Rule 3.4 (Fairness to Opposing Party and Counsel), Rule 4.4 (Respect for Rights of Third Persons), and Rule 8.4 (Misconduct).

The distinction between legitimate witness preparation and guidance versus unethical efforts to influence witness testimony, a practice sometimes known as coaching, horseshedding, woodshedding, or sandpapering,[5] can be ambiguous owing in large part to the concurrent ethical duties to diligently and competently represent the client and to refrain from improperly influencing witnesses.[6] For purposes of this opinion, the term coach is used to signify unethical or ethically questionable conduct. The task of delineating what is necessary and proper and what is ethically prohibited during witness preparation has become more urgent with the advent of commonly used remote technologies, some of which can be used to surreptitiously "coach" witnesses in new and ethically problematic ways.

Analysis

Some quantum of client and witness preparation is appropriate and an affirmative ethical responsibility. But lawyers "must respect the important ethical distinction between discussing testimony and seeking improperly to influence it."[7] There is, in general, a distinction between manipulative conduct during client/witness preparation and active interference with or attempts to influence testimony while a witness is testifying. This opinion addresses both, because either can implicate a lawyer's ethical duties.

With remote proceedings having become commonplace, the sense that brazen witness-coaching behaviors are occurring or could easily occur

5. Black's Law Dictionary 885 (11th ed. 2019) (defining horseshedding as "The instruction of a witness favorable to one's case (esp. a client) about the proper method of responding to questions while giving testimony."). To be sure, a witness can be coached to tell the truth, which would not ordinarily be unethical. The practice of emphasizing continuously the importance of telling the truth, and that truthfully and accurately recounting facts is ultimately the witness's responsibility, is a useful guardrail to avoid coaching. *See* Resolution Tr. Corp. v. Bright, 6 F.3d 336, 341 (5th Cir. 1993) (district court's disbarment of two lawyers for aggressively pushing witness regarding choice of words was an abuse of discretion where there was no evidence that conduct was in bad faith or testimony was false; evidence that lawyers told witness to read the affidavit carefully before signing it undermined allegation that lawyers' conduct was an attempt to cause witness testify falsely under oath).

6. Many commentators have underscored this tension. *See, e.g.*, Tom Barber, *Restrictions on Lawyers Communicating with Witnesses During Testimony: Law, Lore, Opinions, and the Rule*, 83 Fla. Bar Journal 58 (July-Aug. 2009) (noting that "there is considerable disagreement as to the definition of 'coaching' as opposed to legitimate preparation").

7. *See* Geders v. United States, 425 U.S. 80, 90 n.3 (1976) (citing Ethical Consideration 7-26 of the ABA Code of Professional Responsibility (1975)); *see also* Hall v. Clifton Precision, 150 F.R.D. 525, 528 (E.D. Pa. 1993) ("The goal of obtaining the facts of a case is defeated when the lawyer and not the witness is answering questions or influencing the answers to them.").

has been validated by a number of reported instances of misconduct.[8] This development should guide the manner in which courts and lawyers are superintending the use of remote technology.

A. What Preparatory Conduct is Ethical?

Providing a witness with effective preparatory guidance is undoubtedly a component of the "thoroughness and preparation" element of Model Rule 1.1.[9] It is accepted that lawyers can engage in, for example, the following activities:

- remind the witness that they will be under oath
- emphasize the importance of telling the truth
- explain that telling the truth can include a truthful answer of "I do not recall"[10]
- explain case strategy and procedure, including the nature of the testimonial process or the purpose of the deposition
- suggest proper attire[11] and appropriate demeanor and decorum
- provide context for the witness's testimony
- inquire into the witness's probable testimony and recollection

---

8. The risk of witness-preparation misconduct is not particularly augmented in a remote environment because such interactions still occur "behind closed doors," so to speak. Technology-driven efforts to influence in-progress witness testimony—signaling or messaging a witness testifying remotely, out of the sight of opposing counsel and the adjudicative officer—has generated increased scrutiny.

9. *See* Model Rules of Prof'l Conduct R. 1.1 (Competence) & cmt. [5]. Other germane rules include Model Rules of Prof'l Conduct R. 1.3 (Diligence), 1.4 (Communication), and 2.1 (Advisor). *See, e.g.*, Hall v. Clifton Precision, 150 F.R.D. 525, 528 (E.D. Pa. 1993) (an attorney has right and duty to prepare a client for deposition); Maryland v. Earp, 571 A.2d 1227, 1234 (Md. 1990) ("[a]ttorneys have not only the right but also the duty to fully investigate the case and to interview persons who may be witnesses."); John S. Applegate, *Witness Preparation*, 68 Tex. L. Rev. 277, 287-88 (1989), ("The practical literature uniformly views the failure to interview witnesses prior to testimony as a combination of strategic lunacy and gross negligence.").

10. Telling a witness that a truthful answer of "I do not recall" is an acceptable response and ethically distinguishable from telling a witness, "The less you recall the better." The latter is a statement that affirmatively encourages a witness to "forget" information, i.e., to lie under oath about what is remembered. It is the ethical equivalent of telling a witness affirmatively to testify to something that is contrary to fact. *See* Model Rules of Prof'l Conduct R. 3.4(b) (a lawyer shall not counsel or assist a witness to testify falsely).

11. Vanessa Friedman, *Caroll, Clothes and Credibility*, N.Y. Times (May 9, 2023) (noting that witness's attire and demeanor were so effective that people wondered if someone was stage-managing the style: "Well, her lawyers, duh. It has long been understood that appearance is part of any courtroom drama.").

- identify other testimony that is expected to be presented and explore the witness's version of events in light of that testimony
- review documents or physical evidence with the witness, including using documents to refresh a witness's recollection of the facts
- identify lines of questioning and potential cross-examination
- suggest choice of words that might be employed to make the witness's meaning clear[12]
- tell the witness not to answer a question until it has been completely asked
- emphasize the importance of remaining calm and not arguing with the questioning lawyer
- tell the witness to testify only about what they know and remember and not to guess or speculate
- familiarize the witness with the idea of focusing on answering the question, i.e., not volunteering information.[13]

When it comes to preparation of a client or witness for a testimonial event such as a trial or deposition, there is a fair amount of latitude in the types of lawyer-orchestrated preparatory activities that are recognized as permissible.[14]

B. Unethical Pre-Testimony Coaching

Within the broad class of lawyer conduct directed at a client's or witness's future testimony, certain categories of lawyer activity are firmly established as unethically interfering with the integrity of the justice system and unethically obstructing another party's access to evidence. A lawyer violates ethical obligations by counseling a witness to give false testimony, assisting a witness in offering false testimony, advising a client or witness to disobey

---

12. The Restatement (Third) of the Law Governing Lawyers, § 116, cmt. b (2000), emphasizes that in suggesting choice of words "a lawyer may not assist the witness to testify falsely as to a material fact," which would constitute knowingly counseling or assisting a witness to testify falsely or otherwise to offer false evidence. *Id.* (citing Restatement § 120(1)(a)).

13. Many of these techniques are expressly referenced in the Restatement (Third) of the Law Governing Lawyers §116, cmt. b.

14. *See generally* Jonathan L. Rosner, Preparing Witnesses (2022-23 ed.); Daniel I. Small, Preparing Witnesses: A Practical Guide for Lawyers and Their Clients (5th ed. 2020); Video: Jan Mills Spaeth, *Become a Strong and Credible Witness: Witness Preparation for Deposition and Trial* (2019) (streaming HD video); James M. Miller, From the Trenches II: Mastering the Art of Preparing Witnesses (2019); Kenneth R. Berman, Reinventing Witness Preparation: Unlocking the Secrets to Testimonial Success (2018).

a court order regulating discovery or trial process, offering an unlawful inducement to a witness, or procuring a witness's absence from a proceeding.[15]

Prominent among the ethics rules in this area is Model Rule 3.4(b), which prohibits a lawyer from advising or assisting a witness—whether a client or not—to give false testimony.[16] Instigating a witness to lie can occur in ways beyond an outright instruction to fabricate testimony. For example, it is unethical to tell a witness to "downplay" the number of times a witness and a lawyer met to prepare for trial[17] or to encourage a client to misrepresent a location of a slip and fall accident to have a viable claim.[18] Other representative examples of unacceptable witness coaching and influencing behaviors

---

15. *See, e.g., In re* Stroh, 97 Wash. 2d 289, 300, 644 P.2d 1161, 1167 (1982) (disbarring lawyer following conviction for tampering with a witness; "Under no circumstances may false testimony knowingly be introduced into a hearing by an officer of the court.").

16. Model Rules of Prof'l Conduct R. 3.4(b). Such conduct might also constitute assisting the client to engage in conduct that the lawyer knows is criminal, i.e., perjury, in violation of Model Rule 1.2(d), as well as offering false evidence in violation of Model Rule 3.3(a)(3). Model Rules of Prof'l Conduct R. 1.2(d) & 3.3(a)(3). For examples of discipline for transgressing these rules, *see, e.g., In re* Peasley, 90 P. 3d 764 (Ariz. 2004) (lawyer who coached witness to lie disbarred); *In re* Paul Storment, 873 S.W.2d 227 (Mo. 1994) (lawyer disbarred in Missouri and reciprocally suspended for two-years in Illinois for advising client during recess to deny material facts of another witness's testimony that lawyer knew were true and prompting client on redirect to testify to known false testimony); *see also In re* Attorney Discipline Matter, 98 F.3d 1082 (8th Cir. 1996) (affirming reciprocal disbarment of same Missouri lawyer); *In re* Mitchell, 244 Ga. 766, 262 S.E.2d 89 (1979) (disbarring lawyer who had instructed six witnesses to say that a fictitious man by the name of "David Thompson" was the real father of a child whose paternity was disputed); *In re* Oberhellmann, 873 S.W.2d 851, 852 (Mo. 1994) (disbarring lawyer who, during client's deposition, instructed client to lie about a number of things, including client's place of residence).

17. *In re* Meltzer, 21 N.Y.S.3d 63, 64 (2015) (accepting lawyer's resignation and ordering disbarment in matter arising from lawyer's instructions that witness "downplay" the number of times they met to discuss testimony to prepare for trial in the event witness was asked such a question on cross-examination).

18. *In re* Rios, 965 N.Y.S.2d 418, 421, 423-24 (2013) (lawyer disciplined for violation of New York RPC 8.4(c)).

include programming a witness's testimony,[19] knowingly violating sequestration orders,[20] and encouraging a witness to present fabricated testimony.[21]

It is also unethical to compensate a lay witness for the substance of their testimony or to condition such payment on the content of the witness's

---

19. *In re* Brooke P. Halsey, Jr., Case No. 02-O-10195-PEM (State Bar of California Hearing Dep't, Aug. 1, 2006) (prosecutor's secret pre-trial coaching of forensic pathologist who had performed autopsy of victim was so intrusive and extensive that it "tampered with the heart of [the witness's] testimony"). Except in extreme cases of witness programming such as *Halsey*, the extent to which a lawyer can "script" or "prefabricate" otherwise truthful witness testimony has not been definitively resolved. Compare United States v. Welton, 2009 U.S. Dist. Lexis 138113 (C.D. Cal. 2009) ("While directing a witness to use (or avoid using) particular words when phrasing an answer is unacceptable conduct, particularly for a prosecutor . . . there is no evidence that [the witness] testified falsely . . . as a result of the advice she received from the [prosecuting attorney]") with Resolution Tr. Corp. v. Bright, 6 F.3d 336 (5th Cir. 1993) (drawing distinction between asking witness to swear to facts which are knowingly false and placing statements in draft affidavit that have not been previously discussed with witness). *See generally* Matthew Hector, *The Beau Brindley Case: Witness Preparation v. Coaching*, 103 ILL. BAR JOURNAL 11, 11 (2015) (analyzing federal district court for the Northern District of Illinois's decision that use of question-and-answer scripts to prepare witnesses for trial was not prohibited coaching, and noting that there is "no bright line" between rigorous witness preparation and improper witness coaching).

20. Transcript of Evidentiary Hearing Before the Honorable Leonie M. Brinkema, U.S. District Court Judge, United States v. Zacarias Moussaoui, No. 01-692 (E.D. Va. Mar. 14, 2006) (lawyer representing Transportation Security Administration emailed trial transcripts to a group of potential witnesses who were under a sequestration order; the court barred the government from introducing that evidence, and the lawyer was referred to the Pennsylvania Disciplinary Board). *See also* Miller v. Universal City Studios, Inc., 650 F.2d 1365 (5th Cir. 1981) (court ordered exclusion of witness testimony *where* lawyer violated sequestration order by allowing an expert witness to view the transcripts of other witness contrary to an order based on Fed. R. Evid. 615). *But see* State v. Blakeney, 137 Vt. 495, 408 A.2d 636 (1979) (sequestration order excluding witnesses from courtroom in no way restricted the right of counsel to confer with their clients or witnesses; purpose of the order was not to segregate witnesses from counsel who called them, although issuance of such an order would be within the sound discretion of the trial judge in an appropriate case).

21. *In re* Edson, 108 N.J. 464, 471-73 (1987) (lawyer disbarred after providing an undercover detective posing as a client with a memo fabricating facts to be used as the detectives' testimony, in violation of New Jersey RPC 1.2(d), RPC 8.4(a), (b), (c), and (d)). Even merely permitting a client to testify to fabricated evidence is sanctionable as offering false evidence. *See* Attorney Griev. Comm'n v. Elmendorf, 404 Md. 353, 946 A.2d 542 (2006) (leaving person with the impression that they could mislead the court in a divorce action by attesting to compliance with 6-month waiting period violated Rule 8.4(d)); Patsy's Brand, Inc. v. I.O.B. Realty, Inc., No.98 CIV 10175(JSM), 2002 WL 59434 (S.D.N.Y. Jan 16, 2002) (citing Rule 3.3(a)(3), court sua sponte sanctioned law firm for permitting client to submit false affidavit; although client insisted affidavit was true, where "no reasonable lawyer would believe it" in light of other evidence known to law firm).

testimony,[22] even if that payment is for "truthful" testimony.[23] Other types of unlawful inducements are similarly unethical.[24] For example, donating money to a witness's favorite charity was held to be an improper attempt to influence testimony.[25] In addition, offering a witness money or other incentives *not* to testify is a species of witness tampering and flatly prohibited by the Model Rules.[26]

C. Unethical Conduct During Witness Testimony

While the methods of advance witness preparation are variable and there is a broad range of acceptable methods, the equation changes when a lawyer's efforts to refine witness testimony happen during a trial or deposition. Overtly attempting to manipulate testimony-in-progress would in most situations constitute at least conduct prejudicial to the administration of justice in violation of Model Rule 8.4(d). Violation of a court rule or order restricting such coaching behaviors would be knowing disobedience of the rules of a tribunal in violation of Model Rule 3.4(c).[27]

---

22. MODEL RULES OF PROF'L CONDUCT R. 3.4, Comment [3] ("The common law rule in most jurisdictions is that it is improper to pay an occurrence witness any fee for testifying and that it is improper to pay an expert witness a contingent fee."). Most states permit "reasonable" compensation to occurrence witnesses for time and expenses in preparing to testify, although some jurisdictions place restrictions on testimony for actual courtroom time. ABA Comm. on Ethics & Prof'l Responsibility, Formal Op. 96-402 (1996) (nonexpert witness may be compensated for time spent attending trial or deposition or preparing for testimony if payment is not conditioned upon the content of testimony and does not violate any law). *See generally* ABA ANNOTATED MODEL RULES OF PROFESSIONAL CONDUCT, Rule 3.4, at 425-27 (10th ed. 2023) (discussion of Witness Fees).

23 *In re* Discipline of Callister, No. 70901 (Nev. 2017) (lawyer suspended for offering to pay a witness $7,000 for his "honest testimony" in support of certain facts and threatening the witness with personal liability and "the legal implications of perjury" if he testified the other way).

24. *E.g.*, People v. Gifford, 76 P.3d 519 (Colo. O.P.D.J. 2003) (advising client to offer ex-wife real estate in exchange for favorable testimony in criminal case). *See generally* ABA ANNOTATED MODEL RULES OF PROFESSIONAL CONDUCT, Rule 3.4, at 424 (10th ed. 2023) (discussion of Offering Illegal Inducement to Witness).

25. Christopher v. DePuy Orthopaedics, Inc., 888 F.3d 753 (5th Cir. 2018) (granting relief from judgment under FED. R. CIV. P. 60(b) where lawyer had represented that experts were non-retained and serving "pro bono," but lawyer had secretly donated $10,000 to one expert's private school alma mater before trial and collectively paid the two experts $65,000 after trial).

26. *See, e.g., In re* Discipline of Kronenberg, 155 Wash.2d 184, 198 (2005) (disbarment appropriate for lawyer who gave victim-witness $3,000 and a one-way bus ticket to Oklahoma so witness would not testify against defendant in a criminal case, in violation of Washington State RPC 8.4(a)-(d) bribing and tampering with a witness and 8.4(c) for deceiving prosecutors about procuring the witness's absence; lawyer also deemed unfit to practice law).

27. In some cases, such conduct may also be a violation of MODEL RULES OF PROF'L CONDUCT R. 3.4(a) (unlawfully obstructing another party's access to evidence). *See generally* ABA ANNOTATED MODEL RULES OF PROFESSIONAL CONDUCT, Rule 3.4, at 422 & 427-29 (10th ed. 2023) (discussions of Obstructing Another Party's Access to Evidence and Obeying Obligation to Tribunal).

Winking at a witness during trial testimony, kicking a deponent under the table, or passing notes or whispering to a witness mid-testimony are classic examples of efforts to improperly influence a witness's in-progress testimony.[28] Other more subtle types of signaling also implicate ethical obligations and at times result in court-ordered sanctions. A familiar type of covert coaching is the so-called "speaking objection," or "suggestive objection." These are "statements that go beyond just stating the objection or the basis for the objection and are intended—or at least suspected of being intended—to coach the witness and impede the deposing attorney's discovery."[29] The rules in many state and federal jurisdictions prohibit objections that have the effect of coaching a witness, and may also prohibit lawyers from instructing a witness not to answer a question unless specifically authorized to do so.[30] Some jurisdictions have enacted rules for the conduct of depositions that expressly restrict speaking objections.[31]

---

28. *See, e.g.*, Vnuk v. Berwick Hospital Co., No. 3:14-CV-01432, 2016 WL 907714, at *4 (M.D. Pa. Mar. 2, 2016) (finding lawyer violated court rules by conferring with witness over break, passing notes and whispering during deposition). One commentator likened lawyer-to-witness gesturing to the catcher's signal to the pitcher in a baseball game advising what pitch to throw. Holland & Hart, *Witnesses: Don't Rely on 'Catcher Signals'*, JDSUPRA (Apr. 26, 2021), available at https://www.jdsupra.com/legalnews/witnesses-don-t-rely-on-catcher-signals-5364552/.

29. Michael Roundy, *Speaking Objections Risk Sanctions*, ABA LITIGATION SECTION PRACTICE POINTS, *available at* https://www.americanbar.org/groups/litigation/committees/pretrial-practice-discovery/practice/2019/speaking-objections-risk-sanctions/?login (May 31, 2019). Openly asking a witness to correct an inadvertent misstatement when the witness obviously misunderstood a question or simply misspoke is not a coaching concern. In some circumstances involving false witness testimony, a lawyer may have an ethical duty to take reasonable remedial measures to correct the testimony. *See* MODEL RULES OF PROF'L CONDUCT R. 3.3, cmt. [10]. *See generally* ABA ANNOTATED MODEL RULES OF PROFESSIONAL CONDUCT, Rule 3.3, at 412-13 (10th ed. 2023) (discussion of Remedial Measures).

30. *E.g.*, FED. R. CIV. P. 30(c)(2) ("An objection must be stated concisely in a nonargumentative and nonsuggestive manner. A person may instruct a deponent not to answer only when necessary to preserve a privilege, to enforce a limitation ordered by the court, or to present a motion under Rule 30(d)(3)."); Sec. Nat. Bank of Sioux City, Iowa v. Day, 800 F.3d 936, 942 (8th Cir. 2015) (lawyers should not use an objection to instruct the witnesses how to answer or not answer a question); Deville v. Givaudan Fragrances Corp., 419 F. App'x 201, 209 (3d Cir. 2011) (affirming imposition of sanctions upon finding that attorney "testified on behalf of witness by way of suggestive speaking objections"); Goode v. Ramsaur, No. 20-cv-00947-DDD-KLM, 2023 U.S. Dist. LEXIS 80236 *13-24 (D. Colo. May 8, 2023) (finding sanctionable counsel's conduct involving countless speaking objections during deposition); Sec. Nat. Bank of Sioux City, Iowa v. Abbott Laboratories, 299 F.R.D. 595, 604 (N.D. Iowa 2014) (objections must be stated in a non-suggestive manner).

31. Brightman v. Corizon, Inc., 2021 NY Slip Op 50735(U), ¶ 2, 72 Misc. 3d 1213(A), 150 N.Y.S.3d 233 (Sup. Ct. 2021) (referencing New York's Uniform Rules for the Conduct of Depositions, which expressly limit speaking objections: "Speaking objections are thus singled out as undesirable: they are not necessary to preserve an objection to form, they disrupt and impede the conduct of the deposition, and they risk coaching the deponent on how to answer a pending question.").

Relatedly, when a witness's testimony is underway, lawyers sometimes attempt to exercise midcourse testimonial influence and undertake damage control during a break or recess and may even seek or insist upon such breaks while a question is pending for the apparent purpose of coaching the witness in a private conference. Although there is no express ethical prohibition on communications between witness and counsel during a break in testimony, adjudicative officers have, at times, exercised control over these circumstances, including entering specific orders and imposing deposition guidelines and/or sanctions.[32]

Lawyers should both refrain from efforts to physically signal witnesses when testimony is in progress and attend closely to the strictures imposed by court rule, local rule, or court order.

1. Misconduct in Remote Settings

The use of remote communications platforms and other technologies in adjudicative proceedings and depositions, provides opportunities and temptations for lawyers to surreptitiously tell or signal witnesses what to say or not say in the proceedings of a tribunal.

This is not a novel phenomenon. When the ubiquity of cell phone technology made it convenient to communicate with another person covertly, some lawyers began to abuse it. In a troubling example of text-message-based coaching, a Florida lawyer, in a worker's compensation case, was disciplined for sending text messages to a witness regarding the witness's testimony while a deposition was in progress, which texts included coaching and spe-

32. *See, e.g.*, Hall v. Clifton Precision, 150 F.R.D. 525, 528 (E.D. Pa. 1993) (holding that a lawyer and client "do not have an absolute right to confer during the course of the client's deposition"; noting that deposition guidelines restricting private conferences would be undermined "by a lawyer's making of lengthy objections which contain information suggestive of an answer to a pending question," i.e., speaking objections); Brightman v. Corizon, Inc., 2021 NY Slip Op 50735(U), ¶ 2, 72 Misc. 3d 1213(A), 150 N.Y.S.3d 233 (Sup. Ct. 2021) (discussing prohibition in Uniform Rules for the Conduct of Deposition on a lawyer interrupting the deposition for the purpose of communicating with the deponent, as well as the trial court's discretion to bar consultation between a party and counsel while the party is testifying to the extent consistent with the party's constitutional rights). *See also Deville v. Givaudan Fragrances Corp.*, 419 F. Appx. 201, 207 (3rd Cir. 2011) (upholding sanctions for abusive, unprofessional and obstructive conduct during deposition); *Specht v. Google, Inc.*, 268 F.R.D. 596, 598-599, 603 (N.D. Ill. 2010) (imposing sanctions for speaking objections that obstructed deposition); *BNSF Ry. Co. v. San Joaquin Valley RR Co.*, 2009 WL 3872043, *3 (E.D. Cal. Nov. 17, 2009) (imposing sanctions for inappropriate and burdensome objections).

cific directions on how to respond to questions.[33] Similarly, it is improper for a lawyer to text a witness who is testifying at trial.[34]

The logistics of trials and depositions using remote meeting technologies are such that a lawyer and a witness may be in one location, with the opposing lawyer at another location, and, in trial situations, an adjudicative officer in yet another. In these circumstances, many things can happen that cannot readily be monitored by participants in the other remote locations.[35] It would be relatively easy for an off-camera lawyer or someone acting at the lawyer's behest to signal a witness with undetectable winks, nods, thumbs up or down, passed notes, or the like. Surreptitious off-camera activities such as texting the witness or other real-time electronic messaging are possible and easily done.

Allegations of misconduct in remote proceedings have been addressed by regulators and the judiciary. A lawyer has been disciplined for providing a client with answers to questions while off camera during a remote proceeding.[36] Another example involved a lawyer representing the defendant in a federal lawsuit, who, during a remote deposition, was overheard by opposing counsel providing the client with an answer to a question, after which the client repeated the answer as the client's own. After reviewing the deposition

33. When confronted about the text messages by counsel taking the deposition, the lawyer falsely denied texting the witness and stated he was only receiving a text from his daughter. Then, after agreeing to put his cellphone away, the lawyer continued sending texts, and inadvertently sent text messages intended for the witness to deposing counsel. The Florida Bar v. James, 329 So.3d 108, 109-112 (Fla. 2021) (finding violation of Florida Bar Rules 3-4.3 (commission of any act that is unlawful or contrary to honesty and justice), 4-3.4(a) (obstructing another party's access to evidence), Rule 4-8.4(d) (conduct prejudicial to the administration of justice)).

34. *See* Sky Dev. Inc v. Vistaview Dev. Inc., 41 So. 3d 918 (Fla. Dist. Ct. App. 2010) (lawyer who texted witness while witness was testifying at trial constituted a "blatant showing of fraud, pretense, collusion or other similar wrongdoing"); Wei Ngai v. Old Navy, No. 07-5653 (KSH) (PS), 2009 U.S. Dist. LEXIS 67117, at 4 (D.N.J. July 31, 2009) (during remote video-conference deposition with lawyer in one state while deponent was in another, lawyer and deponent exchanged five text messages; because lawyer also accidentally sent a text meant for deponent to opposing counsel, the texting came to light; in ordering production of the text messages, court rejected assertion of attorney-client privilege for the texts, which violated Fed. R. Civ. P. 30(c) ("depositions are to be conducted in the same manner as trial examination") because texts were equivalent to passing notes to client with the intent "to influence the fact finding goal of the deposition process").

35. *See* Wei Ngai v. Old Navy, Civil Action No. 07-5653 (KSH) (PS), 2009 U.S. Dist. LEXIS 67117, at *2 (D.N.J. July 31, 2009) (in dispute over defense counsel's sending of text messages to witness during remote deposition, plaintiff's counsel noted that the deponent and defense counsel were only visible from the "chest up" and that she was unable to observe defense counsel's hands during the deposition).

36. *In re* Claridge, PDJ 2021-9088 (Ariz. Jan. 21, 2022) (suspending lawyer for 60 days by consent where lawyer used chat feature to instruct client during cross-examination at trial using GoToMeeting platform, in violation of Arizona Ethics Rule 3.4(a) ER 8.4(c), and ER 8.4(d)).

footage, opposing counsel found 50 additional circumstances where the lawyer had provided the client with answers to questions while off-camera during the remote deposition.[37]

Lawyers have a duty to comply with the rules of professional conduct and rules of court that prohibit witness coaching, in all testimonial contexts regardless of the format of the deposition, hearing, or trial. Remote coaching, like its historical antecedents, puts the perpetrating lawyer at risk of adjudicative rebukes and court-ordered sanctions,[38] as well as disciplinary sanctions.[39]

2. *Systemic Precautions for Addressing Such Misconduct*

All lawyers have an ethical obligation to understand how relevant technology works.[40] Some degree of sophistication regarding the nature of the technology used in remote proceedings will help avoid inadvertent missteps.[41] An understanding of the coaching-related risks of remote technology will also enable lawyers and adjudicative officers concerned about potential surreptitious coaching to structure remote proceedings in ways that will deter its occurrence and enhance the ability to detect it.

---

37. Barksdale School Portraits, LLC v. Williams, 339 F.R.D. 341 (D. Mass. 2021) (disqualifying lawyer from case, ordering that jurors be allowed to hear both the deposition witness's testimony and the lawyer's coaching and draw their own conclusions regarding the credibility of the testimony, and referring matter to another federal district court judge to evaluate potential discipline); *see also In re* Jeffrey Rosin, No. 21-mc-91571-LTS (U.S. Dist. Ct. for the Dist. of Mass., Jan. 19, 2022) (ordering lawyer in *Barksdale School Portraits* case to contact a group called Lawyers Concerned for Lawyers "for the limited purpose of receiving and completing counseling on better management of emotions and judgment in the face of adversity").

38. *See, e.g., Barksdale School Portraits, supra* note 37; Johnson v. Statewide Investigative Services Inc., No. 20-C-114 (N.D. Ill., March 4, 2021) (magistrate judge accepted lawyer's explanations of questionable conduct during Zoom deposition, finding that what happened during deposition was the result of a lack of professionalism and collegiality rather than an unethical attempt to coach witness).

39. The most severe sanctions to date were the disciplinary suspensions in the *James* and *Claridge* cases, discussed *supra* at notes 33 & 36. *See* Zack Needles, *Ethics Authorities Go Relatively Easy on Virtual Witness Coaching—For Now*, LAW.COM (Feb. 2, 2022) (noting that "ethics authorities have shown a fair amount of mercy to the offending lawyers, perhaps in recognition of the fact that virtual litigation is still pretty weird for everyone involved.").

40. MODEL RULES OF PROF'L CONDUCT R. 1.1, cmt. [8].

41. In Johnson v. Statewide Investigative Services Inc., No. 20-C-114 (N.D. Ill., March 4, 2021), a dispute over what appeared to be remote coaching, the trial judge firmly rejected a lawyer's proffered explanation that the problems occurred because he was not "technologically savvy," noting that at the time of the deposition, lawyers across the country had been primarily conducting their practices using technology for ten months: "This has included a host of different videoconferencing platforms for court hearings, depositions, and appellate arguments. Thus, while [a lawyer's] lack of technology expertise may have sufficed as an explanation at one point in time, it is no longer valid or credible."

What systemic precautions will prove useful in helping to prevent and detect incidences of problematic remote coaching and empower adjudicators to intervene as appropriate to control questionable lawyer conduct during remote trials and depositions? The following suggested approaches—though not ethically required under the Model Rules—provide a starting point:

- Skillful cross-examination[42]
- Court orders directing uninterrupted testimony[43]
- Motions to terminate or limit a deposition or for sanctions[44]
- Inclusion of protocols in remote deposition orders, scheduling orders, and proposed discovery plans[45]

---

42. This remedy was recommended by the United States Supreme Court. *See* Geders v. United States, 425 U.S. 80, 89-90 (1976) ("The opposing counsel in the adversary system is not without weapons to cope with 'coached' witnesses. A prosecutor may cross-examine a defendant as to the extent of any 'coaching' during a recess, subject, of course, to the control of the court. Skillful cross-examination could develop a record which the prosecutor in closing argument might well exploit by raising questions as to the defendant's credibility, if it developed that defense counsel had in fact coached the witness as to how to respond on the remaining direct examination and on cross-examination.").

43. This remedy also was recommended by the United States Supreme Court as a component of the judge's power to control the progress and shape of the trial. *See* Geders v. United States, 425 U.S. 80, 90 (1976) ("[T]he trial judge, if he doubts that defense counsel will observe the ethical limits on guiding witnesses, may direct that the examination of the witness continue without interruption until completed. If the judge considers the risk high he may arrange the sequence of testimony so that direct- and cross-examination of a witness will be completed without interruption. That this would not be feasible in some cases due to the length of direct- and cross-examination does not alter the availability, in most cases, of a solution that does not cut off communication for so long a period as presented by this record. Inconvenience to the parties, witnesses, counsel, and court personnel may occasionally result if a luncheon or other recess is postponed or if a court continues in session several hours beyond the normal adjournment hour. In this day of crowded dockets, courts must frequently sit through and beyond normal recess; convenience occasionally must yield to concern for the integrity of the trial itself.").

44. *See* Fed. R. Civ. P. 30(d); Steven Baiker-McKee & William M. Janssen, Federal Civil Rules Handbook 871 (2022 ed.) (a party may move to terminate a deposition if it is being conducted in bad faith or in an unreasonably annoying, embarrassing, or oppressive manner; a court may impose an "appropriate sanction" on a person engaging in obstructive behavior). *See* Advisory Committee Notes to the Federal Rules of Civil Procedure, 1980 Amendment to Fed. R. Civ. P. 26, Subdivision (f) (1980) ("In the judgment of the Committee abuse can best be prevented by intervention by the court as soon as abuse is threatened.").

45. Such protocols can be agreed to as part of a stipulation to a deposition by remote means or ordered by the court when authorizing that a deposition be taken by remote means. *See* Fed. R. Civ. P. 30(b)(4). Protocols could also be included in a proposed discovery plan. *See* Fed. R. Civ. P. 26(f). A number of courts routinely require that depositions be conducted in accordance with the stringent procedures set forth in *Hall v. Clifton Precision*, 150 F.R.D. 525, 528 (E.D. Pa. 1993). *E.g.*, Kelleher v. Wells Fargo Ins. Servs., No. 10-6247-NLH-KMW, 2011 U.S. Dist. LEXIS 13074, at *2 (D.N.J. Feb. 10, 2011). For an example of a re-

- Administrative orders governing the conduct of remote depositions[46]
- Inclusion of remote protocols in trial plans and pretrial orders[47]
- Development of guidelines and best practices for conduct in remote proceedings[48]
- Professionalism/Civility/Courtesy Codes[49]

Structuring remote proceedings in advance by way of agreement, court order, or collectively adopted behavioral norms will create greater transparency and provide helpful guardrails to guide lawyers away from unethical conduct.

Conclusion

Under the Model Rules of Professional Conduct, a lawyer's failure to prepare and guide a witness would in many situations violate the ethical duties of competence and diligence. Witness preparation becomes unethical when the conduct transgresses Model Rules governing prohibiting interference with the integrity of the justice system and obstructing another party's access to evidence. The use of technology in the profession, particularly

---

mote deposition protocol, see Uniform Civil Rules for New York State Trial Courts, Rule 202.70(g), Appendix G, STIPULATION AND PROPOSED ORDER CONCERNING PROTOCOL FOR CONDUCTING REMOTE DEPOSITIONS, *available at* https://www.nycourts.gov/LegacyPDFS/RULES/trialcourts/202.70(g)%20-%20Rule%2037-Appendix%20G.pdf (last visited Aug. 25, 2023).

46. *See, e.g.*, SUPREME JUDICIAL COURT OF MASSACHUSETTS UPDATED ORDER REGARDING REMOTE DEPOSITIONS (Oct. 23, 2020), *available at* https://www.mass.gov/supreme-judicial-court-rules/supreme-judicial-court-updated-order-regarding-remote-depositions.

47. *See* FED. R. CIV. P. 16(c) & (e). *See, e.g.*, STATE OF NEW YORK UNIFIED COURT SYSTEM, VIRTUAL BENCH TRIAL PROTOCOLS AND PROCEDURES (including Proposed Stipulation and Order for Virtual Bench Trial Protocols and Procedures), *available at* https://www.nycourts.gov/whatsnew/pdf/VirtualBenchTrial-Protocols-2112021.pdf (last visited Aug. 25, 2023).

48. *See* NATIONAL CENTER FOR STATE COURTS, REMOTE PROCEEDINGS TOOLKIT 47-50 (Proceedings Conduct) (2002), *available at* https://www.ncsc.org/__data/assets/pdf_file/0027/82377/Remote-Proceeding-Toolkit-Final.pdf; WASHINGTON STATE SUPREME COURT, REMOTE JURY TRIALS WORK GROUP BEST PRACTICES IN RESPONSE TO FREQUENTLY ASKED QUESTIONS (FAQ) (June 2021) (including links to resources such as sample orders for remote/virtual jury trials), *available at* https://www.courts.wa.gov/newsinfo/index.cfm?fa=newsinfo.remotejurytrialsworkgroup.

49. *See, e.g.*, COLORADO PRINCIPLES OF PROFESSIONALISM, PRINCIPLE 7.2.5 (2011) ("We will refrain from coaching deponents by objecting, commenting, or acting in any other manner that suggests a particular answer to a question."), *available at* https://www.cobar.org/For-Members/Committees/Professionalism-Coordinating-Council/Principles-of-Professionalism#9712573-colorado-principles-of-professionalism (2011). A compilation of Professionalism Codes from around the United States can be found on the ABA Center for Professional Responsibility Resources page of the ABA website, *available at* https://www.americanbar.org/groups/professional_responsibility/resources/professionalism/professionalism_codes/.

remote-meeting technologies, presents distinct opportunities for surreptitious witness coaching. But the Model Rules that constrain unethical witness coaching extend to all testimonial contexts, regardless of format. It is prudent for lawyers and adjudicators to consider prophylactic measures designed for use in remote proceedings to prevent and detect incidences of unethical coaching conduct.